SOCIAL WELFARE IN SOCIETY

SOCIAL WELFARE IN SOCIETY

George T. Martin, Jr., and
Mayer N. Zald, Editors

1981
COLUMBIA UNIVERSITY PRESS
NEW YORK

Clothbound editions of Columbia University Press books are Smyth-sewn and printed on permanent and durable acid-free paper.

Library of Congress Cataloging in Publication Data
Main entry under title:

Social welfare in society.

Bibliography: p.
Includes index.
1. Public welfare—United States—Addresses,
essays, lectures.   2. United States—Social policy
—Addresses, essays, lectures.   3. Welfare state—
Addresses, essays, lectures.   4. Social service—
United States—Addresses, essays, lectures.
I. Martin, George T. II. Zald, Mayer N.
HV91.S624   361.6'0973   81-3837
ISBN 0-231-04922-6   AACR2
ISBN 0-231-04923-4 (pbk.)

Columbia University Press
New York   Guildford, Surrey

To the memory of David Street,
who brought us together and
who died as this project was in progress

PREFACE

OUR purpose in assembling this reader is to present a broad sociological perspective on social welfare institutions and their relation to society. Our intended audience is composed of students of social welfare, social work, and the social sciences, both undergraduate and graduate. We have tried to illuminate critical issues of policy choice, societal support, and agency practice by selected exemplars of sociological research and analysis.

The idea for producing this reader came from the conjuncture of Zald's (1965, out of print) interest in preparing an improved version of an earlier sociology of social welfare reader, and Martin's concern with the inadequacy of teaching materials in the field. Although the analytic structure of both this reader and Zald's earlier effort are similar, there are major divergences. This reader includes sections (none of which was in the 1965 reader) on political economy, race and sex biases, innovation, and the future of social welfare. No selection appeared in the 1965 reader. Over all, the present reader has more material with a national rather than local focus. Also, the analyses here are more sophisticated methodologically than those in the 1965 reader, reflecting a general trend in social science. Finally, social science has become more variegated politically and ideologically. This change is expressed in our readings, which confront policy issues directly.

In putting together this reader, we have had an unusually productive and amicable partnership. Although Martin took the lead in preparing the volume, Zald was involved at each stage. The final product represents our best joint assessment of the scope and contours of the sociology of social welfare.

We thank our friends and colleagues, Joanna Foley, Laura Kramer Gordon, Kirsten Grønbjerg, John L. Hammond, Yeheskel Hasenfeld, Patrick J. Molloy, and Jeffrey Shaffer, each of whom made helpful comments in the preparation of this work. We acknowledge the secretarial assistance of Doris Gale, Montclair State College Department of Sociology, and that of Elizabeth Barlow, University of Michigan School of Social Work. We also recognize the support of the staff of Columbia University Press, especially John Moore, Joan McQuary, and Dorothy M. Swart. We gratefully share the success of our effort with these people but take full responsibility for its shortcomings.

Finally, although our principal interest in social welfare is as sociologists, we are also concerned with social welfare practice, particularly in terms of its human outcomes. In addition to the fact that both of us teach the sociology of social welfare, Martin has an M.A. and experience in social work, and Zald has considerable experience in the evaluation of social welfare programs. We hope that this work ultimately contributes to improving social welfare practice for both clients and workers.

George T. Martin, Jr.
Upper Montclair, N.J.

Mayer N. Zald
Ann Arbor, Mich.

CONTENTS

SOCIAL WELFARE IN SOCIETY

INTRODUCTION

THE practice and analysis of social welfare are reaching a turning point in the United States. The dominant welfare state model, rooted in 1930s reforms and Keynesian economics, can be defined by its stress on state responsibility for the basic material security of citizens. It is being challenged economically by the fiscal crisis, in which state revenues are increasingly falling short of expenditures, and politically by the disintegration of the Democratic Party's New Deal coalition. Socially, the challenge is in accommodating the emergence of client, worker, ethnic, and other groups with new demands. The challenge emerged forcefully with the reform efforts and insurgency of the 1960s. The major lesson of the 1960s may prove to be the welfare state's failure to handle new problems, just as the 1930s demonstrated the inability of laissez-faire welfare to deal with the challenges of that time.

The turning point is evident in the different questions one asks: In a society dominated by welfare state policies, political conflict often focuses on the distribution of increasing resources—who gets what? However, in a society impacted by a fiscal crisis, conflict refocuses on the distribution of increasing costs—who pays? In the 1960s, public welfare recipients organized to demand more of society's resources, challenging its welfare state liberalism to produce more egalitarian benefits. In important ways the society did produce. The "welfare explosion" was real, resulting in larger caseloads, higher benefit levels, and greater welfare rights. In the 1970s, middle-class property owners organized to reduce their increasing costs for welfare state policies, challenging the society to economize. Apparently, the society is responding. Not only did public welfare caseloads and benefits level off after 1975, but total social welfare expenditures declined in 1977 as a proportion of the gross national product—for the first time in over twenty years.

The present turning point has been produced in part by the weakened position of international capitalism and of Western welfare states, posing potential threats to their stability. Stagflation, increasing international competition, and the decline of neocolonialism may have critically weakened the capacity of the United States to ameliorate domestic economic problems by continued expansion of welfare benefits. This may be an even greater problem because of demographic changes; for example, the "aging" of the population.

However, we are not at an apocalyptic crossroads, only an important one. The welfare state model remains dominant in determining the direction of social welfare policy, practice, and analysis. Its inertia is ponderous, while the alternatives offer unknown or even bleaker prospects. It is unlikely that the welfare state will be dismantled by conservative fiscal backlash. Its interest groups (Social Security beneficiaries and bureaucrats) remain politically potent. At most, its progress will be slowed. It is also unlikely that the welfare state will become a full-blown socialist state as a result of insurgency from below, unless economic conditions dramatically worsen and massive political change occurs. But these two pressures—from the right and the left—will considerably narrow the range of options available for the still dominant welfare state liberal center.

The welfare state is well-established, but issues of the equity and humaneness of its services remain principal questions for its clients and workers. Increasing professionalization and bureaucratization may have increased the distance between social welfare organizations and their clients. The welfare state remains vulnerable to the charge of sustaining impersonal and stigmatizing programs. These programs do not provide their beneficiaries with equity or equality, nor do they serve society with humanity or efficiency. This critique recognizes that bureaucratization and professionalization may contribute to client well-being (through enforcement of universalism, for example) but also points to their disabling effects. Although, as Wilensky and Lebeaux (1965:141) indicated, modern social welfare is based on "help given to the stranger," it does not necessarily follow that both the helpers and the helped become alienated.

The study of social welfare can also be criticized. Understanding and explanation, however important as research goals, are not often enough linked to resolution of problems at the interpersonal level. On the one hand, sociological study focuses in a detached way on institutional failures in social welfare—a scientific debunking of discrepancies between the goals and operations of practice. On the other hand, study focuses on societal functioning, a perspective that relates social welfare to other sectors at a broad level. Although both make important contributions, they often leave unattended the unmet or insufficiently met needs of clients and workers.

The sociology of social welfare's unique status as contributor to both sociological theory and social welfare practice is based in its effort to link the structural and personal. As Mills (1959) pointed out, this link is critical to the sociological imagination. Social welfare in important ways is a mediating institution. By linking the personal and structural, it helps to translate human needs into structural modification (reform). (Of course, at the same time it may inhibit structural change, or revolution.) To paraphrase an old adage, for an understanding of a society, one may look to the treatment of its members in need.

Despite its continuing shortcomings, the sociology of social welfare has achieved maturity in the last decade. Now there is a formidable literature and a variety of theoretical and empirical approaches. The field is no longer a neglected stepchild of sociology and social work. However, the kind of professional sibling rivalry pointed to by Street (1967) exists between sociologists and social workers. Although there are mutual respect and need in this relationship, it is marked by differences in perspective. Sociologists often condescend to social workers for being unscientific, while social workers criticize sociologists for being uncaring.

Several emergent areas of study in the sociology of social welfare can be identified as important, including the following:

1. Continued examination of the structural roles and effects of social welfare, especially from a comparative political economy perspective, with a focus on market, centrally planned, and mixed economies

This involves determining the relation between social welfare and the redistribution of social resources, particularly income.

2. Grappling with the issue of accountability, a major source of challenge by client (demands for adequate service) and taxpayer (demands for efficient service)
3. Specifying the nature and extent of continuing racism, sexism, and class bias and their disabling effects on clients and workers

4. Analyzing further the nature and effects of professionalization and bureaucratization, dominant trends in recent years.

For example, there appear to be simultaneous, conflicting trends for social welfare workers—proletarianization at lower levels and professionalization at upper levels. This issue relates to the potential of the politicization of clients (in interest groups) and workers (in unions), separately and in concert.

This reader takes an institutional approach that is both macrosociological, focusing on social structural processes, and microsociological, focusing on role and interpersonal relations. We are particularly concerned with social welfare institutions as they relate to other sectors of society, and with organizational processes such as bureaucratization. Our definition of social welfare is relatively exclusive: social welfare attempts to enable people in need to attain a minimum level of social and personal functioning. This definition excludes the closely related areas of education and medicine. Both represent well-established subfields in sociology and each falls outside our definition—education because its social welfare functions are largely latent and its services are not addressed to people defined as in need; medicine because it principally addresses people's physical needs. However, we include readings which deal with problems in these two fields because of their relevance to social welfare.

Our contributors represent various specializations, pointing to the interdisciplinary nature of the subject. However, most are sociologists or social workers, indicating the centrality of these fields in the study and practice of social welfare. We have attempted to use the best and most representative of contemporary work, and for that reason the reader is inclusive. We include neoconservative and neo-Marxist perspectives; essays, journal articles, case studies, and monograph chapters, as well as original work.

We have attempted to focus the readings on distinctive problems in the sociology of social welfare. These include the conflictual nature of goals and minimum standards, the unique relationship between agencies and their clients, and the interpersonal nature of technologies. The selections highlight issues to which the sociology of social welfare has made significant contributions; for example, in the analysis of goal displacement and client-organization relations.

The organization of material follows from our institutional perspective. We begin with broad historical and comparative issues and then focus on analysis of specific programs and agencies. Finally, we address issues of change at both the societal and programmatic levels. The readings are divided into three general parts, each comprised of several sections. About half of the articles deal with the broader structural level, while the remainder analyze agencies and programs.

PART I

THE HISTORICAL AND SOCIETAL
CONTEXT OF SOCIAL WELFARE

A. SOCIAL WELFARE IN HISTORICAL AND COMPARATIVE PERSPECTIVES

In part I, the focus is on broad analyses of social welfare. The material is macrosociological, having as its primary unit of analysis, society. The purpose is to provide understanding of the structural background in which contemporary social welfare institutions developed and are administered. In addition to historical and comparative analyses in section A, section B examines the influence of values and ideology, in the areas of program development and policy. Because policy formulation has an important impact on the structuring and direction of social welfare, it receives attention on its own, in section C. The formulation of policy, in turn, takes place in the context of political conflict among competing economic interests. The concluding part examines social welfare from a traditional perspective that has been revived recently—political economy.

The first two selections in section A deal with how social welfare evolved in the framework of developing capitalism. The first selection, "Historical Overview of Social Welfare," is by one of the co-editors, George T. Martin, Jr. The welfare state is viewed as a correlate of mature, monopoly capitalism. Social welfare's evolution is considered in terms of two progressions culminating in the welfare state: from poor relief to income maintenance and from charity to social service. Critical processes in these developments are bureaucratization and professionalization. This essay is offered only as a summary of social welfare's evolution.

The second selection, Andrew T. Scull's "Madness and Segregative Control," details the history of a traditional social welfare institution, the insane asylum. This article exemplifies the use of historical methods. It demonstrates an important latent function of social welfare—social control. Scull focuses on the role of capitalism's rationalization, rather than on the processes of industrialization and urbanization, in the asylum's emergence.

The remaining selections in section A are examples of two general types of comparative analysis of contemporary social welfare. The first type is quantitative research specifying cross-national predictors of social welfare expenditures. Phillips Cutright (1965) did early work in this growing field. Here, in another article, "Income Redistribution: A Cross-National Analysis," he presents the finding that egalitarian political pressure, the age and power of the Social Security bureaucracy, and the control of the population over the environment (economic development) accounted for 86 percent of the variance in the proportion of gross national product allocated to Social Security in forty nations.

Subsequent work (Aaron 1967; Pryor 1968) using social welfare expenditures as dependent variable uses more complex statistical models and amends but does not radically alter Cutright's findings. One important addition is Wilensky's (1975; see Miller 1976) focus on age structure: the higher the proportion of aged, the greater the demand on social welfare expenditures. Another related strand of quantitative cross-national research focuses on inequality as dependent variable and aspects of political structure as independent variables (Cutright 1967; Hewitt 1977; Jackman 1974, 1980; Rubinson and Quinlan 1977; Stack 1978). A third line of research uses national position in the world economy as independent variable and inequality as dependent variable (Bornschier and Ballmer-Cao 1979; Chase-Dunn 1975; Rubinson 1976).

The final selection represents another general type of comparative work, qualitative comparison of national programs and policies, especially income maintenance programs and redistributive policies. It is the summary chapter of a two-volume study of public and private social welfare in twenty-two nations. The authors, Daniel Thursz and Joseph L. Vigilante, point to common trends as well as to divergences, in countries that are disparate in their levels of development and types of political structure.

[1]

HISTORICAL OVERVIEW OF SOCIAL WELFARE

George T. Martin, Jr.

SOCIAL welfare has reflected the societies of which it is part and served as a means of innovation in those societies. Its history, at least in the capitalist West, can be viewed as manifesting two underlying themes:

1. Social welfare has an economic function. It is tied to a society's mode of production, particularly its labor supply. The economy's influence is mediated by the social relations of production (such as class relations) and political and organizational processes. Historically, this can be analyzed as the progression from poor relief to income maintenance.
2. Social welfare reflects a moral value to care for the less fortunate. It is an expression of human solidarity and is related to the particular ideologies of societies. This can be seen as the progression from charity to social service.

These themes are separated for this overview; empirically, they are intertwined. Both aspects of social welfare have culminated in the contemporary welfare state.

Modern social welfare has its roots in the dissolution of feudalism and the rise of mercantile and, later, industrial and corporate capitalism. This important historical transition is also variously described in terms of rural to urban, agricultural to industrial, and traditional to modern society. It constitutes the master typology in sociology: *Gemeinschaft/Gesellschaft* (McKinney and Loomis 1970; Tonnies 1957).

I gratefully acknowledge helpful comments made by Joanna Foley, Jerry Kloby, and Mayer N. Zald.

The transition from feudalism to capitalism required a radically different labor force, socially controlled in new ways (from vassalage and artisanship to proletarianization). One important way this was done was by using "poor laws" to force the able-bodied to work at prevailing wages. Marx (1967:737) vividly described this transition period and its poor laws: "Thus were the agricultural people, first forcibly expropriated from the soil, driven from their homes, turned into vagabonds, and then whipped, branded, tortured by laws grotesquely terrible, into the discipline necessary for the wage system."

The break-up of feudalism and rise of capitalism in England played a critical role in the evolution of social welfare. English poor laws, beginning in the fourteenth century, represented early efforts to control labor on a society-wide level. They were in part a reaction to feudal labor's opposition to proletarianization. The first of these laws, the Statute of Labourers of 1349, ordered the able-bodied to work and restricted their movement. As de Schweinitz (1943:1) noted, this law was "an attempt by the English landowners to assure themselves of a supply of agricultural workers" in the aftermath of the Black Death. Later, the 1536 Act for the Punishment of Sturdy Beggars and Vagabonds established residency laws and the 1563 Statute of Artificers fixed wages and hours of work.

The Elizabethan poor laws of the sixteenth century expanded the role of the state in the regulation of labor. Nascent capitalism did not hesitate to use the state in its efforts to control labor, as Marx (1967:737) pointed out: "The bourgeoisie, at its rise, wants and uses the power of the state to regulate wages." The Statute of 1572, for example, provided for taxation to cover poor relief expenses. De Schweinitz (1943:20) refers to these laws as "the beginning of public relief."

Subsequently, in the eighteenth and nineteenth centuries, the development of social welfare reflected the rise of industrial capitalism. English poor law history reached its nadir in the 1834 Poor Law Reform Act, the basis for what has been called the "first recognizably modern welfare system" (Marcus 1975:16). It emerged as industrial capitalism was forcibly proletarianizing its labor force. This punitive law (receipt of relief was contingent upon entry into loathsome workhouses) led to concerted resistance by England's working class.

The extension and systemization of labor-regulating aspects of social welfare proceeded apace under industrial capitalism. In its heyday, during the late nineteenth and early twentieth centuries, social insurance programs began to appear in Europe. They were an advance over poor relief and represented gains for working people. Social insurance guaranteed security against specified interruptions of earning power, such as retirement or disability. Since it is financed by direct contributions or by taxation of employees and employers, it is a "contributory" program. (Poor relief's traditions continue in contemporary public assistance.) Social insurance extended and upgraded coverage, strengthened the role of the nation state (reducing capricious provincial variation), destigmatized receipt of assistance, and rationalized the delivery system. Germany under Bismarck pioneered in this area. A major impetus for social insurance came from below, from the demands of industrial capitalism's burgeoning and increasingly organized labor force. Bismarck's motivations unabashedly included a desire to provide an alternative to socialism within capitalism.

This period in English social welfare history was highlighted by the work of the Webbs and the Fabian Society. It produced the progressive Poor Law Report of 1909. This report reflected the increased political power of workers and reformers; its keynote was not punishment, but amelioration. Soon after its release, England passed the National Insurance Act, its first major social insurance program.

Consistent with other aspects of its social welfare history, the United States lagged behind England and the European continent in the progression from poor relief to income maintenance. This was due to the racial and cultural heterogeneity of the United States, its political decentralization (Wilensky and Lebeaux 1965:xvi–xxv), and its lack of a feudal past, all of which helped to produce less clearly defined class politics. The ideology of laissez-faire (entrepreneurial) capitalism has survived longer in the United States than in other Western nations, even after the economy has undergone a major shift to monopoly (corporate) capitalism, for which welfare state liberalism is the more congenial ideology. The United States did not adopt social insurance until passage of the 1935 Social Security Act, the most important social welfare legislation in its history. This resulted, largely, from the spur created by the economy's collapse during the Great Depression, when a huge surplus labor population posed a major political threat.

The adoption of social insurance has been a major lever by which the welfare state has come to dominate the rhetoric, if not the actuality, of modern social welfare. The welfare state model was first applied to England after World War II and was linked to the Beveridge Report (1942). Its basic premise was cogently stated by Titmuss (1950:506): "It was increasingly regarded as a proper function of government to ward off distress and strain among not only the poor but almost all classes of society." A thrust in the welfare state is toward public sponsorship of universalistic social welfare programs. This, in turn, is tied to increasing centralization and rationalization of administration. The relief of poverty became legitimized as an official state function: income maintenance.

The historical progression from charity to social service begins with the idea of love for humankind. Perhaps as late as the mid-nineteenth century, the practitioners and progenitors of charity were members of the clergy and their organizations. The Webbs (1927:1) make this point in their *History of English Poor Law*: "Throughout all Christendom the responsibility for the relief of destitution was, in the Middle Ages, assumed and accepted individually and collectively, by the Church." Today, social welfare is infused with religious ideals and organizations although, of course, they no longer dominate.

If there is a single starting point for modern charity, it may be the Leisnig, Saxony, Ordinance of a Common Chest in 1519, under the influence of Martin Luther and the Reformation. This and similar efforts to create "community chests" formalized communal responsibility and introduced civil administration of poor relief (Martin 1966). The first nonclerical practitioners of charity were overseers of the poor. Their principal tasks were administration of a "means test" (by which the destitute had to prove they lacked means of support in order to obtain aid) and surveillance of the poor. In England, they were established under Elizabethan poor laws, especially the Statute of 1572. Following overseers were "visitors" of the poor, perhaps more altruistic in their interests. In 1633 in Europe Saint Vincent de Paul founded the Daughters of Charity with the express purpose of visiting the poor.

Modern social work has its roots in the nineteenth-century ascendancy of industrial capitalism. Perhaps the first expression used to denote what was to become the vocation of altruism was "scientific charity" (Chalmers 1832). Combining the old moral imperative of charity (the term was used by a Scottish minister) with the emergent technology (social science) of the post-Enlightenment period, scientific charity became a guiding concept for the development of social work in the nineteenth century.

With the growth of industrial capitalism and urbanization, social problems increased—in visibility if not also in scale and intensity. This was especially true of poverty, a social problem related directly to the labor market. In New York City in 1843, the Association for Improving the Condition of the Poor was established. It was a harbinger of social reform efforts to come.

Perhaps the most noteworthy expression of the science of charity was the Charity Organization Society (COS) movement, which originated in England in 1869 and spread to the United States in 1877. Closely related was the settlement house movement, in which bourgeois practitioners of the new discipline "settled" in working-class districts. The earliest such institution was London's Toynbee Hall, opened in 1884. The most notable settlement in the United States was Chicago's Hull House, founded by Jane Addams in 1889 (see Addams 1961). (The present Jane Addams School of Social Work of the University of Illinois is located at the site of a restored Hull House.) The scientific aspect of this reform period was illustrated by Booth's (1892) study of London, in which he found that about one third of the city's population lived in poverty.

During the progressive period at the turn of the century, efforts to moderate the abuses of industrial capitalism multiplied, as did activities to create a vocation out of these efforts. This in part reflected the growing political strength of the working class, exemplified by advances in unionism. By 1898, the science of charity reached the point at which formal training in social work began, at the New York School of Philanthropy. Its first technology was social casework, pioneered by Mary Richmond, a COS veteran (Richmond 1917). In 1917 the National Social Workers Exchange was founded, and in 1920, the journal *Social Casework* began publishing.

The science of charity became dominated in the 1920s by Freudian approaches, imported from Europe. This was heralded by the formation of the American Association of Psychiatric Social Workers in 1919 and the ascendancy of social casework over the previously dominant social action/reform approach. Successful professionalization in social work has been built on the casework model. However, social work's greatest growth has resulted from massive social upheavals in the 1930s and 1960s. In both periods, huge public social welfare reforms (the New Deal and the Great Society) employed thousands of social workers. This has created recurrent strain in the profession between the traditional casework and the social action (harking back to Jane Addams) tendencies.

The professionalization of social work has been a major impetus for the rise of the welfare state, as well·as reflecting its rise. An important dynamic has been the expansion of public programs, creating a structural basis for a vocation of "helping others." Charity became institutionalized as the expertise of a specified secular vocation: social service.

Today, social welfare in Western capitalist societies is dominated by the welfare state model, and national systems are typically evaluated in terms of how well they approximate its ideals, with the social democratic nations of Northwestern Europe (especially Scandinavia) more nearly complete welfare states, followed by Australia, Canada, New Zealand, and the United States. The United States is widely perceived as the laggard. For example, Wilensky and Lebeaux (1965:xvi–xvii) state:

The United States is more reluctant than any rich democratic country to make a welfare effort appropriate to its affluence. Our support of national welfare programs is halting; our administration of services for the less privileged is mean. We move toward the welfare state but we do it with ill grace, carping and complaining all the way.

In the progression from poor relief to income maintenance, a key process has been bureaucratization along classic lines: proliferation of organizational forms featuring a complex division of labor in a hierarchy of offices governed by written rules (Weber 1946:196–244). However, the central function remains the same: subsidization of those inadequately integrated into the labor force, principally the surplus labor population, ordained by the workings of capitalist production (Marx 1967:628–40). This population includes the underemployed, the intermittently employed, and the unemployed. Progress has resulted from the struggles of workers to gain a better life as well as from the bourgeois state's interest in forestalling cataclysmic social change. The intermediaries between workers and the bourgeois state have often been reformers.

In the progression from charity to social service, an important influence has been professionalization: the process by which an occupation achieves hegemony over a specialized practice (see Greenwood 1957). However, the function, at least in part, remains the same: expression of love for one's fellows. Progress resulted from the desire of reformers to institutionalize their role in society as well as from the bourgeois state's interest in supervising and socializing its labor force.

Perhaps Engels (1972:165), in words first published in 1884, best captured the central contradiction of social welfare in our society: "The more civilization advances, the more it is compelled to cover the ills it necessarily creates with the cloak of love." Presently, the welfare state is increasingly considered an ill because, in part, its bureaucratization and professionalization have produced impersonal social welfare programs, often alienating those seeking and those offering help.

MADNESS AND SEGREGATIVE CONTROL: THE RISE OF THE INSANE ASYLUM

Andrew T. Scull

IN recent years sociologists have rightly come to see deviance and control as essentially symbiotic rather than antagonistic phenomena. Unfortunately, much of the work done pursuant to this basic insight has been marred by its narrow, ahistorical, and nonstructural focus. While the immediate interaction between deviants and control agencies and the etiological significance of deviance-processing have received considerable attention, the historical and structural contexts within which this processing occurs have been largely ignored. We have thus been forced to make do with "an analysis which lacks a sense of history, a sensitivity to institutional patterns, and a range which is wider than a narrow focus upon encounters between deviants and officials" (Rock 1974:145). Adequate theoretical work in this area clearly demands that we develop an historically informed, macrosociological perspective on the interrelationships between deviance, control structures, and the wider social systems of which they are a part. More specifically, we need to clarify the developing relationships between the nature of deviance and its control, and the increasing rationalization of the social order which has been the dominant feature of Western social development since the Middle Ages.

I

Three key features distinguish deviance and its control in modern society from the shapes such phenomena assume elsewhere: (1) the substantial involvement of the state, and the emergence of a highly

From *Social Problems* (February 1977), 24(3):337–51. Reprinted by permission.

rationalized, centrally administered and directed social control apparatus; (2) the treatment of many types of deviance in institutions providing a large measure of segregation from the surrounding community; and (3) the careful differentiation of different sorts of deviance, and the subsequent consignment of each variety to the ministrations of experts—which entails, as an important corollary, the emergence of professional and semiprofessional "helping occupations." Throughout much of Europe, England, and the United States all these features of the modern social control apparatus are a comparatively recent development.

Prior to the eighteenth century, and in many places as late as the early nineteenth century, the control of deviants of all sorts had been an essentially communal and family affair. The amorphous class of the morally disreputable, the indigent, and the powerless—including such elements as vagrants, minor criminals, the insane, and the physically handicapped—was managed in essentially similar ways. Characteristically, little effort was made to segregate such "problem populations" into separate receptacles designed to keep them apart from the rest of society. Instead, they were dealt with in ways which left them at large in the community. Most of the time families were held liable to provide for their own, if necessary with the aid of temporary assistance or a more permanent subsidy from the community. Lunatics were generally treated no differently from other deviants: only a few of the most violent or troublesome cases might find themselves confined—in a specially constructed cell or as part of the heterogeneous population of the local gaol (Fessler 1956).

The transformation of traditional arrangements into what we know today as systems of social control is clearly a subject with a profound sociological significance. I shall comment on some aspects of this transition with respect to one major variety of deviance, by examining nineteenth-century efforts to "reform" the treatment of the mentally ill. More specifically, I shall try to provide an account of the reasons for the emergence of the asylum as the primary, almost the sole, response to the problems posed by insanity.

This explanation will radically challenge David Rothman's (1971) provocative account of the American "discovery of the asylum," probably the study of the history of mental institutions most familiar to American sociologists working in the field of deviance. The account Rothman provides is essentially, despite occasional backsliding, an idealistic one. The rise of the asylum is pictured as the product of a

peculiarly Jacksonian *angst* about the stability of the social order—
together with a naïve and uniquely American utopianism about the
value of the well-ordered asylum. This was to be an institution which
would at one and the same time eliminate the scourge of insanity
and, by correcting "within its restricted domain the faults of the
community . . . through the power of example spark a general reform
movement" (Rothman 1971:133). But while Rothman persuasively
describes this anxiety, he almost entirely neglects to *explain* it—to give
us any understanding of why these persons became anxious about
these things at this time. The structural sources of the concern with
the imminent breakdown of the social order remain unexplored and
unperceived. Similarly, Rothman's account places heavy emphasis on
the uniqueness of American developments. Yet the rise of the asylum
is *not* a uniquely American phenomenon. For example, its emergence
is also characteristic of English society in this period, presenting
obvious problems for a culture-specific theory.

Despite these weaknesses, Rothman's account has appealed to
sociologists: partly because of the resonance its implicitly anti-insti-
tutional message has for an audience reared on Goffman's *Asylums*
(1961); partly because of how easily the model may be assimilated to
the way most sociologists of deviance already "explain" transformations of control structures by reference to the nefarious activities of
"moral entrepreneurs" (Becker 1963). Equally important, its allure
reflects the absence on either Rothman's or his readers' part of a
comparative perspective on American developments; and the crude-
ness and implausibility of alternative explanations. My intent here is
to make use of some of these neglected comparative materials (those
dealing with the parallel and almost contemporaneous lunacy reform
movement in England) to develop a *structurally based* explanation of
the rise of segregative means of managing the mad. In doing so, I
shall endeavor to avoid the mechanistic and historically dubious
assumptions plaguing earlier interpretations of this sort.

II

At the very outset of his book, Rothman engages in a polemic against
a portrait of the asylum as "the automatic and inevitable response of
an industrial and urban society [to insanity]" (Rothman 1971:xi–xii).
The weaknesses of the position he criticizes are so patent that one is
tempted to dismiss it as a straw man, erected to lend an air of greater

plausibility to his interpretation. Yet any such notion is not only
uncharitable, but unfair. For "explanations" of this sort are indeed
to be found, nowhere more prominently than in the brief forays of
sociologists into these areas. David Mechanic (1969:54) succinctly
outlines this position:

Industrial and technological change . . . coupled with increasing urbanization,
brought decreasing tolerance for bizarre and disruptive behavior and less
ability to contain deviant behavior within the existing social structure.

The increased mobility of the population and the anonymity of
existence in the urban slums were combined with the destruction of
the old paternal relationships that went with a stable, hierarchically
organized rural society. The situation of the poor and dependent
classes, huddled together in the grossly overcrowded conditions
accompanying the explosive, unplanned growth of urban-industrial
centers, became simultaneously more visible and more desperate.
There emerged the new phenomenon of urban poverty "among
concentrated masses of wage earners without natural protectors to
turn to in distress" (Perkin 1969:162).

All of this is consistent with the view that the structural preconditions for a system of parochial relief were fast disappearing. The
new class of entrepreneurs could not wholly avoid making some
provision for the "undeserving poor," if only because of the revolutionary threat they posed to the social order. The asylum, and
analogous institutions such as the workhouse, allegedly constituted
the bourgeoisie's response to this situation.

But there are serious problems with this argument; it rests on a
systematic misreading and distortion of the historical record. For,
even in England, when pressures developed to differentiate and
institutionalize the deviant population, the process of urbanization
was simply not as advanced as this line of reasoning would lead us
to expect. In the early stages of the Industrial Revolution, "cotton
was the pace-maker of industrial change, and the basis of the first
regions which could not have existed but for industrialization, and
which expressed a new form of society, industrial capitalism" (Hobsbawm 1968:56).

Though technical innovations introduced into the manufacturing
process in the latter half of the eighteenth century and the application
of steam power soon resulted in factory production, the technology
of cotton production remained comparatively simple; and much of

the industry remained decentralized and scattered in a variety of local factories, as likely to be located in "industrial villages" as concentrated in large urban centers (Hobsbawm 1968:58–65). Consequently, although large towns absorbed an increasing proportion of the English population, city dwellers remained a distinct minority during the first decades of the nineteenth century, when pressures to establish public lunatic asylums on a compulsory basis were at their strongest (cf. Weber 1899). The lack of parallelism in these events casts doubt on the notion that it was *urban* poverty as such which forced the adoption of an institutional response to deviance; a conclusion strengthened when one notes the marked enthusiasm of many rural areas for the asylum solution, an enthusiasm manifested at a comparatively early date (Rothman 1971: *passim*, esp. 130; cf. Scull 1974: chs. 3 and 4).

Instead, I would contend that many of the transformations underlying the move toward asylums can be more plausibly tied to the growth of the capitalist market system and to its impact on economic and social relationships. Prior to the emergence of a capitalist system, economic relationships did not manifest themselves as purely market relationships. Economic domination or subordination was overlaid and fused with personal ties between individuals. But the market destroyed the traditional connections between rich and poor, the reciprocal notions of paternalism, deference, and dependence characterizing the old order, producing profound shifts in the relationships between superordinate and subordinate classes, and of upper-class perceptions of responsibilities toward the less fortunate.

Indeed, one of the earliest casualties of the developing capitalist system was the old sense of social obligation toward the poor (Hobsbawm 1968:88; Hobsbawm and Rude 1969:26; Mantoux 1928:428; Townsend 1786). At the same time, the increasing "proletarianization" of labor—that is, the loss of alternatives to wage work as a means of providing for subsistence—went together with the tendency of the primitive capitalist economy to oscillate unpredictably between conditions of boom and slump. Obviously, these transformations greatly increased the strains on a family-based system of relief (Furniss 1965:211–21; Hobsbawm 1968: chs. 3 and 4; Polanyi 1944:92ff.). There is, despite its simplification and rhetorical flourish, a profound and bitter truth to Marx's comment that the advent of a full-blown market system

has pitilessly torn asunder the motley feudal ties that bound man to his "natural superiors," and has left no other nexus between man and man than naked self-interest, than callous "cash payment". . . . In one word, for exploitation veiled by religious and political illusions, it has substituted naked, shameless, direct, brutal exploitation (Marx and Engels 1968:37–38).

And while the impact of urbanization and industrialization was at this stage geographically limited in scope, by the latter part of the eighteenth century almost all regions of England had been drawn into a single national market economy (Hobsbawm 1968:27–28; Mantoux 1928:74). The impact of the universal market of capitalism was felt everywhere, forcing "the transformation of the relations between the rural rich and the rural poor, the farmers and their labor force, into a purely market relationship between employer and proletarian" (Hobsbawm and Rude 1969: ch. 2).

The changes in structures, perceptions, and outlook marking the transition from the old paternalist order to a capitalist social system triggered a search for an alternative to traditional, noninstitutional methods of managing the indigent. The development of an industrial economy also precipitated a sizable expansion in the number of those receiving temporary or permanent poor relief. This expansion took place at precisely the time when the newly powerful bourgeoisie was least inclined to tolerate it. The industrial capitalists readily convinced themselves that laxly administered systems of household relief promoted poverty rather than relieved it—a position they found well justified ideologically in the writings of Malthus and others (cf. MacFarlan 1782:34–36; Malthus 1798, esp. ch. 5; Rimlinger 1966:562–63; Temple 1770:258). Increasingly, therefore, the bourgeoisie were attracted to an institutionally based response to the indigent. Institutional management would, at least in theory, permit close oversight of who received relief, and, by establishing a regime sufficiently harsh to deter all but the most deserving from applying, would render the whole system efficient and economical (Furniss 1965:107; Poor Law Report 1834; Temple 1770:151–269).

Moreover, just as the vagrancy laws of the sixteenth century had begun to produce the "discipline necessary for the wage labour system" (Marx 1967:737; see also Chambliss 1964), so too the conditions in the new institutions mimicked the discipline necessary for the factory system. The quasi-military authority structure of the total institution seemed ideally suited to the inculcation of "proper" work habits among those marginal elements of the work force most resistant to the monotony, routine, and regularity of industrialized

labor. As William Temple put is, "By these means, we hope that the
rising generation will be so habituated to constant employment that
it would at length prove agreeable and entertaining to them"
(1770:266ff.).

Bentham's (1791) *Panopticon*, which fascinated many of the lunacy
reformers (cf. Stark 1810; Wakefield 1812), was, in his own words,
"a mill to grind rogues honest and idle men industrious" (Bentham
to Brissot in Bentham 1843:226), an engine of reformation which
would employ "convicts instead of steam, and thus combine philanthropy with business" (Stephen 1900:203). And, undoubtedly, one of
the attractions of the asylum as a method of dealing with the insane
was its promise of instilling the virtues of bourgeois rationality into
that segment of the population least amenable to them.

There were, of course, other factors behind the move toward an
institutionally focused, centrally regulated system of social control.
For the moment, however, I will leave further analysis of these
factors to one side and turn to the question of how and why insanity
came to be identified and managed as a unique problem requiring
specialized treatment in an institution of its own, the asylum. For it
should be obvious that before the asylum could emerge as a specialized
institution devoted to the problems of insanity, the latter had to be
distinguished as a separate variety of deviant behavior not found
only among a few upper-class families or confined to cases of furious
mania; but existing more pervasively among the lower classes of the
community as a distinct species of pathology—a pathology unclassi-
fiable as just one more case of poverty and dependency.[1]

The establishment of a market economy and, more particularly,
the emergence of a market in labor, provided the initial incentive to
distinguish far more carefully than heretofore between different
categories of deviance. Under these conditions, it was important to
distinguish the able-bodied from the non-able-bodied poor. A precondition for the development of a capitalist system, as both Marx
(1967:578, 717-33) and Weber (1930:22; 1961:172–73) have emphasized, was the existence of a large mass of wage laborers who were
not "free" to dispose of their labor power on the open market, but
who were actually forced to do so. But to provide aid to the able-
bodied, as frequently occurred under the old relief arrangements,
was to undermine the whole notion of a labor market.

Parochial relief for the able-bodied interfered with labor mobility
(MacFarlan 1782:176ff.; Smith 1776:135–40). In particular, it en-

couraged the retention of a "vast inert mass of redundant labor," a
stagnant pool of underemployed laboring men in rural areas, where
the demand for labor was subject to wide seasonal fluctuations
(Redford, cited in Polanyi 1944:301; see also Hobsbawm 1968:99–100;
Polanyi 1944:77–102; Webb and Webb 1927 *passim*). Social protection
of those who *could* work distorted the operations of the labor market
and, thereby, of all other markets, because of its tendency "to create
cost differentials as between the various parts of the country"
(MacFarlan 1782:178; Mantoux 1928:450; Polanyi 1944:301; Poor
Law Report 1834:43). Finally, by its removal of the threat of individual
starvation, such relief had a pernicious effect on labor discipline and
productivity (MacFarlan 1782:169ff.), an outcome accentuated by
the fact that the "early laborer . . . abhorred the factory, where he
felt degraded and tortured" (Polanyi 1944:164–65; see also Thompson 1963).

Instead of organizing poor relief in a way which failed to take
motivation or compliance into account, it was felt that want ought to
be the stimulus to the capable, who must therefore be distinguished
from the helpless. Such a distinction is deceptively simple; but in a
wider perspective, this development can be seen as a crucial phase
in the growing rationalization of the Western social order and the
associated transformation of *extensive* structures of domination into
the ever more *intensive* forms characteristic of the modern world. In
the precapitalist era, domestic populations were generally viewed as
an unchangeable given, from which to squeeze as large a surplus as
possible. But with the emergence of capitalism and the need for
greater exploitation of labor resources, the labor pool came to be
viewed as manipulable human material whose yield could be steadily
enlarged through careful management and through improvements
in use and organization, rationally designed to transform its value as
an economic resource. As Moffett has shown, during this process
"The domestic population came increasingly to be regarded as an
industrial labor force—not simply a tax reservoir as formerly—and
state policies came increasingly to be oriented to forcing the entire
working population into remunerative employment" (1971:187 *passim*). The significance of the distinction between the able-bodied poor
thus increases *pari-passu* with the rise of the wage labor system.

The beginnings of such a separation are evident even in the early
phases of English capitalism. The great Elizabethan Poor Law, for
example, classified the poor into the aged and impotent, children,

and the able but unemployed (Marshall 1926:23); and a number of historians have been tempted to see in this and in the Statute of Artificers (1563) a primitive labor code of the period, dealing respectively with what we would call the unemployed and unemployable, and the employed. But, as Polanyi suggests, in large measure "the neat distinction between the employed, unemployed, and unemployable is, of course, anachronistic, since it implies the existence of a modern wage system which was absent [at that time]" (Polanyi 1944:86). Until much later, the boundaries between these categories remained more fluid and ill-defined than the modern reader is apt to realize. Moreover, though it is plain that the Tudors and Stuarts did not scruple to invoke harsh legal penalties in an effort to compel the poor to work (cf. Dobb 1963:233ff.), these measures were undertaken at least as much "for the sake of political security" as for more directly economic motives (Mantoux 1928:443; Marshall 1926:17).

Gradually, however, economic considerations became increasingly dominant. As they did, it became evident that "no treatment of this matter was adequate which failed to distinguish between the able-bodied unemployed on the one hand, the aged, infirm, and children on the other" (Polanyi 1944:94). The former were to be compelled to work, at first through the direct legal compulsion inherited from an earlier period (Furniss 1965: *passim*; Marshall 1926:37ff.). However, the upper classes came to despair of the notion "that they may be compelled [by statute] to work according to their abilities" (MacFarlan 1782:105); they became increasingly attracted by an alternative method according to which, in the picturesque language of John Bellers (1696:1), "The Sluggard shall be cloathed in Raggs. He that will not work shall not eat." The superiority of this approach was put most bluntly by Joseph Townsend (1786):

Hunger will tame the fiercest animals, it will teach decency and civility, obedience and subjection to the most perverse. In general, it is only hunger which can spur and goad [the poor] on to labour; yet our laws have said they shall never hunger. The laws, it must be confessed, have likewise said, they shall be compelled to work. But then legal constraint is attended with much trouble, violence, and noise; creates ill-will, and can never be productive of good and acceptable service: whereas hunger is not only peaceable, silent, unremitting pressure, but, as the most natural motive to industry and labour, it calls forth the most violent exertions.

Or, in the words of his fellow clergyman, T. R. Malthus,

When nature will govern and punish for us, it is a very miserable ambition
to wish to snatch the rod from her hands and draw upon ourselves the
odium of the executioner (Malthus 1826:339).

Thus the functional requirements of a market system promoted a
relatively simple, if crucial, distinction between two broad classes of
the indigent. Workhouses and the like were to be an important
practical means of making this vital theoretical separation, and thereby
of making the whole system efficient and economical. But even
though workhouses were initially intended to remove the able-bodied
poor from the community in order to teach them the wholesome
discipline of labor (Bailey 1758:1), they swiftly found themselves
depositories for the decaying, the decrepit, and the unemployable.
And an unintended consequence of this concentration of deviants in
an institutional environment was that it exacerbated the problems of
managing at least some of them (MacFarlan 1782:97ff.). More
specifically, it rendered problematic the whole question of what was
to be done with those who could not or would not abide by the rules
of the house—among the most important of whom were the acutely
disturbed and refractory insane.

A single mad or distracted person in the community produced
problems of a wholly different sort from those the same person
would have produced if placed with other deviants within the walls
of an institution. The order and discipline of the whole workhouse
was threatened by the presence of a madman who, even by threats
and punishment, could neither be persuaded nor induced to conform
to the regulations. By its very nature, a workhouse was ill-suited to
provide safekeeping for those who might pose a threat to life or
property. In the words of a contemporary appeal for funds to set up
a charity asylum:

The law has made no particular provision for lunaticks and it must be
allowed that the common parish workhouse (the inhabitants of which are
mostly aged and infirm people) are very unfit places for the Reception of
such ungovernable and mischievous persons, who necessarily require separate
apartments (St. Luke's Hospital 1750:1).

The local gaol, a common substitute in such cases, proved scarcely
more satisfactory; the dislocations produced by the presence of
lunatics provoked widespread complaints from prisoners and gaolers

alike. General hospitals of the period, facing similar problems, began to respond by refusing to accept lunatic inmates "on Account of the safety of other Patients" (St. Luke's Hospital 1750:2). Clearly, then, the adoption of an institutional response to all sorts of "problem populations" greatly increased the pressures to elaborate the distinctions amongst and between the deviant and dependent.[2]

Initially, with respect to the insane, this situation provided no more than an opportunity for financial speculation and pecuniary profit for those who established private madhouses and asylums. Such, indeed, was the general character of the eighteenth-century "trade in lunacy," a frequently lucrative business dealing with the most acutely disturbed and refractory cases, those who in the general mixed workhouse caused trouble out of all proportion to their numbers. While claims to provide cures as well as care were periodically used as a means of drumming up custom, the fundamental orientation of the system (besides profit) was toward an economical restraint of those posing a direct threat to the social order (see Parry-Jones 1972). In the long run, however, such a differentiation of deviants provided the essential social preconditions for the establishment of a new organized profession, claiming to possess a specific expertise in the management of insanity, and oriented toward a rehabilitative ideal.

On the most general level, the English elite was receptive to the notion that a particular occupational group possessed a scientifically based expertise in dealing with lunacy. This receptivity reflected the growing secular rationalization of Western society at this time; a development which, following Weber, I would argue took place under the dominant, though not the sole, impetus of the development of a capitalist market system. More specifically, it reflected the penetration of this realm of social existence by the values of science, the idea that "there are no mysterious incalculable forces that come into play, but rather that one can, in principle, master all things by calculation" (Weber 1946:139). Linked to this change in perspective was a fundamental shift in the underlying paradigm of insanity, away from an emphasis on its demonological, nonhuman animalistic qualities toward a naturalistic position which viewed the madman as exhibiting a defective *human* mechanism, and which therefore saw this condition as at least potentially remediable.

How the "mad-doctors" of the period were able to exploit this favorable cultural environment to secure for themselves the status of a profession is a question dealt with elsewhere.[3] Here I am concerned with one important consequence of the fact that they were able to do so. The growing power and influence of what was to become the psychiatric profession helped to complete and to lend scientific legitimacy to the classification of deviance; transforming the vague cultural view of madness into what now purported to be a formally coherent, scientifically distinguishable entity reflecting and caused by a single underlying pathology.

In a sense, then, one had here a self-reinforcing system. For while the key to the emerging profession's claims to expertise, the new system of moral treatment,[4] did reflect a fundamental transformation in the basic paradigm or perception of insanity, it was not based on a more scientific understanding of the subject (cf. Foucault 1965; Scull 1974: chs. 5 and 8). Rather, it represented, from one perspective at least, a novel administrative technique, a more efficient means of management. The essence of this innovation lay in its emphasis on order, rationality, and self-control; and much of its appeal, both for the lunacy reformers and their audience, derived from the high value it placed on work as a means to these ends. The new approach could only be fully developed and applied in an institutional setting. So that, just as the separation of the insane into madhouses and asylums helped to create the conditions for the emergence of an occupational group ("mad-doctors") laying claim to expertise in their care and cure, so too the nature and content of the restorative ideal these doctors espoused reinforced the commitment to the institutional approach. Thereafter, the existence of both asylums and psychiatry testified to the "necessity" and "naturalness" of distinguishing the insane from other deviants.

A vital feature of this radically new social control apparatus was how much its operations became subject to central control and direction. As both the Weberian and the Marxist analyses have stressed, precapitalist societies were overwhelmingly localized in their social organization. The mechanisms for coping with deviance in pre-nineteenth-century England placed a corresponding reliance on an essentially communal and family-based system of control. The assumption of direct state responsibility for these functions thus marked a sharp departure from these traditional emphases.

While administrative rationalization and political centralization are not only or wholly the consequence of economic rationalization, it seems inescapable that the advance of the capitalist economic order and the growth of the central authority of the state are twin processes intimately connected with each other.

On the one hand, were it not for the expansion of commerce and the rise of capitalist agriculture, there would scarcely have been the economic base to finance the expanded bureaucratic state structures. But on the other hand, the state structures were themselves a major economic underpinning of the new capitalist system (not to speak of being its political guarantee) (Wallerstein 1974:133).

In a very literal sense, institutional control mechanisms were impracticable earlier because of the absence both of the necessary administrative techniques and also of the surplus required to establish and maintain them.

The creation of more efficient administrative structures, both the precondition and the consequence of the growth of the state and of large-scale capitalist enterprise, possessed a dual importance. On the one hand, it allowed for the first time the development of a tolerably adequate administrative apparatus to mediate between the central and local authorities, and thus to extend central control down to the local level. On the other, it provided the basis for the development of techniques for the efficient management of large numbers of people confined for months or years on end. Without these structures, institutional methods of social control would scarcely have achieved the importance they did. State construction and operation of institutions for the deviant and the dependent were very costly. Hence the importance, as a transitional arrangement, of the state contracting with private entrepreneurs to provide jails, madhouses, and the like. Under this method, the state allows the "deviant farmer" to extort his fees however he can, and turns a blind eye to his methods; in return, the latter relieves the state of the capital expenditure (and often even many of the operating costs) required by a system of segregative control. Movement to a system directly run by the state required the development of large stable tax revenues and/or the state's ability to borrow on a substantial scale. These in turn were intimately tied to the expansion of the monetary sector of the economy and the growth of the sophisticated credit and accounting mechanisms characteristic of capitalist economic organization (Ardant 1975).

Likewise, the development of national and international markets produced a diminution, if not a destruction, of the influence traditionally exerted by local groups (especially kinship groups) in the patterning of social life. More directly, the growth of a single national market and the rise of allegiance to the central political authority to a position of overriding importance undermined the rationale of locally based responses to deviance, based as they were on the idea of settlement and the exclusion of strangers. As local communities came to be defined and to define themselves as part of a single overarching political and economic system, it made less sense for one town to dispose of its problems by passing them on to the next. There was a need for some substitute mode of exclusion. In combination, these developments contributed to "the monopolization of 'legitimate' coercive power by one universalist coercive institution" (Weber 1968:337), and to the development of a state-sponsored system of segregative control.

The struggle to legislate and to implement lunacy reform in England involved just such a transfer of the locus of power and responsibility to the central authority and necessarily took place in the face of fierce local resistance (Scull 1974: ch. 4). This opposition reflected both a parochial defensiveness against the encroachments of the state, and the uneven spread of a new outlook on the insane. Local authorities generally accepted the traditional paradigm of insanity, along with its emphasis on the demonological, almost bestial character of madness. In consequence, they were frequently unable to comprehend why the reformers saw the treatment of lunatics within their jurisdiction as brutal and inhumane; why conditions they saw as unexceptionable produced shock and outrage in others. The reformers had fixed on the fundamentals of a new system for dealing with the insane—asylums constructed at public expense, and regular inspection of these institutions by the central authorities—as early as 1815. But before the plan was given legislative approval in two 1845 acts of Parliament there were three decades of parliamentary maneuvering and compromise designed to placate local opposition; a series of official inquiries producing a stream of revelations of the abuses of the old system (1815–16, 1827, 1839, 1842–1844); and a mass of propaganda in popular periodicals and reviews extolling the merits of their proposed solution.

III

Most historical writing on lunacy reform perpetuates the illusion that the whole process represented progress toward enlightenment, the triumph of a rational, altruistic, humanitarian response over ancient superstitions, the dawn of a scientific approach to insanity. Yet this is a perspective made possible only by concentrating on the rhetoric of intentions to the neglect of the facts about the establishment and operation of the asylum system. Even a superficial acquaintance with the functioning of nineteenth-century mental hospitals reveals how limited was the asylum's concern with the human problems of its inmates.

The consistent structural limitations of the total institution (Goffman 1961) operated from the asylum's earliest years to reduce its ostensible clients to the level of cogs to be machined and oiled till they contributed to the smooth running of the vast apparatus of which they were each an insignificant part. In such a place, said John Arlidge,

a patient may be said to lose his individuality and to become a member of a machine so put together as to move with precise regularity and invariable routine; a triumph of skill adapted to show how such unpromising materials as crazy men and women may be drilled to order, but not an apparatus calculated to restore their pristine condition and their independent self-governing existence (1859:102).

Certainly, the equanimity with which the English upper classes regarded this development cannot have been unrelated to the fact that the inmate population was overwhelmingly drawn from the lower segments of society. Nor can there be much doubt that the influential classes' emphasis on the centrality of efficiency and economy in the daily operations of the asylum (an insistence likewise reflecting the low social status of the bulk of the insane) functioned only to worsen the drab awfulness, the monotonous custodial quality of institutional existence.

Asylums quickly assumed gigantic proportions. Within twenty-five years of the establishment of the first state-supported institution of this sort, the larger asylums already contained between five hundred and a thousand inmates. By mid-century, some had façades which stretched for nearly a third of a mile, and contained wards and passages of more than six miles (*Quarterly Review* 1857:364). Thereafter, wing was tacked on wing, story upon story, building next to building, as the demand grew to accommodate more and more "lunatics." In the words of one critic, they began to "partake more of the nature of industrial than of medical establishments" (Arlidge

1859:123), where "all transactions, moral as well as economic, must be done wholesale" (Browne 1864:18). In such places, the mad-doctors of the period "herd lunatics together in special institutions where they can be more easily visited and accounted for by the authorities" (Bucknill 1880:122).

In addition to the broader sources of the commitment to the asylum model, the activities of a committed group of lay reformers and of that segment of the medical profession with an interest in the mad business obviously played an important role in legitimizing the institutional approach. In the second quarter of the nineteenth century, such men developed an increasingly elaborate pro-institutional ideology. Moreover, the fact that the asylum was presented as an arena for professional practice had much to do with the stress on rehabilitation and the marked utopian strain so characteristic of its early years. In the process, the defects inherent in the asylum's structure were largely, though not entirely, overlooked (see Browne 1837).

The drawbacks of choosing an institutional response were elaborated, with striking prescience, by a few early critics of the asylum (Conolly 1830; Hill 1814; Reid 1816), and were repeated some years later by a handful of disillusioned reformers (e.g., Arlidge 1859; Bucknill 1880). By then, the operation of the system had revealed the basic accuracy of the criticisms; yet their authors continued to be ignored. A major source of the resistance to these objections is undoubtedly to be found in the unattractiveness to the English bourgeoisie of the alternative policies that might have been pursued. In particular, given that many of the conditions which so aroused the lunacy reformers were little or no worse than the conditions large numbers of the *sane* lower classes were forced to endure (see Chadwick 1842; Engels 1969), to have attempted to improve the condition of the insane while leaving them in the community would necessarily have entailed questioning the fundamental structure of nineteenth-century English society.[5] In view of the social background of the lunacy reformers, and their concern with incremental change, it is scarcely surprising that they failed to do this. But in the absence of a coherent alternative plan, their carpings about the defects of the asylum could be (and were) simply ignored (cf. Scull 1977: chs. 6 and 7).

Once the asylum was established, the psychiatric profession sought, without success, to secure a clientele not restricted to lower-class marginal elements of the population. The upper classes displayed an understandable reluctance to confine their nearest and dearest in a total institution. With a few exceptions (which in any event bore little resemblance to the conventional asylum of the period, save in the number of cures they could claim), the expansion of the English asylum system during the nineteenth century was substantially an expansion of the pauper sector.

Undoubtedly, this circumstance is a major explanation for the low prestige of the psychiatric profession throughout this period. The class focus of institutions at this time had a critical impact on the nature of the asylum itself, reinforcing the pressures to develop low-cost custodial warehouses characterized by huge size, routine, and monotony. Under these conditions, moral treatment, never grounded in a well-developed theory of insanity, simply became a system of discipline and a convenient verbal camouflage for the psychiatric profession's questionable expertise.

The formal commitment to rehabilitation remained, but the practical concerns of those running the system were by now far different: the isolation of those marginal elements of the population who could not or would not conform or could not subsist in an industrial, largely *laissez-faire* society. But even as the optimism of the first years evaporated, the usefulness of custody for widely differing segments of society operated to sustain a system that had apparently failed, and helped to prevent the emergence of a constituency objecting to the asylum.

Working-class opposition to the elimination of parish relief and their hatred of the new workhouse "Bastilles" brought only a limited modification of the rigors of the new poor law and not its abandonment (Hobsbawm 1968:229). The poor thus had little alternative but to make use of the asylum as a way of ridding themselves of what, in the circumstances of nineteenth-century working-class existence, was undoubtedly an intolerable burden, the caring for their sick, aged, or otherwise incapacitated relatives. From the bourgeoisie's perspective, the existence of asylums to "treat" the mentally ill at public expense could be invoked as a practical demonstration of their own humanitarian concern with the less fortunate. But far from asylums having been "altruistic institutions . . . detached from the social structures that perpetuate poverty" (Gans 1971), one must realize that they were important elements in sustaining those structures; important because of their symbolic value and as a reminder of the awful consequences of nonconformity.

Ultimately, I contend, we must see the move toward an institutionalized and centralized social control apparatus as primarily the product of closely interrelated structural changes; the main driving force behind these changes being the commercialization of social existence and the advent of a full-blown capitalist market economy. What is crucial about the late eighteenth and the first half of the nineteenth century is that both the need and the ability to organize the necessary administrative structures and to raise the substantial sums required to establish such a control system were present in this period. Returning to the rival account of the rise of segregative control offered by Rothman, one may view the pervasive anxiety about the stability of the social order (which Rothman so persuasively describes but fails to explain) as the anxiety of a specific class. It was the way the bourgeois and professional classes made sense of the corrosive effects of capitalism on such traditional precapitalist social restraints as religion and the family. As such, the fears of the professional and entrepreneurial bourgeoisie were mediators through which structural pressures were translated into "reform"; but they cannot plausibly be regarded as the primary or decisive cause of this change. A break with Rothman's cultural form of explanation has this further and crucial advantage: it moves us decisively beyond the implicit solipsism of his account, and allows us to see developments in England and the United States as part of a single phenomenon.

NOTES

1. Of course, I am not suggesting here that prior to this process of differentiation the population at large were naively unaware of any and all differences between the various elements making up the disreputable classes—between, say, the raving madman and the petty criminal, or the blind and the crippled. (Obviously, on a very straightforward level such distinctions were apparent and could linguistically be made.) The critical question is rather when and for what reasons such perceived differences became rigid and were seen as *socially significant*; that is, began to provoke differential responses and to have consequential impact on the lives of the deviant.

2. For primitive mid-eighteenth-century examples of this process of differentiation, see Marshall 1926:49ff. On the necessity of such a classification, see MacFarlan 1782:2–3. The increasing numbers of the poor "are thought to arise chiefly from the want of proper general views of the subject, and of a just discrimination of the characters of those who are the objects of punishment or compassion. Thus, while at

one time the attention of the public is employed in detecting and punishing vagrants, real objects of charity are exposed to famine, or condemned to suffer a chastisement they have not deserved; at another time, while an ample provision is made for the poor in general, a liberal supply is often granted to the most slothful and profligate. Hence arise two opposite complaints, yet both of them well-grounded. The one of inhumanity and cruelty to our distressed fellow creatures; the other, of a profusion of public charity, and an ill-judged lenity, tending to encourage idleness and vice." For an elaborate late eighteenth-century classification and differentiation of the various elements composing the poor, see Bentham 1797.

3. The negotiation of cognitive exclusiveness on the part of mad-doctors—whereby insanity came to be defined as a disease, and hence as a condition within the sole purview of the medical profession—was necessarily a prolonged and complicated process. As is usual in such cases, "the process determining the outcome was essentially political and social rather than technical in character" (Freidson 1970b:79). Persuasive rhetoric, the symbols (rather than the substance) of expertise, the prestige and ready access to elite circles of the more respectable part of the medical profession—all these resources were employed to secure and maintain a legally enforceable medical monopoly of the treatment of madness. For details, see Scull 1975, 1976.

4. One cannot readily summarize in a phrase or two what moral treatment consisted of, nor reduce it to a few standard formulas, for it was emphatically not a specific technique. Rather, it was a general, pragmatic approach which aimed at minimizing external, physical coercion; and it has, therefore, usually been interpreted as "kind" and "humane." Instead of merely resting content with controlling those who were no longer quite human, the dominant concern of traditional responses to the mad, moral treatment actively sought a transformed lunatic, remodeled into something approximating the bourgeois ideal of the rational individual. Those advocating moral treatment recognized that external coercion could force outward conformity but never the necessary internalization of moral standards. Instead, lunatics must be induced, by playing on their "desire for esteem," to collaborate in their own recapture by the forces of reason and conformity; and their living environment must be reconstructed so as to encourage them to reassert their own powers of self-control. As moral treatment evolved in the large public asylums, it was increasingly simplified and reduced to a set of internal management devices: the crucial elements here were the development of the ward system, and the creation of an intimate tie between the patients' position in the classificatory system and their behavior—still among the major weapons mental hospitals use to control the uncontrollable.

5. Thus, improving the conditions of existence for lunatics living in the community would have entailed the provision of relatively generous pension or welfare payments to provide for their support, implying that the living standards of families with an insane member would have been raised above those of the working class generally. Moreover, under this system, the insane alone would have been beneficiaries of something approximating a modern social welfare system, while their sane brethren were subjected to the rigors of a poor law based on the principle of less eligibility. Such an approach would clearly have been administratively unworkable, not least because of the labile nature of lunacy itself, and the consequent ever-present possibility that given sufficient incentive (or rather desperation) the poorer classes would resort to feigning insanity. (This possibility probably provided an additional incentive for

keeping the conditions in the lunatic asylums as unattractive as possible, as "ineligible" as workhouses.) These obstacles presented an absolute barrier to the development of a plausible alternative, community-based response to the problem of insanity—in fact none of the critics of the asylum was ever able to suggest even the basis of such a program: a *sine qua non* if their objections were to receive serious consideration.

[3]

INCOME REDISTRIBUTION: A CROSS-NATIONAL ANALYSIS

Phillips Cutright

A LTHOUGH sociological theorists have repeatedly stressed the importance of the distribution of material rewards in determining the shape of the stratification system, researchers have been stymied by a lack of comparative data that would allow them to test sociological theory with empirical data.[1] This paper offers a conceptual scheme and an empirical analysis of the efforts by the governments of forty nations to redistribute income through Social Security programs (nonfamily transfer payments).[2] A discussion of the effect of these programs on the income stratification system follows the analysis.

In an earlier paper this writer (Cutright 1967) has offered a preliminary statistical analysis of variation among nations in the equality of the distribution of gross factor income. Gross factor income is the total real earnings plus capital income available to an adult or family through its own work and investments.[3] Gross factor income is the type of income commonly used by sociologists to measure individual or family income. When individuals or families are placed into income intervals according to their gross factor income, the sociologist can produce a chart that graphically displays the shape of the income stratification system. When compared to other systems, such charts can be converted to Lorenz coefficients, and the degree of inequality in income distribution can be compared.[4]

There are two important sources of income that are usually neglected in such analyses, and their neglect results in a misleading picture of the shape of the income stratification system. The first is nonfamily transfer income; ths is computed by adding all money and nonmoney transfers received from sources outside the dwelling unit. With the exception of the well-to-do, nonfamily transfer income to

From *Social Forces* (December 1967) 46:180–90. Reprinted by permission.

most families comes from government Social Security programs. (Among the well-to-do, private insurance programs provide the bulk of nonfamily transfer income.) The second source of income is net intrafamily transfers: any money payments or food and housing donations received from other members of the family, less any such contributions the unit makes to other members of the family.

Data for the United States population clearly show that families with gross factor incomes below $3,000 a year (1959) are helped largely by nonfamily transfers. For example, families with under $500 gross factor income received an average of $709 in nonfamily transfer income and an average of $314 in net intrafamily transfers. In the $500–$999 interval, the average nonfamily transfer was $870, compared to $87 net intrafamily income; while in the $1,000–$1,999 interval, the average nonfamily transfer income amounted to $823, compared to only $12 net intrafamily transfer income.[5]

When nonfamily transfers and net intrafamily transfers are added

Table 3.1. Percent of Adult Units in Gross Factor and Gross Disposable Income Intervals: United States, 1959 (N = 3,396 adult units)

Income Interval	Percent by Gross Factor	Percent by Gross Disposable	Effect of Transfers and Federal Income Tax
Under $500	17.7	3.2	− 14.5
500–999	7.4	8.7	+ 1.3
1,000–1,999	10.6	12.5	+ 1.9
2,000–2,999	8.5	10.7	+ 2.2
3,000–4,999	15.6	22.1	+ 6.5
5,000–7,499	18.2	22.7	+ 4.5
7,500–9,999	10.4	11.3	+ .9
10,000–14,999[a]	8.0	6.7	− 1.3
15,000 and up	3.6	2.5	− 1.1
Total	100.0	100.4[b]	

NOTE: An adult is a person 18 or older, his spouse if married, and any dependent children living with him.
[a] Federal income tax responsible for the downward shift in the $10,000-and-over intervals.
[b] Total does not add to 100 because of slight errors in estimating from bar graphs in original source. Data adopted from Morgan et al. (1962:314, 317).

to the "original" gross factor income (and income tax is deducted in the upper-income groups), the result is the family's gross disposable income. Since it is gross disposable income that determines the family's ability to consume goods and services, it is likely that gross disposable income is a better measure of the family's income status than is gross factor income.[6]

The enormous effect of nonfamily transfers on the shape of the income stratification system can be best appreciated by a graphic display of the figures in table 3.1, but the figures are, by themselves, impressive. Remembering that nonfamily transfers are the major factor that shifts low-income families *up* and across income intervals, we can begin to appreciate the power of government programs to alter the shape of the income stratification system. We see, for example, that nearly 18 percent of all adult units had a gross factor income below $500 in 1959, but only 3 percent had a gross disposable income this low. Over 80 percent of all adult units under $500 gross factor income are moved to a higher income level because of transfer payments. The income status of millions of families is altered by nonfamily transfer payments, and one effect of this change is to make the distribution of gross disposable income more equitable than in the distribution of gross factor income.

Concepts and Indicators

DEPENDENT VARIABLE

Income redistribution through Social Security expenditures. The dependent variable is the effort by government to redistribute a share of the national wealth to persons with low gross factor incomes. This effort will be measured by the percent of the gross national product allocated to national Social Security expenditures in 1960. This measure was developed by the United States Social Security Administration (1965; see Gordon 1963) and allows international comparisons. Government Social Security programs provide the apparatus through which nearly all nonfamily transfer payments are made. Most of these transfer payments go to low-income people who have low incomes because they are not in the labor force. A large proportion of Social Security program funds go to the aged, the retired, the permanently disabled or unemployed, and children in families with low incomes. Nations with well-developed programs also provide medical care for the population.

Social Security programs provide the nonfamily transfer funds that alter the shape of the gross factor income distribution. If the percent of gross national product (GNP) allocated to Social Security programs were near zero it is obvious that the distribution of persons to gross disposable income intervals would be very similar to the distribution of persons to gross factor income intervals. A nation with a relatively high percent of its GNP allocated to Social Security programs will be a nation in which the income distribution will be strongly altered in an equalitarian direction. Conversely, a nation with a low proportion of GNP devoted to Social Security programs will be a nation in which the distribution of gross disposable income is very little altered.

INDEPENDENT VARIABLES

1. *Equalitarian pressure in the political system.* Because Social Security programs are political acts—legislative acts, in fact—it is difficult to imagine that the nature of the political system will not be related to the level of Social Security expenditures. Political systems with a strong equalitarian component will have large Social Security programs.[7] The extent to which this outcome is a function of the attitudes of the citizenry, the political elite, or some interaction between the two groups is speculative. Our measure of equalitarian pressure within the political system is the percent of the voting age population voting in national elections during the 1950s (Russett et al. 1964:84–86). We reasoned that regardless of whether the voting is compulsory or not (and both Communist and non-Communist nations have compulsory voting), the level of voting participation should tell us something important about pressures within the political system to reach a certain level of Social Security expenditures. In systems with forced citizen participation, the government must legitimate its equalitarian ideology through government activity consistent with the ideology. In Communist nations, forced citizen participation is linked to an official ideology of equalitarianism, while in democratic nations, the democratic ideology also demands that, by virtue of their citzenship and shared fate in the social order, the poor and unfortunate be given government aid. A political system that fails to hold elections, or discourages participation by disenfranchising large segments of its population, should be one in which neither the full force of a developed equalitarian democratic ideology nor a developed Socialist or Communist ideology will be translated

into effective government programs involving large transfer payments.

2. *The experience and power of the Social Security bureaucracy.* The experience of agencies responsible for operating government programs will affect the level of Social Security expenditures. A bureaucracy with many years of program experience will have the technical knowledge required to operate a massive program, and it will have the power to implement its internally generated demands for greater coverage of the population by its programs. Further, as programs are initiated, the population becomes a constituency of the bureaucracy, and present and potential beneficiaries are stimulated to act as real or potential pressure groups in support of the bureaucracy's demands for higher benefits and greater coverage.

Our measure of the experience and power of the Social Security bureaucracy is the number of years of Social Security program experience the nation accumulated between 1920 and 1960. Five types of programs (work injury; old age, invalidism, death; sickness and maternity; unemployment; family allowances) are used. If a nation had only one program in 1920 and added no further programs it would accumulate 41 years of program experience between 1920 and 1960. If it had all five programs throughout this time period, it could accumulate 205 years of experience. The Social Insurance Program Experience Index (SIPE) for the 40 nations of our sample ranges between 188 (Belgium) and 20 (Ghana).[8] We expect that the greater the number of years of program experience, the larger the Social Security expenditures.

3. *Control of the population over the environment.* Populations in nations with high levels of modernization have greater control over their environment than do populations in nations low on modernization. There are several subtleties involved in analysis of modernization indicators. First indicators of modernization are intercorrelated, and the choice of one in preference to another does not mean that only one is important. For example, education, the proportion of the population in the industrial labor force, GNP per capita, percent of the population over 65, and urbanization are all intercorrelated.[9] Whatever the dependent variable, the correlations of these indicators taken as independent variables will show a similar level of correlation against *any* dependent variable—if one is positively related, all will be positively related to the dependent variable. But the correlations will not be identical, and for prediction purposes one would normally select the one or two modernization indicators that

yield the best prediction. The interpretation of the correlation should not, however, ignore the fact that the indicator of modernization yielding the best prediction is itself strongly related to a number of other analytically distinct, but empirically correlated, phenomena. For example, in our analysis (below) we find that the percent of the labor force employed in industry yields a slightly better prediction of Social Security expenditures than do other measures of modernization. This does not mean that the age structure, education level, urbanization, and so on are not contributing to this outcome—obviously they are. We will, however, use the percent of the labor force that is employed in industry as our indicator of the control of the population over its environment (Russett et al. 1964:185–86).

A second subtlety in thinking about indicators of modernization is the multiple conceptual meanings we must ascribe to these indicators. The percent of the labor force employed in industry is an indicator of economic organization, but it is more: it is an indicator of the probable *vulnerability* of the population to drastic income status change associated with change from labor force to nonlabor force status. It is also an indicator of the *sensitivity* of the population to its present and future needs for protection against the hazards of nonlabor force status, and its sensitivity to the possibility that *something can be done* about this problem. Also, a modernization indicator describes the probable level of a population's *ability to place effective demands* on government for an income floor regardless of the official equalitarian political ideology. We do not have to ask whether the population has strong equalitarian values, but we only have to assume that the modernized population can and will act in terms of its present or future self-interest. The higher the level of modernization, the greater the control of the population over its environment; and the greater the control, the larger the Social Security expenditures.

We expect, then, that the degree of political equalitarianism, the experience of the bureaucracy, and the control of the population over its environment will explain the differences in the extent to which governments will or will not operate programs that redistribute income.

Preliminary Analysis and Stratification of the Sample

Since we viewed national Social Security expenditure effort as a sociological and not as a simple economic phenomenon, we did not include an "ability to pay" measure such as GNP per capita in our conceptual scheme (Russett et al. 1964:155–57). Was this decision justified? Log GNP per capita correlates .61 against expenditures, but does not contribute to an explanation of the variance when it is placed in competition with the other variables. Log GNP has correlations of .65 and .61 with industrial labor force and SIPE respectively, while these indicators were correlated .78 and .85 against expenditures. In the absence of a theory that could support an analysis that would first remove the variation in expenditures that is linked to GNP and then analyze the remaining unexplained variance with the independent variables specified above, it is not possible to retain GNP in the analysis.[10]

Multiple R using our three independent variables and all 40 nations was .93; each variable entered the regression above the .05 level, providing preliminary confirmation of the usefulness of our conceptual scheme. The errors of prediction based on this single regression

Table 3.2. Actual 1960 Expenditures and Errors of Prediction

| Nation and Stratum | Actual Expenditures[a] | Errors of Prediction[b] | |
		Across Strata	Within Stratum
High GNP			
Australia	7.9	−3.6	−3.6
Belgium	14.2	1.0	0.7
Canada	8.9	0.0	0.7
Denmark	11.1	−0.8	−0.8
France	13.9	1.3	1.1
Great Britain	11.0	−2.4	−2.7
Luxemburg	14.2	2.1	2.2
Netherlands	11.0	−1.3	−1.5
New Zealand	13.0	1.3	1.4
Norway	10.3	−0.8	−0.6
Sweden	12.4	0.4	0.3
Switzerland	7.7	−1.4	−0.2
United States	6.3	−1.1	0.0
West Germany	16.1	3.3	3.0
MEAN ERROR		1.50	1.35
Low GNP			
Austria	14.0	1.1	−0.3
Ceylon	4.5	1.3	1.7
Chile	8.5	0.5	0.2
Cyprus	3.3	−0.6	0.1

Table 3.2. Continued

Nation and Stratum	Actual Expenditures[a]	Errors of Prediction[b]	
		Across Strata	Within Stratum
Czechoslovakia	15.3	3.3	1.6
El Salvador	2.2	0.7	0.0
Finland	9.6	0.7	0.5
Ghana	1.3	0.7	−0.2
Guatemala	3.0	2.2	1.2
Iceland	7.2	−2.5	−2.2
India	1.4	−1.7	−1.5
Ireland	9.4	−0.4	−0.7
Israel	7.1	1.0	1.8
Italy	12.7	0.5	−1.5
Japan	5.2	−3.0	−2.9
Malaya	3.1	0.9	0.9
Panama	6.2	2.3	3.4
Philippines	1.1	−1.8	−1.7
Poland	9.0	−0.3	−0.1
Portugal	5.5	0.9	1.4
South Africa	3.8	−0.5	−0.3
Spain	4.2	−1.4	−1.3
Taiwan	1.2	1.0	−0.5
Turkey	1.3	−2.0	−1.4
Venezuela	2.8	−2.3	−1.5
Yugoslavia	11.0	1.6	1.6
MEAN ERROR		1.38	1.17

[a] Actual expenditures are the percent of total GNP allocated to Social Security expenditures.
[b] A negative sign with an error or prediction means the nation was spending less than predicted, using SIPE, votes, and industrial labor force as independent variables. A positive sign indicates it was spending more. Errors are also in terms of the percent of GNP.

equation are shown in table 3.2. The standard error of these errors of prediction is 1.77 percent.

In spite of this successful application of our data to Social Security expenditures, we stratified nations into those above and below $800 per capita GNP[11] because: (1) The sample was heavily weighted with low-income nations, and statements about the importance of variables for the total universe might be biased. (2) GNP per capita has little predicting value of itself, but does allow us to group nations into two types that are relatively homogeneous on a number of

Table 3.3. Matrix of Correlations, Means, Standard Deviations, and Beta *Weights for Nations Above $800 per Capita GNP (N = 14)*

	Variable Number	2	3	4	Mean	S.D.	Beta Weights
SIPE	1	56	23	72	161.0	22.5	.397
Votes	2	—	−41	54	77.8	16.2	.459
Industrial Labor Force	3	—	—	24	26.0	5.3	.336
Social Security Expenditures 1960	4	—	—	—	11.3	2.9	—

$R_{4.123} = .78$
Average error of prediction = 1.35.
Standard error of prediction = 2.05.

modernization characteristics. (3) We wanted to see whether the same predicting variables worked in nations at different levels of GNP per capita. (4) If the same variables worked in the same manner for two strata, the power of the conceptual scheme would be enhanced.[12]

The Level of Social Security Expenditures in High GNP Nations

Table 3.3 presents the data for the fourteen high GNP societies. The means, standard deviations, and *beta* weights are to the right of the matrix of product-moment correlations. For this matrix, multiple *R* is .78; the average absolute error of prediction around the mean Social Security expenditure of 11.2 percent is 1.3 percent, and the standard error of prediction is 2.05. (Two thirds of the errors of prediction will fall within the range of plus or minus one standard error of prediction.)

The *beta* weight is a measure of the independent effect of each independent variable when the correlated effects of the remaining independent variables are controlled. The *beta* weight of .397 associated with SIPE means that a change of one standard deviation in SIPE (twenty-four years of experience) is associated with a change of about 0.39 percent of the standard deviation in the dependent variable, independent of correlated change in the other variables. Since the standard deviation of Social Security expenditure is 2.8 percent, we can calculate that twenty-four years of program experience are related to an increase in Social Security expenditures of 1.1 percent of GNP.[13] The positive sign with each *beta* weight indicates that the effect of each variable is in the direction predicted by our conceptual scheme.

Detailed inspection of the effects of the three independent variables showed that neither voting participation nor industrial labor force aided in reducing the standard errors of prediction, after SIPE was correlated with expenditures. The standard error of the predictions using only SIPE was 2.06, and the addition of the two other variables resulted in an insignificant reduction to 2.05. This suggests that in this stratum, populations are relatively homogeneous with regard to the conceptual meanings we attached to our indicator of population control over the environment. It also suggests that the pressures within the political systems of these nations are constant, although there is noticeable variation in voting participation rates. An alternative view, however, would note that we have no logical basis in our conceptual scheme that would allow us to place SIPE in a causal order prior to the other predictors. The fact that the *beta* weights for all three variables are similar in size should, therefore, be considered as evidence of the independent effect of each variable on expenditures.

We are working here with "developed" nations, and part of the implicit meaning of that term is that certain characteristics of these nations have changed from the past, but are now relatively stable. We might assume that most of the increases in Social Security expenditures in the stratum occurred in the past, and these nations are now simply holding to some level of expenditures established in the past. If the process that has led to a given level of expenditures in high GNP nations is near its end, we should find that the 1957–60 period would show little if any increase in the level of expenditures. (The measure of the percent of GNP to Social Security in 1957 and 1960 takes into account increases in GNP per capita and population size during this time period.) If the process is still at work, the majority of these fourteen nations should show an increase.[14] In fact, twelve of the fourteen nations do show an increase in expenditures between 1957 and 1960. The mean gain for all fourteen was just over eight tenths of one percent. Change is still underway in this stratum.

Table 3.2 shows the errors of prediction for both high and low GNP nations. (The following discussion of the errors of prediction refers to the column of "within stratum" errors, not the "across strata" column in table 3.2.) West Germany and Australia are deviant cases, the former spending considerably more, and the latter much less on Social Security than our regression equation predicts. It is interesting that the United States is on the prediction line in spite of the recriminations one hears about the inadequacy of our national Social Security effort. (Translating. the percent of per capita GNP allocated to Social Security into dollars per capita spent on Social Security programs, we can show that Luxemburg, Sweden, and Belgium were spending more dollars per capita than the United States; and Canada, New Zealand, and West Germany were very close.) When the Social Security effort is viewed in the relative terms we are using here, the magnitude of the United States effort, given the late start on such programs in the United States, its low voting participation rate, and its labor force in industry, is predictably low.

The Level of Social Security Expenditures in Low GNP Nations

Table 3.4 shows the results of the analysis of the twenty-six low GNP nations. SIPE and votes were analyzed in raw form, while the remaining variables were t-scored to normalize their distributions for the correlation analysis.[15] The raw means and standard deviations are shown, however, to allow comparison against the same variables shown in table 3.3 for high GNP societies.

Multiple R for this stratum is .89, the average error of prediction is 1.2 percent and the standard error of prediction is 1.5 percent. Three of the twenty-six nations have an error as great as 2 percent.

Table 3.4. Matrix of Correlations, Means, Standard Deviations, and Beta Weights for Nations Below $800 per Capita GNP (N = 26)

	Variable Number	2	3	4	Mean	S.D.	Beta Weights
SIPE	1	24	64	79	95.8	52.6	.552
Votes	2	—	39	56	58.7	30.0	.329
Industrial Labor Force	3[a]	—	—	73	14.0	6.5	.244
Social Security Expenditures 1960	4[a]	—	—	—	5.9	4.2	—

$R^{4.123} = .89$
Average error of prediction = 1.17.
Standard error of prediction = 1.51.
[a] Variables 3 and 4 were t-scored to normalize distributions. Raw score means and standard deviations are given to facilitate comparisons with table 3.3.

SIPE takes on the largest *beta* weight—a change of one standard deviation in SIPE (52.6 years) is related to a gain of about 55 percent of the standard deviation in Social Security expenditures, when votes and industrial labor force are controlled. All three predictors are significant (.05 level) when entered in descending order of importance; therefore the standard error of prediction becomes smaller with the introduction of each variable—unlike the situation reported in the high GNP stratum. The positive sign with each *beta* weight indicates that the direction of the effect of each predictor is consistent with the conceptual scheme.

We might expect that low GNP nations would have larger 1957–60 expenditure growth than high GNP nations, because they are so much lower than the latter group. However, we observed that no "ceiling effect" was operating among the high GNP nations, and this may prepare us for the finding that the mean 1957–60 gain in expenditures among low GNP nations was only five tenths of one percent—compared to a gain of eight tenths of one percent in high GNP nations. Change in SIPE in low GNP nations averaged only 10.6 years from 1957 to 1960, compared to 14.6 years in the high GNP nations, and the smaller gains in Social Security expenditures in low GNP nations may also reflect their smaller gains on the other variables as well.

Table 3.2 shows the actual and predicted Social Security expenditure after the *t*-scores used in the low GNP stratum are converted back to the raw data. Inspection of the "within stratum" column reveals that Panama, Czechoslovakia, Yugoslavia, Ceylon, and Israel are "deviant cases" with around 2 percent larger expenditures than predicted, while in Japan, Iceland, and the Philippines, actual expenditures are around 2 percent under our prediction. It will be interesting to follow the 1961–65 series to see whether nations well below the regression line have a more rapid rate of increase than is the case for the whole group.[16]

The "across strata" errors of prediction in table 3.2 allow us to compare the errors resulting from use of a single regression equation for all nations with errors from separate equations from each stratum. The mean error of prediction is given for each stratum, and the two comparisons indicate that a slightly better prediction is gained by using the "within stratum" equations. This may appear to be remarkable at first glance because the multiple correlation across strata was .93, while the multiple correlations within the high and low GNP stratum were only .78 and .89 respectively. But we get only slightly more accurate prediction using within stratum regression equations than we get from the single equation.

Discussion

We have found that the effort to redistribute income is greater in high than in low GNP nations. This is not simply the result of a difference in ability to pay (measured by GNP per capita). In both strata, government effort to redistribute income is linked to differences among nations in the pressures for redistribution within the political system (measured by voting participation), the experience of the Social Security bureaucracy (measured by years of program experience), and the control exercised by the population over its environment (measured by the proportion of the labor force employed in industry). These three variables account for 79 percent of the variation in Social Security expenditures in the low GNP stratum, and 61 percent of the variation in the high GNP stratum. Although an equation using these same independent variables across both strata accounted for 86 percent of the variation in Social Security expenditures, the average error of prediction and the standard errors of estimate were slightly smaller when a separate within stratum analysis was used.

The analysis within strata also revealed that the addition of each predictor in the low GNP stratum yielded continuous improvement in prediction. In the high GNP stratum the addition of voting and industrial labor force added nothing after SIPE was used. However, a simultaneous solution yields *beta* weights of about the same size for each predictor in the high GNP stratum, indicating that all three predictors are contributing to a given outcome. We speculate that the nations in this stratum may be relatively homogeneous now, but past variation in political and economic development accounted for variation in the number of years of program experience—the one variable that can be used as a single predictor in this stratum. We conclude that our conceptual scheme has been tested and found useful.

The effect of large Social Security programs is to make the distribution of income more equitable. This is true primarily because Social Security programs distribute income to people with very low gross factor incomes. If one visualizes the national income stratification system as measured by the distribution of gross disposable income, then it is clear that Social Security programs are having a major impact on altering the shape of the stratification systems in those nations with large programs. Further, previous work in inequality (Cutright 1967; Kravis 1960;. Kuznets 1963; Oshima 1962) indicates that the distribution of gross factor income is more equitable in developed than in underdeveloped nations. One must add to that fact the major finding of this study: government efforts to redistribute income in an equalitarian manner are greatest in the developed nations, the same nations in which the distribution of gross factor income is the most equitable to begin with. Although we lack a comprehensive measure of gross disposable income, we conclude that the distribution of gross disposable income is more equal in developed than in underdeveloped nations.

The impact of income redistribution on the income stratification system in developed nations is probably enormous. (The example of the United States in table 3.1 is, after all, taken from a nation in which only 6.3 percent of the GNP goes to Social Security expenditures.) The manifest function of these programs (to maintain an acceptable income floor among the poor who are in the labor force, and the dependent population that is out of the labor force) is understood by all. Program planners are also aware of the implications of these programs for maintaining social order, occupational mobility, and economic growth. Although the intent of the planners may differ from nation to nation, the social and economic consequences of a more equitable distribution of income may be similar.

NOTES

1. I do not mean to suggest that there is a sociological theory that "explains" redistribution. The topic is ignored in the Davis-Moore theory of stratification and by their critics. See Buckley (1963), Davis and Moore (1945), and Huaco (1963). An effort to integrate the functionalist and the conflict theorist's views of the "distribution process" (Lenski 1966) discusses redistribution, but does not explicitly tie it to a conceptual scheme. Lenski's theory focuses largely on the distribution of wealth and income rather than the redistribution of income.

2. There are, of course, many types of federal government activities that benefit middle- and upper-income groups. For example, the tax laws provide deductions for children to those with high incomes. Certain types of income common to the rich are not taxed at the same rate as wage and salary income. Government aid to education, roads, and housing have benefited the middle- more than the lower-income groups. A comprehensive review (Titmuss 1962) of postwar redistribution in Great Britain held that little if any redistribution of total wealth had occurred.

3. See Morgan et al. (1962:497–507) for definitions of adult unit, gross factor and gross disposable income, net intrafamily transfers and nonfamily transfers. Definitions used here are adopted from Morgan.

4. The Lorenz coefficient measures the extent to which the income distribution departs from a line of perfect equality; the lower the coefficient, the greater the equality. See Morgan et al. (1962:310, 315) for discussion and examples of Lorenz coefficients applied to gross disposable and gross factor income distributions for the same sample of United States adult units in 1959. Morgan demonstrates, for example, that the coefficient for the distribution of gross factor income is .485, and it drops to .402 when gross disposable income is measured.

5. Data are from Morgan et al. (1962:314) and are based on reports from the 3,396 adult units drawn from the United States population in 1959. Above $2,000, net intrafamily transfers are negative, and become larger with increasing gross factor income, reaching a high of negative $179 in the $15,000 and over gross factor income interval.

6. Other characteristics of the spending unit (number of persons, rural or urban residence, age and sex composition) are important. See Orshansky (1965). Morgan et al. (1962:315) notes that the Lorenz coefficient drops from .402 (using gross disposable income) to .346 when the number of dependents per adult unit is taken into account. Kuznets (1963:31) shows that the low-income units have *fewer* members than higher-income units the world over.

7. See Lenski (1966:24–42) for a discussion of human nature and the distributive process. The basic assumption is that people will act in terms of their self-interest, and the next assumption is that they will see Social Security programs as being in their self-interest. See also Coleman (1966) for a discussion of rationality, self-interest, and decisions by groups with competing interests. Although some members of the population do not favor these programs, the programs fit the interests of a heavy majority in all nations.

8. See Cutright (1965) for a discussion of the content of these programs and construction of the SIPE index. The SIPE index is constructed from data from the U.S. Department of Health, Education, and Welfare (1961). Discussion of the characteristics of each of the five types of programs can be found in that document. An earlier analysis (see Cutright 1965) of 76 nations found that by 1960, 71 had begun work-injury programs, 58 had sickness and/or maternity programs, 56 had programs grouped under old age, invalidism, and death, 40 had some type of family allowance plan, and 27 had unemployment insurance programs. The five major types of Social Security programs form a Guttman scale. In all, 63 of the 76 nations were in perfect scale types, and this yields a coefficient of reproducibility of .966. In that study SIPE was taken as the dependent variable, while measures of economic development, education, and political development were used as independent variables. Controlling for economic development, Cutright showed that positive changes in his Political Representativeness Index were related to the introduction of new Social Security programs. Late introduction of programs will, of course, result in low SIPE scores, and low SIPE scores will relate to low levels of economic and political development.

9. See Russett et al. (1964:264-87) for a complete matrix of correlations among these and other modernization indicators for all nations with available data.

10. We have not stated a theory of income redistribution, but have specified a conceptual scheme that we believe will explain the differences among national levels

in expenditures. Obviously, a nation must have some level of economic development and some surplus product before it can redistribute a portion of that product. But the correlation between GNP and expenditures is so weak that we suspect it is not an important variable in the nations on which we have expenditure data. See table 3.2 for actual level of expenditures in high and low GNP nations and later discussion distinguishing the "per person value" of the redistributed income from the our "effort" measure. GNP will have a stronger relationship to a per person value than to the effort measure we have used here. For example, the United States is twenty-fourth in "effort" (the measure we use) but fourth in per person dollar value of the redistributed income.

11. See Russett et al. (1964:293–303) for a similar definition of cut-off points used in separating "mass consumption societies" from societies at lower stages of economic development.

12. The logic of this procedure is similar to that used by survey researchers when they find that their controls have reduced the case base. The power of an independent variable is assessed, in part, by its ability to produce the expected pattern of percentage differences consistently within several "homogeneous" strata (see Stouffer 1963:23–24). If we find that the same variables produce significant effects within two strata, as well as for all nations, our intuitive assessment of the power of the variables would be enhanced in spite of the known instability of correlations using a small number of cases. The empirical evidence, for example, supporting our argument about the effect of high or low levels of voting on expenditure effort will be strengthened if this independent variable has an effect on expenditures within both the high and low GNP stratum. The reader can observe (table 3.2) that all communistic (high-turnout) nations are in the low stratum, and one might "expect" them to have high expenditure effort; but would one also "expect" the democratic nations in the high GNP stratum to show a similar effect? An analysis that does not divide high and low GNP nations might be vulnerable to the charge that the voting variable "worked" simply because both groups were lumped together and the resulting correlations were, for some reason, spurious.

13. The *beta* weights for votes and industrial labor force can also be used in this manner. However, as we note in the next paragraph of the text, there is reason to think that neither votes nor industrial labor force adds significantly to *prediction after* SIPE is entered. The problem in interpretation is whether one wants to look at the results of a simultaneous solution (the *beta* weights) for answers to questions about the importance of each variable, or whether one wants to accept the results of an analysis that removes the effect of the predictor with the largest zero-order correlation with the dependent variable, and then see whether the remaining variables explain anything. In the present case one's conclusions are radically different, depending on this choice. Previous analysis of the correlates of the SIPE index (Cutright 1965) demonstrates that a nation's SIPE score is, in large part, due to its *past* levels of industrialization and political development. For this reason (and other reasons, see text) we show the *beta* weights, and do not claim that votes and industrial labor force are irrelevant.

14. The definition of the "proper" population to be covered by Social Security programs has undergone continual expansion. Many current programs do pay benefits to persons in the labor force (national medical insurance programs, for example), and it is likely that Social Security programs will expand to include large numbers of low earners who are in the labor force. The type of program that would cover this group would be similar to the guaranteed annual wage programs now under discussion.

15. For a single variable, t-scoring the raw data will yield a distribution with a mean of 50 and a standard deviation of 10. See Edwards (1954:107–13, 511).

16. We have this expectation because a nation on the regression line is assumed to be more nearly "in equilibrium" than one off the line. For a discussion of the logic behind this view, see Cutright (1963).

[4]

CURRENT SOCIAL SERVICE ARCHITECTURE: A RETROSPECTIVE APPRAISAL

Daniel Thursz and Joseph L. Vigilante

OUR goal was to bring together the experience of more than twenty diverse countries throughout the globe and to make available a fairly comprehensive view of the social service architecture of these lands. Assembling and analyzing the reports, often written by colleagues overseas, was a difficult task. The comparison of these experiences remains a difficult if not impossible goal. Language differences, for example, make it difficult for American editors to comprehend essential elements and important nuances that are often hidden in translation. The variables that affect the development of structures in different parts of the world, however, are endless. Each country presents a special set of circumstances, and the structure of its delivery system is inevitably affected by its history, economic ability, political ideology, cultural heritage, religious traditions, degree of ethnic heterogeneity, military needs, whether imaginary or real, and so on.

Perhaps one of the most rewarding results deriving from the investment of time and energy in this project has been the opportunity for an intensive overview of what social welfare systems are like in these many places. A part of this reward is the recognition that there is a commonality of understanding among social workers about what is meant by human needs and some of the necessary tools—institutional and individual—required to provide a structured response to need. We have found similarities in programs where we did not

From Daniel Thursz and Joseph L. Vigilante, eds., *Meeting Human Needs: Additional Perspectives from Thirteen Countries* (Beverly Hills, Calif.: Sage Publications, 1976), pp. 273–80. Reprinted by permission; copyright © 1976 Sage Publications.

expect that they would exist. We have uncovered commonalities in need recognition as well as commonalities of omission in response to need in many countries. Our review of the materials suggests to us that there are important identifiable differences and similarities in the varied approaches, new and old, to the development of social service systems throughout the world. Our reading suggests to us that these similarities and differences have significant implications not only for the organization, administration, and manpower development of the social services but also for the possible transferability of services from one country to another.

Predominant among the reports from almost every country is the *importance of human values* in the organization and development of social services systems. Values have been variously described—from those concerned with the dignity and worth of the individual and those concerned with social change to those which emphasize the importance of "solidarity and mutuality" in the development of services. This term "solidarity and mutuality" is identified in the report from Yugoslavia, but, although an emphasis on mutuality tends to be more typical of socialist countries, it was also identified in nonsocialist countries as an important aspect of delivery systems. In the Western countries it is the emphasis of the "social" component of social welfare that illuminates the mutuality connotation. However, it is not without some significance, we believe, that socialist countries like Yugoslavia also refer to the importance of individual "personal" needs. We would suggest some evidence, therefore, of an effort in the development of social welfare delivery systems to bring together individualized services with social responsibility.

All countries further report *relatively wide gaps between needs and services.* This phenomenon apparently is as true of preindustrialized countries as it is of postindustrialized countries. Nowhere, apparently, have nations on this planet as yet achieved a state of grace whereby the personal social needs of the citizenry are adequately met. To make the observation may only beg the question as to whether such a state of nirvana is possible. Be that as it may, the gaps remain quite clear.

In many countries there is a common *trend toward decentralized social services systems.* The move to the neighborhood level as the operational nexus for social service delivery systems is an example. It appears that there is a search for some way to build in services at "a caring scale," and it is strongly suggested by the information we have obtained that large public bureaucratic systems (with some rare exceptions, which will be discussed later) seem not to achieve the goal of delivering massive services "at caring scale." The evidence is to be found in such widely different national cultures as that of the United Kingdom and that of the People's Republic of China. It is not our purpose to illuminate or enunciate all the areas in which we see similarities in the approach to social service systems development but only to illustrate representative cases where they do indeed exist.

There is an enormous wealth of material here that should help reduce the complacency or rigidity that seems to characterize the design of service delivery systems. More accurately, perhaps, is the problem that the *systems have not been consciously designed.* Social services systems are not the result of long-range policy planning; rather, they spring up haphazardly in response to crisis and urgent need. Many programs, established in response to crisis as temporary measures, endure and resist change.

Our study leads us to a deepened awareness that throughout the world there is agreement among social workers and others concerned with the issues of social services about what is meant by human needs and some of the tools—both institutional and individual—required to provide a structure of response to such common needs. At the same time, it becomes abundantly clear that in most countries— regardless of political ideology—*there are divisions among policy-makers as to the role of government and the extent to which such needs can be met or should be met on a universal basis.* Even in Communist countries, one finds continued concern for the "deserving" and "undeserving" members of the society, as illustrated by the action program of the Czechoslavakian Communist party adopted in 1968:

The pursuit of equality has developed in an unprecedented manner, and this fact has become one of the most important obstacles to intensive economic development and higher living standards. The negative aspects of equality are that lazy people, passive individuals and irresponsible employees profit at the expense of skilled ones and those who are backward from the point of view of technology profit at the expense of those with initiative and talent.

The debates which characterize the conflicts in ideology in the United States are reflected in almost every part of the world, including Great Britain and the Scandinavian countries, which have been defined as models to be imitated and emulated by the United

States. The world-wide debate can easily be summarized in a phrase taken from remarks made by Margaret Thatcher, leader of the Conservative party of Great Britain, in a lecture given for the Institute for Economic Studies: "Government must temper what may be socially desirable with what is economically reasonable."

The dream of universal services within nations—desirable as it may seem to most students of social policy and service delivery structure—must also be contrasted with the fact that in most parts of the world those in greatest pain are not served. No review can leave the reader with the sense that we are close to being a world in which all personal social needs are met. On the contrary, one is forced by the evidence to ponder means for establishing priorities on a world-wide basis if we are ever to achieve a sense of peace on this planet. The inequality of services throughout the world parallels or exceeds the lack of equitable distribution of resources within countries.

Another fascinating aspect of the review of the material is the degree to which large delivery systems are defined as inadequate, leading to a search in most countries for decentralized social service systems. However, the decentralization of services without adequate decentralization of decision-making creates enormous problems. This was acknowledged in the United States by one of the study committees created by the Office of Management and Budget, within the Executive Office of the President. The report states:

Taken together, the pressure on the political leaders of State and local government represent a formidable management challenge. What they are being asked to do with limited authority and generally brief tenures is to provide—from a highly complex and nonharmonious mix of programs, fiscal sources and administrative entities—an integrated package of services tailored to the special needs of their jurisdictions.

On the other hand, the assignment of both responsibility and authority to a series of decentralized bodies brings with it the danger of a lack of coherence in the country's over-all policy, lack of accountability, and, in some cases, the vagaries of individual choices and prejudices with the concomitant result of lack of equity for all who need services. In some of the countries the hope of millions depends on a nationally directed and administered thrust. Here again, it is clear that there are enormous differences in the current reality of these countries and the options available to them.

The desire for a "caring system" has led many countries to explore the communal rather than the institutional route for meeting the needs of some of the population, especially those accused of crimes or delinquent behavior or those who suffer from mental illness. For instance, those responsible for the organization and structure of social services in the United States and Scotland are equally concerned with the lack of available halfway houses for adults and youth who are between the institution and the community in rehabilitative systems. However, the concern for reducing alienation and alleviating the impact of bureaucracy goes far beyond the establishment of halfway houses. The report from Yugoslavia emphasizes the importance of "solidarity and mutuality." Volunteers play a crucial role in the delivery of social services in Poland. In the People's Republic of China the small group, in which primary relationships are developed, serves as the basis for most social services, meeting the need for individualized and potentially tailor-made services within the context of a large country with an immense population.

If most countries share the same ideals and are aghast at the difficulties in reaching such goals regardless of the level of their economic and social development, it is fascinating to discover how their more immediate concerns tend also to be similar.

Throughout all the reports received, there is ample evidence of an articulated concern with intrafamily problems characterized by tension in family relationships. Yet those from countries outside the United States who have had even a brief experience with the education at American professional schools of social work have been chastising each other for years that social workers returning to their home countries had little use for family counseling techniques and other interventive methodologies designed to assist individuals or groups with their personal relationship problems.

Another problem area that seems to have reached universal importance is the care of the aged in both preindustrial as well as industrialized countries. For some countries, the aged constitute a new population at risk—notably in Israel, where the founding generation is becoming older, creating essentially novel issues for such innovative institutions as the kibbutz. As health-maintenance efforts meet with some success, death, which essentially has reduced the problem of aging, has been pushed back, creating both a greater population and a vulnerable and needing sector. Coupled with little if any reduction in the birth rate, the population problem puts new pressures on the working population in the middle years to support ever-widening youth and aging segments.

Services to youth generally—and specifically to that portion of the youth population that is deviant, with problems ranging from truancy, vagrancy, and delinquency to drug and alcohol abuse—represent one more area in which there seems to be almost universal concern. To this list must be added care for orphans and for abandoned, neglected, or abused children.

Finally, we must add to this list of common issues that seem to transcend national boundaries an increasing challenge involving minority or so-called native populations. No country seems to be immune to the peculiar problems of meshing various national or ethnic groups, of differentiating services according to the particular needs and folkways of such groups, and of meeting the accusations of having neglected such populations in the development of national policies. There are few long-lasting homogeneous nations these days. In Israel, the issue centers on both the Sephardic Jewish and Arab populations. In the United States, it is the blacks, Spanish-speaking Americans, and Indians. In South Africa, the conflict centers on blacks and those of mixed blood. In Great Britain, the focus is on the immigrants from the Commonwealth countries who often inhabit the slums of the large industrial cities. In many European countries, the migrant industrial and farm workers are pointed to as suffering from neglect in social services, and so on.

Another major area in which one can find a great deal of similarity among the nations is that involving the organization and administration of social services. Almost all countries report the *relative haphazard nature of the organization of social services*. Social welfare experts in the Western countries should not be surprised at this, since it continues to be a major problem for the more advanced countries despite major efforts over the past two decades to reduce the overlapping services of multiple agencies and to clarify the relationship between voluntary and tax-supported agencies. Coordinated planning systems for attacking major social problems remain an elusive goal for most countries. It should be noted that in this regard Sweden and the United Kingdom are perhaps exceptions to the rule. In addition to these two countries, there is evidence that in Australia, the People's Republic of China, and Poland a great deal of concern is being directed toward developing national systems for administering human services. The efforts of these countries—despite their contrasting ideologies—may reveal, upon subsequent evaluations, some desirable directions for other countries to follow. It must be stressed that, in all the countries listed, the social services do become instruments of national policy. This, in turn, raises questions about the political power and influence of social welfare as an institution and the potential use of that power in future socioeconomic political planning.

The dilemma which we noted earlier has a particular significance in the discussion of planning to avoid or reduce fragmentation of services. In most countries, the social welfare responsibility is already spread in a variety of administrative departments at the national and subnational levels. Where social welfare planning does exist, it is usually because the over-all responsibility lies clearly in one top governmental system such as a ministry for social and health affairs. At issue is the desirability of organizing social services in a single central department which acts as a service organization for other departments or governments in contrast to an alternate scheme which calls for establishing social service units in discrete state or federal agencies or ministries such as housing, labor, and the like.

The degree to which income-maintenance programs should be fused with social services continues to perplex most of the architects of such systems. Even United States proponents of a sharp separation are now having second thoughts as they realize the need to provide additional support to families receiving cash benefits. In too many instances, the real needs of a family are ignored because they are "handled" by personnel trained to deal with cash benefits only. On the other hand, many who are seeking social service support also require financial assistance—without the long bureaucratic process of referral to a totally separate agency.

Furthermore, in some countries the availability of both income support and social services is tied to being identified as part of the working force. Once that status has been lost—or if indeed it has never been gained—the individual may not be eligible for any assistance and must depend on the historic but limited charitable efforts of the church and volunteer groups, if not on begging.

Not all countries make an equal commitment to income-maintenance programs as well as social services programs. In some, one or the other may lag considerably behind. In Australia and Canada, for instance, there is considerable recognition of the need for social services; yet the major emphasis is on income-maintenance programs.

Neither of these countries has the long tradition of voluntary social services which the United Kingdom possesses. It is possible to hypothesize that without a history of voluntary services, moving social services into the public sector may be unusually difficult. Furthermore, we find that among all nations, regardless of their level of industrialization, there is considerable confusion as to the relative role of government and the voluntary sector in the delivery of social services. There is little movement toward solving that issue. Whereas the move toward public and government-financed social services has been the trend since World War II, the accomplishments of this trend are being challenged. Alvin Schorr, in delivering the Titmuss Memorial Lecture in Coventry, England, in 1974, questioned whether public responsibility for social services had produced the kinds of humane services that are needed. Although voluntary agencies continue to play a major role, we observe increasing efforts by governments to purchase services from voluntary agencies, if not to provide them with outright subsidies. As with all government support, the private sectors lose a degree of independence and the freedom to innovate. The paradox is that the concept of voluntarism seems to be enjoying a renaissance in many parts of the world, again without regard to the political or economic system of the countries involved. Several of the reports highlight the importance of "self-helpers" or "volunteers." The reliance, for example, on informal, family, and local community groups for the delivery of social services typical in the Soviet Union and the People's Republic of China is being considered by other nations, including the United States and Great Britain. The concept of a service corps such as the Peace Corps or VISTA of the United States is being copied in other lands, notably in Iran and Israel. Volunteers, small self-help groups, ethnically oriented and differentiated services, and neighborhood social service shopping centers are among the innovations that are piercing national and political ideological boundaries throughout the world. At the same time, the trend toward national income-maintenance programs administered centrally or under specific national dictates is continuing.

The training of personnel to conduct the many functions grouped under social services varies considerably from country to country. In some, like the People's Republic of China, the concept of a professionally trained social worker is rejected on both ideological and pragmatic grounds. The local group, with its various actors bridging experience and age, is expected to provide the necessary assistance.

In others, the general level of education remains low and training opportunities in universities are nonexistent. On-the-job training provides the only substitute for professional education. In the United States, where professional social work training has been most highly developed, the issue of the relevance to the provision of concrete services, especially to the low-income population, remains as a critical problem. The interest in therapy based on "conversations with a purpose" continues at a very high level among graduate students in schools of social work, and there is a general antipathy to activities that are designed to provide concrete assistance to poor people looking for jobs, adequate shelter, clothing, or similar needs.

The irony contained in the advancement of social work into the realm of the professions throughout the world is that the new status granted to professional graduate social workers will create more opportunities to provide important services to the middle and upper classes either in voluntary agencies or through private practice. The United States experience may serve to provide some important warnings to other countries that wish to increase the effectiveness of the social service staff through university education.

As we close this retrospective appraisal, it is important to note that from two countries we have reports indicating that the national policy contains an assumption that different systems of social services should be designed for different races and that the services for people with white skin should be inherently superior to those given to persons with black skin. The differentiation is built into all aspects of the social service systems, including benefits to clients and education and salary for workers. This last instance can serve as a powerful reminder that social service architecture depends initially on the policies developed for social welfare in any particular setting and then ultimately rests on a foundation of values held by the majority of the citizenry in democratic lands or the values held by those who rule in nondemocratic countries. Without a commitment to the sanctity of human life and to improving the quality of life for all inhabitants, the architecture of service delivery will have little meaning. However, even with such a commitment, the problems of delivering such services within the resources available loom large and extremely difficult to overcome. We are pledged to using this medium to share the exploits and the failures of our colleagues throughout the world in the hope that some of the experiences reported here will prove helpful to others facing similar issues in other parts of our globe.

B. IDEOLOGY AND VALUES

THE historical development of social welfare has been shaped by
ideology and values. Values are "ends" which denote individual
or collective concepts of what is desirable, or good. They condition
action by influencing the choice of "means" and by serving as
evaluative criteria. An ideology is a value *system* characteristic of a
group, and it is tied to and sustains economic and political interests.
For example, the Protestant ethic (expressing the value of hard work)
has influenced the evolution of income-maintenance programs in
Western society. One may note the difference in legitimacy accorded
to Aid to Families with Dependent Children and to Social Security
in the United States. Those who receive AFDC are "recipients" and
are stigmatized, while those who receive Social Security are "beneficiaries" and suffer no such opprobrium.

In social welfare in the United States, tension between residual
and institutional orientations has produced what Wilensky and
Lebeaux (1965:138–40) refer to as "ideological dualism." The residual approach relies on social welfare to address only the "residue" of
needs not met by private structures such as the family and the
market. However, the institutional perspective favors expansion of
social welfare as an ongoing function, sponsored by the state. This
dualism helps explain why the United States is a reluctant welfare
state. The residual approach reflects the laissez-faire ideology of
entrepreneurial capitalism, while the institutional perspective expresses the ideology of welfare state liberalism.

The two selections in this section highlight the interaction between
ideology and values, and social welfare programs and policies. The
first piece, "The Art of Savage Discovery," is the opening chapter in
William Ryan's book *Blaming the Victim*. His typology of exceptionalist
(conservative) and universalist (liberal) values in social welfare parallels, respectively, Wilensky and Lebeaux's residual and institutional
categories. Ryan critiques both perspectives, noting their essential

similarity in that both ultimately blame the victim of social problems. He says that although programs developed under the dominant liberal perspective point to past social causes of problems, they try to change the victim rather than society.

The other selection, John E. Tropman's "Societal Values and Social Policy," discusses six important values, including individualism and the belief that the United States is the land of opportunity. He argues that these values contribute to the stigmatization of social welfare recipients. This has resulted from the centrality of the "mobility ethic," which views pejoratively those who do not attain upward mobility, or success. Thus, failure to move up from poverty is both a basis for becoming a client and for being stigmatized for moral failure or weakness.

[5]

THE ART OF SAVAGE DISCOVERY: HOW TO BLAME THE VICTIM

William Ryan

TWENTY years ago, Zero Mostel used to do a sketch in which he impersonated a Dixiecrat senator conducting an investigation of the origins of World War II. At the climax of the sketch, the senator boomed out, in an excruciating mixture of triumph and suspicion, "What was Pearl Harbor *doing* in the Pacific?" This is an extreme example of Blaming the Victim.

Twenty years ago, we could laugh at Zero Mostel's caricature. In recent years, however, the same process has been going on every day in the arena of social problems, public health, antipoverty programs, and social welfare. A philosopher might analyze this process and prove that, technically, it is comic. But it is hardly ever funny.

Consider some victims. One is the miseducated child in the slum school. He is blamed for his own miseducation. He is said to contain within himself the causes of his inability to read and write well. The shorthand phrase is "cultural deprivation," which, to those in the know, conveys what they allege to be inside information: that the poor child carries a scanty pack of intellectual baggage as he enters school. He doesn't know about books and magazines and newspapers, they say. (No books in the home: the mother fails to subscribe to *Reader's Digest*.) They say that if he talks at all—an unlikely event since slum parents don't talk to their children—he certainly doesn't talk correctly. (Lower-class dialect spoken here, or even—God forbid!—Southern black. *Ici on parle nigra*.) If you can manage to get him to sit in a chair, they say, he squirms and looks out the window. (Impulsive-ridden, these kids, motoric rather than verbal.) In a word,

From *Blaming the Victim* (New York: Random House, 1976), pp. 3–30. Reprinted by permission; copyright © 1976 William Ryan.

he is "disadvantaged" and "socially deprived," they say, and this, of course, accounts for his failure (*his* failure, they say) to learn much in school.

Note the similarity to the logic of Zero Mostel's Dixiecrat senator. What is the culturally deprived child *doing* in the school? What is wrong with the victim? In pursuing this logic, no one remembers to ask questions about the collapsing buildings and torn textbooks; the frightened, insensitive teachers; the six additional desks in the room; the blustering, frightened principals; the relentless segregation; the callous administrator; the irrelevant curriculum; the bigoted or cowardly members of the school board; the insulting history book; the stingy taxpayers; the fairy-tale readers; or the self-serving faculty of the local teachers college. We are encouraged to confine our attention to the child and to dwell on all his alleged defects. Cultural deprivation becomes an omnibus explanation for the educational disaster area known as the inner-city school. This is Blaming the Victim.

Pointing to the supposedly deviant black family as the "fundamental weakness of the black community" is another way to blame the victim. Like "cultural deprivation," "black family" has become a shorthand phrase with stereotyped connotations of matriarchy, fatherlessness, and pervasive illegitimacy. Growing up in the "crumbling" black family is supposed to account for most of the racial evils in America. Insiders have the word, of course, and know that this phrase is supposed to evoke images of growing up with a long-absent or never-present father (replaced from time to time perhaps by a series of transient lovers) and with bossy women ruling the roost, so that the children are irreparably damaged. This refers particularly to the poor, bewildered male children, whose psyches are fatally wounded and who are never, alas, to learn the trick of becoming upright, downright, forthright all-American boys. Is it any wonder the blacks cannot achieve equality? From such families! And, again, by focusing our attention on the black family as the apparent *cause* of racial inequality, our eye is diverted. Racism, discrimination, segregation, and the powerlessness of the ghetto are subtly, but thoroughly, downgraded in importance.

The generic process of Blaming the Victim is applied to almost every American problem. The miserable health care of the poor is explained away on the grounds that the victim has poor motivation and lacks health information. The problems of slum housing are traced to the characteristics of tenants who are labeled as "Southern rural migrants" not yet "acculturated" to life in the big city. The "multiproblem" poor, it is claimed, suffer the psychological effects of impoverishment, the "culture of poverty," and the deviant value system of the lower classes; consequently, though unwittingly, they cause their own troubles. From such a viewpoint, the obvious fact that poverty is primarily an absence of money is easily overlooked or set aside.

The growing number of families receiving welfare are fallaciously linked together with the increased number of illegitimate children as twin results of promiscuity and sexual abandon among members of the lower orders. Every important social problem—crime, mental illness, civil disorder, unemployment—has been analyzed within the framework of the victim-blaming ideology.

It would be possible for me to venture into other areas—one finds a perfect example in literature about the underdeveloped countries of the Third World, in which the lack of prosperity and technological progress is attributed to some aspect of the national character of the people, such as lack of "achievement motivation"—but I plan to stay within the confines of my own personal and professional experience, which is, generally, with racial injustice, social welfare, and human services in the city.

I have been listening to the victim-blamers and pondering their thought processes for a number of years. That process is often very subtle. Victim-blaming is cloaked in kindness and concern, and bears all the trappings and statistical furbelows of scientism; it is obscured by a perfumed haze of humanitarianism. In observing the process of Blaming the Victim, one tends to be confused and disoriented because those who practice this art display a deep concern for the victims that is quite genuine. In this way, the new ideology is very different from the open prejudice and reactionary tactics of the old days. Its adherents include sympathetic social scientists with social consciences in good working order, and liberal politicians with a genuine commitment to reform. They are very careful to dissociate themselves from vulgar Calvinism or crude racism; they indignantly condemn any notions of innate wickedness or genetic defect. "The black is *not born* inferior," they shout apoplectically. "Force of circumstance," they explain in reasonable tones, "has *made* him inferior." And they dismiss with self-righteous contempt any claims that the poor man in America is plainly unworthy or shiftless or enamored of idleness. No, they say, he is "caught in the cycle of poverty." He is trained to be poor by his culture and his family life, endowed by his environment (perhaps by his ignorant mother's outdated style of toilet training) with those unfortunately unpleasant characteristics that make him ineligible for a passport into the affluent society.

Blaming the Victim is, of course, quite different from old-fashioned conservative ideologies. The latter simply dismissed victims as inferior, genetically defective, or morally unfit; the emphasis is on the intrinsic, even hereditary, defect. The former shifts its emphasis to the environmental causation. The old-fashioned conservative could hold firmly to the belief that the oppressed and the victimized were born that way—"that way" being defective or inadequate in character or ability. The new ideology attributes defect and inadequacy to the malignant nature of poverty, injustice, slum life, and racial difficulties. The stigma that marks the victim and accounts for his victimization is an acquired stigma, a stigma of social, rather than genetic, origin. But the stigma, the defect, the fatal difference—though derived in the past from environmental forces—is still located *within* the victim, inside his skin. With such an elegant formulation, the humanitarian can have it both ways. He can, all at the same time, concentrate his charitable interest on the defects of the victim, condemn the vague social and environmental stresses that produced the defect (some time ago), and ignore the continuing effect of victimizing social forces (right now). It is a brilliant ideology for justifying a perverse form of social action designed to change, not society, as one might expect, but rather society's victim.

As a result, there is a terrifying sameness in the programs that arise from this kind of analysis. In education, we have programs of "compensatory education" to build up the skills and attitudes of the ghetto child, rather than structural changes in the schools. In race relations, we have social engineers who think up ways of "strengthening" the black family, rather than methods of eradicating racism. In health care, we develop new programs to provide health information (to correct the supposed ignorance of the poor) and to reach out and discover cases of untreated illness and disability (to compensate for their supposed unwillingness to seek treatment). Meanwhile, the gross inequities of our medical care delivery systems are left completely unchanged. As we might expect, the logical outcome of analyzing social problems in terms of the deficiencies of the victim is the development of programs aimed at correcting those deficiencies. The formula for action becomes extraordinarily simple: change the victim.

All of this happens so smoothly that it seems downright rational. First, identify a social problem. Second, study those affected by the problem and discover in what ways they are different from the rest of us as a consequence of deprivation and injustice. Third, define the differences as the cause of the social problem itself. Finally, of course, assign a government bureaucrat to invent a humanitarian action program to correct the differences.

Now no one in his right mind would quarrel with the assertion that social problems are present in abundance and are readily identifiable. God knows it is true that when hundreds of thousands of poor children drop out of school—or even graduate from school— they are barely literate. After spending some ten thousand hours in the company of professional educators, these children appear to have learned very little. The fact of failure in their education is undisputed. And the racial situation in America is usually acknowledged to be a number one item on the nation's agenda. Despite years of marches, commissions, judicial decisions, and endless legislative remedies, we are confronted with unchanging or even widening racial differences in achievement. In addition, despite our assertions that Americans get the best health care in the world, the poor stubbornly remain unhealthy. They lose more work because of illness, have more carious teeth, lose more babies as a result of both miscarriage and infant death, and die considerably younger than the well-to-do.

The problems are there, and there in great quantities. They make us uneasy. Added together, these disturbing signs reflect inequality and a puzzlingly high level of unalleviated distress in America totally inconsistent with our proclaimed ideals and our enormous wealth. This thread—this rope—of inconsistency stands out so visibly in the fabric of American life that it is jarring to the eye. And this must be explained, to the satisfaction of our conscience as well as our patriotism. Blaming the Victim is an ideal, almost painless, evasion.

The second step in applying this explanation is to look sympathetically at those who "have" the problem in question, to separate them out and define them in some way as a special group, a group that is *different* from the population in general. This is a crucial and essential step in the process, for that difference is in itself hampering and maladaptive. The Different Ones are seen as less competent, less skilled, less knowing—in short, less human. The ancient Greeks deducted from a single characteristic, a difference in language, that the barbarians—that is, the "babblers" who spoke a strange tongue— were wild, uncivilized, dangerous, .rapacious, uneducated, lawless, and, indeed, scarcely more than animals. Automatically labeling strangers as savages, weird and inhuman creatures (thus explaining difference by exaggerating difference) not infrequently justifies mistreatment, enslavement, or even extermination of the Different Ones.

Blaming the Victim depends on a very similar process of identification (carried out, to be sure, in the most kindly, philanthropic, and intellectual manner) whereby the victim of social problems is identified as strange, different—in other words, as a barbarian, a savage. Discovering savages, then, is an essential component of, and prerequisite to, Blaming the Victim, and the art of Savage Discovery is a core skill that must be acquired by all aspiring Victim Blamers. They must learn how to demonstrate that the poor, the black, the ill, the jobless, the slum tenants, are different and strange. They must learn to conduct or interpret the research that shows how "these people" think in different forms, act in different patterns, cling to different values, seek different goals, and learn different truths. Which is to say that they are strangers, barbarians, savages. This is how the distressed and disinherited are redefined in order to make it possible for us to look at society's problems and to attribute their causation to the individuals affected.

Blaming the Victim is an ideological process, which is to say that it is a set of ideas and concepts deriving from systematically motivated, but *unintended*, distortions of reality. In the sense that Karl Mannheim (1936) used the term, an ideology develops from the "collective unconscious" of a group or class and is rooted in a class-based interest in maintaining the status quo (as contrasted with what he calls a *utopia*, a set of ideas rooted in a class-based interest in *changing* the status quo). An ideology, then, has several components. First, there is the belief system itself, the way of looking at the world, the set of ideas and concepts. Second, there is the systematic distortion of reality reflected in those ideas. Third is the condition that the distortion must not be a conscious, intentional process. Finally, though it is not intentional, the ideas must serve a specific function: maintaining the status quo in the interest of a specific group. Blaming the Victim fits this definition on all counts. Most particularly, it is important to realize that Blaming the Victim is not a process of *intentional* distortion although it does serve the class interests of those who practice it. And it has a rich ancestry in American thought about social problems and how to deal with them.

Thinking about social problems is especially susceptible to ideological influences since, as John Seeley (1967) has pointed out, defining a social problem is not so simple. "What is a social problem?" may seem an ingenuous question until one turns to confront its opposite: "What human problem is *not* a social problem?" Since any problem in which people are involved is social, why do we reserve the label for some problems in which people are involved and withhold it from others? To use Seeley's example, why is crime called a social problem when university administration is not? The phenomena we look at are bounded by the act of definition. They become social problems only by being so considered. In Seeley's words, *"naming* it as a problem, after naming it as a *problem."*

It is only recently, for example, that we have begun to *name* the rather large quantity of people on earth as the *problem* of overpopulation, or the population explosion. Such phenomena often become proper predicaments for certain solutions, certain treatments. Before the 1930s, the most anti-Semitic German was unaware that Germany had a "Jewish problem." It took the Nazis to *name* the simple existence of Jews in the Third Reich as a "social problem," and that act of definition helped to shape the final solution.

We have removed "immigration" from our list of social problems (after executing a solution—choking off the flow of immigrants) and have added "urbanization." Nowadays, we define the situation of men out of work as the social problem of "unemployment" rather than, as in Elizabethan times, that of "idleness." (The McCone Commission, investigating the Watts Riot of 1966, showed how hard old ideologies die; it specified both unemployment *and* idleness as causes of the disorder.) In the near future, if we are to credit the prophets of automation, the label "unemployment" will fade away and "idleness," now renamed the "leisure-time problem," will begin again to raise its lazy head. We have been comfortable for years with the "black problem," a term that clearly implies that the existence of blacks is somehow a problematic fact. *Ebony Magazine* turned the tables and renamed the phenomenon as "The White Problem in America," which may be a good deal more accurate.

We must particularly ask, "To whom are social problems a prob-

lem?" And usually, if truth were to be told, we would have to admit
that we mean they are a problem to those of us who are outside the
boundaries of what we have defined as the problem. Blacks are a
problem to racist whites, welfare is a problem to stingy taxpayers,
delinquency is a problem to nervous property owners.

Now, if this is the quality of our assumptions about social problems,
we are led unerringly to certain beliefs about the causes of these
problems. We cannot comfortably believe that we are the cause of
that which is problematic to us; therefore, we are almost compelled
to believe that *they*—the problematic ones—are the cause, and this
immediately prompts us to search for deviance. Identification of the
deviance as the cause of the problem is a simple step that ordinarily
does not even require evidence.

C. Wright Mills (1943) analyzed the ideology of those who write
about social problems and demonstrated the relationship of their
texts to class interest and to the preservation of the existent social
order. In shifting the material in thirty-one widely used textbooks in
"social problems," "social pathology," and "social disorganization,"
Mills found a pervasive, coherent ideology with a number of common
characteristics.

First, the textbooks present material about these problems, he says,
in simple, descriptive terms, with each problem unrelated to the
others and none related in any meaningful way to other aspects of
the social environment. Second, the problems are selected and
described largely according to predetermined norms. Poverty is a
problem in that it deviates from the standard of economic self-
sufficiency; divorce is a problem because the family is supposed to
remain intact; crime and delinquency are problematic in so far as
they depart from the accepted moral and legal standards of the
community. The norms themselves are taken as givens, and no effort
is made to examine them. Nor is there any thought given to the
manner in which norms might themselves contribute to the development of the problems. (In a society in which everyone is assumed
and expected to be economically self-sufficient, as an example,
doesn't economic dependency automatically mean poverty? No attention is given to such issues.)

Within such a framework, then, deviation from norms and standards comes to be defined as failed or incomplete socialization—
failure to learn the rules or the inability to learn how to keep them.
Those with social problems are then viewed as unable or unwilling

to adjust to society's standards, which are narrowly conceived by what Mills calls "independent middle-class persons verbally living out Protestant ideas in a small-town America." This, obviously, is a precise description of the social origins and status of almost every one of the authors.

In defining social problems in this way, the social pathologists are, of course, ignoring a whole set of factors that ordinarily might be considered relevant—for instance, unequal distribution of income, social stratification, political struggle, ethnic and racial group conflict, and inequality of power. Their ideology concentrates almost exclusively on the failure of the deviant. To the extent that society plays any part in social problems, it is said to have somehow failed to socialize the individual, to teach him how to adjust to circumstances which, though far from perfect, are gradually changing for the better. Mills's essay provides a solid foundation for understanding the concept of Blaming the Victim.

This way of thinking on the part of "social pathologists," which Mills identified as the predominant tool used in *analyzing* social problems, also saturates the majority of programs that have been developed to solve social problems in America. These programs are based on the assumption that *individuals* "have" social problems as a result of some kind of unusual circumstances—accident, illness, personal defect or handicap, character flaw or maladjustment—that exclude them from using the ordinary mechanisms for maintaining and advancing themselves. For example, the prevalent belief in America is that, under normal circumstances, everyone can obtain sufficient income for the necessities of life. Those who are unable to do so are special deviant cases, persons who for one reason or another are not able to adapt themselves to the generally satisfactory income-producing system. In times gone by these persons were further classified into the worthy poor—the lame, the blind, the young mother whose husband died in an accident, the aged man no longer able to work—and the unworthy poor—the lazy, the unwed mother and her illegitimate children, the malingerer. All were seen, however, as individuals who, for good reasons or bad, were personal failures, unable to adapt themselves to the system.

In America health care, too, has been predominantly a matter of particular remedial attention provided individually to the more or less random group of persons who have become ill, whose bodily functioning has become deviant and abnormal. In the field of mental health, the same approach has been, and continues to be, dominant. The social problem of mental disease has been viewed as a collection of individual cases of deviance, persons who—through unusual hereditary taint, or exceptional distortion of character—have become unfit for normal activities. The solution to these problems was to segregate the deviants, to protect them, to give them *asylum* from the life of the community for which they were no longer competent.

This has been the dominant style in American social welfare and health activities, then: to treat what we call social problems, such as poverty, disease, and mental illness, in terms of the individual deviance of the special, unusual groups of persons who had those problems. There has also been a competing style, however—much less common, not at all congruent with the prevalent ideology, but continually developing parallel to the dominant style.

Adherents of this approach tended to search for defects in the community and the environment rather than in the individual; to emphasize predictability and usualness rather than random deviance; they tried to think about preventing rather than merely repairing or treating—to see social problems, in a word, as social. In the field of disease, this approach was termed public health, and its practitioners sought the cause of disease in such things as the water supply, the sewage system, the density and quality of housing conditions. They set out to prevent disease, not in individuals, but in the total population, through improved sanitation, inoculation against communicable diseases, and the policing of housing conditions. In the field of income maintenance, this secondary style of solving social problems focused on poverty as a predictable event, on the regularities of income deficiency. And it concentrated on the development of standard, generalized programs affecting total groups. Rather than trying to fit the aged worker ending his career into some kind of category of special cases, it assumed all sixty-five-year-old men should expect to retire from the world of work and have the security of an old age pension, to be arranged through public social activity. Unemployment insurance was developed as a method whereby all workers could be protected against the effects of the normal ups and downs of the business cycle. A man out of work could then count on an unemployment check rather than endure the agony of pauperizing himself, selling his tools or his car, and finding himself in the special category of those deserving of charity.

These two approaches to the solution of social problems have existed side by side, the former always dominant, but the latter gradually expanding, slowly becoming more and more prevalent.

Elsewhere I (1969; see Wilensky and Lebeaux 1965) have proposed the dimension of *exceptionalism-universalism* as the ideological under-pinning for these two contrasting approaches to the analysis and solution of social problems. The *exceptionalist* viewpoint is reflected in arrangements that are private, voluntary, remedial, special, local, and exclusive. Such arrangements imply that problems occur to specially defined categories of persons in an unpredictable manner. The problems are unusual, even unique, they are exceptions to the rule, they occur as a result of individual defect, accident, or unfortunate circumstance and must be remedied by means that are particular and, as it were, tailored to the individual case.

The universalistic viewpoint, on the other hand, is reflected in arrangements that are public, legislated, promotive or preventive, general, national, and inclusive. Inherent in such a viewpoint is the idea that social problems are a function of the social arrangements of the community or the society and that, since these social arrangements are quite imperfect and inequitable, such problems are both predictable and, more important, preventable through public action. They are not unique to the individual, and the fact that they encompass individual persons does not imply that those persons are themselves defective or abnormal.

Consider these two contrasting approaches as they are applied to the problem of smallpox. The medical care approach is exceptionalistic; it is designed to provide remedial treatment to the special category of persons who are afflicted with the disease through a private, voluntary arrangement with a local doctor. The universalistic public health approach is designed to provide preventive inoculation to the total population, ordered by legislation and available through public means if no private arrangements can be made.

A similar contrast can be made between an exceptionalistic program such as Aid to Families with Dependent Children and the universalistic program of family allowances based simply on the number of children in a family. The latter assumes that the size of a family should automatically be a consideration in income supplementation, since it is in no way taken into account in the wage structure, and that it should be dealt with in a routine and universal fashion. The

AFDC program, on the other hand, assumes that families need income assistance only as a result of special, impoverishing circumstances.

Fluoridation is universalistic; it is aimed at preventing caries in the total population; oral surgery is exceptionalistic, designed to remedy the special cases of infection or neglect that damage the teeth of an individual. Birth control is universalistic; abortion, exceptionalistic. It has been said that navigational aids have saved far more lives than have rescue devices, no matter how refined they might be. The compass, then, is universalistic, while the lifeboat is exceptionalistic.

The similarity between exceptionalism and what Mills called the "ideology of social pathologists" is readily apparent. Indeed, the ideological potential of the exceptionalist viewpoint is unusually great. If one is inclined to explain all instances of deviance, all social problems, all occasions on which help is provided to others as the result of unusual circumstances, defect, or accident, one is unlikely to inquire about social inequalities.

This is not to devalue valid exceptionalistic services. Despite fluoridation, some instances of caries and gum disease will require attention; despite excellent prenatal care, handicapped children will occasionally be born; husbands will doubtless continue to die unexpectedly at early ages, leaving widows and orphans in need. And at any given moment, the end products of society's malfunctioning— the miseducated teenager, the unskilled adult laborer, the child brain-damaged as a result of prenatal neglect—will require service that is predominantly exceptionalistic in nature.

The danger in the exceptionalistic viewpoint is in its impact on social policy when it becomes the dominant component in social analysis. Blaming the Victim occurs exclusively within an exceptionalistic framework, and it consists of applying exceptionalistic explanations to universalistic problems. This represents an illogical departure from fact, a method, in Mannheim's words, of systematically distorting reality, of developing an ideology.

Blaming the Victim can take its place in a long series of American ideologies that have rationalized cruelty and injustice.

Slavery, for example, was justified—even praised—on the basis of a complex ideology that showed quite conclusively how useful slavery was to society and how uplifting it was for the slaves (Newby 1965). Eminent physicians could be relied upon to provide the biological justification for slavery since after all, they said, the slaves were a separate species, just as, for example, cattle are a separate species. No one in his right mind would dream of freeing the cows and fighting to abolish the ownership of cattle. In the view of the average American of 1825, it was important to preserve slavery, not simply because it was in accord with his own group interests (he was not fully aware of that), but because reason and logic showed clearly to the reasonable and intelligent man that slavery was good. In order to persuade a good and moral man to *do* evil, then, it is not necessary first to persuade him to *become* evil. It is only necessary to teach him that he is doing good. No one, in the words of a legendary newspaperman, thinks of himself as a son of a bitch.

In late nineteenth-century America there flowered another ideology of injustice that seemed rational and just to the decent, progressive person. But Hofstadter's (1955) analysis of the phenomenon of Social Darwinism shows clearly its functional role in the preservation of the status quo. One can scarcely imagine a better fit than the one between this ideology and the purposes and actions of the robber barons, who descended like piranha fish on the America of this era and picked its bones clean. Their extraordinarily unethical operations netted them not only hundreds of millions of dollars, but also, perversely, the adoration of the nation. Behavior that would be, in any more rational land (including today's America), more than enough to have landed them all in jail, was praised as the very model for a captain of modern industry. And the philosophy that justified their thievery was such that John D. Rockefeller could actually stand up and preach it in church. Listen as he speaks in, of all places, Sunday school:

The growth of a large business is merely a survival of the fittest. . . . The American Beauty rose can be produced in the splendor and fragrance which bring cheer to its beholder only by sacrificing the early buds which grow up around it. This is not an evil tendency in business. It is merely the working-out of a law of nature and a law of God (Ghent 1902).

This was the core of the gospel, adapted analogically from Darwin's writings on evolution. Herbert Spencer and, later, William Graham Sumner and other beginners in the social sciences considered Darwin's work to be directly applicable to social processes: ultimately, as a guarantee that life was progressing toward perfection but, in the short run, as a justification for an absolutely uncontrolled laissez-faire economic system. The central concepts of "survival of the fittest," "natural selection," and "gradualism" were exalted in Rock-efeller's preaching on the status of laws of God and Nature. Not only did this ideology justify the criminal rapacity of those who rose to the top of the industrial heap, defining them automatically as naturally superior (this was bad enough), but at the same time it also required that those at the bottom of the heap be labeled as patently *unfit*—a label based solely on their position in society. According to the law of natural selection, they should be, in Spencer's (1864:414) judgment, eliminated. "The whole effort of nature is to get rid of such, to clear the world of them and make room for better."

For a generation, Social Darwinism was the orthodox doctrine in the social sciences, such as they were at that time. Opponents of this ideology were shut out of respectable intellectual life. The philosophy that enabled John D. Rockefeller to justify himself self-righteously in front of a class of Sunday school children was not the product of an academic quack or marginal crackpot philosopher. It came directly from the lectures and books of leading intellectual figures of the time, occupants of professorial chairs at Harvard and Yale. Such is the power of an ideology that so neatly fits the needs of the dominant interests of society.

If one is to think about ideologies in America, one must be prepared to consider the possibility that a body of ideas that might seem almost self-evident is, in fact, highly distorted and highly selective; one must allow that the inclusion of a specific formulation in every freshman sociology text does not guarantee that the particular formulation represents abstract truth rather than group interest. It is important not to delude ourselves into thinking that ideological monstrosities were constructed by monsters. They were not; they are not. They are developed through a process that shows every sign of being valid scholarship, complete with tables of numbers, copious footnotes, and scientific terminology. Ideologies are quite often academically and socially respectable and in many instances hold positions of exclusive validity, so that disagreement is considered unrespectable or radical and risks being labeled as irresponsible, unenlightened, or trashy.

Blaming the Victim holds such a position. It is central in the mainstream of contemporary American social thought, and its ideas pervade our most crucial assumptions so thoroughly that they are hardly noticed. Moreover, the fruits of this ideology appear to be fraught with altruism and humanitarianism, so it is hard to believe that it has principally functioned to block social change.

A major pharmaceutical manufacturer, as an act of humanitarian concern, has distributed copies of a large poster warning "LEAD PAINT CAN KILL!" The poster, featuring a photograph of the face of a charming little girl, goes on to explain that if children *eat* lead paint, it can poison them, they can develop serious symptoms, suffer permanent brain damage, even die. The health department of a major American city has put out a coloring book that provides the same information. While the poster urges parents to prevent their children from eating paint, the coloring book is more vivid. It labels as neglectful and thoughtless the mother who does not keep her infant under constant surveillance to keep it from eating paint chips.

Now, no one would argue against the idea that it is important to spread knowledge about the danger of eating paint in order that parents might act to forestall their children from doing so. But to campaign against lead paint *only* in these terms is destructive and misleading and, in a sense, an effective way to support and agree with slum landlords—who define the problem of lead poisoning in precisely these terms.

This is an example of applying an exceptionalistic solution to a universalistic problem. It is not accurate to say that lead poisoning results from the actions of individual neglectful mothers. Rather, lead poisoning is a social phenomenon supported by a number of social mechanisms, one of the most tragic by-products of the systematic toleration of slum housing. In New Haven, which has the highest reported rate of lead poisoning in the country, several small children have died and many others have incurred irreparable brain damage as a result of eating peeling paint. In several cases, when the landlord failed to make repairs, poisonings have occurred time and again through a succession of tenancies. And the major reason for the landlord's neglect of this problem was that the city agency responsible for enforcing the housing code did nothing to make him correct this dangerous condition.

The cause of the poisoning is the lead in the paint on the walls of the apartment in which the children live. The presence of the lead is illegal. To use lead paint in a residence is illegal; to permit lead paint to be exposed in a residence is illegal. It is not only illegal, it is potentially criminal, since the housing code does not provide for criminal penalties. The general problem of lead poisoning, then, is more accurately analyzed as the result of a systematic program of lawbreaking by one interest group in the community, with the toleration and encouragement of the public authority charged with enforcing that law. To ignore these continued and repeated law violations, to ignore the fact that the supposed law enforcer actually cooperates in lawbreaking, and then to load a burden of guilt on the mother of a dead or dangerously ill child is an egregious distortion of reality. And to do so under the guise of public-spirited and humanitarian service to the community is intolerable.

But this is how Blaming the Victim works. The righteous humanitarian concern displayed by the drug company, with its poster, and the health department, with its coloring book, is a genuine concern, and this is a typical feature of Blaming the Victim. Also typical is the swerving away from the central target that requires systematic change and, instead, focusing in on the individual affected. The ultimate effect is always to distract attention from the basic causes and to leave the primary social injustice untouched. And, most telling, the proposed remedy for the problem is, of course, to work on the victim himself. Prescriptions for cure, as written by the Savage Discovery set, are invariably conceived to revamp and revise the victim, never to change the surrounding circumstances. They want to change his attitudes, alter his values, fill up his cultural deficits, energize his apathetic soul, cure his character defects, train him and polish him and woo him from his savage ways.

Isn't all of this more subtle and sophisticated than such old-fashioned ideologies as Social Darwinism? Doesn't the change from the brutal ideas about survival of the fit (and the expiration of the unfit) to kindly concern about characterological defects (brought about by stigmas of social origin) seem like a substantial step forward? Hardly. It is only a substitution of terms. The old, reactionary, exceptionalistic formulations are replaced by new, progressive, humanitarian, exceptionalistic formulations. In education, the outmoded and unacceptable concept of racial or class differences in basic inherited intellectual ability simply gives way to the new notion of cultural deprivation: there is very little functional difference between these two ideas. In taking a look at the phenomenon of poverty, the old concept of unfitness or idleness or laziness is replaced by the newfangled theory of the culture deprivation: there is very little functional difference between these two ideas. In taking a look at the phenomenon of poverty, the old concept of unfitness or idleness or laziness is replaced by the newfangled theory of the culture of poverty. In race relations, plain black inferiority—which was good enough for old-fashioned conservatives—is pushed aside by fancy conceits about the crumbling black family. With regard to illegitmacy, we are not so crass as to concern ourselves with immorality and vice, as in the old days; we settle benignly on the explanation of the "lower-class pattern of sexual behavior," which no one condemns as evil, but which is, in fact, simply a variation of the old explanatory idea. Mental illness is no longer defined as the result of hereditary taint or congenital character flaw; now we have new causal hypotheses regarding the ego-damaging emotional experiences that are supposed to be the inevitable consequence of the deplorable child-rearing practices of the poor.

In each case, of course, we are persuaded to ignore the obvious: the continued blatant discrimination against the black, the gross deprivation of contraceptive and adoption services to the poor, the heavy stresses endemic in the life of the poor. And almost all our make-believe liberal programs aimed at correcting our urban problems are off target; they are designed either to change the poor man or to cool him out.

We come finally to the question: Why? It is much easier to understand the process of Blaming the Victim as a way of thinking than it is to understand the motivation for it. Why do Victim Blamers, who are usually good people, blame the victim? The development and application of this ideology, and of all the mythologies associated with Savage Discovery, are readily exposed by careful analysis as hostile acts—one is almost tempted to say acts of war—directed against the disadvantaged, the distressed, the disinherited. It is class warfare in reverse. Yet those who are most fascinated and enchanted by this ideology tend to be progressive, humanitarian, and, in the best sense of the word, charitable persons. They would usually define themselves as moderates or liberals. Why do they pursue this dreadful war against the poor and the oppressed?

Put briefly, the answer can be formulated best in psychological terms—or, at least, I, as a psychologist, am more comfortable with such a formulation. The highly charged psychological problem confronting this hypothetical progressive charitable person I am talking about is that of reconciling his own self-interest with the promptings of his humanitarian impulses. This psychological process of reconciliation is not worked out in a logical, rational, conscious way; it is a process that takes place far below the level of sharp consciousness, and the solution—Blaming the Victim—is arrived at subconsciously as a compromise that apparently satisfies both his self-interest and his charitable concerns. Let me elaborate.

First is the question of self-interest or, more accurately, class interest. The typical Victim Blamer is a middle-class person who is doing reasonably well in a material way; he has a good job, a good income, a good house, a good car. Basically, he likes the social system pretty much the way it is, at least in broad outline. He likes the two-party political system, though he may be highly skilled in finding a thousand minor flaws in its functioning. He heartily approves of the profit motive as the propelling engine of the economic system despite his awareness that there are abuses of that system, negative side effects, and substantial residual inequalities.

On the other hand, he is acutely aware of poverty, racial discrimination, exploitation, and deprivation, and, moreover, he wants to do something concrete to ameliorate the condition of the poor, the black, and the disadvantaged. This is not an extraneous concern; it is central to his value system to insist on the worth of the individual, the equality of men, and the importance of justice.

What is to be done, then? What intellectual position can he take and what line of action can he follow that will satisfy both of these important motivations? He quickly and self-consciously rejects two obvious alternatives, which he defines as "extremes." He cannot side with an openly reactionary, repressive position that accepts continued oppression and exploitation as the price of a privileged position for his own class. This is incompatible with his own morality and his basic political principles. He finds the extreme conservative position repugnant.

He is, if anything, more allergic to radicals, however, than he is to reactionaries. He rejects the "extreme" solution of radical social change, and this makes sense since such radical social change threatens his own well-being. A more equitable distribution of income might mean that he would have less—a smaller or older house, with fewer yews or no rhododendrons in the yard, a less enjoyable job, or, at the least, a somewhat smaller salary. If black children and poor children were, in fact, reasonably educated and began to get high Scholastic Aptitude Tests (S.A.T.) scores, they would be competing with *his* children for the scarce places in the entering classes of Harvard, Columbia, Bennington, and Antioch.

So our potential Victim Blamers are in a dilemma. In the words of an old Yiddish proverb, they are trying to dance at two weddings. They are old friends of both brides and fond of both kinds of dancing, and they want to accept both invitations. They cannot bring themselves to attack the system that has been so good to them, but they want so badly to be helpful to the victims of racism and economic injustice.

Their solution is a brilliant compromise. They turn their attention to the victim in his postvictimized state. They want to bind up wounds, inject penicillin, administer morphine, and evacuate the wounded for rehabilitation. They explain what's wrong with the victim in terms of social experiences *in the past*, experiences that have left wounds, defects, paralysis, and disability. And they take the cure of these wounds and the reduction of these disabilities as the first order of business. They want to make the victims less vulnerable, send them back into battle with better weapons, thicker armor, a higher level of morale.

In order to do so effectively, of course, they must analyze the victims carefully, dispassionately, objectively, scientifically, empathetically, mathematically, and hardheadedly, to see what made them so vulnerable in the first place.

What weapons, now, might they have lacked when they went into battle? Job skills? Education?

What armor was lacking that might have warded off their wounds? Better values? Habits of thrift and foresight?

And what might have ravaged their morale? Apathy? Ignorance? Deviant low-class cultural patterns?

This is the solution of the dilemma, the solution of Blaming the Victim. And those who buy this solution with a sigh of relief are inevitably blinding themselves to the basic causes of the problems being addressed. They are, most crucially, rejecting the possibility of blaming, not the victims, but themselves. They are all unconsciously passing judgments on themselves and bringing in a unanimous verdict of Not Guilty.

If one comes to believe that the culture of poverty produces persons *fated* to be poor, who can find any fault with our corporation-dominated economy? And if the black family produces young men *incapable* of achieving equality, let's deal with that first before we go on to the tasks of changing the pervasive racism that informs and shapes and distorts our every social institution. And if unsatisfactory resolution of one's Oedipus complex accounts for all emotional distress and mental disorder, then by all means let us attend to that and postpone worrying about the pounding day-to-day stresses of life on the bottom rungs that drive so many to drink, dope, and madness.

That is the ideology of Blaming the Victim, the cunning Art of Savage Discovery. The tragic, frightening truth is that it is a mythology that is winning over the best people of our time, the very people who must resist this ideological temptation if we are to achieve nonviolent change in America.

[6]

SOCIETAL VALUES AND SOCIAL POLICY: IMPLICATIONS FOR SOCIAL WORK

John E. Tropman

ONE of the limitations of the social work enterprise as it has developed in the United States is a lack of understanding about, and concern with, the context of values and beliefs which form the social policy within which it operates. It would be useful to explore the larger context within which we have developed a social welfare structure in this country to understand why it developed as it did. We need to ask, as Heilbroner (1970:15; see Tropman 1971a) asks: "Why is the United States, which is a leader country in so many areas, so far behind in the provision of social welfare benefits?" Indeed, one needs to look at the cultural structure as the largest system within which social policy is made, within which social welfare programs develop and succeed or fail, and within which the social welfare system attempts to provide a variety of kinds of aid to meet a variety of needs (see Schorr and Baumheier 1971:1361–67).

Social Policy, the Social Welfare System, and Minority Groups

The advent of the 1960s brought about the realization that there were subgroups within American society which were cut off in one way or another from access to some of the main benefits offered by the society. Generally, we can consider such groups minorities—whether the basis is racial difference, ethnic identification, regional location (such as Appalachia), or status positions ("lower class"). In a variety of ways the special needs of these groups were brought to the attention of the American public, and were accorded a salience, legitimacy, and identity which had not hitherto been possible. None of these minorities was new, or even recent, to the American scene, so the awakening of interest in them could not be considered acknowledgment of new elements in the system, but rather recognition, through redefinition, of elements always present. Embarrassingly enough, the social welfare profession found itself with as little special knowledge and technology relating to minority groups as anyone else in the system, notwithstanding the fact that social workers had been dealing with the individuals in these groups for fifty years. It seems fair enough to state that there had been a social policy of nonrecognition of minority groups.

It was only as recently as 1959 that the implications of "lower-class culture" for social work practice were considered in any detail (Gursslin, Hunt, and Roach 1959; Miller 1959). It is not surprising in a society which does not like to acknowledge the existence of social classes that the implications of this structure for intervention were slow in coming. Indeed, the forty-year index of the *Social Service Review* (1968:59, 67–68, 80, 83–84) lists ninety-eight entries under "social casework," one under "social class," and two (one article and one letter about the article) under culture. One article and four "notes" appear on the topic of race. Nothing appears on ethnic groups as such, although there are nineteen entries on the topic of immigration, mainly in the early issues.

What accounts for this lack of focus on the part of the social welfare enterprise? Following Schorr and Baumheier, who note that "social policies are . . . influenced by and themselves influence beliefs, values, customs and tradition," we shall argue that there are certain key elements in the American value structure—both structural and substantive—which hindered development in this direction. Indeed, some key American values like equality prevented the social work enterprise specifically, and society generally, from recognizing the special needs of minority groups.[1] We must realize, too, that only certain minorities suffered from the policy of nonrecognition. Minorities of wealth and power were sought by the welfare system in a variety of roles, as they were by the society at large. Hence, we must explore not only the general lack of attention given to certain minority groups, but also the special characteristics of some minority groups which single them out for a combination of inattention and scorn. It is to this effort that we now turn.

The American Value Structure

American values—or American culture, if that term is the more appropriate one—are an immensely complicated set of beliefs, values, norms, laws, and customs, within which we all live and carry out daily tasks (see Williams 1961:415–68). To attempt to capture it in any complete way would be impossible in a short essay such as this, especially if one is attempting to develop implications for the structure of the social welfare profession. It seems more appropriate, therefore, to select aspects of the value system which appear to have had a very salient effect on the development of the welfare enterprise, and to suggest briefly the nature of this effect.

Two aspects of the value system appear worthy of exploration: one key dimension reflects something about the structure of that system, and a second relates to the substance of a particular value pattern. It is important to distinguish between structural and substantive properties here. For example, value systems may be integrated or disparate, applicable or suffering from "cultural lag," explicit or vague, and so on.

These are structural properties which do not involve the analysis of any substantive content. Substantively, values do have particular directions. For example, under certain conditions they may condone or prohibit murder. They may support individual responsibility and "mastery" of the life space, or they may argue that "all is in the hands of the gods." The effect of structural factors is as important as the effect of the particular substantive directions mandated by values. Each has had its effect on the development of social policy, and on the approach of the social work enterprise to minority groups. We shall first consider the structural effects, then follow some of the directions shaped by particular values.

VALUES IN CONFLICT

In any consideration of American values one must immediately note that, perhaps more than anything else, the value system is characterized by conflicting values and a lack of consistency within the value framework. The value of equality is countered by "racism and group superiority themes" within the culture (Williams 1961:466). Moral judgments about those who have somehow failed to "make it" in the success/achievement mobility race are softened by values advocating humanitarian approaches to people. In particular, our view toward the poor is at once mean and compassionate (see Fritchey 1971). Thousands of dollars will be donated to help a poor family if its plight becomes public through the press, yet welfare grants have never been adequate, and welfare officials are criticized as working to undermine "the will to work" (see Weiner et al. 1971). There exists a basic ambivalence within the American value system, an ambivalence which permits differing opposed, yet legitimate, values to be espoused. And nowhere is that ambivalence more acute than in its application to clients of the social welfare enterprise. It is this broad group which bears the brunt of humanitarianism and moral condemnation, of equality and racism, of nationalism and ethnic pride. It becomes obvious that the values espoused by the social work enterprise—concern, understanding, help for people in need—have countervalues which undermine the legitimacy of the effort. It becomes especially difficult to develop policy and programs of any consistency based upon these values because the programs immediately are criticized on the basis of alternative ones. The war on poverty, based upon humanitarian mores, secured only a fraction of the resources of the war in Vietnam which was based upon values of nationalism. Value conflict has presented a special problem for minority groups. As programs were considered which might take account of their special situations, the proposals were countered with invocations to the value of equality.

DOMINANCE, SUBDOMINANCE, AND UNCERTAINTY

To say that values are in conflict, however, does not mean that the conflicting values have the same degree of legitimacy and extensivity. If we regard success, achievement, and progress as dominant themes in the American values structure, then it seems appropriate to regard some of the values which mediate the full force of that value structure as subdominant—important, but of a lesser order of importance (Williams 1961:417, 431). It is for this reason that the value of humanitarianism never seems fully to counter the values of achievement, and it may well be the reason that we can often observe generous and humanitarian acts on an idiosyncratic basis, but find it so difficult to establish continuous and ongoing programs on this basis.

Subdominance does not at all suggest that the values are marginal to the system, but simply that they are not as strongly held. But it is precisely because they have the effect of mitigating the full effect of the main values that they become themselves suspect, and subject to criticism perhaps more than the dominant value cluster.

Finally, the structural property of value heteronomy, the simple fact that one cannot be sure at what times, places, and in what ways it is appropriate to invoke what values, induces its own echelon of difficulties. The uncertainty implicit in value conflict makes us hesitant to advance new programs, especially for unpopular groups. It is particularly problematic for welfare professionals, because we are often dealing with people who did not succeed, or who are having difficulty moving along the normal gradients (Vinter 1963:5).

Value conflict, then, serves to undermine, or at least create ambiguity around, some of the policies and programs developed within the framework of the social welfare enterprise. The conflict alone, however, is not a sufficient basis on which to understand the relationship between the value structure and social policy. One must take into account the fact that the value cluster with which we most often are associated occupies an important, but subdominant, status within the American value system. When "business concerns" square off against humanitarian ones, the adage "business is business" often seems to apply. Finally, the general uncertainty developed by the situation of value conflict and subdominance tended, it seems, to lead to conservatism and entrenchment. When one is uncertain whether something will be acceptable, and there is a possibility of being seriously criticized for undertaking it, the tendency is to remain with the status quo.

Minority groups have suffered from inattention based on some of these structural concerns. As we mentioned, the possibility of developing special programs were countered by other values. Because of their minority status, there was no possibility of building broad support in the system for their interests. Hence, they suffered from a version of the subdominance motif in the system, at the same time that the values invoked to help them would be themselves subdominant. Finally, in the face of uncertainty, we simply did not act, perhaps too secure in the knowledge that there was cultural justification. At this point, we should look at specific values and their implications.

Six Critical Values for the Social Welfare Enterprise

The influence of value conflict, subdominance, and uncertainty would not alone have led to the policy of ignoring the special problems of minority groups within social work, had there not been some positive support for this course in the very nature of the value structure itself. There are, in particular, six major value constellations which have had the effect of encouraging this approach: (1) the melting pot; (2) the land of opportunity; (3) individualism; (4) nationalism/patriotism; (5) problem moralism; (6) religious freedom (Williams 1961). Let us consider each in turn.

THE MELTING POT

The belief and hope that America was a land in which all groups and races "melted" into an American nationality has long been a major value. As early as 1782 Crevecoeur, in *Letters from an American Farmer* noted that "here individuals of all nations are melted into a new race of men" (Glazer and Moynihan 1963:288). By 1908 the notion had been expressed in a famous Broadway play by Israel Zangwill, entitled *The Melting Pot*. Oddly enough, this emphasis continued despite numerous observations over the years that it was not acutally the case (see Fairchild 1926; Hamison 1880; Kennedy 1944; Steinfeld 1970). Withal, it is only recently that minority groups have begun to make a case for themselves as minority groups, rather than on the basis of their similarity to central tendencies in American culture. The slogan "Black is Beautiful" serves as one example. (For a treatment of the middle-European ethnic see Novak 1971b.) Blended with the melting pot idea was the one Williams calls external conformity. He comments (1961:453) that "the very heterogeneity of American culture tends to produce a stress upon external conformity." Naturally, this value made it difficult to mount special programs which would have appeared to be highlighting, rather than suppressing, the differences between minority racial and ethnic groups and the main culture. The goal, particularly for immigrant minorities, was "Americanization" as soon as possible, with emphasis on developing "external conformity" to American values and languages (see Bogardus 1919).

It seems reasonable, then, that policy governing the treatment of minority groups within the social work enterprise would follow "melting pot" ideology and would tend to ignore their special problems and difficulties, focusing, as with the foreign-born, on ways to help them become Americanized.

THE LAND OF OPPORTUNITIES

One very widely valued belief in America is that this is the "land of opportunity." In some sense, it means as well that anyone can be successful. As a practical matter, it has meant a denial, for a considerable period of time, that there was serious poverty in the United States. As late as 1958, John K. Galbraith was arguing that poverty was not a national problem. In 1959, the year after the book (Galbraith 1958) was published, there were 21.5 percent of American families with incomes of $3000 a year or less (U.S. Bureau of the Census 1963b). As late as 1967, about 15 percent of the families in this country were poor, and about 2.5 percent were receiving AFDC (Tropman 1971b). It was not until Dwight MacDonald's (1967) review of Michael Harrington's book *The Other America* that this idea suffered appreciable contradictions. We simply have not recognized in this country the extent of poverty, and have not been prepared to deal with the number of poor, nor to regard them as having any special category of difficulty. The value of equality, which we also hold, further complicated development of social policy which would specifically address the problems of the poor. It is true, of course, that we have had a variety of special programs which meet the needs of some poor, somewhat, at some times, and in some places. But there is certainly no uniformity in this *ad hoc* arrangement of programs, nothing that could be called a unifying policy. Strange as it may seem, social work has tended to ignore the poor. And we have had to struggle, as the problems of the public welfare program so amply attest, to maintain the limited support of others. Part of the reason for this nonrecognition lies in the value of the availability of opportunity.

INDIVIDUALISM

America is a land of individualists. We believe that the individual is the relevant unit, and it is he who makes decisions and must, therefore, stand or fall by those decisions. It is the individual who must prove himself through work, and the individual for whom opportunities are supposedly equal, or at least present. Within the social work enterprise, little is clearer than the effect of the individualistic ethic. For many years, after an initial flirtation with the Social Gospel movement, we became very interested in the individual dynamics of the individual person. Just recall those ninety-eight citations on social casework in the *Social Service Review* as an example. The external conditions, such as sex, social status, racial identification, or ethnic identification, meant relatively less than the person himself, and his internal processes. The social welfare enterprise developed very much toward providing professionals to counsel on an individual basis. The areas which worked on more broadly external matters—community organization and social policy—have been long in coming. There is no better example of the implementation of the ethic of individualism than the structure of the public welfare system—the very thought that casework is the appropriate method provides an example of the focus on the individual. The lack of attention to the logistics of such an enterprise—how many caseworkers we would actually need if most of the poor people in this country were to be assigned one—demonstrates the lack of sensitivity to the extent of poverty. And the focus on individual, interpersonal attention to single "clients" based upon "relationship" tends to exclude such things as race, ethnicity, and so forth.

NATIONALISM-PATRIOTISM

Nationalism/patriotism, as Williams (1961:456) points out, has two key facets. One facet, important enough for social policy, is the simple loyalty to the United States. It had a most serious effect on ethnic groups, making it quite difficult to develop special programs and technologies. It could seem as if one were promoting, however indirectly, loyalty to another nation-state. And it should not be forgotten that within the past sixty years we have been engaged in two wars with Central European countries, something which not only heightens an emphasis on pro-America orientations, but simultaneously makes a focus on ethnicity all the more suspect.

This facet alone would have hampered systematic attention to minority, and especially ethnic, groups on the social policy side, but it was augmented by an evolving identification between "nationalism" and the "central features of American life." In this latter sense, criticism of any feature of "the system" becomes a treasonous offense, provoking the strongest reactions (Williams 1961:456). Hence, recognition of the claims of minority groups which would somehow involve implicit or explicit criticism of at least some major values became a serious offense. In this sense, minority nationals entered the picture. Development of special organizations for blacks could be seen as un-American. In a perverse way, then, recognizing the plight of long-time residents of the country—residents who had indeed been dreadfully wronged by the system—became, somehow, vaguely disloyal.

PROBLEM MORALISM

Americans tend to see the world and, in particular, individual actions in moral terms. Hence, the culture supports the making of judgments about a wide range of situations, and the value of individualism locates a full complement of such judgments at the feet of the individual person. This tendency may account for the repetitive and continuous stigma which attaches to the users of social services. It is, for example, much more acceptable to have a physical problem than a "mental" problem, an ulcer than a nervous breakdown. It is much more acceptable to receive government money for the soil bank than for unemployment relief. Because of other values—land of opportunity, melting pot, equality—the country assumes that everyone can "make it." Indeed, there is even some feeling, based upon the Horatio Alger myth, that one *should* make it despite overwhelming odds. Hence, anyone who seems not to be performing adequately must be in this situation for a reason—his personal inadequacy—and he is judged and scorned because of it. This particular theme is one which is so basic to the development of social welfare policy that we shall subsequently consider it in more detail. Suffice it to point out here that the moral, judgmental apporach to problems is one which tends to focus on inner character, rather than external conditions. Once again, minority status is considered irrelevant.

RELIGIOUS FREEDOM

Thus far we have suggested ways in which key elements of the value structure kept the social welfare enterprise from paying explicit and direct attention to the problems of the various minorities with whom we have come in regular contact. Values, however, also work in a positive way, and encourage development in certain other directions.

One of the important values, and one which seems directly related to the development of social policy within the social work enterprise, is the value of religious freedom. Whereas racial, ethnic, sexual, and other distinctions were suppressed and judged irrelevant to the problems presented by special individuals, the exact reverse was assumed to be the case in religion. While there was great pressure to develop "external conformity" with the main tenets of "the American Way of Life" there was no, or very little, pressure internally to change religion. Hence, we had in effect a policy of recognizing religious difference, rather than suppressing it. This recognition, coupled with its well-accepted cultural legitimation, resulted in the pattern of religious-based social service agencies, known as "sectarian agencies," which we can observe today, following the major breakdown of Protestant, Catholic, and Jewish. It is interesting to note that, in direct contrast to the minority group exclusion, we have embraced, recognized, and legitimated religious differences within the social welfare enterprise.

This development was, in some sense, helpful to the ethnic members of society, for religion could be a "cover" under which they could receive help from at least coreligionists who could be sympathetic. And while Catholic Social Service was not Irish Social Service, and Jewish Family and Children's Service was not Russian or German Social Service, there was some commonality. Glazer and Moynihan (1963:19, emphasis added) comment that "New York organizational life is in large measure lived within ethnic bounds. These organizations generally have religious names. *For it is more acceptable that welfare and health institutions should cater to religious than to ethnic communities.*"

Yet even the doctrine of religious freedom was a mixed blessing. Although helpful and legitimizing to ethnic minorities, it contained a trap for racial minorities. Deep within at least the Christian tradition lies the concept of "pagan," someone who over the years became defined as nonwhite. It is perhaps unnoted, but each of the racial minorities within the United States, blacks (Negroes), reds (Indians), yellows (Chinese and Japanese), and browns (Mexican-Americans) had been subjected within the confines of their original lands to attempts at conversion. It seems reasonable to argue that the presence of at least the Christian ethic in this country prevented, or at least did not encourage, systematic attention to the problems of racial minorities while it did tend to be sympathetic to the problems of ethnics.

Societal Values and Social Stigma: the Mobility Ethic

In the previous section, we have looked at some of the ways in which the structure of the value system in America influenced the development of social policy, and the way in which some specific value constellations affected the treatment of minority groups by the social welfare enterprise. The fact that we tended to de-emphasize minority-related aspects of problems, and did emphasize the religion-related elements, might not have been caused in a direct sense by the value system, but an understanding of that system certainly aids us in understanding the nature of the directions in which we moved.

There remains, however, an important aspect of the relationship of values to social policy which we have only touched upon, yet one which deserves somewhat more systematic attention. Somehow, the client system involved in making use of the programs developed for their aid becomes severely stigmatized in their use. It is almost as if the programs are developed, but like the electric chair, there is the sense that they should remain unused. In the culture as a whole, we can observe a bitterness and vindictiveness toward the users of social programs which deserve attention in and of themselves, especially since these themes exist within a social system which is also characterized, at least in part, by humanitarian values. Furthermore, and paradoxically enough, the enmity is not expressed on the part of have-nots toward the haves, but rather, it seems that those who have much begrudge little to those who have nothing. And to add insult to injury, if the poor or the blacks or other minorities complain, they tend to be seen as a threat to the national security. This state of affairs is certainly curious, and deserves our systematic concern, especially because those people who bear the brunt of the stigma are the ones for whom we in the social welfare field are often working, or at least whom we are serving. The issue involves, but goes beyond the question of, minority groups, to embrace the whole client system. Americans scorn them and flee from them, as if they had something contagious. And we in social welfare have been no less enterprising in trying to redefine, and refine, our client system (Cloward and Epstein 1967). Any consideration of the general problem of values and social policy would be incomplete without some attention to this problem. Basically, it seems reasonable to argue that scorn is reserved for those persons who have seemingly failed in achieving social mobility, because it both represents personal moral failure and becomes a threat to the integrity of the value structure which supports mobility.

MOBILITY AS AN INTEGRATING VALUE

Many analysts of the "value structure" of America list numerous and, as we have indicated, often contradictory values as characteristic of the country. Williams lists sixteen (1961:456). Yet, somehow little is done to emphasize themes and interlinks within the value system and therefore to assess the cumulative and total effect of the value pattern. It seems to us that one of the most dominant themes within the value structure is the emphasis on social mobility. This dominant value touches almost every part of the lives of most Americans, and becomes the vehicle through which many of the other values are expressed. Along with some corollary values, it provides a basis for judging men and women. We have already noted that the American culture tends to be judgmental, yet is silent on the basis upon which judgment would be made. Mobility becomes that basis.

For most Americans, there has existed and still does exist, the hope that their lot is subject to improvement. Lipset (1963) notes the importance of "achievement" in colonial culture. Rischin (1965) has prepared a book of writings drawn from all areas of American life entitled *The American Gospel of Success*. Anecdotal evidence on this point is legendary, from references to America as the land of opportunity to stories about Horatio Alger, and reports about travels from rags to riches.

The mobility value is more than just another "value" for American citizens. It becomes the basis around which much of life and thought is organized. Indeed, it becomes almost a sacred value, an outward expression of the Protestant ethic. Upward mobility, with its implied and actual personal achievement, has religious overtones, but not in the sense in which we were discussing religious differences earlier. In this country, certain tenets have become secularized and widely shared, to the extent that they emerge as national values rather than religious ones, held, albeit, with a religious intensity. It is this wide secularization of these originally religious values that calls the Catholic father to send his son to Notre Dame and the Jewish mother to speak of "my son the doctor" (see Lipset 1963; Slater 1969). People hope, of course, for intragenerational mobility in which their own situation can improve over their own lifetime; but failing that, everyone can certainly expect intergenerational mobility, and parents have even come to expect that their children will occupy a station in life higher than theirs. It is our contention that the mobility ethos provides a common denominator for many Americans—provides for them a common set of assumptions on which there can be wide agreement. It has also provided a way for Americans to look at social welfare programs.

The social mobility ethos involves two corollary values—the value of work and the value of equality. They become assumptions which rule the mobility race. The importance of work has a long history in this country. Hard work, it was thought, was good and would be rewarded. In America's secularized religion, "holier than thou" became "busier than thou." (This point was suggested by Penelope Tropman.)

Equality involved both assumptions about the equality of opportunity (with sly admiration for the man who, in defiance of the norm, made his own opportunity, as in "God helps him who helps himself") and the basic notion that all men are created equal, and are quite capable of making do without any help from anyone else, especially the government.

MOBILITY AS CONTEST

Mobility, then, is open at all times, on the basis of work performed (at least this is thought to be the case). The land of opportunity, however, under this system becomes the land of the trap door. As Ralph Turner has pointed out, the American mobility system can be described as a contest during which people are always "in the game" and continuously being judged. At any moment, failure to perform can cause the lurking specter of downward mobility to materialize. Sometimes this can occur with frightening rapidity, as men who are organized out of new conglomerates after years of service to one of the original firms have come to realize. The effect of such a situation, in which the trap door of achievement can suddenly spring open, dropping a person down the social scale, can perhaps best be appreciated by contrasting it with a system in which there is a tradition of aristocracy. A duke, in a country which has dukes, can become mad, act in an aberrant fashion, and he remains a duke. The Marquis de Sade, despite his unusual proclivites, remained a marquis. No contest there.[2] There is no outsider hammering at your door, so that if you failed to perform in an appropriately ducal fashion someone else would replace you.

In a mobility system based upon the contest mode of selection, the only way one can avoid the game is by removing himself from it by assuming some kind of status outside the parameters of what is generally considered to be "the race" (or, in more depressed moments, "the rat race"). There are certain statuses which are generally recognized to be exempt from expected role performance. Illness is one example (Parsons 1956a).

MOBILITY AND SOCIAL WELFARE POLICY

The ethic of mobility and its correlates have affected the social welfare enterprise in a variety of ways. The secularized, religious nature of the ethic means that it becomes a vehicle through which one proves his personal worth, and hence carries much more social meaning than simply a neutral statement of one's position in a ranking. It provides us with some explanation of why we seem to dislike welfare clients so much—because their apparent failure in the mobility process becomes transposed into a failure of the moral process, something about which judgments are to be made.

Social work implicitly tends to accept this view. We therefore try to develop programs based upon ethics either counter to the mobility ethic, or separate from it. In the first case, the appeal to humanitarian values is common. And we have previously noted that these mitigating values tend to be subdominant. We can now suggest that their subdominance comes from the implicit acceptance of the major values. In essence, we argue that a person should be excused from judgment because he could not be expected to "make it," hence conceding that fact that (a) he did not "make it" and (b) that "making it" is an appropriate value. We tend to develop categories of people who, for one or another reason, are exempt from the mobility process. Hence, the main categories of people who are eligible for federal aid—the old, the blind, the disabled, and mothers and children—have in common at least the fact that they are freed, by reason of that particular aspect of their status, from the mobility process.

There is an additional reason for the dislike of welfare clients beyond the "moral" institutionalization of values within the mobility process. Basically, it relates to the development of support for extant value systems. Given the fact that mobility is at least one of the dominant value constellations within the American system, the culture then has some interest in continuing to maintain commitment to it.

There is good reason to argue that the society generally (and indeed, most social systems) tends to scorn those within it who do not espouse its values. Hence, we stigmatize the poor not only to distinguish clearly between who has "made it" and who has not, but as a way of reinforcing the very value of mobility itself. Hatred of the poor, of people who are at the bottom of the ladder, provides both negative sanctions for being in that position, but tends to reinforce, through solidarity of the haters, support for the mobility value system (see Durkheim 1947).

Still, one might note that moral judgment and the development of support for the norms, though two positive reasons why we dislike the poor, are themselves insufficient to account for the active aversion to poor people, and welfare clients, generally. Surely, whatever else it may be, a stigmatized status is not contagious. One cannot become stigmatized by associating with a stigmatized person. Or is this possible? We act as if it is. Indeed, it becomes, in effect, possible and it is at this point that the "contest" aspect of the mobility system becomes important. In a mobility-oriented society, one often knows where others are located in the system as well as where he is located through association with other persons. In other words, one public indicator of one's position in the system comes from the status level of one's daily associates. Generally, the norm governing association is always to seek to interact with persons of status higher than, or equal to, one's self. In fact, the function of prestigious universities, law firms, hospitals, and so on is often not to insure that their education, legal advice, or medical care is much better, but rather to become the place where prestige persons can be found. Hence, clients of social work practice and those persons and agencies involved in the social welfare enterprise need to be avoided lest some of the stigma, via association, rub off. In a general way, it is then no surprise that programs for poor people become poor programs in often a surprisingly short time.

What is operating here, for the social welfare enterprise, is the subtle implication that by associating with lower status persons through staffing programs designed to help them, the possibility of downward mobility through association will occur. It is, thus, no accident that we seek the legitimacy of "top community leaders." Nor is it any accident that some of the leaders in the development of the welfare enterprise have come through "charitable" organizational routes, and have been high-status persons within the system, relatively, but not completely, immune to the possibility of downward mobility.

Summary and Conclusions

We have tried to suggest some of the ways in which social values influence the development of the social welfare enterprise. We have suggested that conflict within the American value system, plus subdominace of some of the values generally advocated by social workers, tend to create difficulty. Substantively, we have suggested that there are specific American values which have provided directions to the field, and which have directed us away from recognition of the racial, ethnic, and status groups as a basis of specialization. Finally, we looked generally at the stigmatized status of social work clients, and argued that the inclusiveness of the social mobility ethic, plus the contest method of achieving social mobility, becomes important in understanding why we seem to dislike the clients so much.

NOTES

1. Henry J. Meyer has pointed out that the other side to this question, particularly for ethnic group analysis, is to consider why the various ethnic benevolent associations have not sought to formalize their role and mission through developing training in the social work field. Is it perhaps significant that we have Jewish social workers and Irish cops?

2. There is, of course, mobility in lands with aristocracies, but the overall ethics and approaches are different. See Turner (1966).

C. SOCIAL POLICY

THE articulation and implementation of social policy can be viewed as a link between ideology and social structure. In its essence, policy reflects the outcome of competing political constituencies and economic interests. Social welfare policy's political nature is demonstrated by the fact that it has become increasingly a function of government. The three selections in section C focus on contemporary public policy in the United States. For comparative historical analyses of the role of politics in modern social welfare policy, see Rimlinger's (1971) study of Europe, the United States, and the Soviet Union, and Heclo's (1974) study of Britain and Sweden.

The first, "Government Policy and Local Practice" by Paul Attewell and Dean R. Gerstein, is a case study of the impact of federal policy on the operations of local methadone treatment clinics in a California city. It challenges the prevalent view that government policy is ineffective because of the particularism of its local implementation. The Attewell and Gerstein data support the argument that national policy has important effects, even at the microsociological level of local agencies and their client-staff interactions.

In the second article, "Class Power and State Policy," Alexander Hicks, Roger Friedland, and Edwin Johnson use a cross-sectional analysis of forty-eight American states to assess the effect of public policy on income redistribution. They find that income redistribution involves conflicting social class interests, and that labor union presence has a positive effect on state redistributive efforts while corporate presence has a negative effect. Hicks, Friedland, and Johnson use an additive regression model, econometric techniques, and other advanced statistical procedures. Because of its complexity, the article's methodology has been edited and specific terms have been defined in an editor's note to table 8.3.

The final selection represents the neoconservative point of view on social policy. In "The Limits of Social Policy," Nathan Glazer argues that liberal social policy creates different problems which are as serious as the ones it tries to resolve. He suggests that policy should be based, at least in part, on reversion to a residual approach, relying as much as possible on traditional, private structures. This and other neoconservative work can be seen as a reaction to welfare state policies. The Family Assistance Plan discussed in Glazer's article was defeated in the Senate in 1971.

GOVERNMENT POLICY AND LOCAL PRACTICE

Paul Attewell and Dean R. Gerstein

A position currently popular among policy scientists views government policy as relatively impotent in local settings because, it is argued, original policy intentions become diluted in the face of daily exigencies at the local level (Pressman and Wildavsky 1973). It follows from the Pressman-Wildavsky approach that the apparent failure of many government policies stems not from the faults of the policies themselves, but rather from the complexities of implementation at the local level and especially from the diffusion of power among multiple local decision-makers. Such a perspective therefore implies broad discontinuity between governmental policy-making and local program outcomes, as a result of essentially particularistic aspects of local circumstances.

Based on our research on government policy and its implementation in the area of drug abuse, we present a different conceptualization of government policy, which has implications opposite to those of the Pressman-Wildavsky approach. Drawing on organizations theory we demonstrate that under certain specifiable conditions, federal policy can be seen to determine directly local program behavior even down to the microsociological level. The "failure" of local efforts is seen to flow *systematically from the structure of policymaking*, especially in so far as contradictory interests, embodied in policy, undermine crucial resources which local agencies require to gain the compliance of their clientele on a day-to-day basis.

From *American Sociological Review* (April 1979), 44(2):311–27. Reprinted by permission.

Using a case-study approach, we attempt to link the macrosociology of federal policy on opiate addiction to the microsociology of methadone treatment, in order to show how the sociopolitical forces which shape government policy subsequently determine the practical realm of daily clinic life. The link between public policy and the clinical *Lebenswelt* is structured by the managerial responses of treatment agencies to the institutionalization of government regulation.

Our model is developed in the sections below. The material is presented in five stages. The first is an historical overview of United States heroin policy. Secondly there follows a more detailed analysis of the policy toward methadone maintenance implemented in the late 1960s. The purpose here is to examine why policy took the form it did, and what this implied for treatment outcomes. A third section goes into the response of treatment agencies to federal regulations and local pressures. The fourth section analyzes the impact of this process upon the clinic milieu, especially upon the actions of addicts and staff. The final section summarizes the practical dilemmas of gaining compliance in the clinical setting as the ultimate result of the policies involved, and generalizes from the specific case-study findings to a more widely applicable model of governmental regulation and its likely outcome.

We have utilized two kinds of data in this research. First, in characterizing clinic and addict life, we draw upon our own work in several methadone clinics (from 30 to 160 clients in size) in one California city. This included ten months of intensive participant-observation research in three clinics (Gerstein 1975, 1976), detailed, transcribed interviews with a representative sample (N = 100) of present and past clients of the clinics (Attewell, Judd, and Gerstein 1976; Judd and Gerstein 1975), and statistical analyses of program records for five clinics over a four-year period. We obtained comparative data on clinics elsewhere from published ethnographies of treatment settings (Gould et al. 1974; Nelkin 1973; Soloway 1974), materials published by program administrators (Dole and Nyswander 1976; A. Mandell 1971); and from our own discussions with treatment managers and personnel in several other cities.

Second, in characterizing government policy, we have drawn upon government publications and upon historical materials including those published by principal figures (Chambers and Brill 1973; Dole and Nyswander 1976; Finney 1975; Lindesmith 1965; Musto 1973).

Evolution of United States Opiate Policy

Prior to this century, opium and all of its derivatives were available virtually free of legal restriction throughout the United States. Their use for recreational and a broad range of medicinal and quasi-medicinal purposes was widespread. However under pressure from social reformers, and for supplementary reasons stemming from international politics, a series of federal actions between 1906 and 1920 made distribution and use of many opiates illegal (Musto 1973). Even physicians were constrained to use opiates strictly for analgesic purposes. By 1938, some 25,000 medical doctors had been arraigned and 3,000 imprisoned because they attempted to prescribe narcotics to addicts (Brill 1973:11).

Thus with the exception of a few short-lived clinics (1912–24), addiction effectively was taken out of the jurisdiction of private physicians and became defined as a law enforcement rather than a medical problem (Brecher et al. 1972:116). Thereafter, medical involvement was limited to the Public Health Service, especially its Lexington prison-hospital.

Throughout the 1950s criticism grew over a purely law enforcement approach to addiction, culminating in a 1963 recommendation by a presidential commission on drug abuse that medical treatments be reconsidered. A technique was developed in 1964, by Vincent Dole and Marie Nyswander at Rockefeller University, based on earlier work by Isbell and Vogel (1949), which involved weaning an addict off heroin and substituting a daily oral dose of the synthetic opiate methadone. The addict entered an inpatient (later ambulatory) facility, received progressively larger doses of methadone until no heroin withdrawal symptoms were evident, and then was expected to take this dose of daily methadone *indefinitely*. Intensive supportive therapy to reestablish ego integration and normal social functioning—especially a steady paying job—ensued, and patients were put on an ambulatory (outpatient) basis, with renewable prescriptions for methadone, once such normal functioning had been established.

The major achievement of Dole and Nyswander in the mid-1960s was not simply their perfection of this clinical technique. Rather it was their gaining legitimation for the medical approach to addiction as a treatable disease. This legitimation involved a postulated analogy between addiction and chronic diseases such as diabetes. Addicts, it was argued, suffer a permanent metabolic deficiency. Just as diabetics require insulin medication for an indefinite period of time, so addicts require ongoing methadone for an indefinite period, in order to "cure" their disease (Chambers and Brill 1973:350). In addition, it was claimed that methadone (*a*) blocked the addict's craving for heroin, and (*b*) blocked the addict's pleasure from taking heroin (Dole and Nyswander 1965; 1966; 1967).

Government Policy and Early Institutional Regulation

Dole and Nyswander not only were faced with the task of legitimating methadone maintenance treatment in the eyes of the general public and fellow doctors. They also faced a variety of institutional actors: the Food and Drug Administration (FDA), the Bureau of Narcotics and Dangerous Drugs (BNDD), and local political officeholders. The early clinical trials with methadone treatment carried out by Dole and Nyswander took place in a context in which legality was unclear, and early researchers took the risk of prosecution and of censure for practicing unethical medicine. In 1962, the Medical Society of the County of New York partially legitimated the treatment of addicts, including prescribing narcotics to them, by ruling that such treatment in a strict clinical research setting was ethical medicine (Nelkin 1973:41). Such clinical programs later were specifically authorized by a 1965 law passed by the New York state legislature. Nevertheless the legal situation remained ambiguous (Brill 1973:21–22), and both the FDA and the BNDD attempted to secure their jursidiction in the area, as we shall explain below.

Critics of Dole and Nyswander attacked methadone maintenance on two bases. The first was that it was morally wrong to give narcotics to addicts. One medical critic argued that methadone researchers were "openly giving addicts narcotics to gratify and perpetuate their addiction" (Ausubel 1966). The second objection involved the possible diversion or misuse of methadone by addicts. This issue was particularly salient to the BNDD, the federal police agency responsible for controlling illegal drugs. In spite of the New York law, the BNDD maintained that methadone programs were illegal under the 1914 Federal Harrison Act (Nelkin 1973:48). Although the BNDD went so far as to approach certain clinics and make its views known, it did not take the step of prosecuting the clinics (Brecher et al. 1972:164). Hence its jurisdiction remained ambiguous until a later period.

The FDA has no legal power to control the practice of medicine.

However, it does have certain powers to control new drugs, especially to monitor their production, quality, availability, and so forth. As methadone clinics began opening in various hospitals, the FDA asserted its jurisdiction by categorizing methadone as an "Investigational New Drug," this despite methadone's use in the United States and abroad since 1943. This special status of methadone continued well into the 1970s, even after tens of thousands of cases had shown methadone maintenance to be quite safe under clinical management. However, the invocation and protraction of investigational status gave the FDA a continuing mandate to license and inspect clinics prescribing the drug. The latter police function it delegated to the BNDD in 1970.

Initially the FDA simply required physicians wishing to treat addicts with methadone to obtain permission to use this "Investigational New Drug." However, in 1970–71 the FDA promulgated a "model protocol" which specified in considerable detail various constraints on, and procedures to be carried out in, methadone programs. As we shall see, this protocol had a dual function. Firstly it acted to consolidate the practical control of the FDA over physicians wishing to provide methadone treatment, by detailing program regulations and behavior. More important, however, it sought to co-opt or placate significant critics of methadone treatment by casting their objections in the form of FDA regulations. For example, the BNDD was given direct control over medication security, and had veto power over licensing. Similarly the FDA bowed to the interests of medical critics such as Ausubel (1966), and included in the contents of the model protocol a variety of measures (to be detailed momentarily) designed to reassure critics that their specific fears concerning methadone would not be realized.

This response of the federal government, to *insist on its jursidiction* over a new area, and to embody *in policy itself* the views of a variety of interested and often critical parties, was to have crucial consequences for implementation at the local level. This phenomenon is an important element in our general model of government action. We shall return to this in our discussion.

Substantive features of the FDA model protocol included the following stipulations:

1. Minors (under eighteen) were excluded. This was later modified to allow special exceptions.
2. Documentation of prior and present addiction had to be

provided, and a confirmed history of one or more prior failures of treatment, before an addict could obtain methadone.

3. Consideration had to be given to discontinuing eventually the drug for patients who had adjusted well to maintenance.

4. Termination from treatment was required for patients who continued to use narcotics or other drugs, or who exhibited alcoholism or continued criminal activity after entering treatment. Drug use was to be checked by at least weekly collection of urine specimens for laboratory testing.

5. Prior BNDD approval of any methadone program was required (see U.S. Food and Drug Administration 1970).

It is central to our argument that these and other provisions in the FDA model protocol strongly determined the future course of methadone maintenance. To demonstrate this, we shall first make four points concerning these particulars of the protocol, and then we shall consider why the protocol in general had such an impact on program behavior.

1. The protocol resulted in the virtual exclusion from methadone maintenance of the primary vector of heroin "contagion": adolescents who have themselves only started heroin use comparatively recently, and who rapidly introduce their friends to the drug (Hunt and Chambers 1976). FDA item 1 above excluded many of these from treatment on age grounds alone. Moreover, item 2 above, documentation of prior failures at abstinence, requires considerable addiction history. Long-term addicts who have served jail sentences (which constitute "forced abstinence") are easily able to furnish documentary proofs of prior failure. However younger or recently addicted individuals are unlikely to have accumulated such documentation. Consequently this FDA protocol stipulation precluded maintenance programs from treating the recently addicted individuals who keep the heroin system supplied with recruits, and instead limited methadone maintenance to a "treatment of last resort." This bowed to the views of those critics who claimed methadone simply addicted heroin users to a new drug. By allowing only long-term, "hard-core" addicts access to methadone, the FDA staved off the argument that it was turning young drug users into permanent methadone addicts.

2. The diabetes analogy of Dole and Nyswander was effectively struck down. Although item 3 above did not require methadone patients to be terminated after a time, it set up the ideal that a

successful patient be weaned from methadone and end up drug free. This was in direct contrast to the Dole-Nyswander view of methadone as a lifelong medication like insulin, and instead made the drug-free "graduate" the standard of success. This shift in the criterion of successful treatment of a methadone patient was to have strong implications for the future behavior of clinics.

3. The BNDD's institutional interest was to prevent methadone from reaching the illegal market (Dole and Nyswander 1976). It had no responsibility for treatment. Yet in order to obtain and maintain BNDD approval, methadone programs were obliged to institute rigorous control, security, and accounting procedures. Thus security preempted therapy in the design of dispensing procedures.

4. The FDA protocols stipulated a maximum daily dose of 160 mg. Despite assurances that local programs could argue for a higher figure, the FDA succeeded, via this "suggestion," in controlling dosages and making lower doses a measure of better programs. As we shall see below, mean dosage levels were to decrease steadily in subsequent years, eroding yet more of the Dole-Nyswander method. However this FDA protocol item countered charges made by critics of maintenance programs to the effect that methadone would be prescribed in high dosages which would allow addicts to get "high," and hence abet their "moral decay."

At this point we have to raise the issue of why the provisions of the FDA protocol had such a profound and long-lasting effect, even though they were not enforceable as law. The FDA itself was obliged to state that the protocol was "intended only as a guide to the profession," while "modification of the protocol and completely different protocols will be accepted, provided they can be justified by the sponsor" (U.S. Food and Drug Administration 1970). In more general terms, we are raising the issue of why governmental agencies' policies often acquire considerable force even though they are not embodied in law.

First, in the short term, program applicants who were faced with a lengthy and difficult FDA licensing procedure tended to stick closely to the model protocol, rather than risk delay or rejection by diverging from the guide. In the longer term, the FDA guide gained its force because it was adopted by most of the crucial organizational actors who constituted the external environment of the methadone programs. The FDA protocol provided potential criteria for evaluating a program: numbers of drug-free graduates, changes in arrest records, and so forth. State and local agencies therefore took these as standards by which to assess a program's requests for licensing and refunding.

In addition the FDA protocol became a model for permanent state legislation. (The states *do* have jurisdiction over medical practice.) State laws were usually more restrictive elaborations of the FDA protocol. For example, in California, state regulations required *two* or more documented treatment failures, and proof of *two* years addiction prior to entry into a methadone program, compared with one failure and one year in the FDA protocol.

We see here a process not uncommon in situations where federal agencies set technically complex safety standards: less expert political bodies show their concern by toughening up the standards. This often occurs at the behest of state regulatory agencies which increase their areas of jurisdiction and autonomy by arguing for controls which go beyond those already covered at the federal level. Similar phenomena have been discussed in other settings by Becker (1963:147–63). In his analysis of the impact of institutionalization and enforcement upon "moral entrepreneurship," he notes both a tendency for legislators to insert their own interests at the rule-making stage, and the fact that enforcement personnel feel the need to justify their existence and the goal displacement which often results from this (Becker 1963:152, 156–62). One can see both of these processes operating in the case of methadone maintenance.

Thus the FDA protocol, many of whose elements were ideals or suggestions, become elaborated into state law. The protocol and the laws then became the bases upon which authorized inspectors judged programs during site visits. In some cases these inspectors were empowered to revoke program licenses. In other cases, which we will discuss, they simply could discredit programs by feeding negative evaluative findings to the local news media.

In sum, the FDA protocol molded the external environment within which programs operated by providing a standard against which programs could be judged. The ways in which programs responded to this process are the subject of the next section.

Managerial Response at the Program Level

The rapid appropriation of millions of dollars for drug treatment, and the relative paucity of organizations already in the field, led to a proliferation of programs, as universities, hospitals, community groups, and private corporations responded to the existence of funding (Diaz and David 1972; Finney 1975:20–30; A. Mandell 1971). Because the FDA invoked an investigational status for methadone, which required that a potential program show evidence of medical and administrative expertise, community-based groups were hindered considerably in acquiring methadone licenses. This frequently led community groups to develop drug-free addiction treatment modalities. In contrast, university- and hospital-affiliated groups, and private organizations with medical and bureaucratic expertise, did well in gaining FDA authorization and government funding for methadone. Since community-based drug-free treatment agencies and methadone maintenance programs provided alternative approaches to treatment, and often competed for funding and addict clientele, community agencies frequently became pitted against the more medical-establishment methadone agencies for such resources. In cities where community groups were able to wield political influence, this acted to make local government especially cautious over methadone treatment (cf. Nelkin 1973: 90–92).

Even among methadone programs "range wars" erupted, and a process of monopolization or oligopolization later occurred in many cities (cf. Finney 1975:25). In the early years, however, there was something of a funding bonanza, and many agencies sought to enter the field. Typically, programs were set up as pilot projects, subject to continuation only if acceptable performance was demonstrated.

Programs responded to this situation by developing what we shall term a *reality construction* or *presentation of self* in order to convince funding and regulatory agencies that they were doing a good job (Goffman 1959). Waiting lists were adopted as one indicator of the need for a program, its success in the eyes of the addict community, and, of course, the need for more money. Characteristics of addicts in treatment—time in treatment, positive changes in employment status, reduction in criminal activity—also became widely publicized as indicators of success. A program's statistics were compared with others' in order to show its efficiency (*Proceedings of the National Conference on Methadone Treatment* 1971; 1972; cf. Thompson 1967). It took several years to realize that time series data of the type collected by programs were particularly susceptible to statistical "sleight of hand." By 1973, Brill and Chambers (1973:362–63) were complaining: "Unfortunately, not everyone counts everyone when compiling 'retention' or 'attrition' statistics to share with their professional peers, with funding sources, or with the less-than-informed public." Even indices of reduced criminal activity and increased employment proved subject to manipulation or misinterpretation (Holzman and Lukoff 1976:6ff).

In addition to these positive presentational activities, methadone programs also had to manipulate their public image in order to stave off external criticism. This became progressively more important over the years as state and federal laws gave regulatory control to a variety of watchdog agencies. For example, a California Board of Pharmacy inspector complained in the local press of one program: "It is a failure to the agencies monitoring it, to the agencies administering it, to the patients using it, and to the taxpayers." His major complaint was that program administrators would not define "just what constitutes a successful *completion* of the program" (emphasis added).

We see here the impact of the FDA protocol in ignoring Dole and Nyswander's rationale for indefinite methadone treatment (like insulin). Instead of regarding the fact that addicts were in treatment as itself a success, regulators invoked the FDA ideal of a drug-free addict (weaned from methadone) as the measure of success. The newspaper which reported this inspector's complaints subsequently divided the total methadone program budget by the small number of drug-free graduates and headlined their article: "Each 'Cure' Costs Taxpayers $53,000." Thus Dole and Nyswander's original conception of methadone treatment was forgotten.

This perilous external environment (cf. Nelkin 1973:138) and the desire to look good to funding and regulatory agencies increased the importance of manipulating the public image of methadone programs. These presentational needs were reflected in three particular contexts: (1) aggregate movement of methadone dosage levels; (2) numbers of clients admitted and discharged; and (3) staff composition. In each case it will be seen that the programs studied showed increasing sensitivity toward outside regulatory agencies and other potential threats, and hence reorganized or toughened-up clinical practices to avoid any possible external criticism.

1. *Methadone dosage levels.* From the earliest days of methadone maintenance, critics had accused programs of helping addicts get high. Thus one physician attacked Dole and Nyswander: ". . . they are simply substituting the euphoric action of methadone for the

euphoric action of heroin by administering massive dosages of the former" (Ausubel 1966:949). Equally the BNDD pushed for lower dosages in the belief that dispensing higher ones meant a higher likelihood of illegal diversion. In such an environment, programs' mean dosage levels became strategic symbols of their toughness and desire to wean addicts from methadone. High doses came under public criticism from surveillance agencies, and programs responded by further lowering their dispensing averages.

Consequently, methadone dosage became a pawn in an organizational struggle, its individual impact on each particular addict lost in presentational politics. In response to external agencies there was pressure on clinicians from program administrators to deny addict requests for increases, and to lower stable doses. The result was a steady decline in average dose over the years.

An additional matter, manipulated for similar reasons, involved "take-home" methadone. The requirement to attend the clinic seven days a week in order to ingest methadone was first seen as a temporary measure during a client's initial stabilization. Thereafter, in order to encourage more normalized lives, including employment, clients periodically were allowed to take home and self-administer one, two, or more days' worth of methadone. However, this was a security risk, since take-home methadone could potentially be sold illegally. In line with the increasing sensitivity to possible sources of criticism, the clinics studied progressively reduced the take-home privilege over the years, made it available to fewer and fewer individuals, and hedged its use with greater restrictions.

2. *Admissions and discharges.* In the early days of the clinics studied, waiting lists existed, and program success could be demonstrated by burgeoning numbers of clients in treatment. Some clients continued using illegal drugs, but this was not seen as prima facie failure, since the figures showed considerable reductions in drug use relative to untreated addicts (Chambers and Taylor 1971). However, as regulation intensified, as community media became more critical, and as federal and local funding sources grew more begrudging, program administrators pushed harder for stringent enforcement of rules, backed by detoxification (discharge from the program following stepwise reduction of methadone dose). In 1973 a policy shift was undertaken to toughen up clinical behavior, which resulted in a rapid *doubling* of the rate of termination of clients, as those with records of continuing heroin abuse were expelled from treatment. The new

policy caused a precipitous (30 percent) decrease in total caseloads over the year.

The point here is that administrative fiat, oriented toward external regulatory and surveillance agencies, succeeded in rapidly changing program census. There was no indication based on a study of clinical records that these actions resulted from changed patient behavior during that period.

3. *Staffing.* In the early days of methadone maintenance many programs utilized ex-addicts (persons currently presumed abstinent) as front-line staff in the clinics. This pattern of ex-addict staffing was quite common nationwide, as ex-addict peer counseling provided role models for clients, job prospects for ex-addicts, and inexpensive labor for programs, all at one sweep (A. Mandell 1971). In the clinics studied, physicians, as expensive resources, primarily were involved in signing prescriptions and in performing periodic physical examinations. Doctors did wield considerable power by regulating dosages; however, they were seldom involved in therapy, this being the task of the paraprofessional ex-addict counselors.

While some commentators on methadone maintenance have stressed that the impact of government regulation was to limit the role of physicians in treatment (Dole and Nyswander 1976:2119), our data indicate that the most profound change in staffing policy was a movement away from hiring ex-addicts as staff. This has been commented upon at the national level (Espada 1977), and is borne out in the clinics which we studied, where a steady turnover of ex-addict staff in early years turned into a full-scale rout in later years. As we shall describe below, this again took place in response to the program's increasing concerns with rigid adherence to mandated rules, and its need to present an efficient, tough image to the external environment.

In summary, what we see in these several program responses to government regulation is a progressive displacement of organizational goals, away from therapeutic aims per se and toward an increasing concern with manipulation of clinic practices in order to look good to outside agencies, particularly to powerful surveillance and funding agencies. At a more general level we would suggest that this kind of organizational goal displacement is typical of programs heavily dependent on government money or licensing for their continued existence. Since the goal of maintaining the continued existence of an organization is logically prior to that of the instru-

mental task at hand, there is a constant tendency to become preoccupied with the former at the cost of the latter. In the case of detailed
governmental regulation and surveillance this implies the rise of
bureaucratic interests in the organization and the subordination of
other interests to the primary one of adapting to one's external
environment in order to keep the organization safe (cf. Dole and
Nyswander 1976:2119; Thompson 1967).

   We now shall consider the cumulative effect of these organizational
responses upon the experiential realm of daily clinic life.

Clinic Life for Clients and Staff

Once the initial disorientation of entering a new setting has been
dispelled, the experience of a patient within a methadone clinic is
fundamentally one of regulation, of rules, of specified procedures
which have to be carried out: in short, of grown adults in a high
school setting. Everyone knows the rules, virtually everyone present
dislikes the rules, but everyone's behavior is rule-governed, even if
only in grudging ritualistic compliance.

   The fundamental business at hand is the distribution of methadone.
There is no casualness here. Fixed hours are set: a couple of hours
each in the morning and afternoon. Anyone who is late misses his/
her methadone. Persons are called singly to a nurse at an enclosed
dispensing station. Although client and nurse see one another daily,
the client must always produce a special I.D. card, in the ritualistic
fashion of military security, here mandated by BNDD. Methadone
is prepackaged in coded bottles of fruit drink, of fixed volume to
disguise the dosage, which is meant to be a secret to clients and even
counselors. Each client must drink in full view of the nurse, and then
respond to quesions, to assure that the drink has been swallowed; all
this also is mandated by BNDD. Methadone dispensing, the basic
ritual, occurs seven days a week, 365 days per year.

   Other practices are equally mandatory but less regular, especially
the "urine drop." Once a week (he/she never knows quite when) each
client is approached by a counselor for a urine specimen. The
purpose of obtaining this specimen is for detection of illegal drug
use. The urine donation (like the dispensing ritual) is a regular
reminder of distrust. It bears no relation to the euphemistic privacy
of a urologist's office. The addict enters a bathroom, followed by a
counselor. The rules specify that he/she must be watched while

urinating into the bottle. Mirrors are even installed to facilitate this surveillance. Some counselors look away, act indifferently, or dissemble a lack of attention, but the underlying rule is strengthened by such interactional camouflage work.

An important activity occurs when a urine sample has shown "dirty"—evidence of residues of heroin, barbiturates, and so on. The client, confronted with the report, often denies all knowledge: "[I]t's a mistake. The test screwed up. . . . The counselor messed up the bottles"; protests of injured innocence to save face. The counselor must act peeved: warnings that the next time may be the last, threats of future retribution, occasional real retribution, notice of a twenty-one-day "punitive detoxification." Since urinalysis only detects a heroin injection from the prior day or two—and then only if the heroin was relatively pure and the urine not too dilute—injecting heroin becomes Russian roulette. In the context of "probably they won't ask for a drop today," or "I fixed [injected] two days ago, probably it'll turn up negative," being caught is a nasty surprise, an unlucky event, a good reason to be angry.

Another weekly ritual is an interview with the counselor. Again, a degree of interpersonal concern and interest often exists, although counselors have on the average ten minutes per client per week for face-to-face counseling. Occasionally therapeutic relationships blossom. But in each interview a formal mandated agenda of information must be obtained: "Did you work this week? Engage in illegal activities? Were you arrested, convicted, etc.?"

To these repetitive activities are added an occasional group therapy session, extended personal counseling, a doctor's appointment for some physical complaint, and so on. But such activities are only leaven. The essential routines consist of waiting for methadone, giving urine, and checking in with the counselor. Many patients totally ignore voluntary therapeutic offerings. The senior administrator of one program felt obliged to point out to the press in the fifth year of the program's operation: "We put in a rule eighteen months ago that anybody on the program was to participate in counselling. That rule is still in effect for patients until they and their counselors decide sessions are not needed."

While the clinical experience of the typical client is a one-dimensional exchange of weekly urine for daily methadone, the clinical reality of the staff is necessarily more complex. The backstage operation of a methadone clinic can be seen as involving an interpenetration of three different realities, each with its own rationale and interests. The first involves self-definition, particularly for the counselors and clinic directors, who were at first (1970–72) virtually all ex-addicts, though individuals without heroin experience were later hired. The ex-addicts' job credentials were principally their firsthand knowledge of addict behavior, presumed (since Synanon's publicity) to give them special efficacy in drug treatment. Ex-addict counselors had to put this knowledge in a clinical perspective, while shifting their own self-image from down-and-out to upwardly mobile. They had, on the one hand, to convince addict clients of their *savoir faire*, that they could not be "conned," and, on the other, to establish themselves as paraprofessional clinicians. This was accomplished in part by language and style. Counselors and clinic directors dressed and spoke with a streetwise style, but also with a facile psychiatric terminology: "subconscious motivation," "defense and coping mechanisms," "denial," "confrontation," and so on. This combination set them off from the clientele, without sacrificing their claim to an insider's knowledge of addiction.

A second reality, which all staff shared, was a bureaucratic-administrative one. Each clinic director was sandwiched between the top program administrators far from the clinic, and the day-to-day problems of staff and clients. Through the clinic director came administrative directives, the majority involved with getting paperwork done, new government edicts and inspections, and making sure security was kept tight. Since rules were constantly breached or bent in the day-to-day life of the clinic, and were, in any case, so complex and frequently changed that often it was unclear what rule applied, there was always room for criticism (and grounds for firings) by the administration. Getting the paperwork done, and avoiding or patching up administrative upsets, were constant concerns for the staff.

The third reality involved the day-to-day management of addicts as nonmedical, nonbureaucratic, nonpassive people. A typical day of staff concerns would be as follows (using their own terminology): Client X is being a pain about needing more methadone, is kicking up a fuss about being screwed over, loudly telling anyone who will listen. Client Y is a slick S.O.B. whom the staff would like to get rid of, but whom no one can catch making heroin deals in the clinic, or using heroin. Client Z keeps coming up dirty, but her old man has just gotten out of jail, lives with her, and is shooting up all the time. The staff knows she has two kids, cares desperately about staying in the program, and would go back to dope and hooking if kicked off the program.

The experiential immediacy of concerns like these enables them to compete in the minds of staff with bureaucratic and other demands.

Staff Responses to the Clinical Milieu

It is clear that the staff members' *normal* situation, particularly for ex-addicts, was one of profound role conflict. This was exacerbated as bureaucratization progressed, although it was partially "solved" by the steady elimination of ex-addicts. The role conflict drew its power from all of the interests working at cross purposes in the clinic. First and foremost, counselors—particularly ex-addicts—sympathized and even identified with clients. Some knew at firsthand that success in the program meant new life chances: keeping a job, gaining status and self-respect, regaining hope. They also knew what involuntary expulsion from the clinic could mean: the extraordinary mental and physical pressures of hustling, seeking dope, pain, finding dope, shooting, near or actual overdoses. Often superimposed upon this is constant harassment by police and narcotic agents, and emotional and sometimes physiological blackmail as police lock addicts up until withdrawal prompts them to "cooperate." Ex-addict or nonaddict counselors were too close to this reality not to be influenced by it. The cold administrative calculus of punishment broke down when the client was known as an individual and the situation into which he/she would be thrust was viewed as abominable.

The first level of conflict, then, derived from the counselor's proximity to the client world, crossed with demands to enforce punitive sanctions. This conflict was not simply a matter of the counselor's social background, but was *genuinely organizational in its origins.* Counselors qua therapists were expected to establish supportive relationships with clients. The establishment of therapeutic trust was and always is predicated upon notions of care and respect for the individual client. A lack of such particularistic solidarity empties a therapeutic relationship of its meaning and force. Nevertheless, due to the increasing concern with the external environment the counselors were increasingly required to be disciplinarians, enforcers of universalistic rules, organizational moralists. The conflict arose from contradictory demands to be particularistic while universalistic, and trusting while punitive.

While counselor conflict derived at one level from opposition between therapeutic and rule-maintenance interests, a second conflict involved self-image. Counselors wished to see themselves as persons of status, individuals with skills, and more specifically, professionals able to help others. Perhaps the term *altruistic orientation* overstates the real professionalism involved, but counselors were undoubtedly caught in this imagery. Administrative policies increasingly undermined such bases of self-definition. A subordinate force which thought it knew what was best for addicts could not be tolerated, especially as the watchdog and punitive functions of counselors began to overshadow therapeutic concerns. Thus in addition to having to integrate contradictory pressure in their *duties*, counselors had to stave off contradictory definitions of their status. Their role as counselor had positive cultural value; while the role of policeman was particularly abhorrent in addict society, in which police and snitches were loathed. The administration, far from euphemizing the punitive, watchdog functions of counselors, left increasingly little doubt that they were there primarily for that purpose. The most cogent testimony to the assault upon counselors' self-images was the terminology used by a senior program administrator, who began referring to counselors as "urine monitors."

Staff response to these cross pressures in the clinics studied varied between demoralization, acquiescence, and hostility. The importance of these jobs for the ex-addicts gave the process extra poignancy. Counseling paid comparatively little, but it was generally the first white-collar work ex-addicts had had, their first experience of a respectable niche in which they could keep working successfully. Under these cross pressures some ex-addicts left early for other programs. Others dropped out, were kicked out, or acquiesced to demands which redefined their role. For those who did leave, the blow often propelled them directly toward their only other social identity: dope fiend. Completing the circle, some later reappeared as clients in the program.

The Client Point of View

In the preceding sections we have given our sociological view of several changes which took place in methadone maintenance—shifts in dosages, staff changes, sudden changes in program expulsions, and so on,—and have tried to explain these changes in terms of program response to its external environment and mandated policies. It is important to realize, however, that our analytic perspective on these matters is not that of the addicts themselves. While these same topics were constantly addressed in the course of our interviews with addicts, their folk perceptions of these phenomena clustered instead around the apparent arbitrariness of clinic life, especially as regards disciplinary actions against addicts.

We wish to make two points concerning the addict's world view: First, the addict perspective was a rational response to real phenomena; that is, a high degree of arbitrariness did, in fact, exist. Secondly, we wish to show that the addict's world view was readily rendered irrational, and indeed seen as one aspect of addict personality pathologies, by staff members who viewed addict responses through a psychiatric framework. The mutual unintelligibility of addict and staff world views is best illustrated in terms of urinalysis requirements and punitive detoxification (incremental reduction of methadone dose to zero and expulsion from the clinic).

Examining the issue of urinalysis, we find that a high degree of arbitrariness (or luck) is involved in the process. On the one hand, addicts were faced with uncertainty as to what day they would be called upon to give a urine sample. Thus, being caught with a "dirty urine" was not simply a matter of scientifically catching those clients who were illegally continuing heroin use. Rather it was a matter of being the unlucky one who happened to be caught on a certain day for a urine sample. This arbitrariness was intensified by problems in the technique of urinalysis itself, having to do with variations in personal metabolism and laboratory procedure. Residues of heroin used two days previously might be identified in the urine of one individual, while heroin shot hours before testing might not be detected in another addict. Drinking beer prior to giving a urine sample would often dilute the sample so that no heroin was detectable. False positives were also not unknown in urinalysis: even when urines were split into two portions for separate urinalysis, the results rarely agreed (C. Lidz, personal communication). Thus addicts did not experience urinalysis as an objective system of surveillance in which if one had cheated program rules one was caught. Rather, they experienced urinalysis as a form of unpredictable Russian roulette. Staff, however, noting the BNDD licensing of laboratories and the high prices for urinalysis, had to take the official line that urinalysis results were accurate, and a fair method of catching those individuals who broke program rules.

Given the addict experience of the arbitrariness of urinalysis, there was a widespread belief by addicts that staff members switched urine samples, either to protect friends, earn bribes, or hurt enemies. This was often interpreted by psychiatric staff as a magical or paranoid belief system. Similarly, a widespread addict response to urinalysis results was to claim that the outcomes were simply wrong. This was seen by staff as denial in the psychiatric sense. Finally, addicts tended to respond to being caught with a dirty urine by becoming angry. Indeed, anger is a rational response to a situation where a series of low-probability outcomes (day urine requested, metabolism, accuracy of urinalysis) all coincide, causing the addict to be caught. Yet anger was seen by staff as addicts' refusal to take personal responsibility for their actions.

A similar mutual unintelligibility underlay staff and client views of involuntary or punitive detoxification, where again addicts viewed the punitive process as arbitrary and ill-intentioned. Program rules were fairly specific: if a client continued using illegal drugs for long after entering the program, the client would first be verbally warned, and then obliged to sign a contract agreement that more "dirties" would result in detoxification and termination from the program. This organizational rule reflects federal and state regulations.

As indicated, the timing and results of urinalysis exhibit a degree of randomness. But in addition, an examination of program records revealed that the number of dirty urines permitted before one received a contract varied according to counselor, concurrent level of administrative strictness, frequency or imminence of audit, and so forth. Even after a contract was written, the actual number of dirty urines tolerated could vary.

Yet even after the contract was deemed violated and detoxification begun, a further mystification occurred. Clients saw the *process* of the twenty-one-day "detox" as *itself* the punishment, rather than seeing their subsequent *termination* from the program as the *real* punishment, with detoxification merely a technical means of withdrawing methadone prior to termination (Attewell, Judd, and Gerstein 1976). Although federal regulations set the minimum time for detoxification at fourteen days, addicts felt that even twenty-one days was so abrupt that one suffered severe withdrawal pains. Forty-five percent of the clients interviewed in our interview sample (Attewell, Judd, and

Gerstein 1976; Judd and Gerstein 1975) objected specifically to the length of detoxification. Allied to this was the knowledge that expulsion from the program—ostensibly the *real* punishment—was manipulable. Addicts could, and did, return to the program very shortly after being punitively detoxified. Detoxified patients were sometimes on the rolls again within two weeks. Thus, addicts saw the punitive response of the program as centering on the physical pains of detoxification, rather than the moral censure of expulsion or exclusion from treatment.

What, then, was the consequence of this contradiction between staff and addict world views? Given this context of unpredictability concerning detection of illegal drug use, unpredictability of program response, and addict redefinition of the termination process, a significant proportion of clients denied the fairness or validity of the system of punitive governance upon which the clinics operated. Combined with the various humiliating rules, such as viewing one urinating, this led to many addicts taking an alienated and instrumental view of the program. Many began a cyclical revolving-door pattern of program involvement: repeated entries to clinics, detoxifications due to continued drug use, and subsequent reentries to treatment after weeks or months on the street hooked on heroin. This was abetted by federal documentation rules which enabled former patients to reenter rapidly, while new addicts, who never previously had been treated, would often have to hang on for weeks or months, awaiting documentation. The program, meanwhile, was able to keep up its case census by admitting "retreads," some up to six times in a four-year period.

This type of career virtually co-opted methadone maintenance as a complementary adaptation to preexistent street life. Typical street heroin use involves a period of sporadic shooting (injecting) which escalates to a daily fixed-interval schedule, reinforced by the onset or threat of withdrawal. But the body learns to tolerate a given mean level of heroin, and addicts often respond by taking larger doses. This procedure has finite limits, because money and heroin become relatively hard to get in ever-larger quantities. Addicts responded to this, prior to the existence of methadone maintenance, by experiencing withdrawal pains frequently and eventually going cold turkey (withdrawing from heroin), often in jail. Later, the pattern of injecting would start over.

This stereotypical picture of periods of addiction interspersed with periods of abstinence has become modified by the revolving-door methadone maintenance career. Some 37.5 percent of addicts in one program studied showed this career type by late 1974 (Judd and Gerstein 1975). These addicts entered the maintenance program, reduced their heroin use considerably, and ultimately were detoxified and expelled for not quitting completely. They resumed full-time street use of heroin until their tolerance got too high, legal or personal problems grew unmanageable, or their heroin connection dried up. Then they reentered the program. Methadone maintenance provided a cushion for such people, by helping them control their heroin needs, and keeping them out of prison.

This creative co-optation of methadone maintenance did interfere with those addicts in treatment who were motivated to avoid heroin entirely, and was not exactly beloved by revolving-door addicts, since it involved continual harassment and degradation by a plethora of treatment practices. But as a "rational" response to an institutional pattern which preached treatment and practiced control, this career pattern, of using treatment to buffer the more unmanageable aspects of addiction, is strikingly symbiotic. The encumbered institutional attempt at treating a social problem produced its antithesis in addicts' use of treatment to solve their own problems.

The Dilemmas of Compliance

We have indicated that the addict's experience in treatment involved on the one hand a routine of repetitively demeaning rituals, and on the other a series of uncertain and/or irregular surveillance and punitive measures. This combination, we have argued, is demoralizing for addicts, leads to an alienated and instrumental perspective, and does little to encourage respect for the program. One possible explanation for this could be that these negative consequences result from a lack of adequate bureacratization, rather than a surfeit (cf. Perrow 1972). In other words, residual particularistic attitudes (constant bending of rules regarding detoxification and so forth) rendered unpredictable an otherwise rational system of treatment as defined by the FDA.

In countering this "underbureaucratization" thesis we have to demonstrate two things. First we shall show that particularism was not some peculiar aberration of the clinics studied but on the contrary was a necessary consequence of the organizational structure imposed on methadone maintenance. Secondly, we shall argue that clinical practices were not hindered by particularism per se, but rather by the undermining of such particularism resulting from increased attention to FDA and state regulations. In explaining these processes we shall use Etzioni's (1961) work on compliance in which he distinguishes among three types of organizations (coercive, remunerative, and normative), each of which employs a specific set of tactics in gaining the compliance of its participants.

From our preceding review of methadone treatment, it becomes apparent that programs have difficulties in using *any* of the typical organizational constraints or compliance mechanisms to control addict-clients. For example, coercive compliance depends above all upon physically restraining an individual from leaving an institution. Even though addicted to methadone, the addict in treatment does have the option of quitting the program and returning to street narcotics. Thus, methadone programs cannot effectively operate as coercive organizations.

Remunerative compliance requires a set of variable rewards which may be adjusted to match a subordinate's behavior, and hence entice the subordinate to follow organizational rules. Unfortunately, methadone programs' abilities to marshal such rewards were very limited. Therapeutic offerings such as counselling were not perceived as rewards: indeed, we saw earlier that addicts had to be forced to attend counseling sessions. One possible reward structure—allowing methadone dosage to slide up and down according to good behavior—was ruled out by physicians' ethical objections to utilizing medication as a variable reward. The only other meaningful reward, take-home privileges, had been curtailed and made inflexible due to BNDD and other external pressure. Thus there was a paucity of remunerative compliance in methadone clinics.

The third type, normative compliance, was similarly hamstrung. As Etzioni argued, normative mechanisms (rituals of solidarity, prestige and status rewards, exclusion, moral stigmatization) only work in a situation where participants have a high degree of commitment to organizational goals. The various degrading and status-deflating aspects of methadone maintenance, such as I.D. cards, urine monitoring, punitive rules, all acted to destroy any possibility of status or prestige rewards and hence undermined the basis for normative compliance.

Normative control was similarly encumbered in terms of its major negative sanction: expulsion and moral stigmatization. There was a contradiction between the use of exclusion or expulsion as a compliance/control device, and culturally dominant notions of medical treatment. Having successfully defined themselves as providers of medical treatment, programs could not exclude on a long-term basis those expelled former clients who had returned to the street and become readdicted. To do so would be to deny a sick person medical treatment, which bites too deeply into social mores and taboos. Thus, because of the medical definition, programs could neither effectively exclude rule breakers nor, after readmission, deny them any of the treatment provisions of the program. Methadone programs, therefore, had to live with their own treatment failures. Consequently, programs totally lacked any effective negative sanctions for normative control of erring subordinates.

In sum, most of the major mechanisms which complex organizations typically utilize for controlling subordinate participants were absent or unavailable in the case of methadone maintenance programs. Programs were therefore unable to mold effectively the behavior of their addict clients.

In such a situation the only remaining lever for obtaining compliance involved the use of personal loyalties between staff and clients generated in the day-to-day life of the clinic and in counseling sessions. These friendships produced respect and trust, feelings of mutual understanding and personal obligation. To be kicked out of a clinic involved loss of face to some addicts, not because they felt committed to the program per se, but because they had betrayed the personal trust of a specific staff member to whom they felt obligated. To the extent that a counselor believed and acted as though a client was an individual worthy of being trusted—by imbuing the relationship with importance and solidarity—a counselor could impose such a personal commitment upon the client, which might be reciprocated.

The major method of imposing such a commitment and establishing mutual respect involved treating a person individually rather than as a typical case among many. Particularistic behavior thus meant special treatment, making exceptions to rules, doing more than the standard minimum. By being flexible with rules, a counselor could show that he/she cared, understood the client as a particular individual with special problems, and had enough trust to go out on a limb. In a situation where few other bases for gaining compliance existed, for the reasons outlined above, the particularism of program staff became a crucial organizational resource for compliance.

How, then, does this fit into our wider framework? We have shown that particularistic decisions by counselors were made on the basis of, in Weber's term, substantive justice. The historical intensification of bureaucratic routinization in the clinics, in response to external pressure toward strict enforcement of government regulations, favored formal justice—enforcing rules universalistically, without regard to particular circumstances. But the insistence on increasing formal rationality fatally undermined the particularistic basis of clinical compliance. As the counselors were denied discretionary powers, they became simple enforcers of rules, urine monitors, while the clients, treated more and more as cogs in a metered dispensing machine, increasingly were removed from sources of commitment to treatment.

Thus the mounting pressure to comply with the externally mandated rules intensified the contradiction between strict universalistic application of program rules (designed to prevent abuse of methadone), and a particularistic therapeutic outlook designed to change addicts' behavior. As programs attempted to respond to outside agencies by strictly enforcing federal and state regulations they simultaneously became the agents of their own therapeutic demise.

Summary and Conclusion

We have tried to give a developmental perspective on methadone maintenance and to link macrosociological levels to the experiences of participants. Methadone maintenance was an attempt to reintroduce a medical treatment model for heroin addiction after a fifty-year history of punitive prohibition. Government agencies, principally the FDA, succeeded in gaining an early jurisdictional mandate to control these medical interventions. Its model protocol redefined the parameters of methadone maintenance away from the original intentions of Dole and Nyswander, and incorporated the objections of the BNDD and medical critics into its protocol stipulations. Programs had little choice but to accept this redefined model of methadone maintenance. They were in a situation of lopsided dependency upon federal and state licensing, surveillance, and funding agencies, and upon the good will of local media and local government. Since all these institutional actors took the FDA protocol as the template against which to evaluate local programs, such programs had to appear to succeed according to the FDA model. Programs made elaborate efforts at manipulating their public image in order to maintain the support of those external agencies. As surveillance intensified, this involved an increasing attempt at strict compliance with federal and state regulations. These efforts in turn led to intense role conflicts within clinic staff, and alienation and mystification among addict clients. The already limited bases of organizational compliance in the clinics became further undermined, and an adaptational client role—the revolving-door syndrome—grew increasingly prevalent.

Generalizing from the particular case of methadone, we can derive certain insights into the workings of government policy in general, and return to the debate with the Pressman-Wildavsky position described earlier. The first thing to note is that the strength of government policy in this area (in contrast to their notion of federal impotence) derived primarily from the monopsonic position of government as buyer of certain services, such as methadone maintenance. In such monopsonic situations where government is faced with a myriad of competing sellers, and where a nongovernmental market for the services barely exists, one is likely to find a much greater degree of "potency" to government policy than elsewhere.

Secondly, we see that government policy is frequently contradictory in the sense that it embodies conflicting principles of action. In the case of methadone maintenance this involved the multiple goals of limiting methadone to specific subpopulations, and of strictly policing its distribution, while simultaneously attempting to set up a successful clinical milieu. Such conflicted policies are likely to emerge, we would suggest, in many instances of policy-making precisely because of the political context of federal agencies. In our case the FDA, attempting to appease or co-opt both friends and foes of methadone maintenance, allayed the criticism of foes via a hedge of restrictive regulations. This attempt by government policy regulations to appease all interested parties is quite general, especially in contentious areas. It is frequently a prerequisite for obtaining the necessarily broad political support required for the passage of enabling legislation, and also stems from the policy bureaucracy's desire to minimize conflict and opposition to its plans. In most cases this kind of policy-making behavior leads mainly to an excess of regulation and lack of flexibility.

At its worst, it results in quite incompatible demands being included in policy and placed upon local implementing agencies.

The impact of such compromised policies is particularly severe in contexts of monopsony or lopsided dependence of local agencies on national government. Agencies then have to involve themselves in institutional presentation-of-self, which involves actively selling their ability to perform contradictory tasks, in order to obtain central financing. Any attempt to fight the irrationalities in policy would simply result in some other competing organization receiving funding.

Finally, the manner by which these policy demands have their impact at the program level involves a displacement of program goals toward sustaining funding via strict adherence to government regulations and active presentational work. But compromised policies also impact upon programs by restricting their organizational resources for gaining the motivated compliance of subordinates. Many organizations under the best of circumstances find it difficult to develop an effective reward structure and an appropriate form of normative, remunerative, or coercive compliance mechanisms. But under the burden of detailed government regulations such resources may be severely limited, leading to organizational failure due to paucity of rewards. Alternatively, as in the case of methadone maintenance, government policy may mandate the use of quite incompatible compliance mechanisms, that is, normative alongside coercive control, in which case the programs begin to unravel from within as they cannot hold the loyalty or commitment of their members. In either case government policy unwittingly forces programs into presiding over their own demise: the closer the programs attempt to obey the dictates of government, the worse become their problems of organizational control.

Thus, far from conceptualizing government policy as impotent on the local level and regarding outcome as detached from policy, we recommend, at least in the context of governmental monopsony, a model which emphasizes the power of policy and of its consequences, both intended and unintended, upon local practice.

[8]

CLASS POWER AND STATE POLICY

Alexander Hicks, Roger Friedland, and Edwin Johnson

T YPICALLY, it has been argued that poor people in the United States are unorganized and thus denied access to the political system (Schattschneider 1960). Excluded from the relatively high-wage unionized sector of the economy, the working poor are not organized politically via their place in production (O'Connor 1973). As a result, the poor are forced into disruptive tactics outside the limits of American pluralism (Alford and Friedland 1975; Piven and Cloward 1971). In this view, the politics of poverty represent a desperate form of interest group politics which force political elites into co-optive and conciliatory concessions.

The thrust of our paper is that redistribution to the poor through government expenditure and taxation policies is a class issue. We argue that national corporations and labor unions are organizational bases of class power; that the distribution of these class organizations across states will affect the pattern of redistribution to the poor; and that these effects will be consistent with a class conflict model of redistribution to the poor. Specifically, we hypothesize that the presence of national corporations will have a negative and labor unions a positive effect on state redistribution to the poor.

Toward a Class Model of Governmental Redistribution

The potential impact of corporate and labor union power on redistribution to the poor has been virtually ignored in the empirical literature on state policy (for an exception, see DeLeon 1973). We

From *American Sociological Review* (June 1978), 43(3):302–15. Reprinted by permission.

argue that corporate and labor union organizations have class interests in state government redistribution to the poor through public taxation and expenditure. To the extent that corporate or labor union organizations are concentrated in a state, the level of government redistribution to the poor is hypothesized to be more consistent with these class interests.

Interests generally shared between unionized and nonunionized segments of the working class can be conceptualized as class interests. Similarly, interests shared between corporations regardless of their industrial or market position can be conceptualized as class interests. Positive labor union interests in redistribution to the poor might be expected to be minimal given the concentration of labor unions in the most capital intensive, highly productive, monopolistic sectors of the economy, and the concentration of the working poor in labor-intensive, less productive, more competitive sectors (O'Connor 1973). However, while the material condition of the poor is not relevant to the immediate collective bargaining interests of the relatively high-income union membership, it is critical to the political power of organized labor which makes these immediate gains possible. First, organized labor's political power is contingent upon the strength of the Democratic party whose electoral success in turn requires the political mobilization and votes of the nonunionized working class and dependent surplus populations (Greenstone 1969). Second, labor unions are interested in protecting the private incomes of low-income families through progressive taxation and supplementing them through public expenditures to increase the floor under the union wage. Third, labor unions are interested in using the public purse to protect and supplement the incomes of their own membership. Because taxation and social service programs are often organized in universalistic terms, nonunionized members of the working class are also likely to benefit. This is more than a trickle-down effect. On the contrary, because many of the poor are in fact former union members who are retired, disabled, or laid off, much labor union interest in the poor is closely tied up with union members.

Corporate interests in redistribution to the poor, on the other hand, are negative. First, corporate political power is neither tied to the Democratic party nor is it greatly contingent upon electoral mobilization (Alford and Friedland 1975). Second, corporations continue to be interested in the availability of low-income labor, particularly where open-shop legislation and routine, low-skill production make this possible. Third, corporate elites are interested in protecting their profitability and income both by minimizing the progressiveness of the tax structure and by securing the maximum share of public expenditures for programs which are indirectly productive. High levels of redistribution to the poor involve both relatively progressive taxation and high levels of government expenditures which are not even indirectly productive.

Patterns of corporate and labor union elite behavior suggest that these interests are salient political concerns. National labor union elites are as ideologically supportive of welfare expansion and income equalization programs as national corporate elites are opposed (Barton 1975). Labor unions are perhaps more effective in securing broad redistributive legislation benefiting the entire working class than they are in securing regulatory changes that benefit the more particularistic concerns of the union (Lowi 1969). State-level case studies indicate strong, active corporate opposition to redistributive policy changes (see Fischer 1974; Lockard 1959). At the city level, labor unions have played an important role in organizing the Democratic vote of the working and dependent poor (Greenstone 1969).

The resources that labor union and corporate organizations have to translate these class interests into policy are considerable. The potency of corporate elite political participation in state governments is intensified by their well-financed lobbyists (Schattschneider 1960; Ziegler 1969), monopolies over information and expertise required by government (McConnell 1966), control over high-income career paths out of the public sector, and by their discretionary control over investment decisions upon which the efficacy of government policy is dependent (Friedland 1977a; Haveman and Hamrin 1973). Beyond its own lobbying apparatus, the political participation of labor union elites is buttressed by their control over an extensive apparatus for political mobilization of voters at all levels of government (Greenstone 1969). Thus the very presence of corporations and labor unions which command concentrated political and economic resources may structure the range of political coalitions, issues, and public policies without high levels of participation by their elites.

We have specified the proredistributive interests of labor unions and the antiredistributive interests of corporations, and the considerable political resources these organizations can wield in the determination of public policy. Consequently, we hypothesize that *a strong labor union presence in a state will have a positive effect upon governmental redistribution to the poor, while a strong corporate presence in a state will have a negative effect upon governmental redistribution to the poor.*

PAST RESEARCH FINDINGS

Theory and research concerning the causes and consequences of government income redistribution through public expenditure and taxation have developed rapidly over the past two decades (Cutright 1965, 1967; Dawson and Robinson 1963; Fry and Winters 1970; Hofferbert 1972; Jackman 1974, 1975; Key 1956; Lowi 1964; Wilensky 1975). Such policies have been argued to be important for societal integration, business-cycle stability and long-term economic growth (see Galbraith 1958:115–20; Samuelson 1973:805–6; Shonfield 1966:3–18). Recent economic research on the United States, Great Britain, and Sweden indicates that the net redistributive impacts of government spending and taxing upon poverty and income inequality are quite substantial (see Franzen, Kerstein, and Rosenberg 1975; Nicolson 1974; Reynolds and Smolensky 1974, 1977).[1]

Quantitative research on the determinants of governmental redistribution consistently has found that socioeconomic development (per capita GNP and median school years), redistributive need (percent poor), and governmental structure (executive centralization) significantly influence redistributive policies (see Fried 1975; Fry and Winters 1970; Jackman 1975; Peters 1974; Wilensky 1975). The strength of relatively Left parties and the degree of unionization sometimes have been found to influence redistributive policy in Western European nations (Fried 1975; Peters 1974).[2] In the case of the United States, the Democratic party's electoral and office-holding strength has been found to have a positive impact upon redistributive policy outcomes under conditions of high party competition and cohesiveness (Hicks, Friedland, and Johnson 1976).

Development, Poverty, Party, and Governmental Redistribution

Such aspects of socioeconomic development as income, education, industrialization, and urbanization consistently have been found to affect redistributive policy outputs (Cutright 1965; Dawson and Robinson 1963; Jackman 1974; Lineberry and Fowler 1967; Peters

1974; Wilensky 1975). The enlargement of discretionary resources, the decline of kinship-based forms of social security, and the liberalizing effects of increased education are a few of the reasons that have been given for the tendency for government redistribution to increase with greater socioeconomic development.

The level of poverty, as measured by such variables as percent poor, also has been found to have consistently positive effects on redistribution (Fry 1974; Fry and Winters 1970; Wilensky 1975). To what extent such effects are to be attributed to the social control and office-holding interests of governmental elites, to humanitarian responses of governmental personnel, or to perceived human needs has not been established. Whatever the reason for poverty's redistributive effects, past research does suggest that public expenditure will be more redistributive in jurisdictions with a large proportion of poor people.

Political scientists and sociologists have focused considerable attention upon the relation of party and electoral variables to public policies (see Cutright 1965; Dawson and Robinson 1963; Hofferbert 1972; Jackman 1974). Until recently, most evidence on the impact of electoral variables, such as the strength of the Democratic party and interparty competition, upon governmental redistribution suggested they were inconsequential (see Dawson and Robinson 1963; Fry and Winters 1970; Hofferbert 1972). However, Hicks, Friedland, and Johnson (1976) found that Democratic party strength, Democratic party cohesion, and interparty competition interact with one another to generate more redistributive state policy. More precisely, they concluded that Democratic party strength has a positive effect on the level of state redistribution to the poor to the extent to which Democratic party cohesion and interparty competition are also simultaneously high in a state. The rationale is that Democratic party strength denoted by office-holding is not translated into progressive, redistributive legislation without the complementary *capacity* of party cohesion and the *imperative* of interparty competition. This hypothesis will be tested here in the context of new controls for corporate and union presence.

In this section, we have focused upon those variables in the state policy literature likely to affect governmental redistribution. However, a number of additional variables in the literature have been argued to influence governmental redistribution. The majority of such variables are referred to in Fry and Winters (1970) and Booms and Halldorson (1973). A number of variables, most of them drawn from these two sources, will be employed for control purposes in our statistical analysis.

Methodology

THEORY AND TECHNIQUE

Our use of an additive regression model to assess the impact of labor union and corporate presence on redistribution to the poor makes a series of implicit theoretical assumptions. First, holding corporate presence constant, we estimate the effect of labor union presence on redistribution. The implicit conception of power is additive, not interactive. We do not measure directly class conflict, or even the relative organizational presence of corporations and labor unions. We treat a class power as a relation of the class to the state but not as a relationship between classes. Second, by assuming conflicting corporate and labor union interests in redistribution to the poor, and by arguing that cross-sectional variation in redistributive policy is partially and additively determined by class organization, we approach a pluralist theory *cum* class actors. Redistribution to the poor is determined by a vector sum of pressures by organized interests, each of which can have some independent access to the state. Third, we do not specify any functional role for the state, except as it transmits the power of organized interests into policy. The model specifies no variable capacity for states to adjust to general systemic problems generated by social disruption or economic contradictions, which may vary across states. Finally, the structure of the state is taken to be theoretically nonproblematic in that it is assumed not to affect corporate and/or labor union political power vis-à-vis redistributive policies to the poor *across different U.S. states*.

UNITS OF ANALYSIS

The American states have been a principal domain for the testing of hypotheses on determinants of redistributive policies (Booms and Halldorson 1973; Dawson and Robinson 1963; Fry and Winters 1970; Hofferbert 1972). This appears to be the case for a number of reasons. Substantively, the states are important United States political jurisdictions. They have authority over the bulk of public assistance and unemployment and workmen's compensation programs; and they have, on the average, raised nearly a quarter of all governmental revenues and spent nearly a third of total government expenditures in the United States during the past three decades (see Sharkansky 1972). Methodologically, states are rich in data from census sources and past study surveys; they are unusually free from problems of comparability which plague much comparative research; they are numerous enough for the application of fairly sophisticated quantitative techniques; and they are few enough for economical quantitative research.

MEASUREMENT AND DATA

For our measure of state redistribution to the poor, we used a measure of the extent to which the total spending and taxing activities of state governments progressively redistribute income to poor households. This measure of state redistribution for 1961 was constructed by Booms and Halldorson (1973) with data from the U.S. Department of Labor (1965), Bishop (1967), and the U.S. Bureau of the Census (1963). It resembles a number of other indices constructed during the past decade to measure governmental redistribution (Bishop 1967; Reynolds and Smolensky 1974). It operationally defines governmental redistribution as the ratio of estimated net expenditure benefits to estimated net revenue burdens for households with incomes of less than $4,000. Values on this index range from a minimum value of 1.54 for South Dakota to a maximum value of 6.00 for Massachusetts. (See table 8.1 and Booms and Halldorson [1973] for further information on this measure.)

South Dakota's 1.54 value on the redistribution index means that the average poor family received $1.54 in public goods and money transfers for every dollar paid in taxes and user charges. A few figures on transfer payments and tax schemes for this scale's extreme cases may serve to increase the reader's feel for the index. In South Dakota in 1961, $46 was paid out in public assistance payments for every person below the federal poverty line for that year; the corresponding figure for Massachusetts was $171. In the same year, the maximum annual unemployment payment for an individual was $816 in South Dakota and $1,350 in Massachusetts. Similarly, the mixes of (regressive) sales and (progressive) personal income tax revenues were strikingly different for these two states. In South Dakota in 1961, 61 percent of state-raised revenues were raised by means of sales taxes, and 0 percent by means of personal income

138   A. HICKS, R. FRIEDLAND, AND E. JOHNSON

Table 8.1.   Booms and Halldorson's Redistribution Index Values for 48
States, 1961

6.004	Massachusetts	2.995	Pennsylvania	2.184	Wyoming
5.904	Illinois	2.958	Oregon	2.166	Delaware
5.804	California	2.785	Minnesota	2.128	Nebraska
5.385	Colorado	2.774	Nevada	2.126	North Carolina
4.700	Connecticut	2.653	Oklahoma	2.126	Florida
4.680	Washington	2.590	West Virginia	2.123	Louisiana
4.348	New York	2.559	Utah	2.036	Arkansas
4.342	New Jersey	2.522	Wisconsin	1.971	New Mexico
3.900	Ohio	2.522	Georgia	1.910	Montana
3.694	Missouri	2.482	Iowa	1.908	Vermont
3.679	Idaho	2.435	Arizona	1.845	New Hampshire
3.549	Michigan	2.398	Kentucky	1.740	South Carolina
3.501	Kansas	2.304	Alabama	1.728	North Dakota
3.375	Rhode Island	2.216	Tennessee	1.661	Virginia
3.372	Maryland	2.211	Maine	1.574	Texas
3.348	Indiana	2.198	Mississippi	1.537	South Dakota

NOTE: mean: 3.172; standard deviation: 1.226.

taxes. Corresponding figures for Massachusetts were 34 percent and 30 percent (see U.S. Bureau of the Census 1963.)

Corporate and labor union presences were operationalized by the existence of their administrative and/or policy-making centers in a state. The presence of national corporate and labor union centers in a state indicates a variety of things. First, it indicates the presence of capitalists and working-class elites within the state who are available for state-level political participation. Second, it indicates the presence of organizational actors and organizational units of political representation in the state. Third, it indicates the size and diversity of the organizational base for class political action should it occur.

For indicators of corporate presence, measures of the presence of policy-making and administrative centers of large financial and nonfinancial corporations are used. Items employed include the number of headquarters of the top 500 manufacturing corporations and the top 50 commercial banks located in a state, and the number of upper-class clubs located in a state (see Domhoff 1970; *Fortune* 1961a, 1961b). Headquarters were emphasized and corporate plants ignored because headquarters are loci for political activity, while plants are not, due to limited political autonomy (see Aiken 1970:396–97; Friedland 1977a).

A principal components analysis with varimax rotation was run on the corporate items to test for their unidimensionality and covergent validity.[3] Only one principal component with an eigenvalue greater than one emerged from the analysis; and all thirteen corporate items loaded highly on this principal component.[4] The factor score for the component was used to scale our measure of corporate presence.

For indicators of the presence of labor unions we used measures of the number of both union headquarters and locals. Union locals were employed because of their political autonomy (see Greenstone 1969). Union membership seemed an appropriate indicator of union political resources because of the extensive union apparatus for member political mobilization.[5] Principal components analysis was used to establish covergent validity and construct a scale for union presence.

To measure socioeconomic development, we used data on the most common development variables and measures in the American state policy literature. These were median personal income, median years of education, and percent of state population residing in cities with populations greater than 2,000. Several measures were then added to these to broaden the range of development measures. The percentages of state populations residing in central cities and Standard Metropolitan Statistical Areas were added to complement the measure of urbanization noted above. Per capita value added in manufacturing was used as an additional measure of industrialization. Percent white-collar was introduced as a crude measure of socioeconomic status. In order to achieve a parsimonious measurement of development, all items were entered into a principal components analysis. From this, two clear components emerged: socioeconomic development and urbanization-industrialization. Both will be used as development variables.[6]

Poverty is measured by the percentage of state households with incomes of less than $3,000 in 1959. This measure of poverty has been the most commonly used measure of poverty in the state literature on redistributive policies. (See U.S. Bureau of the Census 1963, for source.)

The three party variables—Democratic strength, Democratic cohesion, and interparty competition—were also measured using separate principal components analyses to establish their covergent validity and to generate scales. The principal component for Democratic strength includes items on the average strength of the Democrats in terms of percentages of gubernatorial votes and legislative seats (1948 through 1962) and an item on the number of successive two-year periods during the same period marked by simultaneous Democratic possession of the governorship and Democratic majorities in all legislative houses. The items for interparty competition include two measures of absolute deviations from fifty-fifty party splits in voter support and legislative control (both averaged over the period 1948–62). They also include two measures of interparty turnovers in elective office holding (1948–62). The component for Democratic cohesion contains three items, two measures of Democratic voting cohesion, and a measure of partisan conflict in state legislatures.[7] (For a theoretical and operational elaboration of these measures, see Hicks, Friedland, and Johnson 1976).

Eleven additional variables were incorporated into our statistical analysis as controls in order to check and correct for possible specification bias due to omitted variables. Three sorts of variables were selected. These are presented here in terms of the criteria used for their selection. First, those variables that had partial correlations in Fry and Winters (1970) *and* standardized regression coefficients in Booms and Halldorson (1973) which were greater than 0.20 in absolute value were used. These are income inequality, political participation, governor tenure potential, legislative professionalism

Table 8.2.   Matrix of Zero-Order Correlations for Variables of 48-State Model of Government Redistribution

		X_1	X_2	X_3	X_4	X_5	X_6	X_7
X_1	Corporate presence	1.00						
X_2	Union presence	.85	1.00					
X_3	Poverty	−.30	−.40	1.00				
X_4	Socioeconomic development	.34	.42	−.92	1.00			
X_5	Democratic strength × Democratic cohesion × interparty competition	.04	.08	−.48	.44	1.00		
X_6	Government tenure potential	.28	.29	−.41	.45	.25	1.00	
X_7	Policy innovation	.58	.72	−.62	.59	.30	.21	1.00
Y	Redistribution	.42	.62	−.56	.64	.48	.48	.70

and policy innovation, and percent of the labor force employed in nonagriculture. Second, Democratic strength and cohesion and interparty competition—the three variables composing the party variable interaction—were used. Third, population size (a possible source of spuriousness in the estimates for corporate and union presence) and a dummy variable for the South (a proxy for long-term, institutionalized one-party politics) were used. The procedures which we used to incorporate these variables into our analysis as controls are discussed below.[8]

MODEL AND TECHNIQUES

Our model may be expressed in the form of the following equation:

Redistribution = $a - b_1$ Corporate presence
+ b_2 Union presence
+ b_3 Poverty
+ b_4 Socioeconomic development
+ b'_4 Urbanization-industrialization
+ b_5 (Democratic strength $\times$ Democratic cohesion $\times$ Interparty competition)
+ $b_6 X_6 + \ldots + b_n X_n + e$,

where $X_6, \ldots X_n$ are control variables.

Analysis was performed in three rounds. First, the equation was estimated without the eleven control variables. Second, the equation was reestimated after ejection of those variables which did not have significant effects upon governmental redistribution at the .05 level, as indicated by results of the first round of estimation. Third, tests were run for significant effects of the eleven controls by means of a stepwise regression procedure for which a 0.05 level of significance was designated as a criterion for the incorporation of controls into our model. Ordinary least squares was used for estimation. T-statistics were used for all statistical tests. All tests were one-tailed. In the section on findings, results for the end of the third round of estimation will be emphasized.

FINDINGS

Our hypotheses regarding the effect of labor union and corporate presence are supported by our regression analyses (see table 8.3). Labor union presence has positive effect upon governmental redistribution, while corporate presence has a negative effect upon governmental redistribution. The effect of corporate presence upon governmental redistribution is $-.390$ in raw metric terms and $-.329$ in standardized terms (see $\hat{b}_1$ and $\hat{\beta}_1$ in table 8.3). The effect of union presence is .575 in raw metric terms; it is .484 in standardized terms (see $\hat{b}_2$ and $\hat{\beta}_2$ in table 8.3).

Two of the eleven control variables are found to influence significantly governmental redistribution. These are governor tenure potential and policy innovations (see below). Our model's fit with the data is good. When our model includes governor tenure potential and policy innovations, it has a coefficient of determination corrected for degrees of freedom of .71. When it excludes these two controls, it has a coefficient of determination corrected for degrees of freedom of .65 (see table 8.3). Our presentation of findings is confined to those for the model which includes the two controls since estimates do not vary substantially between the two variants of our model and since the longer model reveals the shorter one to be misspecified (see table 8.3).

Poverty and socioeconomic development both have positive impacts upon governmental redistribution. The effects of poverty are $\hat{b}_3 = .068$ and $\hat{\beta}_3 = .582$. Those of socioeconomic development are $\hat{b}_4 = .755$ and $\hat{\beta}_4 = .635$ (see table 8.3).

The party variable interaction term has a positive impact upon governmental distribution ($\hat{\beta} = .276$).

The control variable, governor tenure potential, has a significant positive effect upon governmental redistribution ($\hat{b}_6 = .222$, $\hat{\beta}_6 = .227$) in our regression analysis of 48 states (see table 8.3). Governor tenure potential has been found to affect positively governmental redistribution on the assumption that (1) a governor's tenure potential, as an indicator of his power over careers in state politics, is an important gubernatorial resource; and (2) the broad constituency support needs for gubernatorial election requires redistributive appeals and action from governors (see Fry and Winters 1970).

The control variable innovations, an index of the overall rapidity with which state governments have adopted a broad range of policy innovations in the period 1870–1960, has a positive effect upon governmental redistribution. Because of its long-time coverage, it was regarded as an exogenous variable. Its effects are $\hat{b}_7 = .0005$ and $\hat{\beta}_7 = .392$. Policy innovativeness was hypothesized to affect positively governmental redistribution on the assumption that it tapped the "equitable, efficient, issue-oriented, progressive tradition in American politics" (Fry and Winters 1970:518).

Table 8.3. Parameter Estimates for Regression Analysis of State Governmental Redistribution[a]

	X_1: Corp. Pres.	X_2: Union Pres.	X_3: Poverty	X_4: Dev't	X_5: Interaction	X_6: G.T.P.	X_7: Innovs.
$\hat{\beta}_1$	−.329 (−.326)	.484 (.742)	.582 (.440)	.635 (.704)	.276 (.331)	.227	.392
$\hat{b}_1$	−.390 (−.387)	.575 (.882)	.068 (.052)	.755 (.837)	.093 (.112)	.222	.0005
SE $\hat{b}_1$	.176 (.194)	.210 (.201)	.025 (.027)	.251 (.274)	.031 (.034)	.089	.0002
p	.016 (.026)	.004 (.000)	.003 (.034)	.005 (.002)	.002 (.001)	.008	.004
a =	−2.918 (.194)	$\bar{R}^2$ = .714 (.647)					

[a] Results for equations run without the control variables governor tenure potential (G.T.P.) and innovations (Innovs.) are presented in parentheses.
$\hat{\beta}_1$ = estimated standarized regression coefficient for variable i = 1, . . . , 7.
$\hat{b}_1$ = estimated unstandardized regression coefficient for variable i = 1, . . . , 7.
SE($\hat{b}_1$) = standard error of $\hat{b}_1$; a = regression intercept; p = probability value of $\hat{b}_1$.
$\bar{R}^2$ = coefficient of determination corrected for degrees of freedom.

EDITOR'S NOTE: Regression is a statistical model in which a dependent variable—in this case, state governmental redistribution—is predicted from an independent variable—in this case, variables X_1-X_7. The unstandardized regression coefficient measures the amount of change in the dependent variable associated with one unit of change in the independent variable. In order to assess the relative importance of several independent variables, a comparable unit of measurement must be obtained. The usual practice is to standardize the scores. Original, raw scores are metric and unstandardized. With standardized scores, the relative importance of independent variables can be determined because all have identical variances (= 1). Standard error is a measure of the variation or scatter about the line of regression. The larger the value, the greater the scatter and the poorer the relationship. The regression intercept is the predicted value of the dependent variable when the standardized independent variable is equal to 0. The probability value is a test of the statistical significance of a relationship between variables. It measures the probability that observed differences can be explained by chance. Probability values of .05 or less are generally considered to indicate statistically significant differences, not chance ones. The coefficient of determination is a relative measure of the degree of association between dependent and combined independent variables. It measures the proportion of the variance in the dependent variable that is explained by the independent variables.

In conclusion to our presentation of findings, let us note that urbanization-industrialization and nine of the eleven control variables were not significantly related to redistribution. This means that variables such as voter turnout, South and population size did not have to be included in our final models in order to obviate specification error.

Discussion

Our findings of significant positive effects of labor union presence and negative effects of corporate presence on governmental redistribution to the poor at the state level suggest, first, that labor unions and corporations are organizational bases of class power and, second, that redistribution to the poor is a class issue. That these findings control for electoral characteristics suggests that corporations and labor unions exert an influence upon state policies which is unmediated by electoral politics. Our findings of net effects of the interaction of Democratic party strength and cohesion and interparty competition on state redistribution to the poor suggests that electoral politics indeed does make a difference where a more progressive political party has *both* the legislative capacity and the electoral imperative to pursue redistributive policies. That these party characteristics affect redistribution independently of corporate and labor union strength indicates that the party system provides the electorate with a partially autonomous means of influencing redistributive policy (see Hicks, Friedland, and Johnson 1976). Class politics and party politics both matter in the determination of redistributive policy. So, in consonance with much previous research, do socioeconomic development, poverty, governor tenure potential, and policy innovativeness (see Findings above).

Research is accumulating which indicates that class power operates on subnational policy-making via the location of policy-making and administrative centers of national corporations and labor unions. Friedland (1977b) has found analogous additive positive and negative effects of corporate and labor union presence on central city responses to the War on Poverty. Research is being conducted on the historical development of corporate and labor union power (Hicks 1979), as well as its impact on state policies which are more directly related to profitability and wage interests of corporations and labor unions (Johnson, forthcoming). A dozen years after Lowi (1964:707) wrote that "issues that involve redistribution cut closer than any others along class lines and activate interests in what are roughly class terms," systematic evidence of class power as a determinant of redistributive public policy is being generated.

The challenge is to begin to develop models of policy determination with appropriate methodologies which specify the relational nature of class power and the impact of state structure and public policy on class power (see Friedland, Piven, and Alford 1977).

NOTES

1. Reynolds and Smolensky (1974, 1977) find that the net impact of the fiscal activities of all levels of government in the United States has tended; over the past three decades, to augment the final incomes of the prefiscal poor by about 100 percent, and to decrease overall income inequality by more than 25 percent. Musgrave, Case, and Leonard (1975) have generated congruent findings for the United States, as have Nicolson (1974) for Great Britain and Franzen, Kerstein, and Rosenberg (1975) for Sweden.

2. Findings on the relation of Left party strength to redistributive policies in Western Europe are not all consistent; they vary from unit to unit and period to period (see Fried 1975).

3. The discriminate validity of this measure and of our measures of union presence, Democratic cohesion, and interparty cohesion were assumed on theoretical grounds. For example, some items for the corporate presence measure correlated more highly with certain union presence items than with certain other corporate presence items. Still, they were regarded theoretically as indicators of *corporate* presence, which was expected to have impacts on governmental redistribution opposite to those of union presence. This expectation, as we shall see, was confirmed by our analysis.

4. The principal component for corporate presence explained 87.3 percent of the common variance in its constituent items. The thirteen items included numbers of headquarters in a state of the 50, 200, 500, and 1,000 largest manufacturing corporations and of the 50 largest banks and the 50 largest insurance companies (*Fortune* 1961a, 1961b, 1963); the number of personnel of, and value added by, administrative and auxiliary enterprises (U.S. Bureau of the Census 1966); the numbers and assets of corporate foundations headquarters in a state (U.S. Bureau of the Census 1963); the assets of all financial corporations headquartered in a state (U.S. Bureau of the Census 1963); and the number of Domhoff's (1970) upper-class clubs located in a state. Loadings ranged between .985 and .843 and had a median value of .934. Only one principal component with an eigenvalue of 1.0 emerged from the analysis of these items. All components referred to have been constructed using varimax rotation.

5. One principal component emerged from the analyses of the four union presence items: 1) number of AFL-CIO members in a state (.955); 2) number of union headquarters (.925); 3) number of union locals (.923); 4) number of AFL-CIO affiliated locals listed in a state (.853). This component explained 83.7 percent of the common variance in the items. (Loadings are listed in parentheses.) Data for these items are taken from U.S. Bureau of the Census (1963) and U.S. Office of Labor-Management and Welfare-Pension Reports (1960). Data for the corporate and union presence measures are not standardized on the size of state (population, economically active population, and so forth) because such standardization would control away corporate and union policy effects entailing the mediation of corporate and union leverage over the national political system (national parties, congressional committees, federal agencies). Thus, nationally mediated effects of a state's large business corporations on unions would be expected to be larger for, say, a 5,000,000 population state with 500,000 union members, headquarters, than for a one million population state with 100,000 union members. In order to control for size effects other than corporate or labor presence effects, population size will be utilized below as a controlled variable.

6. The socioeconomic development principal component explained 81.5 percent of the common variance in measures of median household income (.927), median years

of schooling (.884), and percent of the labor force in white-collar occupations (.881). (The numbers in parentheses are component loadings.) The urbanization-industrialization component explained .95 percent of the common variance in the percentage of state population in noncentral city portions of SMSAs (.889), the percentage of non-SMSA state population in cities with greater than 2,000 inhabitants (.976), and per capita value added in manufacturing (.989).

7. The principal component for Democratic strength explains 90.2 percent of the common variance in its three items. The principal component for Democratic cohesion explains 65.5 percent of the common variance in its three items. The principal component for interparty competition explains 64.5 percent of the common variance in its four items. See Hicks, Friedland, and Johnson (1976).

8. Fry and Winters (1970) and Booms and Halldorson (1973) were our main sources of control variables because these studies alone approached exhaustive use of the principal operationalized variables in the state policy literature and because each of these studies used measures of governmental redistribution. See Fry and Winters (1970) for theoretical and operational discussions of variables in our first set of controls. Measurement of three party controls is discussed above and in Hicks, Friedland, and Johnson (1976). Population was measured as the natural logarithm of 1959 population figures from the U.S. Bureau of the Census (1963). The South was defined as the ten-state region composed of Alabama, Arkansas, Georgia, Florida, Louisiana, Mississippi, North Carolina, South Carolina, Texas, and Virginia.

[9]

THE LIMITS OF SOCIAL POLICY

Nathan Glazer

T HERE is a general sense that we face a crisis in social policy, and
in almost all its branches. Whether this crisis derives from the
backwardness of the United States in social policy generally, the
revolt of the blacks, the fiscal plight of the cities, the failure of
national leadership, the inherent complexity of the problems, or the
weakening of the national fiber, and what weight we may ascribe to
these and other causes, are no easy questions to settle. I believe there
is much at fault with the way we generally think of these matters,
and I wish to suggest another approach.

The term "social policy" is very elastic. I use it to describe all those
public policies which have developed in the past hundred years to
protect families and individuals from the accidents of industrial and
urban life, and which try to maintain a decent minimum of living
conditions for all.[1] The heart of social policy is the relief of the
condition of the poor, and it is in that sense I use the term here.

There are, I believe, two prevailing and antagonistic views of social
policy.

One—I will call it the "liberal" view—operates with a model of the
social world in which that world is seen as having undergone
progressive improvement for, roughly, the past hundred years. The
unimproved world, in this view, was the world of early and high
industrialism. Market forces prevailed unobstructed, or nearly so.
The enormous inequalities they created in wealth, power, and status
were added to the still largely unreduced inequalities of the preindustrial world. This situation, which meant that most men lived in
squalor while a few, profiting from the labor of the many, lived in

From *Commentary* (1971), 52:51–58. Reprinted by permission; copyright © 1971,
American Jewish Committee.

great luxury, was seen by a developing social conscience as both evil and dangerous. It was evil because of the huge inequalities that characterized it and because of its failure to insure a decent minimum at the bottom levels; and it was dangerous because it encouraged the destitute to rebel against industry and the state. Consequently, in Bismarck's Germany, and somewhat later on in England, conservative states grew worried about rebellion and workingmen began to be protected against complete penury in old age or in times of unemployment through industrial accident and illness; small beginnings were also made in helping them cover some of the costs of medical care. Gradually, such measures of protection were extended to cover other areas like housing, and were made available to broader and broader classes of people.

In the liberal view, then, we have a sea of misery, scarcely diminished at all by voluntary charitable efforts. Government then starts moving in, setting up dikes, pushing back the sea and reclaiming the land, so to speak. In this view, while new issues may be presented for public policy, they are never really new; rather, they are only newly *recognized* as issues demanding public intervention. Thus the liberal point of view is paradoxically calculated to make us feel both guiltier and more arrogant. We feel guilty for not having recognized and acted on injustices and deprivations earlier, but we also feel complacently superior in comparison to our forebears, who did not recognize or act on them at all.

I have given a rather sharp and perhaps caricatured picture of the liberal view. Liberals are of course aware that new needs—and not simply new recognitions of old needs—arise. Nevertheless, the typical stance of the liberal in dealing with issues of social policy is blame— not of the unfortunates, those suffering from the ills that the social policy is meant to remove, but of society, of the political system and its leaders. The liberal stance is: for every problem there is a policy, and even if the problem is relatively new, the social system and the political system must be indicted for failing to tackle it earlier.

There is another element in the liberal view. It sees vested interests as the chief obstacle to the institution of new social policies. One such interest consists simply of those who are better off—those not in need of the social policy in question, who resist it because of the increase in taxes. But other kinds of obstructive interests are also there: real-estate people and landlords in the field of housing, employers subject to payroll taxes in the field of Social Security, doctors in the field of medical care, and so on.

Despite the assumption here of a conflict pitting liberals against conservatives, I would suggest that the main premises behind this general picture of social policy are today hardly less firmly held by conservatives than they are by liberals. In the American context, conservatives will differ from liberals because they want to move more slowly, give more consideration to established interests, keep taxes from going up too high. They will on occasion express a stronger concern for traditional values—work, the family, sexual restraint. But on the whole the line dividing liberals from conservatives grows steadily fainter. The Family Assistance Program, the major new reform of the welfare system proposed by the Nixon administration, will illustrate my point. Anyone who reads through the Congressional hearings on this proposal will be hard put to distinguish liberals from conservatives in terms of any naive division between those who favor the expansion of social policy and those who oppose it.

It is not only in America that one sees the merging of liberal and conservative views on social policy, and not only today. Bismarck, after all, stands at the beginning of the history of modern social policy. In the countries of northwest Europe, the differences over social policy between liberals and conservatives are even narrower than they are in this country. In England, very often the issue seems to turn on such questions as what kind of charges should be imposed by the National Health Service for eyeglasses or prescriptions. It was this kind of reduction in the conflicts over basic values in advanced industrial societies that in the 1950s led Raymond Aron and Daniel Bell to formulate their ideas about "the end of ideology." And while in the 1960s all the old ideologies returned to these countries in force, it remains true that ideological battles between major political parties have been startlingly reduced in intensity since World War II.

Having incorporated the conservative point of view on social policy into the liberal, I will go on to the only other major perspective that means much today, the radical. The radical perspective on social policy comes in many variants, but they can all be summed up quite simply: if the liberal, and increasingly the conservative, believes that for every problem there must be a specific solution, the radical believes that there can be no particular solutions to particular problems but only a general solution, which is a transformation in the nature of society itself.

This point of view has consequences, just as the liberal point of view does. If, for example, the conservative proposes a guaranteed annual income of $1,600 for a family of four, and the liberal proposes that the figure be doubled or tripled, the radical will feel quite free to demand an even higher minimum. He knows that his figure is unlikely to be adopted, but he also knows that he can cite this failure as proof of his contention that the system cannot accommodate decent social demands. If, on the other hand, his policy or something like it is taken seriously, he can hope for a greater degree of class conflict as demands that are very difficult to implement are publicized and considered. And even if his policy is implemented, the radical remains firm in his faith that nothing has changed: the new policy is after all only a palliative; it does not get to the heart of the matter; or if it does get to the heart of the matter, it gets there only to prevent the people from getting to the heart of the largest matters of all. Indeed, one of the important tenets of radicalism is that nothing ever changes short of the final apocalyptic revolutionary moment when everything changes.

As against these two perspectives—the one that believes in a solution to every problem, and the other that believes in no solution to any problem save revolutionary change—I present a somewhat different view of social policy. This view is based on two propositions:

1. Social policy is an effort to deal with the breakdown of traditional ways of handling distress. These traditional mechanisms are located primarily in the family, but also in the ethnic group, the neighborhood, and in such organizations as the church and the *landsmanschaft*.

2. In its effort to deal with the breakdown of these traditional structures, however, social policy tends to encourage their further weakening. There is, then, no sea of misery against which we are making steady headway. Our efforts to deal with distress themselves increase distress.

I do not mean to suggest any automatic law. I do suggest processes.

One is the well-known revolution of rising expectations. This revolution is itself fed by social policies. Their promise, inadequately realized, leaves behind a higher level of expectation, which a new round of social policy must attempt to meet, and with the same consequences. In any case, by the nature of democratic (and perhaps not only democratic) politics, again and again more must be promised than can be delivered. These promises are, I believe, the chief mechanisms in educating people to higher expectations. But they are, of course, reinforced by the enormous impact of mass literacy, the mass media, and expanding levels of education. Rising expectations continually enlarge the sea of felt and perceived misery, whatever may happen to it in actuality.

Paralleling the revolution of rising expectations, and adding similarly to the increasing difficulties of social policy, is the revolution of equality. This is the most powerful social force in the modern world. Perhaps only Tocqueville saw its awesome potency. For it not only expresses a demand for equality in political rights and in political power; it also represents a demand for equality in economic power, in social status, in authority in every sphere. And just as there is no point at which the sea of misery is finally drained, so, too, is there no point at which the equality revolution can come to an end, if only because as it proceeds we become ever more sensitive to smaller and smaller degrees of inequality. More important, different types and forms of equality inevitably emerge to contradict each other as we move away from a society of fixed social orders. "From each according to his abilities, to each according to his need"; so goes one of the greatest of the slogans invoked as a test of equality. But the very slogan itself already incorporates two terms—"abilities" and "needs"— that open the way for a justification of inequality. We live daily with the consequences of the fact that equal treatment of individuals does not necessarily lead to "equality" for groups. And we can point to a host of other contradictions as well which virtually guarantee that the slogan of "equality" in any society at all will continue to arouse passions and lead to discontent.

But in addition to the revolution in rising expectations and the revolution of equality, social policy itself, in almost every field, creates new and, I would argue, unmanageable demands. It is illusory to see social policy only as making an *inroad* on a problem; there are dynamic aspects to any policy, such that it also *expands* the problem, *changes* the problem, *generates* further problems. And for a number of reasons, social policy finds it impossible to deal adequately with these new demands that follow the implementation of the original measures.

The first and most obvious of these reasons is the limitation of resources. We in this country suffer from the illusion that there is enough tied up in the arms budget to satisfy all our social needs. Yet if we look at a country like Sweden, which spends relatively little for arms—and which, owing to its small size, its low rate of population growth, and its ethnic homogeneity, presents a much more moderate range of social problems than does the United States—we will see how even the most enlightened, most scientific, least conflict-ridden effort to deal with social problems leads to a tax budget which takes more than 40 percent of the gross national product. And new items are already emerging on Sweden's agenda of social demands that should raise that percentage even higher. For example, at present only a small proportion of Swedes go on to higher education. Housing is still in short supply and does not satisfy a good part of the population. And presumably Swedish radicals, growing in number, are capable of formulating additional demands, not so pressing, that would require further increases in taxation—if, that is, any society can go much beyond a taxation rate of 40 percent of its GNP.

In this country, of course, we still have a long way to go. By comparison with Sweden and with other developed nations (France, West Germany, and England), our taxes are still relatively low, and there is that huge 8 percent of the GNP now devoted to arms and war that might be diverted, at least in part, to the claims of social policy. But social demands could easily keep up with the new resources. We now spend between 6 percent and 7 percent of the GNP on education, and about as much on health. It would be no trick at all to double our expenditures on education, or on health, simply by taking account of proposals already made by leading experts in these fields. We could with no difficulty find enormous expenditures to make in the field of housing. And quite serious proposals (I believe they were serious) were put forward for a guaranteed minimum income of $6,500 for a family of four, with no restrictions.

My point is not that we either could not or should not raise taxes and use the arms budget for better things. It is that, when we look at projected needs, and at the experience of other countries, we know that even with a much smaller arms budget and much higher taxes, social demands will continue to press on public resources. And we may suspect that needs will be felt then as urgently as they are now.

A second limitation on the effectiveness of social policy is presented by the inevitable professionalization of services. Professionalization means that a certain point of view is developed about the nature of needs and how they are to be met. It tends to handle a problem by increasing the number of people trained to deal with that problem. First, we run out of people who are defined as "qualified" (social workers, counselors, teachers, and so forth). Second, this naturally creates dissatisfaction over the fact that many services are being handled by the "unqualified." Third, questions arise from outside the profession about the ability of the "qualified" themselves to perform a particular service properly. We no longer—and often with good reason—trust social workers to handle welfare, teachers and principals to handle education, doctors and hospital administrators to handle health care, managers to handle housing projects, and so on. And yet there is no one else into whose hands we can entrust these services. Experience tells us that if we set up new agencies it will be only a very few years before a new professionalism emerges which will be found limited and untrustworthy in its own turn. So, in the poverty program, we encouraged the rise of community-action agencies as a way of overcoming the bad effects of professionalism, and we already find that the community organizers have become another professional group, another interest group, with claims of their own which have no necessary relation to the needs of the clients they serve.

The third limitation on the effectiveness of social policy is simply lack of knowledge. We are in the surprising position of knowing much more than we did at earlier stages in the development of social policy—more about income distribution, employment patterns, family structure, health and medical care, housing and its impact—and simultaneously becoming more uncertain about what measures will be most effective, if effective at all, in ameliorating pressing problems in each of these areas. In the past, there was a clear field for action. The situation demanded that something be done; whatever was done was clear gain; little as yet was expected; little was known, and administrators approached their tasks with anticipation and self-confidence. Good administrators could be chosen, because the task was new and exciting. At later stages, however, we began dealing with problems which were in some absolute sense less serious, but which were nevertheless irksome and productive of conflict. We had already become committed to old lines of policy; agencies with their special interests had been created; and new courses of action had to be taken in a situation in which there was already more conflict at the start, less assurance of success, and less attention from the leaders and the best minds of the country.

Thus, if we look at the history of housing policy, for example, we will see that in the earlier stages—the 1920s and 1930s—there was a good deal of enthusiasm for this subject, with the housing issue attracting some of the best and most vigorous minds in the country. Since little or nothing had been done, there was a wide choice of alternatives and a supply of good men to act as administrators. In time, as housing programs expanded, the issue tended to fade from the agenda of top government. (Indeed, it has been difficult to get much White House attention for housing for two decades.) Earlier programs precluded the possibilities for new departures, and as we learned more about housing and its effects on people, we grew more uncertain as to what policies—even theoretically—would be best. Housing, like so many other areas of social policy, became, after an initial surge of interest, a field for experts, with the incursions of general public opinion becoming less and less informed, and less and less useful. This process is almost inevitable—there is always so much to know.

Perhaps my explanation of the paradox of knowledge leading to less confident action is defective. Perhaps, as the liberal perspective would have it, more knowledge will permit us to take more confident and effective action. Certainly we do need more knowledge about social policy. But it also appears that whatever great actions we undertake today involve such an increase in complexity that we act generally with less knowledge than we would like to have, even if with more than we once had. This is true for example of the proposed great reform in welfare policy—which I shall discuss below.

But aside from these problems of cost, of professionalization, and of knowledge, there is the simple reality that every piece of social policy substitutes for some traditional arrangement, whether good or bad, a new arrangement in which public authorities take over, at least in part, the role of the family, of the ethnic and neighborhood group, or of the voluntary association. In doing so, social policy weakens the position of these traditional agents, and further encourages needy people to depend on the government, rather than on the traditional structures, for help. Perhaps this is the basic force behind the ever growing demand for social policy, and its frequent failure to satisfy the demand.

To sum up: Whereas the liberal believes that to every problem there is a solution, and the radical believes that to any problem there is only the general answer of wholesale social transformation, I believe that we can have only partial and less than wholly satisfying answers to the social problems in question. Whereas the liberal believes that social policies make steady progress in nibbling away at the agenda of problems set by the forces of industrialization and urbanization, and whereas the radical believes that social policy has made only insignificant inroads into these problems, I believe that social policy has ameliorated the problems we have inherited but that it has also given rise to other problems no less grave in their effect on human happiness than those which have been successfully modified.

The liberal has a solution, and the radical has a solution. Do I have a solution? I began this discussion by saying that the breakdown of traditional modes of behavior is the chief cause of our social problems. That, of course, is another way of saying industrialism and urbanization, but I put it in the terms I did because I am increasingly convinced that some important part of the solution to our social problems lies in traditional practices and traditional restraints. Since the past is not recoverable, what guidance could this possibly give? It gives two forms of guidance: first, it counsels hesitation in the development of social policies that sanction the abandonment of traditional practices, and second, and perhaps more helpful, it suggests that the creation and building of new traditions must be taken more seriously as a requirement of social policy itself.

A nation's welfare system provides perhaps the clearest and severest test of the adequacy of its system of social policy in general. Welfare, which exists in all advanced nations, is the attempt to deal with the distress that is left over after all the more specific forms of social policy have done their work. After we have instituted what in America is called Social Security (and what may generally be called old-age pensions); after we have expanded it to cover widows, dependent children, and the disabled; after we have instituted a system to handle the costs of medical care, and to maintain income in times of illness; after we have set up a system of unemployment insurance; after we have enabled people to manage the exceptional costs of housing—after all this there will remain, in any industrial system, people who still require special supports, either temporarily or for longer periods of time.

In thus describing the place of welfare, or "public assistance," in a system of social policy, I am of course describing its place in an *ideal* system of social policy. I do not suggest for a moment that our programs of Social Security, health insurance, unemployment insurance, housing, are as yet fully adequate (though as I understand these matters, even if they were better, they would still not be seen as fully adequate). The strange thing, however, is that even if we go to countries whose systems of social insurance could well serve as models of comprehensiveness and adequacy, we find that the need for welfare or public assistance still remains, and on a scale roughly comparable to our own. In Sweden, the number of persons receiving public assistance was 4.4 percent of the population in 1959, and it was in the same year less than 4 percent in America. In England, despite the broad range of social policy there, the number of those on Supplementary Benefits—the English welfare, formerly known as National Assistance—is of the same order of magnitude. In Sweden and England, too, we find concern, though much less than here, over the stigma of welfare, over the effects of a degrading means test, over the problem of second- and third-generation welfare families.

Why, then, do we have, or consider that we have, a greater problem than they do? One reason is that, whereas in Sweden the proportion of those on welfare declines as other forms of social insurance broaden their coverage and become more effective, quite the opposite has happened here. In this country, there has been a rise in the number of people on welfare during the past decade. The rise is not phenomenal—from 4 percent to 6 percent of the population. Nor, interestingly enough, despite the increased cost of welfare, does it form a really heavy burden on the budget. The cost of welfare, though rising, still accounts for only a bit more than one percent of the GNP, and 6 percent of the federal budget. However, it forms a greater share of state and local revenues, and in some larger cities up to 15 percent of the population is on welfare. That is one reason it has become a serious problem.

But there are more important reasons. In Sweden and England a high proportion of those requesting public assistance are the aged; in America the aged constitute a smaller proportion of the welfare population, and families a much larger share. Indeed, our increase has been almost entirely concentrated in the family population, those assisted under the federal program called Aid to Families with

Dependent Children (AFDC). Here the situation is quite startling. In 1955, 30 out of every 1,000 American children received welfare; by 1969 this had doubled to more than 60 out of every 1,000. In New York City, where eligibility has always been broad, and where the city and the state provide welfare to families not covered by the federal statute, the increase has been even more dramatic. In 1960 there were 328,000 persons on welfare in New York City, of whom 250,000 were in the family categories (children and their parents). In 1969, there were 1,012,000—about 12 percent or 13 percent of the population—of whom 792,000, or four fifths, were in the family categories. Yet during the same period, there seems to have been a drop in the number of families in poverty—from 13 percent to 10 percent of all families—and the rate of unemployment was halved, from 6 percent to 3 percent.

A second reason why welfare is a more serious matter in America than in Sweden or England is that in those countries it is a problem of the backward areas, whereas here it is a problem of the most advanced. A third and final reason is that welfare has come to be seen in America as a *regular* means of *family* support. In England and Sweden welfare is thought of as emergency aid, provided in response to a special crisis, and meant to put a destitute family back on its feet. In America the situation of the destitute family is increasingly considered a more or less permanent condition for which provision over a very long period of time must be made.

Why should all this be so? One of the most popular explanations is that no jobs are available for the men—mainly unskilled—who would ordinarily support these families. In fact, however, unskilled jobs were widely available in the latter part of the 1960s, just when the number of families on welfare increased so impressively. It is true that these jobs did not generally pay enough to support a family, but it is also true that large numbers of the urban unemployed were young and unmarried men and women who were not as yet required to support families on their own, though they might well have been capable of contributing to the support of the parental household in which they presumably lived. (The majority of American families, as it happens, are supported by two earners, or more.)

There is a modified form of the argument that no jobs are available, which is that since the actually available jobs do not pay enough to support a family, and since there is no way for working husbands to get supplementary assistance, they are encouraged to defect in order to make their families eligible for help. But let us consider the advanced jurisdictions, like New York State, where complete families *are* eligible for support and have been for a long time, and where a working husband *can* have his income supplemented to bring it up to some necessary minimum for the support of his family. It is just in these jurisdictions that we have had the most remarkable increase in the number of families broken up by abandonment. In 1961 there were about 12,000 deserted families on welfare in New York City. In 1968, there were 80,000, a more than sixfold increase during a period when the population of the city, in overall numbers, remained stable. During the same period, there was a more moderate increase in the number of welfare families that consisted of mothers and illegitimate children, from 20,000 to 46,000. In other words, the family welfare population shifted to one overwhelmingly consisting of abandoned women and their children.

Another effort to account for the situation argues that high welfare payments in New York and other Northern cities encouraged migration from the South and from the rural areas. This probably played some role. But there is no evidence that abandoned families in these areas moved to New York in larger numbers in the 1960s than in the 1950s. And if the abandonment took place in New York, in a brisk job market, we would want to know why it took place, and migration would not be the explanation.

Then there is the view which holds that in the 1960s—with the spread of concern about poverty, with the development of community organizations, and with the rise of such groups as the National Welfare Rights Organization—more and more of the poor discovered their entitlement to welfare, more and more became willing to apply for it, and higher and higher proportions of those applying were accepted. According to this explanation, then, it was not the poor who increased in numbers, but only the poor on welfare. This is undoubtedly part of the story. But think once again of that huge increase in the number of abandoned families on welfare. If there were just as many, or almost as many, before, what did they do to stay alive?

Still another interpretation emphasizes the fact that the levels of welfare aid in New York became higher during the 1960s. This would certainly mean that more and more workers could apply for income supplements. But why would it mean a six-and-a-half times increase in the number of abandoned families?

One must take developments in New York seriously because in many respects they can be considered a test run of the Family Assistance Program (FAP), the reform in the welfare system proposed by the Nixon administration. Without going into detail, and leaving aside the fact that welfare would acquire a national floor and a national administration, there are, I believe, four major features that distinguish the Family Assistance Program from the system we have at present.

The most important is that the working poor would be included in the same system as the nonworking poor. The reasoning behind this feature is as follows: Welfare levels cannot be raised if people on welfare get as much as, or more than, people who are working. This would first of all lead to political resistance and resentment on the part of the working poor. Further, they would try to redefine themselves as incapable of work in order to get the higher benefits of the nonworking poor. If, however, the working poor are also included, their resistance to higher levels of welfare will decline, and they will have less incentive to become nonworking.

A second major difference is that a substantial incentive to work is built into the program. Thus, working leads not to the loss of welfare benefits but to an overall increase in the family income. FAP payments are reduced when there is more earned income, but only as a proportion of the increased earnings.

Third, the grant would in part be divorced from services and from the stigma of investigation. It cannot be fully divorced from investigation—it is, after all, a grant based on need—but the hope is that in its administration it will become more of an impersonal income-maintenance program and less involved in the provision of help through services rather than through money.

A fourth feature of the proposal is that, in addition to building in an incentive to work, it contains a *requirement* that everyone capable of work register for job training or for employment. If there is a father, he must register; if there is no father, the mother must register unless she has children still below school age. (This feature has been the target of much criticism because of the element of compulsion.)

What are we to conclude about the prospects of the new system? Since all four of its features are in large measure already in existence in New York State, whose condition is not exactly of the happiest, we can be sure that FAP will not succeed in "solving" the problems of welfare. What it will do is redistribute more income, and put more money into the pockets of the poor. It will raise the abysmally low welfare payments in large areas of the South. It may, by moving some part of the way toward national standards, reduce immigration to the big cities of the North. It will provide some relief—but relatively little—to the states and local jurisdictions that now are heavily burdened with welfare costs. All this is to the good. But what the new system will not do, I believe, is strengthen the family or substantially increase the number of those on welfare willing to enter the labor force. If it does, the accomplishment will be a mystery because similar arrangements have not done so in New York, nor in any of the other states in which families with unemployed males are eligible for welfare, or where a work requirement exists. The forces leading to the breakdown of male responsibility for the family among some of the poor seem greater than those the new program calls into play to counteract them.

This brings us back to my original point, and to a possible answer to the question I posed earlier as to how we can account for the dramatic increase in recent years of abandoned families on welfare. The constraints that traditionally kept families together have weakened. In some groups they may not have been strong to begin with. Our efforts to soften the harsh consequences of family breakup speak well of our compassion and concern, but these efforts also make it easier for fathers to abandon their families or mothers to disengage from their husbands. Our welfare legislation has often been harsh, and its administration harsher. But the steps we take in the direction of diminished harshness must also enhance the attractions of either abandonment or disengagement and encourage the recourse to welfare.

And yet, what alternatives do we have? FAP was, after all, the most enlightened and thoughtful legislation to have been introduced in the field of welfare in some decades.

My own tendency, following from the basic considerations I have suggested, would be to ask how we might prevent further erosion of the traditional constraints that still play the largest role in maintaining a civil society. What keeps society going, after all, is that most people still feel they should work—however well they might do without working—and most feel that they should take care of their families— however attractive it might on occasion appear to be to desert them. Consequently, we might try to strengthen the incentive to work. The work-incentive provision is the best thing about FAP, but we need to make it even stronger. Our dilemma is that we can never make this incentive as strong as it was when the alternative to work was starvation, or the uncertain charity of private organizations. Nor is it politically feasible to increase the incentive by reducing the levels at which we maintain the poor. If anything, the whole tendency of our thinking and feeling is to raise them, as indeed FAP does. The only alternative, then, is to increase the incentive to work by increasing the attractiveness of work. I do not suggest that this is at all simple (we know the ambiguous results, for example, of raising the minimum wage). Could we, however, begin to attach to low-income jobs the same kind of fringe benefits—health insurance, vacations with pay—that now make higher-paying jobs attractive, and that paradoxically in some form are also available to those on welfare?

The dilemma of income maintenance is that, on the one hand, it permits the poor to live better, but on the other, it reduces their incentive to set up and maintain those close units of self-support—family in the first case, but also larger units—that have always, both in the past and still in large measure today, formed the fabric of society. The administration proposal is a heroic effort to improve the condition of the poor without further damage to those social motivations and structures which are the essential basis for individual security everywhere. But does not the history of our efforts to expand policies of income-support suggest that inevitably improvement and damage go together?

In other critical areas of social policy, too, the breakdown of traditional measures, traditional restraints, traditional organization, represents, if not the major factor in the crisis, a significant contribution to it. Even in an area apparently so far removed from tradition as health and medical care, the weakening of traditional forms of organization can be found upon examination to be playing a substantial role, as when we discover that drug addiction is now the chief cause of death—and who knows what other frightful consequences—among young men in New York.

Ultimately, we are not kept healthy, I believe, by new scientific knowledge or more effective cures or even better-organized medical-care services. We are kept healthy by certain patterns of life. These, it is true, are modified for the better by increased scientific knowledge, but this knowledge is itself communicated through such functioning traditional organizations as the school, the voluntary organization, the family. We are kept healthy by decent care in institutions where certain traditionally oriented occupations (like nursing and the maintenance of cleanliness) still manage to perform their functions. I will not argue the case for the significance of traditional patterns in maintaining health at length here; but I believe it is a persuasive one.

One major objection, among many, that can be raised against the emphasis I have placed on tradition has to do with the greater success of social policy in a country like Sweden which shows a greater departure from traditionalism than America does. And it is indeed true that social services in Sweden, and England as well, can be organized without as much interference from tradition-minded interest groups of various kinds (including the churches) as we have to contend with in this country. Certainly this is an important consideration. But I would insist that behind the modern organization of the social services in the advanced European countries are at least two elements that can legitimately and without distortion be called traditional.

One is authority. Authority exists when social workers can direct clients, when doctors can direct nurses, when headmasters can direct teachers, when teachers can discipline students and can expect acquiescence from parents. Admittedly, this feature of traditionalism itself serves the movement *away* from tradition in other social respects. The authority will be used, as in Sweden, to institute sex education in the schools, to insure that unmarried girls have access to contraceptives, to secure a position of equality for illegitimate children.

But then another feature that can legitimately be called traditional—ethnic and religious homogeneity—sets limits in these countries on how far the movement toward a new tradition may be carried away from the traditional. In America, by contrast, it is the very diversity of traditions—ethnic, religious, and social—that makes it so hard to establish new forms of behavior that are universally accepted and approved, and that also makes it impossible to give the social worker, the teacher, the policeman, the judge, the nurse, even the doctor, the same authority they possess in more homogeneous countries.

But there is a more basic sense in which tradition is stronger in the countries of Western Europe than here. Whatever the situation with sex education and with the laws governing illegitimacy, divorce is less frequent in Sweden and England, responsibility for the rearing of children is still consistently placed within the family, and the acceptance of work as a normal pattern of life is more widespread and less challenged. In England and Sweden it is still taken for granted that the aim of welfare is to restore a man to a position in which he can work, earn his living, support his family. And indeed the psychological damage that renders a man unfit for work, and the ideology arguing against the desirability of work, are so little known in England and Sweden that the restoration of family independence is a fair and reasonable objective of welfare. But this is no longer a reasonable view of welfare for substantial parts of the American population. It is in this core sense that America has gone further in the destruction of tradition than other countries. In doing so, America comes face to face, more sharply than any other country yet has, with the limits of social policy.

NOTE

1. This definition excludes measures aimed at influencing the entire economic or physical environment, even though such measures certainly have some claim to be considered as falling within the realm of social policy and may well be evaluated in terms of their effect on those vulnerable elements of the population who are the special target of social policy. Education, too, falls increasingly into the sphere of social policy, particularly when it is seen as a means of protecting people from poverty and destitution. The same is true of the control of crime, particularly if we see it as a response to poverty and destitution. I shall, however, exclude both these areas from my discussion.

D. THE POLITICAL ECONOMY OF SOCIAL WELFARE

THE contemporary revival of political economy reflects the impact of the 1960s' social upheavals and the 1970s' fiscal crisis on the analysis of social welfare. James O'Connor's key work in this revival is included in the final section of this reader. Political economy was a dominant form of intellectual endeavor in nineteenth-century Europe, represented by the writings of Adam Smith (1776) and John Stuart Mill (1848). It then denoted the practical management of national resources to increase prosperity. This classical approach was systematically criticized by Karl Marx; the sub-title of his *Das Kapital*, first published in 1867, is "A Critique of Political Economy." Partly as a result, political economy has come to refer to the theoretical study of the production and distribution of wealth. Its revival introduces new perspectives, particularly neo-Marxist ones, in the study of the relation of economics to other sectors of society. Gough's *The Political Economy of the Welfare State* (1979) is an example of such work in social welfare. (For an example in education, see Bowles and Gintis 1976.)

The first of two selections in section D, "The Political Functions of the Social Services," is a chapter from Jeffry H. Galper's book *The Politics of Social Services*. His neo-Marxist analysis focuses on social work practice. He discusses the relationship between social service and the labor market, arguing that social workers often serve to channel their clients into exploitative work situations. Galper also considers the ways in which the behavior of social service workers is regulated by agencies in which they work. Ultimately, he argues, the social control of social service workers and clients serves the interest of the status quo, inhibiting social change.

The second selection is illustrative of liberal political economy in social welfare. Morris Janowitz's "The Dilemmas of the Welfare State" is a chapter from his book *Social Control of the Welfare State*. He argues that the central problem confronting the welfare state is the end of the high levels of productivity and economic surplus upon which it has been built. Janowitz's "end of cornucopia" perspective is the liberal corollary to the neo-Marxist "end of empire" analysis of the decline of the United States and advanced capitalism in general. In his perspective, this new situation threatens social control and political stability.

THE POLITICAL FUNCTIONS OF
THE SOCIAL SERVICES

Jeffry H. Galper

THE general philosophy of the welfare state is realized through the creation of social policies at the federal level and is eventually operationalized through the provision of the specific social services. Consequently, these services represent a direct link to a larger political philosophy and are strongly influenced by that philosophy. To understand the full meaning and purpose of the social services, therefore, it is necessary to see them both in their own light and in the light of the larger context within which they function.

When we make this dual analysis, the following contradiction in the social services emerges sharply: the social services deny, frustrate, and undermine the possibilities of human liberation and of a just society, at the same time that they work toward and, in part, achieve greater degrees of human well-being. The social services represent the larger duality of liberalism and of the welfare state. They express concern for individual and social welfare, but they do so in a form shaped by limited and distorted values and structures and, thus, ultimately undermine the pursuit of human welfare.

One half of this duality is the fact that, whatever else they do or do not do, public welfare programs do provide resources to people who would otherwise have less. Mental health programs alleviate psychological distress for some of their clients. Those social service workers who struggle to meet human needs and feel that they make some progress in doing so are not fools or charlatans. On the contrary, their commitment to their clients and the real help they are

From *The Politics of Social Services* (Englewood Cliffs, N.J.: Prentice-Hall, 1975), pp. 45-72. Reprinted by permission; copyright © 1975 Prentice-Hall.

sometimes able to provide represent that part of the welfare notion that has remained true to the concept of welfare.

However, social services do not operate in a vacuum. They are established within a political and economic context. This context, we believe, acts to subvert the welfare concept by organizing the role of the social services so that they support and reinforce conformity, among both clients and workers, to the very institutions and values that generate the problems to which the services were addressed in the first place. The services mirror in their internal structures and procedures the kinds of people-denying orientations contained in the larger society. Thus, as they succeed in achieving their mandates, they succeed in denying the greatest potential for life and joy in their clients.

We have two purposes in the sections that follow. First, we explore and illustrate some of the ways in which the social services contain the denial of their own best ideals. Their intimate relationship with people-limiting dynamics in the larger society and their internal absorption of people-denying values are also examined.

Second, we suggest that these patterns are neither accidental nor amenable to piecemeal reform. The services function in a symbiotic relationship with the major institutions of society because, like the welfare state policies of which they are a manifestation, they are generated by the need to shape and contain social reform efforts within the logic and requirements of a capitalistic society. They contain people-denying values because these are consistent with the logic of our major institutions. Were the social services to pursue a fuller notion of human liberation, the consequences would be revolutionary. For example, if mental health agencies single-mindedly devoted themselves to helping people become mentally healthy, they might well encourage people in the view that the proper role of a mentally healthy person in a mentally unhealthy society is to be revolutionary. Such outcomes would create tensions between those facilities and their larger support systems, to say the least. The problems we identify are solvable by nothing short of a radical change in the society as a whole.

Regulating Client Behavior

The social services foster particular behavior patterns in clients both as a condition of usage and as a consequence of service. These patterns require clients to accept behaviors and roles for themselves in which they accommodate themselves to conservative visions of the good society and the good life. These visions perpetuate liberalism's notions of justice and decency, but deny clients the fullest possibilities of their own well-being. In this section, some of the major ways the social services encourage this kind of self-denying conformity in clients are discussed.

SOCIAL SERVICES AND THE LABOR MARKET

We explored and found unconvincing the liberal thesis about the nature of the welfare state. That thesis argued that the welfare state represents a humanistic modification of market forces by progressive state intervention. It saw the welfare state as an alternative to the market and to market principles. The liberal view captures only the rhetoric of this nation's social policies. The reality is that welfare state programs have been so organized that, in practice, they support and nurture market institutions.

One of the ways in which this occurs is through the role the social services play in channeling people into the labor market, thus serving as a support to that market. Once we realize this, it becomes harder to argue that the services can be seen as an alternative system for people who have failed to maintain themselves through labor market participation. Policy developments in the mid-1970s emphasized this pattern. As the 1973 rule revisions to the public assistance regulations put it,

Families and individuals must be free to accept or reject services. Acceptance of a service shall not be a prerequisite for the receipt of any other services or aid under the plan, *except for the conditions related to the Work Incentive Program or other work program under a State Plan approved by the service* (Federal Register 1973:4609; emphasis added).

To many, this observation will be neither a surprise nor a source of distress. After all, in a society in which work must be done, and which is organized according to marketplace principles, it is to be expected that people will work and that systems will be developed to encourage them or force them to work when, for any reason, they are not willing or able to work. From this perspective, the existence of a social service network is a preferable alternative to a Spencerian notion of the survival of the fittest in which those not able to work would simply be allowed to fall by the wayside.

In criticizing the social services as a labor market support, we do not mean to imply that work itself is inherently undesirable. Even if it is true that we are entering an age of nonscarcity or of postscarcity in which work, as we know it, will not be required for our maintenance, we will still have the obligation to relate ourselves to the larger society in some way that facilitates the survival and maximization of that society. In other words, in a better world, work in its present form might be abolished, but we would still require individuals to contribute to the larger whole in some fashion. Contrary to the present reality, the ideal situation would be one in which the individual's maximum contribution to the society as a whole would be, simultaneously, exactly that person's maximum contribution to his or her own self-development. In a truly humanized society the ideal toward which we would strive would be the elimination of the duality between actions which primarily benefit the individual actor and those which benefit others. The work of the society would not be dehumanizing or exploitative of the individuals who perform it, but would facilitate their development as people.

It is around this issue that the role of the social services in shaping clients' work behavior must be criticized. The social services are organized within the context of a society that defines its well-being in terms of economic growth and has its primary expectation of the individual his or her maximum contribution as a worker or as a facilitator of workers to economic growth. This contrasts sharply with the potential of our society. We may always recognize the need for economic achievement, but we can learn to see that achievement as fostering conditions which encourage human fulfillment.

In our own society today, the struggle for economic growth produces neither equitable nor humanistic outcomes. We do not function on the basis of a social view of the meaning of work, and even in our limited economic view we distribute the rewards of satisfying work and high pay inequitably. For many workers, work is a means to an end, the end being leisure time at high levels of consumption.

To the extent, therefore, that the social services buttress the labor market, they move people into a relationship with the means of production that insures their exploitation as producers and, eventually, as consumers. This is the basis of the criticism in our observation that the social services are structured to service the labor market. If work fit the model that serving oneself and serving others were identical processes, then the social services might happily function to reinforce the labor market. Inasmuch as work is, at present, exploitative of workers, inasmuch as it turns human beings against themselves, we need to try to understand as fully as possible the way the social services, which we hope would represent life forces and energy for the liberation of people, have come to represent the opposite.

The income-maintenance provisions of the Social Security system, in some of their facets, provide an illustration of the process by which human needs are met in this society within a market framework. This system represents a social policy response to some rather basic human needs for retirement security and for protection against death of the primary wage earner in a family with dependents. While these needs exist in every society, the need for public involvement is exacerbated in an industrialized society in which more traditional mechanisms for meeting these needs are disrupted. In the United States, it took the crisis of the mid-1930s, with its extraordinary economic dislocations, to bring such a system into existence. The Social Security system obviously operates in close relationship to the market. Receipt of Social Security benefits is contingent on the worker's past participation in paid employment in the labor force. Reforms in the system have so modified it that receipt of Social Security benefits has required progressively less firm attachment to the market, though the principle of prior labor market attachment has been retained. Presently, however, even persons with a rather casual prior relationship to the labor force are entitled to some benefits.

Nonetheless, the Social Security system both compensates for the inadequacies of the labor market and ties people more firmly to it. A recent development in this program is illustrative. In 1972, the Senate Finance Committee began to plan for the provision of higher pension benefits to the lowest paid workers in the labor force (New York Times 1972a, 1972d). On the surface, this seemed like a liberal and generous act and a further departure from rigorous actuarial calculations of benefit entitlement. However, the underlying realities highlighted other motivations. Among these realities was the fact that nearly all of the estimated 340,000 persons to be immediately affected by this provision were persons who were receiving supplemental welfare benefits as well as Social Security benefits. (A total of 1.2 million persons receive benefits from both programs.) These Social

Security amendments, therefore, actually served to shift the financing of some portion of the supplemental welfare benefits to the Social Security system. They also made an estimated 93,000 people ineligible for Medicaid (New York *Times* 1972e). These provisions, in other words, did not necessarily result in increased benefits for recipients. That part of the recipients' benefits received from welfare would now come from Social Security, and many would no longer be at a low enough income level to be eligible for welfare. Furthermore, since public welfare is financed from the more progressive income tax and Social Security from the less progressive payroll tax, the shift would mean that lower paid workers, in general, would pay proportionately more for their future benefits under the new arrangements. What the welfare state giveth, the welfare state taketh away.

In addition, the same provision encouraged the lowest paid segment of the labor force to remain faithfully at work, in that it proposed disproportionately rewarding more stable low-wage workers. The provision suggested, in other words, that if people remain at low-paid work for long periods of time, they will be able to count on marginally more generous retirement benefits. This proposal attempts to encourage the loyalty of a segment of the work force which might otherwise have little motivation to work steadily and stably. The admitted need of low-wage earners for retirement income beyond that which they could normally provide for themselves is acknowledged. Simultaneously, this need is met in a way which encourages workers to buy into the system, and into a level of the system that insures their marginal financial existence both as active workers and as retirees.

A second example of the use of social services as a labor market adjunct is the provision of day care services. We have generally not had a substantial public day care program in the United States. Some relatively few facilities have been provided through the welfare program, and a brief, nonwork-related effort was undertaken, and then largely phased out, during the War on Poverty years.

In 1971, a coalition of forces surfaced with legislation to establish a broad network of day care facilities as a part of a $2-billion-a-year package of child-development legislation (*Social Service Review* 1972a). This legislation was passed by both houses of Congress, but was vetoed by Richard Nixon, then president. At the same time, a day care program, oriented toward custodial care rather than child development, passed with congressional and presidential blessing as part of welfare program revisions. To pressure welfare mothers to work, apparently not so much out of a need for labor as a need to reduce the welfare rolls and as a warning to others not to leave their jobs, an $800 million network of child care and day care center facilities for children of low-income working mothers was envisioned.

The 1973 crackdowns on social service expenditures also reflected these priorities. Social services which had been provided to a relatively broad range of clients, from a base in public welfare programs, were increasingly restricted only to current welfare clients. One of the few exceptions to this restriction was day care, but only "in the case of a child where the provision of such services is needed in order to enable a member of such child's family to accept or continue in employment or to participate in training to prepare such member for employment" (*Federal Register* 1973:4613). (Death or abandonment by the mother is a further exception, later stated.)

The message is clear. We will have a day care program in this country if and when it serves the purpose of making welfare recipients or others work, but not if and when its primary focus is simply the healthy development of children. The provision of services for children is used as a tool to reach the real target, the welfare recipient. Moreover, we must keep in mind that forcing welfare recipients to work speaks as well to a far larger number of the working poor who otherwise might find welfare an attractive alternative to work.

These examples only scratch the surface. The fact that patients in mental hospitals have been exploited for the work they could perform while institutionalized has come to public attention once again (New York *Times* 1973). The variety of ways in which the public welfare system has attempted to pressure clients to work, both in the past and present, has been widely documented (Piven and Cloward 1971). Similarly, for a variety of social service programs, a return to work status might well be taken as the operational definition of success. Mental health programs and alcoholic treatment centers, juvenile delinquency prevention services, and physical rehabilitation workshops come to mind. Recreation programs often have as a stated purpose the inculcation of disciplined attitudes toward work. The value of work and of being a good worker is a cornerstone of the value system of this country, and it has been adopted all too uncritically by the social services. Of course, it would be politically suicidal for the social services to represent themselves as being against the work ethic. Because the services do not understand or address the radical possibility of encouraging a different kind of work—a personally and socially useful work—they have been left in the position of encouraging the typical patterns of work as we have known them. This has not been of the fullest service to clients.

THE SOCIAL SERVICES AND SOCIAL CONFORMITY

The emphasis on work is not the only way in which the services attempt to shape client behavior in conformity with prevailing conservative values. In all programs, a variety of notions about the ways in which people are expected to behave is structured into the rules and regulations. It is very difficult to think of any social service which is available to people simply as a consequence of their human existence.

Public welfare offers an embarrassing wealth of case material. Undoubtedly because welfare involves the direct distribution of cash and, consequently, is involved in competition with the other major cash distribution mechanism, the labor market, its clients are especially subject to behavioral control.[1] Welfare regulations have been used to shape client behavior in every area of life. Regulations attempt to control sexual conduct, family relations, market purchases, the household budget, registration for work and work training, the right to privacy, and so on. To a large extent, being on welfare means a loss of control over one's life. Decisions are made for the welfare client in his or her role as consumer, provider, parent, and citizen (Glassman 1970; B. Mandell 1971; Rauch 1970).

A recent development in welfare, the "brownie-point system," made these dynamics more explicit. Welfare clients, in the several states where this program was implemented, were required to "earn" welfare benefits by accruing points. These points were garnered by meeting certain behavioral mandates: so many points and, consequently, so many dollars for registering for work, for taking one's children to the doctor, for serving as a cub scout or brownie troop leader, and so on (*Social Service Review* 1972b). The efforts to control welfare clients' behavior continue to escalate, as illustrated by the massive efforts to force welfare clients to work (New York *Times* 1972d), the renewed efforts to develop birth control programs to curtail potential welfare roll increases (New York *Times* 1972c), and the increased concern about addicts on welfare which has resulted in plans to curtail benefits to addicts who do not accept treatment (New York *Times* 1972b). Cloward and Piven (1965; see Dumont

1974) have highlighted the role of the social services in socializing clients into an acceptable political stance. They argue that passivity and/or conformity are encouraged by conditional benefits with inadequate, if any, procedures for appeal and by the general debilitation and demoralization of the welfare way of life.

These dynamics in the welfare program are both relatively well known and of wide concern. As such, they may obscure the extent to which such conditions operate in other programs. For example, the receipt of Social Security benefits requires registration of the individual with the government (the Senate Finance Committee, at one point, suggested that this occur when a child entered the first grade) (New York *Times* 1972d), regularized work with a registered employer, and retirement at a specific age on penalty of benefit reduction or complete benefit loss. Similarly, institutional child care in the United States has been and continues to be heavily motivated "by a concern for idleness, lack of productivity, presumed moral depravity, and the protection of society" (Whittaker 1972), with a consequent impact on the services provided. The use of the various behavior-modification techniques likewise makes the behaviors valued in clients more explicit. This was clearly the case in a report of a social service program in a public school system where self-discipline and conformity were encouraged through a token-economy system, a point-exchange system, and a chart system (Wadsworth 1970). Day hospitals for formerly hospitalized mental patients likewise use the positive notion of the therapeutic community "to reactivate the patient's ability to behave responsibly and thus to become capable of maintaining himself independently in the community. Such independence implies the ability to earn a living or at least contribute to his maximum potential" (Scoles and Fine 1971).

A classic demonstration of these dynamics was provided by Kingsley Davis (1938) who argued that individualism and an array of values associated with the Protestant Ethic are inherent in the concept of mental health as pursued by the mental health movement as he observed it in the 1930s. The characteristics of the Protestant Ethic, as he described them, are democracy (in the sense of favoring equal opportunity to rise socially by merit rather than birth), worldliness, asceticism, individualism, rationalism and empiricism, and utilitarianism. The mental health movement, as he was able to demonstrate, utilizes this value schema as its standard of mental health. Consequently, mental health is defined as the active pursuit of a career, the engagement in competition within the rules of the game, the focus on "wholesome" recreation (asceticism) and on purposeful activity in general (utilitarianism). Individualism is reinforced by focusing on the person as responsible for his or her own destiny, the definition of the ultimate good as the satisfaction of individual needs, and the assumption of human behavior as understandable in terms of individuals abstracted from their society. Inasmuch as the values of the Protestant Ethic are intimately tied to the values and behaviors of a capitalist society (Weber 1930), Davis's analysis suggests that the mental health professions operate to reinforce values and behaviors supportive of capitalism.

In a specific case, Leichter and Mitchell (1967) examined the kinship patterns that were reinforced by the family caseworkers in New York City's Jewish Family Service. Although the clients, mostly of Eastern European origin, rarely reported problems with kin, caseworkers, from their perspective, consistently saw a wide array of problems in family patterns and acted vigorously to deal with them. The client population operated within their traditional network of extended family relationships, and the workers saw this as destructive to the nuclear family and as an inducement to maintain immature dependency patterns. The workers saw health as lying in the direction of breaking kinship ties and establishing closed nuclear families, and they focused their casework intervention on achieving these ends. Consequently, a more typical middle-class kinship structure was reinforced. The consequences were twofold. At the least, a sustaining and gratifying pattern of family relationships was weakened. Additionally, as nuclear family patterns were established, the ties of these persons to capitalist structures were reinforced.

The extended family potentially violates the Protestant Ethic and the capitalist values of individualism and self-reliance in the same way that the commune and the counterculture represent such threats. The fewer the nonmarket supports on which the individual or nuclear family can rely, the more they are forced to maintain themselves within the market structures. This means engaging in regular work and not engaging in behaviors that might jeopardize job security. It seems unlikely that the workers of New York's Jewish Family Service saw themselves as agents of capitalism. Nonetheless, the values that they had internalized and that they expressed in their professional practice were values that derive from and reinforce the kind of isolationism, individualism, and conformity which are supportive of capitalist society. The Leichter and Mitchell case study, consequently, serves as a specific illustration of what Walter Miller (1959) has identified as social work's intolerance of class differences and its concern with eliminating those lower-class behaviors that are not seen as functional or useful within the dominant value schemes of the society.

Finally, we should not overlook one of the most obvious, but one of the most important, ways in which the social services carry a message about the behavior that is expected of adults. This message is contained in the fact that the social services are rarely funded at an adequate level. This is so obvious that we may tend to overlook its significance. One cannot escape the reality of this country's wealth, yet social service programs generally operate on marginal budgets. Whatever reasons are presented publicly for this fact, a clear implication is that public services are simply not high-priority items in our society. The message is that people who cannot make it in the private market cannot really count on a public support system for much help.

A few figures will help make this point. It is true that the total amount of funds devoted to social welfare expenditures in the United States has increased over time. Social welfare expenditures (SWEs) as a percent of the gross national product (GNP) rose from 11.8 percent in 1965 to 16.9 percent in 1971 (Skolnik and Dales 1971:9). Over the past thirty years, this pattern has been consistent. However, much of this growth reflects local community input into education, which is included in the government's overall index to welfare state expenditures. It also reflects the Social Security program, which is paid for directly by workers through a generally regressive tax. When expenditures for education and for Social Security were taken out of the SWE figures, SWE as a percentage of GNP went from 4.5 percent in 1949 to 3.1 percent in 1959 to 4.8 percent in 1970. The figures and consequently the measure of this nation's concern for public service look quite different from the more rosy picture of growth and commitment that is usually painted.

Regulating Social Service Workers

As social service workers control clients as a function of the services they provide, so too are they controlled by the conditions of their work. These controls foster discipline in workers, encourage the acceptance of hierarchical and authoritarian structures, and create passivity and disengagement from others. It is necessary to impose on these workers the kinds of controls to which production workers are more easily subjected as a function of their basic conditions of work, inasmuch as the work place is one of the key institutions in which values of conformity and obedience are inculcated. In part, this occurs as a result of fairly straightforward indoctrination, as occurs when professional workers are encouraged to feel that it is inappropriate to unionize. More subtly, however, it occurs as a result of the assumptions of work that are rarely explicit, but are implicit in the daily realities of work. There are several reasons why it is important that the behavior of social service workers be shaped through their agencies.

In the first place, as the number of social service workers grows, they become a more significant part of the total work force in the United States. The growing size of this population makes clearer the dimensions of the problem. In 1900, 4.3 percent of all working people were professional or technical workers. In 1960, 11.1 percent and in 1970, 14.4 percent were in this category (U.S. Bureau of the Census 1970:74; see Syzmanski 1972). In 1960, they represented approximately 7.5 million workers. In 1970, 89 percent of all professional and technical workers were salaried. Within the category of professional and technical workers, 136,000 persons were social welfare and recreation workers, 1.7 million were elementary and high school teachers, and 1.1 million were health workers. In other words, almost 39 percent of the people in this important category of workers were in job classifications largely embraced within welfare state bureaucracies. Not included in these figures are 4.3 million clergymen, one million dietitians and nutritionists who often work in social welfare settings, and 180,000 college teachers. Furthermore, service workers have increasingly become proletarians; that is, the proportion of professionals and technical personnel who function as entrepeneurs has been decreasing steadily since the turn of the century, while the total number of people in these job categories has increased.

Another reason why service workers must be monitored is that they are often asked to perform as workers acts that might violate their deeper impulses as people. In order to insure that workers will perform as required by the social services, they must be pressured, propagandized, or molded into conformity with the role requirements of the job. The social service worker's situation creates some problems of control because accountability is less easy to achieve than in some other kinds of work and because social service workers have, as part of the aura of professionalism, an ideology that values autonomous activity.

However, social agencies have generally mastered the problem of control. They are assisted, in the case of more highly trained workers, by the fact that such workers are less likely than others to be conscious of the extent to which they are not autonomous. The ethics of professionalism encourage such workers to adopt the self-image of independent practitioners. In order to maintain this myth, however, it is necessary for these workers to ignore certain realities of work, especially concerning the lack of input into policy decisions affecting the nature of the services provided and, consequently, the nature of their work. In many respects, professional workers are technicians whose practice requires some latitude. Caseworkers in the more elite private agencies, for instance, have some trappings of autonomy, such as an office, a secretary (shared), dictating machinery, middle-class and respectful clients (often), and a decent salary. These enhance a feeling of well-being, self-respect, and autonomy. The organizer or planner may have even more discretion over work conditions, such as the daily schedule, and may hobnob with higher-status professionals, politicians, and business people. On the other hand, all of these activities take place within a framework that the worker has had little hand in shaping. In many agencies, workers have virtually no control over their assignments and certainly no officially sanctioned input into evaluating the assumptions on which their work proceeds.

Self-regulation, then, is a key to the control of many of the more highly trained workers. However, they are not the majority of the social service work force. (Over 80 percent of direct service positions in public and voluntary social agencies are staffed by workers without professional social work degrees [Loewenberg 1970].) In fact, in social work, the trend is toward greater use of less highly trained personnel, accompanied by increased routinization and structuring of the task of the job. The social work function in public welfare, for example, has been divided into the social service functions, which the smaller number of elite trained workers perform, and the cash eligibility functions, which the eligibility technicians perform. The mental health aide in mental health settings and the army of nurses, technicians, and aides in hospital settings perform routine tasks, while the trained worker does the more complex social casework (Agento 1970; Barker and Briggs 1969). For these workers, it is clear that employment in a service setting shares much with employment in more routinized production settings: control is maintained by the more traditional methods of rigidly enforced hours of work, closely monitored sick leave, watchful supervisors, narrow job definitions, and so on.

For both groups, work is generally structured in hierarchical fashion. The social work tradition of supervision insures a lifetime of boss-worker relationships extending before the worker. One escape is to rise in the hierarchy. The supervisor continues to be supervised and controlled, but in turn can supervise and control others. However, the pressure to rise in the hierarchy, as a mark of one's worth and as a response to the pressures at the line level, give rise to devaluation of the immediate tasks of the line worker—a devaluation which both the line worker and the agency share. The realization that the major rewards come from rising hierarchically as opposed to excelling horizontally is bound to undermine the effort to do the best possible job at the line level.[2]

We have suggested that social services can presently be of very little assistance to people. It is likely that the workers who provide these services will experience some sense of the limited impact of their work. To the extent to which this awareness leads to feelings of powerlessness or to resignation and cynicism, workers will be easily managed and dominated in their work settings; they will be unlikely to feel that any actions they might take would make much positive difference. Cynicism and resignation, as opposed to anger that turns to rebellion, maintain the status quo. Cynicism is reinforced when the worker, feeling inadequate in the face of the human crises that are part of everyday work, finds no sense of crisis and urgency in the agency or profession. Cynicism also flourishes when the worker's performance, which the worker may consider inadequate, is viewed as satisfactory and even helpful by the agency supervisors and is rewarded by promotion.

As a consequence, social service workers typically do not seek hierarchical advancement as a way to find the satisfaction lacking in working directly with clients,[3] and are likely to become cynical about the possibilities of being helpful to others. The few empirical studies that have been done on worker attitudes corroborate this point. Wasserman (1970, 1971; see Tracy 1972) studied welfare workers for a two-year period, beginning with their entry into the welfare system, and found them to be in severe conflict. The workers saw supervision as oppressive bureaucratic control. They had to break rules to try to do a marginally better job for their clients. Breaking rules led, in turn, to feelings of guilt and anxiety. Over time, they became desensitized to their clients' needs and grew increasingly cynical. They were quite aware that they could not do much to help their clients, and they saw their primary options as either leaving the agency or attempting to move up in its hierarchy.

On the other hand, in a study conducted in the early 1960s, Billingsley (1964) found that the 110 caseworkers he studied in two private family casework agencies tended to be oriented more toward carrying out agency policies and procedures than toward what they themselves saw as the needs of their clients and the mandates of their profession. While the consequences for the workers were not specifically explored in the study, some degree of cynicism or, at least, some loss of sensitivity to others would seem to be unavoidable.

Similarly, a research team of the Social and Rehabilitation Services (SRS), Department of Health, Education, and Welfare, reviewed nine empirical studies on the effects on initial entry into the social welfare and rehabilitation fields and found the impact on the workers to be primarily negative. The dominant worker responses were disillusionment, loss of idealism, and loss of interest in staying in the field. While specific causes of these reactions were not analyzed, the report did suggest that the lack of accomplishment of the field in general "may increase the amount of cynicism among workers and decrease the extent to which they will continue to emphasize service goals as opposed to self-serving goals in their behavior" (U.S. Social and Rehabilitation Services 1971:89).

Saucier (1971) studied worker turnover in an empirical analysis of the Franklin County Welfare Department, Columbus, Ohio. Of the 233 caseworkers, 72 percent left the agency within a 26-month period between 1967 and 1969. While the conditions of work were not the primary focus of the study, it was observed that 50 percent of the workers' time was involved with paperwork and only 20 percent in direct communication with clients or in collateral interviews.

The SRS study of manpower cited above extensively analyzed the problem of high turnover among social welfare personnel. Some underlying problems in the field are highlighted by their findings. Their conclusion (1971:50) was that

A standard of acceptable rate of turnover of Social Welfare and Rehabilitation Services workers, based on a smattering of opinions and data on rates of turnover among professionals in other fields, is estimated to be between 10 percent and 15 percent per year. By this standard, the amount of turnover in the Social Welfare and Rehabilitation Services field overall can be characterized as excessive, for it seems about double the acceptable rate.

In their analysis, "much turnover is . . . attributed to efforts (often fruitless) to locate a professionally more challenging and rewarding position" (1971:126).

Ullman et al. (1971) reported on a survey of over 600 National Association of Social Work (NASW) hospital-based social workers and 500 NASW social workers not in hospital practice. (Hospital-based social workers represent approximately one sixth of the entire NASW membership.) Of the hospital-based workers, only 45 percent could say they were generally very satisfied with their work, as opposed to only somewhat satisfied or dissatisfied. The hospital-based and nonhospital-based groups, taken together, reported approximately similar levels of dissatisfaction with specific aspects of work, with 75 percent reporting heavy work loads, 72 percent reporting inadequate community resources for referral, and 56 percent reporting little or no promotional opportunity, as serious or moderate problems in their work. No data were reported on the extent to which workers felt they were effective. It seems unlikely, however, that they would feel they were making a major impact, given that they are overworked and that they do not have adequate community resources to supplement their in-house activities. Specific studies of worker response in dealing with health problems of the poor (Pratt 1970) and with mentally disabled clients in a public welfare setting (Segal 1970) do illustrate how pessimistic many service workers become.

Finally, the services reinforce the larger patterns of social control by their discriminatory responses to female and black workers. The social services have been no exception to the rule that women and blacks have the lower-level jobs in the professional hierarchies and get less money than white males for similar jobs. The situation of the female workers in social work has been reviewed by Scotch (1971;

see Chafetz 1972; Williams, Ho, and Fielder 1974), who found patterns of discrimination against women in social work in salaries, promotions, and job opportunities. The salaries of male social workers are higher than those of females and have risen proportionately faster. More males than females have achieved administrative positions, have published professional articles, and hold honorific and leadership positions in professional organizations. Inasmuch as the service professions support discriminatory practices regarding minorities and women in the profession, they help to support the larger patterns of exploitation in the society.

Thus, the general message to the client that is contained in the fact of underfinanced, inadequate services is also a message to the worker. The worker is providing social services to people who have, for some reason, failed to contain within themselves the symptoms of our social crisis. The worker knows how poorly provided for these clients are. The message must necessarily be that if the worker does not remain properly at work and properly within the accepted standards of behavior, he or she might someday be forced to accept the very kind of inadequate service being provided to present clients. The social service worker knows better than anyone, save clients, that the social services are not what they claim to be and that making it on one's own in the market is the nearest one can come in our society to having security.

The Social Services and the Competition for Scarce Resources

The United States is marked by significant inequalities in the internal distribution of nearly all its resources. By every measure, we are a wealthy nation, and just as clearly our wealth is so distributed that a small fraction of the population receives an overwhelmingly disproportionate share of it. We are so used to hearing the figures that their full meaning can escape us. Nonetheless, it remains a measure of this country's distorted priorities that the top 20 percent of the families in the United States receive over 40 percent of the income of all families and the top 20 percent of all individual units receive over 50 percent of the income for all individual units (U.S. Bureau of the Census 1969:24). This maldistribution creates the potential for discontent and hence for political instability. Unless most people in the country can be convinced that inequalities are nonexistent or, if existent, are inevitable or desirable, they might try to take a larger share of the available resources for themselves. For them to do so would, of course, threaten the established order of the society.

A variety of possibilities suggests themselves as mechanisms for maintaining social stability in the face of both absolute and relative levels of deprivation. The most effective technique is to convince people that inequalities do not exist or are not as great as they really are. In fact, there is a great deal of propaganda to the effect that the United States is a classless society. Those inequalities that do exist are assumed to reflect individual abilities rather than institutionalized or class-based patterns of distribution. Furthermore, it is argued that some inequalities are inevitable in any society and are productive as a stimulus for individual effort. Inequalities also lead to the accumulation of capital, to investment, and, thus, to national economic growth. However the facts are presented, the general problem is the same—to encourage people to accept or at least to live with significant inequalities in the society.

The social services face a similar problem. They are one of the types of resources that the society has at its disposal and that must be distributed in accordance with the political mandates under which other resources are distributed. That is, we must ration them so as to obscure the fact that the amounts of resources being distributed are meager, so that awareness of inequities in the distribution of social services is minimized, and so that challenges to the overall order of the society are diffused. The social services are in fact distributed in a manner that meets these political requirements. In this section, the variety of ways in which this occurs are examined.

MAINTAINING CLASS ANTAGONISMS

One of the most significant political outcomes of the social services and, from a conservative perspective, one of the most functional outcomes, is that they lead to exacerbation of tensions and divisions among sectors of the population. Social services tend to provide benefits on narrowly selective dimensions. The result is that some people, who are essentially similar to those who do receive benefits, do not receive benefits, because of small differences in their income, residence, age, or health. Subsequently, these groups tend to view one another as the primary obstacles to receiving needed services, and competition among groups consisting of equally exploited people is established.

These divisions occur on at least two dimensions. First, the poor must place greater reliance on public social services, and second, there is competition among the poor for control of those services. In each case, need for, and competition over, scarce resources establish internecine warfare, which can only benefit the more advantaged segments of the population who have the private resources to permit them to stand above these conflicts.

One of the outcomes of the development of a more elaborate welfare state structure has been to exacerbate the mutual antagonisms of the working poor, the blue-collar workers, the lower middle classes, and the welfare population (Binzen 1970; Howe 1970). This reflects the first of the divisions created by the patterns of service distribution. The lower middle classes are often not eligible for public service programs such as medical care, income supplements, housing supports, and so on. At the same time, they are able to purchase adequate services on the market only with the greatest difficulty. Close at hand are the poor who receive public assistance, seemingly without expending any effort to achieve that self-reliance so prized by the lower middle classes. The outcomes are antagonism and the subsequent failure of groups like the National Welfare Rights Organization to organize the working poor and the unemployed into coalitions with welfare recipients. This antagonism, while having some basis in reality, is misplaced in that it ignores a more appropriate dimension for political struggle: the extent to which the United States has a dual system of publicly financed services, one for the poor and one for the middle and upper classes.

The services for the poor are the public social services. Expenditures for these programs are usually highly visible and often subject to political attack since they are expenditures on behalf of a group that tends to be politically unpopular, socially scapegoated, and relatively unable to mount a counterattack. At the same time, those with money to purchase private social services are subsidized in these purchases through the tax system. For example, tax deductions for medical expenses and mortgage interest are a public subsidy to those who are able to buy medical care or private housing. So, for example, the poor rely more heavily on the Social Security system for retirement income than the nonpoor, some of whom are able to save for retirement through a private pension plan. Yet, the private system represents a public expense of approximately one billion dollars a year in taxes foregone as a result of the tax deduction privileges built into that system (*Public Policy and Private Pension Programs* 1965; see

Galper 1973). Similarly, public expenditures for medical programs which primarily benefit poor people need to be weighed against tax deduction privileges for medical expenses of which middle- and upper-class people are more likely to make use. In 1970, total gross budgetary costs for Medicare and Medicaid were $4.6 billion, while tax deductions for private medical care and private health insurance in that year resulted in $3.2 billion in taxes foregone by the federal government (Joint Economic Committee 1972:38, 206). Likewise, in 1962, the federal government spent approximately $820 million for housing for poor people, while in the same year it spent approximately $2.9 billion in subsidies for housing for middle- and upper-income people (Schorr 1968:24). Private charity contributions to the poor must be weighed against the value of those contributions to the people who claim them as tax deductions, and so on. Even the dependency allowance system in the tax codes encourages this pattern. The AFDC mother may receive as little as $20 per month in welfare benefits for an additional child, or $240 per year. The person who earns $50,000 per year and deducts the standard deduction of approximately $700 per year for each dependent will avoid over $350 of taxes per year with an extra child, since he or she will be at the 50 percent tax-bracket level. The poor person gets a government grant for another child of $240 per year, and the wealthy person gets a grant of $350 per year.

This reflects the generally perverse effect of the tax system on these patterns of income versus benefits. The higher the income of the taxpaper, the more he or she benefits from a given deduction. While the poor person may claim a $675 deduction for an additional dependent, the actual savings of taxes will be no more than 10 percent of this amount. That is, if taxable income is reduced from $4,000 to $3,325, the tax is reduced from $400 to $332, or by $68. On the other hand, if taxable income is reduced because of an extra dependent from $75,000 to $74,325, the tax may be reduced from $37,500 to $37,162, or by $338. The same pattern prevails for deductions for medical expenses, mortgage payments, and so on.

The reality is that public financing undergirds a great deal of the social services for all classes and, in fact, does not benefit the poor to the exclusion of, or more heavily than, the nonpoor. Nonetheless, the poor serve as a scapegoat for the lower middle and middle classes. That the financial stress felt by working people is not based on the relatively small expenditures for welfare programs is a logical argument, but it is weak in the face of the hysteria that is encouraged by politicians and the press. The dual social service system obscures important commonalities among welfare recipients and working people and isolates them from one.another. Those benefiting most from public financing—the wealthy—escape the most bitter condemnation, or else become targets of far less hostile populist appeals for tax reform. The middle and lower classes go to the boards over the spoils.

Similarly, there is competition among recipient populations for welfare state goods and services and for the control of welfare programs. Grass-roots political organizing around services often takes place along racial and ethnic lines. In the absence of a class analysis, this has had the effect of turning blacks, Puerto Ricans, and white ethnic groups against one another in the poverty program, the Model Cities Program, and in numerous struggles for community control of social services (Mogulof 1970). These struggles among oppressed groups deflect attention from the common enemy and permit the continued allocation of small amounts of resources to these programs, since each group sees the problem in terms of competition with, and victory over, other groups in an essentially similar condition.

The isolation of poor people from one another is reinforced by the manner of benefit distributions in welfare programs. As Cloward and Piven (1965) have pointed out, benefits are generally distributed individually, in a manner which inhibits aggregation of clients. Complex procedures encourage individualized negotiations around eligibility. The structure and arrangements of benefit receipt encourage clients to assume a highly individualistic perspective on the problems, which does not lend itself to unified political action.

Two recent experiences in the city of Philadelphia illustrate these dynamics. An interesting mechanism was developed in Philadelphia in the early 1970s to ration one valuable resource—placement in a progressive high school within the public school system. The Parkway School utilized a city-wide lottery as a device to select students. The effect of this device was to focus a great deal of attention on the mechanisms of choice, on the gambling aspects of the lottery, and on the hope of beating out the other contestants. If the payoff did not come, only chance and other eager parents, not the political system, could be blamed. Consequently, the lottery focused attention away from the reality that the city was offering a very limited quantity of desirable resources and was otherwise offering mediocre educational services. John Cohen, a psychologist of gambling, has identified (1960:190) the general political phenomenon that operates in such cases. He writes:

In the context of a competitive culture, the idea of luck may serve as a convenient stabilizer, convenient, that is, to the "lucky ones," at the same time stultifying initiative and independent thinking. Daily emasculation of the reflective process of millions, whose horoscopes are cast in the daily press, produces a politically pliable mentality that sees the futility of social intervention if everything is foreordained by the stars.

Another plan with potential for stimulating competition among the have-nots was developed by the Philadelphia Housing Authority. "Good" public housing tenants will now have an opportunity to move to more preferable public housing units as they become available (Philadelphia *Inquirer* 1971). A "good tenant" is defined as one having no record of trouble with other tenants. As the tenants themselves will be the judges in these matters, and a favorable rating of one tenant will reduce the possibilities of other tenants moving up the ladder, this plan reinforces the competition of the poor with one another. It is interesting that a city housing administration which has not been noted for its concern for tenant self-determination has suddenly proposed a scheme for self-determination in one facet of its operation. In true colonial fashion, those with power and those who control the resources permit self-determination at a very distant point in the chain of events, under a set of circumstances that assures that self-determination will be, in the long run, an additional mechanism to weaken organized opposition.

This mutual alienation of people and of classes of people is facilitated, often unwittingly, by the social planner whose job is ostensibly to develop criteria for the most rational possible use of existing welfare state resources. In the process, the planner rationalizes and professionalizes some mechanism for distributing scarce resources to competing groups. In the name of rationality, equally valid claims on resources are set against one another, and discriminations are made among competing groups. This process occurs whenever communities or groups apply for funding within the framework of a larger social policy as, for example, in Model Cities, day care, drug treatment, and so on, and within the limits of some overall pool of funds allocated to that category of program. The planner, in these circumstances, professionalizes a process of discrimination despite his or her conscious intentions. In the case of the advocate planner, the worker's role is defined as ally of a community or group. All too often, the reality is that the planner's effort to get "more" of anything for one segment of the community results in a reduction of the resources available for some equally needy group that is without the good fortune of a planner to serve it.

SUBSTITUTING SERVICES FOR HARD RESOURCES

The substitution of inexpensive social services for more vital and critical services is another mechanism by which we make do with scarce resources and simultaneously deflect greater political consciousness. Fully meeting people's needs in any area of service would entail not only more expense than the society is prepared to allow, but, as we have argued, would require a radically altered society. As an alternative, the social services function to encourage people to redefine their needs and their views of what a solution to their problems entails, so that inexpensive and politically accommodating services can replace expensive and politically disruptive services. Hence, the counseling components of social service programs tend to receive more support than those which involve the distribution of harder resources like money, jobs, and houses. This occurs despite continued and substantial evidence that social services cannot take the place of the more substantial goods and resources that people need (Berleman, Seaberg, and Steinburn 1972; Mullen, Chazin, and Feldstein 1972).

This process began the first time that the moral influence of the Charity Organization Society friendly visitor was offered to the poor in the place of cash assistance (Lubove 1969:15). Since that time, the social services have continued to be offered as a substitute for the critical structural changes that our society requires. (Some commentary is offered by Alvin Schorr [1969] in two editorials in *Social Work*.) In the face of a job market that has fairly consistently demonstrated its inability to provide sufficient employment for all, the society has offered job training to the poor and social services to welfare clients. In the face of our inability and/or unwillingness to make our school system responsive to the needs of all, we have tacked on a Head Start program to help children cope with the poor programs they will experience (Romanyshyn 1971). In the face of society's inability to deal with repressive psychological realities of the society, an elaborate network of mental health facilities has been developed.

On the one hand, then, we offer the social services, which have a primary focus on changing people, as a substitute for policies dealing with the structure of the society which has created the people's problems. This is relatively less expensive economically and politically than the massive redistribution that would be required for structural changes, and it keeps the focus on the individual as the target of intervention.

On the other hand, those services we do offer are a conservative and warped version of services that would adequately meet people's needs. Job training services typically train people for low-status, low-paid, low-mobility employment in marginal industries. Sewing machine operators and beauty parlor technicians come to mind.[4] It is not unreasonable to assume that a training program that trained for decent work would require decent inputs. Instead of providing such inputs, we substitute low-level goals which are less expensive to achieve and which do not threaten the established stratification patterns. Likewise, we do not rehabilitate drug addicts by the adequate provision of life supports that would make drug use unnecessary. Rather, we lock them up, further narcotize them with methadone, or do counseling. Similarly, we do not help the mentally ill move toward their own liberation; we maintain them on drugs. The social services, then, have functioned as a substitute, and a poor substitute at that, for the more fundamental kinds of policies and changes required in the society.

INTAKE AND REFERRAL

In a number of ways, we parcel out limited social services with a veneer of rationality and objectivity. We try to make do with inadequate resources, while creating the impression that those with proper claims on resources can have these claims met. Each of the discriminatory mechanisms we employ is rationalized on a variety of groups and so is not always understood as a discriminating mechanism by workers or by clients, though more often clients know full well that they are simply being shut out, regardless of the rationale.

Two of these mechanisms are the social service functions of intake and referral. As we would expect, they are not generally understood in this way by those who staff them. Intake is seen, in professional terms, as serving the function of determining the extent that agency resources and client need match and as preparing the client for further use of the services. Elaborate diagnostic categories have been developed to assess clients, and on this basis precise discriminations are attempted. However, when intake is examined in the light of its role in resource distribution, it becomes clear that it serves in part to screen out some number of clients to prevent overload of the system, thus insuring that the agency will be more successful with those cases it does accept (Hallowitz and Cutter 1954).

The rationale of this process from within the profession generally concerns the desire of the profession to use itself with the population group with whom it feels most effective. The client populations so selected will have the most chance of using a service well. One effect of this process is that the population so selected is likely to consist of those persons already somewhat advantaged. The capacity to make use of help is itself a mark of strength. This process of selecting those clients most able to use a service leads to a systematic neglect of those who may be most in need of help (Cumming 1968:122; Lichtenberg, Kohrman, and Macgregor 1960:190–94; Rein 1964). It also leads to a higher probability that the service will be able to demonstrate higher success rates. Intake, therefore, both excludes the most needy clients and builds in the higher success rate required by the service structure to strengthen its competitive hand in the struggle with other services for funding (Steger 1931).

Referral, likewise, takes the pressure off the service system, but in a somewhat different manner. The client is taken into the service structure and is given a referral which is itself defined as a service. The nature of that service is that the client is sent elsewhere for service. Referral, in professional terms, is something more than a shove out the door. It may involve a diagnostic intake interview, an advance contact with the service structure at the receiving end, and some discussion with the client about the referral. Inevitably, some number of clients will get lost in the transfer, some will never get into the service structure to which they are sent, some will get in and will be referred out again, and some will get sent to services that do not exist or that exist in name only. An analogy is the parking problem in most large cities: there are never enough spots for all in need, but at any one time some cars are cruising the streets, looking. Referral is a way of dealing with clients in need without really dealing with them. Whatever its ostensible justification, it serves the function of rationing scarce social service resources to a population that needs more services than are available.

Similarly, waiting lists serve a number of functions for social agencies. They permit social agencies to deal with more people than they can actually serve. At the same time, as Perlman (1963:201) suggests, a waiting list may

stand as a reminder to board and community that more people need help than the agency can accommodate and that, therefore, it needs more money to employ professional staff. . . . One may also wonder whether some prestige has become attached to an agency's having a waiting list. Not only is a waiting list a declaration that casework service is in great demand, but it duplicates the usual pattern of private psychiatric and psychoanalytic intake.

STIGMATIZING SERVICES

There are a variety of additional ways employed to ration services. Making the receipt of services unpleasant surely helps to dissuade some eligible and needy people from using them. The stigmatizing effects of public welfare are not inevitable concomitants of an income distribution system. They are built into the intake processes and the ongoing conditions of benefit receipt, and they serve as one of the ways that eligible persons are discouraged from becoming clients.

Another mechanism employed to keep people away from services is keeping services a secret. The systematic publishing of information on Social Security through employers and the mass media, in comparison with the absence of information on the availability of public welfare, should tell us that selective processes of information dissemination are at work.[5] People are also kept out by rigid eligibility criteria, including age (old age assistance and Social Security), sex (AFDC, in large part), residence (welfare residency laws, until the courts declared them unconstitutional, and such devices as mental health catchment areas, target populations, service districts, and the like), income, and others.

MAINTAINING HIGH CLIENT TURNOVER

Finally, social services are rationed by "bouncing"—moving people who are recipients of services out of the service system as quickly as possible. A number of mechanisms for bouncing are utilized. For some services, like unemployment insurance, the straightforward device of a set number of weeks of eligibility is employed. For welfare, demands for behavioral conformity are made on the client, and clients are dropped from the service if these demands are not met. In mental health centers, elaborate rationales have been developed for emergency short-term service, after which the client may have to enter another network to continue treatment. In each case, some professional-rational-scientific overlay is developed for a process of exclusion. These mechanisms enable the service to come closer to giving an appearance of meeting need. In reality, the function served is the rationing of a scarce resource in such a way that the underlying reality of scarcity if obscured is a barrage of regulations and professional rationales.

NOTES

1. Hagith Shlonsky (1971) has argued that the distribution of any money or in-kind benefit that would influence the prevailing stratification system will operate on the basis of the principle of minimums as opposed to the principle of optimums. The welfare system does have a potential influence on the stratification system and operationalizes the principle of minimums through behavioral constraints, as well as other mechanisms. This is a useful distinction, though it minimizes the extent to which the adequate provision of any social service would have such an influence.

2. Bertha Reynolds (1963), a social worker whose life and work were informed by Marxist thinking, has identified in her autobiography the suspicion with which she was regarded when she attempted to return to direct practice after a distinguished career as teacher and author.

3. This is reinforced by the advice given the worker in the professional literature. For example, a prominent casework theoretician has written that when agency policies are unfair, unwise, or unnecessary, a desirable course is to try to work for change in policy, recognizing that workers can bring about improvements in policy and its administration, or at least can try to keep things from getting worse, "especially at the supervisory and higher administrative levels" (Hollis 1972:144).

4. For example, in 1971, clerical, service, and machine workers constituted 43 percent of Manpower, Development, and Training Act trainees. Of the remainder, 13 percent were in the professional-technical-manager category, 16 percent in construction-related work, 7 percent other, and 21 percent unknown (*Manpower Report of the President* 1972:267).

5. It is estimated that approximately one half of those eligible for public welfare are not recipients (James 1972:42). Even programs ostensibly designed with outreach purposes are often undermined if they prove too successful (Brody, Finkle, and Hirsch 1972).

[11]

THE DILEMMAS OF THE WELFARE STATE

Morris Janowitz

O NE does not have to be doctrinaire to recognize the profound dilemmas confronting the welfare state. Even the strongest advocates of welfare will attest to its failure to eliminate poverty. Its strongest critics will contend that it has been accompanied by a persistence and even an escalation of domestic sociopolitical conflict rather than the increase in consensus that it was supposed to achieve. On a very pragmatic basis, the welfare state has been accompanied by disruptive political struggles over the appropriate level of expenditure for welfare and by unresolved debate about the fraction of the gross national product (GNP) required for capital investments to sustain economic growth.

Of course, it is possible to speak of the difficulties of the welfare state under advanced industrialism in economic terms. Since 1970, the growth of the welfare system has been accompanied by both high levels of inflation and chronic unemployment. We speak of real unemployment, not measured unemployment. The key indicator of inflation has been added to that of unemployment. Inflation in and of itself creates new forms of social tension and human misery; it also introduces pervasive elements of uncertainty in the outlook of most of the citizenry. The combination of unemployment and a high level of inflation underlies the inability of the political institutions under the welfare state to resolve economic and social conflict. The new economic condition of stagflation raises the prospect of very low rates of economic growth—rates that strain and limit the aspirations of the welfare state.

Although the roots of the welfare state push far back in history, its extensive growth and its resulting dilemmas, for the purposes of this

From *Social Control of the Welfare State* (New York, N.Y.: Elsevier, 1976), pp. 1–16. Reprinted by permission.

essay, are encompassed by the period 1945 to 1975 in Western European parliamentary democracies, the United States, Canada, Australia, and New Zealand. The normative and institutional dimensions of the welfare state are set forth below. At this point the "welfare state" refers to government practices of allocating at least 8 percent to 10 percent of the GNP to welfare. The definition of welfare includes all public expenditures for health, education, income maintenance, deferred income, and funds for community development, including housing allocations.

In quantitative terms, the United States has lagged behind as compared with selected major industrialized nations. By 1935, welfare expenditures had reached close to 10 percent of the GNP. The figure dropped to a low point of 4.4 percent during World War II and returned to 10 percent by 1966. On a comparative cross-national basis, the United States has expanded its welfare expenditures more slowly than the major Western European nations, but the gap has been closing. By 1970, welfare expenditures in the Federal Republic of West Germany had reached 19.5 percent of the GNP, in France, 20.9 percent, while the comparable figure in the United States was 15.3 percent, reaching 17.0 percent in 1971 (European Communities Statistical Office 1972; U.S. Bureau of the Census 1973:286; 1974:273). Since 1971 the gap has continued to close.

The welfare state and welfare expenditures are not synonymous. The welfare state rests on the political assumption that the well-being of its citizens is enhanced not only by allocations derived from their occupations and the marketplace but also from grants regulated by the central government. It is necessary to point out that the welfare state involves at least two additional elements. First, under the welfare state, the extent and nature of welfare expenditures are conditioned decisively by parliamentary regimes; that is, they reflect political demands and consent and not authoritarian decisions. Second, it is accepted as a legitimate goal of the political system to intervene through governmental institutions in order to create the conditions under which its citizens can pursue their individual goals.

Paradoxically, the difficulties of the welfare state cannot be thought to be the result of a lack of achievements. Industrial development and the institutions of the welfare state have in fact reduced human misery. In retrospect, there does not appear to have been any alternative strategy compatible with a high degree of political freedom. In the most general terms, the failure of the welfare state rests in its failure to increase its flexibility and to confront its limitations. In this sense, the predicament of the welfare state extends beyond economic formulations. It did not succeed in generating a political, social, and intellectual basis for sustaining and transforming itself. Its accomplishments have not been accompanied by a system of self-generating and self-reinforcing legitimacy. The welfare state is not different from other historical accomplishments (Dahrendorf 1959; Schumpeter 1942). Each epoch brings with it the requirements for social change and adaptation.

However, given the enormous expansion of higher education under the welfare state and the equally extensive allocations of resources for organized "intelligence" and collective problem-solving, it had been expected that the welfare state would carry with it, to a greater degree than other epochs, the mechanisms and the capacity for self-redirection and self-generation in institution building. Despite the amount of intellectual effort, this has not been the result, although contemporary dilemmas may well have been deeper and more disruptive without these self-critical standpoints. (For the alternative point of view see Horkheimer 1947.)

Instead, as a result, the essential difficulties of the welfare state have come to rest in its direct effect on the political regime and the resulting inability of the political elites in democratic regimes to govern and effectively modify basic institutions. In each of the parliamentary political systems of the West, the expansion of the welfare system has been accompanied by the emergence of weak political regimes. One of the purposes of this essay is to explore this proposition in some detail. With striking uniformity, the Western parliamentary systems have been unable, during 1965 to 1975, to create governments that command a decisive majority of the electorate. Minority and coalition governments have become a chronic reality. The fragility of the national political consensus can be measured by the instability of the party in power as well as by popular mood and sentiment. The minority and the fragile political regimes are unable to govern effectively. This trend has emerged throughout the Western parliamentary democracies regardless of any differences in their commitments in foreign policy.

No doubt, the changes in social structure and administrative organization are at the root of this process of sociopolitical change. However, it is necessary to assess the extent to which the institutions and practices of the welfare state contribute to political instability.

Although there is every reason to assume that the central features of the welfare state will endure and that welfare expenditures will increase, the political mechanisms for administering it will undergo important adaptation if parliamentary regimes are to "master" the stagflation. The problem is whether authoritarian solutions can be avoided; for even a limited increase in authoritarian sanctions would destroy the moral basis and the goals of the welfare state.

Welfare in the Sociological Tradition

Thus, it is necessary to view the difficulties of the welfare state as rooted in economic dimensions—in the new economics—but at the same time to explore these dilemmas as central in the macrosociology of advanced industrial society. In the sociological tradition, there is a core of writings that supply a base for such an agenda. Of course, the classical figures in sociology, from August Comte to Karl Marx to Lester Ward, were concerned with the effect of urbanism and industrialism on the "welfare function" (Commager 1967). But it was in the 1930s, with the emergence of the new mass programs of welfare, that sociological writings focused on the impact of welfare institutions on social structure. T. H. Marshall (1950; see Shils 1962), the British sociologist, in *Citizenship and Social Class* traced out the historical process by which citizenship was enlarged and redefined to include the political rights of social welfare. In *Man and Society in an Age of Reconstruction* (1940), Karl Mannheim, the exiled German sociologist, used the awkward phrase "fundamental democratization" to analyze the instabilities of parliamentary rule involved in the expansion of the electorate.

In the post-World War II period, Richard Titmuss (1958) in Great Britain and Harold Wilensky (Wilensky and Lebeaux 1965; Wilensky 1975) in the United States have been the chief figures pursuing the analysis of the effect of social welfare institutions on social structure. The basic argument has been offered—and there is every reason to accept it, but only as a point of departure—that the size of national welfare expenditures is a direct function of the size of the per capita gross national product, the length of time that the welfare system has existed, and the size of the old-age population. The thrust of this argument is that among industrialized nations, the form of government and the content of political ideology are not overriding factors in the amount of welfare expenditures. However, our problem goes beyond such statistical analysis into the consequences and limitations of the welfare state.

Sociologists have therefore been concerned with the extent to which welfare services, plus educational expenditures, have redistributed income. They have assumed that an effective system of social welfare would increase social equality and thereby strengthen the mechanisms of a political democracy. However, increased social welfare payments and more extensive social service expenditures have not been accompanied by a drastic or even marked redistribution of income. It has become inescapable that an important aspect of this issue is the incidence of taxation as well as the resulting incidence of welfare payments.

Social welfare involves both transfer payments of money and the rendering of a variety of services. In recent years, sociologists have been concerned with the quality of welfare services and in turn with the increasing demand for welfare services. The administrative agencies created to administer a variety of welfare programs have not performed up to expectation in the quality and effectiveness of services offered. Contrary to expectation, the increase in the supply of welfare services has not decreased the demand. The demand for welfare, especially for medical services, has grown enormously and has the potential for continued marked growth. It is almost as if the demand for welfare services in an advanced industrial society is self-generated.

As a result, the issues of social welfare have emerged as a central theme of political debate and protest. In the 1960s, the drama of student protest against the war in Vietnam and against conscription produced a visible state of explosive tension. The de-escalation of the United States involvement in Vietnam defused that focal point of conflict; but the underlying tensions associated with the problems of the welfare state constitute the central points of political conflict, even though these have been less likely to erupt in symbolic expressions of protest and/or violence.

In the perspective of sociological analysis, the amount, content, and quality of social welfare services, as much as the level of industrial and economic production, are the central issues of the social order under advanced industrialism. Social welfare has served as a crucial dimension in posing for "modern" sociologists the classical problem: how is it possible for men and women with competing interests and goals to create a social order? The advent of the welfare state only serves to redefine the content and substance of the sociological tradition.

In essence, the dilemmas of the welfare state are expressions of the strains and limitations on the system of social control. "Social control" refers to the ability of a social group or a society to engage in self-regulation (Park and Burgess 1921:766; Turner 1967). The obverse of social control is coercive control. The macrosociology of an advanced industrial society raises the question of how to organize and manage a system of social welfare without a resort to, or with a minimum of, coercive control. In the intellectual tradition of sociology, social control transformed sociological inquiry at the turn of the century from a speculative enterprise to an empirical research effort (Janowitz 1975). The notion of social control carried with it philosophical implications—concern with higher moral principles—the basis on which social control would be created and the ethical principles and goals to which social groups would aspire. Suddenly, in the 1930s, under the impact of the Great Depression, sociologists departed from these formulations of social control as they became fascinated and preoccupied with issues of power. The result was not an effective sociological perspective for analyzing the complexities of the social structure and its relation to political power. Instead there emerged an emphasis on oversimplified "power" theories often grounded in gross economic determinist arguments. The idea of social control was temporarily transformed into a pejorative term which came to mean conformity and social repression. But the contemporary problems of the welfare state focus attention on the underlying character of the social order and the issues of social control. Sociologists have been forced to focus increasingly on the total social order of modern society; the conception of social control supplies an indispensable perspective for linking economic processes to the difficulties of welfare institutions. Throughout this essay, the term "social control" will be used in its "classical" and enduring sense, although this is not the fashion in which it is used by many writers.

Welfare and Economic Growth

In essence, the welfare state rests on the availability of some form of economic surplus, or economic profit—individual or social—that can be reallocated in terms of a set of principles. (The issue of mutual self-help, including community self-help, is also crucial and is not overlooked in this formulation.[1]) An economic surplus is calculated according to some notion of profit. Of course, the components of profit and the system of calculating economic transitions are arbitrary. But having pointed this out, we must recognize that the conception of profit remains indispensable for analyzing the systems of regulation and self-regulation of the welfare system. The sociologist cannot proceed without a notion of profit, however it is defined. The welfare state rests on the idea that industrial enterprise creates a profit—an economic surplus—that supplies the material basis of the welfare function.

In the contemporary setting, we speak of a system of national accounts rather than profit. National accounts are the total sum of the economic transactions in both private and public sectors. The new terminology does not obscure the observation that the system of national accounts requires some conception of profit that is compatible with the various traditions of economic thinking. In fact, it makes little difference whether one draws on classical economic formulations or on those specifically offered by Marx.

The dilemmas of the welfare state can be and must be analyzed in the terminology of profit and the resulting economic surplus. One can speak either in terms of the labor theory of value or of the exchange theory of value. Industrial and commercial enterprises generate profit and an economic surplus, which can be used for social welfare purposes. In the case of Marx, the allocation of this economic surplus is central to his perspective, since it reflects the social relations of society and influences the patterns of social conflict. In simplest terms, "capitalist" societies produce surplus profit that cannot be utilized effectively for the workers' welfare. Instead, surplus profit produces disruption because of the economic business cycle and the pressure for imperialist expansion and imperialist war, both of which create the conditions for political conflict and the transformation of capitalism to socialism and socialism into communism.

However, the structure of the national economy—that is, the pattern of national accounts—for advanced industrial societies under parliamentary regimes has been modified by the welfare state. During the period from 1945 to 1965, these nations were able to produce high rates of economic development and to limit fluctuation in industrial and employment levels as described below. Since 1945 and particularly since 1965, the significance of military expenditure to maintain economic growth and full employment has declined and can hardly be considered basic for the vitality of the economy. To the contrary, the burden of military expenditures has led to limited economic growth. This is not to underemphasize the impact of military establishment on domestic and international affairs.

The available estimates of the relation between military spending and welfare spending, as well as the problematic issue of the impact of capital investments, economic growth, and welfare expenditures are discussed below. It is necessary to point to the pattern, magnitude, and scope of growth in welfare expenditures. The data for selected years from 1929 to 1974 are presented in table 11.1. Total expenditures in constant 1974 prices rose from over $10.9 billion to $241.7 billion from 1929 to 1974. In per capita terms, the growth was from $88 in 1929 to $1,125 in 1974, with the level of expenditures more than doubling in the decade since 1965.

The underlying assumption of this analysis is that progressively the relative availability of economic resources with which to underwrite the development and maintenance of the welfare state has declined. In fact, the trend has been toward creating a "negative" surplus in Western industrialized societies.

It needs to be emphasized that obviously we are dealing with the summation of the economic transactions of the private and the public sectors. To speak of a decline of economic surplus is to indicate that the national society (as measured by its national accounts) has come to consume relatively more than it produces. (In this formula the requirements of reinvestment for capital goods are taken into consideration and are crucial.) It is necessary, as will be done below, first to examine the patterns of public accounts and then to proceed to the private sector. The pattern of spending since 1945 indicates the emergence of a chronic deficit in spending by federal as well as by state and local government. But the resources available for welfare—relative and absolute—rest on the articulation of the public sector accounts with those of the private sector.

The economic transactions of the private sector operate to generate economic resources required to pay economic costs (wages, materials, interest) and to produce profit. A portion of the profit is allocated for reinvestment in capital goods and part is available for transfer by taxes to the system of public accounts. To speak of a decline of economic surplus reflects both the long-term, relative decline in rates of profit and the level of private investment; these indicators again imply the relative decline of available economic surplus.

Table 11.1. Growth in Welfare Expenditures in the United States, 1929-1974: Total and Per Capita Social Welfare Expenditures under Public Programs in the United States in Actual and 1974 Prices

| Fiscal Year | Per Capita Social Welfare Expenditures in Current Prices[a] | | | | | | | | Constant Fiscal Year 1974 Prices | | |
| | Total[b] | Social Insurance | Public Aid | Health and Medical Programs | Veterans' Programs | Education | Other Social Welfare | All Health and Medical Care[c] | Total Social Welfare Expenditures | | Implicit Price Deflators (1974-100) |
									Amount (in Millions)	Per Capita	
1929	$31.80	$2.78	$0.49	$2.85	$5.31	$19.75	$0.62	$3.87	$10,882.4	$88.83	36.0
1950	152.56	32.19	16.26	13.34	44.18	43.47	2.92	19.97	44,107.0	287.31	53.1
1955	194.66	58.71	17.98	18.58	28.46	66.68	3.71	26.47	53,916.7	322.82	60.3
1960	285.42	105.35	22.46	24.45	29.52	96.43	6.24	35.03	78,237.6	428.56	66.6
1965	391.15	142.29	31.95	31.76	30.31	142.73	10.50	48.48	109,118.6	554.82	70.5
1970	701.78	262.47	79.48	47.01	42.99	245.23	21.24	121.65	176,472.6	850.64	82.5
1971	818.61	315.28	101.47	52.09	49.08	271.62	24.07	136.51	199,453.2	951.87	86.0
1972	906.72	351.88	123.25	58.71	53.59	286.14	26.86	156.07	216,044.3	1,021.08	88.8
1973	1,001.65	401.83	134.58	59.28	60.13	305.91	29.71	167.98	232,410.9	1,089.93	91.9
1974	1,125.59	456.41	156.58	65.44	64.19	838.66	32.29	192.35	241,736.9	1,125.59	100.0

SOURCE: From *Social Security Bulletin* (Washington, D.C.: U.S. Government Printing Office, 1975), p. 10. Per capita figures are based on January 1 data from the Bureau of the Census for total United States population, including armed forces and federal civilian employees and their dependents overseas, and the civilian population of territories and possessions. Deflators are based on implicit price deflators for personal consumption expenditures prepared for the national income accounts by the Bureau of Economic Analysis, Department of Commerce.

a Excludes expenditures within foreign countries for education, veterans' payments, and OASDHI and civil service retirement benefits.
b Includes housing, not shown separately.
c Combines health and medical programs with medical services provided in connection with social insurance, public aid, veterans' payments, vocational rehabilitation, and antipoverty programs.

The negative surplus is described below in terms of the language and categories of national accounts. The emergence of a negative surplus or a chronic economic deficit in the public sector has been a long-term trend. It reflects the system of internal management of investment, profits, and wage allocations. But it also reflects the increased rates of increased social welfare expenditures. The welfare state has become a permanent, or rather a chronic, deficit economy in the public sector accounts. Therefore, the system of social control comes under fundamental strain. The essential dilemmas of the welfare state are those of ineffective social control or self-regulation. The resulting internal political conflict derives in part from the decline of an effective surplus for social welfare and the profound escalation of demand for social welfare.

The difficulties of the welfare state cannot be resolved by increases in the supply alone; a restructuring of the demand for social welfare is required. But at this point there is no need to be limited by economic language. The issue is the potential for institution building to refashion human needs. The content and the definition of the "good society" and the moral order are directly involved.

NOTE

1. Mutual self-help implies the availability of some economic surplus, in the form of either manpower or economic resources, which is administered on a local basis without reference to marketplace considerations but is utilized on the basis of commercial norms. There is often a multiplier element in that self-help makes use of external resources or is able to be effective because it can mobilize economic resources. The notion of self-help has particularly important consequences in welfare because of its symbolic content.

PART II

THE ORGANIZATIONAL CONTEXT
OF SOCIAL WELFARE

A. SOCIAL WELFARE ORGANIZATIONS IN THE COMMUNITY

THE welfare state is rooted in expansion of the role of national government in social welfare. However, there remains considerable local and organizational variation in its implementation. Within parameters set by national policy, these variations are important in determining the extent and quality of social service delivery. The selections in part II address these and related issues of organizational process and client relations.

Part II contains four sections, the first of which, "Social Welfare Organizations in the Community," is discussed below. Section B, "Goal-setting and Organizational Theory," addresses special organizational issues in the sociological study of social welfare, including goal displacement. Section C, "Client Relations," focuses on the problematic nature of client-organization interaction. Material in section D, "Race and Sex in Social Welfare," is concerned with the issue of bias in the functioning and delivery of social welfare.

Despite the fact that the welfare state has eclipsed local and private efforts, the community context of social welfare remains important, especially in efforts to develop new service approaches. The political decentralization of the United States assures the continuing influence of the community context of its social welfare, the focus in section A. The first selection, "Community Structure and Innovation," by Michael Aiken and Robert R. Alford, is a national study of local urban renewal programs. Their findings indicate that the dependent variable, local innovation, is substantially affected by variations in city age and size, educational and income levels, unemployment rate, and other independent variables. Aiken and Alford offer the idea that interfaces, or networks, between interorganizational power centers increase the opportunity for innovation.

Mayer N. Zald, one of the co-editors, contributed the second selection, "The Structure of Society and Social Service Integration."

He applies interorganizational analysis to the traditional problems of coordination and integration of social welfare programs. This requires a special focus on organizational environments. Zald points out that greater social and social welfare structural differentiation has increased the demand for coordination. He makes the additional point that social service integration cannot simply be a matter of efficiency. In the United States, for example, it has been easier to create new programs than to eliminate older ones. The latter have constituencies which support them.

The final selection in section A is "Resource Allocations in United Funds," by Jeffrey Pfeffer and Anthony Leong. Based on a national sample of sixty-six United Funds, this study supports the "power-dependence" framework of interorganizational relations. The major finding is that United Fund allocations are determined largely by agency power. This power, in turn, is a function of agency and United Fund mutual dependence. This work by Pfeffer and Leong highlights a recurring policy problem in social welfare—to the extent that funding bodies are tied to established agencies, innovation becomes more difficult.

[12]

COMMUNITY STRUCTURE AND INNOVATION: THE CASE OF URBAN RENEWAL

Michael Aiken and Robert R. Alford

T HE search for determinants of public policy innovation in American cities has received little attention from social scientists. The controversy over "community power structure" focused almost entirely upon case studies of "who governs" in particular cities and barely at all upon the policy consequences of different configurations of power in the local community (Aiken 1970; Alford 1969; Jacob and Lipsky 1968). However, a number of comparative studies have appeared recently focusing upon such policy outputs as urban renewal, fluoridation, and desegregation. The data used in these studies, often rather crudely, indicate the concepts they allegedly represent. Such slippage between available data and theoretical constructs has resulted in the proliferation of diffuse explanations of public policy innovations and identical or even contradictory empirical indicators.

We shall review a number of theories of community policy innovation, examine some empirical findings about innovation in urban renewal, and conclude by suggesting an alternative theory which conceives of the community as an interorganizational system. Articles parallel to this one analyze innovation in public housing and in poverty programs (Aiken and Alford 1968, 1970).

The Nature of Community Innovation

Little attention has been given to innovation in communities, although they are continually introducing new ideas, activities, processes, and

From *American Sociological Review* (August 1970), 35(4):650–65. Reprinted by permission.

services. In the comparative perspective utilized here, we are interested in not only those structures and processes in communities that are associated with the *adoption* of an innovation, but also in the *speed* of the innovation and the *level of output* or performance of the innovative activity. In particular, we are interested in identifying the underlying structural properties and community processes that explain why some communities moved quickly to enter the urban renewal program while others were either slow to innovate or have never participated at all in this federal program. At least five theories of innovation which are relevant to this question can be found in the social science literature. Nowhere have these various explanations of community innovation been brought together. In part this lack of theoretical integration is due to the diverse concepts used; what we consider to be innovation has also been called community decision-making, community decision outcomes, and policy outputs.

Some Theories of Community Innovation

The five general hypotheses of community innovation are as follows:

1. *Political culture.* Cities with majorities holding "public-regarding" values are more innovative with respect to policies benefiting the community as a whole than cities dominated by groups with "private-regarding" values (Wolfinger and Field 1966; cf. Wilson 1966).

2. *Centralization of formal political structure.* Cities with centralized administrative arrangements and a strong mayor, that is, cities with city manager or partisan mayor-council governmental structures, are more innovative (Crain, Katz, and Rosenthal 1969; Greenstone and Peterson 1968).

3. *Concentration or diffusion of community power.* There are two aspects to this argument: concentration of systemic power (Hawley 1963) and diffusion of power through mass citizen participation (Crain and Rosenthal 1967). In both cases the hypothesis is the same: the greater the concentration of power, the greater the degree of innovation.

4. *Community differentiation and continuity.* Older and larger cities are more bureaucratic and consequently less receptive to policy innovations than younger and smaller cities (Dye 1968).

5. *Community integration.* Cities in which community integration breaks down or is extremely low have a lower probability of innovation or other collective actions. Consequently, innovation should be highest in integrated communities (Coleman 1957; Pinard 1963).

We have presented these five explanations separately because it is possible to conceive of them as five independent factors. However, one or more of these factors may be either spurious or intervening variables for the operation of another more fundamental factor, such as the sheer need for a program. Also, as we shall see, the indicators of the theoretical variables have been quite diverse, overlapping, and are sometimes used for quite different concepts. This diversity in the use of the same empirical indicators is partly a result of the great "distance" of the easily available quantitative indicators from the theoretical variables of greatest concern to most scholars.

Most of the data we use are no better, but we have the advantage of bringing together most of the various indicators used in the previous literature, as well as adding several measures which have the merit of being considerably closer to the theoretical variables to which they refer, although they have defects of their own.

Data and Methods

Urban renewal programs have been the most frequently studied aspect of public policy-making in American cities in recent years. In the scholarly literature, the aspects studied have been diverse, including whether or not a program had reached a planning or execution stage in a given city, urban renewal expenditures, and the number of years a city took to enter the program. The problems which have led to its study include community power structure, the political ethos of the city, and the capacity of shrewd political leaders to generate support. (There seems to be little doubt that the main effect of the program has been to reduce the stock of low-cost housing, since the original legislation explicitly forbade local governments to use income from the sale of land to build new low-rent housing, and relatively few cities have built public housing with other funds, whether federal or nonfederal.)

The findings of this study are based on the universe of 582 American cities in 1960 with the following characteristics: (1) incorporated urban places of 25,000 population or more, (2) location in states that had state enabling legislation prior to 1958 permitting cities to enter the urban renewal program, and (3) cities in existence in 1950. Of the 676 incorporated urban places with 25,000 population or more in 1960, 74 are omitted because they were located in 11 states which did not get enabling legislation until 1958 or later

(Idaho, Montana, New Mexico, Utah, and Wyoming), or which had highly restrictive enabling legislation, reversals of decision, or no enabling legislation at all as of June 30, 1966, or had a combination of these (Florida, Louisiana, Maryland, Mississippi, Oklahoma, and South Carolina). Another 20 cities that did not exist in 1950 are also omitted.

Since the cities that are included in this study constitute the population of all eligible cities of 25,000 or more, one may question the appropriateness of using statistical tests of significance. The use of statistical tests of significance when the data do not meet the assumptions of those tests (as is the case here) has been a continual problem for sociologists (cf. Gold 1969; Morrison and Henkel 1969; Winch and Campbell 1969). Even though we have exhausted all the units in the universe, there is still the possibility that the observations were produced by errors of measurement. In addition, because we have no other criteria, we utilize significance tests to distinguish between negligible and appreciable correlations, although we recognize that this test, strictly speaking, is not one of statistical significance, nor does it provide assurance of substantive significance (cf. Gold 1969).

The various measures of community structure were taken from the *Municipal Year Books* of 1963 and 1964, the 1950 Census of Housing, and the 1960 Census of Population. Information about the innovation measure, that is, participation in the urban renewal program, was taken from the *Urban Renewal Directory: June 30, 1966* (Department of Housing and Urban Development, U.S. Government, Washington, D.C., 1966).

We shall ignore changes in federal urban renewal legislation from 1949 on, although such changes may alter the incentives of different cities to obtain such resources. The original 1949 act required that 55 percent or more of the project area be residential either before or after renewal in order to qualify for federal assistance. This requirement was gradually eased by subsequent legislation. Undoubtedly, the incentives of local industrialists, real estate investors, and local groups of residents to initiate, support, or oppose urban renewal were altered by these changes, and therefore the probabilities of a given program being carried through, but we do not have the data to investigate this possibility (Ventre 1966).

We measure the presence or absence of innovation by whether or not a community has ever participated in the urban renewal program.

Table 12.1. Relationships among Indicators of Community Innovation

| | Presence of Innovation | Speed of Innovation | | Level of Output |
	Presence of Urban Renewal Program	Number of Years after 1949 before Entering the Urban Renewal Program	Number of Years It Took after State Enabling Legislation Was Present	Number of Dollars Reserved Per Capita (Natural Log)
Presence of participation in the urban renewal program	—	-.69***	-.62***	.86***
Number of years after 1949 before the community entered the urban renewal program	—		.88***	-.80***
Number of years it took after state enabling legislation was present	—			-.71***
Number of urban renewal dollars reserved per capita (natural logarithm)	—			—

NOTE: The number of cases is 582 except for the proportion of registrants voting, which was 370. The presence of urban renewal programs of one or another form of political structure was treated as a "dummy" (binary) variable for purposes of correlations and regressions in subsequent analysis. The natural logarithm of four highly skewed variables was used for correlation analysis, in order to produce an approximately normal distribution.
***p < .001.

Of the 582 cities in the analysis here, 372 (or 64 percent) had innovated an urban renewal program, although 32 of these later dropped out of the program. Among the remaining 340 cities, 187 had completed at least one urban renewal program as of June 30, 1966; 130 others had reached the execution stage of the program; and the other 23 were still in planning. There were 210 communities that had never innovated an urban renewal program.

The speed of community innovation is measured by the number of years after 1949 before the city entered the urban renewal program. This is similar to a measure developed by Straits (1965) in his critique of Hawley's (1963) work, although Straits used 1951 to calculate the speed with which a community entered the urban renewal program. The distribution of this variable was slightly skewed toward the lower end of the distribution, but skewness was not of sufficient magnitude to warrant a transformation of this variable.

Since some cities were located in states that did not enact enabling legislation until after 1949, another measure of speed in innovation was constructed: the number of years it took the city to enter the program after state enabling legislation was enacted.

The level of output measure is the number of urban renewal dollars reserved per capita as of June 30, 1966. This measure is similar to those used by Wolfinger and Field (1966) and Clark (1968), although not strictly comparable. The measure used here was computed by determining the total number of dollars reserved for all urban renewal projects as of June 30, 1966, and then standardizing this figure by the population size, thus yielding a dollar amount reserved per capita for all urban renewal projects. This distribution was highly skewed toward the upper end of the scale so that a natural logarithm transformation of this variable (which was approximately normally distributed) was used in the computation of correlation coefficients.

The relationships among these measures of innovation are quite high, as shown in table 12.1, although not so high as to make them equivalent measures. Nor are they logically the same.

Findings

A preliminary test of the several different theories of community innovation is found in table 12.2. We have classified each indicator under only one theoretical concept, although it may have been used to measure more than one concept.

1. *Political culture.* There is some question about the authorship of this theory. Wilson (1966) has written that he and Banfield (Banfield and Wilson 1963; Wilson and Banfield 1964) never developed the theory that Wolfinger and Field (1966) attributed to them. In spite of the question of exactly whose theory this is, we still include it here as an alternative theory of community innovation. According to this theory, a low proportion of foreign born in the city's population, a small proportion of Catholics, and a high proportion of the population that is middle class have been regarded as indicators of a likelihood that a community is composed of a majority of individuals and groups holding "public regarding" values. The consequence should be a high level of performance on policies which do not directly benefit the persons voting. While it can be argued that urban renewal directly benefits downtown businessmen rather than the poor, at least one study has tentatively accepted the appropriateness of measuring the consequence of public-regarding values by urban renewal outputs (Wolfinger and Field 1966).

In addition, we have added the percent voting for the Democratic candidate for president in 1964 as an additional indicator of the presence of a population holding private-regarding values. Cities that are heavily Democratic (as measured by the Democratic vote in 1964) are likely to be highly ethnic (r = .32), have many Catholics (as measured by the proportion of school children in private schools, r = .23), and have many working-class persons (r = .22). This is surely a more direct political measure than any of these demographic characteristics. Thus, if the political culture theory works, we should find that Democratic communities are less likely to have urban renewal.

Table 12.2 shows that of the sixteen relationships between the four indicators of community innovativeness, only one is in the expected direction. Most of the relationships between percent in private schools, median family income, and percent voting Democratic in 1964 are in the opposite of the predicted direction. In the case of percent of foreign stock, one of the indicators of speed of innovation is significant and in the predicted direction, but the others have no relationship with this measure of political culture. The political culture theory is thus (with one exception) not supported by any of the indicators and is contradicted by an additional one percent voting Democratic in 1964.

2. *Centralization of formal political structure.* This argument has two

Table 12.2. Relationships Between Indicators of Innovation, Speed, and Outputs and Various Measures of Community Structure and Culture

Theoretical Categories and Empirical Indicators	Presence of Innovation	Speed of Innovation		Level of Output
	Presence of Urban Renewal Program	Number of Years after 1949 before Entering the Urban Renewal Program	Number of Years after Enabling Legislation	Number of Dollars Reserved Per Capita (Natural Log)
Political Culture				
Percent of native population of foreign or mixed parentage[a]	-.01	-.04	.10*	.02
Percent of elementary school children in private schools[a]	.06	-.08*	.05	.08*
Median family income[a]	-.33***	.26***	.37***	-.29***
Percent voting Democratic, 1964[b]	.09*	-.13***	-.10*	.08*
Political Structure				
Presence of a city-manager form of government[c]	-.16***	.14***	.05	-.14***
Presence of nonpartisan elections[c]	-.14***	.14***	.04	-.18***
Percent of city council elected at large[c]	-.04	-.04	-.10*	-.02
Number of members of the city council[c]	.16***	-.13***	-.04	.14***
Centralization of Community Power MPO ratio[a]	-.30***	.29***	.21***	-.32***
Citizen Participation				
Percent of adult population with four years of high school education[a]	-.38***	.36***	.32***	-.38***
Percent of registrants voting[d]	.18***	-.20***	-.10*	.18***

Community Differentiation and Continuity				
Age of the city (census year city reached 10,000 population)[a]	−.48***	.54***	.46***	−.48***
Size of the city (natural logarithm)	.33***	−.49***	−.49***	.33***
Community Integration				
Percent unemployed[a]	.23***	−.25***	−.24***	.25***
Percent migrant[a]	−.23***	.25***	.12***	−.24***
Poverty				
Percent of housing dilapidated, 1950[a]	.20***	−.14***	−.28***	.13***
Percent of families with less that $3,000 income per year, 1959[a]	.26***	−.22***	−.34***	.21***
Percent adults with less than five years education (natural logarithm)	.36***	−.36***	−.40***	.34***
Percent 14-17-year-olds in school[a]	−.33***	.29***	.35***	−.30***
Percent of population that is nonwhite (natural logarithm)	.37***	−.44***	−.46***	.39***

Sources of the data are as follows:

[a] U.S. Census of Population, 1960.

[b] *County and City Data Book*, 1967. The county Democratic vote in 1960 was coded as follows: 60% or more Republican, 55–59% Republican, 50–54% Republican, 50–52% Democratic, 53–58% Democratic, 59% or more Democratic, to create six nearly equal groups. The two cities for which data were not available (Washington, D.C., and New York) were assigned to the mean category.

[c] *The Municipal Year Book*, 1963 (International City Managers' Association, 1963). Four or five cities with missing data on one or more of the measures of political structure were assigned to the mean category. The categories for the number of members of the city council were collapsed as follows: 3–4, 5, 6, 7, 8, 9, 10–19, 20–29, 30–50.

[d] Data are from a survey taken by Eugene C. Lee, Director, Institute of Governmental Studies, University of California at Berkeley. For further details and analysis of the voting data, see Alford and Lee (1968).

*p < .05.
**p < .01.
***p < .001.

aspects, one based on centralization of formal power, the second related to the political culture argument. In the first place, the thesis in the literature is that the more centralized the formal political structure, the more innovative it should be and the more capable it is of policy outputs (Crain, Katz, and Rosenthal 1969). There is some disagreement on what the indicators of centralization should be, since the usual conception of "reform" government is that its structural devices—the city manager form, nonpartisan elections, at-large elections, small city councils—were intended to centralize power in the hands of a small executive and a professional manager at the same time that potential power in the hands of citizen groups was fragmented and dispersed by removing the instruments of political party and ward organization. On the other hand, some have argued that strong political parties were the most effective device for centralizing power. But in either case there was agreement that administrative or political centralization should lead to a greater capability for innovation and greater policy outputs, regardless of the institutional form which centralization took.

The second aspect of political structure is related to the political culture argument, because it has been argued that reform political institutions were part of the array of policies favored by groups with public-regarding values, and presumably the instruments of such values should produce consequences similar to that of sheer demographic composition.

In most respects, the predictions of innovation which would be made by either the administrative centralization or political cultural interpretation of the indicators of political structure would be the same. The prediction is ambiguous only in the case of the form of elections. If nonpartisan elections are regarded as decentralized, then, according to this line of reasoning, they should be associated with less innovation. But if they are regarded as instruments of groups with public-regarding values, then nonpartisan elections should be associated with more innovation.

Table 12.2 shows that the relationships of urban renewal innovation and output with political structure contradict the centralization of formal political structure hypothesis completely. Manager, nonpartisan, at-large, small council cities are with one exception either *less* likely to innovate, or there is no relationship. The relationship between at-large elections and the modified speed of innovation measure is in the predicted direction, but this is the only one. The centralization argument is also contradicted, unless one wishes to accept the argument that partisan elections lead to administrative centralization, and therefore greater innovation. The data support the latter proposition.

3. *Concentration or diffusion of community power.* We refer here to two related explanations of community structure and consequences for the distribution of power: the ecological or systemic theory which sees power as a property of dominant institutions; and a mass participation theory which argues that those structural features which reduce mass participation will, as a consequence, concentrate power. We cannot test with our data a third, an "elite-participation" hypothesis, which argues that the smaller the number of elite participants and the more homogeneous their interests, the more centralized the power structure and the greater the policy outputs (cf. Clark 1968). While these theories differ in the feature of community organization which they single out as the critical measure or cause of concentration of power, they share the general assumption that the fewer the actors, whether mass or elite, and the more those actors represent dominant institutions, the more concentrated the power. The further inference that concentrated power leads to greater innovation is not always explicitly stated, but we believe that it is a justified extension of the theories.

In his study of urban renewal, Hawley (1963) argued that communities with a greater concentration of power will have a high probability of success in any collective action affecting the welfare of the whole. Hawley used participation in urban renewal programs as his measure of a successful collective action, and he used the MPO ratio (the proportion of the employed civilian labor force that are managers, proprietors, or officials) as his measure of the degree of concentration of community power. He reasoned that system power is exercised through managerial functions, and that those functions can be more readily coordinated if there are few positions performing those functions relative to the number of all other positions.

The data in table 12.2 support Hawley's empirical prediction: cities with high MPO ratios are less likely to innovate in all respects that we have measured than cities with low MPO ratios.

Other data drawn from case studies raise questions about the meaning of the MPO ratio, however. Aiken (1970) classified thirty-one case studies of community power on a four-point scale of concentration of power ranging from "monolithic" to "pyramidal" to "pluralistic" to "dispersed-power" arrangements, using qualitative judgments of the number of groups involved in major issues in the community as the measure of degree of dispersion of power. The results show a tendency for less centralized communities to have higher levels of innovation and outputs, and for cities having high MPO ratios to have higher concentrations of power than cities with low MPO ratios. Another study of fifty-one cities (Clark 1968) found that the greater the decentralization of community power as measured by the number of persons involved in decision-making in four issues (urban renewal, air pollution, poverty programs, and the selection of the mayor), the greater the number of urban renewal dollars per capita secured from the federal government.

Thus, cities with high MPO ratios are found to have little urban renewal, as Hawley predicted, but few active power centers, which finding appears to be inconsistent with his thesis. But since centralization for Hawley referred to the distribution of systemic power while the meaning of centralization here refers to elite participation, this does not mean that Hawley's thesis is necessarily wrong. Systemic power may be highly dispersed, yet few actors or power centers may be active. Still, such an inconsistency does raise interesting questions about the meaning of centralization and about an adequate explanation for this inconsistency.

The second aspect of the concentration of power theory refers to citizen participation. Crain and Rosenthal (1967) argued that the higher the level of education in a community, the higher the political participation, which in turn leads to higher conflict, then stalemate, and consequently less innovation in urban renewal. Their hypothesis links a high level of educational attainment with a low degree of community innovation and output, and posits an intervening process of heightened political participation and consequent community conflict and blockage. The relationship between the percent of adults with a high school education and the four measures of innovation supports this hypothesis (see table 12.2).

While the empirical relationships between these variables are clear, the meaning of this educational variable and the intervening process may be questioned. Does a high level of educational attainment in a community reflect the presence of many well-educated, relatively affluent persons? Or does it reflect merely the absence of a poor population and less urban decay? Do cities with many well-educated persons have greater citizen participation and consequently more stalemate and inaction, or do they simply have a less apparent need for urban renewal? Among cities over 25,000 population, the correlations between median education and the upper extremes—percent of adults who have completed college and percent of families with incomes of $10,000 or more per year—are 0.62 and 0.63 respectively. But cities with high median education also have fewer adults with less than five years of education (r = −.77), fewer families with incomes of less than $3,000 per year (r = −.53), less housing built before 1929 (r = −.48), and less dilapidated housing (= −.39). The interpretation of educational level clearly depends on which end of the stratification scale one wants to emphasize, the degree of poverty, low educational attainment, and poor housing stock, or the degree to which an articulate middle class is present.

In the analysis of thirty-one case studies of community power (Aiken 1970), it was found that there were fewer power centers active in cities with high educational levels than in those with low educational levels, although the relationship was not a strong one. Similarly, Clark (1968) found a positive relationship between the median educational level of a city and the degree of centralization (i.e., fewer elites participating in the four decision areas he examined). If centralization refers to the degree of elite participation, middle-class cities appear to be more centralized than working-class cities. Even if this is true, it is still possible that citizen participation is greater in highly educated cities, thus accounting for less innovation in urban renewal. They, like us, lack direct data on the key intervening variable of participation. Unfortunately, adequate data on political participation do not exist for a large sample of cities. If voting turnout can be regarded as a crude indicator, a study (Alford and Lee 1968) has shown that better-educated cities have lower voting turnout than less well educated cities. We find among the 381 cities in our study for which data on voting turnout are available that *higher* voting turnout is associated with greater innovation, although the relationship is not a strong one (see table 12.2).

Our empirical relationships between level of education and innovation in urban renewal are quite consistent with the findings of Crain and Rosenthal, although empirical indicators vary slightly. Middle-class cities have less urban renewal, but they also apparently have *less* elite participation. If centralization means elite participation, then we find that there is less urban renewal in centralized cities. If centralization means citizen participation (as measured by educational levels) or dispersed systemic power (as measured by the MPO ratio), then we find that there is less urban renewal in decentralized systems. We do not mean to suggest that the well-reasoned theories of Hawley and Crain and Rosenthal are incorrect; we do not have the evidence to demonstrate that. But we do wish to point out the various usages of the term centralization in the literature on comparative community decision making and to call attention to an inconsistency in conclusions about the relationship between centralization of power and innovation. Clearly, greater conceptual refinement and additional research using more direct measures of mass participation and distribution of systemic power will be necessary to unravel the meaning of an inconsistency such as this.

4. *Community differentiation and continuity.* As noted at the outset, the few articles that have used the variables of age and size of cities have disagreed about their interpretation, arguing on the one hand that older and larger cities would be more rigid, more set in their ways, more complex, and therefore more incapable of action, and, on the other hand, that such cities should be more adaptable, more experienced, more flexible (Dye 1968; Mohr 1969).

The data of table 12.2 show that older and larger cities are in fact more likely than younger and smaller cities to have innovation in urban renewal. The correlation coefficients of these two character-istics with the various innovation measures are the largest of any in table 12.2. Whether or not age and size are merely a reflection of a high level of structural degradation of the housing and building stock, and hence only a reflection of need for urban redevelopment, is a question which will be addressed later.

5. *Community integration.* The argument here is that more highly integrated communities, those with highly developed networks of communication and contact among social groups, should suffer less from paralyzing conflict in the case of a new issue requiring decision, because, on the one hand, channels of communication to work out compromises exist and, on the other hand, isolated factions standing fast on their own positions would not be present (Pinard 1963). The indicators used for community integration are quite diverse, and include several already mentioned under other headings, but two additional variables—the unemployment level in the community and the amount of migration—are also included in this argument. Pinard's thesis is that high unemployment levels will produce disin-tegration of community life by reducing attachments to community

institutions resulting in high conflict levels and low innovation capabilities. High levels of city growth and in-migration reduce integration because they disrupt long-standing networks of communication and interchange among the organizations comprising the community. He also argues that racial and ethnic diversity and large city size indicate low community integration and that high political participation indicates the bringing into the political system of those least attached to the community, therefore those most likely to oppose innovation.

Table 12.2 shows that in the case of urban renewal these theoretical expectations, with one exception, are not supported. As already seen, highly ethnic and large cities are *more* likely to innovate, as are cities with high voting turnout. And cities with high unemployment are more likely to have urban renewal, contradicting the hypothesis. Cities with high levels of in-migration have less urban renewal, in accordance with the hypothesis.

Few of the hypothesized relationships drawn from the literature are borne out completely; in the case of those that were supported, we have noted some inconsistencies in the meaning of the concept of centralization. Our main empirical findings are that older and larger cities and those with low levels of education and income, high unemployment, fewer managers and officials, and low levels of in-migration and growth are more innovative.

The first question which these results raises is whether or not a community's innovation in urban renewal is simply a function of the poor quality of the housing stock, the deterioration of the central business district, and the generally lower levels of economic growth in older cities. To answer this question, we have included some additional measures of poverty and housing conditions in table 12.2. Cities with more dilapidated housing in 1950, more poor families, fewer well-educated families, and more nonwhites were far more likely to have entered the urban renewal program, entered it faster, and have higher levels of participation in the program.

Given the strong and consistent relationships between city size and these need measures and innovation in urban renewal, we may pose the question whether or not many of the previously discussed relationships, regardless of the concepts they were alleged to represent, are not simply functions of a high degree of community need for urban renewal. To answer this question, we computed a series of partial correlations between two measures of innovation and most of the variables in table 12.2, controlling for city size and level of dilapidated housing. As shown in table 12.3, the relationships between the variables that were strongly related to the innovation measures in table 12.2 are still relatively strong when city size and the amount of dilapidated housing are partialed out.

Stepwise, regression analyses which introduced the five "need" measures were first performed, and showed that approximately 18 percent of the variance was accounted for by those measures. Additional variables, each accounting for at least one percent of the variance, were age of city, city size, percent migrant, percent foreign stock, and median family income (listed in order of selection).

A few words are necessary on the relationships between both the independent and dependent variables and the regional location of a city. Cities in the Northeast are most likely to have urban renewal, followed in order by cities in the South, the Midwest, and the Far West, as shown in table 12.4. Similarly, Northeastern cities were faster in applying for and more successful in obtaining money for urban renewal. But these cities are also likely to be older, poorer, and have higher levels of ethnicity and out-migration. The question can be raised whether all of these relationships are accounted for by regional location of a city.

Although we cannot present the data in detail, the major findings hold up when they are examined within the four regions. Age and size of the city are closely related to all four measures of innovation in all four regions, as are education, income, MPO ratio, and nonwhite composition, with only a few exceptions. Almost all of the original relationships that were low remain low in all four regions, except for a few cells for which we have only ad hoc explanations. Political structure, Democratic vote, and voting turnout are significantly associated with innovation only in the Far West, for example. Our general conclusion, however, is that the findings previously discussed are, with some exceptions, also true even within regions in spite of strong regional variations in innovation rates (see Aiken and Alford, 1970).

We have also examined the correlation coefficients between the various independent variables and the speed and output measures among the 372 cities that had ever entered the urban renewal program. This is a very conservative procedure since it excludes cities that never innovated in urban renewal. We would expect the correlations between the various independent variables and the speed and

Table 12.3. Partial Correlations Between Community Characteristics and Speed of Innovation (After Enabling Legislation) and Level of Output, Controlling for Size of Community and Percent of Housing Dilapidated in 1950

	Speed of Innovation (after Enabling Legislation)	Log N Urban Renewal Dollars Per Capita
Political Culture		
Percent of native population of foreign or mixed parentage	−.04	.09*
Percent of elementary school children in private schools	−.02	.11**
Median family income	.23***	−.24**
Percent in the county voting Democratic, 1964	−.03	.02
Political Structure		
Presence of a city-manager form of government	.01	−.12**
Presence of nonpartisan elections	.04	−.18***
Percent of city council elected at large	−.10*	−.03
Number of members of the city council	.09*	.06
Concentration and Diffusion of Community Power		
MPO ratio	.14***	−.28**
Percent of adult population with four years' high school education	.21***	−.34***
Community Continuity		
Age of city (census year city reached 10,000 population [log n])	.26***	−.38***
Community Integration		
Percent unemployed	−.14**	.21***
Percent migrant	.08*	−.21***
Poverty and Need		
Percent of families with less than $3,000 income per year	−.19***	.18***
Percent of adults with less than five years' education (log n)	−.24***	.28***
Percent 14-17-year-olds in school	.17***	−.22***
Percent population that is nonwhite (log n)	−.25***	.29***

*p < .05.
**p < .01.
***p < .001.

Table 12.4. *Means of Indicators of Innovation in Urban Renewal within Region*

Region[a]	Number of Cities	Presence of Urban Renewal Program	Number of Years after 1949 before Community Entered Urban Renewal Program	Number of Years after State Enabling Legislation Was Present	Number of Dollars Reserved per Capita (Natural Log)
Northeast	164	82%	9.1	8.9	7.25
South	191	62%	11.5	8.0	5.18
Midwest	219	48%	13.5	12.7	3.86
Far West	102	36%	13.9	13.0	3.10
All cities	676	58%	11.9	10.6	4.97

[a] The states included in each region are as follows:

Northeast: Maine, New Hampshire, Vermont, Massachusetts, Connecticut, Rhode Island, New York, New Jersey, Pennsylvania, Maryland, Delaware, and District of Columbia.

South: Texas, Oklahoma, Kansas, Missouri, Arkansas, Louisiana, Alabama, Mississippi, Florida, Georgia, North Carolina, South Carolina, Virginia, West Virginia, Kentucky, and Tennessee.

Midwest: Ohio, Indiana, Illinois, Michigan, Wisconsin, Minnesota, Iowa, North Dakota, South Dakota, Nebraska, Montana, Idaho, Colorado, Utah, Wyoming, Arizona, and New Mexico.

Far West: California, Oregon, Washington, Nevada, Alaska, and Hawaii.

output measures of innovation to be attenuated. While the size of the correlations among this subset of 372 cities that have ever innovated is indeed reduced, the major findings remain intact. Age, size, nonwhite composition, low income, and low education are still related in the same direction to the speed and output measures. Evidently the same factors that contribute to innovating in the first place also affect the speed with which innovation cities enter the urban renewal program and their level of outputs in the program.

But even if we know which are the best predictors or that our results are not simply a function of the size and level of need, regional variations, or results produced by including noninnovating cities in our study, we still do not know why and how some communities enter the urban renewal program and others do not. The mind is not set at rest by such findings. In the first place the relationships are not strong. In the second place the condition of housing or the age of a city does not tell us anything about the intervening processes which enabled some cities to displace its blacks for new businesses or expensive apartments while others did not use urban renewal in this way.

Structural Differentiation and Community Innovation

Let us start negatively by reviewing the rejected explanations. Global properties of the political ethos of majorities and integration seemed to fare most poorly. While the zero-order predictions of Hawley and Crain and Rosenthal were as predicted, we have shown that even these relationships can be removed by partialing procedures. That is, hypotheses referring to properties of the city as a whole rather than properties of groups or organizations making up that city seemed (1) to use concepts most distant from the available data and (2) to be supported most weakly by the data. If anything, the data point in the opposite direction. Cities that appear to be heterogeneous, differentiated, and fragmented—as indicated by ethnicity, a large working class, nonwhite composition, size, and the qualitative data on centralization (elite participation) in the works of Clark (1968) and Aiken (1970)—are most likely to have innovated in urban renewal. The same studies show that the more groups and actors participating in current decisions, the higher is the level of innovation and outputs.

Additional and more directly relevant data support the proposition that the more differentiated the organizational structure of a city, the more innovative it will be. A more direct measure of organizational complexity than simply city size would be a count of the number of organizations of various types which play some role in community life. We have data on three such types of organizations—manufacturing firms, banks, and trade unions—although only for a subsample of cities in each case. Unfortunately, we lack data on other more crucial types of organizations such as political parties, voluntary associations, or the local government.

Not only the sheer number of organizations may be important, but also the number having sufficient resources to affect critically the course of community innovation. For this reason we have chosen the number of manufacturing establishments with 100 or more employees and the number of independent banks with assets of at least $50 million as our measures of organizational complexity and differentiation. Unfortunately, the unionization data cannot be treated in exactly the same way. But because larger firms are more likely to be unionized and because the data include all establishments in which a majority of the plant workers are unionized, we believe that this measure is an appropriate indicator of the organizational complexity of a community.

Table 12.5. *Differentiation of Economic Structure and Innovation in Urban Renewal in American Cities*

	Manufacturing Number of Establishments of Size 100 or More	Banking Number of Independent Banks with Assets of $50 Million or More	Unionization Percent of Plant Workers Unionized among All Industries	
			North	South
Innovation				
Presence of urban renewal	.27***	.33***	.22*	.33**
Speed of Innovation				
Number of years after 1949 it took the city to enter the urban renewal program	−.42***	−.46***	−.15	−.48***
Number of years it took after state enabling legislation	−.33***	−.37***	−.03	−.03
Outputs				
Log N urban renewal dollars reserved per capita	.32***	.36***	.24**	.40**
N = (217)	(217)	(77)	(35)	

SOURCE: Manufacturing and banking data are available for the 217 nonsuburban cities in the size range 25,000 to 250,000 population which had 20% or more of their labor force in manufacturing in 1960. The unionization of manufacturing establishments is available for 84 metropolitan areas, which provide an estimate of unionization in 112 cities within them. See Michael Aiken, "Economic Concentration and Community Innovation," unpublished manuscript, 1969, for details on the construction of the measures. The banking data were taken from *Polk's Bank Directory* (Nashville, Tenn.: R. L. Polk and Co., 1966). The data on unions are drawn from Bulletin No. 1465-86, Bureau of Labor Statistics, U.S. Department of Labor, Washington, D.C., October 1966, entitled *Wages and Related Benefits: Part I, 84 Metropolitan Areas, 1965–66.* The measure is the approximate percent of all plant workers employed in establishments in which a union contract covered a majority of workers during the period July 1964 to June 1966. We have assigned the degree of unionization in the SMSA to the urban place as the best estimate we have of the unionization of the city itself.
*p < .05
**p < .01
***p < .001

These data relating structural differentiation and community innovation are presented in table 12.5. Because the level and character of unionization can be presumed to be different in the North and the South, the data for that variable are presented by region. The results are consistent with our expectations. The more manufacturing establishments, the more independent banks, and the more unionized plants that a city has, the more innovative it is.

These measures of structural differentiation can be regarded as ways of spelling out more precisely what it means to be a large city as far as capacity to innovate is concerned. Large cities have a greater diversity of social organizations, and they also have greater innovation.

An Alternative Explanation

Because we find none of the previously discussed theories completely satisfactory, we here propose one approach that seems to be more consistent with the previous findings. Our alternative explanation of the findings can be only a suggestion since we do not have the empirical data to test directly our ideas. Therefore, we shall only suggest here some of the concepts that appear to us at this time to be most relevant in explaining innovation in such decision areas as urban renewal, public housing, and the War on Poverty.

Our tentative alternative explanation is that such innovations are a product of the nature and state of interorganizational networks in communities (cf. Turk 1970). Such networks are properties of community systems that have developed historically through the interaction of organizational units and their leaders. If the population of a community is relatively stable, these interorganizational networks are not likely to be disrupted by the continuous influx of new citizens and organizations, and thus greater potential exists for increasing their capacity for coordination over time.

The degree of historical continuity in a community structure—especially as it affects interorganizational networks—may also influence innovation. Presumably, older cities have had a longer time for existing organizations to work out patterns of interactions, alliances, factions, or coalitions. In such communities the state of knowledge in the community system about the orientations, needs, and probable reactions to varying proposals for community action is likely to be quite high, thus increasing the probability of developing a sufficiently high level of coordination in order to implement successfully a community innovation.

The degree of structural differentiation and complexity of a community may also influence innovation for two reasons. First, larger cities are likely to have more organizations devoted to specific kinds of decision-areas; that is, more likely to have a redevelopment agency, a housing agency, a community action agency, a city development agency for Model Cities, welfare councils, and other community decision organizations. Such organizations are likely to have larger, more specialized, and more professional staffs to provide the technical, administrative, and political knowledge required to innovate successfully, not only within their organizations, but also in the activation of interorganizational relationships and establishment of critical coalitions (cf. Mohr 1969). Second, it is precisely in the larger, more structurally differentiated communities that coalitions that can implement an innovation will be easiest to establish. If we assume that only a limited number of organizational units need to be mobilized to bring about a successful innovation, then it follows that in large, highly differentiated communities a lower proportion of the available organizations will participate in such decisions, and that there will be wider latitude in selecting organizations for these critical coalitions. In other words, the "issue arena" involved in the innovation will require the participation of only a few of the organizations that exist in the community system. In one sense, this proposition is simply a spelling out of what is meant by "structural differentiation" or "functional specialization." The more highly differentiated or specialized a community system, the higher the proportion of decisions that are likely to be made by subsystems and the less likely the entire system will be activated on most issues.

The extent to which the interorganizational field is "turbulent" may also influence innovation (cf. Terreberry 1968). Where many people are moving out of the city, the existing historically developed network of organizational relationships may be relatively undisturbed, except in so far as out-migration indicates an economic or perhaps political crisis which existing institutions cannot handle. Conversely, where many people are moving in, bringing with them different ideas about the appropriate functions of local government, and perhaps creating demands for new services, newly established organizations may be severely limited since they are less likely to be in an organizational network which can aid in achieving an adequate level of coordination for a proposed community innovation.

We thus suggest that three properties—structural differentiation, the accumulation of experience and information, and the stability and extensiveness of interorganizational networks—may contribute to the capacity of a community to innovate. Let us turn to more concrete concepts and hypotheses that might be consistent with this particular approach.

Community systems can be conceived of as interorganizational fields in which the basic interacting units are *centers of power*. A center of power can be defined as an organization which possesses a high degree of autonomy, resources, and cohesion. The linking mechanisms among centers of power in a community system we call *interfaces* (see Mott 1970). Interfaces are not only the current set of interorganizational relationships in the community, but more important include the historical accumulation of knowledge and experience among various centers of power. An *issue arena* is the organization set (Evan 1966) of centers of power which must be activated on a given issue in order to effectuate a decision.

We hypothesize that the greater the number of centers of power in a community and the more pervasive and encompassing the interfaces, the higher the probability of innovation in a given issue arena. In other words, the more choice among acting units in the system—centers of power—and the greater the state of information about organizational actors, the higher the probability that a minimum coalition can be formed. For many issues this will mean the creation of an organization whose specific task is the implementation of the decision to innovate. Warren (1967a; 1967b) refers to these as "community decision organizations," and he cites community action agencies, housing authorities, welfare councils, and health departments as examples. The community decision organization is a special type of center of power whose mission is to supervise the planning, coordination, and delivery of the innovated activity. The professional staffs of such organizations are likely to generate further innovations.

The structural conditions in the community that lead to the introduction of an innovation in a given activity—organizational differentiation and historical continuity—may not be the factors that are most conducive to high levels of performance by community decision organizations. Once the innovation has been introduced, the community decision organization may seek to develop relatively tightly controlled relationships with cooperating organizations in their issue arena and thus gain legitimacy for an exclusive mandate from other community decision organizations. If so, communities with high levels of performance in various community action activities may well be those in which relatively autonomous issue arenas have emerged. It may be that the structures of relationships within such subsystems are indeed "centralized" in the sense of a given organization having strong control over units within that issue arena. If this is true, it would suggest that Hawley's thesis may be appropriate if a community subsystem is taken as the unit of analysis.

It is possible, however, that this model is only applicable to decisions for which the major actors are organizations. To the extent that private citizens are mobilized on a given decision—as in the case of fluoridation—this model may not be appropriate, or at least it may be incomplete.

What we have suggested is a two-stage process in which the overall state of a community system may be most important for understanding the community's propensity for innovation across a wide spectrum of issues, but that the appropriate analytic unit for understanding specific innovations, as well as performance in such innovations, is a subsystem of a community in which the central actor is the community decision organization. Our data do not permit us to test the validity of assertions such as these; that would require a completely different type of comparative study. But this particular approach appears to us to be as consistent with the data presented in this paper as any of the theories we have examined, if not more so.

13

THE STRUCTURE OF SOCIETY AND SOCIAL SERVICE INTEGRATION

Mayer N. Zald

A s America became an urbanized society in the second half of the nineteenth century, its churches, governments, women of compassion, and social movement leaders began to recognize that the streets of gold had gutters of slime; that the open road of opportunity also contained dead ends of despair, disease, injury, isolation, and poverty (Bremner 1956). The response to perceived social problems was the creation, in the public and private sectors, of a plethora of programs, services, and organizations. Almost as soon as those early entrepreneurial agents of mercy defined and organized services to meet the needs, they began to recognize the problems of coordination and integration of services. The Social Services Exchange (now almost dead) and welfare councils are not products of the post-World War II era, but were products of the very first large-scale welfare efforts in our cities.

The proliferation of services in our own times has intensified the demands for coordination and integration, and there have been recurring attempts to achieve better coordination. The modern emphasis on comprehensive planning has had two main goals: the provision of an adequate level and range of service and program elements and the effective *integration* of the elements of the service or program network, both within and between communities. Yet often the earlier attempts failed to solve problems of fragmentation, and no one viewing the present scene can be sanguine about the orderly relations among our attempts to solve major social problems. Problems of coordinating urban development and service also have preoccupied political scientists and public administrators. Although

From *Social Science Quarterly* (December 1969), 50(3):557–67. Reprinted by permission.

this essay focuses on the social welfare agency, much of its analysis applies to the coordination and integration of other urban services as well (Wheaton 1964).

Since so many of the modern-day intervention strategies do involve comprehensive service plans and integrative networks, it is well worth our while to understand the sources of resistance to coordination and integration—especially since in the world of public officials and social service executives, "coordination" and "integration" are much like the words "competitive marketplace" to the business executive. In both cases they are treasured words, but the actual conditions they represent are hardly pursued with vigor. It is easily understandable why the business executive would want to avoid the rigors of the competitive marketplace: in a fully competitive market he would not make much profit. But it is less clear why executives of agencies for the public weal would attempt to avoid coordination and integration. After all, is not that the route to efficient and effective service?

Instead of analyzing why executives and their organizations resist bringing nirvana to the welfare world, we have typically impugned their motives—they are empire builders, or conservatives (read "fuddy-duddies"), or they are trying to protect their own jobs. In particular instances each of these charges might be correct, but a serious examination will indicate, in many cases, a sound logic behind the resistance to integration and coordination. No argument is made *for* fragmentation and low coordination; instead, there are costs and benefits to *both* integration of services and autonomy of services. Only if these costs and benefits are seriously weighed can anyone estimate the value of different *degrees* of coordination and integration under varying *structural* arrangements.

Our largely theoretical analysis attempts to link up several threads of recent sociological analysis, theories of social differentiation, the "new look" in social problem analysis, and interorganizational analysis. First, we analyze the relationship of changes in social structure and societal differentiation to the perception and definition of "social categories at risk," the target of social problems solutions. Second, the perception and definition of social problems lead to the creation of agencies and programs to cope with them. Each differentiated agency or program presents a new interface for coordination and integration. Third, agencies develop a character and set of commitments that lead to a shifting set of enmities, alliances, and coalitions. With this as our background framework we then turn to a crude, qualitative cost and benefit analysis of various integrative and coordinating mechanisms.

Social Structure and the Emergence of Social Service Programs

There are many kinds of programs that few would have imagined a century ago, or even, in some cases, thirty years ago: crisis (suicide) prevention centers, comprehensive neighborhood health units, community mental health clinics, group treatment units in our prisons, half-way houses, street workers' programs in our largest cities, Medicare, Medicaid, consumer education leagues, and so on.

Where do these programs come from? How are they related to the changing social structure of modern society? There are three, partially interrelated, processes involved. First, the changing composition and structure of society divide the society into social categories. Second, processes within society and within relevant professions lead to definitions of social categories as social problems, creating the potential for new services or changes in existing ones. Third, new technologies, knowledge, and beliefs about how to treat or handle specific problems create the need for new organizations and structures to utilize them.

CHANGING COMPOSITION AND SOCIAL STRUCTURE

For organized services to come into existence there must be a perception of a fairly widespread social category requiring a service. A certain (undefined) minimum population mass must be in a specific category. Thus, only as the society differentiates into recognizable and sizable groups—divorcees, adolescents, alcoholics, senior citizens—can a social problem even begin to be defined. The greater the differentiation, by definition, the greater the number of social categories.

These social categories become potential service receivers as groups within the society begin to define categories as "deficit," as not measuring up to some standard of performance. The changing social structure creates and makes salient the definition of a social category as being in some sense deficient. For example, no one thought of school dropouts as a group or, for that matter, as a problem in the nineteenth century. Only as the age of voluntary school leaving was raised did the category called "dropout" emerge. Furthermore, only as schooling was perceived as a key route to occupational success did

the category become defined as a social problem. Similarly, defining
old age as a social problem is caused by a combination of mortality
rates, changing family structure and retirement policies, not by
changing mortality rates alone. The point is that, in conjunction with
values or standards of "adequate" living, it is the changing structure
of society that creates social categories needing service (Titmuss
1958).

SOCIAL DEFINITIONS OF PROBLEMS

Not only are the social categories for service created by the structure
of the society, but the very definitions of a social problem, of deficit,
are determined by the processes of organizational and professional
growth and interaction. The "new look" in deviance research has
focused on the way in which members of society, professional groups,
and "moral entrepreneurs" create the definition of deficient functioning (Becker 1963; Scheff 1966). Moral entrepreneurs have a
stake in the perception of deficient operation. Problems are created
by societal rules—bookmaking becomes a crime when the society
decides to regulate gambling. No regulation, no crime. (Marijuana
usage as a social problem is exactly of this created kind.) Different
groups with different values "create" social problems (Gusfield 1963,
1967). The problem of positive mental health exists only to the extent
that professional groups convince others to spend money to attempt
to achieve positive mental health in the society. The general sociological point is that increasing differentiation leads not only to a
greater range of social categories at risk, but to an increasing number
of groups and organizations having a stake in defining groups at
risk.

CHANGES IN TECHNOLOGY, KNOWLEDGE, AND BELIEFS

Finally, new organizations and services are created as a variety of
solutions are proposed based on beliefs and knowledge about how to
solve problems. Halfway houses are created as mental health and
penological practitioners come to believe that people who are not
fully incapacitated are better off outside our institutions. Adoption
agencies are made regulated services when it is believed that children
can have better lives this way than when placed in homes through
unregulated services. A behavioral conditioning unit is introduced in
a hospital when these techniques are believed to be more efficacious
for certain disorders than other techniques.

The general thrust of this argument is that the creation of new large and definable categories in society, the growth and change of professional groups, and changing technology create the ever-growing possibility of new organizations and services. (Note, however, that these same processes, though more rarely, can lead to the elimination of "need" for a given type of service. For instance, the need for orphanages declined as a result of: [1] increasing longevity; [2] welfare provisions to support single parents; and [3] the emergence of adoption services.)

Thus, the fragmentation of services and the lack of integration of services is, ultimately, a result of some of the basic processes of modern society creating literally hundreds of specific purpose programs. Each new program is a planned intervention to affect some problematic category. The addition of each new program or agency multiplies the problem of coordination with every related funding, governmental and civic organization serving similar or related clientele groups. Each interface shared between organizations becomes a potential coordination area.

Organizations and Their Environment

Of course, if all agencies existed in a world of sweetness and light, in a world without scarcity of time, money, and motivation, in a world of consensus on values and priorities, the problems created by the existence of hundreds of agencies might easily be overcome. If organizations were machines, complete in themselves and made up of mechanized parts, their interadjustment might be relatively easy. Turn a screw here, adjust an interagency linkage there. But it is precisely because they are made up of a number of groups of people with different conceptions of purpose and commitment and because they are in a constant state of flux asking for support from the multiple constituencies of the larger society that they do not lend themselves to easy integration. Essentially, the argument is that organizations are dynamic entities operating in a world of scarcity and more or less constantly faced with problems of motivating support in the community, and within themselves (Clark 1960; Selznick 1949).

As each new organization comes into existence, it must define its goals and opening procedures. Although some social service organizations come into existence with clear-cut goals, target populations, and operating procedures, for most organizations each one of these aspects requires definition. For both public and private organizations, official charters are phrased in ambiguous or general language; scope of mission remains to be determined. A correctional institution is told to "rehabilitate inmates," a children's psychiatric service is given preventive goals and told to have residential and outpatient service. Note that relative priorities and financial allocations are rarely considered. Even in a governmental program like Medicare, although the financial base was specified by law, operating procedures were worked out through an administrative give-and-take. These goals, priorities, and target groups are worked out between executive and staff, other agencies, and key board members and constituencies (Thompson and McEwen 1958). There is an organizational give-and-take as, over time, "turf" is defined, and programs are adjusted to perceived need and to organizational competence.

If these evolving goals and programs were value-neutral, that is, if the people did not have strong feelings about the social worth and importance of these programs, there would be much less problem in changing and coordinating social service progress. But social welfare programs are not like a line of groceries; various groups inside and outside the specific agencies have strong feelings about the purposes of different agencies, the client to be served, and the procedures or technologies of the organization. Attempts to change them often run into stiff opposition based on these strong values and attachments.

Furthermore, the funding patterns of service-welfare organizations contribute to the maintenance of organizational autonomy. Most, if not all, social service organizations, unlike businesses, depend for most of their finances on getting funds and general support from groups who are not the direct recipients of services. Whether they are public or private agencies they are dependent on the good will of funding agencies. Since good will is a sometimes tenuous thing, social service agencies often attempt to "lock in" good will by developing external constituencies and alliances that will work for them and with the various funding agencies. These constituencies (which in specific cases may be board members, the local mental health association, key members of legislative committees, associations of judges or of police chiefs) also develop commitments supporting various goals and modes of operation. Thus, to change organizations in the social service arena is also to neutralize or change the perspectives and operations of a lot of other groups related to the organization.

The discussion of funding arrangements leads to another point: although social service organizations are usually not thought of as operating in a competitive marketplace, because they do not price their products to meet a competitor's price, in fact they operate in an extremely competitive environment (sometimes disguised) in which they compete for the allegiance and financial support of key groups. Unlike the competition of business, the competition is frowned upon in our public rhetoric, yet within and without government, the competition goes on.

What is the consequence of all this for the coordination and integration of agencies? It comes to this: the process of organizational formation and development leads to a host of agencies and services, each with partisans within and without the organization. These organizations may collaborate with others for some specific purposes, but not for other purposes (Long 1958). Given our earlier argument about the increasing differentiation of organizations and social categories, comprehensive planning emerges as an attempt to establish guidelines and integrative nets for the operation of an increasingly fragmented (differentiated) agency-program scene. Whether it or any integration-coordination mechanism is successful depends upon its reckoning with the realities of organizational dynamics and operation.

Coordination and Integration: Costs and Benefits

The words "coordination" and "integration" apply to a wide variety of proposals for changing the authority structure, communication channels, and synchronization of programs and purposes. These proposals run from major structural reforms in which previously separate, private organizations become part of one superagency, to units of government being given a common central authority, to common fund-raising efforts, to relatively minor exchanges of information about a particular case or project.

A dramatic example of the problem of one kind of agency coordination has been presented by Miller (1958). Miller observed a continuing situation in which increasing delinquency in Roxbury, Massachusetts, led to calls for a coordinated preventive program.

Although several *ad hoc* community committees proposed a program, and finally a committee representing concerned agencies was appointed, the committee rarely met. Following the slaying of a rabbi, the Jewish community groups started pushing for a program; the committee began to meet regularly, and a program was funded and in operation. Yet, within two years the program fell apart. Miller explained the failure of the program in terms of differences among the agencies in their conceptions of the *etiology* of delinquency; of the *disposition* of the delinquent; of the *approach priority*; of the appropriate *organizational method*; and of the proper *status of personnel*.

This example, while extreme, indicates the multitude of commitments that leads to difficulty in coordination and integration of services. Overcoming each commitment and conception costs time, energy, and even organization integrity. The costs are often too high. But there are cases where coordination and integration do operate successfully. The problem is to specify the costs and benefits of different levels of coordination and integration.

There are two major classes of argument used in arguing for integration and coordination. One involves issues of *efficiency*—savings in money, time, and personnel—and the other involves *effectiveness*—the ability to accomplish ends.

Efficiency arguments have been involved in several major integration movements in recent times. Two of the most prominent examples are the development of state commissions of higher education and the development of coordinated fund-raising in the private sector (United Fund).

In our time, one of the major cases of integration has been the federated fund-raising drives of United Funds. There are two sources of efficiency here. First, administrative costs in raising money are reduced for each agency. Second, businessmen were saved the time and effort of their own personnel who were involved in the multiple solicitations within the business (Carter 1961).

Note, however, the costs. Individual agencies participating in the drives have not been able to raise their own dollar volume as fast as those agencies with specialized appeals (national health groups like the Cancer Society) which have refused to participate. Furthermore, involvement and lay support have to some extent been lessened.

The development of state commissions (boards) of higher education has come about as the growth of mass higher education has placed an increasing strain on state finances and as the complexity of the system has made it difficult to evaluate alternatives. Often the commissions have been imposed on the universities by the legislature and taxpayer groups seeking efficiency or by a coalition of the weaker and less prestigious schools who want a larger share of the pie. In some cases, the established institutions want to be protected from newer ones. In any case, the commission often insulates the legislature from the job of establishing priorities and weighing multiple appeals. The commission does this by formalizing criteria and rules for allocational incisions (Glenny 1959).

While the development of commissions helps the legislature solve *its* decision-making problems, there is no evidence that it leads to better education. It may stop duplication of facilities, but it also may lead to a slower rise in the quality of education as intra-university competition within a state is cut down. The commissions do not lead to smaller educational budgets, though they may lead to a more efficient use of the money that is allocated.

This should not be read as an argument for the demise of the joint drive. Many people would resent violently a return to the old system. A return to the old system would also hurt newer groups that have muscled in with their own campaigns, and the new groups—including civil rights groups as well as the health associations—deserve attention.

The efficiency principle is seen in a negative case, the decline of social services exchanges. The social services exchanges were established early in the century to coordinate services among private agencies. Each agency listed its cases and the services, including money, that were being given. Ostensibly such a service would still be valuable for the information exchanged. As public welfare increased, however, the real reason for the exchanges declined. The exchanges had stopped beneficiaries from obtaining grants from several agencies. As money was no longer saved by the service, most communities have dismantled their social services exchanges (Litwak and Hylton 1962). (It may be that today modern computers, sharing information, would be less costly.)

EFFECTIVENESS ARGUMENT

In the social welfare arena there are three major effectiveness problems that are supposed to be solved by increased coordination and integration. The first is the problem of uniform services, the second may be labeled the pinball problem, and the third is the problem of partial solutions.

The problem of uniformity of services is a false issue for, in almost every case, people arguing for better integration of services to achieve uniformity of standards are talking about uniform higher standards. For instance, no one argues that New York's welfare payments should be uniformly reduced to Mississippi's. Except for a few people who think rule standardization is a good in itself regardless of the *quality* of the rules, few would pay the cost of lowering some persons' welfare to achieve uniformity.

The pinball problem is that with so many agencies and individuals offering services, the clients may bounce from agency to agency without getting "proper" service. Cumming (1967) described this well in the mental health field. People with problems become "pinballs" which are bounced from friend to minister, to doctor, to one agency or another, without being "properly" treated. If there were only one agency, would not the services be allocated more effectively? The answer is, No! On the one hand, there is no possibility of eliminating the interpersonal and informal network of friends, doctor, and minister. On the other hand, each new agency, private and public, has identified a new set of needs. One only has to note that without significantly affecting suicide rates the development of suicide prevention centers has provided important services to troubled people. Frightened and anxious people who are not calling the police and who are not going directly to established agencies have a new route into the system.

The argument about partial solutions concerns the multiproblem family or client. A host of agencies deal on a fragmented basis with one client or group; would they not be more effective if there were one organization? Let us note that this problem applies as well between the range of government agencies as between private agencies. Robb (1961), for instance, has discussed this very problem in New Zealand where the various units of the Public Service relate on an individual basis to families. If one had just one unit, all of the benefits of specialization and commitment would disappear. It may be that for that section of the population that is multiproblemed, special units are needed. But the largest part of our total social service potential does not really fall into this category. Handling the simple case through one elaborate coordinated service structure would be fantastically costly in money and time. The problem becomes one of finding mechanisms of integration and coordination in which costs are low relative to benefits.

Coordination proposals, as noted earlier, range from simple and *ad hoc* arrangements to the total reshuffling of organizations (see Litwak and Hylton 1962). *Ad hoc* case coordination involves a decision by a worker in one agency to contact another agency concerning a shared client. Just as long as an agency policy does not forbid such contact (if the agencies have a history of enmity such contact may be forbidden), if both workers are willing and have the time and inclination, one-shot coordination may take place. Agency policy may even encourage such sharing, but there is a cost to the workers involved. There are costs in communications time, and the workers may have to pick up new responsibilities.

Information exchanges are also relatively simple coordinating devices usually handled through meetings of top executives or, where a large audience is to be reached, through formal newsletters.

If two agencies share a large common caseload or interests, two integrating devices may be proposed: liaison teams or procedural integration. Procedural integration requires developing a formal set of rules and decision criteria; it is more costly than *ad hoc* case relations because it requires overall organizational adjustment and commitment—records have to be changed, routing procedures adjusted, and the like. At some point, procedural integration will usually involve upper-level executives and the weighing of consequences of the new procedures from the point of view of overall organization as well as for the specialized clientele.

Liaison personnel or teams are likely to be proposed when the volume of agency exchange is high and the exchange involves continuous interagency adjustments and communications about specific cases (Thompson 1967:51–82). This solution leads to increased role specialization within each agency. For instance, in one case a social service agency that had considerable court work turned one worker into a full-time court liaison person. All agency cases involving the court were channeled through this person (oral communication with Roger Lind).

A fifth type of coordination is program integration which involves the joint administration of coordinated staffs (Reid 1964). A coordinated program of this type is quite costly in manpower and time. Since we can assume that most personnel are already engaged in organizationally meaningful tasks, it is most likely to come about either when new finances are made available or under duress (Miller 1958).

New programs at the federal level have had a real impact on program coordination and integration. These programs often require joint community planning. Part of this emphasis on comprehensive planning stems from bureaucratic reasons: (1) the federal agencies would find themselves faced with a fantastic number of applications to evaluate if joint applications were not encouraged; and (2) insisting upon comprehensive planning forces the collecting of data which helps the federal agencies in evaluating need. From the local community side, this emphasis represents a cost. Time and money are spent on collecting data and demonstrating need; however, the cost is usually more than matched by the benefits of money that allow better services, programs, and organizational expansion. But it is not necessarily accompanied by greater actual integration of service. Each new government program in itself contributes to the differentiation of social categories and the creation of new organizational interfaces.

Finally, organizational integration may take place through the creation of one superagency, the placing of separate organizations under one head. For instance, several cities have created human resources administrations. If the major goals and perspectives of the various organizations included are quite different, the costs of such integration may be very high, at least as perceived by respective constituencies, executives, and the like. Usually, such integration will be achieved only if the integration is seen as part of a larger social movement in which large numbers of people are involved and power is mobilized.[1] On the other hand, if goals and norms are similar, if large cost efficiencies are possible, integration may be more easily achieved.

Conclusion

We have stressed that there are a number of hidden costs to integration and coordination that are often ignored. The growth and development of agencies and services in modern society are related to basic changes in the social structure of the society, increasing differentiation of social categories, emerging professions, and new definitions of service needs and means. Organizations develop commitments and internal and external constituencies to support their goals, territories, and procedures. As a consequence they relate to each other like semiautonomous states and engage in coalitions and alliances for specific purposes. Coordination and integration have both benefits and costs, and coordination proposals can be compared in terms of these costs and benefits.

In weighing costs and benefits, it is necessary to use economic, political, and social standards. Many coordination and integration programs have high overall dollar benefits while being extremely costly to specific groups or organizations. Analysts of costs and benefits have to examine the organizational, political, and professional costs as well. Thus, in American society it is easier to add new services than to eliminate old ones, to create new compacts than eliminate total structures.

There is a deep, pervasive strain between the search for equity and equal treatment of all citizens and the increasingly complex, differentiated, and interdependent structure of urbanized and industrialized society. Coordination and integration mechanisms are in part aimed at providing equitable, uniform, and effective services. But, on the one hand, they often entail costs which make them prohibitive and, on the other, the underlying processes of specialization and technological changes create new facets of interdependence and new interfaces of service. Leviathan and a fantastic computer system might solve the problem. But in the meantime we shall continue to add categories and devices dealing with the problematic categories and to worry about means to control and integrate the devices.

NOTE

1. Here may be found one of the reasons that the movement to metropolitan forms of government has largely failed while advisory regional development groups and specific problem compacts (such as sewage disposal) have been created between cities. On the one hand, the broad mass of population is not highly dissatisfied with their own governmental forms, and many people are positively attached to present forms. On the other hand, officeholders have vested interests in preserving the status quo. Purely technical criteria can be used in specific problem areas, and regional development boards do not directly attack either the officeholders or value-identities of their constituents.

14

RESOURCE ALLOCATIONS IN UNITED FUNDS: EXAMINATION OF POWER AND DEPENDENCE

Jeffrey Pfeffer and Anthony Leong

T HERE are several similar statements in the literature outlining a theory of dependence and power between social actors (Blau 1964; Emerson 1962; Jacobs 1974; Thompson 1967). Furthermore, the importance of the concept of power for understanding formal organizations has been emphasized in the political economy approach to the study of organizations (Benson 1975; Zald 1970b). It seems remarkable, therefore, that in spite of the consistent articulation of theories of power and dependence relations, and despite the importance of power and dependence as concepts in the literature on the sociology of organizations, there have been remarkably few studies conducted to test such ideas empirically.

The United Fund provides an appropriate context in which to investigate the effects of power and dependence on resource allocation decisions. As an organization whose principal function is the raising and distribution of money, resources are a critical part of the United Fund's operations. Member agencies typically consist of organizations performing a wide variety of services, ranging from recreation and character building to the delivery of medical services. Thus, the problem of resource allocation is complex, since different goals and values must be compared in the process. As a confederation of independent social service agencies, the United Fund has some of the characteristics of a cartel, in that membership is voluntary and the umbrella organization must be concerned with the possible withdrawal of important members. The United Fund is an interor-

From *Social Forces* (March 1977), 55:775–90. Reprinted by permission.

ganizational coalition, and provides a setting in which interorganizational decision-making (see Tuite, Chisholm, and Radnor 1972) may be empirically examined.

The question of who gets what in an organization has been posed by political theorists (Gamson 1968; Lasswell 1936) and is an issue that is highlighted by the conceptualization of organizations as coalitions (Cyert and March 1963) or political systems (Zald 1970b). The allocation of resources within organizations affects the allocation of resources within society as a whole (Pondy 1970), and the rewards and status achieved by individuals participating in organizations. Thus, examination of the determinants of resource allocation decisions in United Funds provides the opportunity both to explore models of organizational decision-making and empirically examine some of the basic propositions in the power-dependence literature.

The United Fund

The recent interest in interorganizational behavior (Aldrich 1974; Benson 1975; Marcus, Sheldon, and Adams 1974) makes the examination of decision-making within interorganizational associations important. While the studies cited have tended to concentrate on explaining dimensions of interorganizational activity (Marrett 1971), the operations of coordinating interorganizational agencies are important because of the impact on flows of resources among organizations.

The United Fund is distinguished from some other public coordinating agencies in that membership is voluntary. As in a cartel or industry association, each participating organization must decide whether the benefits to be gained from joining the organization are greater than the costs incurred. Litwak and Hylton (1962) argued that coordinating agencies would develop if organizations were partly interdependent, agencies were aware of this interdependence, and the interdependence could be defined in terms of standardized units of action. They argued, further, that interdependence would be most critical in times when resources were either very plentiful or very scarce, and attempted to account for variation in United Funds operations over time using this framework.

The United Fund is based on the belief that with a single fund-raising organization, greater public interest and participation can be achieved, and economies of fund raising can be realized to provide more net funds for the social service agencies. Seeley, Junker, and Jones (1957) and Litwak and Hylton (1962) both note that consolidation of fund raising to reduce donor complaints and to achieve economies of time and other resources is frequently mentioned as a reason for the United Fund coming into existence. Richard Carter (1961) saw the United Fund as an attempt to centralize the funding, and consequently the control, of social services in the hands of a small business elite. Certainly, business has been an important supporter of the United Fund movement.

The original Community Chest organizations encompassed only local agencies. But with the advent of United Funds there was an attempt to consolidate both the local agency and national agency fund-raising drives into a single annual campaign. Both Community Chests and United Funds combined the principles of budgeting and fund raising. The organization not only seeks to raise money for agencies, but also allocates the funds raised. The United Fund has defined its activites in terms of the allocation of resources for community social services.

The United Fund has come to define one of its important goals as including as much of the local solicitation for fund raising as possible.

Under the Community Chest, approximately 60 percent of all funds raised locally through *personal solicitation* in community-wide campaigns came through the Chest . . . today about 95 percent of such funds come through the United Fund. It is doubtful that the United Fund will ever include 100 percent of all such funds raised; nevertheless, the goal is to *further reduce* fund-raising drives which can qualify for United Fund leadership (United Fund of Greater Chattanooga 1973:5).[1]

Agency participation in the United Fund is voluntary. For its participation, the agency receives an allocation from the United Fund from the resources raised during the annual campaign. In return for these funds, the member agency is proscribed from engaging in the personal solicitation of funds, and must comply with the United Fund's budgeting requirements. The agency can continue to raise funds from special events such as sales or auctions, charge for memberships, and receive funds from endowments, sales of publications, foundations, of from city, county, state, or federal tax funds. The United Funds see the budgeting procedures as an advantage, causing individual member agencies to plan programs more carefully.

Agencies receiving resources, however, are subject to external control. The United Fund may request, and then require, that agencies merge in order to receive funds, and control over the agency's services and programs is exercised by approval or withholding of funds based upon proposed programs and budgets.

Hypotheses

The coalitional model of organizations suggests that decisions are made on the basis of relative influence rather than by such bureaucratic criteria as profit maximization, efficiency, or effectiveness. Such a result occurs because of the needs to resolve uncertainty over the connections between actions and consequences and disagreements over goals and preferences (Thompson and Tuden 1959). There is some support in the literature for the coalitional perspective. Cyert, Dill, and March (1958) studied four business decisions in three firms, and found that expectations were developed to justify the decision that was desired, rather than having the decision based on the forecasts. Stagner (1969) surveyed business executives and found that they reported that strong subunits within the organization could get their way without regard to total organizational welfare. E. E. Carter (1971), in another case study of a firm, also found support for Cyert and March's (1963) behavioral theory of business firm decision-making. Pfeffer and Salancik (1974) found that, even after controlling for objective bases of allocation, the use of power was evident in the allocation of the budget at the University of Illinois, and Baldridge (1971) has argued for the applicability of coalitional models of organizational functioning. Our first argument, then, is that given the uncertainty associated with the goals and technology of social service organizations, it is likely that the United Fund decisions concerning resource allocations are made on the basis of subunit power.

The emphasis on dissension and the use of power implied by the political economy and coalitional perspectives leads to the next question, the source of power and influence within social structures. Two perspectives on the determinants of power, related but somewhat distinct, can be found in the literature. One perspective argues that power accrues to those subunits or individuals that can cope with critical organizational uncertainties (Hickson et al. 1971). The sub-unit, to have power, must be able to cope with uncertainty, the uncertainty must be important or pervasive in its effects, and the subunit coping capability must be difficult to replace. The strategic contingencies theory, an extension of concepts developed by Crozier (1964), Thompson (1967), and Perrow (1970) has found empirical support in a study of manufacturing subunits in Canada (Hinings et al. 1974).

The second perspective, and the one adopted for this study, argues that power arises because of the differential dependence existing among actors or subunits in a social context. Emerson (1962) and Blau (1964) developed the idea that power arose because of the dependence of actor A on another actor B. A was dependent on B, or B had power over A, to the extent that B controlled something that A wanted and to the extent there was no way for A to get it except from B. Blau (1964:119–25) has written of ways of maintaining independence that address these two components of power. Coleman (1966) has noted the interrelationship between the concepts of power and the value of some act or resource in the social system being examined. Thibaut and Kelley (1959), in an individual exchange context, have investigated how dependence can lead to control over another's behavior, while Jacobs (1974) has extended Thompson's (1967) formulation to examine the external control of organizational behavior. Our second theoretical argument, then, is that the power of an agency in the United Fund is negatively related to the agency's dependence on the Fund, and positively related to the dependence of the Fund on the agency. Such an argument is a straightforward extension of the power-dependence framework.

The connection between uncertainty reduction and resource interdependence can be seen if we say that one critical resource affecting dependency is the extent of ability to cope with critical organizational uncertainties. The perspectives have, however, led to somewhat different empirical emphases. The Hinings et al. (1974) study addresses directly the problem of measuring uncertainty and the coping capacity of various organizational subunits. Salancik and Pfeffer (1974) found subunit power in a university to be a function of the subunit's provision of outside money and prestige to the total organization. This latter position, that power is a consequence of a unit's relative resource dependence position in the social structure, is the one examined in this study.

Wenocur (1975) has suggested that a political model of organizational behavior is applicable to the United Fund. The United Fund's own literature suggests that the United Fund is interested in maximizing agency participation or keeping as many of the local agencies in the Fund as possible. Each agency, in deciding to join or remain in the Fund, must trade off the resources received against both the loss of program discretion and the constraints on its individual fund-raising efforts. It is plausible to argue that agencies will remain in the United Fund only as long as the resources received do not fall too far below what the agency believes it could raise on its own in a separate fund-raising campaign.

Since community needs and the services provided by agencies are uncertain and difficult to evaluate, power and influence affect United Fund allocations to member agencies. The individual agency's power within the United Fund is a function of its importance to the United Fund and its ability to articulate a credible threat of withdrawal. The ability to threaten withdrawal is determined by the agency's ability to raise funds on its own outside the Fund. If we can view the amount of money raised outside currently as a proxy for the agency's ability to raise money in an independent fund-raising drive, the hypothesis would be: the greater the amount of outside funds raised, the higher the allocation from the United Fund.

The agency's importance to the Fund derives from the consequence of withdrawal for the United Fund's own fund-raising efforts. It is likely that the larger and more visible agencies are more critical to the United Fund. The Fund's dependence on the agency, then, is a function of the proportion of the total United Fund allocations going to the agency. The agency's dependence on the Fund, as described above, is a function of the proportion of the agency's own budget received from the Fund.[2] The dependence of the agency on the Fund, and the dependence of the Fund on the agency, together determine the power of the agency and the Fund vis-à-vis each other. Our argument suggests, therefore, more than just a simple positive relationship between outside fund raising and United Fund allocations. Our argument suggests that this causal relationship will be stronger (a) the smaller the proportion of the agency's budget received from the United Fund (the less dependent the agency is on the Fund), and (b) the larger the proportion of the United Fund's budget that goes to a given agency (the larger, and hence, the more important, the agency is to the Fund).

Data

Data on United Fund allocations to member agencies were sought for the years 1962, 1967, and 1972 in a letter addressed to the executive directors of 130 agencies in cities of over 25,000 population, randomly sampled from the United Fund's listing of United Fund organizations (United Way of America 1971). Two follow-up letters were sent, but because of the work involved in compiling this information, responses were received from only 66 cities. A comparison of responding and nonresponding cities revealed no differences in average size or in geographic location. Of the 66 United Funds responding, not all provided data for all three years. In addition to furnishing United Fund allocations to member agencies, the United Funds supplied data either on each participating agency's total budget or its non-United Fund acquired resources. Since, by definition, the agency's budget is the sum of its United Fund allocations and other receipts, knowing any two enables us to compute the third.

In addition to budget data, demographic variables measuring community characteristics were collected (National Center for Health Statistics 1964, 1972; U.S. Bureau of the Census 1962b, 1973b; U.S. Department of Justice 1961, 1967). These variables were collected on the Standard Metropolitan Statistical Area where possible, since most Funds serve an entire metropolitan area. These data are, for the most part, based on the 1960 and 1970 census.

The measure of the agency's ability to raise funds independently is the amount of funds outside the United Fund it already raises. While this variable might cause problems if we compare agencies with different outside funding sources, if we compare the same agency across cities the validity of this comparison should be high. While the data from three points in time enable us to see if the empirical results are consistent over time, a cross-lagged path analysis is not appropriate. There are five-year intervals in the budget data, and the argument specifies that it is the agency's current ability to attract outside support that affects its allocation from the United Fund, not its support five years ago. As a final analytical point, we note that the best predictor of an agency's allocation, when we examine the same agency across cities, is the size of the city. Since the population of the city was very highly correlated with the total United Fund budget,[3] the total United Fund budget is introduced as a control variable in the analyses. This explicit introduction of city/

budget size as a control is probably preferable to the alternative of transforming the data into proportions by dividing by total budget or city population. The analysis, then, is of a given agency across cities, asking what accounts for the allocation received, controlling for total United Fund budget.

Results

The correlations of agency allocations with non-United Fund resources are presented in table 14.1. The different sample sizes result from the fact that not all agencies are either present or necessarily in the United Fund in each city, as well as from missing data on total agency budgets. Any agency present in fewer than ten cities was

Table 14.1. Partial Correlations Between United Fund Allocations and Non-United Fund Resources, Controlling for Total United Fund Budget

	1962	1967	1972
Family Service	r = .65	r = .48	r = .40
	n = 21	n = 29	n = 36
	p < .001	p < .003	p < .01
YWCA	r = .24	r = .54	r = .57
	n = 25	n = 28	n = 37
	p < .11	p < .005	p < .001
Salvation Army	r = .54	r = .48	r = .64
	n = 22	n = 29	n = 42
	p < .005	p < .005	p < .001
Mental Health	r = .22	r = .21	r = .02
	n = 13	n = 19	n = 29
	p < .25	p < .20	p is n.s.
YMCA	r = .68	r = .41	r = .79
	n = 22	n = 26	n = 35
	p < .001	p < .02	p < .001
Boys Club	r = −.14	r = .40	r = .20
	n = 10	n = 15	n = 22
	p is n.s.	p < .10	p < .20
Boy Scouts	r = .25	r = .52	r = .13
	n = 24	n = 28	n = 38
	p < .11	p < .002	p < .25
Girl Scouts	r = .17	r = .17	r = .40
	n = 23	n = 26	n = 38
	p < .25	p < .20	p < .01
Cerebral Palsy	—	r = −.08	r = −.24

Table 14.1 Continued

	1962	1967	1972
		n = 16	n = 18
		p is n.s.	p < .20
Legal Aid	—	r = −.47	r = −.62
		n = 11	n = 16
		p < .10	p < .005
Goodwill Industries	—	r = .60	r = .50
		n = 12	n = 17
		p < .02	p < .02
Urban League	—	r = .49	r = −.08
		n = 11	n = 18
		p < .05	p is n.s.
Traveler's Aid	—	—	r = −.16
			n = 12
			p is n.s.
Visiting Nurse Association	r = .44	r = −.13	r = −.12
	n = 17	n = 20	n = 20
	p < .05	p is n.s.	p is n.s.
Red Cross	r = .19	r = .28	r = .60
	n = 13	n = 21	n = 30
	p < .25	p < .10	p < .001
Jewish Community Center or	r = .64	r = .74	r = .77
Family Service	n = 0	n = 13	n = 18
	p < .02	p < .001	p < .001
Big Brothers	—	—	r = .19
			n = 10
			p is n.s.
Arthritis	—	—	r = .21
			n = 11
			p < .25

omitted from the analysis. Correlations displayed are partial correlations, controlling for the total United Fund budget, and the tests of significance are one-tailed.

The coalition or bargaining model of organizational decision-making does receive some support from the analyses. Recall that the prediction was that the ability of an agency to raise funds outside the United Fund would lessen its dependence on the Fund, and hence give it more power and a stronger bargaining position to negotiate for more resources within the Fund. In 1962, 5 out of the 11 correlations were in the expected direction and statistically significant at less than the .10 level of probability, while 10 of the 11 correlations were in the predicted direction. In 1967, 10 out of 15 correlations were in the positive direction and statistically significant, while 12 of the 15 correlations were in the positive direction. In 1972, 8 out of 18 correlations were in the predicted direction and statistically significant, while 14 of the correlations were in the expected direction. There is consistent evidence, then, that in controlling for the total United Fund budget there is a positive relationship between outside funding and the agency's United Fund allocation.

THE EFFECT OF DEMOGRAPHIC VARIABLES

The effect of variables that may assess community characteristics was also examined, to explore whether the introduction of such demographic factors might change the relationships previously presented. In table 14.2, the various measures of community context and the sources for the variables are provided. Census data from 1960 were used to account for 1962 allocations, and 1970 data for the 1967 and 1972 allocations.

To give the community demographic measures every chance of being supported, and to avoid using up the limited degrees of freedom available for most agencies, the following analytical procedure was employed. Partial correlations were computed between the allocation to the agency and various demographic variables, controlling for the total United Fund budget. In this first step, few variables emerged as statistically significant. In those instances where a significant relationship was found, a second analysis was performed. Multiple regression equations were estimated including total United Fund budget, the amount of non-United Fund support, and the demographic variable or variables as explanatory variables related to the agency's allocation from the United Fund. In only one instance was a demographic variable statistically significant in these equations. In the equation for the allocation to the Boy Scouts in 1967, the proportion of the population that was nonwhite entered with a positive sign. In no case did the statistical significance of the non-United Fund resource variable disappear with the introduction of demographic variables.

There is, then, strong evidence that United Fund allocations to member agencies are not predicted by various measures of demographic characteristics of the community. Furthermore, the positive relationship between outside fund-raising ability and allocations from

Table 14.2. Demographic Variables

Variable
Population in 1960, 1970[a]
Percent nonwhite
Percent foreign born
Percent urban
Percent over 65 years old
Percent under 5 years old
Income, 1960, 1970[a]
Median income
Percent income over $10,000
Percent income under $3,000
Education, 1960, 1970[a]
Median education
Percent in high school
Percent in kindergarten and elementary school
Employment 1960, 1970[a]
Unemployment rate
Percent in white-collar occupations
Percent owner-occupied housing, 1960, 1970[a]
Crime rate (100,000 population) 1960, 1970[b]
Robbery
Burglary
Auto theft
Larceny-theft
Divorce rate (100,000 population), 1960, 1969[a]

[a] U.S. Bureau of the Census (1962b, 1973b).
[b] U.S. Department of Justice (1961, 1967).
[c] National Center for Health Statistics (1964, 1972).

the Fund remains when demographic variables are introduced as statistical controls.

POWER-DEPENDENCE PREDICTIONS

The power-dependence literature suggests not only that allocations will be responsive to the ability of agencies to raise funds on their own, but in fact that the ability of the agencies to use their outside fund-raising capability, and the related threat of withdrawal, to obtain resources will depend on the relative dependence of the agencies on the Fund and the Fund on the agencies.

It might be argued that the reason outside funds are related to allocations inside the Fund is not because the United Fund is a coalition and power affects decision outcomes, but rather that in a situation of uncertainty, outside support provides the best measure of community demand and need for specific social services. However, the argument that outside funds represent community demand for the services of various agencies does not specify any difference in this relationship across agencies. On the other hand, the power-dependence argument hypothesizes that the ability to translate outside fund-raising into allocations from the Fund depends on the relative position of dependence between the Fund and the agencies. Consequently, a comparison of regression coefficients across agencies will enable us to distinguish between the two arguments.

Agencies were ranked in terms of their dependence on the United Fund, assessed by the proportion of each agency's budget obtained from the United Fund. Agencies were also ranked in terms of the United Fund's dependence on them, assessed by their relative size in the Fund and measured by the average proportion of United Fund budgets allocated to a given agency. Two methods of ranking agencies in terms of their relative power-dependence positions were employed. In the first, only the relative size of the agency was taken into account. Since most of the agencies received, on average, more than 50 percent of their budgets from the United Fund, it is possible that each is so dependent on the United Fund that this dimension is not meaningful in distinguishing among them. Using this first procedure, the argument is that agency power is solely a function of the agency's size and prominence, and the larger and more prominent the agency in the Fund, the more important a threat of withdrawal and, consequently, the greater the relationship between outside funding and allocations from the United Fund.

The second method of computing power-dependence positions used both the agency's importance to the Fund and the Fund's importance to the agency. Agencies were ranked first in terms of the proportion of budget obtained from the United Fund, from 1 for the lowest. The agencies were then ranked in terms of their share of the total United Fund budget, again from 1 for the lowest. The former ranking was subtracted from the latter, giving an estimate of how the agencies compared to each other in terms of net dependence on the United Fund, assuming both components of dependence were equally weighted.

In table 14.3, the unstandardized regression coefficients for the outside funds variable are displayed for the agencies categorized by

Table 14.3. Comparison of Unstandardized Regression Coefficients for Non-United Fund Resources Variable Across Agencies

Agency Power Position Based Solely on Its Size in United States[a]			
More Powerful Agencies		Less Powerful Agencies	
Agency	b	Agency	b
1962			
Red Cross	.929	Mental Health	.115
Boy Scouts	.133*	Jewish Community Center	.323*
YMCA	.653*	Visiting Nurse	.141*
Family Service	.461*	Girl Scouts	.042
Salvation Army	.384*	Boys Club	−.094
YWCA	.084*		
Average	.441	Average	.105
1967			
Red Cross	.319	Legal Aid	−.215
Boy Scouts	.196*	Goodwill	−.0087
YMCA	.091*	Urban League	1.964*
Family Service	.816*	Mental Health	.021
Boys Club	1.34*	Cerebral Palsy	−.130
YWCA	.202*	Jewish Community Center	.303*
Salvation Army	.316*	Visiting Nurse	−.025
Girl Scouts	.097		
Average	.422	Average	.272
1972			
Red Cross	2.02*	Legal Aid	−.032*
Boy Scouts	.260	Arthritis	.036
YMCA	.141*	Traveler's Aid	−.067
Family Service	.353*	Mental Health	.0025
Boys Club	.173	Goodwill Industries	.038*
Salvation Army	.355	Big Brother	.056
YWCA	.195*	Jewish Community Center	.086*
Girl Scouts	.145*	Cerebral Palsy	−.112
Visiting Nurse Association	−.011	Urban League	.022
Average	.403	Average	.0033

[a] Agencies were classified as more or less powerful based on the Fund's dependence on the agency, measured by the average proportion of United Fund allocations that each agency received. The assumption was that larger agencies that received more United Fund allocations were more important to the Fund and its ability to continue to attract contributions.

* p < .15

Table 14.4. Comparison of Unstandardized Regression Coefficients for Non-United Fund Resources Variable Across Agencies

Agency Power Position Determined Both by Its Dependence on the United Fund and the Fund's Dependence on the Agency[a]

More Powerful Agency	b	Less Powerful Agency	b	Intermediate Power Agency	b
1962					
Jewish Community		Boys Club	−.094	Girl Scouts	.042
Center	.323*	Mental Health	.115	Visiting Nurse	.141*
YWCA	.084*			Red Cross	.929
YMCA	.096*				
Boy Scouts	.133*				
Family Service	.461*				
Salvation Army	.384*				
Average	.247	Average [b]	.011	Average	.370
1967					
Jewish Community		Legal Aid	−.215	Girl Scouts	.097
Center	.303*	Cerebral Palsy	−.130	Goodwill Industries	−.0087
YWCA	.202*	Mental Health	.021	Visiting Nurse	−.028
YMCA	.091*	Urban League	1.964*	Red Cross	.319
Boy Scouts	.196*	Boys Club	1.34*		
Family Service	.816*				
Salvation Army	.316*				
Average	.321	Average	.600	Average	.095
1972					
YMCA	.141*	Boys Club	.173	Girl Scouts	.145*
YWCA	.195*	Cerebral Palsy	−.112	Goodwill	.038*
Jewish Community		Legal Aid	−.032*	Visiting Nurse	−.011
Center	.086*	Mental Health	.0025	Red Cross	2.02*
Boy Scouts	.260	Urban League	.022		
Salvation Army	.355*	Arthritis	.036		
Family Service	.353*	Travelers Aid	−.067		
		Big Brother	.056		
Average	.232	Average	.0098	Average	.548

[a] Agencies were classified as to power by considering both the Fund's dependence on the agency, as described in table 14.3, and the agency's dependence on the Fund, assessed by the proportion of the agency's budget which, on the average, was obtained from the Fund.
* $p < .15$

the degree of power with respect to the United Fund using only the importance of the agency to the Fund. The results in that table are consistent with the hypotheses. In each year, the average of the regression coefficients for the more powerful agencies is much larger than the average for the less powerful, and a higher proportion of the regression coefficients is statistically significant in the case of the more powerful agencies. This means that the amount of outside funding received is more likely to have a statistically significant effect, and more likely to have a larger effect on allocations from United Funds in the case of the more powerful agencies. This result is predicted by a political perspective on resource allocation, but is not explained by the argument that outside funds measure community demand.

In table 14.4, the unstandardized regression coefficients are displayed for the agencies, this time categorized according to their dependence on the Fund and the Fund's dependence on them. While the results are not as consistent, the data still tend to support the power-dependence argument. The principal changes in categorization are the movement of Red Cross into the intermediate category, as the agency with the highest dependence on the Fund and the one that receives the largest share of Fund allocations, and movement of Jewish agencies into the high power category, receiving a relatively smaller proportion of their budgets from the Fund.

Tables 14.3 and 14.4 together suggest that dependence of the Fund on an agency, deriving from the agency's prominence and importance, is a more significant factor affecting the relationship between outside support and the ability to obtain allocations within the Fund than the agency's dependence on the Fund. This finding makes sense because as previously noted, the proportion of agency budgets obtained from the United Fund is quite high, typically well over 50 percent. At this level of dependence, variations in proportion of support received from the Fund are, perhaps, not meaningful in discriminating among agencies. Rather, what is significant is the importance of the agency to the Fund.

Discussion

In the examination of resource allocations to member agencies within United Funds, we have found some empirical support for the conceptualization of organizations as coalitions (Cyert and March 1963; Wenocur 1975) and, more important, empirical support for the power-dependence framework which has been proposed to explain interorganizational relations (Jacobs 1974). These results, furthermore, were not affected by the introduction of measures of community demographic variables as statistical controls and, indeed, there was no evidence that such variables were significantly correlated with United Fund allocations. As predicted, power was related to the dependence relationships existing between the agency and the United Fund, and was a function of both the agency's ability to attract outside resources and the importance of the agency to the Fund. Resource interdependence helped account for allocation decisions within this organization, a result which is consistent with the coalitional or political perspective on organizations and with Wenocur's (1975) conceptual analysis of the United Way.

As Benson (1975) has cogently noted, interorganizational researchers, particularly those dealing with public organizations, frequently have proceeded from an assumption of cooperation and have sought to determine how coordination can be maximized. Benson further stated that a more appropriate model might be that of individual organizations competing for funds, and in this competition, staking out claims to domain, using arguments of legitimacy, and engaging in either cooperative or competitive relationships as strategically appropriate. The results of this study are consistent with Benson's position. The United Fund seeks to maximize participation, and in the bargaining between the Fund and member agencies, each agency is willing to use its power to obtain the maximum possible allocation.

This willingness to undertake action when agencies' allocations are threatened was dramatically illustrated by the following series of events which occurred in one small city not included in the sample. As predicted by the results of the study, the United Fund had tended to allocate funds to those agencies that received the most community support, the Y's and the Scouts. However, around the country, the United Fund had been criticized for funding agencies which primarily served middle-class clients and which therefore might be self-supporting. Responding to this pressure, the United Fund in this particular community developed new budget procedures, emphasizing service to the local community, community need, and the ability to obtain alternative funding. As a consequence of these new criteria, allocations for the Y's and the Scouts were reduced. These agencies, as a group, went to the United Fund and asked to have their allocations restored, with the partially explicit threat that if funding were not restored to its previous level, the agencies would withdraw from the United Fund and conduct their own fund-raising drive as a group. The United Way, while never changing the expressed criteria for budget allocation, responded by restoring the allocation to these agencies.

The contest for resources plays an important part in determining organizational and interorganizational behavior. In this competition, given unclear standards of assessment and uncertain technologies, power and influence become important in determining the final decision outcomes. It seems that in terms of accounting for variance in behavior, the political perspective on organizational behavior has much to recommend it, particularly as a balance to the cooperative, coordinating view of interorganizational activity that has tended to predominate.

NOTES

1. Emphasis in original. This particular publication both summarizes and articulately states points made in many other local United Fund publications.

2. These two variables are conceptually and empirically independent. The amount received from the United Fund may be a large or small part of the total United Fund allocations to all agencies independently of the relative magnitude of the amount as a proportion of a given agency's budget.

3. The correlation between population in 1960 and the total United Fund budget in 1962 was .90; the correlation between population in 1970 and the total United Fund budget in 1967 was .94; and the correlation between population in 1970 and the total United Fund budget in 1972 was .89.

B. GOAL-SETTING AND ORGANIZATIONAL THEORY

MODERN social welfare functions through formal organizations; its agencies and programs are fruitful terrain for the sociological study of organizational processes. An early example was Peter Blau's (1955) *The Dynamics of Bureaucracy*, a study of a public employment agency. Social welfare agencies, like other formal organizations, are characterized by specific goals. However, there are major differences between goal-setting in such agencies and other large-scale organizations. One difference is that goal-setting in social welfare involves ideological conflict. Vinter and Sarri (1966) detailed how this process works in juvenile courts.

The first of two selections in this section, Robert A. Scott's "The Factory as a Social Service Organization," is a study of organizational goal displacement. In his research on agencies serving visually impaired people, Scott found that the original goal of integrating clients into the regular labor force (in order to promote their independence) was displaced over time by the goal of organizational maintenance. The root cause of the displacement was the economic exigency faced by these private social welfare agencies in a market economy. In order to survive, the sheltered workshops had to maintain high levels of worker productivity. They hired skilled workers who were not visually impaired and retained visually impaired workers who became skilled. Thus, the agencies fostered client dependency. Scott's work extended the goal displacement concept, earlier analyzed by Michels (1949).

The other selection in this section is a hitherto unpublished essay, "Welfare Administration and Organizational Theory," contributed by David Street. (Sadly, this is one of the last things he wrote before his death.) It applies some of the ideas, including the "loose-coupling" concept, from organizational theory to welfare administration. Street develops an integrated model which can be of value in analyzing problems in welfare administration. Although this is a theoretical essay, it relies on empirical work produced by Street and others in recent years.

[15]

THE FACTORY AS A SOCIAL SERVICE ORGANIZATION: GOAL DISPLACEMENT IN WORKSHOPS FOR THE BLIND

Robert A. Scott

A major theme in the sociological literature on formal organizations is a documented tendency for day-to-day policy decisions of an organization to modify, transform, and occasionally even to subvert the objectives for which the organization was established (Blau and Scott 1962; Etzioni 1964; Messinger 1955; Perrow 1961; Selznick 1949). Systematic descriptions and analyses of such discrepancies between official and operative goals continue to be important and theoretically meaningful sociological tasks. At the same time, it is also necessary to analyze the consequences which they may have. Such analyses are important for two reasons. First, the fact that discrepancies occur between official and operative goals is of theoretical and practical interest only if they make a difference to the organization, to the persons whom it employs and processes, and/or to the original problem situation which led to its establishment. These consequences indicate the theoretical and practical significance of the discrepancies. Second, by focusing on the consequences of goal discrepancies, rather than on the fact of their occurrence, the various terms which are used to label the process are transformed into useful tools of conceptual analysis.

There are several studies of goal displacement in which the effects of this process are described and analyzed. Some of these studies deal with the impact of goal discrepancies within organizations and conditions which the organizations were created to solve (Michels 1949; Selznick 1949). Other studies describe the effects of goal

From *Social Problems* (Fall 1967), 15(2):160–75. Reprinted by permission.

displacement upon such things as types of activities which organizations come to sponsor (Messinger 1955), on the behavior of persons in organizationally relevant contexts (Merton 1957), and on the values and value system of the larger environment of which the organizations are a part (Clark 1956). The findings of these studies provide an excellent base of knowledge concerning the consequences of discrepancies between official and operative goals. The purpose of the present paper is to broaden this base by analyzing the consequences of goal discrepancies in one type of social welfare organization which I have studied, namely, sheltered workshops for the blind.

I will be concerned with two consequences of this process. The first I have already referred to in my discussion. It concerns the effects which goal displacement in sheltered workshops for the blind had upon the problems and conditions which first led to the establishment of these organizations. The second concerns the effects of goal displacement upon the belief systems which are shared by workers for the blind. In order to deal with this it will be necessary to clarify this aspect of organizational behavior.

All organizations which process people, and especially people who have been labeled "problems," maintain complex systems of beliefs about those whom they try to help. These belief systems consist of explanations as to why a particular trait or condition is a problem in the first place, what ought to be done about it, how human nature operates, and how to change it in desired ways. Such beliefs serve as guidelines for establishing the official goals of the helping organizations. They also serve a number of other functions as well. They often become the "window dressing" which convincingly explains and legitimates the organization's activities to the public. For individual workers, these systems of beliefs infuse the otherwise mundane and often distasteful activities of a job with a sense of purpose and nobility. As such, workers experience them as personal, deep-seated convictions about the rightness, goodness, and nobleness of their work.

Initially, systems of beliefs are simply expressions of commonly shared values and convictions about persons who fall into the problem group that concerns the organizations. Official organizational goals are derived from these shared values, and the tasks of workers in them are defined in terms of the specific contribution which they can make toward implementing these goals. If discrepancies and contradictions between official goals and operative policies of an organization arise, these belief systems are subjected to severe stresses and strains. Among the workers who perceive these discrepancies, they are experienced as psychological conflicts. There are several ways in which these conflicts can be reduced.[1]

The first, and most obvious alternative is to establish new operative policies which are consistent with the official goals of the organization. This strategy is seldom possible since operative policies are themselves determined by complex economic, social, and political forces in the environment over which organization members can exercise little influence. Indeed, in many instances the operative policies which conflict with official goals are essential for the organizations' survival. Consequently, attempts to modify operative policies so as to reduce belief system strains may have the effect of running the organization itself out of business.

A second alternative involves the development and use of collective mechanisms of defense. Organization members may simply deny or ignore contradictions and discrepancies between what the organization says it is doing and what it is in fact accomplishing. While some workers may be able to do this for sustained periods, it is unlikely that it will be a successful means for tension resolution for all organization members for the reason that reality impinges upon at least some of them, and sooner or later one of their numbers is bound to give into it.

A third, and more workable, alternative is to change beliefs about the problems which the organization is trying to solve so as to make them consistent with operative policies. This strategy of deriving belief systems about problems of employment of the blind from the concrete policies which are necessary to keep a sheltered workshop in existence requires a periodic reconceptualization of ideas about what the blind do or do not wish to have; what they do or do not need; or what is or is not good for them. The success of this method for reducing the strains of goal discrepancies hinges on simple processes of persuasion, and on extracting testimonial evidence from workshop clients that the derived beliefs about them are in fact correct.

A fourth and equally workable alternative is to change beliefs about the contribution of "normals" to the problems of the deprived group. This involves altering basic conceptions about such things as the willingness of normals to be tolerant toward the blind, and their receptivity to employing the blind. As with beliefs about the problems of persons that organizations attempt to solve, beliefs about the feelings of "normals" are also easily changed since they, too, hinge on processes of persuasion and the accumulation of testimonial evidence.

In this paper I will show how goal displacements which occurred in sheltered workshops produced marked changes in the belief systems of workers for the blind about the problems of employment of the blind and of the part that "normals" play in creating these problems.

Official Goals of Sheltered Workshops for the Blind

Sheltered workshops for the blind were originally conceived as one element of an overall attack upon the problem of employment of the blind. The essence of this problem was that while there were many blind persons who had the demonstrated capacity to work as productively as sighted workers in commercial factories, there were almost none who had the opportunity to do so. Out of a conviction that work is ennobling, and that the integration of the blind into the sighted community through work is good, workers for the blind set out a philosophy which would provide for the implementation of these beliefs.

This philosophy stated as its primary objective the full-time employment of blind persons in competitive industry. A secondary objective, in the event that competitive employment was unfeasible, was employment in sheltered workshops. Still another alternative was the program of home industries. Under this program seriously disabled blind persons could earn a modest income by assembling and finishing products brought to them at their homes by a representative of the state commission or local agency for the blind. Historically, this program has played a marginal part in employment programs for the blind. For this reason, no further mention of it will be made in this paper. Sheltered workshops specialized in the manufacture of a few standard products selected both for the ease with which they could be assembled and for their marketing potential. In sheltered workshops blind persons were taught broom and mop making, rug weaving, chair caning, willow work, and similar crafts. The program of commercial placement rested on the assumption that in every factory and industrial plant there are a number of jobs which do not require sight and which trained blind persons can perform as ably as sighted persons. Commercial employment programs had placement officers whose job was to locate such positions in industries in the community, to find interested and qualified blind persons who might fill them, and to train such persons for the positions. After employment was secured, the placement officer was expected to act as a liaison among the blind worker, his employer, and the sponsoring agency (Obermann 1965).

The goal of full-time employment of blind persons in commercial industry was first formally stated at the annual meetings of the American Association of Workers for the Blind in 1905 by Charles Campbell, head of the Massachusetts State Commission for the Blind. Mr. Campbell states that the purpose of the Massachusetts Commission was "to enable blind persons to become selling agents, and when possible, to become wage earners in shops or factories for the seeing." It was his belief that "every able bodied blind person . . . can find work of some kind side by side with seeing people if efforts are persistently made in this direction" (*AAWB Proceedings* 1905:32). These views which were reiterated by Mr. Campbell and others during the early 1900s have been continually expressed through the years in major policy statements by influential people in the field of work for the blind. (See *Outlook for the Blind* April 1907:10–12, April 1909:13, March 1926:36–39, September 1931:83; *AAWB Proceedings* 1907:101, 1950:59, 1962:186).

It was recognized, however, by most employment specialists that this goal was not always attainable. Some blind persons were so disabled that they could not compete in commercial industry; others were blinded later in life and could not make a good enough adjustment to their visual loss to be considered for commercial work. For these persons sheltered workshops were seen as most appropriate places for work. In sheltered workshops production norms were less stringent than they were in commerical industry; equipment was specially adapted to the requirements of blind operatives; piece rates were generally higher per unit of production then in commercial industry; and a minimum wage was guaranteed regardless of the worker's productivity level. (The minimum wage paid was ordinarily quite low and did not correspond to minimum wage levels established by federal legislation.) The principal intended function of the sheltered workshops was to provide a *social service* to blind persons. This fact was emphasized by a leading employment specialist, J. N. Smith, in the 1937 issue (pp. 105–6) of the *Outlook for the Blind* (a major journal of work for the blind): "While following the methods of industry to some extent, the sheltered workshops are not and never can be businesses or industries; the welfare of the client, and not profit, is the goal."

Sheltered workshops had two secondary functions. They were expected to serve as laboratories for evaluating and training blind persons for placement in commercial industry; and they were expected to absorb blind men and women who were competent to work in commercial industry but who were unable to find jobs because of adverse economic conditions.

Displacement of Goals in Sheltered Workshops for the Blind

In so far as their social service function is concerned, sheltered workshops appear to have been doomed from their inception. This was so for several reasons.

First, because of the fact that they were created in order to provide therapeutic activity for commercially unemployable blind adults, sheltered workshops were bound to operate at a deficit. Yet, workshop founders made no systematic provision for subsidizing these deficits. The question of who would pay the difference between costs and income was either ignored or brushed off as a mundane and practical problem which would somehow solve itself. As we will see shortly, the failure of sheltered workshops to find reliable and long-term sources for subsidizing their operation was a major contributing factor to the displacement of their goals.

The programmed annual deficit of sheltered workshops was aggravated by a second fact. While workshops were not created for the same reasons that commercial factories are built, they were nevertheless subject to many of the same economic principles of supply and demand as commercial enterprises. A manufacturer does not ordinarily build a factory unless he has very sound reasons for believing that there is substantial demand for his product. If his judgment is correct, his operation will expand; if he is in error, his enterprise will be liquidated. The planning of sheltered workshops was not based on this line of reasoning. They started with the premise that a social service function would be fulfilled in a factory. The items which were to be manufactured had to be easy to produce because of the physical deficiencies of the workers. The selection of goods was further constrained by the fact that there was very little capital available for the purchase of equipment and inventories. The selection of goods to be produced in sheltered workshops was not, therefore, determined by their demand or marketability, but by the contingencies of a social service function and the absence of funds for capital investments. The sale of manufactured goods was, however, very much influenced by the principles of supply and demand. Workshops originally produced items such as brooms, mops, and caned chairs. The market for caned chairs was very small indeed; the market for brooms and mops was substantially larger, but the margin of profit was very slight. In their sales campaigns, workshops were therefore forced to emphasize the fact that the products were "blind-made" in the hope that by so doing, the charitable impulses of the public would prevail over their visible disinterest in the items produced. In general, this type of appeal did not succeed.

Third, even though sheltered workshops were supposed to be social service organizations, the general agencies for the blind of which they were usually a part had to hire industrially trained individuals to run them. Workers for the blind simply did not have the know-how to set up and run an orderly manufacturing concern. The necessity for using qualified persons with industrial experience to manage the shops was heightened by the fact that standard broom- and mop-making equipment had to be modified in order to make them operable by a blind worker. This required engineering modifications, the design of special safety equipment, and the rearrangement of standard production line activities. Only a person with training and experience in industrial factories could successfully manage such an operation. Consequently, while the primary goal of workshops was social service to industrially unemployable blind adults, the persons who were hired to implement the goals were ones whose major interest and abilities were in the operation of industrial enterprises. This situation had a number of implications. For one thing, the authority to make operative policy decisions of all types, and especially those of pay, promotion, and standards of production, was placed in the hands of workshop managers who were guided by commercial rather than social service standards. A worker's earnings were calculated on a piece-rate basis. A pay-incentive system was used so that the more a worker produced, the more he earned. A worker had to produce goods at a reasonable rate in order to make any money, or even to make his going to the workshop worthwhile in the first place. In addition, high standards of production were stressed at all times, some workers being docked for producing poorly made items. Moreover, workshop managers measured their success by commercial standards. Their challenge was to make sheltered workshops for the blind "going operations." While they seemed to adopt the abstract concept of work as therapy, their concrete policies were based on concepts and practices which govern commercial factories.

The incompatibilities contained in the basic concept of a factory as a social service organization ultimately resulted in the displacement of the goals of this program. The story of that process is as follows.

Directors of agencies for the blind and workshop managers attempted to make up annual deficits in a number of ways. Attempts were made to prevail upon state legislators to subsidize the workshops regularly. Though subsidies were occasionally made during the early years of the shops' operation, the idea of making a permanent annual appropriation to sheltered workshops was an idea that became increasingly unpopular among legislators. This arrangement was not always welcomed by the agency and workshop personnel either, since it required constant negotiations with the frugal and sometimes capricious politicians. Many workshops conducted annual fund-raising campaigns to make up the difference, but this policy was quickly abandoned because it brought workshops into direct conflict with the fund-raising activities of parent agencies. One commonly adopted policy was for workshops to charge a price higher than the fair market value of the items which they produced. This policy did help to offset some of the annual deficits, but from their inception in 1900 up through World War I, sheltered workshops resembled "shoestring" operations in every respect.

Despite these problems, sheltered workshops did make some modest progress toward implementing their goals. It was generally possible for a blind person of limited abilities to secure a position somewhere in a sheltered workshop; at the same time the energetic and resourceful efforts of those responsible for the placement of more capable blind persons in commercial industries made it possible for at least some blind persons to work "on the outside." Both the commercial placement and the sheltered workshop programs enjoyed moderate success and mutual cooperation up to, during, and shortly after World War I. The Depression, however, pretty thoroughly vitiated programs of commercial placement; at the same time, it had the effect of grossly magnifying all of the basic incompatibilities contained in the idea of a factory as a social service organization. The very existence of sheltered workshops for the blind was threatened during the Depression. The policies which workshop managers had to adopt in order to save the shops eventually resulted in a displacement of their goals. In addition, these policies subverted the goals of the commercial employment program, with the consequence that the sheltered workshops ultimately exacerbated the very problems which the entire employment program for the blind had been established to alleviate.

With the depression employment opportunities for the blind collapsed. As unemployed blind workers began to flock to agencies for the blind for assistance, they were referred to workshops for whatever jobs they could get. The workshops, however, were no better off. The bottom had dropped out of the already limited market of their products, and they were unable to find new products which could be widely sold. The policy of relying upon the charitable impulses of the public as a means for selling products and for meeting deficits became impracticable. People no longer had extra income to buy brooms and mops out of sympathy for the blind. Former commercial consumers of blind-made products were themselves out of business or no longer in need of very many products of the workshops. The workshops, therefore, were caught in the center of a series of cross pressures. The market for their goods had declined at the same time that they were being pressured to find positions in the shops for those blind persons who were laid off in industry. In addition, as their annual deficits rose, it became more and more difficult to obtain public subsidy for them. Under these circumstances the workshop managers were forced to concentrate less upon providing social services to their employees, and more upon keeping the workshops in existence. The concern of the shops shifted from social service matters to a preoccupation with business affairs. The idea of employing industrial incompetents was transformed from a cause to a luxury. Very basic economic problems had to be solved and solved quickly if the shops were not to close down completely.

In order to survive, it was essential for the workshops to find and insure for themselves a dependable market for their goods. The effects of the Depression on sheltered workshops drove home a very basic lesson to their managers. It was that an industrial organization of this type could ill afford to rely upon the general public as its only outlet for goods. A more dependable and predictable consumer had to be found. It was in the federal government that workshop managers found their buyer. Through an intriguing lobbying process, workshop managers succeeded in having an economic platform constructed upon which existing sheltered workshops could begin to build. This platform was the Wagner-O'Day Act, which was passed by Congress and signed by the President in 1937. The act provided that "brooms and mops and other suitable commodities hereafter procured in accordance with applicable federal specifications by or for any Federal department or agency shall be procured from such non-profit agencies for the blind" (*AAWB Proceedings* 1939:145). A critical phrase in the wording of this act was "and other suitable commodities," for within six months of the bill's passage five additional commodities had been added to the list, and within a few years this number was increased to thirty-two items (*AAWB Proceedings* 1948:17). This act also became the model of sixteen similar laws passed by state governments.

This legislation had the intended effect of guaranteeing the shops at least a minimum amount of business each year in standard inventory items such as mops and brooms. Since the government was now bound by law to buy the products that the shops made, so long as these products met its specifications, the shops had a guaranteed outlet for many more goods than just mops and brooms. It was now possible to diversify and expand operations, and consequently to fill up the deficit which the shops were annually running. The principal unintended effect of this legislation was brought about by the fact that the government expected the commodities of the workshops to meet minimum specifications and to be delivered according to a time schedule.[2] The consequence of these specifications was to make it necessary to employ competent and efficient workers. The specifications were such that only industrially competent workers were able to produce the items in the quantity and with the quality which were necessary for government orders. The employment of industrial incompetents, therefore, became increasingly impractical. Moreover, the workshops were forced to adopt a more stringent set of business principles. The acceptance of a government contract introduced a new predictability into the schedule of workshops. Managers could now begin to anticipate and plan production schedules as these came along. This in turn led them to run the shops in a more businesslike fashion than ever before. Consequently, as a result of the Wagner-

O'Day Act, the social service function for which the shops had originally been established was gradually pushed further and further into the background.

Dramatic evidence of this displacement is supplied by a report which was presented to the American Association of Workers for the Blind (AAWB) by the manager of a sheltered workshop in the New York metropolitan area. The data which were reported were responses to a questionnaire mailed out to twenty-five of the major workshops throughout the country. It inquired about the policies of the management concerning matters of employment and business. It was reported that

The consensus of opinion of 25 employers of blind workers is that the maximum age at which workers should be hired should be set at 45 with an outside limit of 50 for exceptional men and women. When we take into consideration the months and even years that it takes to train a blind person to be a topnotch producer, we realize that any higher age limit would tend *to reduce the years of usefulness to the workshop to such an extent that it might well be a losing proposition* (*AAWB Proceedings* 1935:83; emphasis added).

The report went on: "Still another strong argument for *eliminating the incompetents* from our shops is the breakdown in morale of the whole force which is sure to follow if these incompetents are allowed to remain" (*AAWB Proceedings* 1935:82; emphasis added). One can see emerging in this report a striking tendency toward giving precedence to what is good for the workshops over the managers' avowed responsibility to the group of people for whom the workshops were established as a social service.

The report states that the operation of the workshop should be governed by strict business standards—efficiency, production, and cost. Only competent workers should be employed. Some managers pointed to the possibility "that the saving effected in reduced costs of operation will allow for the establishment of auxiliary craftshops in which the less skilled and less competent workers may be given employment in which they might at least be partially self-supporting" (*AAWB Proceedings* 1935:84). Though this suggestion was followed by some agencies, the saving made by the workshops were more often used to expand the workshops than to create special craftshops.

The strength of these sentiments is revealed in some of the correspondence which accompanied the questionnaires which had been sent out. One manager observed: "We are anxious to improve the character of workers and do away with the idea that our shop is a retreat for unemployable blind who foment trouble and do not want to produce anything" (*AAWB Proceedings* 1935:92). Another person took the position that "the blind who are physically and mentally unable to produce sufficiently to take care of their needs should not be employed in a workshop whose *main object is producing marketable merchandise*" (*AAWB Proceedings* 1935:92; emphasis added). The implications of this position are that the shop should *employ industrial competents*, that is, the persons who in ordinary times worked in commercial industry. The seed of a nasty conflict between advocates of workshops and advocates of commercial employment for the blind was planted at this time.

These sentiments of workshop managers were accompanied by a belief that anything that improved the economic position of the workshops was acceptable. The extremes to which this view was taken are revealed in a speech given by S. S. Catell to workshop managers at the 1935 AAWB meeting. Mr. Catell asked the following question of shop managers:

Would it be advisable for this shop to employ a few extra broom makers *who have normal vision*, at times, when needed; to enable the shop to take larger orders, fill them promptly, and give better satisfaction to customers? The shops would then make a special effort to secure larger orders resulting in more employment for the blind worker (*AAWB Proceedings* 1935:191; emphasis added).

Mr. Catell was not alone in proposing this idea. Others had mentioned this matter in the report:

In the consideration of the question of who shall be employed in sheltered workshops, some thought an investigation should be given to the hiring of more sighted workers in our shops. . . . Those who have put this policy into practice say that production is speeded up, costs are kept down, and more blind workers can be put to work (*AAWB Proceedings* 1935:83–88).

In the first few years after its passage, the Wagner-O'Day Act had only a modest impact upon the amount of business which was done by the workshops. In 1939, for example, government orders accounted for only about 10 percent of the total business of workshops participating in the program. It was assumed that this figure might increase somewhat, but that it would probably never exceed 20 percent to 25 percent of total production. The lobbyists for this preferential legislation failed to anticipate World War II, and the enormous increase in demands by the government for workshop-produced goods.

Within the four-year period 1940–43, 80 percent of all business done by sheltered workshops for the blind was devoted to filling government orders (*AAWB Proceedings* 1943:18). During that period the government business with the shops amounted to more than $17 million. Moreover, increased industrial demands, coupled with the generally favorable economic conditions which were brought about by the war resulted in over $8 million in additional sales. In a period of a few years, sheltered workshops were transformed from social service organizations to big businesses (*AAWB Proceedings* 1947:78).

The Consequences of Goal Displacement

The fact that operative policies subverted the official goals of sheltered workshops for the blind had two principal consequences. The first related to the original problem which led workers for the blind to establish a formal employment program for blind persons; the second related to the belief systems of workers for the blind about the blind and about the general public.

The economic boom during the war years, which brought about an acceleration of business for sheltered workshops, had additional consequences for employment opportunities for the blind. When World War II erupted, there was an acute labor shortage in the country. Employers sought every able man and woman for work in factories, shops, and industrial plants in order to meet production orders. Consequently, many opportunities developed for the commercial employment of blind workers (*AAWB Proceedings* 1941:61; 1943:26; Chevigny and Braverman 1950).

These circumstances provided an opportunity for workshops to give consideration to their original function of providing social services to commercially unemployable blind persons. The market for goods was now guaranteed; there were plenty of commercial employment opportunities for the able-bodied blind, and general economic conditions would have made it comparatively simple to raise funds in order to overcome the deficits the workshops would inevitably run. The workshops did not follow this course.

Faced with the prospects of expanded orders for merchandise from federal and state governments, and with an improved commercial market for blind-made products, the workshops began to increase their production, drawing upon the pool of skilled and competent blind workers who had come to them during the Depression. The changing conditions were reflected in the enthusiastic statements of workshop managers concerning the business prospects of the workshops. In 1941 one manager told AAWB members: "Our workshops are now engaged in big business, and they should conduct this business in accordance with the same principles as those observed in the management of private commercial enterprise" (*AAWB Proceedings* 1941:17–18). Discussions at the 1941 and 1943 conventions of the American Association of Workers for the Blind largely consisted of suggestions of ways to implement formal procedures for running the workshops as "big business." One manager was moved to comment:

I want to come directly to the special significance which with the advent of war has come to the workshops for the blind. In a sense, it is a rather curious significance; curious in that it is new to the workshops, and perhaps as yet a bit unfamiliar. But it is also a great thing, and it may be summarized in these five words: you are doing "big business" (*Outlook for the Blind*: April 1942, p. 121).

Despite the generally improved conditions there nevertheless remained a disparity between production and sales. In an attempt to remedy this disparity, the services of sales experts were retained. At no point, however, did workshops have more orders than they could fill.

It seems reasonable to assume that if the shops were outproducing the markets, and there were employment opportunities for the blind in commercial industry, workshop managers would encourage their better workers to get jobs on "the outside." If the essential problem of the workshops was the sale of their items, and not their production, one could adjust the balance of production and sales by encouraging the better workers to leave. This consideration, coupled with the philosophy which originally brought the sheltered workshops into being, leads us to ask: What efforts did agency personnel and workshop managers make to find jobs for their more productive employees? What attitude did they take toward skilled blind men and women leaving for "outside" jobs?

A characteristic attitude (in terms of the considerable support it received) was expressed by one placement manager who remarked:

Without question, I am sure that the primary purpose of every worker for the blind is consideration for the welfare of his client. This being true, every effort should be made to secure for the client the type of work for which he is best fitted and which provides the greatest remuneration. One of the fundamental principles of economics is that labor always seeks the highest bidder for its service—this is true of the blind as well as the sighted worker. We cannot therefore, *blame the blind worker when he deserts the sheltered workshop for more lucrative employment*. . . . In my capacity as Placement Manager, I am responsible not only for the placement of workers in private industry, but the employment of blind labor in the various departments of our own workshops, as well as in our concession stands. It is true *we have lost a number of our best workers to private industry*, but there has not been a general exodus such as that experienced in other cities and which has had such a crippling effect upon workshops, especially those engaged in filling Government orders (*AAWB Proceedings* 1943:124; emphasis added).

National Industries for the Blind (NIB) itself was constantly being approached by industrialists making requests for skilled and able-bodied blind men and women. In relation to these requests the president of NIB gave the following statement of policy:

Of late there has been much discussion regarding the placement of the blind in private industry. This is a service which should be provided by the individual agencies, and it is up to each to formulate its own policies in this connection. Any inquiries which we receive relating to placement are always referred back to the agency in the territory from which the inquiry came. We have tried to devote our efforts strictly to the field of production and merchandising of blind-make products, and we expect to continue this policy in the future (*AAWB Proceedings* 1943:58).

This ostrich-like stance assured NIB that its supply of skilled workmen could go untouched since the only men the agencies could offer were newly blinded persons who were untrained in industrial work. It is clear that this attitude, which was shared by a considerable number of other workers for the blind, mitigated against the placement, by the agencies, of blind workers in commercial industry (Chevigny and Braverman 1950:278–79).

In short, the fundamental incompatibility contained in the idea of a factory as a social service organization was grossly exaggerated by the economic upheaval of the 1930s. The existence of the workshops was threatened by the Depression, so that managers were forced to adopt policies which ultimately led the workshops to prosper, but which also subverted their official purpose. The operative policies which were instituted in order to preserve the shops also had the effect of vitiating the primary objective of employment of the blind in commercial industry, and of exacerbating the conditions which were responsible for the establishment of the employment programs in the first place.

The second consequence of the developing discrepancy between official and operative goals was that belief systems of workers for the blind changed so that by the end of World War II, the basic notions which were expressed about blind persons (what they needed, what they wanted, how to alleviate their plight) were different from, and often contradicted the beliefs of the pioneers of employment programs for the blind.

The first fact to be recognized is that the original, official goals of employment programs, as these were stated in the early 1900s, remained the official goals through this entire process, and continue to serve this function at the present time (Clark 1956). Even during the period when sheltered workshops were enjoying their greatest expansion, workshop managers and others continued to espouse the original and official doctrines of integration of the blind with the sighted in work settings, and of the virtues of such commercial employment. For example, the Director of the Office of Vocational Rehabilitation (a federally sponsored program for retraining handicapped persons for employment), in a major address before the AAWB convention of 1941, stated:

In view of the present emergency in which employers are clamoring for qualified workers, there is presented to all rehabilitation workers, and especially to the workers in the field of work for the blind, not only a golden opportunity, but also a challenge to do their part in seeing that every blind person, who is or can be made employable, finds his proper place in our efforts to meet the defense needs of our nation (*AAWB Proceedings* 1941:60).

These sentiments were accepted and restated by many others who were centrally concerned with employment of the blind. The discussions of special sections on commercial and workshop employment at AAWB conventions from the time of the Depression through the end of World War II suggest a widespread recognition of the fact that operative policies were not entirely in keeping with the official objectives for which employment programs were established. The frequency with which such discussions occurred and the spirited rehashing of old issues underscored the fact that workers at that time were experiencing the strains which were the products of goal discrepancies (*AAWB Proceedings* 1933, 1935, 1937, 1939, 1941).

One of the ways in which these strains were minimized was through a gradual change in beliefs of employment specialists, and most especially workshop managers, concerning the blind, the sighted, and employment problems of the blind. These changes were related to two general issues.

First, beliefs about the desirability of integration of the blind into work settings with sighted persons gradually began to change. At the beginning of this movement there was wholehearted endorsement of the idea of integration of the blind, with an elaborate set of accompanying notions about the ways in which blind and sighted persons would benefit from working together. The proceedings of AAWB meetings of the 1900–1920s reflect these beliefs in many ways. In addition to abstract and highly emotional statements of the integration philosophy, individual workers who had obtained employment in commercial establishments were invited to give testimonial statements as to the virtues of their positions. These were supplemented with statements of the experiences of commercial placement specialists (*Outlook for the Blind* 1907, 1908, 1909, 1911, 1913, 1915).

These beliefs began to undergo changes as the effects of the Depression were felt by the workshops. More and more one heard it said that while integration was a noble ideal, its applicability varied from blind person to blind person; and that there were always going to be some blind persons for whom integration was simply undesirable (*AAWB Proceedings* 1937, 1939, 1941). During and after the war, these beliefs were further transformed, so that managers were now arguing that while there was no doubt that integration was desirable for some blind workers, a majority of the blind were simply happier with their own kind. The most complete statement of this view was expressed by the manager of one of the largest sheltered workshops for the blind in the country, who compared the virtue of employment in sheltered workshops to that in commercial industry. He stated:

In the well-organized blind workshops, year round employment is practically assured, whereas in commercial industry employment quite often is seasonal, and in the case of labor curtailment, the blind worker, being less versatile, is very apt to be the first to go. The efficiently managed workshop . . . can afford to pay higher piece work rates or day labor rates for the work performed, thus offsetting in a measure, the handicap of the individual. In sighted industry, by comparison, the blind individual would have to adapt himself to the equipment at hand and accept the prevailing rate of pay. In an industrial workshop the blind worker is competing at his own level so that when he does a better job than his fellow worker, it gives him a definite lift to know that he can improve himself, increase his earning power and perhaps eventually take over a job with greater responsibility. Everything in a well-organized workshop is created to minimize the blind individual's handicap. The staff has been trained to deal with blind people. In most cases, the workers are collectively producing completed articles which are sold under the agency's label. He can, therefore, take a just pride in the things he creates. By contrast, as an employee among sighted workers, his handicap must be brought home to him in many ways—in his contacts with co-workers, in the equipment he uses, in the facilities of the factory, etc. Unquestionably, in many cases he realized that he is just plainly being tolerated (*AAWB Proceedings* 1950:68–69).

One way in which the strains created by the disparity between official and operative goals in sheltered workshops were minimized was, therefore, to change beliefs about what employment arrangements blind persons needed or preferred to make.

A second change which occurred related to beliefs about how sighted persons, and especially sighted employers, felt about the blind. Initially, the blind took the view that sighted individuals were kindly but misled persons whose misconceptions could be erased if they were taught the "true facts" about the blind. These beliefs were manifested in the content of AAWB programs during the first two or three decades of this century. Employers who had agreed to hire blind workers were invited to discuss their experiences; employment specialists described the success with which they had applied the "hard sell" to factory owners; and the view of blind employees about their treatment at the hands of sighted employers were also solicited. The views of workers for the blind toward the sighted were generally favorable and forgiving; no one questioned the fact that most sighted employers could be reeducated in exactly the same way and with the same success that most sighted workers for the blind had been reeducated (*Outlook for the Blind* 1907, 1908, 1909, 1911, 1913, 1915).

This view of the public and of its attitude toward the employment of the blind changed over the years. The idea began to emerge that the public in general, and employers in particular, were abysmally ignorant about the condition of blindness and the way in which it affected individuals. There emerged over time the notion that there was in the mind of a sighted person a stereotype of the blind. This stereotype consisted of a complex set of erroneous ideas, such as the notion that the blind lived in darkness, or that they were gifted in special but undefined ways, or that they were evil, or alternatively that they were good and noble. These ideas acted as barriers which directly impeded the efforts of commercial employment specialists to place blind workers in industry. It was, therefore, the stereotype of the blind which accounted for the discrepancy between official and operative goals (Gowman 1957; Himes 1951).

There is no doubt that the stubborn, and often irrational, fears and misconceptions about blindness among sighted individuals had a sobering effect upon those who first tried to obtain industrial positions for blind persons. Many employers rejected out of hand the idea of hiring a blind person, without giving workers for the blind so much as an opportunity to present their case. Others agreed to give blind persons a chance, but then reneged at the last moment. These bitter experiences suggested that stereotypic ideas about the blind were indeed real barriers to their placement in commercial industry.

It is not the presence or absence of a stereotype which is at issue, but rather the extent of its pervasiveness. Over the years, workers for the blind have developed an increasingly rigid and elaborate conception about how sighted persons view the blind. The idea has emerged that sighted persons are unenlightened individuals, whose rigid and erroneous ideas are simply unchangeable. In fact, however, the research evidence throws this whole conception into some considerable doubt. Studies by Lukoff and Whiteman (1963) and by Paske and Weiss (1965) have shown that there are individual stereotypic ideas which are held by some, but not all, sighted persons; but that the idea of a stereotype of the blind, in the sense of an aggregate of misconceptions, simply does not exist. That there are particular stereotypic ideas about the blind is clear; it is equally clear that these ideas are not nearly so pervasive, elaborate, and rigid as workers for the blind would have us believe them to be.

One explanation for the development of increasingly unrealistic ideas about the feelings of sighted persons toward the blind is that such beliefs served to minimize the strains which accompanied the discrepancies between official and operative goals. By convincing themselves, and others, of the existence of the stereotype, it was possible for workers for the blind to account to themselves and others for the disparities between their official goals and the effects of the day-to-day policies which they made. In short, they argued that commercially employable blind persons had to be placed in sheltered workshops because commercial employers refused to hire them.

Summary

This paper has described an instance of goal displacement and analyzed two consequences which this process has had. The first concerned the effects of goal discrepancies upon the original problem of employment of the blind; and the second concerned the implications of these discrepancies for the belief systems of workers for the blind about the blind, the feelings of the general public toward the blind, and the best means by which to resolve the plight of the blind. Changes in these belief systems were interpreted as responses to ideological strains which were created by discrepancies between official and operative goals.

NOTES

1. The alternatives described in the following discussion, and the fundamental logic upon which the discussion itself is based, are parallel to the basic formulations of dissonance theory in social psychology. See Festinger (1957).

2. These requirements were explained to workshop managers by C. C. Kleber, President of National Industries for the Blind, at the 1939 AAWB meeting as follows: "Practically every article purchased by the Federal departments is covered by a set of rigid specifications and it is of the utmost importance that these specifications be met in every detail before we can hope to supply any particular article" (*AAWB Proceedings* 1939:92).

[16]

WELFARE ADMINISTRATION AND ORGANIZATIONAL THEORY

David Street

W ELFARE administration has long resisted straightforward description, explanation, and prescription by those who would
apply to it one or another of the major theoretical perspectives on
organizations. For example, efforts at the application of rational
system or neo-Weberian approaches have faltered at the ambiguities
and inconsistencies of goals, technologies, and outcomes that exist in
human service organizations. Similarly, attempts to apply natural
system or human relations approaches to welfare administration have
suffered in the face of the fiscal and structural limitations that exist
on the exercise of leadership or the enhancement of participants'
commitments. The result has been in large part the production of a
series of "goal displacement" studies of welfare organizations. One
thinks of research—often very good in itself—on agencies for the
blind that enlarge rather than reduce dependency (Scott 1969), on
organizations treating alcoholism that cycle their clients through a
closed alcohol-related social network (Wiseman 1970), or on psychiatric institutions that adjust their diagnostic categories in ways that
seem to keep up caseload sizes (Byrd 1974). Such studies have tended
not to cumulate, and they may attract the criticism that the "institutional school" of organizational analysis wallows in an exposé tradition
and a fixation on "trivial" organizations (Perrow rev. 1979:177–83,

An earlier draft of this paper was presented at the annual meeting of the American
Sociological Association, San Francisco, 1978. Subsequently it was part of the working
paper series of the Committee on Sociological Research and Social Policy, Department
of Sociology, the University of Illinois at Chicago Circle. Helpful comments were
received from many persons, including particularly Doris Elaine Byrd, Kathleen
Crittenden, Yeheskel Hasenfeld, Morris Janowitz, John Meyer, Baila Miller, Michael
Moch, James Norr, Gerald D. Suttles, and Mayer N. Zald.

193–94). At the extreme, the student of human service organizations may give up on conventional theories altogether, moving to a completely cynical view of goals as but a smokescreen for efforts to regulate the clients, provide employment for organizational personnel, and facilitate chicanery and aggrandizement by parasitic interests both inside and outside the organization (Perrow 1978). More tempered approaches seek to use conventional theories as starting points but must recognize the limits of these theories in the face of organizational realities and can only look hopefully toward reformulations. Hasenfeld and English express this view nicely:

Looking back over the series of issues and problems that human service organizations encounter as a type of bureaucracy, we can recast them as structural barriers to the pursuit of norms of rationality. It is not surprising, therefore, that human service organizations have benefited only marginally from the "new science of management" and the development of sophisticated management tools such as operations research, and management information system. These . . . techniques are based on assumptions which often cannot be met in human service organizations. Recent efforts to apply such tools to human service organizations—hospitals, police departments, and schools— point to the immense organizational complexities and uncertainties to which they must address themselves. The success of these tools has been limited to the more routine and peripheral aspects of the organization. However, full cognizance and understanding of the unique parameters that shape the service delivery system of human service organizations may enable the development of a "new science of human service management" that is applicable to these organizations (1974:22).

This paper will, in a preliminary fashion, address the value for analyzing welfare administration of using a number of conceptions that have been embodied more or less explicity in recent writings on organizational theory. The major conceptions of interest will be those of *political economy, loose coupling, organized anarchy,* the *caldron model,* and *organizational ritual.* In the end I will work toward a synthetic model that might ultimately be of use to the study of welfare organizations. Empirically, the paper will follow in the tradition of speculation about the ill-defined and diffuse social institution of welfare, although from time to time I will refer rather specifically to some recent studies of urban public welfare with which I have been associated (Street, Martin, and Gordon 1979) along with my involvement with studies of juvenile corrections (Street, Vinter, and Perrow 1966).

Political Economy

As a start, we will need a model of welfare organizations that does not treat departures from a single unified and rationalistic bureaucracy as unnatural. The political economy framework developed by Zald (1970a, 1970b) in connection with his study of the YMCA offers an excellent starting point, one we shall largely assume without much elaboration here. This perspective embodies a *realpolitik* that happily eliminates the tendency to recurrent *weltschmerz* over the fact that organizational goals have been displaced once again. Zald stresses the importance of the relationship of the organization to its environment, particularly as the latter provides or withholds money or other incentives, and also emphasizes the politics of the internal allocation of personnel, money, and facilities. From this perspective, organizational goals become realized largely not because they are important or are internalized by the actors but because their accomplishment is facilitated by the draw of incentives, the exercise of power, or the aggregation of demands. The workings of political and economic processes can accompany substantial differentiation within the organization, such that subunits may take on the characteristics of a social movement (or social movement organization) while other subunits are engaged with routine business (McCarthy and Zald 1973; Zald and Ash 1966).

Loose Coupling

The perspective of Zald and associates does not necessarily assume an organization that is highly politicized and strongly engaged in conflict if a pattern of hegemony has not been achieved. Yet the terms involved in the analysis may imply such a situation, and in so doing may signal a highly determined system. This is why the political economy framework might profitably be paired with a conception more recently given currency, that of the loosely coupled system. The notion refers to disconnections among elements of choice such as cognitions, actions, and response (March and Olsen 1976:15–16), among events (Weick 1976), and among structures, activities, and effects (Meyer and Rowan 1975). It also applies to loose couplings among offices, actors, and subunits. The general conception is not merely that coupling may be loose but that the actual degree of coupling between any two elements of an organization is problematic. Further, as we shall understand when we look into a caldron shortly, elements may be closely or weakly coupled for reasons less related to the state of the political economy than to elements of happenstance involving incompletely articulated histories and agenda.

The relevance of both the political economy and loose-coupling concepts to the American welfare system is readily apparent. The system is highly fragmented into federal, state, and local efforts and under both public and private auspices, with programs highly differentiated by type and showing incredible variation in the degree of coupling of program elements one to another. Similar to the way Weick (1976) sees both positive and negative functions played by loose coupling in educational institutions, we can easily point to many ways in which differentiation among welfare programs on the one hand makes for adaptation and survival of subunits while on the other it weakens the capacity of the welfare system for any genuine reform (on the fragmentation from top to bottom of public assistance, see Street, Martin, and Gordon 1979; on the dilemmas of adaptation through ecological differentiation of welfare programs, see Pearce and Street 1979). And efforts to change the system that are to go beyond rhetoric must address the reassemblage of couplings through incentives and sanctions as analyzed under the political economy model.[1]

Organized Anarchy and the Caldron Model

Closely coupled to the discussion just completed are the conceptions of organized anarchy and the caldron model as developed by March, Cohen, and Olsen in the past few years (Cohen and March 1974; Cohen, March, and Olsen 1972; and March and Olsen 1976).[2] The existence of an organized anarchy is revealed in all organizations sometimes and in some organizations often on those occasions when decisions must be made despite the ambiguities that exist because preferences are problematic, the appropriate technology unclear, and the roster and involvement of participants in the decisions uncertain. Under the circumstances, participants are not able to move logically from premise to conclusion and often must work to

arrive at an interpretation of what they are doing and what they have done while doing it. From this point of view, an organization is a collection of choices looking for problems, issues and feelings looking for decision situations in which they might be aired, solutions looking for issues to which they might be the answer, and decision makers looking for work (Cohen and March 1974:81).

More formally, this view is captured in the metaphor of organizational choices emerging from a caldron into which various components of a stew are more or less arbitrarily poured and stirred. Into the caldron go three streams that—it is most important to note—are relatively independent of one another: streams of *problems* as perceived by the participants; waves of *solutions*, often answers in search of questions; and streams of *choice opportunities*, or occasions that call for an organizational decision, such as deadlines for settling the budget or hiring personnel. Also, a passing parade of *participants* is more or less involved at one time or another. In the caldron, loose coupling is carried to the extreme, for the results of the entry of an element into the caldron may depend as much on what we can call the "luck of the mix" as on any logic of the relationship among elements.

As provocative metaphors, the organized anarchy and caldron conceptions have *prima facie* application to welfare administration. To take the public aid example, even the existence of a consensual preference for survival and extension of the organization seems in question. From the outside:

Public assistance institutions and the roles and reputations of both their functionaries and recipients are suffused to the extreme with the moral ambiguities that in America surround governmental welfare programs and their participants. The extension of social insurance benefits for the aging through the "middle mass" (the middle class together with the solid working class) has attained widespread popularity, and there has come wide acceptance of the provision of temporary unemployment compensation as it, too, is defined as the earned product of an insurance plan. However, the spectre of the welfare state continues to loom large, particularly when it is perceived as furnishing the essence of programs for what can be seen as the "undeserving poor" aided by the categorical or public assistance programs. . . .

Where traditional stereotypes of the poor (e.g., explaining them as lazy, undisciplined, hedonistic, crooks, or whores) begin to pass from the scene, new sophisticated code words (e.g., understanding them as creatures of a culture of poverty or as losers in a complex and changing economic system) hardly can give them reputations and self-images of a more positive, proactive character than that of the "victim." The explanations adduced reinforce the concept of the recipient population as a permanently impoverished underclass, ignoring the fact that for many public assistance is a temporary matter. Further, suspicions about the underclass generalize to a skepticism about the welfare personnel and programs that serve this class (Street, Martin, and Gordon 1979:24–26).

Inside the organization, ambiguities abound as well, particularly as young welfare employees quickly gain "cynical knowledge" of the agency (Goldner, Ritti, and Ference 1977).

To understand public assistance in the contemporary period one must recognize that its crucial opponents are not only those from without, particularly on the political right; they also include functionaries within the system and members of liberal and left political circles within and without the system. These are the middle classes that Schumpeter anticipated, disenchanted with advanced capitalism, and therefore critical and cynical about welfare. Their skepticism is more or less informed by an implicit Marxist critique of capitalist welfare that has seeped into the general consciousness of the well-educated and that is made more salient or generated afresh each day within the welfare agency. They come to see public assistance in a great variety of negative ways: they perceive it as a "people-processing" agency trying to pass itself off as a "people-changing" one; they view it as less oriented to helping than to controlling the personal behavior of members of the underclass and containing their potential for rebellion; they tend to see the proliferation and complexity of welfare regulations, the penuriousness of welfare benefits and the artificiality of agency claims that they offer casework services as concessions, intended or not, to the political right; they see any efforts at incremental improvement of the system as self-deceiving illusion avoiding real change while actually standing in its place; and of course they perceive the keepers of the traditional social work faith as naive at best. Hostility from the conservative side combines with cynicism from the liberal-left side to undercut the middle ground (Street, Martin, and Gordon 1979:26–27).

Such extreme cynicism enlarges the disconnection of preferences, solutions, participants, and choices. The public welfare system is so fragmented by divisions among the federal, state, and local levels and so dependent on decision-making at levels once or twice removed that it is unclear which bureaucratic agencies and which political actors are the necessary participants in any decision-making addressing reform. Further, turnover of caseworkers is high, or at least was when we did our studies, and caseworkers show substantial variations in their perspectives toward the agency and the recipients. Some act strongly as "advocates" on behalf of selected client groups, while some are "bureaucrats," "apathetics," or "mediators." Yet over time, processes of selection out of agency employment along with "hardening" in the caseworker role lead to a disconnection between caseworker views and caseworker behavior and a homogenization of behavior. The homogenization over time comes not just from selection out and not so much by design as by the long-term accretion of a variety of agency practices involving supervision, the use of bureaucratic forms, elaborated regulations, large caseload sizes, and decoupling of supervisory structure and caseworker roles (Street, Martin, and Gordon 1979).

Another example of the functioning of the caldron is that proposals for change like the guaranteed annual income and national health insurance solutions have floated for years without finding the occasion for clear-cut choice and without attaching themselves persuasively to need. Variations in the character of these solutions and in the degree of support and opposition they have attracted have varied dramatically as the forum for discussing these reforms has enlarged and contracted and as various groups (for example, professional groupings, organizations of welfare recipients) have gained and lost prominence in the forum. The relative independence of the caldron streams is illustrated by Grønbjerg's (1977) finding that changes in the welfare rolls across states from 1960 to 1970 reflected much less the many conscious efforts to change the rules for eligibility that occurred during this period than glacial demographic changes in the population composition. A coherent pattern among the streams may be discerned only retrospectively, and in reviewing their study of changes in public aid caseload Ritti and Human (1977:173) caution us that such an understanding is likely to be gratuitous:

In giving interpretation. . . , it is difficult to avoid the assumption that the actors had specific ideas of consequences in mind, as opposed, say, to taking expedient actions simply to "put out the fire" of some immediate problem. Yet the best description of the administration of poverty is one of an emergent process, neither planned nor unplanned, issuing from the confluence of competing social, political, economic, even personal, forces. Federal initiatives translated through state and local organizations may result in consequences far different from those envisioned by their originators. Yesterday's crash solution becomes today's policy, and probably tomorrow's abandoned program.

Further, as Wagner (1977) has described in reporting a study of an innovative school for black dropouts, old priorities do not have to be altered but can simply be allowed to drift out of attention as new matters come to center stage. This comes through a process he calls "serial advocacy."

Organizational Ritual

The caldron model assumes that choices must often be made in the absence of sufficient bases for decisions, and thereby it implies that much organizational behavior is but ritual. In welfare organizations ongoing activities and efforts at reform may often be but symbolic displays—as for example, in the Mobilization for Youth experiment in New York City in the 1960s, so widely touted as radical. There, the hiring of Spanish-speaking professionals, many from Latin America, provided for the "symbolic representation of the poor," that is, of the local poor population of Puerto Ricans living on Manhattan's Lower East Side (Helfgot 1974). Such efforts symbolize as well the "professionalization of reform" of social workers and other groups competing for a piece of the antipoverty pie or for resources available in other fields slated for social improvement (Grønbjerg, Street, and Suttles 1978). In general, welfare organizations that have any professional personnel have always shown a tendency to elaborate and celebrate professional rituals. These are expressed perhaps most completely in the highly professionalized child welfare agency where such rituals as the "case conference" provide a symbolic laying on of hands around a decision on adoption or foster placement.

Although these rituals may deflect or deflate efforts to make welfare organizations more faithful to their announced goals, their utilization is not necessarily cynical—nor is it unnecessary. Meyer and Rowan (1977), seeking to interpret the substantial amount of ritual behavior observed in schools and similar organizations, note that obviously this behavior cannot be accounted for purely in terms of a search for efficiency in goal satisfaction. Instead, the organizations are searching for legitimacy—for symbols that signify their conformity to the changing institutional order. Their analysis is complicated a bit by the fact that they posit that in the modern period legitimacy attaches to the symbols of an increasingly rationalized institutional form. Thus, organizations seek not so much rationality as rationalistic symbols. The resulting ritual activities can serve both expressive and instrumental purposes, the latter as legitimacy is a prerequisite to increments in external resources.[3] Thus to obtain necessary resources modern organizations must elaborate bureaucratic rituals that will be visible to those outside while keeping from view practices that would discredit the rationalistic image. And rationalistic behavior thus engendered can come to embody a set of operating principles that give the organization continuing precedents, practices, and structure.

Not only organizational rituals but both tight and loose couplings can buffer organizations from external challenge. Tight coupling manipulates what might be questioned concretely, and in addition the development of an elaborate form of internal governance may tend to generate informal norms shielding insiders from outsiders (Katz 1977). Loose coupling protects from the outside too by making less visible that which would be difficult to defend. In this regard welfare organizations seem very similar to the schools, where the loose coupling of instruction and results protects against the external pressure which likely would arise if the true effectiveness of teaching were to become known (Meyer and Rowan 1975). These buffering and ritual activities can have other external effects as well, for they may not only express the urge for human improvement but they may also exhaust it.

Variations within and between Organizations

In using the conceptions just discussed, however, we would deeply mislead ourselves if we saw welfare organizations as loosely coupled across the board, if we reified the imagery of the organized anarchy, or if we saw little in these organizations but ritual and little in ritual but emptiness. Streams of solutions, personnel, problems, and choice opportunities do not in fact chase each other perpetually into limbo. If an important property of the conception of loose coupling is to make the degree of coupling problematic, then a promising strategy in organizational analysis is to seek to distinguish the strongly from the loosely coupled components of organizations. We have suggested that across the welfare system organizations tend to be very loosely coupled one to another. Within welfare organizations, however, considerable variation exists in the extent to which different components are tightly or loosely coupled. This distinction is shown nicely for public schools by Meyer and Rowan (1975), who see very loose coupling among organizational structures, classroom instruction, and the results of instruction, and very tight coupling among categories of participants, certifications, and allocations. Thus while the structure of the school is little attentive to what actually goes on in the classroom and to what actually results from this activity, it expresses deep concern with classifying teachers and pupils by type, with recording the formal topics of instruction, units of credit given, and grades, and with judiciously allocating funds, workloads, and supplies.

Analogous patterns are readily apparent in many welfare organizations, where the organizational structure closely attends to the accounting of the caseload registry and the massing of the documentary records while loosely coupling actual staff activities with clients. The contrasts seem heightened in welfare when we distinguish between people-changing processes, which seek altered behavior, and people-processing functions, which produce altered statuses (Hasenfeld 1972).[4] Frequently both functions are pursued within the same welfare organization, and in this case the people-changing activities often are loosely coupled while people-processing activities often are highly coupled. One must distinguish between unintentional and intentional patterns of loose coupling; sustained efforts at people-changing seem to require the latter. Thus in the juvenile corrections system such efforts at rehabilitation as are attempted tend to be treated as so specialized that they must be handled through private professional practice or in separate professional units, lost from sight in the broken coupling of organizational bifurcation. Alternatively, rehabilitation may be assumed to involve so holistic and diffuse a set of "milieu" or "community" activities that no specified oversight can be given. In either case, loosely coupled rehabilitation efforts contrast sharply with the tight coupling that attends intake, allocations to different living units and school or work programs, records or rule infractions that might pertain to discharge, and so on.

Similarly, in public assistance, the provision of "services" even where it is spoken of seriously is largely left to the invisible caseworker-recipient exchange or else decoupled from the core of the agency altogether through referral to other subunits or to outside units. Meantime, the agency very tightly controls the keeping of the books, the enumeration of who is coming on and who is going off the rolls, the creation of records to be utilized to justify decisions under challenge, and the amounts, timing, and addressing of checks. Actual people-changing may never occur, but despite the problems of the United States Postal Service the vast majority of welfare checks arrive when they should and in amounts that are properly justified in the bureaucratic records. Dramatically, the last decade has shown many efforts to decouple the caseworker from himself or herself, through the "separation of services" reform wherein a college-educated "caseworker" handles "services" while a high-school-educated "clerk" handles the matters of "eligibility" and income for the welfare poor. In balance, the more popular changes in public assistance have not been those which emphasize people-changing but instead those that involve adopting practices for processing people which symbolize modern, rationalized organization—as through the use of elaborate systems of regulations and paper work, computerization, and the form if not the substance of modern cost-accounting procedures. In addition to such benefits as may come from a general increment of legitimation, such practices specifically buffer the organization from external accusations of softness on welfare fraud. Importantly, they also protect the reputations of welfare recipients by seeming to insure against welfare chiseling, and they may contribute as well to the notion that people receive welfare as a legitimate right—thus enlarging the citizenship as well as the numbers of the welfare poor (Grønbjerg 1977).

Across welfare organizations generally, any enlargement in organizational legitimacy tends to occur in just such an unexciting way as that described for public assistance. There is truth in the conservative image of a "boring welfare state." After any initial periods of active political leadership, increments in the legitimacy of welfare programs involve bureaucratic routinization rather than the charisma of reformers, and increments grow more often out of the fortuitous workings of loosely coupled changes than from tight plans envisioned by reformers. Legitimacy for welfare does not presume a consensus. Programs survive as much on the presumed demerits of alternative programs as on consensus over their own merits. A splendid example of the ambiguity of claims for welfare solutions can be found in the use of the concept of "deinstitutionalization." This concept on the one hand seems to denote a form of rehabilitation while on the other it appears to be a crass cover for saving funds by closing down institutions. The fact that no one is certain of how to achieve the presumed benefits of the reform has not kept the concept from achieving status as a "policy aim" in the Department of Health and Human Services and from being used to justify a mass emptying out of mental patients into host communities.

Finally, across welfare organizations there are variations in the extent to which organizational practices, once formed however randomly through the luck of the mix in the caldron, actually remain open to further change. In a given caldron the recipe for the organizational stew may become quite fixed, as seen for example in the many social service programs that become highly institutionalized around a given physical plant such as a gymnasium. The agency thus develops a character which disables it in adapting programs to changing populations and changing times. Also, the development of a given recipe for organizational practice may create strong constituencies (such as veterans' organizations acting as interest groups to support Veterans Administration hospitals) that make the continuation of present patterns of operation in effect a necessity. Further, as indicated earlier, placing an emphasis upon certain rationalistic rituals may be generally prerequisite to acquiring and maintaining legitimacy and resources in the contemporary period. The making of such adaptations will make some welfare organizations much less open to change than others, and also much less open to alteration than the organized anarchy model implies.

Propositions

I have argued that there is substantial utility in analyzing welfare administration in starting with the perspective of political economy and then teasing out notions of loose coupling, a caldron model, and organizational ritual. However, I have also reacted against the overkill that comes when decoupling is seen as anarchy and have pointed to some of the complications entailed in applying these concepts to welfare. Now we turn to stating the beginnings of a synthetic analytic model, using the conceptions discussed here by stating some propositions, repeating and expanding some of what has been said so far. From the outset we can complicate the problem a bit further in the shortrun but perhaps simplify it in the long run by introducing the fundamental notion of hierarchy explicitly into the analysis. We can do this by requiring that the analysis proceed somewhat separately for each of the three levels of formal organization listed by Parsons (1956b). These are the *institutional* level (relating the organization to, and legitimating it within, its environment); the *managerial* level (coordinating; developing, and using the organizational structure); and the *technical* level (performing the organization's technology upon the raw material). With this complication in place, we can proceed to state a few preliminary propositions:

1. Welfare organizations show strongly the pattern of loose coupling across hierarchical levels that Parsons implicitly perceived in his theory of organizations.

2. Proposals, personnel, and problems will take on different roles in welfare (and other) organizations depending on the level at which they enter.

   a) When organizational legitimacy or programs are under attack, proposals and personnel may be quite fluid at the institutional level without there being effects upon other levels. Indeed, a high rate of flow of both plans and consultants may simply symbolize a progressive or modern style of operations in the face of external criticism, with few other effects.

   b) Proposals and personnel may also be highly fluid at the technical level, for most people-processing welfare tasks require relatively low skills and replacement of personnel is relatively easy. Proposals are fluid too as personnel at the technical level place their idiosyncratic constructions on their jobs without really affecting the operations of basic organizational routines.

   c) Frequently the diffuse coupling of people-changing activities or their delegation out of ready visibility buffers these activities from scrutiny and thus protects the organization from attack. At the same time, such arrangements can permit strong efforts at people-changing by highly committed personnel who are protected by the buffering arrangements.

   d) Problems can loom heavy at the institutional level, but their existence can be used either to attack the organization or to justify increments in resources so that solutions can be attached to the problems that are seen. Often the problems provide a permanent justification for ineffectiveness.

   e) Problems at the technical level may seem pervasive, too, but they may not come at all to the attention of personnel at other levels unless scandal or protest challenges legitimacy and resources at the highest level.

3. In general, welfare organizations will be more tightly coupled at the managerial level than at the other levels. This statement borders on truism. However, it is important to recognize that problems, personnel, and solutions tend to alter organizational operations in some consistent direction only if they force or attract choices at the managerial level. The continuity of the operations at this level is much less dependent on any tight coupling of proposals and/or of the social networks of participants than on the successive accommodations among choices made in the organization past and present.

Planned Change

The thrust of our analysis may seem to suggest the existence of a highly disordered system of welfare, or at least one in which an extraordinarily complicated series of adaptations or an "ecology of games" (Long 1958) and perhaps many idiosyncratic adjustments play the major role. Indeed, the conception of "negotiated reality" (Strauss 1979) might seem necessary to any attempt at understanding behavior in such a system. Given the fragmentation of the welfare system, planned change in welfare might seem almost an impossibility except in the case of single organizations that are highly buffered from the rest of the system.

The "ecology of games" perspective is useful and impressive, but without qualification it can carry the conceptions we have discussed too far. First, as we have implied, specific efforts at change in the welfare system have often been idiosyncratic and ephemeral, but underneath such patterns has been a gradual but glacial movement to an enlargement of welfare programs and an increase in transfer payments—the growth of the welfare state. Such a growth may have been highly dependent on the existence of a great era of American prosperity, which in turn may help account for the fact that innovations could be so loosely coupled to the underlying extension of welfare. The end of the period of perpetually heightened prosperity might force a great tightening of the coupling of resources to aims to programs, with more firmly ordered priorities.

Second, to some unknown extent loose coupling across the welfare system has reflected the conscious efforts of various interest groups that have worked to keep welfare programs fragmented, and also the activities of particular welfare organizations that are doing well within the existing fragmented arrangements and oppose coordination or other change. Some scenes of great fragmentation may be more or less planned by powerful political units; one thinks of the disarray of the antipoverty program as in part well orchestrated by the often contradictory actions of government. If this be the case, then to some extent the organizational conditions that we have discussed are subject to alterations in the political economy, including alterations that could promote change. Such alterations presumably would require much emptying out of the caldrons of the old stew and starting again with new recipes. The most prominent of such efforts has been the effort by reformers for over a decade to get the public assistance caldron emptied in favor of a recipe for guaranteed incomes. The reasons for the failure so far of this reform are complex, but include the reluctance of some bureaucratic and professional functionaries well situated in the present caldron to fight for a reform that would seek to cut out the "caseworker middlemen" and attached supervisory staffs. Yet a change to a guaranteed-income program, or some other major change, seems possible should there develop a new aggregation of interests and consensus under altered political and economic conditions in the society at large.

Finally, we can consider planned change in a different way, through mentioning the possibilities of organizational improvement as it might involve a heightened conscious and positive use of loose coupling within welfare organizations. Moch and Pondy (1977) have suggested that organizations that deal with complex problems may be in need of developing a strategy to *absorb* uncertainty through becoming loosely coupled internally, rather than to *buffer* uncertainty by exporting problems (and, in welfare, clients) to other organizations. Moch (1978, personal communication) suggests that we need to design organizations explicitly to deal with ambiguity, something he says might be pursued by taking seriously the law of requisite variety (variety is required to deal with and even to perceive variety) and seeking to arrange organizations to maximize variety. Such a conception would extend the notion of "debureaucratization" with which Katz and Eisenstadt (1960) described how Israeli bureaucrats learned how to deal with persons not socialized into Western ways. The purpose would be to help organizations deal creatively with uncertainty rather than to deflect it—and the people who do not quite fit in—back onto the streets. Certainly the conception is attractive; however, discussion of the means to its implementation cannot be attempted here.

NOTES

1. Kirsten A. Grønbjerg is doing a study of the history of private welfare efforts in metropolitan Chicago, and her preliminary findings seem to imply that in recent years the goals of insuring interagency cooperation and overall coordination have become more important than any substantive ends.

2. March and colleagues developed the term "garbage pail model" in studying higher education. I substitute the metaphor of stew in a caldron to avoid any implication that there is anything derogating or unnatural about the processes.

3. Argument can be made that this is a point at which the political economy approach to organizations falls short, for humans seek honor as well as cash. A reply is that honor buys cash and vice versa. The matter is akin to the questions of the

differences between class politics and status politics and of whether there is in addition a "value politics" which seeks what is deemed correct regardless of self-interest. In any event, the political economy approach, which tends to trace actions to incentives even if dimly perceived, is not completely ready to handle the search for conformity where extrinsic rewards may be totally unperceived or nonexistent.

4. The distinction between people-changing and people-processing is not everywhere clear-cut, although it seems relatively straightforward in welfare. John Meyer (1978, personal communication) writes: "It can be argued that the rituals of education status-changing (the welter of little and big initiation ceremonies) *are* the critically effective technology of education: that is, if everybody gets together and believes firmly in education, kids will actually learn a lot. In such an instance, the institutional exoskeleton of the organization *is* its effective technology. Such arguments are harder to make about the welfare system." Further, the relationship of coupling and people-changing varies across different settings. This is illustrated in Wagner's (1977) study of an experimental school for dropouts where the action seemed to be largely social-political and socioemotional but where a major payoff for people-changing came from a quiet and closely coupled program for self-instruction.

C. CLIENT RELATIONS

IN the three selections here, a distinguishing characteristic of social welfare agencies is examined—their unique client relations. The relations between workers and clients in social welfare institutions have served as the basis for sociological research, including Goffman's influential *Asylums* (1961). Gubrium's *Living and Dying at Murray Manor* (1975) is a more recent example.

The first selection is Yeheskel Hasenfeld's "Client-Organization Relations," in which he develops his continuing concern with clients of human service organizations. Hasenfeld here applies a systems perspective and elements of exchange theory to the analysis of client-organization relations and develops a series of propositions to guide research. He argues that a potential contribution of this approach is that it simultaneously considers both organizational and client characteristics.

The second selection is Julius A. Roth's "Some Contingencies of the Moral Evaluation and Control of Clientele," in which he presents data from participant observation in six public, urban hospitals. His findings indicate that major differences exist in the type and extent of professional service extended to patients, depending on the moral evaluation made of them by staff. The evaluation is based on a limited set of superficial patient characteristics. This is contrary to the professional value of universalism, according to which service is based on medical need. Roth found that the patients most likely to be negatively evaluated included drunks, hippies, and unmarried pregnant women. This selection is concerned with health care but has relevance for the client-stigmatizing process in social welfare.

The final selection in section C is "Professional Autonomy and the Revolt of the Client" by Marie R. Haug and Marvin B. Sussman. The authors argue that an important basis for the client revolt of the 1960s was the effort by professionals to extend their authority into areas beyond their specific expertise. Reactions to the revolt included efforts by professionals to co-opt their critics.

17

CLIENT-ORGANIZATION RELATIONS: A SYSTEMS PERSPECTIVE

Yeheskel Hasenfeld

HUMAN service organizations have been distinguished from other types of bureaucracies by the centrality of client-staff transactions as the core activity in such organizations. Unlike the public of other bureaucracies, the clients in human service organizations not only assume the role of consumers, but also serve as raw material to be worked upon; and occupy a quasimembership role in the organization (Hasenfeld and English 1974; Lefton and Rosengren 1966; Parsons 1970; Wheeler 1966). The essential character of any human service organization will be manifested through the patterned relations between its clients and staff, relations which are the *raison d'être* of the organization. It is not surprising that much of the research on human service organizations focuses on identifying the parameters which determine and shape the transactions between the clients and the organization (for a review of these studies see Katz and Danet 1973; McKinlay 1972; Rosengren and Lefton 1970). In general, such studies fall into two broad categories. First, a long-standing tradition of research, particularly in the health field, looks at the attributes of clients as the major determinants of the use of human services and the role the client will assume. McKinlay (1972) identified three specific research approaches in this category: (1) the sociodemographic approach, which explores the effects of such variables as sex, age, race, education, and socioeconomic status of the client; (2) the sociopsychological approach, which focuses on such client attributes as motivation, perception, and learning; (3) the sociocultural ap-

proach, which explores the effects of cultural and social class affiliations, kinship, and friendship networks on the client's role.

Second, a growing body of research focuses on organizational
determinants of client-staff relations. These studies examine the
effects of such organizational variables as goals (Scott 1969; Street,
Vinter, and Perrow 1966), technology and professional ideology
(Perrow 1965; Rapoport, Rapoport, and Rosow 1960; Strauss et al.
1964), organizational resources (Scott 1967), and professionalization
(Cloward and Epstein 1967; Freidson 1970a; Walsh and Elling 1968).
Nevertheless, both categories of research, while advancing our understanding of various facets of human service organizations and
their clients, have failed to provide systematic and, most important,
cumulative knowledge of the parameters that determine client-organization relations.

Problems in Studies of Client-Organization Relations

I contend that the major reason for the current "state of the art" is
a result of the failure to consider *both* client attributes and organizational variables and the interaction between them as determinants
of client-organization relations. Thus, for example, numerous studies
suggest that clients from low socioeconomic background are less
likely to initiate service requests; they underutilize services and they
terminate their transactions with organizations prematurely (Mc-
Kinlay 1972; McKinlay and McKinlay 1972). These actions are
attributed to cultural factors, socialization patterns, and social network
characteristics. In contrast, several studies indicate that the difficulties
clients from low socioeconomic background experience with human
services are attributable to organizational variables, such as professional biases, inappropriate technology (Cloward and Epstein 1967;
Walsh and Elling 1968), ideological biases (Sjoberg, Brymer, and
Farris 1966), and the like. Yet, because both sets of variables are not
studied simultaneously, one cannot draw systematic conclusions from
either set of studies regarding the conditions that affect the relations
between lower-class clients and human service organizations. Neither
of these research strategies allows the investigator to estimate the
relative importance of each set of variables, or to ascertain whether
certain interaction effects between specific client attributes and
organizational variables account for important patterns of client-staff
exchanges.

The problem is not strictly methodological but is also substantive. With few exceptions, to be noted below, most studies lack a theoretical framework or a causal model that interrelates both client and organizational attributes. The difficulties in doing so are obvious. First, one faces the problem of relating two different units of analysis, each of which has distinct structures and processes. Second, there is no apparent efficient way to select the relevant variables from each unit of analysis. Finally, the dependent variable itself—client-organization relations—must be so defined as to be compatible with, and appropriate to, both units. Nevertheless, a major contention of this paper is that a theoretical framework relating both units of analysis is a basic prerequisite for effective research on client-organization relations, particularly in the human services.

One of the earlier attempts in this direction has been provided by Thompson (1962), who proposed that the interaction between the degree of client discretion and the specificity of organizational control over members will produce differential transaction structures. Carlson (1964) developed a similar typology based on the client's discretion to participate in the transaction and the organizational control over its intake. Wheeler (1966) identified several client-related variables, such as social composition and social context, and several organizational characteristics, such as goals, processing technology, and organization-environment relations as determinants of client careers in socialization setting. Nevertheless, these attempts and other similar ones have been fragmentary and limited in scope. The most systematic effort to develop a comprehensive scheme relating client attributes and organizational variables to transactional outcomes has been conducted by Katz and Danet (1968, 1973). Viewing the staff-client encounter as a social system, they identify its input as consisting of the environment, the organization, and the situation, the through-put as the interaction itself; and the output as consisting of the evaluation of outcome re: (1) manner; (2) procedure; and (3) resources (Katz and Danet 1973:22). There are several important contributions that such a framework offers. First, it systematically articulates the components of the encounter following the logic of an open-system perspective. Second, it identifies more clearly the clusters of variables that shape each facet of the encounter, thus enabling a more systematic ordering and classification of the research on the subject matter. However, the model suffers from several limitations: (a) it does not differentiate clearly between client attributes and organizational variables; (*b*) it does not include a finite set of variables and is global in scope; and (*c*) it does not inform on how the variables relate to each other, thus making it difficult to generate specific hypotheses from it.

The model developed here takes off from the work of Katz and Danet (1968, 1973) and attempts to overcome the various limitations cited above. It also adopts the open-system perspective and its logic as a foundation; within this perspective it articulates a common set of client and organization dimensions as determinants of the encounter; and it shows how the model can be used to generate specific hypotheses, linking variables from both systems to elements of the encounter. It should be noted, in this context, that I use the term client simply to denote a person who finds it necessary to interact with human service organizations and, therefore, becomes their raw material. As I shall point out later, such interaction may be either voluntary or involuntary. Moreover, it is not assumed that the services provided by these organizations are always beneficial to the clients. In fact, there may be settings in which clients experience only costs (for example, prison). Finally, the model focuses on clients relating to the organizations as individuals rather than as organized collectivities, since the former is the more predominant mode of interaction with human service organizations.

Client-Organization Relations as Interaction of Two Systems

The starting point in the model building is to view both clients and organizations as purposeful and open systems with analogous functional components. That is, clients and organizations as units of analysis share similar system characteristics in the sense that each is an open system with the following characteristics: (1) a cyclic exchange of energy-information through input, throughput, and output; (2) negative entropy; (3) negative feedback; (4) steady state and dynamic homeostasis; (5) differentiation; and (6) selection of goals and means (Ackoff and Emery 1972:31; Katz and Kahn 1966:19–26). Client-organization relations are therefore a manifestation of the interaction between the two systems whereby there is an exchange of energy-information between the two which is essential to their self-maintenance and purpose. This is depicted schematically in figure 17.1 where both elements *d* and *j* represent the boundary subsystems of the client and the organization respectively. It should be noted that

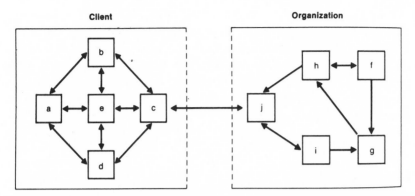

FIGURE 17.1 Client-Organization Relations as Interaction of Two Systems.

the interaction is not confined to elements *d* and *j* since through the course of interaction other elements from each system do exchange energy-information.

The central proposition that underlies the model is that the values assumed by the elements (that is, subsystems) in each system will determine the characteristics of the interaction between the organization and the client. Therefore, the first task is to identify the elements in each system relevant to the interaction. I will do so by viewing organizations and clients as analogous systems. The second task is to define the components and dynamics of the interaction. This will be done through the use of exchange theory (Blau 1964; White 1974).

CLIENT AND ORGANIZATIONS AS ANALOGOUS SYSTEMS

Following the systems perspective, the client and the organization can each be conceptualized as consisting of a similar set of functional subsystems essential to their self-maintenance and pursuit of objectives. These subsystems can be specified as follows:

1. *The boundary subsystem.* This is the set of transactional exchanges at the system boundaries aimed at procurement of needed inputs and disposal of output (Katz and Kahn 1966:89). For the client, these include affiliations with various social networks and activities to obtain personal resources and social status. For the organization, the subsystem functions to provide raw material, fiscal and manpower resources, marketing of output, and attainment of institutional legitimation.

2. *The normative subsystem.* This is the set of values and norms that enables the system to define its purpose and guide its choices. For the client, the subsystem is manifested in his cultural background, personal beliefs, and priority of needs. For the organization, it is expressed through domain consensus and organizational ideologies.

3. *The throughput subsystem.* This set of activities transforms the input of energy into a specified output. For the client, this is the repertoire of skills and competences needed to perform a particular behavior (Morely and Sheldon 1973). For the organization, it is the set of technologies used to transform the raw material (Perrow 1965).

4. *The learning and adaptive subsystem.* This set of activities enables the system to monitor and respond to a changing environment through information processing, feedback, and memory. For the client, this is expressed by such processes as perception, learning, and knowledge development (Kuhn 1974). For the organization, it includes intelligence activities, research and development, and planning.

5. *The control and coordination subsystem.* This set of activities is aimed to manage, control, and coordinate the various components of the system. For the client, it encompasses his decision-making processes, including preference ordering, search behavior, assessment of perceived costs and benefits, and choice based on a "satisficing" principle (Kuhn 1974). For the organization, this is the managerial component or the decision-making aspect of the organization (Katz and Kahn 1966) and involves the coordination of organizational components, decisions about major resource commitments, resolution of conflict, and coordination of external demands with organizational resources and needs.

THE COMPONENTS OF THE INTERACTION

Viewing organization-client relations as an exchange between two systems suggests that the central issue concerning these relations has to do with the ability of each system to optimize its interests. Put differently, I assume that the client will enter the relationship with the objective of getting needed resources and services and/or minimizing personal costs from the organization; while the organization aims to obtain from the client the resources needed to accomplish its objectives, enhance its self-maintenance, and minimize its costs in doing so. Thus, the ability of each system to obtain a favorable outcome from the exchange will depend on the amount of control each can exercise over the other.

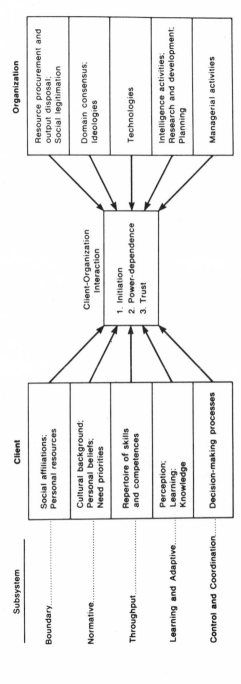

FIGURE 17.2 A Systems Model of Client-Organization Interaction.

From this perspective, three components of the interaction can be identified, each of which measures a particular facet of the underlying control dimension. The first component of interaction refers to the extent to which each system can control the initiation of the interaction (Carlson 1964). Clients who have complete control over the initiation of the interaction operate as consumers in the free market, while clients who lack any control are said to be involuntary subjects of organizational action. Similarly, organizations may vary in the degree of control they have over intake. The second component of the interaction refers to the power-dependence relations between the client and the organization. It focuses on the degree to which the two systems are interdependent in order to optimize their respective interests. The third component refers to the norms that govern the interaction, specifically the degree of trust the client and the organization have in each other (Bidwell 1970). Clearly, these components of the interaction are interrelated and affect one another. For example, when clients do not have control over the initiation of the interaction, the problem of establishing trust between themselves and the organization becomes greater. Similarly, the greater the dependence of the organization on client resources, the more will the organization attempt to induce clients to initiate the interaction. The entire model is presented schematically in figure 17.2.

Determinants of Client-Organization Interaction Patterns

The proposed model attempts to identify systematically *both* the client attributes and the organizational variables which may determine the characteristics of the interaction itself. In this section I will show how the model enables us to generate some specific hypotheses in guiding research and in evaluating existing studies on this subject. In doing so, two basic principles must be kept in mind. First, the cause-effect relations between client and organizational variables and the patterns of interaction are shaped by the exchange of energy-information between the two systems. Thus each system, in the pursuit of its purpose and self-maintenance, attempts to obtain needed resources and services controlled by the other system at minimal costs to itself. Second, each component of the interaction will be influenced primarily by those subsystems which are functionally relevant to it. (Since the control and coordination subsystem intersects all other subsystems, for much of the analysis it will be treated as a constraint.)

What follows are illustrations of the utility of the model in articulating the causal relations among the variables.

INITIATION OF THE INTERACTION

In general, the ability of clients and organizations to control the initiation of the interaction will be a function of their respective goals and values, their other boundary transactions, and their accumulated knowledge and intelligence. Specifically:

The larger the personal resources and the greater the organizational need for client resources, the greater the client control over the initiation of the interaction. Clients who possess many personal resources have a greater choice in the range of organizations they can approach and are less constrained by the costs involved in crossing organizational boundaries. Rushing (1971), for example, noted that rates of involuntary to voluntary commitment to mental hospitals were positively correlated with lower-class positions and unstable marital status, both measures of lack of individual resources. Similarly, Anderson and Anderson (1972) noted a positive relationship between financial security (through personal income or insurance) and utilization of health care services. However, this is a necessary but not a sufficient condition, since the lesser the dependence of the organization on the client's resources, the greater its ability to control its intake (Greenley and Kirk 1973). Similarly, as the need of the client for the organization's services increases, such need lessens his ability to control the initiation of the interaction. For this reason, for example, personal resources may be relatively unimportant in initiating requests for medical care when facing a serious medical problem (Suchman 1965).

The greater the congruency between the client's personal beliefs and organizational ideologies, the greater the willingness of both systems to initiate the interaction. Numerous studies have suggested that the failure to use services may be due to the fact that the client's cultural background, belief system, or need priorities are at variance with the predominant value orientation toward clients in the organization. Cloward and Epstein (1967) noted that the disengagement of family service agencies from the poor was partly due to the middle-class orientation of the professionals, who favored and sought out clients who shared a similar orientation. Similar conclusions were reached by Osofsky (1968) and Strauss (1969). McKinlay and McKinlay (1972) suggested that failure to use free prenatal care services by women of lower socioeconomic status might be due to the incompatibility between the need priorities of the women and the objectives of the clinics. Finally, Berkanovic and Reeder (1974) cite several field experiments by neighborhood health care centers which deliberately attempted to increase the cultural congruency of the organizational mode of service delivery. These experiments brought about a significant increase in the use of the centers.

The greater the amount of client knowledge about organizational services and the greater the dissemination of information by the organization, the greater the client's control over the initiation of the interaction. Knowledge of alternative organizational services, quality of services, eligibility criteria, and the like enable potential clients to make choices and to assess the outcome of alternative courses of action. For this reason the client's social network or lay referral system assumes an important role in the initiation of interaction. The more knowledgeable the lay referral system, the greater the effectiveness of the client in selecting appropriate and better quality human services (Freidson 1961; Kadushin 1969). In contrast, as shown by Levine and Taube (1970), clients lacking knowledge of the availability of organizational services and the procedures to obtain them were less likely to receive adequate housing-related services. The rise of numerous consumer advocacy groups can be seen in part as an attempt to provide clients with better knowledge of organizational services and thus help them to gain some measure of control over the initiation of transactions with public officials (see, for example, Kahn 1970). Similarly, I suggest that some of the effectiveness of client rights organizations, such as the National Welfare Rights Organization, in enabling clients to initiate effectively and receive services from public bureaucracies has been due to the bureaucratic knowledge they have provided clients (Cloward and Elman 1966).

Nevertheless, the client's knowledge is clearly constrained by the willingness of the organization to disseminate and share information about its services. In fact, organizations that wish to control their intake are likely to be highly selective as to the nature of the information they provide and to whom they give it. As Kadushin (1969) points out, psychoanalytic therapists and clinics use a carefully controlled information dissemination process—primarily through persons who are part of the "psychoanalytic system"—to control the flow of "appropriate" patients.

Similarly, one of the most effective mechanisms utilized by human service organizations to control their intake is through the designation of selected referral "gatekeepers" who receive privileged information about the nature of the services offered, and the desired clientele, while the potential clients and other agencies may be kept in ignorance regarding effective referral procedures (Greenley and Kirk 1973).

It should be noted, in this context, that organizational intelligence activities aimed at identifying environmental developments and changes affecting the supply and demand for services will affect the initiation of client-organization transactions. Organizations sensitive to the changing needs of the population and the developments in other human services can adapt and adjust their own service delivery systems so that congruency between the client's needs and values and the organizational goals is preserved. Moreover, such intelligence activities are also likely to assist potential clients and referring agents by informing them about the actual services offered.

POWER-DEPENDENCE RELATIONS

The power-dependence relations between the client and the organization will determine the ability of each to direct the interaction in a manner congruent with its interests. Paraphrasing Thompson (1967:30), a client is dependent on the service organization: 1) in proportion to his need for resources or for the performances the organization provides, and 2) in inverse proportion to the ability of others to provide the same resources or performances. The same, of course, can be said about the organization's dependence on the client. Interdependence, therefore, implies that both systems control important resources needed by each that cannot be easily obtained elsewhere. The advantage of such a perspective is not only in avoiding the "zero-sum" concept of power relations but also in indicating that each system may exercise power in very specific and delineated areas. The frequently espoused cliché that clients are powerless vis-à-vis bureaucracy may result from the failure to recognize this important fact.

It can be deduced from the paradigm (figure 17.2) that the power-dependence relations will be determined by the resources or performances available or needed by each subsystem. That is, to carry out its function, each organizational subsystem may need certain client resources or performances, while the client depends on the resources and activities of various organizational subsystems to satisfy his service needs. This further attests to the multidimensionality and complexity of these relations.

For the sake of brevity I will illustrate how the paradigm can be used to generate hypotheses concerning the conditions under which the power-dependence relations between the client and the organization will be characterized as interdependent. It will be assumed, unless otherwise specified, that the clients have a high need for the organization's services, and therefore seek to interact with it.

The more the client provides important resources and/or sources of legitimation to the organization the greater the degree of interdependence between them. Clients may be important suppliers of income, of scarce "raw material," and be important legitimators of the organization's performance and existence. This is aptly demonstrated in the case of private schools (Bidwell 1970:53–54). Both the study by Clark (1956) of the transformation of the adult education program and that by Zald and Denton (1963) of the changes in the YMCA indicate that as the dependence of these organizations on income generated by clients increased, programmatic changes occurred that reflected more closely clients' demands. An extreme example of organizational dependence on clients as instruments in the solicitation of funds is presented in a study by Scott (1967) of agencies for the blind. In this instance, the dependence on blind children and employable adults to launch effective fund-raising campaigns resulted not only in competition for such clients, but also in the reluctance of such agencies to let these clients exit.

Similarly, organizations may seek out clients who possess the appropriate attributes to insure success on those performance criteria used by key legitimating units in assessing the organization. For example, vocational rehabilitation programs evaluated on the basis of successful employment placement of clients are likely to avoid clients least attractive to employers and seek out potentially successful cases, resulting in a high degree of interdependence between the rehabilitation workers and "attractive" clients (Krause 1966).

The greater the match between the technological requirements of the organization and the attributes and behavioral repertoire of the client the greater the interdependence between them. The hypothesis is based on the fact that every human service technology, in order to be operative, requires that clients possess a certain set of attributes and behavioral repertoire. For example, the success of the conventional educational technology is predicated on having pupils with an acceptable level of intelligence, motivation to learn, and a middle-class behavioral repertoire. As a result, there is a high degree of interdependence between teachers and children possessing these attributes, while children lacking them are rejected (Rist 1970). In the same vein, it has been argued by several writers that psychotherapeutic technologies favor clients who possess middle-class attributes, thus leading to the rejection and disengagement of clients from lower socioeconomic status (Cloward and Epstein 1967; Ryan 1971; Teele and Levine 1968). Furthermore, the attributes of the clients and the technological requirements may be such that they necessitate close interdependence between the client and the practitioner in order to achieve successful results. This is analogous to what Szasz and Hollender (1970) term the mutual participation model, as exemplified in the treatment of diabetes mellitus. Henry (1957), in a classic analysis of the Orthogenic School, suggests that extraordinary interdependence between workers and children was achieved because the workers' own personal growth and development were tied to the therapeutic progress of the child.

In the human services there are intimate linkages between service technologies and organizational ideologies and the distinctions between the two are frequently blurred (see, for example, Perrow 1965). Specifically, organizational ideologies regarding the moral worth of the client, attribution of responsibility to the client, and beliefs about desired outcomes are major determinants of how staff define their role, how they relate to clients, and how they assess service outcomes. Consequently, the affirmation of these ideologies may often depend on the behavioral and normative responses of the client. Therefore:

The greater the reliance of staff on the client's beliefs and behaviors to affirm service ideologies, the greater the interdependence between them. Rapoport, Rapoport, and Rosow's study (1960) of the therapeutic milieu clearly demonstrates that the need to confirm this treatment ideology through the attitudes and behavior of the patients resulted in a high degree of interdependence between therapists and patients. Similarly, the study by Scott (1969) shows that workers in agencies for the blind could work only with clients who have accepted and behaved in accordance with the organization's rehabilitation ideology.

Finally, in this context, it should be noted that the exercise of power by the organization (and the client) is constrained by a normative system that defines the conditions under which such power can be exercised and that is expressed through policy and administrative regulations, law, and professional codes. These in turn may be invoked and enforced when clients perceive inappropriate use of such power. Therefore, the greater the knowledge that clients have of this normative system, the better the likelihood that they could protect themselves from the abuse of power by staff. It is in this sense that one can perhaps explain why clients with bureaucratic competence are likely to have greater success in dealing with bureaucracy (Gordon 1974). And, as Katz and Danet (1966) have demonstrated, successful appeals to public officials occur when the appeals are addressed to the normative basis upon which the organization rests.

TRUST

Trust is an attitude and a belief about the outcome of the interaction *and* the manner in which it is conducted. That is, client trust in the staff of the organization is a belief in the quality and desirability of their performance and confidence in their methods and mode of conduct (Bidwell 1970). Concomitantly, the trust that the staff have toward the client is a belief that the client will not abuse the relationship and attempt to exploit it for illegitimate purposes (for example, obtaining drugs for faked symptoms, receiving aid via falsified information). Clearly, without trust the staff cannot hope to gain access to the client's life space and employ intervention techniques that require exposure of the client's private domain, and the client cannot hope to obtain the moral commitment of the staff to respond to his needs. In both instances, each system uses trust as a mechanism of control over the other system. Thus, for example, the greater the client's trust in the organization, the greater its potential control over him.

The establishment and maintenance of trust relations between clients and organizations is an exceedingly complex and vexing issue and beyond the scope of this paper. Rather, I will attempt to show how the paradigm presented here can be used to begin identifying some of the parameters that may set the broad conditions for the emergence of trust. It should be noted that there is a conspicuous dearth of empirical research on this variable, which further limits the scope of this inquiry. Since trust involves beliefs about outcomes and the means to achieve them, it seems that the subsystems most relevant in this context will be the normative, and the throughput. Thus:

The greater the perceived congruency between the client's personal goals and the organization's output goals, the greater the degree of trust between them. For the client, such congruency assures him that the outcome of the organizational intervention in his life will serve his needs and therefore provide him with a positive impetus to put himself in the hands of the staff (Conviser 1973). Similarly, the organization is less concerned that the client will use it for side transactions (Thompson 1962). It is partly for this reason that clients express greater satisfaction with fee-for-service medical practice, since in such a system physicians are motivated to foster the congruency between the patient's personal goals and the treatment objectives (Freidson 1970b:305–6). In contrast, clients who attempt to use emergency rooms for routine medical problems experience considerable mistrust from the medical personnel (Roth 1972).

Street, Vinter, and Perrow (1966) found that in those correctional settings where staff were more attuned to the personal needs of the inmates, greater trust and positive interaction between staff and inmates developed. And David (1968) found that patients' compliance with doctors' advice (a sign of trust) was partially based on the congruency of values and expectations between them.

An important facilitator of the development of trust relations is the ability of both the client and the organization to control the initiation of the interaction. That is, to the extent to which both systems can select and control the specific systems they interact with, they are able, among other things, to insure that such congruency will be attained. Put differently, trust relations are much more likely to emerge if the relationship is voluntary.

The greater the prestige and reputation of the organization and the more diffused the client's knowledge of the organization, the greater the client's trust in the organization. To the public, the prestige and reputation of the organization are indicators of excellence of the services provided by the organization and of the competence of its personnel—the major ingredients in the establishment of trust (Bidwell 1970). Yet, much of the potency of the organization's prestige and reputation is based on the fact that it provides diffused and selective knowledge about itself. As clients gain more specific knowledge about the organization through past experiences and the lay and professional referral systems, they are less likely to accept the prestige of organizational staff at face value. Rather, the client is more likely to withhold his trust until concrete actions by staff point to their trustworthiness. Hence, clients who possess technical knowledge about the intervention techniques of the organization are more likely to question the decisions made by staff and to challenge their authority, which is why, argues Freidson (1970b), physicians like to control all communications to their patients.

The more the organizational technology treats the client as a subject and the more the client is capable of active decision-making, the greater the trust between the two. The assumptions about the client incorporated in the human service technology vary along a continuum ranging from the client as a subject to the client as an object. In the former, the client is perceived as a person who can actively participate in decision-making about himself, a person who can control his fate. In the latter, the client is seen as passive and incapable of participating in making decisions about his fate. Howard (1975) reviewed a large body of literature on physician-patient relations and concluded that a humanizing and trusting relationship can emerge only when the patient is treated as a subject rather than as an object (see also David 1968; Freidson 1970b). Studies of the "therapeutic community" model in the treatment of mental patients, in which patients are encouraged to participate actively in decisions about their treatment, also point to increased trust and openness in the relations between staff and patients (see, for example, Jones 1968).

Similarly, studies of teacher-student interaction patterns, although not measuring trust directly, seem to suggest that when teachers encourage students to participate in decision-making and to make choices in curricular matters, there is greater acceptance of the teachers and improved classroom morale (Larkin 1975).

For trust to emerge, organizational orientation toward clients as subjects is a necessary, but not sufficient, condition. Surely, the client needs to be equipped with the necessary behavioral repertoire that will enable him to become an active participant in the decision-making process concerning the intervention technology. When the technology sets behavioral expectations for the client which cannot be met, he is likely to experience frustration and to develop mistrust toward the staff. Rapoport, Rapoport, and Rosow (1960) noted this problem in their study of the therapeutic milieu, where patients were expected to participate in decisions for which they lacked competence. Thus, for example, clients who are accustomed to accept passively the authority of officials may react quite negatively and with mistrust when asked to participate actively in decisions about their treatment. Moreover, when patients are unexpectedly asked to participate in decision-making about their course of treatment, they may perceive this as a manipulative device by the organization to insure compliance rather than a way of sharing the power to decide (Etzioni 1960). Finally, *trust will be a function of the interaction between the form of compliance used by the organization in conjunction with its intervention technologies and the client's cultural orientation toward compliance.* Following Etzioni (rev. 1975), one can distinguish among three forms of compliance—normative, utilitarian, and coercive. The organization can use persuasion, inducements, and constraints to achieve each form of compliance respectively (Gamson 1968). Similarly the client, depending on his socialization, social affiliations, and personal experiences, will develop a cultural orientation toward compliance (that is, how compliance should be achieved) along the same categories. It is clear that trust relations cannot be established under conditions of coercion (for example, prison), but through inducements or persuasion. Assuming that the client's cultural orientation toward compliance may be either normative, utilitarian, or coercive, it is possible to predict the effects on trust of the deployment of the three means of control by the organization, following the principle suggested by Gamson (1968). See table 17.1.

That is, when the correspondence between the client's orientation and the organization's means of control is along the diagonal, the initial level of trust will remain unchanged, while the interaction between the two below the diagonal will increase trust and above the diagonal will decrease trust, based on the proposition that trust increases with the movement from coercive to normative compliance.

Table 17.1. Effects of Client's Cultural Orientation and the Organization's Means of Control on Client Trust

Client's Cultural Orientation	Organization's Means of Control		
	Persuasion	*Inducements*	*Constraints*
Normative	M	–	–
Utilitarian	+	M	–
Coercive	+	+	M

M = Maintain current level of trust.
+ = Increase level of trust.
– = Decrease level of trust.

Conclusion

This paper attempts to formulate a framework for the study of client-organization relations, based on open-system concepts and exchange theory principles. Both the client and the organization are viewed as open systems, each with an analogous set of subsystems. The interaction between the client and the organization is conceived as an exchange of energy-information, whereby each system attempts to obtain needed resources from the other system in a manner that optimizes payoff and minimizes costs. Three major components of the interaction are treated as dependent variables: (1) control over the initiation of the interaction; (2) power-dependent relations; and (3) trust. These variables measure the amount of control that each system exercises over the other. It has been shown how the model can be used to generate specific hypotheses that focus on the interaction between organizational variables and client attributes as predictive of client-organization relations.

Hence, it is believed that a major contribution of the proposed framework is its emphasis on the simultaneous effects of *both* sets of variables on client-organization relations, thereby enabling us to test the relative contribution of variables from each set as well as their interaction effect in explaining variance in these relations. In particular, the utilization of the social exchange theory enables us to generate specific hypotheses about the causal relations between client attributes, organizational variables, and the components of client-organization interaction. Moreover, should these hypotheses prove to be correct, as the review of the literature seems to indicate, they have important implications for the practitioners who are committed to enhance the responsiveness of human service organizations to their clients. The model points to the type of organization variables *and* client attributes that need to be changed in order to increase the congruency between human service organizations and their clients.

Nevertheless, the framework is not without its shortcomings that must receive attention as it is being further developed and refined. First, there must be greater specification of the relevant variables in each of the subsystems. An inherent problem in the use of a systems approach is the high level of abstraction that it forces on the investigator and the use of system dimensions that are too encompassing. Hence, as research continues on the subject, it should be possible to tease out the key variables from each system and develop more specific causal models. Second, the interaction between clients and organizations is viewed from a social exchange theory. Nevertheless there are limitations in such an approach, particularly in its applicability to public organizations. In such organizations, client-staff transactions are more likely to be controlled by universalistic norms that severely constrain the discretion of officials (Kroeger 1974). Thus, more attention must be given to conditions external to the client and the organization that constrain their exchange relations. Put differently, the social context in which both clients and organizations are embedded will set some definite boundaries as to the structure and the content of their interaction. Thus it must be explicitly defined and incorporated in study of client-organization relations.

18

SOME CONTINGENCIES OF THE MORAL EVALUATION AND CONTROL OF CLIENTELE

Julius A. Roth

THE moral evaluation of patients by staff members has been explored in detail in the case of "mental illness" (Belknap 1956; Goffman 1961:125–70, 321–86; Hollingshead and Redlich 1958; Scheff 1964, 1966, ch. 5; Strauss et al. 1964, chs. 8 and 12; Szasz 1960). The assumption is made by some (especially Thomas Szasz) that mental illness is a special case which readily allows moral judgments to be made because there are no technical criteria to be applied and because psychiatric concepts in their historical development have been a pseudoscientific replacement of moral judgments. Perrow (1965) stresses lack of technology as a factor which forces psychiatric practitioners to fall back on commonsense concepts of humanitarianism which open the way to moral evaluations of the clientele.

I contend that the diagnosis and treatment of mental illness and the "care" of mental patients are not unique in incorporating moral judgments of the clientele, but are only obvious examples of a more general phenomenon which exists no matter what the historical development or the present state of the technology. Glaser and Strauss (1964) put forward such a notion when they demonstrated how the "social worth" of a dying patient affects the nursing care he will receive. I would add that moral evaluation also has a direct effect on a physician's diagnosis and treatment recommendations. This is obvious in extreme cases, such as when a monarch or the president of the United States is attended by teams of highly qualified diag-

From *American Journal of Sociology* (March 1972), 77:839–56. Reprinted by permission.

nosticians to insure a detailed and accurate diagnosis and has outstanding specialists flown to his bedside to carry out the treatment. I will discuss some aspects of this same process as it applies on a day-to-day basis in a routine hospital operation involving more "ordinary" patients.

The data are taken from observation of six hospital emergency services in two parts of the country—one Northeastern location and one West Coast location. My coworkers and I spent several periods of time (spread over two or three months in each case) in the emergency department of each of the hospitals. In one hospital we worked as intake clerks over a period of three months. At other times we observed areas in the emergency unit without initiating any interaction with patients, visitors, or personnel. At other points we followed patients through the emergency service from their first appearance to discharge or inpatient admission, interviewing patient and staff during the process. During these periods of observation, notes were also kept on relevant conversations with staff members.

The hospital emergency service is a setting where a minimum of information is available about the character of each patient and a long-term relationship with the patient is usually not contemplated. Even under these conditions, judgments about a patient's moral fitness and the appropriateness of his visit to an emergency service are constantly made, and staff action concerning the patient—including diagnosis, treatment, and disposition of the case—are, in part, affected by these judgments.

The Deserving and the Undeserving

The evaluation of patients and visitors by emergency ward staff may be conveniently thought of in two categories: (1) the application by the staff of concepts of social worth common in the larger society; (2) staff members' concepts of their appropriate work role. In this section I will take up the first of these.

There is a popular myth (generated in part by some sociological writing) that persons engaged in providing professional services, especially medical care, do not permit the commonly accepted concepts of social worth in our culture to affect their relationship to the clientele. An on-the-spot description of any service profession—medicine, education, law, social welfare, and so forth—should disabuse us of this notion. There is no evidence that professional training succeeds in creating a universalistic moral neutrality (Becker et al. 1961:323–27). On the contrary, we are on much safer ground to assume that those engaged in dispensing professional services (or any other services) will apply the evaluations of social worth common to their culture and will modify their services with respect to those evaluations unless discouraged from doing so by the organizational arrangements under which they work. Some such organizational arrangements do exist on emergency wards. The rapid turnover and impersonality of the operation are in themselves a protection for many patients who might be devalued if more were known about them. In public hospitals, at least, there is a rule that all patients presenting themselves at the registration desk must be seen by a doctor, and clerks and nurses know that violation of this rule, if discovered, can get them into serious trouble. (Despite this, patients are occasionally refused registration, usually because they are morally repugnant to the clerk.) Such arrangements restrict the behavior of the staff only to a limited extent, however. There remains a great deal of room for expressing one's valuation of the patient in the details of processing and treatment.

One common concept of social worth held by emergency ward personnel is that the young are more valuable than the old. This is exemplified most dramatically in the marked differences in efforts to resuscitate young and old patients (Glaser and Strauss 1964; Sudnow 1967:100–109). "Welfare cases" who are sponging off the taxpayer—especially if they represent the product of an immoral life (such as a woman with illegitimate children to support)—do not deserve the best care. Persons of higher status in the larger society are likely to be accorded more respectful treatment in the emergency ward just as they often are in other service or customer relationships, and conversely those of lower status are treated with less consideration. (The fact that higher-status persons are more likely to make an effective complaint or even file lawsuits may be an additional reason for such differential treatment.)

Of course, staff members vary in the manner and degree to which they apply these cultural concepts of social worth in determining the quality of their service to the clientele. The point is that they are in a position to alter the nature of their service in terms of such differentiation, and all of them—porters, clerks, nursing personnel, physicians—do so to some extent. Despite some variations, we did in fact find widespread agreement on the negative evaluation of some categories of patients—evaluations which directly affected the treatment provided. Those who are the first to process a patient play a crucial role in moral categorization because staff members at later stages of the processing are inclined to accept earlier categories without question unless they detect clear-cut evidence to the contrary. Thus, registration clerks can often determine how long a person will have to wait and what kind of treatment area he is sent to and, occasionally, can even prevent a person from seeing a doctor at all. Some patients have been morally categorized by policemen or ambulance crewmen before they even arrive at the hospital—categorization which affects the priority and kind of service given.

In the public urban hospital emergency service, the clientele is heavily skewed toward the lower end of the socioeconomic scale, and nonwhite and non-Anglo ethnic groups are greatly overrepresented. Also, many patients are in the position of supplicating the staff for help, sometimes for a condition for which the patient can be held responsible. With such a population, the staff can readily maintain a stance of moral superiority. They see the bulk of the patients as people undeserving of the services available to them. Staff members maintain that they need not tolerate any abuse or disobedience from patients or visitors. Patients and visitors may be issued orders which they are expected to obey. The staff can, and sometimes does, shout down patients and visitors and threaten them with ejection from the premises. The staff demands protection against possible attack and also against the possibility of lawsuits, which are invariably classified as unjustified. There is no need to be polite to the clientele and, in fact, some clerks frequently engage patients and visitors in arguments. The staff also feels justified in refusing service to those who complain or resist treatment or refuse to follow procedures or make trouble in any other way. From time to time the clients are referred to as "garbage," "scum," "liars," "deadbeats," people who "come out from under the rocks," by doctors, nurses, aides, clerks, and even people who sweep the floor. When we spent the first several days of a new medical year with a new group of interns on one emergency service, we found that an important part of the orientation was directed toward telling the interns that the patients were not to be trusted and did not have to be treated politely. At another public hospital, new registration clerks were told during their first few days of work that they would have to learn not to accept the word of patients but to treat everything they say with suspicion.

Despite the general negative conception of the clientele, differentiations are made between patients on the basis of clues which they present. Since this is typically a fleeting relationship where the staff member has little or no background information about the patient, evaluations must usually be made quickly on the basis or readily perceivable clues. Race, age, mode of dress, language and accents and word usage, and the manner in which the client addresses and responds to staff members are all immediate clues on which staff base their initial evaluations. A little questioning brings out other information which may be used for or against a patient: financial status, type of employment, insurance protection, use of private-practice doctors, nature of medical complaint, legitimacy of children, marital status, previous use of hospital services. In the case of unconscious or seriously ill or injured patients, a search of the wallet or handbag often provides informative clues about social worth.

Some characteristics consistently turn staff against patients and affect the quality of care given. Dirty, smelly patients cause considerable comment among the staff, and efforts are made to isolate them or get rid of them. Those dressed as hippies or women with scanty clothing are frowned upon and are more likely to be kept waiting and to be rushed through when they are attended to. We observed hints that certain ethnic groups are discriminated against, but this is difficult to detect nowadays because everyone is extremely sensitive to the possibility of accusations of racial discrimination. If a woman with a child is tabbed a "welfare case" (from her dress, speech, and manner, or in the explicit form of a welfare card which she presents), the clerk is likely to ask, "Is there a father in the house?" while better-dressed, better-spoken women with children are questioned more discreetly.

Attributes and Categories: a Reciprocal Relationship

On one level, it is true to say that the staff's moral evaluation of a patient influences the kind of treatment he gets in the emergency room. But this kind of causal explanation obscures important aspects of the network of interrelationships involved. On another, the definition of devalued or favored categories and the attributes of the patient reinforce each other in a reciprocal manner.

Take, for example, patients who are labeled as drunks. They are more consistently treated as undeserving than any other category of patient. They are frequently handled as if they were baggage when they are brought in by police; those with lacerations are often roughly treated by physicians; they are usually treated only for drunkenness and obvious surgical repair without being examined for other pathology; no one believes their stories; their statements are ridiculed; they are treated in an abusive or jocular manner; they are ignored for long periods of time; in one hospital they are placed in a room separate from most other patients. Emergency-ward personnel frequently comment on how they hate to take care of drunks.

Thus, it might seem that the staff is applying a simple moral syllogism: drunks do not deserve to be cared for; this patient is a drunk, therefore, he does not deserve good treatment. But how do we know that he is drunk? By the way he is treated. Police take him directly to the drunk room. If we ask why the police define him as drunk, they may answer that they smell alcohol on his breath. But not all people with alcohol on their breath are picked up by the police and taken to a hospital emergency room. The explanation must come in terms of some part of the patient's background—he was in a lower-class neighborhood, his style of dress was dirty and sloppy, he was unattended by any friend or family member, and so on. When he comes to the emergency room he has already been defined as a drunk. There is no reason for the emergency room personnel to challenge this definition; it is routine procedure and it usually proves correct in so far as they know. There is nothing to do for drunks except to give them routine medications and let them sleep it off. To avoid upsetting the rest of the emergency room, there is a room set aside for them. The police have a standard procedure of taking drunks to that room, and the clerks place them there if they come in on their own and are defined as drunk on the basis, not only of their breath odor (and occasionally there is no breath odor in someone defined as drunk), but in terms of their dress, manner, and absence of protectors. The physicians, having more pressing matters, tend to leave the drunks until last. Of course, they may miss some pathology which could cause unconsciousness or confusion because they believe the standard procedure proves correct in the great majority of cases. They really do not know how often it does not prove correct since they do not check up closely enough to uncover other forms of pathology in most cases, and the low social status of the patients and the fact that they are seldom accompanied by anyone who will protect them means that complaints about inadequate

examination will be rare. There are occasional challenges by doctors—
"How do you know he's drunk?"—but in most cases the busy schedule
of the house officer leaves little time for such luxuries as a careful
examination of patients who have already been defined as drunks by
others. Once the drunk label has been accepted by the emergency-
room staff, a more careful examination is not likely to be made unless
some particularly arresting new information appears (for example,
the patient has convulsions, a relative appears to tell them that he
has diabetes, an examination of his wallet shows him to be a solid
citizen), and the more subtle pathologies are not likely to be
discovered.

Thus, it is just as true to say that the label of "drunk" is accepted
by hospital personnel because of the way the patient is treated as it
is to say that he is treated in a certain way because he is drunk.
Occasional cases show how persons with alcohol on their breath will
not be treated as drunks. When an obviously middle-class man
(obvious in terms of his dress, speech, and demands for service) was
brought in after an automobile accident, he was not put in the drunk
room, although he had a definite alcohol odor, but was given
relatively quick treatment in one of the other examining rooms and
addressed throughout in a polite manner.

Most drunks are men. A common negative evaluation for women
is PID (pelvic inflammatory disease). This is not just a medical
diagnostic category, but, by implication, a moral judgment. There
are many women with difficult-to-diagnose abdominal pains and
fever. If these women are black, young, unmarried, lower class in
appearance and speech, and have no one along to champion their
cause, doctors frequently make the assumption that they have before
them the end results of a dissolute sex life, unwanted pregnancy and
perhaps venereal disease, illegal abortion, and consequent infection
of the reproductive organs. The label PID is then attached and the
patient relegated to a group less deserving of prompt and considerate
treatment. This is not the same thing as saying a diagnosis of PID
leads to rejection by medical personnel.

We observed one patient who had been defined as a troublemaker
because of his abusive language and his insistence that he be released
immediately. When he began to behave in a strange manner (random
thrashing about), the police were promptly called to control him and
they threatened him with arrest. A patient who was not defined as
a troublemaker and exhibited like behavior prompted an effort on

the part of the staff to provide a medical explanation for his actions. Here again, we see that the category into which the patient has been placed may have more effect on determining the decisions of medical personnel than does his immediate behavior.

Thus, it is not simply a matter of finding which "objective" pathological states medical personnel like or dislike dealing with. The very definition of these pathological states depends in part on how the patient is categorized in moral terms by the screening and treatment personnel.

The Legitimate and the Illegitimate

The second type of evaluation is that related to the staff members' concept of their appropriate work roles (Strauss et al. 1964, ch. 13). Every worker has a notion of what demands are appropriate to his position. When demands fall outside that boundary, he feels that the claim is illegitimate. What he does about it depends on a number of factors, including his alternatives, his power to control the behavior of others, and his power to select his clientele (more on this later).

The interns and residents who usually man the larger urban emergency services like to think of this assignment as a part of their training which will give them a kind of experience different from the outpatient department or inpatient wards. Here they hope to get some practice in resuscitation, in treating traumatic injuries, in diagnosing and treating medical emergencies. When patients who are no different from those they have seen *ad nauseam* in the outpatient department present themselves at the emergency ward, the doctors in training believe that their services are being misused. Also, once on the emergency ward, the patient is expected to be "cooperative" so that the doctor is not blocked in his effort to carry out his tasks. Nurses, clerks, and others play "little doctor" and to this extent share the concepts of the boundaries of legitimacy of the doctors. But, in addition to the broadly shared perspective, each specialty has its own notions of appropriate patient attributes and behavior based on its own work demands. Thus, clerks expect patients to cooperate in getting forms filled out. Patients with a "good reason," unconsciousness, for example, are excused from cooperating with clerical procedures, but other patients who are unable to give requested information or who protest against certain questions bring upon themselves condemnation by the clerks who believe that a

person who subverts their efforts to complete their tasks has no
business on the emergency ward.

A universal complaint among those who operate emergency services is that hospital emergency rooms are "abused" by the public—or
rather by a portion of the public. This is particularly the case in the
city and county hospitals and voluntary hospitals with training
programs subsidized by public funds which handle the bulk of
emergency cases in urban areas. The great majority of cases are
thought of as too minor or lacking in urgency to warrant a visit to
the emergency room. They are "outpatient cases" (OPD cases), that
is, patients who could wait until the outpatient department is open,
or if they can afford private care, they could wait until a physician
is holding his regular office hours. Patients should not use the
emergency room just because it gives quicker service than the
outpatient department or because the hours are more convenient
(since it is open all the time). Pediatricians complain about their day
filled with "sore throats and snotty noses." Medical interns and
residents complain about all the people presenting long-standing or
chronic diseases which, though sometimes serious, do not belong in
the emergency room. In every hospital—both public and private—
where we made observations or conducted interviews, we repeatedly
heard the same kinds of "atrocity stories": a patient with a sore throat
of two-weeks' duration comes in at 3:00 A.M. on Sunday and expects
immediate treatment from an intern whom he has got out of bed (or
such variations as an itch of seventy-five days' duration, a congenital
defect in a one-year-old child—always coming in at an extremely
inconvenient hour).

Directors of emergency services recognize that some of their
preoccupation with cases which are not "true emergencies" is not
simply a matter of "abuse" by patients, but the result of tasks imposed
upon them by other agencies—for example, giving routine antibiotic
injections on weekends, caring for abandoned children, giving routine
blood transfusions, receiving inpatient admissions, giving gamma
globulin, providing venereal disease follow-up, examining jail prisoners, arranging nursing home dispositions for the aged. But the
blame for most of their difficulty is placed upon the self-referred
patient who, according to the emergency room staff, does not make
appropriate use of their service.

The OPD case typically gets hurried, routine processing with little
effort at a careful diagnostic work-up or sophisticated treatment

unless he happens to strike the doctor as an interesting case (in which case he is no longer classified as an OPD case). Thus, pediatric residents move rapidly through their mass of sore throats and snotty noses with a quick look in ears and throat with the otolaryngoscope, a throat swab to be sent to the laboratory, and if the child does not have a high fever (the nurse has already taken his temperature), the parent is told to check on the laboratory results the next day, the emergency ward form is marked "URI" (upper respiratory infection), and the next child moves up on the treadmill. If a patient or a visitor has given anyone trouble, his care is likely to deteriorate below the routine level. Often, doctors define their task in OPD cases as simply a stopgap until the patient gets to OPD on a subsequent day, and therefore a careful work-up is not considered necessary.

Medical cases are considered illegitimate more often than surgical cases. In our public hospital tabulations, the diagnostic categories highest in the illegitimate category were gynecology, genitourinary, dental, and "other medical." The lowest in proportion of illegitimate cases were pediatrics (another bit of evidence that children are more acceptable patients than adults), beatings and stabbings, industrial injuries, auto accidents, other accidents, and "other surgical." Much of the surgical work is suturing lacerations and making other repairs. Although these are not necessarily serious in terms of danger to life (very few were), such injuries were seen by the staff as needing prompt attention (certainly within twenty-four hours) to reduce the risk of infection and to avoid scarring or other deformity.

It is not surprising that in surgical cases the attributes and behavior of the patients are of lesser consequence than in medical cases. The ease with which the condition can be defined and the routine nature of the treatment (treating minor lacerations becomes so routine that anyone thinks he can do it—medical students, aides, volunteers) means that the characteristics and behavior of the patient can be largely ignored unless he becomes extremely disruptive. (Even violence can be restrained and the treatment continued without much trouble.) Certain other things are handled with routine efficiency— high fevers in children; asthma, overdose, maternity cases. It is significant that standard rules can be and have been laid down in such cases so that everyone—clerks, nurses, doctors (and patients once they have gone through the experience)—knows just how to proceed. In such cases, the issue of legitimacy seldom arises.

We find no similar routines with set rules in the case of complaints

of abdominal pains, delusions, muscle spasms, depression, or diges-
tive upset. Here the process of diagnosis is much more subtle and
complex, the question of urgency much more debatable and uncertain. The way is left open for all emergency ward staff members
involved to make a judgment about whether the case is appropriate
to and deserving of their service. Unless the patient is a "regular,"
no one on the emergency service is likely to have background
information on the patient, and the staff will have to rely entirely on
clues garnered from his mode of arrival, his appearance, his behavior,
the kind of people who accompany him, and so on. The interpretation
of these clues then becomes crucial to further treatment and, to the
casual observer, may appear to be the cause of such treatment.

It is also not surprising that "psychiatric cases" are usually considered illegitimate. Interns and residents do not (unless they are
planning to go into psychiatry) find such cases useful for practicing
their diagnostic and treatment skills,[1] and therefore regard such
patients as an unwelcome intrusion. But what constitutes a psychiatric
case is not based on unvarying criteria. An effort is usually made to
place a patient in a more explicit medical category. For example, a
wrist slashing is a surgical case requiring suturing. An adult who
takes an overdose of sleeping pills is a medical case requiring lavage
and perhaps antidotes. Only when a patient is troublesome—violent,
threatening suicide, disturbing other patients—is the doctor forced
to define him as a psychiatric case about whom a further decision
must be made. (In some clinics, psychiatrists are attempting to
broaden the definition by making interns and residents aware of
more subtle cues for justifying a psychiatric referral and providing
them with a consulting service to deal with such cases. However, they
must provide a prompt response when called upon, or their service
will soon go unused.)

It is no accident either that in private hospitals (especially those
without medical school or public clinic affiliation) the legitimacy of
a patient depends largely on his relationship to the private medical
system. A standard opening question to the incoming patient in such
hospitals is, "Who is your doctor?" A patient is automatically legitimate
if referred by a physician on the hospital staff (or the physician's
nurse, receptionist, or answering service). If he has not been referred,
but gives the name of a staff doctor whom the nurse can reach and
who agrees to handle the case, the patient is also legitimate. However,
if he does not give a staff doctor's name, he falls under suspicion.

The hospital services, including the emergency room, are designed primarily to serve the private physicians on the staff. A patient who does not fit into this scheme threatens to upset the works. It is the receptionist's or receiving nurse's job to try to establish the proper relationship by determining whether the case warrants the service of the contract physician or the doctor on emergency call, and if so, to see to it that the patient gets into the hands of an attending staff doctor for follow-up treatment if necessary. Any patient whose circumstances make this process difficult or impossible becomes illegitimate. This accounts for the bitter denunciation of the "welfare cases" and the effort to deny admission to people without medical insurance or other readily tappable funds. ("Welfare cases" include not only those who present welfare cards, but all who are suspected of trying to work the system to get free or low-priced care. Most physicians on the hospital staff do not want such people as patients, and feel they have been tricked if a colleague talks them into accepting them as patients; neither does the hospital administration want them as inpatients.) Also, such hospitals have no routine mechanism for dealing with welfare cases, as have the public hospitals which can either give free treatment or refer the patient to a social worker on the premises. Such patients are commonly dealt with by transferring them to a public clinic or hospital if their condition permits.

The negative evaluation of patients is strongest when they combine an undeserving character with illegitimate demands. Thus, a patient presenting a minor medical complaint at an inconvenient hour is more vigorously condemned if he is a welfare case than if he is a "respectable citizen." On the other hand, a "real emergency" can overcome moral repugnance. Thus, when a presumed criminal suffering a severe abdominal bullet wound inflicted by police was brought into one emergency ward, the staff quickly mobilized in a vigorous effort to prevent death because this is the kind of case the staff sees as justifying the existence of their unit. The same patient brought in with a minor injury would almost certainly have been treated as a moral outcast. Even in the case of "real emergencies," however, moral evaluation is not absent. Although the police prisoner with the bullet wound received prompt, expert attention, the effort was treated simply as a technical matter, an opportunity to display one's skill in keeping a severely traumatized person alive. When the same emergency ward received a prominent local citizen who had been stabbed by thugs while he was trying to protect his wife, the staff again provided a crash effort to save his life, but in this case they were obviously greatly upset by their failure, not simply a failure of technical skills but the loss of a worthy person who was the victim of a vicious act. One may speculate whether this difference in staff evaluations of the two victims may have resulted in an extra effort in the case of the respected citizen despite the appearance of a similar effort in the two cases.

Staff Estimates of "Legitimate" Demands

As is common in relationships between a work group and its clientele, the members of the work group tend to exaggerate their difficulties with the clients when they generalize about them. In conversations, we would typically hear estimates of 70 percent to 90 percent as the proportion of patients who were using the emergency service inappropriately. Yet, when we actually followed cases through the clinic, we found the majority were being treated as if they were legitimate. In one voluntary hospital with an intern and residency training program, we classified all cases we followed during our time on the emergency room as legitimate or illegitimate whenever we had any evidence of subjective definition by staff members, either by what they said about the patient or the manner in which they treated the patient. Among those cases suitable for classification, forty-two were treated as legitimate, fifteen as illegitimate, and in twenty-four cases there was insufficient evidence to make a classification. Thus, the illegitimate proportion was about 20 percent to 25 percent depending on whether one used as a base the total of definite legitimate and illegitimate cases or also included the unknowns. In a very active public hospital emergency room we did not use direct observation of each case, but rather developed a conception of what kind of diagnostic categories were usually considered legitimate or illegitimate by the clinic staff and then classified the total census for two days according to diagnostic categories. By this method 23 percent of 938 patients were classified as illegitimate. This constitutes a minimum figure because diagnostic category was not the only basis for an evaluation, and some other patients were almost certainly regarded as illegitimate by the staff. But it does suggest that only a minority were regarded as illegitimate.

The numbers of specific undesirable or inappropriate categories of patients were also consistently exaggerated. Thus, while in the public hospital the interns complained about all the drunks among the men and all the reproductive organ infections among women ("The choice between the male and the female service is really a choice between alcoholics and PIDs," according to one intern), drunks made up only 6 percent of the total emergency room population and the gynecology patients 2 percent. Venereal disease was also considered a common type of case by clerks, nurses, and doctors, but in fact made up only about one percent of the total emergency room census. Psychiatric cases were referred to as a constant trouble, but, in fact, made up only a little over 2 percent of the total. Some doctors believed infections and long-standing illnesses were common among the emergency room population and used this as evidence of neglect of health by the lower classes. Here again, however, the actual numbers were low—these two categories made up a little more than 3 percent of the total census. In two small private.hospitals, the staffs were particularly bitter toward "welfare cases" whom they regarded as a constant nuisance. However, we often spent an entire shift (eight hours) in the emergency rooms of these hospitals without seeing a single patient so classified.

Workers justify the rewards received for their labors in part by the burdens which they must endure on the job. One of the burdens of service occupations is a clientele which makes life hard for the workers. Thus, the workers tend to select for public presentation those aspects of the clientele which cause them difficulty. Teachers' talk deals disproportionately with disruptive and incompetent students, policemen's talk with dangerous criminals and difficult civilians, janitors' talk with inconsiderate tenants. A case-by-case analysis of client contacts is likely to demonstrate in each instance that the examples discussed by the staff are not representative of their total clientele.

Control of Inappropriate Demands for Service

When members of a service occupation or service organization are faced with undesirable or illegitimate clients, what can they do? One possible procedure is to select clients they like and avoid those they do not like. The selecting may be done in categorical terms, as when universities admit undergraduate students who meet given grade and test standards. Or it may be done on the basis of detailed information about specific individuals, as when a graduate department selects particular students on the basis of academic record, recommendations from colleagues, and personal information about the student. Of course, such selection is not made on an unidimensional basis, and the selecting agent must often decide what weight to give conflicting factors. (Thus, a medical specialist may be willing to take on a patient who is morally repugnant because the patient has a medical condition the specialist is anxious to observe, study, or experiment with.) But there is an assumption that the more highly individualized the selection and the more detailed the information on which it is based, the more likely one is to obtain the desirable clientele. Along with this process goes the notion of "selection errors." Thus, when a patient is classed as a good risk for a physical rehabilitation program, he may later be classed as a selection error if doctors uncover some pathology which contraindicates exercise, or if the patient proves so uncooperative that physical therapists are unable to conduct any training, or if he requires so much nursing care that ward personnel claim that he "doesn't belong" on a rehabilitation unit (Roth and Eddy 1967:57–61).

Selectivity is a relative matter. A well-known law firm specializing in a given field can accept only those clients whose demands fit readily into the firm's desired scheme of work organization and who are able to pay well for the service given. The solo criminal lawyer in a marginal practice may, for financial reasons, take on almost every case he can get, even though he may despise the majority of his clients and wish he did not have to deal with them (Smigel 1964; Wood 1967). A common occupational or organizational aspiration is to reach a position where one can be highly selective of one's clientele. In fact, such power of selection is a common basis for rating schools, law firms, hospitals, and practitioners of all sorts.[2]

If one cannot be selective in a positive sense, one may still be selective in a negative sense by avoiding some potentially undesirable clients. Hotels, restaurants, and places of entertainment may specifically exclude certain categories of persons as guests, or more generally reserve the right to refuse service to anyone they choose. Cab drivers will sometimes avoid a presumed "bad fare" by pretending another engagement or just not seeing him. Cab driving, incidentally, is a good example of a line of work where judgments about clients must often be made in a split second on the basis of immediate superficial clues—clues based not only on the behavior and appearance of the client himself, but also on such surrounding factors as the area, destination, and time of day (Davis 1959; Henslin 1968:138–58). Ambulance crewmen sometimes manage to avoid a "bad load," perhaps making a decision before going to the scene on the basis of the call source or neighborhood, or perhaps refusing to carry an undesirable patient if they can find a "good excuse" (Douglas 1969:234–78).

Medical personnel and organizations vary greatly in their capacity to select clients. Special units in teaching hospitals and specialized outpatient clinics often are able to restrict their patients to those they have individually screened and selected. The more run-of-the-mill hospital ward or clinic is less selective, but still has a screening process to keep out certain categories of patients. Of all medical care units, public hospital emergency wards probably exercise the least selectivity of all. Not only are they open to the public at all times with signs pointing the way, but the rule that everyone demanding care must be seen provides no legal "out" for the staff when faced with inappropriate or repugnant patients (although persons accompanying patients can be, and often are, prevented from entering the treatment areas and are isolated or ejected if troublesome). In addition, the emergency ward serves a residual function for the rest of the hospital and often for other parts of the medical-care system. Any case which does not fit into some other program is sent to the emergency ward. When other clinics and offices close for the day or the weekend, their patients who cannot wait for the next open hours are directed to the emergency service. It is precisely this unselective influx of anyone and everyone bringing a wide spectrum of medical and social defects that elicits the bitter complaints of emergency service personnel. Of course, they are not completely without selective power. They occasionally violate the rules and refuse to accept a patient. And even after registration, some patients can be so discouraged in the early stages of processing that they leave. Proprietary hospitals transfer some patients to public hospitals. But compared with other parts of the medical-care system, the emergency service personnel, especially in public hospitals, have very limited power of selection and must resign themselves to dealing with many people that they believe should not be there and to whom in many cases they have a strong aversion.

What recourse does a service occupation or organization have when its members have little or no control over the selection of its clients? If you cannot pick the clients you like, perhaps you can transform those you do get somewhat closer to the image of a desirable client. This is particularly likely to occur if it is a long-term or repeated relationship so that the worker can reap the benefit of the "training" he gives the client. We tentatively put forth this proposition: The amount of trouble one is willing to go to to train his clientele depends on how much power of selection he has. The easier it is for one to avoid or get rid of poor clients (that is, those clients whose behavior or attributes conflict with one's conception of his proper work role), the less interested one is in putting time and energy into training clients to conform more closely to one's ideal. And, of course, the converse.

Janitors have to endure a clientele (that is, tenants) they have no hand in selecting. Nor can a janitor get rid of bad tenants (unless he buys the building and evicts them, as happens on rare occasions). Ray Gold (1964:1–50) describes how janitors try to turn "bad" tenants into more tolerable ones by teaching them not to make inappropriate demands. Tenants must be taught not to call at certain hours, not to expect the janitor to make certain repairs, not to expect him to remove certain kinds of garbage, to expect cleaning services only on given days and in given areas, to expect heat only at certain times, and so on. Each occasion on which the janitor is able to make his point that a given demand is inappropriate contributes to making those demands from the same tenant less likely in the future and increases the janitor's control over his work load and work pacing. One finds much the same long-term effort on the part of the mental hospital staffs who indoctrinate inmates on the behavior and demands associated with "good patients"—who will be rewarded with privileges and discharge—and behavior associated with "bad patients"—who will be denied these rewards (Belknap 1956, chs. 9 and 10; Stanton and Schwartz 1954:280–289). Prisons and schools are other examples of such long-term teaching of clients.[3]

The form that "client training" takes depends in part on the time perspective of the trainers. Emergency ward personnel do not have the long-time perspective of the mental hospital staff, teachers, or janitors. Despite the fact that the majority of patients have been to the same emergency ward previously and will probably be back again at some future time, the staff, with rare exceptions, treats each case as an episode which will be completed when the patient is discharged. Therefore, they seldom make a direct effort to affect the patient's future use of their services. They are, however, interested in directing the immediate behavior of clients so that it will fit into their concept of proper priorities (in terms of their evaluation of the clients) and the proper conduct of an emergency service, including the work demands made upon them. Since they do not conceive of having time for gradual socialization of the clients, they rely heavily on demands for immediate compliance. Thus, patients demanding attention, if not deemed by staff to be urgent cases or particularly deserving, will be told to wait their turn and may even be threatened with refusal of treatment if they are persistent. Visitors are promptly ordered to a waiting room and are reminded of where they belong if they wander into a restricted area. Patients are expected to respond promptly when called, answer questions put to them by the staff, prepare for examination when asked, and cooperate with the examination as directed without wasting the staff's time. Failure to comply promptly may bring a warning that they will be left waiting or even refused further care if they do not cooperate, and the more negative the staff evaluation of the patient, the more likely he is to be threatened.[4]

Nursing staff in proprietary hospitals dealing with the private patients of attending physicians do not have as authoritative a position vis-à-vis their clients as public hospital staff have; therefore, the demands for prompt compliance with staff directions must be used sparingly. In such a case more surreptitious forms of control are used. The most common device is to keep the patient waiting at some step or steps in his processing or treatment. Since the patient usually has no way of checking the validity of the reason given for the wait, this is a relatively safe way that a nurse can control the demands made on her and also serves as a way of "getting even" with those who make inappropriate demands or whom she regards as undeserving for some other reason.

In general, we might expect that the longer the time perspective of the trainers, the more the training will take the form of efforts toward progressive socialization in the desired direction; the shorter the time perspective of the trainers, the more the training will take the form of overt coercion ("giving orders") if the trainers have sufficient power over the clients, and efforts at surreptitious but immediate control if they lack such power.

Conclusion

When a person presents himself at an emergency department (or is brought there by others), he inevitably sets off a process by which his worthiness and legitimacy are weighed and become a factor in his treatment. It is doubtful that one can obtain any service of consequence anywhere without going through this process. The evidence from widely varying services indicates that the servers do not dispense their service in a uniform manner to everyone who presents himself, but make judgments about the worthiness of the person and the appropriateness of his demands and take these judgments into account when performing the service. In large and complex service organizations, the judgments made at one point in the system often shape the judgments at another.

The structure of a service organization will affect the manner and degree to which the servers can vary their service in terms of their moral evaluation of the client. This study has not explored this issue in detail. A useful future research direction would be the investigation of how a system of service may be structured to control the discretion of the servers as to whom they must serve and how they must serve them. This article offered some suggestions concerning the means of controlling the inappropriate demands of a clientele. The examples I used to illustrate the relationships of power of selection and the nature of training of clients are few and limited in scope. An effort should be made to determine whether these formulations (or modifications thereof) apply in a wider variety of occupational settings.

NOTES

1. The authors of *Boys in White* (Becker et al. 1961:327–38) make the same point. A "crock" is a patient from whom the students cannot learn anything because there is no definable physical pathology which can be tracked down and treated.

2. I am glossing over some of the intraorganizational complexities of the process. Often different categories of organizational personnel vary greatly in their participation in the selection of clientele. Thus, on a hospital rehabilitation unit, the doctors may select the patients, but the nurses must take care of patients they have no direct part in selecting. Nurses can influence future selection only by complaining to the doctors that they have "too many" of certain kinds of difficult patients or by trying to convince doctors to transfer inappropriate patients. These attempts at influencing choice often fail because doctors and nurses have somewhat different criteria about what an appropriate patient is (Roth and Eddy 1967:57–61).

3. Of course, my brief presentation greatly oversimplifies the process. For example,

much of the teaching is done by the clients rather than directly by the staff. But, ultimately, the sanctions are derived from staff efforts to control work demands and to express their moral evaluation of the clients.

4. Readers who are mainly interested in what happens on an emergency ward should not be misled into thinking that it is a scene of continuous orders and threats being shouted at patients and visitors. Most directives are matter-of-fact, and most clients comply promptly with directions most of the time. But when the staff's directive power is challenged, even inadvertently, the common response is a demand for immediate compliance. This situation arises frequently enough so that on a busy unit an observer can see instances almost every hour.

19

PROFESSIONAL AUTONOMY AND THE
REVOLT OF THE CLIENT

Marie R. Haug and Marvin B. Sussman

T HIS paper uses the conceptual scheme of professional-client relationships in an analysis of the phenomenon of social unrest. Students, the poor, and the black community no longer accept uncritically the service offerings of the establishment. Our purpose is to interpret this social phenomenon as a new stage in the interaction between professionals and the society, a stage we have called the revolt of the client. This discussion may also help untangle some theoretical issues in the nature of professional autonomy.

In normative terms, a profession may be defined as an occupation based on a unique scientific body of knowledge whose practitioners have a service orientation, and autonomy in the performance of their work (Goode 1961; Hughes 1963). These three core characteristics have been taken as interrelated, with autonomy granted only through public acceptance of the profession's twin claims to expertise and altruism.

The public in this analysis is not, however, the undifferentiated mass. Elsewhere we have marshaled some evidence to show that the general public tends to stereotype occupations and professions without understanding the specific knowledge required or the real nature of the tasks performed. Segmental publics, on the other hand, such as clients utilizing services or colleagues employed in related tasks and fields, are in a position to recognize the skills of the professional and grant the necessary autonomy (Haug and Sussman 1969). The composition of client publics varies by profession. The practitioner-public sets to be considered in this paper are physicians and chronic hospital patients, social workers and welfare cases, college professors

From *Social Problems* (Fall 1969), 17(2):153–61. Reprinted by permission.

and students, and school teachers and ghetto parents. These have been selected for analysis because each represents a different facet of the revolt of the client.

The power of the professional to determine what is best in a particular case, and the autonomy to carry out various remedial, treatment, socializing, or advisory activities, depends on the consent of the client. Although empirically this consent may be based on fear, ignorance, or habit, in a broader sense it is a consequence of the client's implicit acceptance of the professional's expertise and good will, and the understanding that in accepting the authority of the professional the client in turn will be rewarded. Supposedly the doctor knows why it hurts, the social worker knows why the check didn't come, the school teacher knows why Johnny has trouble reading, and the college professor knows the why of all these "whys." The professional can be trusted to apply or transmit his knowledge with the client's interest rather than his own private concerns at heart. The payoff for the client is a solution to one of his problems, and this is the basis upon which the client grants the professional a mandate and authority to proceed.

This idealized model is not now, if it ever was, isomorphic to reality. Provisions for licensure and codes of ethics show that group pressures were found necessary to enforce practitioner approximation to the ideal. Malpractice suits and dropout rates are evidence of individual recognition of poor fit between professional norms and the facts of life. Moreover, professionals discovered that being other-oriented too much could be costly in relation to satisfactions of economic, status, and power needs. Like others in competitive societies professionals have organized around a common interest in order to maintain and enlarge their privileged position in society.

Furthermore, the meeting between professional and client now generally occurs in an organizational context which adds an entirely new dimension to the situation. The "free" professional with a private relationship to an individual in need of service is a vanishing breed. Given bureaucratic delivery systems for professional services, the client is faced not only with the authority of the professional as practitioner, but also as administrator, armed with the regulations and rules of the institutional setting.

At the same time, the professional himself is limited by the organizational milieu in which he performs. Freidson (1970a) questions the impact of such limitations on professionalism; he argues that the delivery system does not seriously impair autonomy, since the core of the professional's power is his control over the actual treatment tasks. Yet decisions concerning use of options best suited to a client's development or problem are affected by a number of organizational imperatives. A clinic doctor bends to the institutional rules of the hospital pharmacy in choosing between recommended medications for his patient. The professor's range of course offerings is shaped by administration budgets and evaluations of such matters as class size or teaching loads. The professional's power, even over specific task performance, is contained with the territory allocated by his institution.

More important for our purposes, however, is the fact that the professional, whether he wishes to admit it or not, has become implicated with the established structure because he uses it to his own ends. In effect, he draws upon organizational power as well as the power of his expertise to control the circumstances under which service is given. This aspect of professional autonomy is a function of the structural links between practitioner and administrator in any institutional setting. Officially, the doctor is the "guest" in the hospital, and the professor is isolated in his ivory tower. Practically, the doctor has a great deal to say about whom the hospital admits and how it is run, while faculty are deeply involved in the same organizational aspects. In this sense the professional shapes institutional practice (Freidson 1970a).

In hospitals, schools, colleges, and the ghettos the clients are rejecting these two aspects of professional power, and are in revolt against both the practitioner's work autonomy and his organizational authority in the role of the administrator. This revolt is in a new dimension because it is a group rather than a personal rejection phenomenon. Heretofore, clients evaded constraints by manipulation of the system, or by leaving it altogether. Nowadays individual clients do not drop out; they get together, sit in, and confront the functionaries of service organizations. The critical difference is that client counteractions are now social and organized. This is the reason we can speak of client revolts only in areas where clients have had an opportunity to be together over an extended period of time, such as patients in long-term treatment hospitals, students in colleges, or welfare cases and residents hemmed in crowded ghetto areas.

Also, one should not overlook the current struggle between the administrator and practitioner in service organizations over control of the work situation and the subsequent polarization of occupational and client groups and enhancement of potential conflict between them. In those instances where the administrator-professional conflict is unresolved the client revolt may be abetted by a sympathetic ally who uses or is used by the client in the struggle for power and control.

Before examining the utility of professionalism as an explanatory framework of client revolt in more detail, it will be useful to dispose of some other current interpretations of social unrest. One such is essentially a nonanalysis. This is the claim that client actions are irrational, the journalistic stance which labels demands as impossible and tactics as irresponsible. While this may be a popular value judgment and even a valid statement if the sole criterion of rationality is conformity to prior norms, it is not an adequate analysis of the social phenomenon. Neither student seizure of buildings nor ghetto marches can be explained as the actions of anomic crowds. Similar challenges to institutional power a generation ago can be considered rational by current perspectives because they were successful: sit-down strikes and demonstrations were among the techniques used to achieve unionism.

This should not be taken to mean that the labor-management frame of reference is fully explanatory either. This model is most suited to situations where there is a conflict over scarce resources: one party to the struggle has what the other party wants. The embattled resources are material and tangible, or at least can be cashed in for these values. Although the issues in current confrontations may have long-term material consequences, the immediate concern is not the extraction of goods from their possessor. The problem is power and its appropriate limits.

Clients engaged in a battle against authority have several possible grounds for challenge. Professional autonomy may be called into question because (1) the expertise of the practitioners is inadequate; (2) their claims to altruism are unfounded; (3) the organizational delivery system supporting their authority is defective and insufficient; or (4) this system is too efficient and exceeds the appropriate bounds of its power. In short, the client revolt attacks the basic legitimacy of the occupational and institutional claims to power of the professional.

There are varying emphases and configurations among these elements of legitimation, depending on the setting and the situation.

In the hospital, organized client resistance has generally remained in the incipient stage. Covert group pressures, such as reported in *Timetables* (Roth 1963), implicitly reject the physician's expertise and professional judgment in pressing for shared definitions of the right moment for hospital discharge. Already reported, however, are more open group efforts, such as those seeking to reject the spread of a chronic hospital's domain over wider areas of the patient's life. (For a discussion of laterality as a form of client-organization relations see Lefton and Rosengren 1966). Thus in one long-term facility in the East, patients have organized to resist hospital meddling with their Social Security, disability, or welfare income (Pilati 1969). Here the claim is not that medical know-how is missing, but rather that it gives no license to handle patients' finances as well as their physical needs. Our own conjecture is that patients in general will resist expansion of hospital professional control to areas not defined as legitimately medical. Patient-clients consider themselves just as competent in social relations as their doctors.

Clients of welfare caseworkers, on the other hand, question even the special professional knowledge of the social worker. He—or more probably she—is apt to be viewed simply as a person "with authority to determine whether or not there is going to be four or five dollars more in a budget" (Harris 1967:47). Marches on welfare offices, sit-ins, sleep-ins, and other group demonstrations are aimed at extracting more benefits from the professionals. Here it might be argued that there are labor-management analogues in the situation, except that the caseworkers do not themselves possess the goods which the clients are demanding, even though they are perceived as agents of the establishment who presumably control the distribution of means. In our framework it is, even more explicit than in the instance of the hospital, a situation where the client feels fully as qualified as the professional to determine what is best for him, and to demand that it be supplied (for a similar stituation in the religious field see Braude 1961).

The revolt of black parents against a ghetto school system dominated by white teachers presents a somewhat different set of factors. In this instance it could be argued that *both* the expertise and the good will of the professional are being challenged. The articulate poor charge that the middle-class ghetto teacher is blind to their particular problems, does not understand their children, is ignorant of black history and innovative teaching methods, and is only waiting to escape to a suburban school system anyway (for substantiation of this stance in an earlier era see Becker 1952). In addition, the ghetto dweller finds that the whole delivery system of education is inadequate and inefficient. Here there seems no charge that the system goes too far, but rather that it does not go far enough.

In the university setting the revolt of the student-client finds grounds for disaffection in all four authority factors. Professional expertise is questioned: black students point to gaps in knowledge of black history, life, and culture, while diverse groups challenge the faculty's knowledge of teaching methods or ability to relate course content to current social concerns. The latter charge suggests a critique of professional humanitarianism as well. A more direct denial of service orientation is the claim that professors are more interested in their own research and consulting opportunities than in teaching students, and moreover that both research and consulting are in the service of immoral ends, such as war or colonialism. Ideas about the inefficiency and inadequacy of the delivery system are seen in demands to "restructure" the university, modify curriculum, revise teaching practices, and the like. Finally, the old notion that the college administration stood *in loco parentis* has been rejected by students who consider this an illegitimate extension of organizational power into personal lives, as witnessed by the ongoing battles for off-campus housing, elimination of separate male and female dorms, and open visiting, among others.

Undergirding some of this revolt is an intergenerational struggle for power. Those of the middle generation hold sway too long, according to the young, and the rebellion functions as a catalyst to speed the process of change of power or to obtain accommodations which provide a rationale for tolerating the rule of elders. This is seen most clearly among the student rebels, and to a certain extent also explains the vigorous rejection by young blacks of the older "Uncle Toms" in their communities.

The situation, then, is that professional knowledge, service, autonomy, and organizational authority are being challenged at various levels of society and among widely diverse groups. Students, predominantly middle- and upper-class, deny the expertise and good will of their educators, while they demand an end to administration and faculty power to meddle in their private lives. Poverty group members, arguing that they know more about their community needs, problems, and solutions than the professional social workers and are more concerned, have organized for a voice in welfare benefits and their distribution. Cutting across social class lines, the blacks confront professors, teachers, and social workers with their demands for more adequate services while hospital patients organize to hold professional control over their lives in bounds.

The slogan for all groups is "Don't call me, I'll call you." The client seems to be rejecting what he considers institutionalized meddling under the cover of professional concern. Outreach programs, from the client perspective, have become outgrab. Students want to organize their own courses and call in the professional as consultant (Shenker 1969). The "whole man" approach in medicine infringes on areas of social relations where clients consider themselves competent; patients want to turn to the doctor when in trouble, but not to be bothered otherwise. This suggests that the client is demanding the right to define the problem, and then call upon the professional only as specialist in a narrow domain. The breadth of professional prerogative, the lateral dimension (Lefton and Rosengren 1966) of professional-client relationships, is the most widely rejected.

The professional's response has generally been heated resistance. The emotional pressure that has been generated seems excessive on logical grounds, but is understandable in social-psychological terms. The professional's authority is precious because it verifies his superior status and shapes his self-image. The client's refusal to perform in a dependent, subadult role relation to the "wise expert" destroys the underlying assumptions of the professional's own position as a man of knowledge, compassion, and power. In this sense the revolt of the client is more devastating than the revolt of the unionized worker because it directly involves the social self-conceptions of the authority figures, not just machines and money.

The professional's tactic for dealing with the situation has been in the classic conflict vein, covering the usual spectrum from outright repression to subtle and not-so-subtle cooptation. The modal pattern, however, has been cooptation. Hospitals form "patients councils," poverty programs include "indigenous" community representation on governing boards, while students are added to curriculum committees, university senates, even boards of trustees. The objective is to socialize the dissidents into the special organizational knowledge of the inner professional circles, even if the specific *scientific* body of knowledge of the professional remains sacrosanct. In this way the autonomy of the professional is preserved at the cost of sharing only a small portion of his institutional power.

The "new careers" movement, although probably not developed as cooptation, may be discussed from this perspective also. This employment scheme initiated by Pearl and Riessman (1965), has now become so institutionalized as to appear in much legislation. On the basis that helping others is a means to one's own therapy, the new careers concept provides that members of poverty groups be employed by social agencies as paraprofessional links between social work practitioners and the community. The outcome is to be improved relations between agency and client, with better understanding of each side of problems and programs, and new opportunities for the untrained poor to embark on a subprofessional career sequence to pull themselves out of the poverty syndrome. Objectively, one might conclude that the process would result in cooptation, with poor careerists eventually identified more with their new employers than their old neighbors. Indeed, it has been explicitly stated that the "new careers" approach "might provide an essential deterrent to the alienation which lies behind various forms of protest in our society, including ghetto upheavals" (Riessman 1969:30).

More direct evidence of the cooptation threat is the growth of an *anti*cooptation movement among new careerists. Sparked by the new careerists themselves, this movement is attacking "professionalism," "credentialism," and "ideas of hierarchy." The ideology is *"highly critical of the professional*: he doesn't understand the community, he is elitist and distant and not willing to accept accountability from consumers." The traditional picture of "a distant and peer-responsible professional and a humble ministered-to client" must be replaced by "new forms of participation and a new responsive professional practice" (Gartner 1969).

This sounds like cooptation that failed, and may indicate a poor prognosis for similar attempts in other fields. Cooptation, after all, assumes that the client is really ignorant and uninformed, and that by being made aware of the professionals' rationale he will come to accept it. But the shoe may be on the other foot. As pointed out by the director of the New York State Health Planning Commission,

The professionals must, for their own sake, accept the realization that the patient—the client—the consumer—is much more sophisticated and aware of his needs than ever before. . . . he will increasingly be more involved in how services to meet these needs will be provided. It may be that . . . we can learn something (Van Ness 1967:78).

Where the clients claim equal or superior knowledge in a whole area of the expert's supposed domain, they may win over the professional instead of the other way around. Some of this has already occurred. A few faculty members help seize buildings and often social workers join the march on welfare offices.

We are reminded of the comment of Everett Hughes that "social unrest shows itself precisely in questioning the prerogatives of the leading professions. In time of crisis, there may arise a general demand for more complete conformity of professionals to lay modes of thought, discourse and action" (1958:83). One may argue over how "general" the demand for reducing professional authority has become, or the extent to which professionals are willing to retreat from the use of previously held power, but if the argument of this paper is accepted, it seems that the process of respecification of legitimate authority has begun to occur.

Given the viability of our interpretation, what are the consequences for professional autonomy in particular and professionalism in general? It seems fair to say that a return to old definitions is largely out of the question, so that in *this* sense a revolution is in progress. If nothing else, the rising level of general education and of expectations will prevent a return to former patterns of client-practitioner relations. Furthermore, since the major thrust of the client revolt has been against the institutional concomitants of professionalism, including the tendency of the professional to extend his authority beyond the limits of his legitimated special expertise, one might predict a narrowing of professional authority to the most limited and esoteric elements of his knowledge base. This is unlikely to mean, despite client-revolt rhetoric, that the professional will fully lose the core of his autonomy, the right to define the nature of the client's problem. Even if the client exercised his right to pick and choose the time and place of his use of the professional's expertise, once the client enters the interaction, the expert's knowledge of cause-effect will permit him to diagnose and respecify the original complaint or need into his terms.

A corollary of this hypothesized development could be change in the prestige accorded the professional. If our empirical evidence as derived from a different context (Haug and Sussman 1969) can be projected into other times and conditions, the expectation is that the prestige-grantors—the clients in revolt—will denigrate the professional's social status as well as the extent of his authority claims, and that this downgrading will shape new, less prestigious stereotypes of the professions.

Thus we project, as one possibility, that the tension between society and professional can lead to a process of deprofessionalization, involving both narrower bounds for autonomy and lowered status. On the other hand, what the client demands—the professional as a limited consultant—may be less a curse than a blessing in disguise. It could enable the professional to give up the "whole man" approach to service and treatment, and enable him to revert to a more specialized expert role. All individuals in complex societies require the services of the expert in order to survive. In the future, as in the past, this should provide the professional with sufficient power, prestige, and financial return. What is lost in diffuse power and prestige would then be compensated for by more focused autonomy within the specialized range. All these issues remain problematic, and are presented less as predictions than as guideposts for future study.

D. RACE AND SEX IN SOCIAL WELFARE

THE manifest function of many social welfare programs is to mitigate the discrimination that some groups of people suffer in the United States. However, these programs perpetuate three major forms of bias—those based on social class, race, and sex. Poor and working-class people, nonwhites, and women are the victims of persistent and structural discrimination which puts them in a disadvantageous position compared to rich and middle-class people, whites, and men. The middle-class bias in social welfare has been recognized for nearly four decades, and has been analyzed by a number of social scientists, including Mills (1943), Hollingshead and Redlich (1958), and Cloward and Epstein (1967). A recent example in health care is Dutton's (1978) finding that inadequate delivery systems rather than subcultural differences account for the low use of health facilities by the poor. Social class bias permeates social welfare as it does other aspects of life in the United States. Many selections in this reader deal with social class issues, including the contributions by Hicks, Friedland, and Johnson; O'Connor; and Ryan. For this reason, the two selections here focus on racism and sexism.

The first article in section D is Carlton E. Munson's "Evaluation of Male and Female Supervisors," based on data from a random sample of twenty-five social welfare agencies in three Eastern states. His findings cast doubt on the stereotypical notion that men work better with male supervisors. Other gender stereotypes are contradicted by the data, including the contention that females are more relationship-oriented and males, more task-oriented. This belief has been used to justify retaining women in practice positions while men are promoted into administration.

The second selection is "Differences in the Provision of Mental Health Services by Race" by Joan Cole and Marc Pilisuk. This is a study of a sample of ninety-four clients of a mental health "crisis clinic." The findings support the argument that an institutional bias discriminates against black men, in both diagnosis and treatment. Although the Cole and Pilisuk selection deals with health care, it has direct relevance to problems of racism in social welfare practice.

20

EVALUATION OF MALE AND FEMALE SUPERVISORS

Carlton E. Munson

ISSUES in social work supervision related to the sex of the workers have never been studied empirically, and there has been little theoretical writing on the subject. This neglect is ironic, since supervision is the arena in which many of the issues that have been raised recently regarding sex discrimination are usually encountered and handled. For example, granting salary increases, evaluating performance, making employment decisions, and granting promotions are all components of supervision that have been identified as the major source of discrimination against women in the profession (Scotch 1971). Discrimination in these areas is related to hierarchial organizational arrangements in which supervisors get paid more than caseworkers, administrators get higher salaries than supervisors, so that "unless women are free to move up in supervisory and administrative positions, the hidden inequities become apparent" (Scotch 1971:7). Women have fared badly in this hierarchial process, and this has generally been attributed to processes of socialization with respect to sex roles (Williams, Ho, and Fielder 1974).

Much speculation exists regarding how men and women feel about working with and for women, but no empirical study has been done to support this speculation.[1] One research study found that men obtain fewer responses in interviewing than women, and female interviewers obtain the highest responses from men, except in situations in which the interviewer and interviewee were both young (Webb et al. 1973:21). Another study that did not explore sex variables directly found that dissimilarity of the parties in an interview

From *Social Work* (March 1979), 24(2):104–10. Reprinted by permission; copyright © 1979 National Association of Social Workers.

led to greater verbal accessibility (Tessler and Polansky 1975). Since supervision in part involves interviewing strategies, these studies demonstrate the need for research on the impact of sex differences on supervision.

Social work has lagged behind other disciplines in investigating and documenting expectations and performance that are based on sex-role stereotypes of men and women in organizational positions. In business and management, research on perceptions of leadership styles has demonstrated that both men and women stereotype females as possessing characteristics that are considered inappropriate for management positions (Bass, Krusell, and Alexander 1971; Schein 1973, 1975). Research that has gone beyond attitudes to evaluate actual performance has not supported the stereotypes. No differences have been found in male and female leadership styles, particularly when leaders were evaluated by their subordinates. Most studies have found no significant difference between workers who had a male or female for a superior in job satisfaction, satisfaction with salary, satisfaction with supervision, or promotional opportunity (Bartol and Wortman 1976).

Literature on Supervision

Historically, there has been little exploration of the roles of males and females in social work supervision. In an early text Robinson (1936:36) merely mentioned that a majority of supervisors in social work were women, and in a revised edition (1949:40) of the same book this reference was eliminated. Reynolds, emphasizing that a majority of social workers were women, identified seven variations of the supervisory situation based on the sex, age, education, and experience of the worker. Reynolds places more emphasis on the problems associated with supervising males than females. She (1965:191) depicts males as more interested in administration, and holds that women excel "in the fine points of personal relationship" that characterize casework practice. Reynolds (1965:193) summarizes the problem of the female supervisor of a male worker as follows:

A woman supervisor . . . has a special hazard to overcome in relation to a man worker whom she supervises. She may tend to enjoy association with him more than women workers, and to "mother" him, with loss of objectivity as to his educational needs, or to look up to him, unconsciously, as "the young prince" who is destined to rule some day—and that very soon as compared to the time it would take a woman to reach a similar position.

She goes on to argue that this situation can be a problem for a man attempting to adjust to a profession that Reynolds saw as "unhealthily feminized" and for males having to deal with some female supervisors who are understandably resentful of promotional opportunities offered men.

Since Reynolds's time, a larger proportion of males have entered the profession. In a recent study of males in social work, Kadushin (1976) found that only 21 percent viewed being supervised by a female as a problem, but 37 percent preferred to be supervised by a male. Kadushin considers the movement of males in social work toward administration in part as an attempt to resolve the problems associated with being supervised by a female. He concludes that his findings support Caplow's (1954) contention that males resist subordination to women, and Vinter (1974:467) also cites Caplow in making the point that stress is created for the male who is assigned a female supervisor. Wilensky and Lebeaux (rev. 1975:322–25) also hold this point of view, arguing that men do not remain in direct service positions and women are seldom assigned top administrative posts because of the conflicts that are created when males are subordinate to females. They point out that strains are created for both sexes in such positions, and they attribute the stress to cultural socialization processes that are carried over to the work relationships. Chafetz (1972:14) has summarized this orientation in an extreme fashion by stating: "In short, no one seems to want a woman boss!"

Although there has been a partial shift toward equality of the sexes and emancipation of women in this society, it is not clear what impact these changes are having on social welfare organizations and the attitudes and behavior of employees of such organizations (Heraud 1970:256; Wilensky and Lebeaux rev. 1975:322–25). Greenfield (1976:31) has observed that men who complain about women supervisors usually have never worked for a woman. She cites research in which 75 percent of males and females who worked for female managers evaluated them favorably, and those who rated women as inferior demonstrated a cultural bias. More research is needed to test empirically the theoretical assumptions about the problems of men working for women in light of the changes that are occurring.

The research to be reported in this article was undertaken, therefore, to explore sex-role issues in social work supervision. It considered the effect of the sex of the supervisor and supervisee on a number of variables related to the worker's satisfaction with, and interaction, in supervision. This research was designed to explore several questions: How do male and female supervisors fare, based on the ratings of the workers they supervise? Do males resent being supervised by females? Are female supervisors perceived as relationship-oriented and men as task-oriented? Do supervisees interact differently based on the sex of the supervisor? What proportion of supervisors is female?

Methodology

A cluster sampling technique was used to select a random sample of social welfare agencies in three adjoining states in the Eastern United States. Using community service directories, all agencies were categorized according to whether they were public or private and whether their area of service was mental health, family and children's services, or social services (public welfare). This resulted in six categories, from which twenty-five agencies were selected at random. Fifty-four percent of the agencies were public and 46 percent private. Among the service areas, 31 percent were mental health, 40 percent family and children's services, and 29 percent social services. Nineteen of the twenty-five agencies selected (76 percent) agreed to participate in the study.

A random sample of practitioners was selected in each agency based on the agency's size, and sixty-five of the seventy workers selected (93 percent) agreed to participate. This resulted in a cross section of social workers with various levels of education and experience. Sixty-six percent of the workers were female, and 34 percent were male. Fifty-seven percent of them had supervisors who were female, and 43 percent had males. Forty-three percent of the workers held MSW degrees, 51 percent had BA degrees, and 6 percent had BSW degrees. Seventy-five percent of the supervisors held MSW degrees and 25 percent BA degrees. None of the supervisors were BSWs. The workers had on the average just under six years of work experience, and an average of three of those years were spent in the worker's current agency. The average age of the workers was 34, and the average age of the supervisor was 44.

The sampling technique used selected one worker for each supervisor, resulting in a sample consisting of sixty-five supervisors and sixty-five supervisees. Each practitioner was given an eighteen-page structured questionnaire regarding his or her supervisor through face-to-face interviews that averaged one hour in length. An interview was used to gather the data because it allows more in-depth responses than a mailed questionnaire, which has been the type of instrument used in most social work research into sex differences (Fischer et al. 1976; Kadushin 1976; Zietz and Erlich 1976).

The questionnaire contained items that measured the respondents' satisfaction with the supervision they received and the type and amount of interaction between supervisors and supervisees. The instrument was pretested, and the split-half method was used to test reliability by comparing odd and even items, yielding a coefficient of .91 ($p < .01$).

Satisfaction with supervision was divided into four areas: (1) general satisfaction, (2) administrative satisfaction, (3) teaching satisfaction, and (4) helping satisfaction. General satisfaction represents an overall rating, and the components of administration, teaching, and helping were based on classic definitions of the social work supervisor's role (Pettes 1967; Williamson 1961). Each of these variables was broken down into specific subcategories, which will be reported in the section on findings.

The variables defining interaction in supervision consisted of friendliness of the supervisor, openness of the supervisor, expression of appreciation by the supervisor, amount of informal contact between the supervisor and supervisee, clarity on the part of the supervisor in giving directions, agreement of values between the supervisor and supervisee, avoidance of confrontation on the part of the supervisor, supervisee's avoidance of contact with the supervisor, and sharing of clinical material between the supervisor and supervisee for professional development. The latter refers to the amount of process recording, audio tapes, videotapes, and joint live interviewing used in supervision.

The supervisees' perceptions of satisfaction with supervision and interaction in supervision were chosen as the variables because these two areas are the major sources of assessing what takes place in supervision and attitudes toward it. If past theories about male and female subordination were valid, then they should be reflected in differences in the scores for male and female supervisors.

The data were analyzed by computer through the use of a breakdown procedure that allowed comparisons of mean scores on each variable on the basis of the sex of the supervisor and the sex of the supervisee (Nie et al. 1975). The t-test of significance was used

Table 20.1. Mean Scores on Satisfaction with Supervision

Characteristics of Supervisors	Sex of Supervisor		t	p^a
	Male (n = 28)	Female (n = 37)		
General satisfaction				
Nondirective	4.6	5.2	−2.35	.02
Helpful	3.7	4.8	−2.54	.01
Fair	4.6	5.1	−1.57	ns
Performance evaluation	4.2	4.9	−2.72	.01
Administrative satisfaction				
Administrative knowledge	4.6	4.7	−0.40	ns
Priority-setting ability	4.2	4.8	−2.04	.05
Organizing ability	4.0	4.2	−0.64	ns
Regulation oriented	3.7	4.9	−3.12	.01
Teaching satisfaction				
Clinical competence	4.1	4.9	−2.15	.05
Theory-oriented	4.7	5.1	−1.59	ns
Underestimating worker's knowledge	4.4	5.0	−2.17	.03
Helping satisfaction				
Developing self-awareness in workers	3.6	3.8	−0.61	ns
Avoiding therapy with workers	4.6	5.2	−2.66	.01
Avoiding analyzing worker's motives	4.2	4.9	−2.56	.01
Improving effectiveness of workers	3.4	4.3	−2.47	.01

[a] Two-tailed probability; ns = not significant.

to analyze the difference in mean scores between male and female supervisors, and the two-way breakdowns by sex of worker and sex of supervisor were analyzed through use of the *F*-ratio analysis of variance.

Findings

Table 20.1 contains scores for male and female supervisors in the four areas of satisfaction with supervision. In every category the mean scores were higher for female supervisors, and for ten of the fifteen variables the differences were significant at the .05 level or better. Female supervisors achieved significantly higher scores than males for being nondirective, helpful, accurate in evaluating the worker's performance, able to set priorities, and clinically competent. They also scored significantly higher in the areas of being regulation-oriented regarding the agency's rules, tending to underestimate the worker's knowledge about practice, avoiding therapy in supervision, avoiding analyzing the worker's motives rather than those of the client when the client dropped out of service, and assisting in improving the worker's effectiveness. Apparently female supervisors more than their male counterparts are conforming to the recent trend to supervise the position rather than the person (Munson 1976). The findings in the various areas of satisfaction with supervision consistently demonstrate that when supervisees were asked to rate their supervisors, female supervisors received higher evaluations than males.

Since there has been much theorizing about males' resistance to being subordinate to females in organizations that are based on cultural attitudes and socialization processes, it was decided to analyze further the data by breaking down the variables regarding satisfaction with supervision according to the sex of the supervisor and the sex of the supervisee (see table 20.2). These findings do not conform to past theory. In thirteen of the fifteen categories, female supervisors of female workers received the highest scores, and in fourteen of the fifteen categories, male supervisors of male workers received the lowest scores. The highest scores on nondirectiveness and fairness were received by female supervisors of male workers. In the remaining areas, the female supervisor of male workers received lower scores than the combination of a female with a female, but in no case did they attain lower scores than the male supervisors of male workers. Eleven of these variables resulted in significant differences at the .05 level or better. The pattern of these significant differences was that the female workers rated both female and male supervisors higher than did the male workers, with the female supervisors of female workers receiving the highest scores on every variable. Also, in all but one of the areas that showed significant differences, the male workers rated female supervisors higher than male supervisors. For the variable of avoiding therapy with the worker in supervision, male workers showed a slightly higher tendency to view female supervisors as doing therapy with them. However, female workers were much more likely to view the male supervisor as placing emphasis on therapy than female supervisors.

The supervisees were also asked to rate their supervisors on a number of variables regarding interaction in supervision (see table 20.3). Females received significantly better scores in four categories. They were reported to be more friendly, more likely to express

Table 20.2. Mean Scores on Satisfaction with Supervision, by Sex of Supervisee and Supervisor

Characteristic of Supervisor	Male Supervisor/ Male Supervisee (n = 10)	Female Supervisor/ Female Supervisee (n = 25)	Female Supervisor/ Male Supervisee (n = 12)	Male Supervisor/ Female Supervisee (n = 18)	F	p^a
General satisfaction						
Nondirective	4.9	5.2	5.3	4.7	2.0	ns
Helpful	2.2	5.0	4.3	4.6	8.1	.01
Fair	4.3	5.0	5.2	4.7	1.2	ns
Performance evaluation	3.6	5.2	4.3	4.6	7.3	.01
Administrative satisfaction						
Administrative knowledge	4.1	4.8	4.7	4.8	1.0	ns
Priority-setting ability	3.1	4.9	4.5	4.8	8.1	.01
Organizing ability	3.3	4.6	3.5	4.4	3.6	.05
Regulation oriented	2.7	5.1	4.5	4.2	6.1	.01
Teaching satisfaction						
Clinical competence	3.2	5.1	4.4	4.7	4.6	.01
Theory-oriented	4.3	5.3	4.8	4.9	2.1	ns
Underestimating worker's knowledge	3.9	5.2	4.5	4.7	4.2	.01
Helping satisfaction						
Developing self-awareness in workers	2.4	4.1	3.4	4.2	3.4	.05
Avoiding therapy with workers	4.8	5.4	4.9	4.6	3.3	.05
Avoiding analyzing worker's motives	3.4	4.9	4.7	4.6	5.6	.01
Improving effectiveness of workers	2.4	4.6	3.8	3.9	5.9	.01

^{a} ns = not significant.

Table 20.3. Mean Scores on Interaction in Supervision

Interaction in Supervision	Sex of Supervisor		t	p^a
	Male $(n = 28)$	Female $(n = 37)$		
Friendliness	4.9	5.4	-2.67	.01
Openness	4.9	4.9	-0.06	ns
Expression of appreciation	4.0	4.7	-2.08	.04
Informal interaction	2.6	2.6	-0.01	ns
Clarity	3.8	4.0	-0.77	ns
Agreement of values	3.8	4.6	-2.45	.01
Avoidance of confrontation	3.0	2.4	1.75	ns
Avoidance of supervisor	2.8	2.0	2.21	.03
Sharing clinical material	1.3	1.4	-0.45	ns

[a] Two-tailed probability; ns = not significant.

appreciation for good work, less likely to be avoided by their supervisees. (In the areas of avoidance of confrontation and avoidance of the supervisor, lower scores indicate a positive outcome.) No significant differences in the performance of male and female supervisors were found in the areas of openness to discussion of problems, informal interaction, clarity in giving directions, avoidance of confrontation, and sharing of clinical material for professional development. Again, these findings do not give any indications that female supervisors are less highly regarded than male supervisors, and in some areas female supervisors appear to be more sensitive to the needs of their supervisees than their male counterparts.

Table 20.4 provides the breakdown of the interaction variables by the sex of the supervisor and the sex of the supervisee. As was the case with the variables regarding satisfaction, female supervisors of female workers received the highest rating in a majority of the categories. However, there were fewer significant differences with the interaction variables. Significant differences were found in the areas of expression of appreciation, agreement of values, avoidance of confrontation, and avoidance of the supervisor.

In the areas of expression of appreciation and agreement of values, female and male supervisors of female workers received significantly higher ratings than supervisors of males, and in both cases female supervisors of male workers received higher scores than male supervisors of male workers. Male workers with male supervisors experi-

Table 20.4. Mean Scores on Interaction in Supervision, by Sex of Supervisor and Supervisee

Interaction in Supervision	Male Supervisor/ Male Supervisee (n = 10)	Female Supervisor/ Female Supervisee (n = 25)	Female Supervisor/ Male Supervisee (n = 12)	Male Supervisor/ Female Supervisee (n = 18)	F	p^a
Friendliness	4.8	5.4	5.4	4.9	2.4	ns
Openness	4.6	5.2	4.5	5.1	1.4	ns
Expression of appreciation	2.9	5.2	3.8	4.6	8.0	.01
Informal interaction	2.5	3.0	2.0	2.7	1.1	ns
Clarity	3.2	4.3	3.5	4.0	1.8	ns
Agreement of values	2.9	4.9	4.2	4.7	5.9	.01
Avoidance of confrontation	3.4	2.1	3.0	2.8	2.7	.05
Avoidance of supervisor	4.0	2.0	2.8	2.6	3.1	.05
Sharing clinical material	1.2	1.4	1.4	1.2	1.3	ns

[a] Two-tailed probability; ns = not significant.

ence lower levels of expression of appreciation and agreement on values and avoid their supervisors more than males who are supervised by females. These findings do not support the contention that males are less satisfied or more threatened when supervised by a female.

The breakdowns of the results by sex reported in tables 20.2 and 20.4 provide the basis for some analysis of the proportion of male and female supervisors. Twenty-eight (43 percent) of the supervisors were male, while thirty-seven (57 percent) of the supervisors were female. These statistics reveal that females are not represented in supervisory positions in numbers equal to their proportions in the profession as a whole, as reflected by the 67 percent of the total sample who were female. Although there are no comparable statistics from past decades, the proportion of female supervisors appears to be increasing, but it is still not equal to the proportional sex distribution in the profession as a whole.

Discussion

In regard to the questions raised at the beginning of this paper that served as a basis for the research, the findings reveal that female supervisors function quite well, regardless of the sex of their supervisees, but male supervisors of male workers do not fare well; that males do not resent being supervised by females; that men and women supervisors do not differ on task and relationship orientations; and that the proportion of female supervisors appears to be increasing. The findings clearly reveal a pattern of satisfaction with supervision and interaction that is not consistent with much of the theoretical speculation about women in supervisory positions or men who are supervised by women. On the simple breakdowns, female supervisors received significantly higher scores on nondirectiveness, helpfulness, evaluation of performance, ability to set priorities, being role-oriented, having clinical competence, contributing to the improvement of workers' effectiveness, being friendly, expressing appreciation, and engaging in informal interaction. When these scores were broken down further according to the sex of the worker, a pattern emerged of female supervisors receiving higher scores regardless of the sex of the worker. On a majority of variables, the lowest scores occurred with the combination of male supervisors of male workers. These findings contradict Brager and Michael's

(1969:596) observation that "men are usually believed to be more effective in working with other men."

Although the theoretical literature cited previously has emphasized the culturally induced stress and threat produced by placing a male in subordination to a female, this view is not supported by the findings. In fact, such speculation has perhaps blinded us to the apparent difficulties that result when males supervise males. Clearly, this is the most problematic area when analyzing the participants' satisfaction with supervision. It is quite possible that the effort to attract more males to the profession and their rapid movement into supervisory and administrative positions have left them ill-prepared for the roles they assume with such rapidity.

Although males in his study had minimal difficulty in working with female colleagues and supervisors, when Kadushin (1976:442–43) reports that over one third preferred a male supervisor, he does not state what percentage of these males had actually experienced supervision by females. In light of the findings presented here, preferences expressed by males might be quite different from what they actually experience in the supervisory situation. An important possibility that remains unexplored is that males for cultural reasons would prefer poor supervision by a male to any type of supervision by a female. This position is consistent with Greenfield's (1976) argument that complaints from men about female supervisors are usually raised by men who have never worked for a woman. However, the study findings suggest that when men do have female supervisors they rate them higher than male supervisors. The results presented here transcend the theoretical situation and demonstrate that when research is based on what actually takes place in supervision, the old myths do not hold.

There is no support in the findings of this study for the contention that females are more relationship-oriented and intuitive, and men are more task-oriented. This has been a long-standing and subtly applied myth used to justify women's predominance in practice positions while men move into supervisory and administrative positions (Bartol 1977). The findings reveal instead that there was no difference for males and females on the variables associated with administrative aspects of supervision, and in some instances females scored higher than males. The variables that related to practice competence followed the same pattern.

The author has encountered interesting responses on the part of female supervisors in workshops where these findings have been presented. They are reluctant to accept the findings as evidence that they are viewed as equally effective as—and often superior to—male supervisors. They often construe the findings as reflecting passivity, acceptance, tolerance, and a positive attitude on the part of female workers rather than a real difference in their evaluation of supervisory performance. Schein (1975) has received similar responses in her study of female managers. Such responses are culturally induced through the traditional socialization processes. Only when findings such as those presented here and those being reported by other studies on women in administrative positions are accepted as having genuine validity will true progress be made in overcoming the old ways of viewing women. This study can be considered as empirical support for Scotch's (1971:9) statement that "there is nothing to suggest that either nature or nurture produces males in our society who are inherently superior to females as far as administration is concerned."

The findings have implications for the practice of supervision. More knowledge is needed about patterns in the proportion of male and female supervisors as well as in their styles of interaction, such as the ones identified in this study. We need to know whether becoming a supervisor is a step to higher administrative positions for both sexes, or whether it tends to be more of a terminal position for females. The position of social work supervisor is not a clearly defined organizational role. For some, supervisor is a full-time position, and for others it is merely an additional responsibility assumed along with that of practice. It is important to determine whether such assignments are made differentially for males and females. This study confirms findings of studies in other fields that it is time to put to rest the old myths that stereotype the sexes and begin to address the hierarchical issues that serve as barriers to equality in organizations.

NOTE

1. For a discussion of how men feel, see, for example, Brager and Michael (1969); Greenfield (1976); Vinter (1974:467–68); and Wilensky and Lebeaux (rev. 1975:322–25). For a discussion of how women feel, see, for example, Chafetz (1972) and Sherif (1976:16).

[21]

DIFFERENCES IN THE PROVISION OF MENTAL HEALTH SERVICES BY RACE

Joan Cole and Marc Pilisuk

DEMOGRAPHIC studies of mental health have dealt with social class more often than with racial differentials (Hollingshead and Redlich 1958; Remmen et al. 1962; Srole et al. 1962). People of lower socioeconomic status have been found to have proportionately more psychiatric problems, and different and more severe types of mental disorders, for which they receive far more custodial care, psychosurgery, and other harsh treatments than do those of the middle and upper classes.

Blacks, Chicanos and other Third World people are most apt to be poor. We, therefore, expect that they will receive fewer mental health services while having higher rates of mental illness than whites. In a study of 594 admissions to Los Angeles County General Hospital for psychiatric treatment, it was found that 11 percent of white patients, compared with 3 percent of black patients, were seen more than ten times in individual treatment. White women were seen longest, and black men were seen for the shortest time period. Nine months after a first appointment, twenty-two of the twenty-eight patients still in active individual therapy were Caucasian. No black men were in individual treatment. In an effort to determine whether patient or worker was responsible for these differences, the investigator interviewed the psychotherapists and found that those who were rated high in ethnocentricity were less likely to select minority clients for treatment.

From *American Journal of Orthopsychiatry* (July 1976), 46(3):510–25. Reprinted by permission; copyright © 1976 American Orthopsychiatric Association. The authors acknowledge the research assistance of Thea Hambright.

Recent studies support the following contentions:

1. Third World people usually receive more serious diagnoses of mental illness (Crawford 1969; Thomas and Sillen 1972).
2. When they are given treatment at all, Third World clients receive supportive or mechanical therapies more often than intensive psychotherapy (Cohen 1969; Krebbs 1971; Thomas and Sillen 1972).
3. Their treatment is shorter in duration (Crawford 1969).
4. They are unlikely to be offered the range of services extended to white clients (Crawford 1969; Fischer 1969; Kramer, Rosen, and Willis 1973; Thomas and Sillen 1972).

Third World clients encounter greater difficulties in the mental health system than do whites, particularly when the deliverers of service are white. Although many techniques of therapy apply to all ethnic groups, the transracial therapy situation demands an additional strategy: consideration of the specific social context of the client in assessment, treatment, and patient-worker relationship (Cohen 1969; Cole 1975; Goodman 1972; Jones et al. 1970; Stiles et al. 1972; Thomas and Sillen 1972; Vontress 1971; White 1970). In some cases, failure to consider the culturally determined social context results in limited or poor services being offered to Third World people. In other cases, the client, hurt and insulted when his or her culture is misunderstood, simply terminates therapy.

This study examines the dispensation of cases seen in a county mental health service. Eighteen months before the present study the service had been changed from an outpatient psychiatric clinic to a crisis clinic. Changes included the addition of a walk-in clinic where a person may be seen without appointment, the institution of limited community education and consultation services undertaken by several staff members, and the addition of an outreach team of a half-time psychiatrist and a psychiatric nurse to make home visits. The other sixteen clinical workers see patients in the clinic. Of these, one staff member is Chicano. There are also two Third World students, one black and one Chinese. The rest of the staff of psychiatrists, psychologists, and social workers are white.

The change to a crisis clinic reflected an overt mandate submitted in the district's proposal to the National Institute of Mental Health for a service that "aims further at active involvement in the local community and neighborhood concerns with care giving." The change was surely not a complete one: Agency administrators did not in fact clarify the new mandate, nor did the agency institute new policies such as in-service education for outreach services, for brief psychotherapy or crisis intervention, or for race relations generally. Hence, some of the intended change was not implemented. Still, the organization, at certain levels, had mandated a change to improve clinic services to poor Third World clients.

While the prescribed change would suggest a possibility of reducing the differential treatment customarily afforded white and Third World clients, the authors postulated that major differences in the dispensation of care would still be found. The premise is based upon three assumptions. First, cultural stereotypes of race are slow to change. The ambiguity between recognition of cultural differences and the stereotyping of such differences create discomfort in verbal therapies between Third World clients and white clinicians (Thomas and Sillen 1972). Second, changes in overt mandate would not provide clinically trained persons with the skills needed to help Third World clients in actual stressful conditions created by their environment. Third and last, it was believed that disturbed minority males would be more easily perceived as dangerous and not suited to traditional therapies.

Method

The handwritten records of mental health workers supplied the information for the study. Records for 94 persons, half the population appearing for the first time at the crisis clinic between August and December, 1973, were included in the sample. A total of 180 cases was arranged by date of admission. Half of these were selected on an every-other-case basis. In six cases, inadequate information was supplemented by reviewing files of patients who had, at some earlier date, been seen as psychiatric outpatients.

The indices selected to determine whether race influenced the type and quality of treatment were, as far as possible, objective measures. To further minimize researcher bias, the coding was done in two stages. The first coding of the case report was a long form (three pages), and the treatment summaries were copied as verbatim highlights on the third page. In the second coding, the first page (which contained the demographic information) was physically separated from the other pages and recorded after the verbatim highlights were coded. Thus, when the coders were making judgments about the treatment variables, they were unaware of the race or socioeconomic status of the client, unless (and this was remarkably rare) this information was explicit in the summaries. Our subjectivity was minimized by relying heavily upon the actual words used by the worker in the records. For example, if the tone of verbatim highlights implied that the worker viewed the client as very intelligent, but the worker never actually wrote that the client was intelligent or bright, the variable on our coding form, "client described by worker as bright," would be coded "not indicated."

The first eight items on the coding schedule are the independent variables: ethnic group, age, sex, presence of telephone in residence, occupation of self and spouse, annual family income, number of dependents, and education of client.

Seven indices were chosen to analyze the various treatment options which patients in the clinic could receive. The seven categories were as follows: diagnosis; case disposition; medication; descriptive labels; number of visits and termination of treatment; worker's opinion of the patient; case management and supplemental services. Standard diagnostic categories were employed in making diagnoses, and these were accepted by the study. Case disposition was divided into four categories:

1. *Psychotherapy.* Any attempt by the worker and the client to solve the client's problem through talking is considered to be psychotherapy. Categories of intensive analytic therapy, group or family therapy, and directive, short-term intervention are combined; the records did not provide enough information to make reliable distinctions among the various talk therapies offered. The client may also receive medication.
2. *Referral.* The client is seen once at the clinic, and is then referred to another agency for treatment. He or she may or may not also have received medication at this clinic on the first visit.
3. *Medication only.* The client is given a prescription for drugs and is either told to return at some future date for more medication, or is not told to return.
4. *No recommendation.* The client is seen at the clinic, is not given medication, is not referred for treatment elsewhere, and is not

offered psychotherapy. The records do not indicate that any treatment is being offered to the client, and there is only one clinic visit.

Similarly, four categories of medication are chosen to distinguish potency of the drugs (Remmen et al. 1962): Prolixin, other phenothiazines (such as Thorazine), benzodiazepines (such as Librium and Valium), and "other." Only the most potent drug prescribed is scored.

Termination was considered to have been initiated by the client or by the therapist. Opinions of the patient were based upon descriptive words (and then synonyms) selected from verbatim transcripts. Terms used to describe fewer than 10 percent of the sample were dropped.

The seventh treatment index, case management and supplemental services, is a summary of three separate variables. Supplemental services include any kind of extension of service beyond psychotherapy and medication, such as worker sending letters or filling out forms for client; worker consulting with agency staff or outside the agency about client; worker giving extra time to client, perhaps offering an extra weekly session for an allotted time to overcome some crisis; or worker referring client to other clinics while client continues present clinic treatment. The second part of this variable is outreach, which is defined to mean the effort made by the worker to reestablish contact with a client who has come to the clinic at least once but fails to show up for further appointments; possible modes of contact include letters, phone calls, and home visits. (The records for this study are dated prior to the hiring of the clinic's outreach team; therefore, only one instance of a home visit was recorded.) The final variable is follow-up, defined as the worker's contact with a client whose active treatment at the clinic is terminated, but who left with prescriptions for medication to be refilled at the clinic at a future date, or instructions to return to the clinic to see how he or she was getting along.

Results

The client population in the sample included thirty-two whites, fifty blacks, nine Chicanos, two Asians, and one Arab. Because of the small numbers, the nine Chicanos and those of other races were combined with the black clients in a Third World group to facilitate comparisons with the white group. Data for blacks and Chicanos are listed separately in the tables but discussed together except when the pattern between these two groups is noticeably different. The sample contained nearly as many women as men, and data are presented separately by sex because of the strikingly different ways in which they were treated at the clinic.

The sample includes fifteen white males and seventeen white women, thirty-six Third World males, and twenty-six Third World women.[1] At least two thirds of the clients seen in either group were between the ages of twenty-one and thirty-nine. Just over 60 percent were reported as unemployed among both white and Third World groups. In fact, recent loss of employment was a common precipitant for coming to the clinic. With two exceptions, the variables of age, education, occupation, and annual family income had a remarkably similar distribution among the two ethnic groups. The major exception is the disproportionate number of white men with some college education and the relative paucity of Third World men with any college education. The other exception is the number of white women with moderate family incomes. This seems to reflect their parents' or spouses' incomes, since most of the women were unemployed. Income data are not considered reliable, as the agency's fee policy encourages falsification of income, frequently with tacit approval of the therapist.

DIAGNOSIS

The first broad area of treatment examined concerns the hypothesis that Third World clients are more likely to be diagnosed as psychotic or more seriously ill than white clients. The literature suggests that this occurs because white workers, failing to consider the differences between their own cultural environments and those of their Third World clients, view differences in behavior as pathological when, in fact, they may be realistic and adaptive (Thomas and Sillen 1972). Labeling black people as paranoid in cases where they are justifiably suspicious of white people is an example of such psychologizing (Grier and Cobbs 1968). Table 21.1 shows the actual distribution of diagnoses by race and sex.

A male client was more than twice as likely to be diagnosed in the most severe category—psychosis—than a woman. Black men in this sample were even more likely to be so diagnosed than white men. No men were diagnosed "adjustment reaction," the one category indicating a reaction to situational stress rather than enduring psychopathology. However, four white men (23 percent) and seven black women (30 percent) were so diagnosed. The data suggest that race

Table 21.1. Diagnosis of Ethnic Groups by Sex

| | White | | Third World | | | | | |
| | | | Black | | Chicano | | Total | |
Diagnosis	Male	Female	M	F	M	F	M	F
Psychotic	7	4	16	3	3	0	21[a]	3
Neurotic	3	4	2	7	0	0	2	7
Personality disorder	5	3	5	2	3	1	8	3
Adjustment reaction	0	4	0	7	0	1	0	9[b]
Other	0	2	4	4	1	0	5	4
N	15	17	27	23	7	2	36[a]	26[b]

[a] Includes two men of other races diagnosed as psychotic.
[b] Includes one woman of other race diagnosed as an adjustment reaction.

may be a factor in severity of diagnosis for black men seen at the clinic (supporting our hunch) but not for black women. A conservative factor in the rating of severity of diagnosis may be seen in the fact that nearly half of the cases are referred by a psychiatric emergency service that screens cases and sends only the less disturbed cases to the crisis clinic.

CASE DISPOSITION

We hypothesized that Third World clients, particularly males, would be less likely to receive psychotherapy and more likely either to receive more mechanical forms of therapy, such as medication or vocational rehabilitation, or be denied treatment altogether. Table 21.2 shows the service received by white and Third World clients.

More white clients received psychotherapy than did their Third World counterparts, the difference being observable among both men and women. There were a few instances of Third World clients receiving "only medication" as the form of treatment. The practice is usually considered inappropriate in a psychological clinic, where drug usage is most often considered adjunctive or facilitative in therapy. Conversely, no white patients were treated with medication alone, nor were any denied treatment (i.e., no recommendation).

It is interesting to note that of the sixteen black men who were diagnosed as psychotic, only six were offered psychotherapy, compared with all three Chicano men and six out of seven white men who were similarly diagnosed.

The importance of these differences in disposition is heightened by an examination of our summaries of case records in greater detail. The following Third World people had no recommendation for treatment:

P. is a 37-year-old black man diagnosed as paranoid schizophrenic. He came into the clinic unusually dressed with a leopard skin hat, vest, and left armband, carrying an English translation of the Koran. He said he needed codeine regularly to prevent pain and depression. When the worker asked about his mental health, he said that some people seemed concerned about it, that he was not. The worker wrote: "I pointed out that I, and probably nobody else, would provide him with narcotics. He is receiving welfare and has things to do daily and seems happy with life. I told him I would not intervene." The patient was dismissed.

S. is a 20-year-old Chicano man diagnosed as having a passive-aggressive personality disorder with depressive features. He said he was awaiting sentencing for a hit-and-run accident which occurred while he was drunk. The accident followed a fight with his parents in which he struck his mother. The worker wrote: "He fears a heavy sentence and spending time in jail. He feels his main problem is not drinking but relating to people. It was suggested that he return to court and once he has been sentenced (providing he does not go to jail), he return to the clinic."

Table 21.2. Case Disposition of Ethnic Groups by Sex

| | White | | Third World | | | | | |
| | | | Black | | Chicano | | Total | |
Disposition	Male	Female	M	F	M	F	M	F
Psychotherapy	12	15	15	17	6	2	22[a]	20[b]
Referral elsewhere	3	2	7	4	0	0	7	4
Medication only	0	0	2	1	0	0	2	1
No recommendation	0	0	2	1	1	0	3	1
Unknown	0	0	1	0	0	0	2[a]	0
N	15	17	27	23	7	2	36[a]	26[b]

[a] Includes two men of other races, one given psychotherapy and the other unknown disposition.
[b] Includes one woman of other race given psychotherapy.

The recommendation in this last case contrasts sharply with the recommendation made under similar circumstances for a white client:

C. is a 21-year-old white man diagnosed as having a neurotic depression. The worker wrote: "He has rape charges pending and wishes psychiatric treatment to cope with the anxiety about possible results of the hearing and also to obtain a more favorable judgment from the court." The clinic referred him to a private psychiatrist and gave him a referral for legal assistance.

In addition to the above cases, there were three Third World clients who were given medication only, with no other treatment or recommendations. Two are described below:

M. is a 22-year-old black man diagnosed as paranoid schizophrenic. He came in because he is anxious and tense about his wedding in two weeks to a girl who is six months pregnant. He had been hospitalized once five or six years ago for mental disorder. The worker wrote: "His hearing voices was the beginning of a relapse of schizophrenia either under the stress of his impending marriage or because he had not taken any medications for the last half year or so." She gave him a two months' supply of phenothiazine and told him to come back when the supply ran out.

J. is a 39-year-old black woman whose diagnosis was deferred. The worker said she gave her a month's supply of phenothiazines because "she does seem to need it." The patient is described as "cheerful, looking well, and feeling fine but has pressured speech and trembling hands."

Case disposition is obviously critical in understanding the suitability of treatment offered to actual client needs. The cases uncovered suggest that nonintervention or prescription of drugs without psychotherapy are the options available to manage cases that would be difficult.

TYPES OF MEDICATIONS

We expected that Third World clients would be more likely to receive medication than would white clients, and that this would reflect not only the greater seriousness of diagnosis of the mental disorders but also the tendency for lower socioeconomic classes to receive custodial types of care rather than active psychiatric intervention (Hollingshead

Table 21.3. Medications of Ethnic Groups by Sex

| | White | | Third World | | | | | |
| | | | Black | | Chicano | | Total | |
Medication	Male	Female	M	F	M	F	M	F
Prolixin	1	0	4	1	2	0	6	1
Other phenothiazines	6	6	15	8	1	0	17[a]	8
Benzodiazepines	0	2	0	6	0	1	0	7
Other drugs	1	1	0	2	1	0	1	2
None	7	8	8	6	3	1	12[a]	8[b]
N	15	17	27	23	7	2	36[a]	26[b]

[a] Includes two men of other races, one given other phenothiazines, one given no medication.
[b] Includes one woman of other race given no medication.

and Redlich 1958). Following this, it was assumed that stronger drugs would be more frequently given to Third World clients. Table 21.3 shows the distribution of different categories of drugs prescribed to clients. More than half of all the clients in our study received some form of medication. Half of the white men and women received drug therapy, while thirty-six of fifty black men and women (72 percent) received such treatment. Corresponding to the greater prevalence of psychoses among men than women, men are more likely than women to receive the more potent drugs such as Prolixin and the other phenothiazines. Since we coded only the more potent drug in cases of multiple medications, although men were prescribed Valium and Librium (the benzodiazepines), this fact is not reflected in the table. Apparently they were never given these medications without also being given the stronger phenothiazines. One case is worth noting here, as it suggests the degree to which a therapist may become dependent upon drugs for managing poorly motivated, ethnically different clients.

G. is a 23-year-old black man diagnosed as drug dependent. He came in because of difficulty sleeping, and feeling things closing in. He has a history of using a wide variety of drugs. The worker wrote: "His parents (who came in with him) are as vague as patient in terms of describing reason for such extensive drug use and such a purposeless life. Patient explains very little about himself spontaneously, tries to answer questions but seems not to have the vocabulary to do so very thoroughly. The parents wanted hospitalization today to keep him away from drugs. I refused it. We must assume patient will use thorazine for sleep only—parents may hope for more magic from it."

DESCRIPTIVE TERMS

In developing a diagnosis and treatment plan for clients, workers make various judgments about the client's personality, including possible "ego strengths." We hypothesized that more white clients would be described as intelligent and verbal than Third World clients. Workers would see them also as motivated, insightful, pleasant, and cooperative more often than they would Third World clients. Conversely, workers would more likely view a disproportionate number of Third World clients as hostile, paranoid, childish, dependent, and as tending to somatize their psychological problems (Jones et al. 1970). As seen in table 21.4, the pattern of remarks is less clear than expected.

As expected, white men were more likely to be labeled bright and verbal, and Third World men were more likely to be called paranoid. There were few appreciable differences between terms used to

Table 21.4. Descriptive Terms Applied to Ethnic Groups by Sex

| Descriptive Term | White | | Third World | | | | | |
| | | | Black | | Chicano | | Total | |
	Male	Female	M	F	M	F	M	F
Bright	5	2	1	4	0	0	1	4
Verbal	8	5	4	7	0	1	4	8
Cooperative	3	1	5	5	1	0	6	5
Pleasant	5	0	4	4	1	0	5	4
Somatizing	2	1	5	6	0	0	5	7[a]
Paranoid	2	2	15	6	1	0	17[b]	6
Hostile	0	0	7	3	1	0	8	3
Dependent	4	7	6	5	1	0	7	5
Not motivated	2	4	5	4	2	1	8[b]	6[a]
N[c]	15	17	27	23	7	2	36[b]	26[a]

[a] Includes one woman of other race described as somatizing and not motivated.
[b] Includes two men of other races, one described as paranoid, the other as not motivated.
[c] Descriptive categories are not mutually exclusive, thus N is less than the sum of the columns.

Table 21.5. Number of Visits of Ethnic Groups by Sex

| | White | | Third World | | | | | |
| | | | Black | | Chicano | | Total | |
Visits	Male	Female	M	F	M	F	M	F
One	4	3	12	9	1	1	14[a]	10
2–5	3	9	8	6	4	1	13[a]	7
6–12	3	2	6	3	0	0	6	4[b]
13–19	1	2	1	5	2	0	3	5
20 or more	4	1	0	0	0	0	0	0
N	15	17	27	23	7	2	36[a]	26[b]

[a] Includes two men of other races, one with one visit, the other with 2–5 visits.
[b] Includes one woman of other race with 6–12 visits.

describe white and Third World women although, as with men, Third World women in this sample were more likely to be described as hostile and paranoid than were white women. In contrast, and contrary to our expectations, the workers labeled more whites than Third World clients as childish or dependent.

DURATION OF TREATMENT AND TERMINATION

Although therapists might give Third World clients psychotherapy, we hypothesized that their treatment would be of shorter duration than that given to white clients, for one of two possible reasons: 1) the worker would be unable to identify with the client and his or her problems; or 2) perhaps the worker would be uninterested or unable to change or affect the environmental stresses facing the client. Table 21.5 shows that black men and women were more likely to have only one clinic visit than were white men and women, and that no Third World men or women were seen in the clinic more than twenty times. Was this the choice of the client or of the worker? That is, did the client fail to show up for further appointments, or did the worker terminate treatment?

Termination is scored for all clients who were seen at least one time and were no longer being seen at the end of the study period. It includes, therefore, all cases not recommended for further visits (whether or not medication was prescribed), those referred elsewhere, and those who were seen again for any length of time.

From table 21.6 we see that black men are more than twice as likely as white men to be terminated by the worker. The differences

Table 21.6. Termination Status of Ethnic Groups by Sex

| | | | Third World | | | | | |
| | White | | Black | | Chicano | | Total | |
Termination	Male	Female	M	F	M	F	M	F
Client	10	9	6	11	0	2	6	14[a]
Worker	3	3	13	6	2	0	15	6
Current	2	3	4	5	2	0	7[b]	5
Other	0	2	4	1	3	0	8[b]	1
N	15	17	27	23	7	2	36[b]	26[a]

[a] Includes one woman of other race who terminated treatment herself.
[b] Includes two men of other races, one currently in therapy, the other of unknown status.

among women are minimal. Perhaps the differences among women were not larger because black women are considered more verbal and "self-disclosing" (Vontress 1971) than black men and are, therefore, more amenable to the kind of treatment in which the worker is interested. They are also not as threatening and frightening to white mental health workers as many of their male counterparts.

The twenty-one Third World clients terminated from treatment by the worker include seven who were either medicated or not recommended for treatment, another seven who were referred elsewhere for treatment after one clinic visit, and a third group of seven who had been offered psychotherapy. Of these, five were abruptly terminated after fewer than five visits, and the other two terminated after a dozen visits found them unresponsive to talk therapy. The following is an example of abrupt termination by the therapist:

D. is a 28-year-old black woman diagnosed as having a personality disorder. She came to the clinic after her two-year-old twins were removed from her home because she had physically abused and injured the girl twin several times. She is described as "attractive, obese, articulate, intelligent and pleasant." During the third visit, the worker said, "we discussed intrapsychic vs. extrapsychic tensions. The client stated that her most pressing problem was extrapsychic." The worker wrote: "My impression is that the court has told her she has problems and they must be solved because if they are not solved, the court will see and treat her as a criminal." The worker went on to say, "The problem seems clear; it is a repetition of her own childhood experiences (of severe punishment) which she was acting out on her own children, but it isn't clear that anything can be done to change these patterns in brief psychotherapy." Therapy was terminated after only three visits.

This same worker saw two white men more than twenty-five times. Both were diagnosed as chronically psychotic, so that it is not at all clear whether it was his commitment to brief psychotherapy, his inability to affect change in the patient, or his lack of interest which prompted the early termination of D.

Four of the five white clients in treatment for more than twenty-five visits were extremely verbal, introspective, and involved in working on the therapeutic relationship. They all had some college education and were between the ages of twenty-two and thirty-one. Only one black client, a woman who was a college graduate with a good income, was kept in treatment for as long as nineteen visits. All six of the white clients who were terminated from treatment by the worker were referred for treatment elsewhere after one clinic visit, which was a screening interview. None was terminated by the therapist after brief psychotherapy.

In an effort to rule out the social class influence on duration of treatment and termination, we examined the data for white and Third World clients with roughly the same level of education, excluding those who were college graduates (mostly white clients) and those with less than high school degrees (mostly Third World clients). The results show that the differences between white and Third World men are even greater for those with similar education than for the group as a whole. Thus, at least for these two variables of treatment, we conclude that ethnic differences, rather than social class, were important in determining length of treatment and who was responsible for termination of treatment.

CASE MANAGEMENT AND SERVICES

The various types of services offered in addition to drugs and psychotherapy were also investigated. These included services such as outreach, follow-up, extra time, referrals to other agencies during treatment, and filling out forms (Crawford 1969). We hypothesized that white clients are more likely to receive a wider range of these services than Third World clients. In the absence of clear clinic policies about what services are to be offered by the staff, those extended are a result of interest on the part of the worker or sophistication on the part of the client in requesting such services. It was assumed that white clients would receive more ancillary services because workers' identification with them might engender greater interest. Whites have also had more success in generating institutional responsiveness; hence, they may be less cynical about making requests and having these requests honored than are the majority of Third World consumers.

Table 21.7 shows that for the services described the data do not support our hypotheses, and in some cases show more services for Third World clients. However, the data also show that few people, white or Third World, receive these extra services. To the extent that Third World people are in greater need of such extensions of care, they might still be receiving proportionately less. But some indeed are receiving these services. What is most interesting in this connection is a comparison of some outstanding cases of service and nonservice which occurred across ethnic groups. The cases studied show examples among white clients of both good and bad service. The inadequacies included failure to contact a suicidal patient who missed two appointments, failure of referral to homemaking services in the case of a teen-ager suffering under the load of caring for five step-siblings, failure to check records indicating prior suicide attempts, and failure to assist client or immediate family members to obtain services for alcoholism or for drug addiction after the problem was made known to the therapist.

Table 21.7. Case Management and Supplemental Services of Ethnic Groups by Sex

	White		Third World					
			Black		Chicano		Total	
Supplemental Service[a]	Male	Female	M	F	M	F	M	F
Services	4	6	13	4	5	0	18	5[b]
Outreach	4	3	5	5	4	2	9	7
Follow-up	0	0	2	0	1	0	3	0

[a] Service categories are not mutually exclusive; unaccounted-for-cases are excluded.
[b] Includes one woman of other race given service.

The services extended to Third World clients were not necessarily better or worse than those extended to white clients. Besides the seven who received no treatment or were only medicated, fourteen additional clients appeared in need of services that were not forthcoming. In some cases, poor case management is obvious. For example, in a few cases there was no attempt to phone or write clients who failed to return for their appointments. The following example suggests case mismanagement and discontinuity in service:

A. is a 16-year-old Chicano diagnosed as schizophrenic. He was brought into the clinic by his mother because he is withdrawn. He dropped out of school and watches TV all day. During his five visits to the clinic, he slowly began to "open up." His worker consulted with various people and spent considerable effort arranging an appropriate high school program for him. However, the program in which he was accepted was not scheduled to begin for two months. The worker dismissed the client, telling him to return in two months when his school program was scheduled to begin. Two months later, the client did not appear. Nor did he enter school. The worker commented, "His cooperation apparently is ended now."

The records provided two notable examples of white workers failing to deal with the excessive environmental stress confronting the client:

B. is a 36-year-old black woman with five children. She receives AFDC, as she is unemployed, and her former husband, to whom she was married for fourteen years, is incarcerated. The client's presenting complaints are that she is having a great deal of trouble sleeping and that she is suicidal. She described her sense of helplessness, ineffectiveness, and sadness. The worker described her as "childlike and of limited intelligence," explaining that she had to take a strong educational approach with her—attempting to empathize with her infantile side and her dependency needs. At no time during this treatment did the worker mention the real life difficulties facing this woman.

R. is a 40-year-old Chicano who has recently separated from his wife, and is having difficulty "getting her out of his mind." He is "depressed and suicidal, and has few social resources." His treatment consisted of five individual therapy sessions in which the psychiatrist medicated him and noted merely that "he wants marriage and a wife to play into." Although it is noted on his background record that he was one of three survivors in a unit of several hundred men all of whom were killed in Korea, this was not dealt with. Neither was the fact that he has worked twelve hours a day, including weekends, for twenty years in order to maintain his own business.

The data show five cases where some form of advocacy, active intervention on the part of the worker for the good of the client, occurred. In two situations, letters were written by workers to employers explaining a client's absence or disability. In a third case, a worker arranged for a reduced fee for dental treatment for a black client's son. There were two other instances of remarkable extension of service, both involving young Chicano men:

E. is a 23-year-old Chicano diagnosed as a latent schizophrenic. He recently moved from the South, describing his life as "moving from failure to failure." He was seen six times by one worker who tried to place him in a board-and-care home. The worker also referred him for more vocational rehabilitation, helped him to apply for Social Security, and accompanied him to another clinic which would provide him daily treatment. Finally, the interested worker called him daily, to give him support for going to day treatment.

H. is a 23-year-old Chicano diagnosed as a chronic undifferentiated schizophrenic. His mother came to the clinic to get help for the son, as he refuses to leave the house and talks to himself. The worker made a home visit and described the client's symptoms as "using ritualistic hand motions, inappropriate laughter and making repetitive statements about having to be satisfied with the way the country is going." He did not respond to any questions. "His father showed me the scrapbook of newspaper clippings of FBI, CIA, and police activities. His father said he appeared normal until he was 18 when he and his friends had to register for the draft at which time he began to withdraw from social contacts." The worker made the next home visit with a nurse and a psychiatrist, in order to evaluate the client's need for medication. He then made two subsequent home visits until the parents decided to sign a petition to have him admitted for hospitalization.

Some white therapists appear quite willing to extend themselves to Third World clients when they do not show up for appointments and when they appear overburdened with environmental problems. It must be noted that in most of the cases in which unusual services were offered to Third World clients in this sample, the clients were Chicano rather than black. Finally, while the records indicate that more Third World than white clients received these services, the great majority of the clinic's clients receive no such services at all.

DEALING WITH RACE IN PSYCHOTHERAPY

There was no need for examination, in any quantitative way, of instances in which the issue of racial difference between therapist and client was noted in the records. In only one case was the difference in race mentioned, and the issue was raised by the client. In this case, the refusal on the part of the worker to acknowledge the importance of the racial difference between the worker and the client, and to comprehend and respond to the patient's point world view, lost the client to the clinic.

K., a 28-year-old black woman with two years of college, came to the clinic seeking counseling concerning her recent marriage. Her stated goal was that she wanted to learn to be "submissive" to her husband. However, when she was assigned a young, white woman therapist, she requested a transfer to an older man, for she felt that the woman worker was too interested in women's liberation, an attitude which she believed would interfere with her treatment. Her request for transfer was denied when the white worker told her that "her lack of confidence in the worker was related to her lack of confidence in her husband and everyone else." The client asserted that this wasn't the problem; rather, the worker's theories about women's liberation conflicted with what she wanted from therapy. To this the worker replied that "her own theories were irrelevant and that her problem was that she was afraid to give up control." K. allowed that this was an interesting conjecture, but it is not surprising that she never returned to the clinic.

While the purpose of psychotherapy is surely not to teach women to be more submissive, it is clear that the ethnocultural disparity did effect the ability of the therapist to convey understanding of the patient's problem, or even to acknowledge hearing it.

The only other data we have on the issue of dealing with race in psychotherapy come from interviews with the staff regarding their preferences in clients and their perceptions of the importance of racial differences to their work.[2]

In general, therapists prefer treating clients with whom they identify and whom they consider good candidates for treatment. This favors patients with the fewest environmental (reality-based) difficulties that the workers feel impotent to change. This conclusion is supported in material provided by direct interview with clinic staff members. For example, when asked, "If poor, Third World people do get to the clinic, is there something about their attitudes or problems which makes them difficult to treat?" one therapist responded: "Their problems tend to be more often psychotic and difficult to treat. They're not motivated to help themselves. The concept is you go to a doctor and he fixes you, not you fix yourself."

Another responded: "They have less psychological sophistication." And a third said: "You can work with the attitude. The thing you can't always work with is the problem—that's the auxiliary service thing. Poverty is something that's hard. You have to prove yourself to them, especially if they're more deprived."

When asked, "What kind of problems do you most enjoy handling?" one worker replied: "If someone comes in and can talk about events, and I can help them clarify them. . . . If a person's problems are centered in his outside world, I can't help him change his problem or lack of job. I am more uncomfortable with that kind of client. I enjoy working with problems I can solve."

And another described her favorite cases as follows: "Intrapsychic problems that involve a minimum of environmental stress contributing to them."

Some of the therapists at the crisis clinic did not consider race an important issue among their Third World clients. One worker commented: "My assessment is that black consciousness is not a big issue or a main problem."

Another made this comment about the need for more Third World staff: "More racial balance? It might make the clinic more appealing. But I believe that a therapist must be objective. I think that the allegation of racism is a fairly naive interpretation."

Some of the workers are, of course, more sensitive to racial issues. Many are in accord with one who spoke of the need for more minority staff: "This place is like a fortress, underrepresentation of

Third World staff is problably felt by people who come once and not again."

Summary and Discussion

Clear and consistent differences are found in psychiatric treatment between white and Third World men. White men in this sample are more likely to be diagnosed as neurotic or less seriously ill, to receive psychotherapy, to be treated without medication, to receive long-term therapy, to terminate treatment themselves, and to be described as bright or verbal. Third World men are more likely to be described as hostile or paranoid. Supportive services, outreach, and follow-up, while uncommon, were however given as frequently to Third World clients as to whites.

The patterns for women did not support the hypothesis of racial differences. There are similarities in the treatment of white men and women and Third World women that are more obvious than the differences. The treatment for Third World men, particularly black men, fell far short of what others received.

If we combine the various options open to the worker, we find that over 40 percent of the white men who come to the crisis clinic were given psychotherapy, compared with 20 percent of the black men. While we had hypothesized substantial differences for men, the lack of a general pattern of difference in treatment for the women was not expected. Surely there were specific instances in which the racial difference between client and therapist affected the course of treatment. It may also be that cultural differences, stereotypes, suspicions, or uneasiness may emerge at any time to interfere with therapy. It is likely that the moderately disturbed black woman presented little immediate threat. Still, her duration of therapy tended to be shorter, suggesting some factor, perhaps race-related, affecting the relationship.

While psychotherapy is surely considered the preferred mode of treatment among the staff of the crisis clinic, the failure to provide it as frequently to black men is understandable if not justifiable. Psychotherapy requires good rapport. There are several factors inhibiting the development of effective therapeutic relationships between black men and white therapists. Surely the elements of black rage and white fear are operative, particularly when the black men are considered psychotic. The combination of severe psychological disturbance with differences in cultural or racial backgrounds may frighten the workers into medicating or immediately referring these clients elsewhere for treatment.

The literature suggests that, in treating Third World patients, a special understanding and attitude are of primary importance, but that new techniques are not always necessary (Cohen 1969). Therapists must maintain a delicate balance between perceiving problems of Third World groups as all psychological or as all social. Third World people need to be viewed as people—not only as individuals with a unique constellation of attributes, but also as members of a group with distinct cultural experiences. In this crisis clinic study, 90 percent of the Third World clients were treated by white workers, who had received no special training for their work with this client population.

In none of the reports of these therapeutic encounters did the worker initiate discussion of race or ethnic differences between client and worker. Successful psychotherapeutic relationships demand an atmosphere of mutual trust and respect. How can such a process be attempted without the mention of such a significant factor as the difference of ethnicity between client and therapist? Thomas and Sillen (1972), remarking on the widespread lack of inquiry into the cultural backgrounds of patients, said that perhaps this is a hyper-sensitive concern to avoid being discriminatory; more likely it is a lack of understanding on the part of the therapists.

The purpose of this investigation is not to place blame. The crisis clinic stands among mental health facilities that have taken some steps toward accessibility and service to their Third World clientele. A number of staff members support this move and an official, if dusty, mandate sanctions the direction. It is clear, therefore, that an official statement and the presence of sincere hopes for change in this area are not sufficient for its accomplishment. Therapists still receive, typically, no special training in community outreach, advocacy, consultation, organizing, or coordination with other services. Neither do they receive extensive training or experience in matters of racial and cultural differences and similarities. The findings suggest a shortcoming in professional education of psychotherapists, as well as need for in-service training programs to assist staff in their work. There is a clear need for the clinic to hire a greater number of Third World, including bilingual, therapists. In the psychothera-peutic endeavor, in which the trust between client and professional is a critical ingredient, suspicions arising out of racial differences should not have to be an added burden. The client's selection of a psychotherapist with whom he or she can feel comfortable is an important beginning of what is probably the most difficult and sensitive of health facilitating services.

NOTES

1. The Third World sample was largely black. Of thirty-six Third World males, there were seven Chicanos, one Near Eastern, and one Asian. Of twenty-six Third World women, there were two Chicanos and one Asian in the sample.

2. The interview material quoted is excerpted from a larger study (Cole 1975). The material selected is for the purpose of highlighting those differences in treatment found to be related to race. This is not an inclusive report of interview statements obtained from the staff.

PART III

CHANGE IN SOCIAL WELFARE

A. INNOVATION

BECAUSE the co-editors believe that social welfare in the United States is at a turning point, a part of the reader is devoted to the subject of change. Since the major upheavals in the society and in social welfare in the 1960s, exemplified by the massive but essentially failed War on Poverty, change has been a dominant focus in the field. It is important to note that impetus for change comes not only from the federal government, as was the case with the War on Poverty, but also from indigenous sources. The three sections in this final part make that amply clear, in their analyses of self-help, insurgent, and other grass-roots pressures for change. Section B focuses on reform and insurgency, while section C examines social welfare's future.

Section A, "Innovation," includes three selections which discuss and analyze programmatic innovations in social service delivery. The first selection, "Responding to Skid Row Alcoholism" by Lincoln J. Fry and Jon Miller, is a case study based on participant observation of an alcoholism treatment clinic. The study identifies several reasons for the program's failure, including a generic source of problems for social welfare agencies—ambiguous and conflicting goals. Perhaps the most interesting finding by Fry and Miller is that large public expenditures contributed to the problem by attracting people to skid row. This was an unintended and self-defeating consequence of the program.

A major innovative concept in social welfare that grew out of the ferment of the 1960s is the guaranteed annual income. The unrealized Family Assistance Plan of the Nixon administration was a conservative version of this idea. A principal reservation about such a program is its possible negative effect on the work incentive of beneficiaries. Sonia Rosenbaum and James D. Wright, in "Income Maintenance and Work Behavior," address this question with data from the New Jersey-Pennsylvania Negative Income Tax Experiment.

They conclude that such a program does not necessarily create work disincentives for those who receive income.

Groups such as Alcoholics Anonymous have been practicing self-help for decades (see Gellman 1964). However, it has lately become an increasingly common phenomenon. Social movements of the 1960s featured many self-help endeavors, including health care groups generated by the feminist movement (see Boston Women's Health Book Collective 1976). The growth of such groups can be explained, in part, by the dissatisfactions produced by impersonal and authoritarian social welfare programs. Alfred H. Katz did early work analyzing the nature of self-help groups. In the final selection in section A, "Self-Help Organizations and Volunteer Participation in Social Welfare," he examines the characteristics of groups composed of parents of the handicapped. Katz points out that self-help groups are usually composed of peers, minimizing the role of professionals.

[22]

RESPONDING TO SKID ROW ALCOHOLISM

Lincoln J. Fry and Jon Miller

BASED upon twenty-seven months of participant observation in a skid row mission, this study explores some of the factors that contributed to the ineffectiveness and ultimate failure of what began as a highly promising alcoholism rehabilitation program. The program was very generously funded from state and local resources; it was technically and philosophically innovative; it was highly professionalized and staffed by young, bright, eager practitioners. Further, it was located in the treatment quarters of an established, highly regarded religious organization that could add stability and experience to this impressive array of financial and professional resources. Despite these advantages the experiment could be credited with almost no positive impact on the alcoholism problem surrounding it, and its professional staff could be seen to change from confidence, to desperation, and finally to disengagement as the failure of the program became apparent.

The study describes how the initial optimism generated by this program was eventually overwhelmed by internal and external considerations. The program began with ambiguous and conflicting goals which led to organizational conflicts involving the competing vested interests of participants. A related factor was the absence of workable technologies for achieving stated objectives.

Before we describe the evolution of the program in more detail, a brief comment on the difficulty of defining and measuring organizational goals and effectiveness seems useful. Assessing the effectiveness of organizations has always been an elusive task. Perhaps in reaction, Warren (1973) has taken social scientists to task for contin-

From *Social Problems* (June 1975), 22(5):675–88. Reprinted by permission.

uing to support ineffective large-scale comprehensive and coordinating strategies designed to alleviate urban social problems. These strategies increasingly consist of interorganizational and interdisciplinary networks designed to present a "unified" attack on a specific problem. They often have vigorous advocates, yet clear guidelines have not been established to measure or promote effectiveness, at either the organizational or interorganizational level. Organizational effectiveness is usually conceptualized in terms of the degree of goal-achievement (Etzioni 1961, 1964; Thompson 1968); however, goals have proved hard to identify. As a result, Etzioni (1964) finds it necessary to distinguish between "real" and "stated" goals while Perrow (1961) identifies "stated" as distinct from "operational" goals. When goals are stated imprecisely they may provide little insight for the observer to record the operation of the organization and measure its effectiveness. However, it is equally important to remember that when goals are imprecisely defined this fact may itself be a factor preventing the organization's participants from moving in any consistent direction. More than any other single factor, the inability clearly to specify and implement its objectives condemned the project we are about to describe to failure.

An Innovative Treatment Program

A major piece of state legislation made funds available for counties in California to create "comprehensive" alcoholism treatment systems. This legislation was designed to promote cooperation between different levels of government and agencies involved in alcoholism treatment; its major impact was to create interorganizational treatment ventures, especially between the state department of vocational rehabilitation and county health departments. Prior to this legislation, alcoholism treatment was offered by a number of separate local, county, and state government agencies, and by private organizations. In the system we studied, one county-wide treatment system was developed with the new funding which centered on services previously offered by the health department. Four clinics made up the system; three of the four clinics were joint ventures between the county health department and the state department of vocational rehabilitation. The fourth clinic was located in a skid row mission operated for a number of years by a large philanthropic religious organization. Data for the present study were collected primarily within this unusual mixed clinic and mission setting. The study involved twenty-seven months of participant observation, supplemented by questionnaires and strategic interviews (see Fry and Miller 1975).

THE MISSION

The mission, which could accommodate 235 residents, occupied the first five floors of a building originally built as a hotel. (The physical location of the clinic and some of the residents changed toward the end of the study when a new wing was opened in the building.) The first floor contained office space, kitchen and dining areas, and a chapel. The second floor housed a medical clinic, a detoxification unit, and further office space. Residents lived in single, double, and dormitory style rooms on the upper floors.

The mission's management structure consisted of a titular head, charged with responsibility for the spiritual well-being of residents, and a business manager responsible for financial affairs. Resident responsibility rested with the house manager and his assistant. These two, both recovered alcoholics, supervised the house staff recruited from the resident alcoholic population. The house manager was an employee of the religious organization and could be moved from one facility to another. The manager had been in this mission six years when the study began. House staff, on the other hand, were attached only to a particular facility, and their employment was transitory.[1]

Located on the main thoroughfare of a major metropolitan skid row, the building which housed the mission appeared more modern than the typical structures lining the street; these were primarily other missions, old hotels, pawnshops, and cheap bars. Men in various stages of intoxication populated the street, some sleeping in doorways. The major visible activity conducted on the street appeared to be drinking, primarily wine from bottles in brown paper bags. Periodically, paddy wagons appeared and took some of the men to jail, usually those who appeared unable to care for themselves.

The other missions on the street offered the traditional "three hots and a cot" as their major service to alcoholics. In contrast, this facility had always stressed long-term residency and treatment. Whether recruiting from the street, "walk-ins," or through its court program, the mission had traditionally admitted residents based upon an assessment of the individual's determination to stop drinking and to show a commitment to the work ethic. Treatment involved religious meetings and employment services; Alcoholics Anonymous meetings were held in the facility once a week. Employment consisted of "day work," with some hope of eventually finding steady work allowing a resident to leave the mission altogether. Most treatment activities were scheduled in the evening and focused on the religious activities and the residents' commonly shared drinking problem.

THE CLINIC

The clinic added to this mission was not a completely new venture. Previously, several professional and clerical personnel had been housed in the mission, including a social worker, a part-time physician for physical examinations, a social service aide, and a clerk. As a result of new funding, increased resources were provided by the agencies involved in the program and, most important, an interdisciplinary treatment team was added. The purpose of this team approach was to concentrate the technical expertise of several fields on the single problem of alcoholism and to coordinate this effort with that of the mission.

The health department provided a number of members for the interdisciplinary team, including several social workers and nurses, a public health investigator, a recreation therapist, and several part-time counselors. The state department of vocational rehabilitation provided the team with a rehabilitation counselor, several part-time physicians for physical examinations, a part-time job developer, and several social service aides. Both the county and the state provided clerical staff. In addition, the state provided the rehabilitation counselor with a budget which included money to be used for room and board for selected patients as well as for training and educational expenses. This vital financial resource in the hands of the treatment team was to become an important factor in the evolution of the program.

The clinic expansion began when a rehabilitation counselor was assigned to the mission. At this time, those professional personnel employed in the mission prior to the increased funding were replaced by other professional personnel recruited specifically to staff the interdisciplinary team. This made clear from the outset that the clinic was to be committed to a counseling technology dispensed through the team method, a group practice in which a number of professionals (four or five, in this setting) meet with a single patient (Horwitz

1970). Through their mutual interaction consensus theoretically develops between patient and team as to the course of treatment.

Alcoholics who entered the mission had a choice. They could become clinic patients or they could be designated just as residents of the mission facility. Nonclinic residents were to be under the sole jurisdiction of the religious organization. Both types of patients were live-ins, and were not segregated within the mission. The clinic facility provided minimal outpatient services. The planning which provided for the expanded services offered in the mission was intended to broaden the mission's sources of patients. In addition to the surrounding skid row, the sources of recruitment became the probation department, the court system, hospitals, other clinics within the county system, and walk-ins. The mission had received residents from the criminal justice system before the team-oriented clinic was added, but the public health investigator attached to the team had a formal responsibility to work with the court system and to expand the number of alcoholics sent to the mission by the courts.

Emerging Difficulties

EARLY ORGANIZATIONAL PROBLEMS: AMBIGUOUS GOALS AND COMPETING INTERESTS

The clinic became operational with the usual optimism expressed by the county treatment system and by the religious organization. Initially, everyone agreed that the clinic represented a change from the old method of alcoholism treatment on skid row and that the clinic was a harbinger of the future. This consensus was largely illusory and short-lived because the immediate changes created by the clinic expansion were more far-reaching than the simple addition of another treatment modality would warrant. The team approach affected all aspects of the mission environment in fundamental ways and the unanticipated sources of contention were many.

The clinic team immediately began to recruit its own patients, to establish training, education, and job development programs for these patients, and to acquire some degree of influence over how the mission operated. As a result, the first problem that emerged was establishing working relationships and mutual objectives for the mission and the clinic. These relationships had not received much attention until after the clinic began to function, and the consequence was the alienation of the mission's resident staff at the very outset of the program when it was least prepared to tolerate strain. In the beginning, a series of meetings was initiated between the mission's management and clinic personnel in order to establish mutually acceptable policies. These meetings took place primarily between the titular head of the mission and the rehabilitation counselor attached to the interdisciplinary team, with the house manager and his staff excluded for several months. The house staff's anger over this exclusion was further accentuated because all the professionals replaced in the transition to the clinic's team treatment had been considered friends by the house staff because they had rarely interfered in the internal operation of the mission. Both the clinic and mission's management became aware, belatedly, that the exclusion of the house staff from policy-making was a major source of resentment but not until there was serious damage to the working environment. In fact, after this point the clinic personnel never enjoyed the full confidence of the house staff. The house staff found a major source of support gone and in its place a new group of professionals who threatened all their time-tested procedures.

Within weeks, a second problem arose over the proper role of medical treatment in the mission and clinic. Both the clinic and the mission indicated that alcoholism treatment was their primary goal, but there was no agreement over the proper approach to take. This was another problem not fully aired before the venture began. The mission's management stressed the medical aspects of alcoholism and requested that a medical director be appointed to head the clinic. The clinic personnel refused to endorse the medical approach to alcoholism treatment or the call for a medical director because they defined the interdisciplinary team model as an alternative to medical treatment. They thought counseling was a more promising approach, and the medical services provided by the clinic were ideally relegated to a supplementary role.

This debate over approaches to alcoholism treatment led to a basic disagreement over the use of drugs in the mission. Consistent with their stress on the medical model, the mission's management was adamant that all of the residents, clinic and nonclinic, be required to take antabuse (a substance which makes alcoholics violently ill if they drink alcohol). The clinic was at best ambivalent about the use of antabuse and related medications, including tranquilizers, which they considered inconsistent with the counseling treatment approach.

They thought patients heavily medicated were not as likely to "get in touch with themselves." The clinic compromised by requiring antabuse for all mission residents, while it understood that the medical director issue would be reconsidered at a later date. In fact, a medical director was never appointed during the course of the study, an outcome representing a considerable victory for the bureaucratic autonomy of the treatment team. However, the agreement to prescribe antabuse was a high professional and philosophical price to pay for this concession.

A third source of early disagreement between mission and clinic involved general personnel procedures. Since the clinic primarily hired recent graduates for regular positions and filled part-time positions with graduate students, the professional staff was unusually young. The house staff and the residents complained bitterly that these new professionals were simply not old enough, despite their training, to understand resident problems. (A common complaint from the residents was that they had been on skid row before some of the staff were born.) At the same time, the mission's management had complaints about the clinic's young staff, with a miniskirted graduate student a major source of consternation.

PERSISTENT STRAINS: EMPLOYMENT, SOCIAL CONTROL AND RECRUITMENT

The problems we have described so far would seem sufficient to drain off much of the initial enthusiasm for the program. Yet, in the face of these early sources of strain, the interdisciplinary team members continued to show enthusiasm for their work. Before long, however, an instance of open conflict developed in the area of employment that went to the heart of the program. Employment was the core element of the treatment effort. The state department of vocational rehabilitation to which the clinic was accountable defined success strictly in terms of employment. This agency provided all of the case service monies in the clinic, and this money was used legitimately only if related to employment potential. As a result, successful rehabilitation was initially defined by the clinic as ninety days working and not drinking. The mission also relied on employment as the major indicator of success, but without a specified time period. The mission relied on the residents' ability to leave and become self-supporting as the major indicator of success. Neither the clinic nor the mission was actually concerned with alcoholism treatment per se as the primary operational criterion determining success.

The clinic and the mission had separate employment programs that began to compete for residents who appeared to be likely candidates for rehabilitation. Each side was critical of the other's approach to the role of employment in the rehabilitation process. The clinic stressed steady work. Day work was not steady work and therefore could not contribute to the rehabilitation of clinic patients. The mission, on the other hand, felt that the clinic's approach to employment was a clear indicator that no realistic conception existed of the type of people who populated the mission. The mission staff thought taking a job in a strange location with a steady work routine spelled disaster for skid row alcoholics. The clinic stressed employment away from skid row and had an employment arrangement with an outside industrial firm. The mission staff thought this would leave the resident isolated, alone in a room in a strange location, and the alcoholic's immediate reaction would be to begin drinking again. A return to skid row would quickly follow and the mission would be defeated once again.

The clinic personnel were antagonistic toward the day labor program of the mission for several reasons. First, day labor is characteristic of the skid row scene. Referred to as "slave markets," day labor offices usually provide skid row residents with just enough money for wine and a "flop" for the night. The clinic felt residents should change their life style and that day labor merely kept them on skid row. Furthermore, the religious organization collected room and board from each resident's day labor effort while the residents were not charged anything if they did not work. Clinic personnel considered this "negative reinforcement" for working. The dispute over the proper role of employment in rehabilitation was never really resolved, and it remained an inescapable source of strain between the clinic personnel and the mission staff.

Several of the persistent sources of strain appeared by the close of the first holiday season after the clinic team was introduced. The holidays were a significant rite of passage for most of the clinic personnel. There was a huge turnover and loss of patients in the facility over Christmas and New Year's because of drinking associated with this period. This devastation of the clients had an effect upon the staff and their attitudes toward the clients as well as their work role within the mission because it demonstrated just how ephemeral the effects of their efforts could be. After these heavy patient losses, the clinic became much more defensive, and less confident, about its approach to treatment and its role in the mission.

Many team members began to complain that their patients were forced to leave the mission because of arbitrary decisions made by the house staff. A more general controversy arose over whether both the clinic and the mission staff tried to "protect their own." Team members accused the house staff of allowing certain individuals to drink in the mission with immunity from the rule that this was an automatic reason for dismissal. The clinic staff believed this questionable privilege was reserved for special (nonclinic) patients. At the same time, the house staff raised a similar complaint about the clinic staff: the professionals were accused of not recognizing minor drinking as an infringement upon the rule against drinking. They were also charged with giving their patients second and third chances to remain in the facility once caught drinking. In short, both the clinic and the mission staff accused the other of subverting the established primary goal of the mission: alcoholism treatment based upon total abstinence in an alcohol-free environment.

The house manager had almost sole power to dismiss residents from the facility. In principle, he could be overruled by the titular head of the mission, but this rarely happened. As a result of the controversy over dismissal of residents, the mission's management was pressured to agree to a policy put forward by the clinic that dismissal of clinic patients should only be by mutual agreement. The clinic gained this concession primarily because of the money paid for the room and board of clinic patients. This was an important financial resource for the mission, and it gave the clinic leverage not otherwise available. Management's agreement to share social control with the clinic was interpreted by the mission's staff as a sellout, an indication that money was more important to management than its own responsibility to maintain order in the mission.

The conflict between mission staff and the clinic over these issues became so severe that residents began to have to take sides, and distinct camps emerged within the patient population based upon these allegiances. Employment again became the crucial factor in this polarization. The residents were caught in a bind. Since day labor was the only reliable source of ready cash, they were reluctant to offend the head of the day labor office by fraternizing with the clinic personnel, for this might mean being turned away from the day labor office. Clinic personnel also put pressure on the residents: continuing on day labor jobs indicated a patient was not sincere about changing his life style, and this activity could bring him into disfavor with the clinic personnel. It was not unusual for team members to request residents to quit the day labor office and formulate a workable training or job development plan in order to receive the special benefits the clinic could offer.

As distinct camps among the residents became visible, a distinct recruitment pattern emerged. The clinic began to recruit surprisingly highly qualified patients through its linkages with various referring agencies. When the clinic began its operation, recruits had been more or less pot luck. As time passed, clinic patients became differentiated from the typical house nonclinic resident as well as from the alcoholics who populated the surrounding streets. The educational levels of some of these patients were impressive. The list included engineers, accountants, data-processing specialists, white-collar workers, and numerous skilled craftsmen. Some unique skills were represented, including a former college mathematics professor and a herpetologist. Individuals with high levels of education and skill are not unknown though uncommon among the skid row alcoholic population. The clinic actively recruited this type of client.

The clinic's recruitment pattern can be explained by the need to demonstrate the superiority of its approach to alcoholism treatment. The clinic not only tried to prove its superiority to the mission, it also felt pressure to meet the expectations imposed by the larger county clinic system. They recruited atypical clinic patients because such patients seemed "easy rehabs," if the major problem for the practitioner was to find work for the client, not to train and then place him. This impression was mistaken because all major employment efforts met with failure. Yet the clinic continued to recruit this type of patient. A common request at patient assignment session was: "Please give me someone with at least a high school education or preferably some college: they do much better in my group." Given the very low incidence of success with these patients, it is not clear what "doing better" meant. Nevertheless, the preference for skilled and previously successful clients persisted.

A number of clinic patients had little or no previous skid row experience. One reason was the increasing number of recruitment efforts within the criminal justice system (the probation department and the courts) rather than within the surrounding skid row area.

Other clinics in the county-wide treatment system but outside the skid row area also referred clients to the mission clinic because it was the only live-in facility available in the county system. Because of this pattern of recruitment and referral, many men were brought to skid row who otherwise might not have come there.

The mission's recruitment pattern also began to change at about the same time, for much the same reason. Admittance from the street came to resemble a referral system. House staff began to screen and admit "walk-ins" only on the basis of personal acquaintance or prior residence in the facility. Those obviously drunk and likely to be troublesome were turned away even though the facility had its own detoxification unit. Skid row residents, and especially those most obviously in need of detoxification and treatment, found it more difficult to gain access to the facility.

While the mission and the clinic came to resemble each other more in terms of the selectivity of their recruitment systems, their relationship with each other grew worse. The mission staff felt the clinic was a waste of time and money, and no longer took pains to hide this opinion. They justified their hostility by claiming the clinic was actually hurting rather than helping residents, that the handouts of training, education, transportation, and clothing money the clinic could provide only gave alcoholics wine money. The mission thought the professionals were allowing the patients to con them, thus retarding rehabilitation. Mission staff felt if alcoholics really wanted help, they would come to the mission staff and not play the "clinic game." The mission approach was defined as both morally and technically superior, and the clients who opted for the mission approach were seen as better, more deserving individuals.

As the study drew to a close, both the clinic and the mission staff withdrew from their positions of open conflict, and their relationship may be characterized as one of avoidance and indifference. The only continuing positive overlap between the clinic's program and the rest of the mission's treatment efforts was in the area of recreation. The residents reacted positively to bingo, ping-pong, and other forms of recreation provided by the clinic, but little else. The original goal of interorganization cooperation between the public clinic and the private mission never really became operational.

Internally, the clinic began to concentrate more on perfecting the functioning of the interdisciplinary team, even though the patients in the mission rarely reacted in a positive manner to meeting with the team. Success, always elusive in the mission environment, became harder to achieve, and the tenor of the team sessions began to change as more clients were rejected and as the team became steadily more dictatorial with those clients it retained.[2] The team began to withdraw from the treatment arena and began to meet more and more often without patients. On several occasions the team shut down the clinic completely to go on day-long retreats. The stated purpose of each of these trips was to "get the team together."

TECHNOLOGICAL DEFICIENCIES

In time there came a period of evaluation of the role of the clinic in the mission. The religious organization was of little help in this respect because it had never kept records designed to measure program effectiveness. The clinic staff felt at a professional disadvantage because they were saddled with the same success criteria as the rest of the county treatment system, and at the same time had to work with the worst (least employable) clients in the system. Most of the other clinics served more middle-class clients. Much discussion arose in the administration of the county clinic system about eliminating the "unproductive" mission clinic from the treatment system. It is in this context that the technological deficiencies of alcoholism rehabilitation became apparent.

Support for the notion of technological failure came from the role medication played late in the study. Fairly early in the program, as the initial optimism began to wane, the clinic personnel had joined the administrators and staff of this mission in approving the use of antabuse. This reliance on drugs eventually expanded to other kinds of medication, including tranquilizers, and by the time the study ended, thirty-six different kinds of medication were dispensed to house residents. The clinic personnel, so confident of the interdisciplinary team technique earlier, began to abandon this approach to treatment and to rely on medication as a means to control (if not permanently alter) patient behavior, especially drinking behavior. Ironically, a new problem appeared when the abuse and misuse of medication became a major problem in the facility.

The residents reacted negatively to all of the treatment technologies used in the mission environment including the clinic's team approach, the mission's religious program and the Alcoholics Anonymous meetings. The majority of residents saw treatment as something they had to bear in order to stay in the mission.[3] They were acutely aware of the distribution of power, and especially their own lack of power. From their perspective, the major payoff from treatment was determined not by its therapeutic (technological) effectiveness, but by the way it affected the individual's position in the mission in terms of privileges and advantages. For instance, when queried about the role Alcoholics Anonymous played in his own rehabilitation, the secretary of the house meeting replied, "I hate A.A." When asked why he was the secretary (house leader) of the A.A. meeting in the mission, he replied, "It was the only good job open, the only one of importance I could get."

Interpretations

Many of the problems besetting this relatively small organization are probably also endemic to large-scale treatment and social change efforts. For this reason our observations have implications that could lead to a better understanding of massive program failure. Most such programs begin with an ill-defined problem to solve, and have difficulty in agreeing on a consistent technological approach. There is little agreement on how to conceptualize or treat alcoholism, a problem that also characterizes other problem areas such as mental illness, criminality, and poverty.

Planning and coordination efforts typically proceed with little understanding of the internal organizational problems likely to be encountered. In the situation analyzed here, for example, the clinic was opened even though the professional staff lacked several vital pieces of information. The clinic personnel did not know how their services would affect the local treatment population, originally intended to be the alcoholics found on this particular skid row. The mission had provided services to some of these alcoholics for a number of years and they were not an unknown group. Yet for reasons that were more financial, organizational, and political than therapeutic, the clinic initiated practices that excluded the local treatment population from the mission. Referrals came more and more from the criminal justice system and other agencies even though the local skid row population was a target population in the planning strategy. A system of funding used by the clinic which provided more money for referrals helps to explain this divergence from a major stated goal. Increased availability of money to the organization inadvertently served to exclude many members of the target population from treatment.

Clinic staff were also ignorant of what the mission resident wanted in the way of services and therefore did not anticipate their lack of response to the program. They reacted with bewilderment when the residents rejected their treatment efforts and extensive vocational rehabilitation program. Staff idealism and compassion were steadily eroded by disappointment and cynicism. When surveyed, the residents indicated they wanted medical services, not counseling services, and demonstrated throughout the course of the program that they did not want to return to the world of steady work. Yet the clinic did not abandon its initial strategy in order to reflect these patient preferences. When the team members did change their approach, they turned to medication as a mechanism of control (an indirect confession of failure) more than as a mechanism of treatment. The inference is that the patients' definition of the problem is a key variable in the success of a treatment program.

The clinic entered the mission environment without an understanding of the mission staff and its existing power structure. The failure to comprehend the power and legitimacy enjoyed by the house manager was a major oversight. There never really was a honeymoon period, and the failure to negotiate a working relationship with the house staff contributed to the conflict which lasted for the duration of the study. The elimination of those professionals who had established an unobtrusive relationship with the mission's staff before the clinic started exacerbated this situation.

Looking at the situation from the other side, the house staff became increasingly hostile toward the clinic. This hostility arose partly from the failure of the professional staff to negotiate with them and the feeling that the clinic personnel did not legitimate their skill in dealing with alcoholics. The professional staff never asked them for advice, and the clinic disrupted their position in the power structure of the organization. House staff had to share power over residents with the clinic staff and at the same time did not control the new sources of reward, especially the financial rewards, available to the clinic staff. House staff felt that a ticket to a baseball game, which they could provide, could not compete with offers of long-term training and education, transportation, and clothing allowances.

The clinic team members were unprepared for this hostility, and as a result their performance changed dramatically over the course of the study. Resentment toward the religious organization grew as the team came to believe that the religious organization, especially its management, placed little value on them as a treatment resource. The constant plea by the mission for a medical director to oversee the team's activities was crucial here.

The result was that the clinic and the mission staff worked frequently at cross purposes, each attempting to make the other look bad in the eyes of the patients. Each expressed the belief that the other was callous and not using the proper approach to the residents' problems. The factionalism between the two staffs in turn was a source of tension for the residents. They all lived together and exchanged their grievances because no distinction was made between clinic and nonclinic residents in room assignments. The mission did have a high retention rate for this type of facility. Patients averaged slightly over five months in terms of total residence and most were likely to be in their second stay within the facility. Despite its problems, the mission still compared favorably with other facilities on skid row even though residents did not see either the mission or the clinic as an avenue to reintegration into the outside world.

Added to these internal problems the clinic was required to accept unrealistic performance criteria imposed by the larger clinic system. Certainly the initial criterion (ninety days working without drinking) was clear, but the clinic was able to achieve this standard only in rare cases. Actually, keeping patients from drinking was even more difficult than finding them work. This fact explains why alcoholism treatment per se was progressively deemphasized while control occupied more and more attention. The change of the clinic staff's attitude toward antabuse was a reflection of their lack of viable treatment technology.

The clinic team also became much more selective in accepting patients in an attempt to provide better performance indicators. At the same time a harshness and dictatorial tone entered into their contact with patients. Patients who did not accept the team's definition of the seriousness of their drinking problem, or the team's plan for treating the problem, were dismissed as "not ready" for treatment. This view was certainly a turnaround from the altruistic and optimistic attitude of the professional staff when the study began. The house staff also became perceptibly harsher in their interactions with patients; and in this respect the clinic and mission staffs became more alike in their relationships with residents.

Eventually, the clinic did manage to have the performance criterion lowered. Ninety days working and not drinking became sixty days of the same. However, the clinic found this criterion no easier to live with and ultimately began to disregard the drinking criterion and to concentrate on work only. They actually had no real way of determining whether the client had complied with the official standard unless the client lost his job *because* of drinking or reentered the mission for being drunk.[4] There were never any clear statistical indicators of success regardless of the criterion utilized. Records were poor, with little cooperation between agencies. Decriminalization of alcoholism made police records unreliable indicators, and the changing success criterion meant that individuals could be readmitted and processed as new cases after being previously closed as rehabilitated.

Conclusion

This paper described factors contributing to the ineffectiveness of a skid row alcoholism treatment organization. Problems involving ill-defined goals, conflicts over resources and vested interests, and inadequate technology were discussed, and the section just concluded has indicated how these problems were intensified by a lack of background planning, coordination, and cooperation between subgroups in the organization. The findings support the conclusions reached by others who have reported on the overwhelming ineffectiveness of efforts to intervene in the skid row alcoholism problem (Rubington 1973; Spradley 1970; Wiseman 1970). We can now say with some confidence that part of the reason for failure of ambitious planning and coordinating strategies is the failure to credit these research findings. Certainly, the kinds of problems the clinic encountered in the mission environment were well-documented in the literature before the program began, and some of these problems could have been minimized or avoided by learning from the mistakes of previous ambitious but ineffective programs.

If any single finding in this study stands out, it is that where the problems discussed here exist and where they are not anticipated and taken into account by planners, no amount of funding will produce an effective program, nor will the recruitment of a young, expert, and committed staff, nor the adoption of a model of inter-organizational (public and private) cooperation, guarantee success. In fact, these ambitious strategies may have directly counterproductive effects. In the present case, the program established an avenue to skid row for clients who might not otherwise have found their way there and at the same time, it deflected the mission from the treatment of many of the alcoholics in the area surrounding the mission, a consequence which seriously questions the wisdom of locating new and largely untested treatment services in an established facility. The consequences may be to erode an established (and, at least partially effective) treatment strategy without creating the conditions of success for a new strategy. In fact, the final conclusion to be drawn from this case history is that the planning and coordinating strategy responsible for creating the clinic actually contributed to the skid row alcoholism problem.

NOTES

1. Another type of mission personnel was found in the mission environment. Known as salvationists, these individuals engaged in street missionary work and in the spiritual program within the facility. They did not have direct control over the residents.

2. For further discussion of team-patient interaction, see Fry and Miller (1974). We do indicate that patients in the entire county system reacted unfavorably to the team approach and that the entire system experienced problems in delivering service. However, the mission patients appeared to have the most negative reaction among the system client population.

3. An exception to the negative reaction to treatment is the residents' feelings toward medical services. When surveyed, physicians and nurses were overwhelmingly chosen as the occupational groups most qualified to treat alcoholism.

4. The success criterion was an irritation in another way. Clinic personnel were faced with the problem of maintaining contact with patients who began working. Once they received a paycheck, residents tended to want to move out of the facility. Since outpatient services were minimal, the resident who moved out lost support from, and contact with, the clinic. The staff were faced with the necessity to verify employment status in order to record a success, which was sometimes difficult. As a result, conflict developed between clients and clinic because of the staff's insistence that they not move out until they had been working for whatever time period met the success criterion at that time. Yet the clinic never advocated extended outpatient services.

INCOME MAINTENANCE AND WORK BEHAVIOR

Sonia Rosenbaum and James D. Wright

ACCORDING to official government figures and definitions, as of 1970 there were approximately 26 million persons in the United States living in poverty, about 13 percent of the total population. Of this group, about 40 percent were children under sixteen, another 20 percent were citizens aged sixty-five and up, and still another 25 percent were women, largely heading their own families. Since it is unreasonable to expect or require persons in any of these groups to "make their own way" in the society, national poverty policy with respect to them is well defined and scarcely debatable; they are to benefit from direct income transfers without stipulations concerning work. The picture for the remaining 15 percent, however, is not so clear-cut; about two thirds of this group are able-bodied men who presumably could work if they "wanted to." Thus proper poverty policy with respect to them is a matter of considerable national debate. On the one hand, it seems cruel and inhuman to expect any family of four to subsist on a yearly family income of $3,970 (the official 1970 poverty cutoff line); hence, there is considerable sentiment and justification for direct income transfers to this group as well. On the other hand, the society does not apparently wish to support "welfare chiselers" who are believed to take advantage of income transfers and drop out of the labor force altogether, content just to "get by on the dole."[1] Hence, national attention has recently turned to income-maintenance schemes which would provide the income necessary to live a decent life without removing all incentives to work.

From *Social Policy* (September/October 1975), 6:24–32. Reprinted by permission; copyright © 1975 Social Policy Corporation.

The Negative Income Tax

One such scheme which has received considerable attention is the negative income tax (NIT), which can be described in terms of three variables. First, all such schemes employ a basic guarantee level (g) below which incomes are not allowed to fall; this level is maintained by direct transfer payments from the government. Second, a tax rate (t) is imposed on earned incomes. Many present welfare schemes in essence employ a 100 percent tax rate, since support must be foregone whenever any income is earned, hence fostering the widely feared "work disincentives." Third, the program has a break-even or cutoff point at which the transfer payment is zero. The formula for computing the transfer payment (p) is as follows: $p = g - tl$, where g is the guarantee level, t the tax rate, and l the gross earned income. For example, if the guarantee level is $4,000 for a family of four, the tax rate is 50 percent, and the family earns $3,000, the transfer payment would equal $4,000—.50 ($3,000) or $2,500, and the family would have a total income of $5,500. At the same guarantee level and tax rate, if the family earned $5,000, the transfer payment would be $1,500 and the total income $6,500. In most cases the tax rate is progressive: the more families earn, the more they get to keep, up to the break-even point (which can be calculated from the above formula and equals g/t). In the example above, the cutoff point would be $4,000/.50 or $8,000. The family would continue to receive supplemental income until it reached that level; beyond that the family enters the "positive" tax brackets.

A major policy concern, then, is the establishment of the right combination of guarantee and tax levels in order to minimize national costs, maximize benefits, and maintain the incentives to work among those who are able. It should be noted that Nixon's proposed but unimplemented Family Assistance Plan was basically a NIT plan with a guarantee of $1,600 for a family of four and a 50 percent tax, hence a $3,200 break-even point.

Proponents of NIT measures claim that they provide the best of all possible worlds. Via the income guarantee, persons are kept out of poverty; via the negative tax rate, they are given incentives to work. Thus, it is hoped that the massive labor force withdrawal predicted for most direct transfer schemes will be avoided. It should also be mentioned that other benefits are also often claimed for NIT arrangements, among them ease and reduced costs of administration, avoidance of the stigmas usually attached to public assistance, and the mere fact that they allow a single policy to cover all aspects of the poverty situation, without regard to health, disability, age, family composition, or employability.

Granting the obvious theoretical advantages of the NIT proposals, there is nonetheless an empirical question which should be raised before any such program is adopted as national poverty policy: will it work? Although on paper the work incentives aspects of NIT look promising, it is also true that these proposals do establish an income floor or guarantee below which incomes will not fall, regardless of work activity. Perhaps, as many fear, poor persons will simply resign themselves to living at the guarantee level, and thus drop out of the labor force, thereby ignoring whatever work incentives are built into the NIT scheme. The possibility has been explored by several federally funded NIT experiments, one of which is reported below.

New Jersey-Pennsylvania NIT Experiment

EXPERIMENTAL DESIGN

The New Jersey-Pennsylvania NIT experiment was designed to assess the work behavior of the working poor as it is affected by an income-maintenance program. The sample was drawn from poverty tracts of Trenton, Paterson-Passaic, Jersey City, and Scranton. Each family in the sample was assigned to one of two groups: an experimental group whose incomes were maintained via NIT, or a control group whose incomes were not. The mean transfer payment to those in the experimental group was $298 per quarter, with a minimum payment of $4.38 and maximum of $1,464.

Quarterly interviews were administered to each group for a total of three years, and information was obtained on various aspects of work behavior as well as other relevant economic and sociological characteristics. The main thrust of the experiment was to ascertain whether work behavior differences would emerge between controls and experimentals as a result of the latter group's incomes having been maintained at a predetermined level by NIT. Of particular interest, of course, was the question whether labor force participation would decrease in the experimental group—whether, that is, those whose incomes were being maintained used the opportunity to cut back on labor force participation.

Part of the experimental design included variations in guarantee level and tax rate. All told, there were four guarantee levels (50 percent, 75 percent, 100 percent, and 125 percent of poverty-line income, adjusted yearly and also adjusted for family size) and three tax rates (30 percent, 50 percent, and 70 percent). The question being raised by this design was which of the several guarantee/tax rate combinations offered the optimal mix for work incentives. Preliminary analyses by the NIT researchers have so far uncovered no consistent differences in response by type of plan, so in the analysis which follows, we have collapsed all experimental families into a single experimental group.

Several points should be noted and emphasized. First, the data indicate no sharp differences between the control and experimental groups: both groups have approximately equal median levels of education, are of about the same age, and are employed in roughly the same types of jobs. More important, both groups had very similar labor force histories prior to the start of the NIT experiment: equal hours worked in the week prior to the pre-enrollment interview, equal average earnings in that same week, and approximately equal rates of labor force participation. The close similarity between controls and experimentals inspires confidence that significant differences observed after the three-year experiment will have been due to the experiment itself, not to extraneous uncontrolled factors.

Second, the absolute situation of the experimental group should be noted, since it confirms that the study deals with the working poor. In the week prior to the pre-enrollment interview, average hours worked among experimental males were about thirty-four; some 84 percent were employed and at work in that week; and only about 12 percent were on welfare. Median earnings for the week in question averaged about $90. Median education was just over nine years; median status of occupation (Duncan Socio-economic Status) was 17, corresponding to the status accorded semiskilled and unskilled labor. In short, the sample is not representative of the hardcore poor; rather, it represents that group which resides just beyond the hard-core poverty line—in sum, the working poor. The sample is also unrepresentative in at least one other important aspect: it is drawn exclusively from the urban, central-city poor, whereas in 1970 only about a third of the poor lived in similar-sized urban areas.

In specific terms, then, we are addressing the question: How is the labor force behavior of male, urban working poor persons affected by the NIT income-maintenance program?

LABOR FORCE PARTICIPATION

Two measures of labor force behavior are used for this analysis: number of hours worked in the week preceding the quarterly interview and total earnings for that same week. Both measures depend on respondent self-reports, although the experiment did make validity checks on these measures by examining payroll stubs and the like. In all cases "income" means earnings prior to any experimental payments. To control for the effects of seasonal variations in the economy, the measures reported are yearly averages; that is, hours worked in, say, the second year, are merely an average of the reported hours worked in each of the four weeks preceding the four quarterly interviews taken during the second year.

Mean earnings among families whose incomes were being maintained rose from $82 prior to the start of the program to about $102 during the last (third) year of the experiment. These figures reflect an inflationary economy during the period, and the increases are less dramatic when adjusted for inflation rates. Similarly, incomes of control group persons rose from $82 to $99 in the same period. Both groups also show a small decline for hours worked in the same three-year period, amounting in each case to about two hours. Further analysis indicates that rising unemployment in the period accounts for the small declines in hours worked. The aspect of the evidence which is most important from present perspectives, however, is lack of significant differences between experimental and control groups. In the statistical aggregate, having one's income maintained by this particular NIT scheme had no measurable effect on labor force activity. If anything, there appears to be a slightly larger increase in earnings among the experimentals.

There are two ways to read this evidence. The optimistic reading is that a guaranteed income does not depress the incentive to work; once a guarantee is established, in short, the working poor do not appear to resign themselves to living at that level and then simply stop working altogether. The other, more pessimistic reading is that there are also no positive incentives present either. Although we believe that the former reading is more appropriate, some comments are nonetheless warranted concerning the latter.

First, it must be mentioned that the "hours worked" figures are somewhat misleading in that they average together two very distinct groups: those working a normal forty-hour week and those not working at all (the unemployed). Hence, any increase in "average hours worked" for the experimental group would necessarily mean fewer numbers of unemployed, not a few more hours per week being worked by each person in the sample. (In any case, voluntary overtime in addition to the basic forty-hour work week is not among the work incentives predicted by proponents of NIT.) Hence, the question must be raised: What is to be made of the concept of "work incentive" among a group of working poor, some 85 percent of whom are already working a forty-hour week? In the present context, "work incentive" cannot simply mean an incentive to participate more; most of the poor persons in the sample are already "participating" as much as one could reasonably expect. What it must mean is simply "incentive *not* to participate *less*," or in other words, incentive not to drop out of the labor force altogether. And this incentive, judging from the evidence just discussed, is clearly present in this particular NIT scheme.

As for the minority group of unemployed among the working poor sample, any "labor force activity" on their part will quickly encounter a major structural inhibition, namely, that officially designated and federally maintained "acceptable unemployment rate" of about 5 percent. This group, moreover, is also affected by a variety of health disabilities, poor education and job training, and so on; and it is unreasonable to expect *any* incentive programs to have much of an effect on their labor force participation. Their nonparticipation, for the most part, is simply not a matter of personal choice.

Thus, the answer to the main question being posed—How is the labor force behavior of male, urban, working poor persons affected by an NIT program?—is, not at all. This group works neither more nor less as a result of its income being maintained by an NIT scheme. This, we would suggest, establishes an empirical base upon which further debate concerning the merits and demerits of NIT as a national welfare program can build.

VARIATIONS IN RESPONSE BY ETHNICITY AND RACE

Thus far our analysis has treated the poor population as a single undifferentiated group. This treatment is consistent with the current literature on poverty, where theories about a "common culture of the poor" are rife. However, there are lines of cleavage within the poor population, and one such cleavage which has received some attention are differences between white, black, and Spanish-speaking poor people. It is conceivable, in short, that persons from these subgroups within the poor might respond differently to the NIT program, reflecting their divergent cultural heritages and more recent occupational and socioeconomic experiences.

Two features of these data bear attention. First, comparisons between experimental and control groups *within* each racial and ethnic category show no significant experimental-control differences. Focusing on whites, there was a $17 increase in average earnings for experimentals and a $21 increase for controls; for hours, the respective figures are two- and zero-hour declines. Neither of these differences has statistical or substantive significance. Essentially similar conclusions hold for both the black and Spanish-speaking contingents: black experimentals, for example, show a $20 increase in earnings; black controls, a $12 increase; similarly, Spanish-speaking experimentals show a $23 increase; Spanish-speaking controls, a $15 increase. In sum, the response of the urban working poor to this NIT program does not vary according to the race or ethnicity of the person.

The second feature of the data which warrants attention is comparisons among the three experimental groups. Again no substantial differences appear in response to the program by race or ethnicity: we find increases of $17, $20, and $23 in average earnings for white, black, and Spanish-speaking experimentals, respectively. For hours worked, the comparable figures are two-, two-, and zero-hours per week declines. In sum, there are no significant or consistent differences by race or ethnicity in response to this NIT income-maintenance program.

NIT and "The Culture of Poverty"

A major theory of poverty is the "culture of poverty" thesis, a phrase first used by Oscar Lewis. This view directs attention to the "common culture" of the poor, and to the various personality and social-psychological pathologies which that culture allegedly embraces, as constituting the ultimate cause of poverty. Since these psychological characteristics of the poor lie at the base of their poverty, since they are relatively permanent features of the social psychology of the poor, and since they are transmitted via socialization from one poor generation to the next, the implication is that any policy is bound to fail if it does not deal with these alleged social-psychological "deficiencies."

The elements of this alleged pathological syndrome have been more precisely specified. First, the poor are thought to suffer from a pervasive sense of anomie, to lack integration into the values, norms, and orientations of the larger culture. Hence, they subscribe neither to the work ethic nor to the consumption and status norms which provide work incentives for the rest of the nonpoor population. Closely related to their alleged sense of anomie is an equally pervasive fatalism: they believe the world is not of their own making, that events are beyond their control, that fate or blind luck rather than hard work and thrift are what determine one's success in this life. Hence, they are also inefficacious, they doubt that events will be influenced by their own intervention. Coupled with their pervasive anomie and fatalism is a low sense of self-esteem; the poor, so the account runs, do not consider themselves as worthy persons, do not take pride in their accomplishments, and have negative self-concepts. Finally, and perhaps most important of all, the poor are said to lack a future-time orientation. Hence, planning for one's future, delaying gratification, preparing oneself now for a better job later, making present sacrifices for greater future gains—all behaviors necessary for upward mobility in the larger society—are activities which are alien to the poor.

Lacking the ability or inclination to plan for the future, unsure of their own actual or potential worth, dubious of their ability to influence events, and hobbled by a state of anomie, the poor are thought necessarily resistant to any social welfare program which makes no provisions for breaking into the vicious cycle of psychological pathology which in reality lies behind their impoverished condition.

Thus, from the culture-of-poverty perspective, the prospects of a successful NIT program do indeed seem bleak. Not included in the program, of course, are those necessary provisions for arranging to transmit a new and different culture, no provisions for breaking into the vicious circle of personality and cultural deficiencies. Surely, the response of the poor to an income-maintenance scheme will be negatively affected by these various social-psychological pathologies.

The evidence discussed so far, however, does not support the rather pessimistic predictions of the culture-of-poverty thesis. Despite their alleged social-psychological detriments, the poor persons in this NIT sample did not merely drop out of the labor force once their incomes were guaranteed. In the statistical aggregate, then, the predictions of poverty-culture theorists are not borne out in these results.

On the other hand, and despite the implications of the culture-of-poverty thesis, it is possible that the poor population is not homogeneous with regard to these alleged personality disorders. It may be that some poor persons are afflicted by these disorders while others are not. Those that are, moreover, may show just the response predicted by the culture-of-poverty thesis: a cessation of labor force activity, and an adjustment of aspiration and need to the guarantee level. Those who are not afflicted may show the opposite response. Consider, for example, the question of time orientation.

It is conceivable that some of the poor embrace a strong present-time orientation, as predicted by the thesis. Not inclined to plan for the future, this group might be expected to live off the guarantee for the duration of the experiment and worry about the future once it gets here. But there may also be another subgroup within the poor which has a strong future-time orientation, contrary to the predictions. The latter group might be expected to use the temporary security provided by NIT to obtain new job training, to search for better jobs, or to exercise other labor force options which are opened up by this temporary security.

Suppose, then, that both these responses are present; and suppose, additionally, that both groups are of approximately equal size. The results so far presented could have merely averaged two very distinct and analytically separate groups. Such a situation would account for the lack of significant differences so far reported. Hence, a more compelling presentation of the evidence, one sensitive to the claims of the culture-of-poverty theorists, would be to break down the labor force response among the poor according to the presence or absence of various social-psychological traits.

These data are reported in table 23.1 which considers four social-psychological characteristics. The first, anomie, was measured by combining five items taken from the McCloskey-Schaar anomie scale, of which a representative example is: "Everything changes so quickly these days that I often have trouble deciding what is right and what is wrong." The second variable is self-esteem, and was measured by combining three items from the Rosenberg self-esteem scale. A typical self-esteem question is: "I feel that I have a number of good qualities." Third is the sense of fatalism or personal inefficacy, measured by combining three items of the following sort: "Planning only makes a person unhappy since your plans hardly ever work out anyhow." Finally is time orientation, measured by three items developed by the NIT researchers for the study, of which an example is: "The present is more important to me than the future."

In each case, the resulting attitudinal indexes have been collapsed into high, medium, and low categories; to facilitate the presentation, however, only the comparisons between the low and high groups are shown in the table. One final and summary variable is included, which combines the four other variables being considered. Those high on the summary measure are those scoring high on three or four of the preceding traits. In every case, the high category in table 23.1 represents the "pathological" response, and hence the group in which the disincentive to work will be most apparent.

The following discussion focuses on the income data, since the "hours worked" differences between groups are neither large nor consistent. Looking first at the anomie variable, for experimentals we notice an increase of some $34 in average earnings for those low on anomie, contrasted with a $16 increase for the highly anomic. In contrast, the control group averages a $14 increase regardless of anomie. Similar results are indicated for the remaining social-psychological variables for those in the experiment: those with positive self-esteem register a $26 gain, contrasted to a meager $3 gain for those with negative self-esteem; the nonfatalistic register a $20 gain, the fatalistic, an $11 gain; the future-oriented register a $25 gain, the present-oriented a $16 gain. Control group differences, on the other hand, are less consistent. Taking all these measures collectively, we can note a $21 total increase in earnings during the three years of the experiment among those with the fewest culture-of-poverty pathologies, and an $11 increase in the same period for those exhibiting three or four of the culture-of-poverty pathologies. The corresponding figures for the control group are $17 and $14, respectively. Once corrected for inflation, what these results mean is essentially no change in labor force behavior for the "pathological" groups in response to NIT, and small increases for each of the "nonpathological" groups.

The data reported in the table should be interpreted with care: the figures for the control group suggest that some of the changes may not be due simply to the experiment as such. Of particular concern is that the control group did not have pre-enrollment earnings comparable to the experimental group, especially for anomie and self-esteem. In short, it seems that the experimental and control groups did not start out with comparable earnings, and hence any

Table 23.1. Work Response to the NIT Experiment by Culture-of-Poverty Traits

	Earnings					N	Hours				
	Pre	1	2	3	Change		Pre	1	2	3	Change
ANOMIE											
Low											
Experimental	82	90	106	116	+34	39	36	35	35	36	0
Control	96	94	96	110	+14	26	37	37	33	37	0
High											
Experimental	84	93	96	100	+16	200	35	33	32	31	−4
Control	80	83	88	94	+14	192	34	33	32	32	−2
NEGATIVE SELF-ESTEEM											
Low											
Experimental	82	96	101	108	+26	223	34	34	33	33	−1
Control	87	89	94	101	+14	132	35	33	33	33	−2
High											
Experimental	75	75	73	78	+3	26	30	26	26	25	−5
Control	66	73	80	90	+24	21	32	30	31	32	0

FATALISM

Low											
Experimental	86	95	97	106	+20	131	34	32	30	31	−3
Control	84	91	93	106	+22	83	32	34	32	33	+1
High											
Experimental	83	93	95	94	+11	124	35	34	33	31	−4
Control	80	82	94	97	+17	90	35	33	34	34	−1

PRESENT-TIME ORIENTATION

Low											
Experimental	88	98	104	113	+25	59	37	36	34	34	−3
Control	90	94	97	97	+7	27	40	36	35	34	−6
High											
Experimental	82	89	94	98	+16	265	33	32	31	31	−2
Control	82	85	91	98	+16	179	34	32	32	32	−2

SUMMARY

Low											
Experimental	83	93	98	104	+21	412	34	33	32	32	−2
Control	83	88	93	100	+17	259	35	34	33	33	−2
High											
Experimental	80	89	88	91	+11	73	33	33	30	30	−3
Control	78	78	89	92	+14	49	34	31	32	32	−2

analysis of experimental changes due to psychological characteristics must be assessed in the light of control group differences. One possibility is that the figures are unstable due to the small number of respondents in some of the groups.

Summing up, the data offer limited support for the culture-of-poverty claims: social-psychological characteristics do apparently influence the individual's response to the NIT program. Beyond that simple assertion, however, the received support for the theory is more limited. Contrary to implication, even the most "pathological" of the working poor do not show massive labor force withdrawal as the result of income maintenance; adjusted for cost of living increases, total weekly earnings of this group are nearly constant throughout the course of the experiment. Coupled with this are some rather obvious positive incentives evidenced among the "nonpathological" groups. In short, there is some variability in response to the experiment according to the social-psychology characteristics of the persons involved, but this variability ranges from "no effect" upward toward what appear to be positive incentives, rather than from massive disincentives up to "no effect."

The policy implication is that NIT could be instituted as a national social welfare program without regard to the social-psychological characteristics of the poor whatever they may be. Among those relatively "unintegrated" into the culture-of-poverty syndrome, some positive incentives may be expected: this may be in the form of looking for and taking better-paying jobs, improved performance on the current job, or perhaps even job training and other educational efforts. Among those who show some of the detrimental social-psychological characteristics, such expectations seem unfounded: this group is apparently most likely to continue working as always, neither decreasing nor increasing labor force involvement. In neither case is a prediction of massive labor force withdrawal supported by these results.

Further Considerations and Policy Implications

In our final remarks, we respond to the more obvious and compelling objections which may be raised against the procedures and inferences reported above, and then consider the policy implications of these data.

Perhaps the most obvious charge to be leveled against the NIT experiment is that it only covers a three-year span, hardly sufficient time to elicit major changes in labor force activity. Persons in the experiment, after all, were told at the outset that it was a three-year program, and that supplemental payments would cease once the experiment had run its course. Hence, labor force withdrawal for this short three-year period would be in essence irrational. Would the results be different if a permanent NIT plan were instituted? Would a more obvious, spectacular labor force withdrawal occur then?

Several points can be made in response to this charge. First, such claims do require a strong "future-time orientation" among a group allegedly characterized by strong attachments to, and preferences for, living in the present. According to the current depiction, the poor live for the here and now; they do not, it is claimed, plan for the two- or the three-year future. If this is the case, then what would prevent them from taking a three-year absence from work and letting the future take care of itself? In short, current depictions of the social psychology of the poor, however accurate they may be, militate against this interpretation of the results.

Second, one might just as easily argue that a three-year experiment is insufficient to elicit positive incentive effects as well. One positive aspect of NIT is that it affords some income security, which may be used for advancing one's education or job training. Since these possibilities are not likely to be short-term, it is conceivable that a permanent income guarantee would elicit more of this type of behavior than would a three-year experiment. There is a related question concerning health—rather the lack of it—which is a major deterrent to labor force participation among the poor. One of the long-range benefits of any income guarantee is that it insures available income that may be spent on health care. As incomes are raised among this group, health-care usage might also increase. In the long run, the increments to health occasioned by an income guarantee may be a major spur to labor force participation, yet any such effects will not be evident in a three-year experiment. Finally, a permanent income guarantee may also have an effect on the various personality and social "disorders" which now allegedly characterize the poor: for example, anomie, self-esteem, and the other traits mentioned above, as well as family patterns, values, aspirations, and so on. Once insulated from the crushing burden of poverty by some sort of income guarantee, it is again possible that the long-run effects on variables of this sort will be positive.

In short, the relatively brief time span of the experiment can be seen in either a positive or negative light: both positive and negative consequences, that is, can be equally well predicted for a longer-running program.

A second plausible objection to the experiment is that the guarantees were not sufficiently liberal to elicit the withdrawal phenomenon. After all, the mean transfer payment to experimental families was only $298 per quarter, or an average of about $25 per family per week. And the highest guarantee level in the experiment was 125 percent of the poverty line, which in 1970 amounted to $4,960 for a family of four—not a sum calculated to send the urban poor off for a three-year vacation in Florida. Moreover, most of the families were at a guarantee considerably less than the 125 percent figure, some as low as 50 percent, or a guaranteed annual income of $1,985 per year. Despite any predispositions to drop out of the labor force, any family of four would have difficulties adjusting to a permanent existence at less than $2,000 per year. Hence, it is possible that the relatively low guarantees provided by this NIT scheme are insufficient to produce the labor force withdrawal phenomenon.

It is unlikely, however, that any nationally instituted NIT plan would be more generous than the most liberal provision included in this experiment, a guaranteed payment of 125 percent of the poverty-line income. The plans chosen for this NIT study were those considered most relevant for actual policy measures. Perhaps more important, as mentioned earlier, variation in the generosity of plan was introduced into the original NIT experimental design, and researchers have not been able to uncover consistent effects. In short, labor force response was approximately equal regardless of the generosity of the income guarantee, which contradicts the suggestion that the more liberal plans would result in more obvious labor force withdrawals.

Although opposition to income-redistribution programs has usually centered on the assumption that, as David Macarov (1970) puts it, unearned income will invariably create disincentives to work, the data reported here have indicated that this is not necessarily the case. Experimental families were given unearned income in the amount of some $25 per week on the average which, although a seemingly trivial sum, did constitute a 30 percent increase in income over the average weekly earnings at pre-enrollment. Despite this 30 percent increase, however, there was scant evidence of disincentives to work among either the poor as a whole, or among racial or ethnic groups within the poor, or among groupings by social-psychological characteristics. Income maintenance of the sort described here, in short, does not appear to lead inevitably to labor force withdrawals.

NOTE

1. Contrary to stereotypes, this situation does not describe the majority of the poverty population. Of these four million men age sixteen to sixty-four living below the poverty levels in 1970, about 60 percent were employed and only 5 percent unemployed, with the remaining third outside the labor force (due for the most part to disability or illness). Further, three-fourths of those who were employed worked full time.

[24]

SELF-HELP ORGANIZATIONS AND VOLUNTEER PARTICIPATION IN SOCIAL WELFARE

Alfred H. Katz

NTEREST in self-help organizations has been rather conspicuously lacking in American social science and social welfare literature. Although a few writers have found intriguing aspects of organizational behavior in self-help groups and believe that they raise important questions for study, especially with regard to citizen participation, there is generally a dearth of studies, and in most works that deal with voluntary agencies and volunteers in social welfare, self-help groups are given short shrift. Only a handful of studies has come to light that analyze self-help groups in health and welfare from the standpoint of organizational or small group theory or consider such questions as the motivations of their members and their relationships with professionals and professional agencies from a social science viewpoint.

This article will discuss these aspects of self-help groups and will go on to consider them as a focus of, and an opportunity for, volunteer participation. An attempt will be made to relate self-help groups to some theoretical formulations in social science and to place the groups within the structure of community organization thinking in social welfare.

The Nature of Self-Help Groups

Self-help groups in the health field were defined in a study by the writer (1961:3) as "those which originate through the activities of parents and relatives seeking to bring about greater knowledge and

From *Social Work* (January 1970), 15(1):51–60. Reprinted by permission; copyright © 1970 National Association of Social Workers.

better physical and socio-psychological treatment for their ill or handicapped child." This definition stresses the "self-organized" and "mutual aid" origin, as compared with the more conventional establishment of social agencies by philanthropic interests.

On sheer magnitude alone, there can be little doubt that organizations formed in this fashion comprise an important segment of voluntary social welfare and health agencies. For example, the National Association for Retarded Children, founded in 1949, had no fewer than 1,300 local units by the end of 1968, embracing a membership of more than 130,000 persons, all of whom were said to perform active volunteer service. The United Cerebral Palsy Associations of America, a national organization founded in 1949, had some 260 local units, a membership of over 100,000, and more than 50,000 year-round active volunteers plus several hundred thousand additional volunteers during fund-raising drives. The Muscular Dystrophy Association of America, originating on a self-help basis in 1950, today claims over 400 local chapters and 500,000 volunteers, active at one time or another, mainly in fund-raising campaigns.

Among other health agencies that have emerged in recent years, usually to promote professional and public interest in a newly diagnosed or relatively little-known health problem, are found the National Cystic Fibrosis Foundation with 152 local chapters, the National Multiple Sclerosis Society with 210 chapters, the National Hemophilia Foundation with 53 state units, and a host of others.

But the disease-specific health agencies alone do not exhaust the list of groups significant to social welfare that have been constituted and function along self-help lines. Groups range from small, local, *ad hoc* efforts to large aggregates. Indeed, in reviewing the roster of national organizations in the health and welfare fields, one might list at least forty such groups that *inter alia* conduct fund-raising campaigns, provide local service programs, maintain research and public information activities, and thereby embody volunteer services. Therefore, it would not be an exaggeration to estimate that more than a million individuals in the United States are involved in health and welfare through membership and volunteer service in self-help groups.

Somewhat in contrast to philanthropic or conventionally established agencies, self-help groups provide a wider variety of volunteer activities than participation in fund-raising campaigns alone. Thus, one finds the parents of children with cerebral palsy involved in the maintenance of activity centers for school-age youngsters who are physically too handicapped to attend regular public schools. Parents of the mentally retarded staff recreation programs, sheltered workshops, and the like, in addition to participating in more common forms of volunteer service such as providing transportation.

In addition to the formal voluntary organizations that participate in local community fund drives, are affiliated with national organizations, and generally employ one or more professional staff workers, a whole host of organizations has grown up in recent years formed by persons with a common problem and usually performing multiple services to their members on a local level, outside the framework of the usual community services.[1] In 1961–62 Jackson (1963) compiled a directory of groups of this kind numbering 265; undoubtedly their numbers have grown since that time. Among such groups, the activities of the Synanon Foundation are well known nationally; less publicized, but of considerable magnitude, are organizations of former mental patients, both those affiliated with the American Federation of Therapeutic Self-Help Clubs and others. Another significant organization is Parents without Partners, composed of single parents concerned with the problems of child-rearing and personal adjustment for divorced or widowed individuals of both sexes. This national organization claimed 106 local units and a membership of 12,000 in 1964. Further, a significant number of ad hoc self-help groups were organized to combat problems of addiction to gambling, to promote weight loss or weight control, and for many other purposes. As the writer said (1965:680–83) some years ago, "These groups are growing so rapidly that no catalog of them is practicable. The proliferation of new groups outstrips the tempo of data collection."

We are thus concerned with a social phenomenon, a new kind of social agency that performs many social welfare planning and programming functions. To be complete, any analysis of voluntary agencies, voluntarism, and volunteers in the health and welfare field should take this large aggregate into account.

In federal legislation, especially that dealing with the antipoverty programs, the importance of enlisting the participation of persons affected by a particular social problem, and therefore presumed to have a stake in its solution, has been recognized. In antipoverty programs, the principle of "maximum feasible participation of the poor" is not only established, but has led to considerable differences and controversy on the local level. In recent years a number of programs have experimented with the enlistment of the poor through their neighborhood representatives in campaigns of social action around the amelioration of local problems. The programs led by Saul Alinsky in Chicago, Rochester, and other localities; the extensive neighborhood development activities of Mobilization for Youth and HARYOU-ACT in New York City; and self-help programs in Syracuse under the leadership of Warren Haggstrom all exemplify this principle, although they differ in details of philosophy and approach.

Taken together, these programs are a form of community action with great inherent significance both for their participants and for the wider health and welfare scene. One line of sociological analysis would hold that in seeking out opportunities for face-to-face interaction with peers and other individuals with similar problems, many persons who participate in these activities are counteracting anomic and isolating tendencies of society. The depersonalizing trends in industry, large academic institutions, and suburban life are to some extent countered by the innovation of a social form that allows people to group themselves according to common interests and common problems and to attain a sense of cooperative activity for common purposes, thereby promoting a sense of social identification.

Social scientists would probably suggest that such activity has become necessary to compensate for the decline of the extended family in contemporary life. When there was a large-scale, multigenerational family, it was not crucially important for the individual to affiliate with others outside the family for purposes of mutual aid and support. But the small nuclear family, which has emerged as the modal type in the United States under the stresses of industrialization, urbanization, and greater population mobility, requires a supplement since it can no longer sustain the total burden of socialization and support hitherto carried by the extended family.

Structural Features of Self-Help Groups

Eight essential structural features that characterize the self-help group and distinguish it from other types of social agencies can be schematically isolated for analysis.

1. *Self-help organizations share the properties of small groups.* Cartwright and Zander (1960:75) define a group as

a collection of organisms in which the existence of all [in the given relationship] is necessary to the satisfaction of certain individual needs in each. That is to say, the group is an instrument toward the satisfaction of the needs of the individual. Individuals belong to the group because they achieve certain satisfactions made possible by its organization which would not be readily possible for them through any other device.

2. *Self-help groups are problem-centered, organized with reference to a specific problem or problems.* This characteristic is implied in the term self-help—the "help" refers to activities on behalf of meeting common needs or common problems. Thus, these groups are not merely for social or recreational purposes, although they may incidentally fulfill such functions.

3. *Members of such groups tend to be peers.* This is usually true with regard to at least one major factor, the central problem. It is the fact of sharing a central problem that defines membership status in self-help groups, despite many individual differences. A peer in a self-help group thus has a commonality or mutuality of problems with others.

This attribute does not exclude the possibility that self-help groups may include members who are not peers, who do not share the common problem. For example, Charles Diedrich, the charismatic leader and founder of Synanon, is not a peer in the sense of being himself addicted to narcotics. A professional who is a member of the group is not a peer, but he may be accepted on a basis of quasi-equality after demonstrating the depth of his concern, sympathy, and knowledge of the problem. In fact, professionals do not often reach this stage of acceptance or identification with the group, and therefore their status and activities remain somewhat outside it. In the quality and nature of professional participation, one may also differentiate between self-help groups and similar forms of organization in which professionals play a leading role, such as a therapeutic community or milieu in a mental hospital ward.

4. *Self-help groups hold common goals.* They are group goals, and the groups are self-consciously goal-oriented with respect to the perceived central problem or problems. Goals emerge from the group rather than being applied to it or given to it from the outside. Whatever the

origin of the group goals, group acceptance of them is requisite to having a true self-help group, and group identification with the goals is essential.

5. *Action is group action.* The self-help group is conceived of as a dynamic whole greater than the sum of its parts. The action of individual members is seen as a part of the whole, having a bearing or effect upon it. Thus, the individual acts in coordination with the goals and sanctions of the group and with the expressed intent of group benefit.

6. *Helping others is an expressed norm of the group.* This is a key aspect of the definition of self-help groups. Perhaps the term "self-help" in this context is somewhat misleading, since the "self" aspect here includes help to others. Self-help through a group should be differentiated from self-help in other contexts. The student instructing himself in a language through the use of a teaching machine is performing self-help, but not in the sense in which we define self-help groups. In the latter the emphasis is on helpfulness to the other or to the group, on the factors of mutuality and cooperation.

7. *The role of the "professional" is not clear-cut, if it exists at all, in the self-help group.* Self-help groups, in fact, tend to minimize the role of the professional, as compared with more conventionally structured social agencies. Some self-help groups have deliberately and systematically excluded professionals from leadership roles—Synanon, for example. The professional may be accepted in such a group as an observer, but unless he shares the common problem, he is not considered to be a member, nor does he generally participate in decision-making processes. Other groups may include the professional as a member, but his role tends to be more that of a rank-and-file participant than that of a leader, decision-maker, or teacher. If he functions as a professional at all, rather than as member-participant, his functions are those of a consultant, resource adviser, evaluator, or expediter. In short, the professional's role may vary along a dimension of no involvement to small involvement in terms of power and leadership.

8. *Power and leadership in self-help groups are on a peer or horizontal basis.* Leadership is an accepted rather than an inherited or a status attribute. Leadership generally has to be earned and justified over a period of time.

Functional Attributes of Self-Help Groups

From these defining structural characteristics flow more general functional attributes of self-help groups, which again serve to differentiate them from conventional social agencies.

1. *Communication.* This is horizontal rather than vertical.

2. *Personal involvement.* Such involvement becomes a requirement in all self-help groups, with activity and personal engagement the keynotes in defining membership. Thus, in contrast to most social agencies and many organizations, the concept of membership does not fully include members who are mere passive recipients or financial supporters. Each member is expected to involve himself in, and to work for, the good of the group to his best capacity at the time. There are indications that within such peer groups a special sensitivity develops to the present capacity of fellow members. In Synanon, for example, it is understood when a member is not ready to perform a certain action; thus, sympathy, leniency, and tolerance may be extended. Yet, at the same time, the converse is true, and group members can be more stringent and even punitive with a laggard member than would be possible with a nonmember. The issue here is that of peer identification and peer influence.

Motivation to join the group is partly individual and partly social. While the primary motivation may be self-improvement, it is generally understood that group goals and group welfare must come first and self-improvement comes as a by-product of working for the group welfare. With respect to motivation for volunteer participation, which will be discussed later, this adds a dimension that is not always present among volunteers in other types of organizations.

The personal help the individual gains may not necessarily be of the type he had anticipated. For example, Wittenberg (1954) writes of a woman working for a neighborhood committee concerned with housing and street beautification, who improved her own mental health in the process. Such unanticipated consequences of altruistic activity probably occur frequently among self-help groups.

3. *Personal responsibility.* The individual member of the self-help group is considered and is held responsible for his own actions. He is expected to give, produce, and act to the best of his ability in accordance with group definitions and standards of what is acceptable or unacceptable. Such a level of personal responsibility is not generally required of other volunteers or members of social welfare organizations.

4. *Action orientation.* Groups are action-oriented, their philosophy being that members learn by doing and are changed by doing. "Do, don't think" is one of the precepts of Synanon philosophy. To put it in other terms, experiential fulfillment, rather than didactic instruction, is frequently an explicit aim of certain self-help groups, and it is sometimes achieved. A result of the emphasis on action is that the groups afford an opportunity for enhancing members' self-esteem by successful or useful endeavors. Achievement by the group can enhance individual self-esteem, since every member is expected to be involved and to contribute.

Processes of Self-Help Group Influence

Review of sociological, psychological, and small group literature, coupled with studies and observation of small-group activity, suggests that a series of mechanisms or processes occur that may usefully be applied in the analysis of self-help group phenomena. These are the following:

1. Peer or primary group reference identification
2. Learning through action; attitude and knowledge change through experience and action
3. Facilitation of communication because members are peers
4. Enhanced opportunities for socialization
5. Breaking down of individual psychological defenses through group action, open discussion, and confrontation
6. Emotional and social support of members by one another; reduction of social distance among them as compared with the distance traditionally maintained from agency staff or professionals
   This enhances the therapeutic qualities of group participation.
7. Provision of an acceptable status system within which the member can achieve his place
   Status is defined according to group goals and needs, and the individual's status within the social system of the group can be relatively clearly defined.
8. Simulation of, or proximity to, conditions of the outside world in the groups, as compared with the institutional setting or professional client-practitioner relationship
9. The "helper" principle enunciated by Riessman (1965), which holds that in helping others, group members achieve personally therapeutic goals for themselves

Dimensions of Volunteer Activity in Self-Help Groups

The phases through which self-help groups pass in their evolution toward a more sophisticated and professionalized type of organization can be outlined as follows: 1) origin, 2) informal organizational stage, 3) emergence of leadership, 4) beginnings of formal organization, 5) beginnings of professionalization.

The idea of these stages is, of course, an abstraction: the stages do not exist in pure form. They may overlap one another in time and they are certainly not similar from one group to another. Nor should they be thought of as involving reference to any particular time period (Katz 1961:110–11).

1. *Origin.* The first phase comes about when two or more persons are motivated to perform a remedial action regarding a common problem. Frequently, such individuals advertise in the public press, attempting to reach others who share the problem. A public meeting may be organized as a means of getting started and attracting publicity through the communications media. All the initial work of planning and conducting the meeting is, of course, carried out by the volunteers who initiate the project.

2. *Informal organizational stage.* In this phase the movement begins to spread through friends and acquaintances; face-to-face group contacts occur, further public meetings are held, and volunteers engage in enlarging the circle of participants through personal contact, newspaper advertising, and exchange of information with one another. They also develop rudimentary program ideas and community contacts and begin to cultivate a few prominent or "strategic" people, professionals or influential laymen. In this phase volunteer activity is varied, nonspecific, and pragmatic, representing innovative or improvised responses to new situations.

3. *Emergence of leadership.* Each group, at an early stage, presents the opportunity for strong leadership to emerge in the person of a single individual or small group of close working associates. These leaders assume the most important tasks in the organization. Part of their leadership function is expressed in their ability to involve other volunteers in routine tasks, and innovative activities become the prerogative of the leaders. Eventually, a division of labor appears, and certain functions become identified with certain persons both within and outside the leadership group. Rank-and-file volunteer activities become routinized and defined in this period.

4. *Beginnings of formal organization.* As a definite leadership core emerges, the group enters the stage of more formal organization. An overall organizational structure is usually developed and codified in rules or bylaws. In the process, the respective roles of the actual leaders, strategy planners, and member volunteers are more clearly defined and established through practice and trial and error.

Structural changes begin to become necessary by reason of the increasing volume and complexity of the functions undertaken by the group. There are increases in program activities, a more ramified administrative structure is needed to enlarge and keep track of membership participation, and an expansion of the group's contacts with community agencies, other groups, and professional workers occurs.

5. *Beginnings of professionalization.* After some time, the leadership group may find it necessary to give up some of its own routine organizational functions to paid staff workers. With the growing complexity of organization, membership, and program, it becomes necessary to shift administrative functions, with the leadership group retaining its primary responsibility for policy and program. As increasingly professional activities are undertaken, professionally qualified staff members may be added. At the latter point, a gradual shift of functions results. Tables 24.1–24.3 indicate the organizational functions carried out by staff workers and volunteers at the end of one, three, and five years of activity in four self-help groups.

Table 24.1. Organizational Functions Carried Out by Staff Workers and Volunteers at End of First Year

Function	Organization A	Organization B	Organization C	Organization D
Fund-raising	V	V	V	V
Public relations	V	V	V	V
Planning meetings	V	V	V	V
Contacts with governmental agencies	V	P	V	V
Contacts with medical profession	V	P	V	V
Social service program	—	P	—	—
Recruitment	V	V	V	V

Source: The source of this and the following tables is Alfred H. Katz, *Parents of the Handicapped*, p.101.
V = Volunteer   P = Paid worker   — = No function at time

Table 24.2. Organizational Functions Carried Out by Staff Workers and Volunteers at End of Third Year

Function	Organization A	Organization B	Organization C	Organization D
Fund-raising	P	V	P	P
Public relations	P	V	P	P
Planning meetings	PV	PV	V	P
Contacts with governmental agencies	PV	P	V	PV
Contacts with medical profession	V	P	V	PV
Social service program	V	P	V	–
Recruitment	V	V	V	P

PV = Both paid staff and volunteers active.

If one were to repeat this analysis of the same groups, no doubt there would still be significant volunteer participation in some of the functions listed, while the process of professionalization would have advanced markedly.

Among self-help groups, participation by volunteers in these functions clearly varies with the phase of the organization, especially with the incorporation of paid professional staff. The generalization can be made that, despite professionalization, volunteer functions in these groups remain broader, more intensive, and more varied than in the more conventional private social agency.

Table 24.3. Organizational Functions Carried Out by Professionals and Volunteers at End of Fifth Year

Function	Organization A	Organization B	Organization C	Organization D
Fund raising	P	V	P	P
Public relations	P	V	P	P
Planning meetings	PV	PV	PV	P
Contacts with governmental agencies	P	P	P	P
Contacts with medical profession	P	P	P	P
Social service program	P	P	P	P
Recruitment	V	V	V	P

Activities usually reported for volunteers in conventional agencies can be classed under the following headings:

1. Fund-raising: a predominant emphasis, but usually under professional direction
2. Board service (policy-making): restricted to relatively few persons (see below)
3. Patient service: usually in a role adjunctive to professionals
4. Public relations: often under professional direction.

In contrast, volunteer activities found among the self-help groups include the following:

1. Fund-raising: frequently without professional direction
2. Policy- and program-making: usually more broadly spread than in the conventional agencies involving more opportunities for participation
3. Social action activities: lobbying, pressure groups, and so forth
4. Public relations participation: including widespread public interpretation to a variety of audiences
5. Patient service: often assuming more significant and less adjunctive "professional-helper" roles (staffing professional services as teachers, social-recreation leaders, vocational counselors, participation in group education); discussion of adjustment problems such as finding a job, preparing a resume; discussion of relationships, as with relatives; discussion of social actions the group can take; provision of transportation, baby-sitting, and other concrete services.

Characteristics of Volunteers

As noted earlier, self-help organizations in health and welfare have been little studied in relationship to the differentials they present in volunteer participation as compared with conventionally organized agencies. A number of sociologists, however, have concerned themselves generally with participation in voluntary associations, including social agencies.

A major conclusion from a variety of such studies is that the class variable is a controlling one. Volunteers in most social welfare organizations are drawn primarily from the middle and upper classes. Persons having sufficient wealth to devote leisure time to agency affairs or for whom volunteering is a path to upward social status predominate. For example, a large majority of the volunteers in Hausknecht's (1962) study held managerial or professional positions. Sills (1957) found the latter motivation especially among such professionals as lawyers, physicians, and accountants, many of whom readily admit that they seek, in volunteer work such as service on the boards of social agencies, opportunities for contact both with wealthy and influential members of the community in general and potential clients or patients in particular.

For those persons affected by a problem who join with others for mutual aid, the careerist motive, however, has lesser importance. In these organizations, social class stratification does not determine participation. Such conditions as mental retardation, cerebral palsy, and alcoholism cut across class, socioeconomic, and occupational lines. In the truest form of self-help group, such as Synanon, a wide variation in educational background and occupation has been observed.

Motivation for volunteer participation is clearly a complex phenomenon; social agency volunteers' participation may be usefully analyzed under the headings of ideological, social, and personal motives. In a study of volunteers at the Council House Mental Health Services in Pittsburgh, Roberts and Eaton (1964) proposed a classification differentiating "service orientation" and "self-orientation." These writers found that volunteers who were self-oriented related better to the program as a whole than did the service-oriented, even though most of the volunteers were middle-aged housewives whose children were grown and who sought self-fulfillment and gratification through volunteer service. A considerable number of these volunteers had been brought to awareness of, and interest in, the program by means of personal contact with mental illness through a friend or relative.

Roberts and Eaton (1964) found that the dissatisfaction of these volunteers arose largely from lack of direct contact or personal involvement with clients. The volunteers who rated highest in terms of satisfaction were those who were in direct contact with groups of former patients as club leaders, resource consultants, and so on. This observation squares with those reported from other groups of former patients in which the volunteers were drawn from various strata of society. Thus Wilder (1963), reporting on the work of the Psychiatric Rehabilitation Association in England, estimates that one out of every three club leaders for that group was a former patient.

Thus, one conclusion that can be drawn from various studies of volunteer motivation is that a high and compelling motive for participation is found in seeking solutions to personal problems. Once contact with the group has been made for this purpose, however, a displacement of goals can occur. In such instances, the volunteer originally seeking personal help is able to pass to a stage of altruism in which he no longer seeks help for himself (or if so only incidentally), but obtains satisfaction through helping others. This dynamic in volunteer motivation is not usually reported from studies of the middle- and upper-class volunteer in conventional social agencies, but its embodiment may be observed every day in self-help organizations and it constitutes a powerful social force. A self-help committee of rehabilitation clients was formed in Alameda County, California, with the purpose of intervening with the State Rehabilitation Service to insure that the clients of that agency receive their maximum entitlements under the law (see Committee for the Rights of the Disabled 1966). Similar self-help organizations of public assistance recipients have now become quite familiar.

There seems little question that self-help organizations are here to stay and will continue to provide extensive opportunities for one important type of volunteer service. Social scientists and students of social welfare should increasingly utilize the rich laboratory setting that these organizations provide for the study of organizational behavior and small social systems and for the analysis of pertinent and inventive volunteer participation.

NOTE

1. A beginning typology for classifying self-help groups has been developed by the writer: assimilative, separative, and mixed. This typology refers to the goals of self-help groups in terms of their relationships with, and use of, other community agencies and professionals. Under this scheme, Synanon might be categorized as separative, United Cerebral Palsy as assimilative, and Alcoholics Anonymous as mixed.

B. REFORM AND INSURGENCY

THE 1960s gave inpetus to new reform and radical efforts to revitalize social welfare. These efforts came from above, as in the War on Poverty; from clients, as in the National Welfare Rights Organization; and from workers, as in efforts to unionize and to create a radical social work practice. The material in this section considers these important phenomena.

The first selection, "Notes toward a Radical Social Work," is co-authored by Richard A. Cloward and Frances Fox Piven. Their work on the labor-regulating aspect of public welfare (Piven and Cloward 1971) and the political organization of poor people (Piven and Cloward 1977) is well known in the field. Here, they use case material to bolster their argument for the need to radicalize social work practice. They argue that in order to respond better to client needs, it is necessary to work for social change. Cloward and Piven define radical social work by demonstrating how it functions. This selection has particular relevance for those engaged in practice, especially social work students.

The second selection, "Welfare Reform from Above and Below," is an empirically based analysis of the effects of 1960s reform and insurgency. George T. Martin, Jr., one of this reader's co-editors, and David Street, adapted it from their book with Laura Kramer Gordon, *The Welfare Industry* (1979). They argue that reform from above and insurgency from below took on attributes of profession-alization and bureaucratization, accounting in part for its lack of success. The becalming of these efforts, Martin and Street propose, has created an ambiguous situation, which has been compounded by the emergence of the fiscal crisis in the 1970s.

25

NOTES TOWARD A RADICAL
SOCIAL WORK

Richard A. Cloward and Frances Fox Piven

THERE is no doubt that social welfare doctrines have become unsettled in the last decade or so. One only has to remember how liberals generally, and the professionals in the social services in particular, once confidently defined the social services as the progressive and humanitarian sector of American society. Services in health, education, welfare, housing, child care, and corrections were taken as the institutional proof that the American state had reached the stage where it was ready and able to intervene in the so-called free-enterprise economy, and ready and able to protect people against some of its worst abuses. In other words, the United States, mainly through its public programs, and to a lesser extent through the voluntary sector, no longer tolerated the vagaries in human welfare produced by a capitalist economy, and no longer left the victims of the economy to fend for themselves. One had only to look at our splendid array of legislation, and the multitude of agencies spawned by the legislation, to know that this was so.

To be sure, liberals acknowledged that there were problems in the social service sector. Great progress had been made, but there was still a distance to go. The problems were largely attributed to the underfunding of social service programs. The agencies were inhibited by lack of money from doing what they knew how to do and urgently wanted to do to help people. Underfunding, in turn, resulted from the still backward attitudes of the American people who, the argument went, retained an old-fashioned skepticism about "big government,"

From Roy Bailey and Mike Brake, eds., *Radical Social Work* (New York: Random House, 1975), pp. vii–xlviii. Reprinted by permission; copyright © 1975 Random House.

along with a lot of unenlightened hostility toward the poor and other unfortunates. But liberals always have unbounded faith in the educative force of their own beliefs, and there was not much doubt in the minds of those who defended the welfare state, and who pressed for its expansion, that Americans would in time come to appreciate the value of the social services and would provide political support for budgetary allocations on the required scale. Slowly but surely, then, progress would occur in the United States; the forces of capitalism would be curbed, their effects buffered by the gradual expansion of the social welfare sector.

The 1960s forced many of us to rethink this faith. We learned a great deal about how the social service agencies on which we rested our hopes for fundamental progress really worked, and about their effects on the lives of people. We did not learn this willingly. We did not re-educate ourselves. We were forced to learn by the turmoil that shook the United States, a turmoil generated by the black movements in the South and in the North, and by the student movement on the nation's campuses. Those movements forced issues of racism, poverty, and imperialism to the top of the American political agenda, and by doing so, made us open our eyes to, among other things, the widespread hardship and suffering that still prevailed in this country. And if there was still much hardship, then we had to wonder about the social service programs which we had so confidently believed were working to ameliorate the condition of the poorest and most exploited people in the United States.

We became at least skeptical. Skepticism opened the way for some of us to develop a different and more realistic way of understanding the agencies of the welfare state. We began to see that social welfare had not curbed capitalist institutions; it had supported and even enhanced them. And we began to understand some of the specific ways in which the social services had played this role. Let us quickly recapitulate some of our criticisms to show how fundamentally they broke with the conventional liberal faith.

We learned, for example, that the government health programs we had fought for, and had believed would make possible decent health care for all Americans, were not providing decent health care at all. More important, we realized that merely allocating more funds to health care, as liberals had advocated, did not improve the programs; it may even have worsened them. We had been fundamentally mistaken in our belief that health care institutions, and the professionals attached to them, knew how to help people and urgently wanted to do so. We began to understand that these institutions were shaped by quite different impulses, by the impulses for expansion and profit. We slowly deciphered the outlines of a health care industry composed of apparently neutral "not-for-profit" hospitals and medical schools, which in turn were linked to profiteering drug and equipment producers, and to profiteering private entrepreneurs called doctors (the highest earning occupational group in the United States).

In other words, we began to understand—we could not help but understand because the evidence was so overwhelming—that public expenditures for health had in fact been absorbed by the industry in ways which subsidized bureaucratic expansion and vastly enlarged profits, but did not much improve medical services. Health care institutions did not buffer capitalist institutions; they *were* capitalist institutions; they differed mainly in the extent to which they de-pended for their profits on the public sector. The arguments we had made, the campaigns we had waged for decent health care, had turned out in the actual world to be advertisements that smoothed the way for the expansion of a profit-based industry.

Similarly, we learned that the government housing programs initiated in the 1930s and expanded in 1949 under the legislative banner of "decent and standard" housing for all Americans were dominated and directed not by the housing needs of Americans, but by the construction and real estate industries and the downtown businesses. The vast government subsidies that we had promoted in the name of those who needed housing had gone to profiteers and speculators in urban land and to construction firms. Instead of modifying free enterprise by redirecting its activities toward the poor, public programs in housing have been a major source of profits for an important sector of free enterprise. Meanwhile, the subsidy programs, such as urban renewal, actually worsened the housing conditions of poor and working-class people, especially black people, by making it profitable to destroy their homes and neighborhoods so that their land could be turned over to private developers at costs underwritten by the public.

In other programs we came to see a less direct but not therefore less essential relation between the social services and what Marxists call "processes of accumulation." The public schools have been defined in liberal doctrine as vehicles for opening up the class structure, for equalizing opportunities among different strata. But we recognized that schools did nothing of the sort. Those who were poor or working-class were also at the bottom of the ladder of school achievement. More funds, more special programs, and more specialists of different kinds were needed, it was said. But these had simply not changed the failure and dropout rates among children at the bottom of society. Dimly, a new explanation began to emerge. Perhaps the schools were not institutions for equalizing opportunity. Perhaps they were institutions which mainly served to legitimate the low status to which many children were consigned by proving to them and to all around that it was they who had failed, not the society. Perhaps for many children the schools simply engrain and legitimate failure, meanwhile instructing them not in the skills and manners that would allow them to rise in the class structure, but in deadening rules of bureaucracy and in docility before bureaucratic authority—the proper education for the lower classes.

Similarly, we learned that public welfare programs inaugurated during the New Deal, that golden age of social welfare, were quite different in practice from what we had believed them to be. The introduction of a national system of public welfare had been regarded as a major step forward by social service professionals. American society had presumably advanced to the point where it was ready to insure at least a minimal level of subsistence for its citizens, or so the legislation said. Thus consoled and deluded by the existence of legislation and of agencies that had the formal mandate to implement it, we did not pay much attention to what our public welfare agencies actually did. But in the 1960s, we were forced to learn that the public welfare system in fact reached very few of the poor, and that it exacted penalties of intimidation and degradation from those few it did reach. With these facts laid bare, a new explanation began to emerge, of public welfare not as a mechanism of state philanthropy, but as a mechanism by which the state enforced work and the search for work on those at the bottom, either by denying aid outright or by making the receipt of aid so degrading as to intimidate most of the poor into surviving as best they could given the vagaries and hardships of the low-wage labor market.

We also learned something about the apparatus of institutions the state had created for the criminal and mentally ill. We had been inclined to think of these institutions as places where a deviant was treated and thus rehabilitated, or at least that treatment and rehabilitation were slowly becoming the predominant focus of prisons and asylums. How we could have entertained such notions in view of the actual conditions in these institutions is puzzling, but at any rate, in the 1960s we began to understand that what had been created was an apparatus for stigmatizing and exiling those who could not cope with the stresses of lower-class life—those who protest their circumstances in bizarre ways full of flight, or in fearsome ways full of rage. As a "cure," these people were consigned to institutions of medieval awfulness, where the culture of the stigmatized enveloped and destroyed them. More recently, a new and perhaps more dangerous addition has been made to the arsenal of mechanisms for dealing with the casualties of capitalism: the promiscuous administration of drugs by the health, education, and social service bureaucracies. The drugging of the American underclass has taken on the dimensions of a social movement, with the twin goals of social control and billion-dollar profits, and it is being led by the pharmaceutical industry and the psychiatric profession, with the unwitting acquiescence of other service professions.

Overall, the lesson we learned was shattering. We had now to deal somehow with the simple fact that during the forty years in which the social service sector in the United States had expanded, during forty years of progress, the incidence of crime, of mental illness, of school dropouts, all had risen, while the income of the lowest 20 percent of the population had hardly changed. In the United States, then, welfare capitalism had turned out to mean new areas of profit underwritten by the public sector and an enlarged state responsibility for disciplining the labor force. For the victims, welfare capitalism was capitalism, not welfare.

The Quandary of Radical Practice

These new perspectives on the welfare state did not tell us, however, what we as professionals should do. The quandary was a difficult one, not only because the perspectives were too general to yield practical solutions, but because the criticism was focused on the agencies to which we as a profession were committed, if only because our livelihoods depended on them. Various solutions emerged among the more critical and radical groups in social work, most of them designed to evade rather than deal with the quandary.

One way in which the dilemma was popularized in the late 1960s was to state it as a stark dichotomy. Radicals in the social service professions (not just in social work), and particularly students entering these professions, became fond of boldly proclaiming that if we were politically committed, we would forsake our professions and become revolutionaries dedicated to a basic overhaul of American institutions. And if we were not prepared to do that, then we ought to resign ourselves to working within these professions and within the agencies, easing a little by our therapeutic efforts the hardships produced by the modern capitalist state. While this dichotomy reflected the depth of our disenchantment, it was foolish nevertheless. It was foolish because it posed an unreal alternative. Very few of those who took satisfaction in posing the stark choice had much idea about how to make a revolution in the United States or, more important, what specifically one would do if one chose to become a revolutionary.

It was foolish for another and more important reason. It encouraged us to ignore the actual political struggle for the rights of the poor, for the rights of those who were down-and-out, for the rights of the victims of American capitalism who were also frequently victims of the social service agencies. It encouraged us to ignore the unspectacular day-by-day strivings of particular people with particular problems, strivings in which we as employees of the social service agencies play a very large role. Our daily activities, our time, and our energies are all expended in the social agencies. The false choice—of whether we should become revolutionaries or merely be social workers—allowed us to avoid a series of much more important choices: more important because they were choices about actual and possible avenues of action, and about areas of activity in which we as social workers might make a difference. The issue was whether we were going to take sides with the agencies and further our careers, or with the victims of an aggressively cruel capitalist society. Were we in our daily work going to defend the practices and policies of the hospitals, courts, prisons, foster care agencies, welfare departments, and mental institutions for which we worked, or were we going to use our jobs to defend and protect the poor, the sick, the criminal, and the deviant against these agencies? That is the real and difficult challenge. It is not easy to be a professional, to lay claim to professional authority and esteem, and side with ordinary folks, especially poor folks. It is not easy to be a bureaucrat, intent on rising within the bureaucracy, and side with the clients and victims of that bureaucracy.

There were other false solutions, false because they helped us to avoid paying attention to the kinds of action which we might most effectively take, and helped us to avoid taking the professional risks of such action. One solution developed in the aftermath of disappointed revolutionism, as it often has before: the study group. Some among us urged that we should acquire a thorough grounding in Marxist theory and elaborate it in ways which would comprehend and explain the institutions of welfare capitalism.

Presumably this effort to develop and clarify an analysis was a precursor to developing guidelines for action, but the guidelines were not forthcoming. Instead, some among us became preoccupied with mastering the abstract and convoluted theoretical schemes produced by academic Marxism (paying obeisance to our special commitment as social workers by reiterating such general notions as the need for a "reserve army of labor" to explain the public welfare system), and satisfied themselves that by identifying with an intellectual tradition that had links with revolution, they were somehow becoming revolutionaries. But the more abstract the studies, the more elaborate the explanations; the more intense the preoccupation with differences of doctrine among Marxist scholars, the less we had to concern ourselves with the question of what social workers should do. We were doing something, after all; we were educating ourselves, so that some day we would know what to do. But that day did not and has not come, and meanwhile one cannot help but suspect that the preoccupation with an academic Marxism so abstract as to have no implications for action has led some of us not closer to struggle but, by a circuitous route, back to an inoffensive professionalism.

Other solutions to the quandary were adopted by those more firmly grounded in the profession. They tried to find new doctrinal footings with a minimum of professional upheaval, such as the turn toward community development or social planning. Presumably the failures of the welfare state could be accounted for by the limited role of professionals. Instead of working with individuals and families, we should work with entire communities; instead of working as the operatives of the social agencies, we should work as planners and administrators.

Both of these developments ought to be understood as efforts to take advantage of the assault on social welfare by expanding the jurisdiction of social workers, a not uncommon response by professions to crises in their institutions. In fact, whether we work with individuals or with community groups is not the issue; the issue is what we *do* when we work with them. When social workers in welfare departments shift from doing casework to doing community relations work, they do not necessarily change the relationship of domination and subordination between the agency and its clients. In fact, they may well enhance domination—for example, by allowing themselves to be assigned the function of smoothing out relations with groups of clients who might otherwise become insurgent.

The problems for practice posed by a radical critique of the agencies of the welfare state are surely not solved by what is called social planning, either. In fact, the premises of this false solution are totally at variance with the critique. Social planning is based on two key doctrines, both wrong. The first asserts that the planner is politically neutral, not taking sides in group and class conflicts; she or he works for something which is sometimes called "the community as a whole." The second belief concerns what planners do to advance the goals of the community as a whole. Social planners are presumably the rational decision-makers in the social services. It is their special role to assess the needs and goals of the community over time, to survey relevant action alternatives in the areas of program development or agency organization, and to assess the future impact of these alternative strategies on the community's needs and goals. Quite aside from the dubious assertion of a unitary public interest, it is surely not revealed in social planning activities. Rather, planners are committed to the bureaucracies and, more important, they are committed to the functions the bureaucracies perform in a capitalist society for a capitalist class. Nor is it true that social planners play a large role in these bureaucracies. The key decisions are made elsewhere. Meanwhile, the studies and proposals produced by the planners constitute a kind of technocratic public relations for the ongoing activities of the agencies. Social planning is extremely seductive as a remedy for our dissatisfactions with the social services, and it is everywhere expanding as a professional specialty, not because it comes to grips with those dissatisfactions, but because it promises to raise the status of social workers in the bureaucracies.

A third effort to establish new doctrinal footings has emerged in the training of those who provide direct services to individuals and groups. It is called "systems theory," and is now being taught in many classrooms. The chief virtue of this approach is that it modifies somewhat the emphasis on psychoanalytic theory which has long dominated the field of social work. But systems theory is not an analysis of bureaucratic power, or of the relation of social welfare agencies to capitalist ideology or institutions.

The systems theory approach invites social workers to view clients as "interacting" with a variety of "systems" in which we should ostensibly "intervene." The very blandness of the language denies any recognition of the realities of power. We learn that inmates "interact" with prisons; that mental patients "interact" with state mental hospitals; that recipients "interact" with welfare departments; that children "interact" with foster care agencies; that slum and ghetto dwellers "interact" with urban renewal authorities. But most clients do not interact with these systems, they are oppressed by them; and social workers ought not to intervene in these systems, they ought to resist them. In other words, this perspective—like earlier perspectives which dominate the field of social work—serves to conceal the true character of the agencies of the welfare state.

In these different ways, then, we have avoided the actual and important political choices that arise every day of our professional lives. And we have also avoided the risks to our careers which these choices pose for us.

Education for Bureaucratic Acquiescence

The kind of training we receive in the schools of social work does not make it easier to recognize these choices, or to understand concretely how to act on them in agency settings. There are few respects in which we can look to the schools for guidance, for they cannot afford to endorse perspectives that run counter to the needs of the bureaucracies of the welfare state. No school wants a reputation for training obstreperous students. It wants instead to insure access for its students to field work placements, and access for its graduates to the best jobs. Consequently, professional training is itself a large part of the problem we face. The schools shape our ways of thinking and acting to insure that we will fit into the agency scheme of things, and will accept the general dictum that what the agencies do is, finally, "in the best interests" of the client.

One striking feature of professional socialization is the frequent presumption that students know virtually nothing. No matter what their undergraduate preparation, no matter what their life experience (social work students are often older than students in other graduate departments) or work experience (which often exceeds or is at least more current than that of their instructors, many of whom have not practiced for many years), students quickly sense that they are often credited with very little. Although they may be mature, resourceful, and committed adults, they are frequently not assumed to bring much to the learning process, except perhaps personality traits that are "barriers" to learning. The dominant tendency is to infantilize students. One student described the reaction when she complained about the way in which she and other students were being treated in a unit:

I made an appointment with my faculty field adviser to complain. I was the first student in the unit [of six] to do so. I was met with what I unfondly call caseworking. My faculty adviser told me I was overly anxious and that I wasn't professional when I entered the school, but I would be when I left. She told me I have a lot to learn and asked me if I thought I knew everything. I tried to tell her what was going on at the agency but it was turned against me. I walked out of that office feeling verbally beaten up.[1]

The infantilization of students is a fundamental mechanism by which the agents of oppression in the welfare state are created. Graduates of schools of social work, having been deprived by their training of much dignity of self-worth, often come to cope with this gnawing self-doubt by according the same treatment to others as was accorded to them.

Infantilization serves another purpose as well. Students educated to mistrust their own judgment, life experience, and feelings are then ready to be trained to acquiesce to the authority of others. Professional education is, in no small part, training in submission to bureaucratic authority, and to the supervisors who represent bureaucratic authority. In other words, we are educated to submit to the policies of our employers.

The Tenets for Radical Action

First, we have to break with the professional doctrine that the institutions in which social workers are employed have benign motives: that the purpose of hospitals is to provide health care for the sick; that the purpose of welfare agencies is to provide assistance for the impoverished; that the purpose of child care agencies is to protect children. We must break with such beliefs as matters of doctrine, taking nothing for granted, and, using our common sense and humanity, look at what agencies actually do.

Once freed from a belief in the benign character of the social agencies, we can free ourselves from a second item of doctrine that follows logically enough—that what is good for the agency is good for the client, that the interests of the agency and the interests of the client are basically identical. If the agencies were in fact benign, committed primarily to the well-being of their clientele, this might be true. But if we pay attention to actual agency practices, a very different reality emerges. That reality should make us constantly alert to the possibility that the agency is the enemy of the client, not only because it is committed mainly to its own perpetuation, but because its perpetuation is often conditional on the systematic neglect or abuse—material or psychological—of the lower class and the deviant. Thus agencies for the blind "cream" the more youthful and educable for rehabilitation in order to improve their record of "success." Public housing agencies try to reject "problem" families so as to enhance the image of the bureaucracy. Urban renewal authorities seal neighborhoods from the poor. Foster care agencies all too often keep children in foster care families or in institutions, refusing either to return them to their parents or to place them for adoption even when these are viable alternatives, because each child adds to the public subsidies they receive.

In other words, there is often a profound conflict of interest between the welfare of the agencies and the welfare of clients. But it is a fundamental objective of professional education to deny this conflict, to teach students that the agencies of the welfare state are *their* agencies. In the countless field evaluation reports which we have read in our capacity as teachers, students are rated on the degree to which they have developed an "appropriate identification" with the agency. We have seen many evaluations in which students were faulted for failing to identify adequately with an agency, but we have never known a student who was criticized for overidentifying. By contrast, students are quite regularly given negative evaluations for "overidentifying" with clients—more often than not because they were seized by the sense that clients were being mistreated.

This emphasis in our socialization clearly serves the interests of our employers. We are, quite simply, being taught to identify with the prisons and asylums, with the welfare departments and the urban renewal authorities, and we therefore develop a "learned incapacity" to perceive our own interests or those of clients. It is a remarkable achievement, reminiscent of the achievements of the era of industrial paternalism and company unionism, when many workers were induced to identify with their employers. But assembly-line workers have since learned that General Motors is not "their" company. We have yet to learn that lesson.

Third, we have to break with the professional doctrine that ascribes virtually all of the problems that clients experience to defects in personality development and family relationships. It must be understood that this doctrine is as much a political ideology as an explanation of human behavior. It is an ideology that directs clients to blame themselves for their travails rather than the economic and social institutions that produce many of them. Students are measured both by their ability to "reach for feelings" in clients and by their ability to provide Freudian interpretations of those feelings. There is little professional literature that instructs students to reach for their clients' feelings about their lot in life, or to provide socioeconomic interpretations of those feelings. This psychological reductionism—this pathologizing of poverty and inequality—is, in other words, an ideology of oppression, for it systematically conceals from people the ways in which their lives are distorted by the realities of class structure. Many teachers, supervisors, and agency administrators are teaching students to throw sand in clients' eyes. And this ideology is all the more powerful because, thanks to the authority of the "helping" professions, it appears to be grounded in the "science" of Freudian psychology.

If many professors and employers encourage us to ignore the ways in which various socioeconomic forces contribute to the personal and family problems of our clients, it is for the obvious reason that clients might then become obstreperous or defiant; that is, they might become a serious cause of embarrassment to the bureaucracies. One student reported the following conflict with her supervisor over just this point. She was assigned to the special services division of a welfare department. Her general responsibility was to reach out to clients who appeared to have problems of various kinds, and to give help by providing liaison with other agencies and resources, as well as to engage in treatment. One of her cases, D., lived in a tenement rattrap, with falling plaster and stopped-up plumbing. D. had refused to pay her rent for a number of months, and the student expressed wholehearted sympathy.

When the student informed her supervisor about the condition of the apartment and the action which D. had been taking to fight the landlord, he was outraged. The student was told, in no uncertain terms, that it was contrary to agency policy to encourage rent withholding by clients. "No professional would encourage such irresponsible behavior. What about her anger? Did you get her anger out? Your job is to help her express·her feelings about the situation, not to encourage her to conduct a rent strike!" The supervisor then insisted that he and the student role-play, so that the student could learn how to help a client express anger. "And so we played that game about feelings," the student said. Students who are taught only to reach for feelings are taught to protect the bureaucracies, and by doing so, to protect important economic groups, such as rapacious landlords, on whose good will the bureaucracies depend.

But once we break with this third tenet of professional doctrine, we will become aware, and be able to help clients to become aware, of the multiple links between economic problems and the problems defined as pathology, as when men out of work grow discouraged and drift away from their families. Men who cannot earn a living have always deserted their families in our society, not because of problems originating in family relationships, but because the humiliation of not being able to support women and children erodes family relationships. When people do not have steady jobs or income, they are deprived of a chief source of self-esteem, which may lead in turn to the kinds of behavior we label personality deterioration—to the listless men hanging on street corners, to alcoholism, addiction, and to other forms of retreat. In a sense these are psychological problems, but in a profounder sense they are the products of an economy that requires a chronically high rate of unemployment and underemployment, and that therefore denies many people access to a livelihood, and to the building blocks of self-respect.

In the same vein, it should be recognized that the mothers who turn out to be incompetent and irresponsible often have these deficiencies because of the overwhelming discouragement of trying to raise children alone, in crowded and deteriorated quarters, without the income to feed and clothe them properly. When these children reach the age of six or seven, mothers then watch helplessly as they lose them to the life of the streets. These women cannot be helped much by therapy. A small part of their tragedy is that often they cannot even turn to us for human sympathy and support without being stigmatized.

My supervisor only supervised us with reference to those cases which interested her. The clients had to have either interesting pathology or some secretive events in their lives. The cases she refused to discuss were those she considered "hopeless." For example, I was seeing a fifty-nine-year-old black woman whose husband was an alcoholic, whose son was on heroin and involved in a day program for drug rehabilitation, and whose daughter was in college. This mother was working as a salesclerk to support her family and keep her daughter in college. She was also involved in many church activities, one of which was taking adolescents on trips out of New York. This was to give them a chance to see other things besides the "ghetto." My supervisor decided that this was a very "masochistic woman" and there was nothing I could do for her. She told me to let her ventilate and refused to discuss the family with me any further. I had to call friends in social work to get needed information—such as how to obtain disability benefits for her husband and job programs for her son. I felt alone with the weight of my client's problems on my shoulders. My supervisor further stated, when I pressed her, that this woman had "no ego." No ego! From my perspective, this was a woman who was keeping her family together precisely because she did have a strong ego [quoted with the permission of Debra E. Pearl].

What lower-class mothers in this society need most is the means to survive: the means to feed their children, to take care of them, in ways which allow women to recapture pride in their role as mothers and as people. Once we stop locating all problems in personality adjustment and family relations, it will become clear that adjustment depends in the most fundamental way on resources. This is not a surprising assertion, except perhaps to many members of the helping professions. In a sense, it is an unprofessional assertion, merely for being so commonplace. It runs counter to long-standing trends by which social work has tried to remove itself from the concrete and urgent needs of poor people, and has instead become preoccupied with psychological needs. These trends have their origins partly in our desire to gain status by elaborating our expertise in esoteric clinical methods. We should reject such professional opportunism and accept the burden of asserting the obvious. If a client has no food in the house, he or she needs money. If a client lives in overcrowded and squalid housing, he or she needs money. Money in American society is, quite simply, the root of all normalcy.

K. came to this country a few years ago from Puerto Rico. She was separated from her husband. She just had her second baby and was trying to arrange for a friend to baby-sit so she could return to work. The babies were often ill, and that required numerous visits to clinics. Few baby-sitters were willing to undertake these chores. The clinics were also costly, and she had little money. Although K. had previously worked double shifts she had used up her money during the pregnancy, and had been advised by a social worker to apply for public assistance. But no one had given her any help in dealing with the application process.

Anyway, K. didn't get assistance, and she came to the social service department of the hospital where I am in training. She was very upset; she always cried and appeared extremely nervous. She was diagnosed by the team as being a "depressive neurotic" and therapy was recommended. The case was then given to me by my supervisor.

During our early interviews, K. always cried; her hands shook nervously and she was constantly depressed. Her physical appearance began to deteriorate. Her clothes were dirty and she had extremely bad body odor. This is important, for when she was originally seen at the clinic she was described as being neat, clean, and attractive.

As I saw it, K. had a great deal to be nervous and depressed about. The world she had created for herself was gone. She had lost her job; her husband was gone; she had two babies that she could not care for if she were going to work; she had been evicted; and she had no money.

I soon realized that K. could not read English well. She was extremely embarrased about this, and tried to hide it from me. This turned out to be one reason why she had so much difficulty with the welfare department. She didn't understand what they were talking about when they told her to get various documents and she could not read the instructions given to her. She was illiterate in a bureaucratic society. Consequently, I gave K. a great deal of help with her housing and welfare problems.

I don't know what I think about the diagnosis of "depressive neurotic." K. certainly had all of the symptoms that the people on the clinic team pointed out to me. But a funny thing has happened. Now that K. has gotten public assistance and a place to live, her behavior has changed. She is now neatly dressed when she comes to see me, and she doesn't cry and wring her hands nervously any more.

Clearly, if there are any systems of programs and agencies with which we ought to be intimately familiar, they are those that provide concrete benefits—Supplemental Security Income, Aid to Families with Dependent Children, food stamps, and the like. But we are not. And professional education is largely the reason that we are not, for the English Poor Law commissioners still haunt our classrooms. We no longer talk about encouraging immorality; instead we worry about encouraging dependency among the poor. The rhetoric has changed, but the pieties persist; it is the psychologically unworthy who must now be protected from their defects of character. Consequently, students are not taught about the world of the waiting rooms and the long lines, nor about how to help their clients deal with that world. The faculty members of the schools of social work generally do not know that world, and many do not want to know it. But a student can ask a casework teacher to describe the general differences between neurosis and psychosis and be quite confident of obtaining an extended answer of some kind. Students are taught "social policy"—those grand schemes defining how the world ought to be. Such knowledge is a source of academic and professional prestige. But if a student asks for a description of the differences in criteria of eligibility between AFDC and food stamps, nine out of ten teachers of casework and social policy will stand mute.

Fourth, and finally, it follows from what has been said that we ought to become aware of the ways that "professional knowledge and technique" are used to legitimate our bureaucratic power over people. The professional dedicated to serving people will understand that his or her most distinguishing attribute ought to be humility. The doctrine that "we know best" must be exorcised; there is simply no basis for the belief that we who have MSW degrees or similar university credentials are better able to discern our clients' problems than they are, and better able to decide how to deal with these problems. In fact, we know next to nothing about the problems we claim to understand. A potpourri of dubious propositions drawn from the social and psychological sciences has been dignified as knowledge, when the most charitable thing to be said about them is that they are speculations.

None of this would be so important were it simply that we do not know very much. But thinking we know a great deal, we often ignore what clients say they need. Even worse, we invoke this witches' brew of "professional knowledge and technique" to brand people with horrendous psychiatric labels, and impose on them the loss of efficacy and self-esteem that inevitably follows. The ultimate absurdity occurs when we persist in stigmatizing people even when our own "diagnostic techniques" fail to disclose evidence of pathology. One student reported a case of a thirteen-year-old boy who was referred to a child development clinic for hyperactive children because of behavioral and academic difficulties in the public school. The psychologist examined the youngster first and reported:

He related in an appropriate manner . . . did not display very much hyperactive behavior . . . his approach to work was not impulsive. Rather, he tended to work persistently and was appropriately involved in the tasks even when they were difficult for him. Recommendation: James should be considered for our treatment program for hyperactive children.

Next the psychiatrist examined him and said:

James showed no hyperactivity either in my office or in the waiting room. He was not restless or fidgety. His attention and concentration were good, and he wasn't distractable. There was no evidence of thought or affect disorder. Recommendation: acceptance for treatment program as well as pharmacotherapeutic treatment based on the diagnosis of hyperkinetic reaction of childhood.

Finally, the neurological examiner noted:

Throughout the interview there was a moderate amount of movement, both body and small hand movement, but this was never excessive nor was there any evidence of distractibility or decreased attention span. Diagnosis: hyperactive reaction of childhood. Recommend admittance.

The final diagnosis and recommendation appear in the case record as follows:

Although James was not found to be excessively active either during psychiatric or neurological examinations, nor during psychological testing, he does fulfill the criteria for our program; both school and home describe him as being hyperactive. He will therefore be admitted to our program for hyperactive children with a diagnosis of: hyperactive reaction of childhood.

Technocratic power is dangerous in other ways as well. When clients, who often desperately need a humane and supportive human contact, tell us their troubles (almost always in the mistaken belief that their confidence will be protected), we interpret the meaning of these not only to them, but to the agencies through the records we keep. These records are the dossiers of the state, by which clients are victimized. It is often records that lead agencies to remove children from their homes and mothers unjustly; that provide the justification for parole revocation; that lead to the incarceration of juveniles for "offenses" as harmless as truanting or running away. We mindlessly allow ourselves to comply with the doctrine that record-keeping is a "professional method." One student placed in a parole agency reported that social workers serving as parole officers record everything, and that parole is regularly revoked as a result. One parolee was sent back to prison because he confided that he was living with a woman; another because he did not consult with his parole officer before getting married; and another because there was the smell of liquor on his breath. The agencies have made us into policemen. In this, as in so many other ways, we remain oblivious to the actual results of professional doctrines and agency policies. There is a cardinal rule of resistance: record nothing that will harm a client! You cannot know how your agency will use the information, or to whom they will make it available.

Resistance

Having rid ourselves of some of the obfuscations of professional doctrine, we have to begin to learn about the concrete activities of the agencies, but in an entirely different way, for an entirely different purpose. We have to become intimately familiar with the rules and regulations, with the rituals and the jargon, and with the way these affect the day-by-day actions of agency personnel. And we have to learn these things not to serve the agencies, but to penetrate them, manipulate them, defy them, and expose them. We have to learn the bureaucratic ropes in order to learn the bureaucratic vulnerabilities. In other words, we have to understand precisely how the agencies work in order to develop the tactics to fight them in the interest of clients. We have to learn how to exploit whatever discretion is available to us in our jobs; how to challenge effectively the bureaucratic and professional authority of those above us; how to short-circuit the bureaucratic runarounds through which the urgent needs of people are defined away as someone else's function; how to get around the rules, and even how to break them. We have to become excruciatingly aware of the role designated for us, and of every facet of the agency's activities on which we impinge, because that is how we will learn to convert our jobs into weapons to defend people against the agencies.

The unemployed and the subemployed in American capitalism turn for subsistence to the public welfare or Social Security or food stamp agencies. When we deal with these agencies, we have to clear our heads of the confusions generated by proclamations that they aid the needy, and always remember that it is in the interest of these agencies to fend off the poor so as to keep costs down and insure continued support from dominant political and economic interests. Accordingly, we will scrutinize agency procedures with keen skepticism, always asking how many people will get how much money as a result of this or that legal or bureaucratic arrangement. To do this, we will have to educate ourselves thoroughly about regulations and practices (this is something we will have to do very much on our own, for we are taught more in the schools of social work about the English Poor Laws than about the rules and regulations of the contemporary welfare programs on which so many clients depend for their existence). In particular, we must learn about the intake procedures which are always justified as discriminating the truly needy from the not-so-needy, but which are really barriers erected to ward off the poor. Thus if a welfare department designs new application procedures—substituting a twelve-page form for the two-page form previously in use, for example—we ought to recognize immediately that the object is not "greater efficiency" and "better management" (as the commissioner and top policy-makers will proclaim), but greater inefficiency and worse mismanagement. They will generate more burdensome work for the intake personnel, so that fewer applicants can be processed; create additional requirements for documents (birth certificates, marriage licenses, rent receipts, pay stubs, and so forth), so that fewer applicants can survive the application process; and make the waiting lines longer and the waiting rooms more crowded, so that more applicants will grow discouraged and abandon the effort to obtain benefits. Accordingly, those few of us who have something to do with the design of such procedures ought to resist them when they are introduced, never succumbing to the familiar argument that if the agency is able to win public confidence by its improved "efficiency," the poor will be better off in the long run. And the many of us who deal with these procedures as they affect particular clients ought always to be ready to challenge the regulations, or to evade them. To do this, we must read the manuals, visit the intake offices, harass the staff, and continually invoke the appeals procedures. We ought to arm ourselves for this resistance with a special urgency now, for higher and higher levels of unemployment and underemployment are being defined by ruling groups as "normal" even while inflation has severely eroded the limited incomes of many families.

Obtaining medical treatment for people is often as much a problem as the way they are treated by medical personnel. The supervisor of one student placed in a hospital setting learned of a patient in the waiting room who was only nineteen, pregnant, and lonely. She instructed the student to "let her ventilate her feelings" [quoted with the permission of Arlene Hagan]. The student established contact, and learned that the young woman had been thrown out of the house by her grandmother because of the pregnancy, and was living with a friend who gave her twenty dollars a week to perform baby-sitting services. The student told her that she was eligible for public assistance as an emancipated minor, and inquired whether she had Medicaid. The patient replied that she had two letters, one saying she was eligible and the other saying she was ineligible. The student told the patient to go to the Department of Social Services and try to get things straightened out.

On the next visit to the hospital, the patient was in tears. She had been told that she was not eligible for public assistance or for Medicaid because she was an "illegal" (from a Latin American country). The patient was now upset both because she had "disgraced" her grandmother and because she might be deported, for the irate Department of Social Services worker had called the immigration authorities to report that an illegal alien was trying to obtain public relief. The student promptly called several legal defense organizations. She was advised to do everything she could to stall any action until the baby was born, since it was unlikely that a deportation proceeding would be instituted if the patient was the mother of a citizen.

The student then told her supervisor of her plan, and made it clear that the patient needed prenatal care even though she had no Medicaid card. Her supervisor became quite defensive, and expressed regret that she had assigned the case. She also insisted that the student prepare a written statement saying that the supervisor did not know the patient was an illegal alien, and said she doubted that care could be provided. The student expressed disgust, but made the necessary notation in the hospital chart. The hospital charged $1,000 for a delivery, and the supervisor did not want to be responsible for a case of nonpayment. The student later learned from the financial office, however, that Medicaid provides coverage for thirty days in the event that an illegal alien is admitted on an emergency basis. Each time the patient came in for care, the student managed to get the admitting department to treat it as an emergency. On one occasion, she slipped the patient in by saying that she had lost her Medicaid card.

The patient then received a notice to report for a deportation hearing. The student told her supervisor that she was going to write a letter saying that the patient could not appear because of her pregnancy. "When I told my supervisor this, she was completely dumfounded but she didn't know how to get out of the situation, so she had to go along." Luckily, the baby was born on the same day that the hearing was scheduled, and the student left the field placement in May feeling that the deportation question had become moot. She planned to continue seeing the patient on her own, however, in order to be certain that the immigration authorities took no action.

In the criminal justice system, social workers have been made into something resembling the police agents of the state. In that role, we make life-determining decisions to revoke probation or parole and to place people in institutions. Ostensibly, we make these decisions as social workers committed to rehabilitation. But do we really believe that penal institutions of any kind rehabilitate people? And if we do not, then we are permitting a lot of professional and technical mumbo jumbo to obscure the fact that we are incarcerating people, not rehabilitating them.

In the juvenile courts, the banner of treatment flies even higher. Under the guise of treating parents and the presumed deficiencies of their children, we have participated in the institutionalization of children for such behaviors as truancy, incorrigibility, or sexual promiscuity. In effect, we have participated in the criminalization of children for offenses for which no adult could be arrested or confined. An important form of resistance is to use our discretion to keep adults out of prisons and children out of the reformatories and "residential treatment centers" whenever we possibly can. If we use our common sense, we know that children are almost always better off even as runaways than in institutions.

A case was referred to the private counseling service in which I am placed. The mother, Mrs. X., reported that her daughter Joan had gotten in trouble with the police when she and a friend went into a truck and stole seventy dollars. Mrs. X. stated that her daughter had been in trouble a few times in the past, and was spending too much time with "bad girls." Both she and her husband felt that the child was disrespectful to them, and they both spend a lot of time yelling at her.

Mrs. and Mr. X. are white, lower-class, and Irish Catholic. Mr. X. has been hospitalized and is now medically disabled. He has been unemployed for some time, and the family has had to go on welfare. They have applied for Supplemental Security Income benefits. Mrs. X. used to be a domestic worker and she is planning to resume that kind of work.

There are several stresses on the family in addition to the father's illness and unemployability. They had to move to a cheap apartment, and of course they have lost a lot of social status because of their poverty-stricken state. With these changes, communication in the family seems to have broken down. Anger and disappointment seem to have taken over. I have been working with various family members around these angers and communication problems, and I have also become Joan's advocate in dealing with the courts.

I received a call from Joan's probation officer who wanted information about the family, since she is making out a report for the judge. She said there were two choices for Joan: residential treatment or some kind of continuing counseling. She told me that if we could come up with a good plan, the judge could be persuaded to keep Joan out of an institution. So I began to work on the case.

After I had seen Joan several times to talk things over, I got a call from her mother that they were canceling their various sessions with me. The message also said that their Medicaid eligibility had run out, and they could no longer pay the agency's fees. I tried to reach them by telephone and letter, but they did not respond. I then contacted the probation officer and explained the situation. She said she would get in touch with them and tell them to call me. I felt strongly that the reason they had discontinued coming was because they had no money. Mrs. X. is a very proud woman.

A few days later, the probation officer's supervisor called me and bawled me out for getting her supervisee involved in any problems with my clients. She said it was perfectly obvious that Mrs. X. does not want any kind of counseling for her daughter, that she is resisting, and that the only answer for Joan is to put her in a residential placement. Since the parents can't control Joan, she said, the child needs a "structured setting."

I could not believe what I was hearing. Once I had calmed down, I told her off. I began by saying that she didn't know anything about the family and all they've been through because of the father's unemployment and illness. She finally backed down and she said she would consider a plan if I could develop one. I figured I had won round one.

A few days later, Mrs. X. called because the probation officer had been in touch with her. It soon became apparent that the reason for her discontinuance was that her Medicaid card had run out, just as I had thought. With a little effort, I was able to get that problem straightened out, and then Mrs. X. agreed that the family would continue.

I then worked out a plan for Joan to have a "Big Sister," and I arranged to continue seeing various family members on a regular basis.

When I spoke to the probation officer, she was quite embarrassed. She explained that her supervisor always thought institutional placement was the best remedy for kids. She explained to me that she was a student in training and didn't feel secure arguing with her supervisor. We agreed to continue working together around the pending court appearance, and we both felt confident that the judge would listen to us. As it happens, he did. Things are going much better with Joan now, and with her family.

If we work in mental institutions or have dealings with them, we will dismiss treatment claims for what they are—doctrines that are utterly unsubstantiated. Mental institutions do not treat people, and they rarely cure them. With our heads cleared of doctrine, we can see that what hospitalization actually does is deprive people of ordinary liberties and of any vestige of self-esteem or competence. And we play a role in that process—as social workers in intake offices, as members of psychiatric teams, in discharge departments and in referral agencies. We can use the opportunities afforded by these positions to resist decisions to commit, to challenge capricious diagnoses, to question the stupefaction of people by drugs. We need to remember that while people may need counseling, mental institutions do not provide it. What they do provide, almost no one needs. No one needs stigmatization; few people need medication; and even fewer need institutionalization.

One student resisted his supervisor over the question of whether a veteran in an outpatient veterans' facility should be drugged. M. had been diagnosed as schizophrenic, but at the time the student began seeing him, he had obtained a job as a truck driver, was earning more money than ever before, and found the job enormously rewarding. He showed some signs of nervousness, however, and the student's supervisor suggested that M. be seen by the agency psychiatrist in order to obtain medication so that he "wouldn't fall apart." The student replied that far from falling apart, he was doing fine, and that medicating him would interfere with the performance of a job that had come to be extremely important to him. The student stressed that if this veteran lost his job, then he would indeed fall apart. Consequently, the student refused to refer M. to the psychiatrist for medication. Afterward, the student commented that he felt gratified about the whole matter, noting that the price he paid was insignificant—a sentence in his field evaluation saying that he was having difficulty with authority and that he had dogmatic views about drugs and psychiatrists.

The key decisions that lead to the institutionalizing of people occur in many settings where social workers are employed, or to which they are related, not just in the mental health agencies and the courts. The incarceration process can be set in motion in the public schools, for example.

A. and her seven children live in one of the most rundown sections of the South Bronx. The A. family moved to the United States from Puerto Rico in 1970. The case was referred to the Bureau of Child Welfare by the guidance counselor at P.S. ____ because George was having serious behavior problems at that school. When the case was first transferred to me, the guidance counselor called me to inform me that George was a "recalcitrant" child who should be placed immediately in an institution. I visited the family and learned that A. was vehemently against placement for her son. A couple of weeks later, I received a call from the guidance counselor informing me that George had been suspended because he had been involved in a fight with a school employee.

I went out to visit the family again. George told me that the school employee had hit him over the head with a broom because he had refused to get out of his way when he had been ordered to do so. A. was furious with the school and threatened to sue.

I called a meeting to discuss with the school officials what could be done to help George. The consulting psychiatrist was present at this meeting, together with the school principal, George's former teacher, the guidance counselor, and some big-shot administrator from the school district. It became clear to me and to the psychiatrist (we became allies during this battle) that the school officials were not interested in helping George; they had only one objective—to get rid of him. The teacher and the guidance counselor repeated again and again that George was an "impossible" child and that the school could do nothing to help him. The school principal made it clear that he was mainly concerned with the school's image in the community. Because George had once cut his wrist in a fit of anger (both the psychiatrist and I doubt that his incident could in any way be construed as a "suicide attempt"), the principal talked about her concern that George might try to commit suicide in the school. Her concern was not for the child, but for herself. She mentioned at least five times during the meeting that she could already envision the "screaming New York *Times* headlines" if George were to kill himself in "her" school.

The meeting was tense. I flatly stated that the Bureau of Child Welfare would not place the child unless the mother and the child voluntarily requested placement. The psychiatrist urged the principal to arrange for George to be placed in a "grade B" class, which is a special, small class that caters to the needs of "problem children." The principal said that she could not guarantee admission to one of these special classes because there are so many "disturbed" kids in the South Bronx. But finally we won, and George was not sent to a residential setting. He got the special class instead [quoted with the permission of Laura Nitzberg].

The way people are treated in institutions provides countless occasions for resistance.

I am placed in a residential treatment institution for field training. During the course of the year, I became aware of many instances of child abuse, especially by the cottage staff. Others knew about these practices, but everyone was afraid to take action. The chief victimizer of the children was the head of child care who was a former matron in the women's prison. She had hired several retired prison guards as cottage parents. Children were intimidated, demeaned, and physically abused. At first I was frightened— these were frightening people, and I was afraid for my own safety. Veiled threats were made. I also had doubts about whether it was proper to accuse another staff member. The doctor was also abusive. One of my clients thought she might be pregnant and wanted a test, which had to be approved. At first the doctor refused: "Miss Tureff, I am the doctor around here. This is a medical, not a social decision." Then the doctor asked, "Has your client been diagnosed? I find her behavior most age-inappropriate. I think she is more than just psychoneurotic, she is definitely prepsychotic. How long has she been promiscuous?" I replied that she had been seen by a psychiatrist, but no label had been attached. I also said that she was not promiscuous, just sexually active.

As the weeks passed, I became increasingly concerned with reports of child abuse, especially physical beatings. Teachers in the school told me of children with bruised lips. Children told their natural parents about beatings. A number of children told me directly. And other professionals on the grounds had their own sources of information regarding such practices. One of the natural parents came in to complain to the director, after I had encouraged her to do so. But the director dodged the problem, saying, "Look, Ms. J., there are some suspicions about the cottage parents, but I can't just run in there and fire them. I need concrete evidence. They are under surveillance, and that's all I can do for now."

Fortunately, a new director was hired toward the end of the year. I had been talking with my supervisor about the whole problem. She knew what was going on, but she too was frightened. However, she spoke with the new director, and after some trepidation, agreed that I (and several other students in placement) could do the same. The director subsequently suggested that the children be asked to provide testimony, but the children were too terrified. By now the new director was concerned. He called a meeting of the child care staff and lectured them on child abuse. Someone had also anonymously informed the state board of social services, and an investigator had come to the agency.

Once things got stirred up, things began to happen. Several child care workers have resigned, the head of child care is going to be terminated, and everyone is more aware now that child abuse cannot always be concealed, so they are more careful. Although I (and my supervisor) were both afraid that she might lose her job because of what I had been doing, I think now that she is glad that I protested these conditions [quoted with the permission of Susan Tureff].

In the struggle against agency practices, it is often necessary to bring external pressure to bear, such as organizing clients to protest or threatening litigation. A mother and three children were burned out of their apartment in the South Bronx. The mother desperately sought housing for several weeks, but could find nothing that welfare officials would approve and for which they would advance a security deposit. She then went to the public housing authority. When she was shunted aside, she began to scream and refused to leave the office until something was done to insure housing for her and her children. The police were called, with the result that she was placed in a mental hospital, and her children sent for placement. The mother was promptly diagnosed as "schizophrenic—paranoid type," medicated, and involuntarily detained for several months. When she was released, she went to the child care agency to demand her children. The student assigned to the case had to tell her that the children could not be released until an appropriate apartment was found that met the agency's criterion of adequacy. To make matters worse, it turned out that the welfare department would not approve a rent allowance adequate for the family until the children were returned—a case of "catch 22."

When the woman flew into another angry rage, the student protested to her supervisor that the agency should help find housing for the family. "That," she was told, "is not our function." The mother subsequently broke down again, and was returned briefly to a mental hospital. The student again protested to her supervisor, saying that if the agency's housing standards were universally applied, there would be no children left in the South Bronx. The supervisor would not relent.

Because of the cost of visiting the children, who were in an upstate institution, the mother had difficulty seeing them, although she tried to do so as often as possible. On these visits, she screamed and cried and raged that she wanted the children back, all of which was used by agency personnel to discredit her emotional health and maternal "fitness." Her visits to the children became more sporadic and more enraged. The student was also enraged; she argued that the agency was receiving thousands of dollars for the care of the children, but still she could not persuade her supervisor to authorize payment for the mother's travel.

Finally, the student herself visited the children and reported that she could find no reason why they should not be returned to their mother. Her supervisor disagreed: where but in a professional child care institution, the supervisor asked, could such children receive the best of clinical services and other forms of care? The student saw it differently; she saw an agency enriching and maintaining itself by kidnapping children.

Since all else had failed, the student decided to get legal assistance for this mother. She ran down a civil liberties lawyer who called and wrote the agency, making it clear that litigation would follow. There was quite a flap at the agency, but the student stood her ground. Finally, the agency director decided he did not want to go to the trouble and cost of a court action, and so the student was allowed to help the mother find housing, and the children were subsequently released.

Finally, a few words of warning are in order. Anyone who undertakes to fight for client interests must be prepared to be discredited. One of the main lines of attack mounted by the agencies is that their clients need no advocates; what is done to the client is for the best. Sometimes, when the evidence of abuse is too blatant to be dismissed—for example, when desperately needy families are summarily turned away from welfare departments—the line of attack shifts. Now the claim is not that the agencies are above reproach, but rather that the client is "dependent," for otherwise he or she would be able to overcome the obstacles generated by faults in agency practice. If one gives actual assistance—telephoning on behalf of the client or accompanying a family member to some agency, or whatever—the charge will be leveled that this help actually exacerbates the client's problems by inducing dependency. Presumably, clients should fend for themselves, the theory being that otherwise they will not acquire the competence to cope.

These assertions are designed, of course, to prevent agency procedures from being resisted or disrupted. To argue that clients can, one by one, successfully fight the huge, centralized, and powerful agencies of the welfare state solely with the weapon of their egos is, of course, to render them helpless while appearing to render them strong. By this sleight-of-hand, problems of power are converted into problems of personality: it is not the power of the agencies that needs to be fought, but the strength of the client's ego that needs to be buttressed.

Serious forms of retribution may also ensue, although we typically exaggerate the punishments that will be meted out if we run afoul of our superiors (these exaggerations enable us to avoid any action at all). Still, we have to develop tactics not only to defend clients, but to defend ourselves. Clearly, the more of us in any agency who are joined together and committed to mutual support, the stronger we will be, not only ideologically—although that is important—but because we will be able to counter bureaucratic efforts to discipline us with job actions of our own. Some of us will find ourselves too isolated to develop collective tactics of self-defense, and some of us may even be fired. But most of us can get other jobs. In any case, we delude ourselves if we think that any serious political action—in social work or elsewhere—is possible that does not entail some risk and sacrifice.

At best, if we seriously decide to resist on behalf of the poor and the victims, we are not likely to be rewarded with professional esteem, and we probably will not advance rapidly in the bureaucracies, simply because those who side with the sick and the deviant, the poor and the criminal, are not usually rewarded for their troubles.

But if we choose such a course, we will become social workers in fact and not just in proclamation. And we will accomplish something important. If we manage to get people who are hungry a bit of bread, or to protect the weak against the assaults of the courts or the mental hospitals, then we will have gone a short way toward redressing the wrongs of a harsh society. Which of us is so arrogantly unfeeling, or so confident of the prospects for revolutionary transformation, as to think these small gains not important?

In the longer run, moreover, if we fight for the interests of the people we claim are our clients, then we will also be waging a struggle against the institutions of the capitalist state. There is a kind of tautological trick inherent in some Marxist arguments, to the effect that any actual effort to deal with the contradictions created by capitalism will produce reforms that paper over the contradictions. The trick is a professionally convenient one, for it enables us to say that no action short of the final cataclysmic action ought be taken.

But revolutions are not made all at once. If we believe that the maintenance of wealth and power in the United States depends in part upon the exploitation, isolation, and stigmatization of the victims of capitalism by the agency of the welfare state, then our role is to resist these processes, and all the more fiercely because we now understand that the practices of these agencies are not accidental, but are central to the operation of capitalist society. If we believe our analysis of the welfare state, then it follows that if any struggle is important, then so is this one, for it is a struggle to make contradictions explicit, not to obscure them.

NOTE

1. The case materials used throughout this paper were taken, with permission, from term papers. Some students wished to be acknowledged, and so their names have been cited; others preferred to remain anonymous. Names, places, and agencies have been disguised when appropriate.

26

WELFARE REFORM FROM ABOVE AND BELOW

George T. Martin, Jr., and David Street

M OST welfare reform efforts in America since World War II have come from above, originating in liberal, middle-class, and professional circles. With each of these efforts a variety of conditions has resisted reform. Reform efforts from above usually work through public agencies, which recurrently experience severe problems of goal-setting and implementation. Goals are often multiple and ambiguous, making it difficult to set priorities and leading to bifurcated organizational structures. The public welfare agency faces ambiguities and conflicts over goals because it is charged on the one hand with helping the poor, and on the other hand with exercising surveillance over them. The agencies also have problems in recruiting support, maintaining legitimacy, and achieving the freedom to act independently. Like prisons, public welfare agencies derive a lowered reputation simply by working with a disesteemed clientele, disabling them in obtaining resources and support for genuine reform. Further, structures of decision-making and command tend to be weak in organizational efforts to implement reform. This is often the result of administrative fragmentation into a variety of agencies, each of which is incomplete, and of the existence of statutory requirements that prescribe and circumscribe practices and roles so that the organizations can make little change. Thus, while public welfare agencies can be fateful for thousands of people, and in this sense are powerful, this does not make them masters of their own actions.

From David Street, George T. Martin, Jr., and Laura Kramer Gordon, *The Welfare Industry: Functionaries and Recipients in Public Aid* (Beverly Hills: Sage Publications, 1979), drawn from chs. 5, 7, and 8. Reprinted by permission; copyright © 1979 Sage Publications.

THE PROFESSIONALIZATION OF REFORM

Reform from above is critically disabled by processes involved in the professionalization of reform. Professionalization implies a process by which occupational groups progressively work to establish a publicly recognized monopoly of expertise in dealing with aspects of behavior considered important. The most clearly professionalized occupation is medicine, in which practitioners exercise a high degree of control in making practice of many kinds of health care illegal for any but MDs. For self-interested and altruistic reasons, all other white-collar and some blue-collar occupations aspire to be more professional by moving toward the medical model. In so doing, they unevenly work to develop theories of practice, ideologies of service, training schools, licensing procedures, professional associations, and codes of ethics along the lines that doctors have pursued so successfully.

Professions have a clientele for which they purport to speak. The American Medical Association (AMA) claims, with considerable success, to speak for patients. Indeed, a source of power for professional groups is their claim to speak authoritatively for a special constituency. One result of the professionalization of reform has been creation of a constituency of welfare recipients and of the poor for whom middle-class social welfare bureaucrats and professionals speak. These people work in professional associations such as the National Association of Social Workers, public bureaucracies such as the Department of Health and Human Services (HHS), and private organizations such as the Ford Foundation. When Congress wants to hear about the situation of welfare recipients and the poor, it calls on representatives of such organizations, just as it calls on the AMA when it inquires into health. Even the insurgent organization of recipients, the National Welfare Rights Organization (NWRO), was dominated to some extent by middle-class professionals. For example, of the twenty-seven Chicago recipient groups in 1969, the majority were organized by social workers, caseworkers, lawyers, and other professionals. One NWRO organizer in Chicago was heard to remark that at local meetings there were often "twice as many caseworkers and lawyers as there were recipients."

By professionalization of reform we refer to efforts to define social problems as the special and exclusive province of particular professionalizing occupational groups. Moynihan (1965, 1969) first made this term well known, pointing to the fact that during the Kennedy and Johnson administrations, particularly during the antipoverty program's development, a host of specific reforms was proposed and implemented at the behest of social workers, educators, social scientists, lawyers, and psychiatrists. Important to this concept is the observation that in contrast to earlier reform periods in America, these programs were designed in the relative absence of prior political coalitions. For example, academic centers for the study of welfare rights preceded both public concern with the issue and political mobilization of recipients. An important legal article on welfare rights was published two years before NWRO emerged (Reich 1965).

There were expectations at large for reform at the broadest level (the *end* to poverty), but they did not compel specific reform programs. Thus, professionals inside government and without emerged in the context of generalized political demands, brandishing heretofore hidden but detailed reform agendas that were suddenly defined as imperative. It is important, too, as McCarthy and Zald (1973) argue, that the existence of the political demands was in large measure dependent on "professional social movements" in which foundations and affluent groups played a leading role by providing support.

Our use of professionalization of reform is not limited to the period of the antipoverty program or to Moynihan's conception of the process. We refer instead to the broad tendency in this century to develop professional ideologies that seek to define certain remedies as appropriate and expert. To clarify our conception, we can refer to aspects of what Lowi (1969) describes as "interest group liberalism" in the design of the antipoverty program. Lowi suggests that the principal problem to which the antipoverty program responded was elimination or reduction of injustice, something that might have been addressed, for example, by straightforwardly making racial discrimination illegal. Rather than taking such steps, however, the government dealt with injustice indirectly, by "delegating good intentions" and money in the hopes of creating a poverty constituency parallel to others such as labor or business. Congress appropriated millions of dollars to eliminate poverty, without making careful specification of the uses to which the funds could be put—money thenceforth available to competing professions to implement their definitions of reform.

The individual service model. Perceiving poverty as rooted in individual preparation and functioning has been central to reform in America. Of crucial importance for the poor is the fact that ideologies of professional educators have been omnipresent. Problems of inequality and poverty are conventionally redefined as problems of effort and opportunity, and the corrective measures prescribed typically involve improving and expanding the educational system. That the United States developed a mass secondary school system long before the nations of Europe did so may be crucial to understanding why this country has been more reluctant to develop a welfare state than have those countries. The United States institutionalized a set of structures and beliefs that embodied a conventional wisdom in which changes in the social and economic system were deemed unnecessary; all that was needed was for individuals to develop the motivation to take advantage of expanded educational opportunities.

The strength of this commitment to education as *the* solution can be seen in its dominance throughout the antipoverty program. Even during the period in which community action programs (CAPs) were center stage, demanding fundamental change in the system, the predominance of resources was going to educational programs for preschool children (Operation Head Start), job training (Job Corps), and parallel programs devoted to improving individual functioning. Although it had become clear that extension of equal educational opportunity does not produce equality of results, its proponents continued to act as if it did.

Education's closest competitor as the profession that defines the problem of poverty has been social work. In its central thrust, social work, too, acts as if it would solve problems of inequality but fails to provide a technology. Social work's principal input to the solution of social problems has been to suggest the curative value of social casework addressed to putting the client in contact with resources and to ministering (sometimes) to his psyche. However helpful this may be to individuals, it cannot address the general problem of inequality. This professional technology is, however, largely compatible with the educational strategy: counseling people to take fuller advantage of such opportunities as are available and diverting attention of change-oriented publics from questions of direct revision of the system.

Education, social work, and other professions addressing social problems have shared a commitment to the service strategy in which the diagnosis of needed change is to fund new programs that hire professionals to provide individual services. Educators teach about the need for more teachers, social workers counsel the provision of additional caseworkers, doctors prescribe new clinics, lawyers advocate legal aid for the poor, police command an enlarged patrol capacity, psychiatrists bring to consciousness the need for new community health centers, and city planners draw blueprints for additional public housing. Thus, whatever the profession making the diagnosis, reform becomes a definition of the poor as clients and of trained, paid practitioners as the "engine of change." Where professions are weak in their assertion of expertise in a given area of reform, new specialties may be developed, as when community psychology arrived as an offshoot of psychology to compete with community mental health professionals from psychiatry and social work.

Competition, coalition, and mutual discrediting. Acting in the interest of social improvement, reformers become "moral entrepreneurs" (Becker 1963); during competition for increasing resources available in a period of high attention to reform, they can easily become entrepreneurs. Efforts at large-scale change, no matter how grandly phrased, frequently consist only in aggregation of existing service strategies rather than in development of new approaches. This is the case with often-ballyhooed "comprehensive programs" that involve some combination of "service packages" as a compromise in a coalition of the professions included. As social problems surface to widespread public attention, professions immediately come forward with proposals for new combinations of service programs. Most dramatic in recent years has been development of the drug-service industry, consisting of large numbers of medical doctors, psychiatrists, social workers, clergy, and others who seek legitimacy and money for new comprehensive drug programs—whatever these are (Helfgot 1974). Despite the frequent willingness of competing professions to compromise by including themselves in comprehensive programs, the ideologies of professions act to discredit reformist claims of other professions and thus ultimately the credibility of their own demands and reform programs. This has nowhere been seen more dramatically than in the controversies of the late 1960s in New York City between those who sought to decentralize the system (often led by social workers who, dissatisfied with casework, had become community organizers) and teachers who (through their union) fought to preserve their professional prerogatives against parent and community groups, and social workers.

This example provides as well indication of how discrediting of reformist claims can occur within a single profession—social work. At varying times, social work has emphasized each of the world views that Lofland and Stark (1965) propose as basic to defining life's problems: religious, psychological, and political. Nineteenth-century social work showed a mix of the religious and political world views, professional social work has always emphasized the psychological view, and 1960s community organizers came to stress the political view once again. To some proponents of the latter perspective, the concept of help became anathema; an individual in difficulty is not to be helped but educated that she is being "screwed by the system"— without effective political organization, information about as helpful to the poor as the earlier doctrine that poverty was self-inflicted.

Across professions, mutual discrediting wreaks havoc. Proponents of community control see community mental health practitioners as naively apolitical; community mental health people in turn see the mental health establishment as tied to an obsolescent medical model; members of that establishment see the others as unprofessional. The accumulation of discrediting of professions' reformist ideologies no doubt heightens apathy and cynicism about the potential for change among officials and the public. Paradoxically, the effort to improve society induces competition that is strikingly capitalist in character. To many Americans reformers become understandable only when their zeal translates into a marketing technique. Americans have little grounds for trusting the altruism of others, even the reformers among them. Indeed, reformers often show an unrealistic position and tone that seem arrogant (Novak 1971a). Lack of trust for those who espouse public improvement, expressed in the invidious tone with which the term "do-gooder" is used, is found among professionals as well, and embodies a self-reinforcing prophecy that may be critically inimical to genuine reform.

Competition and pork-barreling of programs also discredit the poor themselves. Professional competition to define their situation often serves to blur, reinforce, and multiply stereotypes so that their condition is seen as even more hopeless and deviant. Consider the case of poor, black, urban pupils, as educators sought additional resources for innovation to help them and to work with other professions in comprhensive service strategies in the 1960s. The schools and cooperating agencies tended toward a proliferation of interrelated categories for describing the pupils' problems. Thus, while it is difficult to be poor and black, these pupils became defined as being *culturally deprived, emotionally handicapped, problem children, acting-out children, from a broken home, slum residents, subject to gang pressures, children of junkie communities*, and the like. Diagnoses, however well-intended, can multiply to create a single powerful stereotype that makes Claude Brown's (1965) heroic escape from the ghetto seem the only exit possible. Such stereotyping can be particularly pernicious when a social scientific approach to understanding the poor, that of the "culture of poverty," is selected for prominent display as an explanation of why the stereotype persists. The "culture of poverty" approach holds that the poor really *want* to live as they do, or at least they know no other way to live. This theory is uniquely suited to a contemporary reinforcement of the individualistic service strategy, for while seeming to take structural explanation (historical forces and the culture) as the heart of the problem, individuals receive the blame in practice and require resocialization, if redeemable at all (Ryan 1971).

Definitions of inequality that challenge the individual service strategy recurrently emerge within professions, but ultimately lose their force as they come to be discredited as more political than professional. It is widely recognized that during the period of the antipoverty program, efforts to break out of the standard service model—particularly by social workers not oriented to casework—fell prey to opposition by established political, business, and civil service groups. Opposition came not only from traditional opponents of change but also from *within* reform-oriented professions. Once it is agreed that the solution to a social problem is a professional matter, processes of discrediting between and within professions arise, and the usual victor—understandable, given its entrenchment in the culture—is the standard professional model embodying the individual service strategy. Professions are probably incapable of anything other than a service orientation, and the alternatives make them claim to be authorities on human values as well as on their technology.

THE PERPETUAL EFFORT TO REFORM WELFARE FROM ABOVE

The effort to reform welfare from above continually confronts the fact that the institution is spread in a confused, fragmented fashion across federal, state, and local levels, and operates in omnipresent political conflict or stalemate. The first major reform was one initially established in the 1930s that provided substantial federal funds to lower levels of government for the provision of cash and services to the poor. The programs produced by this New Deal reform proved more substantial and long-lived than originally intended. Public assistance was seen mostly as a temporary appendage to Social Security, a subprogram destined to dry up with the end of the Great Depression. Instead, the need for public assistance continued to grow to the present, slowly producing a recognition that for some classes of persons it would constitute a more or less permanent operation. This fact guaranteed as well public unpopularity, for while Social Security was intended positively and in perpetuity for the "deserving poor," public assistance seemed to give tenure to the "undeserving poor."

A second major reform sought to address the question of permanence on the public assistance rolls through upgrading of services—an ambiguous term, denoting on the one hand professional help and on the other hand manipulation that can become coercive (e.g., pushing recipients into work training programs regardless of their situations). This reform came in the 1962 amendment to the 1935 Social Security Act, when the federal government sought to extend, clarify, and firm-up services. Additional legislation in the early 1970s reinforced service requirements further. The caseworker had always served a dual function, checking eligibility and enforcing rules as one task, and providing information and advice as another. Under the new legislation, the federal government provided additional subsidies to states that would insure that their welfare workers routinely provided substantial services. This reform culminated the agitation of professional social workers over the years, and it celebrated the traditional and dominant social work technology: casework.

Social work's potential to make substantial inroads in poverty has been limited by the weakness of the formulation of casework as *the* professional model while income distribution is the critical problem. This was exacerbated in public assistance by the difficulty of reconciling provision of help with the authoritative role of surveillance and eligibility determination. The centrality of the casework model is understandable, however, given the history of the profession. For decades, social workers principally consisted of "ladies bountiful," often upper-class women attempting to help the poor. After the turn of the century, it became possible for practitioners setting up professional schools to begin developing an esoteric theoretical base which would indicate that social work had at least a partial expertise in helping people. (It is easier to claim a monopoly over the desire to help people than over the means of doing so.) That base consisted of psychological theories derived from, or reacting to, Freud. These theories provide a rational for counseling on a one-to-one basis in order to help the person, even the poor one, in regard to pathology or difficulties. Often the lesson for the poor is that they must learn to cope with poverty. It is problematic whether or not the social worker can help the poor person as the psychotherapist can aid the affluent (Cloward and Epstein 1967). Clearly, the treatment will not by itself raise income or provide employment.

The casework model has perhaps its least useful though most widespread application in legislation that mandates substantial individual services. Realities of agency operation, including the shortage of resources and high caseloads of the 1960s, meant that this service model would become superficial or symbolic, and thus the object of derision. In several cities, the services consisted solely in the caseworker routinely indicating on a form that services (completely undefined) had been provided the preceding month. This reform only aggravated the conflicts and ambiguities of goals that haunt public welfare, especially the strain among the multiple goals of providing financial resources, services, and surveillance.

The upshot was that by the late 1960s the welfare system seemed unworkable and ready for another round of reform (Naparstek and Martin 1968). It contained an elaborate number of unmanageable programs. It lacked resources to provide adequate help for people, and those working in the system knew this. Staff spoke of a double standard, wherein middle-class employees recognized they were enforcing living standards on recipients that would be unthinkable for themselves. However, the next round of reform, in the late 1960s and early 1970s, also meant relatively little change for the welfare bureaucracy. By mid-decade public assistance agencies were essentially the same as they had been after implementation of the 1962 legislation, except: (1) the dilemma of combining eligibility determination with service had been addressed—however unstably—by splitting the two functions between separate personnel; (2) certain categories of recipients had been destigmatized by inclusion with Social Security beneficiaries; (3) judicial opinions had restricted surveillance procedures and rules making people ineligible; and (4) the federal government was footing more of the bill. The principal technology remained the allocation of money; the subsidiary window-dressing procedure remained the provision of services—casework or labor-compelling, depending on the audience to be impressed. Interlarded in the services were programs involving such matters as job training and literacy, utilizing the traditional educational strategy once again. The professional claims for casework services had been generally discredited in public assistance, but they had not been replaced or reformed.

Indeed, the big news about public assistance and the poor in the early 1970s was the failure of welfare reform—this time rather basic reform. The change proposed in Nixon's Family Assistance Plan or in guaranteed annual incomes in various forms had offered to eliminate the "social work middleman" and the welfare bureaucracy by moving to an impersonal system of mailing out checks on a universalistic basis. Congress at length failed to adopt such a plan. A variety of explanations, ranging from Nixon's true motives to the possibly self-defeating positions taken by liberal Democrats, has been adduced to explain the failure. Important also is the apparent fact that public suspicion will be high for any plan that does not boast frequent surveillance of the poor. Relatively unnoticed is the fact that despite support from some bureaucrats and professionals, it was basically a plan seeking to eliminate bureaucracy and reduce professional claims. Thus, the lack of sufficient support is no surprise in an era of the bureaucratization of poverty and professionalization of reform. President Carter proclaimed a new round of reform, but we got more stalemate.

THE WAR ON POVERTY

The most drastic developments promising to reshape welfare came in the rise, peak, and passing of the War on Poverty. These phases were marked by the Equal Opportunity Act of 1964, the implementation of hundreds of programs in the years immediately following, and a sharp reduction in programs preceding dismantling of the Office of Economic Opportunity (OEO) in 1973. The War on Poverty was an all-embracing battle offering an array of programs ranging from quite traditional or revitalized ones (job training or extension of educational opportunities to young children through Head Start) to the controversial CAPs that featured rhetoric of structural change, tactics of conflict and confrontation, and ideology hostile to the establishment. The antipoverty program was extraordinary in the extent to which it sought actual or "maximum feasible" participation of the poor, sponsoring reform from below, and in the degree to which it tried to elicit participation (with appropriate financial incentives) of the full array of public and private welfare agencies, schools, and community organizations that relate to the poor.

A complex series of explanations can be offered for the ultimate decline of the program.[1] Fundamentally, it sought both bureaucratization of inequality and professionalization of reform, attempting to create a federal agency that could develop a comprehensive and rational ordering of programs emphasizing a total strategy for elimination, or at least dramatic reduction, of poverty. In its bureaucratic aspects the program suffered from a familiar weakness: its command of expenditures and programs was too weak to control decision-making and innovation from the top. Indeed, centralization was made impossible by the ideology of the War on Poverty, which emphasized the benefits of decentralized and local decision-making.

In its professionalization of reform, however, the antipoverty program is most intriguing. The professionalization of reform became the repoliticization of reform. Contrasting earlier periods, in which the specifics of reform were proper subject of legislative debate, with the War on Poverty period, in which reforms become professional prerogatives, the latter era is seen as one in which high levels of professional competition ultimately transformed and repoliticized reform. While the air was filled with glowing pronouncements that the federal government was directing a comprehensive and integrated attack on poverty, in reality public and private agencies and groups were engaged in fierce political infighting to gain resources and public support.

To understand the repoliticization of reform, one can extend Lowi's (1969) analysis of "interest group liberalism." Lowi suggests that the 1930s New Deal did not lead to the end of capitalism but to its salvation. It was saved, he asserts, by acceptance of the necessity of statism, or large-scale government intervention, and of pluralism as the conventional wisdom of politics. Interest group liberalism thus becomes the dominant form of politics, following pluralist philosophy in assuming that all relevant interest groups should be party to political decisions. Further, where there are no identifiable interest groups, they must be created. As a result, those practicing interest group liberalism acquiesce in, or even honor compromise of, the traditional distinction between administrative agencies, including regulatory units, and the interest groups which they control. In

Lowi's terms, interest group liberalism elevates conflict of interest from a criminal act to a principle of government. Thus, logrolled decisions are legitimate so long as they involve all relevant parties. The formula of involving interested parties to bargain out lines of action becomes a solution to all kinds of problems, ranging from settling on inflation and pollution controls to arranging programs to ward off recurrence of race rioting.

The antipoverty program was an example *par excellence* of interest group liberalism in action. Programs were developed at different levels and in varying jurisdictions on the basis of negotiations of professors, social workers, lawyers, ministers, and some poor people—all said to speak for the poor. It was in such a fashion that competing professions and agencies repoliticized reform during the War on Poverty. Agencies came to be seen not merely as bureaucracies administering certain programs but as agencies *identified* with specific parties (e.g., professions) that were instrumental in getting those programs approved. Rather than being seen as rational Weberian bureaucracies and impersonal instruments of policies, the agencies came to be identified with certain interest groups. As with federal regulatory agencies like the Federal Communications Commission, HEW and the Department of Housing and Urban Development came to be seen as providing a necessary partisan element in drawing the poor into pluralistic politics. Thus, the poverty program came to be identified with the poor and employees of the program came to see themselves in this way. The agencies tended to become interest groups in themselves. They became parties to political decisions, seeking to "get theirs." To do so, they became programmatic chameleons: during the War on Poverty, agencies lined up to get whatever resources they could for whatever kinds of programs were marketable to the federal government. Community-oriented organizations would become interested in individual counseling and counseling agencies would develop an interest in community organization, keying their pitch to the market of antipoverty funds.

Further, in becoming interest groups, agencies often lost sight of questions of long-run accountability and looked only to short-run success. The result was to undercut whatever prospects they had for being granted a professional mandate. As was the case with school reform, agencies came to accept the popular version of pragmatism, requiring immediate demonstration of successful effects on clients. The loss of long-run accountability in the interest of short-run success was inimical to autonomous operation of the bureaucracy as well as to professional integrity. Neither bureaucracy nor professionalism can be implemented given the day-to-day changes required by political bargaining with external publics.

The antipoverty program's dramatic failure must be understood not simply as reform whistling in the wind of reaction but also as a prime example of the weakness of the American notion of reform and the problems of bureaucratization of inequality and professionalization of reform. The government sought to eradicate poverty by giving funds to a great variety of bureaucratic organizations but it did not exercise the strength of command to change, rather than merely subsidize, these agencies. The rationale for programs came from a variety of competing and coalescing professional groupings, together nowhere producing a consensus of purpose much more specific than endorsement of change.

Expressing the bureaucratization of inequality and reflecting the professionalization of reform, the recent history of welfare shows great growth and a plethora of minor alterations. However, over a decade of efforts at change from above came to nought, and the fundamental operating principles of welfare were little changed even by the War on Poverty. With reform from above professionalized, the public assistance agency and its functionaries, whatever else they do, play a key symbolic role: they show the public something is being done about the poor.

Reform from Below: the Effects of NWRO

Not all welfare reform efforts have come from above. Some have been, at least in part, insurgent efforts from below, as with the welfare rights movement (Bailis 1972; Levens 1968; Martin 1972; Piven and Cloward 1971, 1977; Whitaker 1970). To a considerable extent, NWRO grew as a genuine effort at collective initiatives on the part of public assistance recipients. The potentials and problems of reform from below can be assessed by an analysis of NWRO's effects. We shall see that reform from below involves many of the same problems as reform from above. We shall also see that whereas NWRO contained strong indigenous elements, it also expressed reformism from above and it faltered on the problems of bureaucratization of inequality and professionalization of reform.

LOCAL EFFECTIVENESS IN TWO CITIES

To some extent NWRO was organized from the bottom up and was a confederation of local welfare recipient groups. Certainly, what went on locally was important and at least partially determined the course of the national organization. Here, the experiences of recipient groups in two cities where NWRO was active, Chicago and Detroit, will be examined.

Recipient groups in both cities were only somewhat effective, but for different reasons. In Detroit, effectiveness was inhibited because of the overpowering domination by a single group; in Chicago, because of lack of cooperation among highly localized groups. These differing situations were described by informants in 1969 as follows: "in Detroit, welfare rights equals West Side Mothers and both are run by the same two organizers"; in Chicago, "power struggles and squabbling over turf take all the people's time."

One notable achievement of Chicago's groups was their enhancement of recipients' status. On the other hand, in Detroit, this was one criterion of effectiveness on which recipient activities failed. In contrast with Chicago, where groups tended to develop or to be developed by outspoken indigenous leaders, in Detroit not only was activity dominated by one group, but that group was effectively dominated by its nonrecipient organizers' tendency to speak for the group and to inhibit development of recipient leadership (and its consequent status rewards). An example of status enhancement in Chicago occurred in 1969 when an indigenous recipient leader played a prominent role in a large fund-raising affair for a state legislator sympathetic to welfare rights. The benefit featured columnists Mike Royko and Jimmy Breslin and was covered extensively by local media. On the other hand, in Detroit in 1968, when a recipient leader was asked to make a television appearance, she met opposition from two nonrecipient organizers. They wrote a speech for the recipient and when she refused to use it, they succeeded in having her removed from office. Informants commonly viewed the incident as an example of the repression of indigenous leadership.

Welfare rights groups in Chicago were noticeably less effective than in Detroit in providing services. Detroit's city-wide organization, Detroit Metropolitan Welfare Rights Organization (DMWRO), in 1969 was providing the following services to recipient members: workshops in leadership training, personal budgeting, and organizational financing; legal advice; mimeographing; meeting space; and technical assistance with regard to welfare, housing, health care, and other issues. In addition, DMWRO had a program to assist members purchase homes by securing mortgage credit. At the same time, the Chicago Welfare Rights Organization provided little service, although virtually all local groups provided some modest services. With a few noteworthy exceptions, these services were limited in scope and offered irregularly. The exceptions were groups affiliated with larger, more powerful groups such as the West Side Organization (WSO) and the Woodlawn Organization (TWO). These groups could afford the overhead necessary to support more extensive services. The better services provided by DMWRO can be traced in part to the centralization of activity there and to its closer relations with the national organization.

Differing political ecologies contributed to the variations in recipient activity. Chicago has a stronger ethnic-turf orientation, a political machine, and a more concentrated and segregated black population (Greenstone and Peterson 1968; Taeuber and Taeuber 1965). (NWRO's principal constituency was urban, black recipients of Aid to Families with Dependent Children.) There, aldermen are elected in local wards based to a considerable degree on boundaries of ethnic and racial communities. In Detroit, elections are at-large, and the political style has been based less on ethnic-turf considerations and more on reform and interest group politics. These factors helped produce localized, factional groups in Chicago and centralized, nonfactional groups in Detroit.

Relations between local groups and NWRO were characterized by conflict, although it was more serious and of longer standing between Chicago groups and NWRO. A pronounced attitude of recipient organizers in both cities was that whatever success they achieved was without NWRO's help and, in some cases, despite it. The primary grievances against the national organization were its (1) mishandling of finances and lack of financial support for local groups, (2) authoritative decision-making, and (3) use of nonrecipient staff and organizers, many of whom were paid.

Groups in both cities were rather unsuccessful in the critical area of securing changes in welfare practices. In neither city were recipient groups formally recognized by the welfare department. Groups in both cities emphasized individual service and problem-solving, an ironic replication of the casework model. Of course, it is difficult for local groups to obtain change in welfare policy, much of which is made in Washington and state capitals. City-wide groups in the cities had little influence with local government, even when they mounted coordinated action among local groups. During several years of field work, only one clear example of change in policy was found in each city. Chicago groups got a raise in· the welfare department's rent ceiling for FHA-financed apartments from $90 to $150 per month in 1969. In Detroit, groups obtained in 1970 a retroactive raise of $8 per person in the monthly grant.

MOBILIZATION AND VISIBILITY

Recipient groups organized a relatively small proportion of their potential membership bases. Only about one in forty adult recipients was "claimed" as a member by groups in Chicago or Detroit in 1971.[2] Fifty-three groups in the cities claimed about 3,000 members, while the number of adult AFDC recipients was about 115,000. NWRO claimed 100,000 members in 1971, while the total number of adult AFDC recipients was about 2.9 million.

More surprising than the low membership rate is evidence that the welfare rights movement had little visibility among recipients. We interviewed a cross section of recipients in a northside Chicago district. Of a sample of 194 recipients, just 24 percent said they had *heard* of recipient groups. This percentage seemed especially low considering the fact that the area in which the random sample was drawn had recently experienced a great deal of publicized recipient activity sponsored by several groups, including a sit-in at the district welfare office.

DIFFERENTIAL SELECTION AND ORGANIZATIONAL SOCIALIZATION

The issue of whether or not NWRO had any measurable effect on its activists can be addressed in more general terms as a question of some interest to social scientists. Two apparently divergent explanations have been suggested to account for activism: differential selection and organizational socialization (Erbe 1964).

Thirty Chicago activists were asked when they became involved in recipient organizations and in other types of voluntary groups, indicating a temporal relationship. Forty-seven percent of activists had participated in neighborhood-based voluntary organizations prior to their participation in recipient groups. These neighborhood organizations were manifestly political and included WSO, TWO, and Jobs or Income Now. Other data—in table 26.1—resulted from

Table 26.1. Percentage Distribution of Auspices
and Dates of Activists' Original Involvement in
Recipient Groups

Auspices of Involvement	Before NWRO Emerged[a]	After NWRO Emerged[a]	Total
Civil rights	33	23	57
Social work[b]	3	23	27
War on Poverty	–	10	10
NWRO	–	7	7
Total	37	63	(100)
(N)	(11)	(19)	(30)

[a] Before or after June 1966.
[b] Unrelated to civil rights or the War on Poverty and usually a public welfare caseworker.

asking activists the dates and auspices of their original participation in recipient organizations.

The data indicate that a sizable proportion of Chicago activists had organizational experience prior to involvement in recipient activity. That this experience politicized activists was indirectly indicated by their responses to other questions. When asked why they had originally participated in a recipient organization, only 10 percent said the reason was because they had problems with welfare. The most frequently mentioned response (33 percent) was that participation was based on political considerations. An example of this response included: "I think it's helping the lower class people on welfare. I think it's a start. The poor have to help the poor. The rich sure ain't gonna help. It's important to fight for your rights. Nobody else will do it for you."

In addition to political considerations, activists reported they first participated in recipient groups because of personal characteristics; for example, because they liked people. Moreover, when activists did mention a welfare problem or issue in their response to this item, they often did so within a political context. Following is one example:

The welfare tried to cut me off. They said I didn't need the money, that I could get by. It's just like everything else. The rich get more than they need and the poor don't get nothing. They never say anything about all the people like Senator Eastland down in Mississippi who lives on welfare. And they get lots of money, not nickels and dimes like poor people get.

Rather than focusing on welfare as reasons for participation in recipient groups, most activists focused instead on general political beliefs. Although they could have acquired these attitudes through participation in recipient organizations, it seems more likely the attitudes were acquired in previous experience and served as a stimulus for their involvement in recipient organizations.

Thus, this limited data indicate that many activists in Chicago recipient organizations were selectively recruited by the welfare rights movement on the basis of prior politicization in other voluntary groups, particularly groups related to, or part of, the civil rights movement. NWRO's effects on its local leadership can be viewed as having been limited in Chicago to providing yet another means of political expression, although perhaps a critical one. Political activism was a behavior pattern already developed by many recipient activists.[3] Thus, in addition to its limited direct effect on the welfare population, NWRO's effects on its membership were somewhat limited.

EXTERNAL EFFECTS

If our interpretation is correct, NWRO was more a stage on which selected activists could perform than a school to educate recipients about their rights. This does not deny the importance of this stage, however, once one recognizes the audience intended. NWRO's greatest effectiveness seemed to lie in its symbolic and national activities. Its leaders, particularly George Wiley, Johnnie Tillmon, and Beulah Sanders, gained considerable attention in the mass media. They appeared before Congressional committees and other bodies to represent recipients. Through demonstrations, such as occupation of the Office of the Secretary of HHS in the spring of 1970, NWRO became publicly identified as representing recipients. Its leaders figured prominently in major commentaries about welfare, as in *Time* and *Newsweek* cover stories in 1971. Indeed, it is probable that NWRO was much better known among representatives of the media, academicians, liberal politicians, and professionals—especially social workers—than among recipients.

THE BUREAUCRATIZATION AND PROFESSIONALIZATION OF INSURGENCY

Although reasons for NWRO's limited effects are complex, one internal reason was the organization's tendencies toward bureaucratic and professional control. Other social movement organizations have similar tendencies. NWRO's principal internal cleavage developed around the issue of nonrecipient control versus local autonomy. On the whole, those who favored centralization and national office expansion were nonrecipient staff and organizers, while those who favored more local control were recipient members.

Indications of professionalism were evident in the organizing impetus for NWRO and many of its local groups and in the organization's staffing. Nationally, its emergence was influenced significantly by intellectuals, organizers, social workers, and students. Many were veterans of the civil rights movement and the War on Poverty. George Wiley, for example, had been a national officer of the Congress on Racial Equality. Locally, groups were organized with participation of middle-class professionals, especially social workers. In addition, several liberal and professional groups supported or inspired NWRO's organizing efforts, including New York City's Mobilization for Youth and students at the University of Chicago's School of Social Service Administration. Indeed, NWRO's emergence was based in good measure on the actions of individuals who could be described as "entrepreneur activists." These were people, generally middle class and often with professional training and organizational experience, who were full-time organizers, moving from group to group, and issue to issue within the context of the civil rights movement and the War on Poverty.

In ongoing operations, NWRO's national staff had a decidedly professional cast for a social movement organization of welfare recipients. In addition to entrepreneur activists, lawyers, social workers, and students were frequently staff members. For example, the National Association of Social Workers underwrote the costs of forty social work graduate students to work in NWRO's national office in 1969. Related to the tendency toward professionalism was a move toward bureaucratization. By the time of NWRO's founding convention in 1967, the organization already had a national office in Washington with a staff of nine, a tax-exempt foundation, a newsletter, and a membership system. By 1969, NWRO had moved into its third and largest office, with a staff of about fifty people. The evident trend toward centralization and specialization accelerated in 1968, when NWRO signed a $450,000 contract with the Department of Labor to provide information to recipients about the job-training program, WIN (Work Incentive Program). Accepting the contract led NWRO to hire more professionals at relatively high salaries, as compared to other organizational salaries and especially to the incomes of members.

At the same time that NWRO's national staff was expanding and taking on specialized functions, its decision-making began to reflect a top-down, bureaucratic quality. The national staff made important decisions about organizational policy, sometimes with approval of elected recipient officers, but often independently. One example occurred in Detroit in 1969 and was related by a local leader: "They hired some student to be our statewide organizer. We had already voted to have a welfare mother as the first choice for the job and the national office hired this student without clearing it with us. She finally got fired after we protested a lot."

Although race was the salient factor in the emergence in 1969 of a black caucus in NWRO's national office, a principal complaint of its members was the bureaucratic and professional characteristics of the office. In its literature, the caucus criticized "middle-class professionals" and "administrative staff" in the national office for ignoring recipients and for making policy on their own. One of the caucus slogans at NWRO's national convention in Detroit in 1969 was: "End Professional Control!"

After its conflict-ridden 1969 convention, NWRO attempted reforms in the face of internal criticism. However, much damage was already done, and there were problems and disadvantages in reform. For example, in 1970, two recipients were hired full time in the national office. Following is an account by a staff member of the conflict which resulted:

One of the recipients felt the staff didn't care about people because of their lack of interest in individual problems. She tried to talk at length on the phone about recipients' individual problems when they called in. We wanted to refer them if they had personal problems but she didn't see it that way. The staff tends to de-emphasize individual problems and focus on organizational things. But the recipients who worked in the office tended to take a personal interest in people's individual problems and let organizational things slide. The recipients would try to help people with things like their family problems and slide by the fact the person had called the office because she needed this or that organizing material.

Other disadvantages in reform included the drying up of significant funds from foundation and government sources.

The reforms failed, and NWRO entered a period of increased internal conflict, slackening growth, and decreased public visibility.

In several respects, of course, these were the result of external forces and paralleled similar developments in other movement organizations. Due primarily to demands for recipient control, Wiley, the nonrecipient director, stepped down in 1972. Continuing his career as a movement activist, he began organizing the Movement for Economic Justice, aimed at mobilizing a general poverty level constituency.[4] Wiley's departure was followed by more factionalism over whether NWRO should have a local or national focus. Also, the organization faced challenge on the left from local members, principally in New York City and Philadelphia, over its reform ideology. At the 1973 national convention in St. Louis, one of NWRO's founders who supported a national focus was ousted in mid-term. Finally, the organization experienced serious financial problems and by late 1974 had reduced its staff to two and had its phone cut off because of payment delinquency (Holsendolph 1974).

UNDERSTANDING THE DECLINE

NWRO's decline and demise can be traced to factors involved in its emergence: the "welfare explosion," the War on Poverty, and the civil rights movement. The data in table 26.2 indicate that NWRO's decline coincided with the tapering off of the welfare explosion and OEO's dismantling. Between 1965 and 1970 (NWRO's growth period), the average annual increase in the number of AFDC families was 28.4 percent, while between 1970 and 1975 (NWRO's decline) the increase was only 7.8 percent. The sharpest drop in OEO employment was 1969–70, Nixon's first year in office, when it fell 15.5 percent. In addition, it is commonly recognized that the civil rights movement has been in decline since the late 1960s.

NWRO's demise can also be traced to its inability to resolve several internal dilemmas. The organization developed along lines of national centralization and professional leadership, as opposed to local control and indigenous leadership.[5] Also, given its ties to ongoing local welfare rights efforts, NWRO was never able to generate a poverty-diffuse (as opposed to its welfare-specific) strategy, and thus was limited largely to material incentives (e.g., pursuit of an increment in the monthly check) as opposed to ideological appeals. For these and other reasons, the organization encountered local resistance, internal factionalism, competition and cooptation from other movement organizations, and difficulty developing sustained commitment from members.

Table 26.2. NWRO Families, AFDC Families, OEO
Employees, 1965–1975 (in thousands)

Year	Estimated NWRO Families	OEO Employees	AFDC Families	Percentage Increase in AFDC Families over Previous Year
1965	0	1.3	1,054	4.2
1966	1	2.1	1,127	6.9
1967	5	3.0	1,297	10.3
1968	10	3.5	1,522	17.3
1969	25	3.3	1,875	23.2
1970	30	2.8	2,553	36.2
1971	30	2.7	2,918	14.3
1972	20	2.3	3,123	7.0
1973	5	1.6	3,156	1.1
1974	1	1.1	3,312	4.9
1975	0	0.5	3,401	2.7

SOURCES: *Social Security Bulletin*, Annual Statistical Supplement, 1975; *Statistical Abstract of the United States*, 96th ed., 1976; George T. Martin, Jr., "The Emergence and Development of a Social Movement Organization."

Finally, structural factors led to NWRO's demise. Paramount among these were Nixon's election, conservative reactions to the gains of the 1960s, and economic recession. One impact of these changes was to reduce the resources available to the organization's members. For example, the AFDC monthly payment increased at an average annual rate of 7.8 percent between 1965 and 1970, but only 3.3 percent between 1970 and 1975 (U.S. Bureau of the Census 1976).[6] NWRO's demise has not meant the end of welfare rights. Local groups—for example, the Welfare Action Coalition in New York City—continue to organize recipients. Other local groups, such as Chicago's TWO, continue to maintain welfare rights components. NWRO's demise does not rule out the possibility of other national organizing efforts. However, no such efforts appear on the horizon at present.

We can assess NWRO's efforts at reform from below as follows. First, the concrete effects of welfare rights groups on the practices of public assistance appear to have been real but modest. Second, under some circumstances NWRO groups were effective at providing services to recipients and enhancing the status of recipients. Third, welfare rights seemed relatively invisible to nonactivist recipients, while for a period NWRO increasingly became the visible interest group speaking for recipients nationally. Fourth, activisim in welfare rights reflected differential selection into the movement. And last, NWRO faltered in large part because of an inability to handle the processes of bureaucratization of inequality and professionalization of reform that had been necessary to its growth.

Effects on the Poor

The failure of reform came during a period in which great increases in government expenditures apparently reduced the absolute deprivation of the welfare poor. This occurred crescively as the numbers of persons on welfare and levels of payments increased in state after state, and particularly in the most populous and wealthiest states (Grønbjerg 1977). In addition, there came sizable federal expenditures on new programs such as Medicaid and food stamps that serve, among others, the public assistance population. Changes in absolute deprivation are, of course, not the same as changes in relative deprivation—in fact, improvements in the former can sharpen the bite of the latter. And whereas the changes of the 1960s and early 1970s may have raised the general level of living of the poor and improved the relative positions of certain subclasses of poor persons, their general effect was less to reduce inequality than to transform the ways in which people became and lived as unequals. Thus, reform attempts in recent years in public welfare, together with the changes attempted under the antipoverty program, in some ways enlarged and certainly complicated the problems of coping with life among the poor. To the economic disadvantages and social stigma attached to poverty were added the tasks of dealing with bureaucracies that administer inequality, professions that seek to reform it, and social categories that are produced by it. Professional groups engaged with poverty furnish additional social definitions that can catch the poor in a web of multiple reifications. At the extreme, bureaucratization and professionalization could theoretically provide an unprecedented threat to the poor, as in a Weberian/Kafkaesque nightmare in which organizational definitions become all-powerful, embodied in scientific dossiers providing elaborate and fateful official public reputations alterable only by the master professional-bureaucrat. Fortunately, the same conditions which had the defect of undercutting major governmental reform for the poor have the virtue of making this imagery mainly a bad dream. The structural weakness of public bureaucracies and the strong processes of competition and mutual discrediting among the professions that deal with the poor serve as strong limits on their accretion of power or the plausibility of their pronouncements.

The most important effect seems ambiguous: the further confusion wrought in the social construction of poverty by the continuous ebb and flow of competing bureaucratic, professional, political, and social definitions of the poor. This construction becomes especially problematic and important for the ways in which the poor come to view themselves. Over time, what may have been most difficult for the poor was the fact that within less than a decade reform efforts could produce high levels of optimism about reducing inequalities and then could so soon take an aborted turn. No wonder that within this period groups of poor persons were reported at various times to show such divergent reactions as high levels of obsequiousness, rioting, feelings of stigmatization, involvement in instrumental self-help, politicization and militance, self-aggrandizement and "mau-mauing," and general apathy.

For AFDC clients, the events of the 1960s and NWRO may have played a positive role in legitimizing their reputations as ordinary members of yet another interest group—that of welfare recipients. This perspective is compatible with a viewpoint that sees the increases in numbers of welfare recipients and in the level of payments as reflecting extension of citizenship (Grønbjerg 1977). However, the overall and lasting public effects of the various diagnoses presented with respect to the poor are probably mixed.

Professional labels sometimes make little difference, as they can be translated quickly back into traditional terms, as when "culturally deprived" became seen as a euphemism for poor black. Despite elaborate terminology, both poor and nonpoor groups often know who is really being talked about and who is really to benefit from a program. Generally, professional labels are likely to be meaningful more for any warnings they seem to contain than for any understanding they connote, as when residents of a poor neighborhood become more wary of street crime once they learn a methadone clinic has opened in their area. Some labels may have the intended effects, as when members of a generation of Americans raised after the Great

Depression learned of the notion of structural poverty signified by the term underemployment.

The public definitions of bureaucracies and professions engaged with the poor are mixed as well. They are seen simultaneously as trying to help the poor and as ready to cater to the poor, to give universalistic aid but also to provide benefits to favored minorities, to design new programs but also to bootleg support for tired ones, and to recruit talented staff but also to furnish jobs to cronies. In practice as well as image, the agencies and professions do all these things. Reform has both a genuine and an appearance side. Reform efforts do seek to do something about the poor, and thus try to meet and exhaust the demands of those genuinely interested in change. Simultaneously, the professionalization and politicization of reform tend to discredit notions of change, thus feeding cynicism about these efforts in the public and among the poor and professionals. Discredited, reforms do not reach a threshold of comprehensive effort at which they can have progressive and reinforcing effects.

At least some of the efforts that emerged out of the 1960s met with some success for categories of poor people. Clearly, some formerly poor persons moved up in such fields as education, social work, and public administration. The great increase in completion of junior college training among poorer populations probably compensates for the correlated decrease in the meaning of the high school diploma, and presumably it signifies an increment in "bureaucratic competence" for dealing with the vicissitudes of relating to health, governmental, and other agencies. An increase in bureaucratic competence seems crucial for coping with the modern world; unfortunately, as the poor tend to inherit the cities there is a diminution of attention to, and optimism about, the possibilities of the urban school system. Bureaucratic competence has its limits and dangers as a solution, however, for it continues to place responsibility on the poor rather than on the organizational structures with which they must deal, and its tendency to facilitate "creaming away" the most talented of the poor may increase the passivity of the rest (Gordon 1974).

Finally, with regard to the professionalization of social service, the reforms during the War on Poverty have given way to a return to normalcy. Having been jarred and revitalized in the 1960s by the great excitement over poverty, social work now seems to be separating itself from concern with the poor. This occurs as it did in the 1920s, although for different reasons, as evidenced now by reductions in community organization offerings, movements toward an increasingly middle-class clientele, private practice, and third-party payment, and increasing emphasis on behavioral modification of phobias, sex therapy, and other amenities-oriented aspects of help. The result has been largely stalemate. Ultimately, reform has been insidious by being largely symbolic, standing for doing something about the poor while little challenging—and sometimes reinforcing—the fateful dichotomy between poor and nonpoor.

Impact of the Fiscal Crisis

The fiscal crisis is here to stay. In a recent essay on the welfare state in America, Janowitz (1976) implies a demise of the possibilities for undifferentiated reform. Neo-Marxists talk of the end of empire and the decline of monopoly capitalism. New York City may be the harbinger of America's future. Whatever its other ramifications, that city's fiscal crisis is important in illustrating how thin can be the line between the politics of abundance and the politics of imminent bankruptcy. As a result of this crisis, the federalization of public welfare is more likely to be accomplished. It is one step in the direction of recognizing that the fiscal crunch is both long-term in its effects and national in its scope. Such action is both necessary and appropriate, assuming that it involves some form of guaranteed incomes program that reduces the role of capriciousness on the part of the bureaucracy and functionary and decreases the burden on the poor to exercise extraordinary bureaucratic competence. Even when public programs cannot adequately address income problems they can extend citizenship, but that goal is incompatible with gratuitous treatment.

Yet, given the general rise in the cost of living, the need to make some differentials in payments between the urban North and rural South, the rise in numbers on welfare and the escalating fiscal crunch, any income program implemented could not produce the general boon to big city recipients foreseen a decade ago. Indeed, a universalization of welfare payments might hurt most those urban poor who have special competencies—whether "bureaucratic" or "hustling"—for maximizing their situations. For the majority of the poor, welfare reform will little affect their relative social or political positions. Universalization could free recipients somewhat from

oversight by functionaries. However, given both the American suspicion of "welfare chiselers" and the power of the process of
professionalization of reform, it is more likely that a new class of
functionaries would be created to oversee the recipients' new-found
freedom.

The immediate economic impact of the fiscal crisis appears to be
inhibiting professionalization and bureaucratization. Social welfare
programs are normally targets of budget pressure, and the crisis can
only accelerate and deepen the pressure. In New York City, those
most affected and attacked the most conspicuously include welfare
recipients and functionaries, and teachers. There is the possibility of
new political alignments, of which the "McGovern coalition" may
have been an early sign: an alliance among public service professionals, bureaucrats, and clients that could develop as the crisis continues
(O'Connor 1973). The coalition developed in rudimentary fashion
during the late 1960s. The unusual alliances between local caseworker
unions and welfare rights organizations that occurred in some cities
are the key examples of the possibilities.

Prospects

At least some of the failures of the 1960s reform efforts can be traced
to what Wilensky and Lebeaux (1965) refer to as the "ideological
dualism" of American social welfare. On the one hand, we have a
liberal welfare state perspective, from which vantage point the 1960s
reform efforts did not go far enough. On the other hand, we have
a *laissez-faire* conservatism, from which vantage point the reforms
went too far. This dualism often devolves into pseudoreform, in
which political compromise produces reformist rhetoric and goals
without generating the commitment and resources necessary to effect
real change. Importantly, this dualism takes place within the context
of the dominant political establishment and between its competing
liberal and conservative sectors. It does not involve meaningful input
from poor and working people, who are either forgotten, repressed,
or for whose interests others purport to speak.

The prospects for the immediate future center on further ambiguity. The present becalming can represent a lull before the storm,
or a lull before more lull. A general tendency to national economic
decline, expressed through many ups and downs, may be the long-
term prospect—and a long-term political decline seems unmistakable.

Social scientists may want to forecast major changes as a result of the situation, but in fact the news may be a rather unbearable lack of news. For the welfare poor, prolonged economic crunch and national slippage threaten tougher competition and thus more severe deprivations, perhaps leading to insurgency and reform.

NOTES

1. The antipoverty program failed in its specifics, particularly with regard to widespread reduction of poverty and enlargement of community participation. However, overall assessment requires seeing it as closely related to the civil rights movement. This movement involved major accomplishments, including incorporation of blacks into politics, improvement of the positions of Chicanos and Native Americans, change in the legal status of the poor, and an opening of effort to enlarge the rights of correctional inmates.

2. Membership claims usually overstated reality by about 50 percent. In addition to the fact that record keeping was inadequate, it was in a group's interest to claim a larger membership. Carrying members on the rolls who had ceased being active appeared to be the greatest source of error. Group membership claims may represent the number of recipients who had ever belonged, not the real number of members at a given time. Membership estimates—as opposed to claims—are based on delegation strengths at national meetings (determined by local membership levels), observation of attendance at meetings and other activities, and informant reports (see table 26.2).

3. In her study in New York City, Levens (1968) concluded that AFDC recipients were not selectively recruited by welfare rights groups. The difference with the finding here may be accounted for by the fact that her research did not differentiate between members and leaders. Thus, rank-and-file members could be politically socialized by their participation, while leaders could have been socialized previously and then selectively recruited (Maccoby 1958). The finding here applies to leaders only.

4. Tragically, Wiley was lost in Chesapeake Bay while boating some months later, in 1973. For an excellent biography, see Kotz and Kotz (1977).

5. An alternative tactic unsuccessfully argued for NWRO by Piven and Cloward (1977:284)—"mobilization" instead of "organization"—would probably not have resolved this dilemma. It appears that their approach would also have placed emphasis on leadership that was national ("a national network of cadre organizations") and professional (i.e., clergy) rather than local and indigenous.

6. Perhaps the most appropriate conceptual framework for analyzing this phenomenon is that of "resource mobilization" (McCarthy and Zald 1977).

C. THE CHOICES AHEAD

I N this final section of the reader, the three selections examine recent trends in social welfare and its future, particularly in light of current challenges to the welfare state model. It is important to note that the selections included do not exhaust the available trends and options. However, they are representative of the range of choices and include those which deal with two major pressures for change—the fiscal crisis and demographic trends.

The first selection in this section is an essay prepared for this volume by one of the co-editors. In "Social Welfare Trends in the United States," George T. Martin, Jr., describes major changes that have occured since the 1930s, including the federalization of social welfare. He also discusses the impact of demographic changes and the fiscal crisis on social welfare. (For further analysis of the influence of demographics on the welfare state, see Zald 1977.)

The second selection, "Social Services for All?" is the concluding chapter in a book by Alfred J. Kahn and Sheila B. Kamerman, *Not for the Poor Alone*. They discuss social trends in the United States, including the rise in the "dependency ratio." This and other changes are putting greater fiscal pressure on social welfare programs. Kahn and Kamerman indicate that the United States might learn from the experiences and perspectives of European, especially Swedish, social welfare.

The final selection in the reader is James O'Connor's "The Fiscal Crisis of the State." His is among the best known of neo-Marxist work on the political economy of the United States. The fiscal crisis of the state is the increasing discrepancy between public expenditures and revenues, threatening the fiscal collapse of a number of munic-ipalities, including New York City. As O'Connor points out, this crisis has important implications for the welfare state, especially for its clients and lower-level workers. One consequence is the threat to social welfare budgets. However, the fiscal crisis also offers the potential for increasing political organization by clients and workers, separately and collectively.

27

SOCIAL WELFARE TRENDS IN THE UNITED STATES

George T. Martin, Jr.

IN 1976, social welfare expenditures in the United States were an estimated $453 billion, 27.5 percent of the gross national product (GNP) (see table 27.1). Public expenditures were approximately three fourths of the total. Income-maintenance programs accounted for nearly two fifths of expenditures.[1] An estimated 58.3 million people, over one fourth of the population, received public income-maintenance benefits (see table 27.2). Looking at social welfare from the vantage point of the early 1980s, there are several points to discuss:

1. Sizable increase in expenditures, beneficiaries, and workers
2. Changing balance between private and public auspices and, within public, among federal, state, and local auspices
3. Accelerated expansion in 1965–75, especially in AFDC
4. Slackening of growth in the late 1970s.

Growth

As a percentage of GNP, social welfare expenditures doubled between 1950 and 1975, rising from 13.4 percent to 26.7 percent. Between 1890 and 1976, expenditures under public programs rose from 2.4 percent to 20.4 percent of GNP (see table 27.3). As a percentage of government outlays, social welfare expenditures rose from 38.0 in 1890 to 60.2 in 1976. Per capita expenditures have also increased substantially, rising from $98 in 1929 to $319 in 1950 and $1,319 in 1975, in constant 1975 prices (Skolnik and Dales 1976:10).

I gratefully acknowledge helpful comments made by Joann Foley, John L. Hammond, Alma McMillan, and Mayer N. Zald.

Table 27.1. Social Welfare Expenditures, Selected Fiscal Years, 1950–1976

	1950	1955	1960	1965	1970	1975	1976[a]
Total ($ billion)[b]	35.3	50.0	78.7	117.9	211.0	395.9	453.0
Percent	100.0	100.0	100.0	100.0	100.0	100.0	100.0
Income maintenance	30.1	34.2	37.2	35.5	33.8	38.5	39.6
Public	27.4	30.4	32.8	30.5	28.4	33.3	34.6
Private	2.7	3.7	4.4	5.0	5.4	5.3	5.0
Health	33.7	34.2	32.3	32.4	32.3	30.9	30.8
Public	8.6	8.7	8.0	7.9	11.8	12.9	13.0
Private	25.1	25.5	24.3	24.5	20.5	18.0	17.8
Education	30.6	28.1	27.1	28.5	29.1	24.4	23.6
Public	26.3	23.4	22.5	23.5	24.3	20.8	20.3
Private	4.3	4.6	4.6	5.1	4.9	3.6	3.3
Welfare and other	5.6	3.5	3.3	3.6	4.7	6.2	6.1
Public	3.7	1.9	2.0	2.4	3.6	5.5	5.3
Private	1.9	1.7	1.4	1.2	0.9	0.8	0.8
Percent	100.0	100.0	100.0	100.0	100.0	100.0	100.0
Federal	29.6	28.9	31.2	31.4	36.2	42.2	43.8
State and local	36.4	35.6	34.1	32.9	32.0	30.1	29.4
Private	34.1	35.5	34.7	35.7	31.8	27.6	26.8
Percent of GNP, Total	13.4	13.2	15.9	18.0	22.1	26.7	27.5
Income maintenance	4.1	4.6	6.0	6.5	7.6	10.5	11.1
Health	4.6	4.6	5.2	5.9	7.2	8.4	8.6
Education	4.1	3.7	4.4	5.2	6.5	6.6	6.6
Welfare and other	0.8	0.5	0.5	0.7	1.0	1.7	1.7

SOURCES: Alfred M. Skolnik and Sophie R. Dales, "Social Welfare Expenditures, 1950–75," p. 19; U.S. Bureau of the Census, Statistical Abstract of the United States, 1977, pp. 316–17.
[a] Preliminary.
[b] Adjusted to eliminate duplication.

The number of people who receive social welfare benefits has also increased substantially. In 1940, the 9.1 million beneficiaries of federally funded income-maintenance programs represented 6.9 percent of the population. In 1975, these beneficiaries represented 27.3 percent of the population, totaling over 58 million people (a greater number than the populations of all but 12 nations in the world).

The number of social welfare workers has also increased. For example, between 1960 and 1979 the proportion of civilian federal employees who worked for the Department of Health, Education, and Welfare (HEW) more than doubled, from 2.6 percent to 5.7

Table 27.2. Estimated Cash Beneficiaries of Federal Income-Maintenance Programs, Selected Years (December), 1940–1978 (in millions)

Category	1940	1945	1950	1955	1960	1965	1970	1975	1976	1977	1978
Total[a]	9.1	9.0	14.2	19.1	29.1	35.2	48.0	58.1	58.3	58.5	58.2
Social Insurance[b]	2.1	5.5	8.3	13.8	22.9	28.8	35.8	43.4	44.0	44.8	45.1
OASDI	0.2	1.3	3.5	8.0	14.8	20.9	26.2	32.1	33.0	34.1	34.6
Railroad retirement	0.1	0.2	0.4	0.7	0.8	0.9	1.0	1.1	1.1	1.1	1.0
Civil service	0.1	0.1	0.2	0.3	0.5	0.7	1.0	1.4	1.5	1.5	1.6
Veterans	0.9	2.2	3.4	3.9	4.5	5.1	5.5	5.5	5.5	5.5	5.4
Unemployment	0.7	1.8	0.9	1.0	2.3	1.1	2.1	2.9	2.5	2.1	2.0
Public Assistance[c]	7.0	3.6	6.1	5.8	7.1	7.8	13.8	16.7	16.4	15.9	15.3
OAA	2.1	2.1	2.8	2.5	2.3	2.1	2.1	2.3	2.1	2.1	2.0
AB	0.1	0.1	0.1	0.1	0.1	0.1	0.1	0.1	0.1	0.1	0.1
APTD	—	—	0.1	0.2	0.4	0.6	0.9	1.9	2.0	2.1	2.2
AFDC	1.2	0.9	2.2	2.2	3.1	4.4	9.7	11.4	11.2	10.8	10.3
GA	3.6	0.5	0.9	0.7	1.2	0.7	1.1	1.0	0.9	0.8	0.8
Percent of Resident Population	6.9	6.8	9.3	11.6	16.2	18.2	23.5	27.3	27.2	27.0	26.7

SOURCES: U.S. Social Security Administration, Social Security Bulletin, June 1979, pp. 31, 44, 55, 73; U.S. Bureau of the Census, Statistical Abstract of the United States, 1977, p. 5; personal communication with U.S. Bureau of the Census, August 24, 1979.
[a] Adjusted to eliminate duplication.
[b] Beginning in 1975, includes "black lung" program.
[c] In 1974, OAA, AB, and APTD became Supplemental Security Income (SSI).

Table 27.3. Social Welfare Expenditures under
Public Programs, Selected Fiscal Years,
1890–1977

Year	Total ($ billion)	Percent of All Govern- ment Outlays	Percent of GNP	Percent Federal
1890	0.3	38.0	2.4	36.2
1913	1.0	34.0	2.5	19.6
1929	3.9	36.3	3.9	20.4
1935	6.5	48.6	9.5	49.0
1940	8.8	49.0	9.2	39.2
1945	9.2	8.4	4.4	47.1
1950	23.5	37.4	8.9	44.8
1955	32.6	32.7	8.6	44.8
1960	52.3	38.4	10.5	47.7
1965	77.2	42.2	11.7	48.9
1970	145.9	48.2	15.2	53.0
1975	290.1	57.9	19.9	58.4
1976	331.9	60.2	20.4	59.5
1977[a]	362.3	59.7	19.7	60.5

SOURCES: U.S. Bureau of the Census, *Historical Statistics of the United States*, 1975, pp. 340–41; Alma McMillan, "Social Welfare Expenditures Under Public Programs, Fiscal Year 1977," pp. 4, 10, 12.
[a] Preliminary.

percent. The absolute increase was from 61,641 to 156,582 employees (U.S. Bureau of the Census 1979:277–78). In fact, the creation of HEW in 1953 reflected social welfare's growth. In 1980, a separate Department of Education was created and HEW was reconstituted as the Department of Health and Human Services. These changes were another sign of continuing growth in social welfare.

Despite these substantial increases, the United States lags behind other nations in terms of social welfare expenditures. For example, in 1966, the United States spent 7.9 percent of its GNP on Social Security. Among 64 countries, this figure ranked 31st (Wilensky 1975:122–24).

Changing Composition

The 1930s witnessed the first major change in social welfare, as noted by Wilensky and Lebeaux (1965:148): "Although by 1700 governments had already accepted responsibility to aid the poor, the orphan, the widow, the aid must be minimal, deterrent, local, and it remained so with remarkably little change in the U.S. until the depression thirties." During the Great Depression, social welfare began its shift from *laissez-faire* to welfare-state principles. (This shift reflected, in part, the economic transition from competitive to monopoly capitalism.) Since then, the federal government has increased its role in social welfare at the expense of the private sector and local government.[2] Although the pre-1950 data are sketchy, the overall trend is apparent. Between 1950 and 1976, the federal portion of social welfare expenditures rose from 29.6 percent to 43.8 percent. In the same period, the state and local share declined from 36.4 percent to 29.4 percent and the private portion dropped from 34.1 percent to 26.8 percent. Private expenditures outweigh public in only one category—health—but it also demonstrates increasing federalization. Between 1929 and 1975, the private share of health expenditures declined from 86.7 percent to 57.9 percent, while the federal portion rose from 2.7 percent to 28.5 percent (Skolnik and Dales 1976:15, 17).

Federalization of social welfare began to displace not only the private sector in the 1930s but local government as well. As Musgrave and Culbertson (1953:104) noted: "The meteoric rise of the federal and the relative eclipse of the local budget during the thirties was indeed a revolutionary change in our fiscal structure." In 1929, the federal share of public expenditures on social welfare was 20.4 percent. By 1940, it had climbed to 39.2 percent. The state share of public expenditures on social welfare remained stable in this period, while the local portion dropped (Musgrave and Culbertson 1953:105).

Perhaps the key category responsible for social welfare increases *and* federalization has been income-maintenance programs. Musgrave and Culbertson (1953:104) commented on this continuing process: "Considering the broad trends in the development of social welfare expenditures, the most important factor of change in recent decades has been the rise of public assistance payments and social insurance benefits since 1929." These programs in 1929 accounted for only 7.0 percent of federal social welfare expenditures, 1.8 percent of all federal outlays, and 0.1 percent of GNP. By 1976, these programs represented over three fourths of federal social welfare expenditures, over two fifths of federal outlays, and one eleventh of GNP (McMillan 1979:4–5; U.S. Bureau of the Census 1975:224, 340–41, 1114; U.S.

Bureau of the Census 1977:247, 440). Social insurance has dominated
income-maintenance programs, accounting for nearly four fifths of
their expenditures in 1976. As Skolnik and Dales (1976:11) noted:
"The enormous and growing preponderance of social insurance
programs among the social welfare expenditures fairly leaps to the
eye."

Accelerated Growth in 1965–75

Largely because of the "welfare explosion," the 1965–75 period was
one of increased growth in social welfare, especially public assistance.[3]
If the 1930s was the original decade of change and expansion in
social welfare, then the late 1960s and early 1970s may represent a
second important period of growth. In the years 1950–65, the
average annual percentage increase in social welfare expenditures
was 15.6 percent; in 1965–75, this increased to 23.6 percent. Much
of the increase can be attributed to public assistance and its largest
program, AFDC. Between 1965 and 1975, the percentage of public
social welfare expenditures that went to public assistance increased
from 8.1 percent to 14.0 percent. In 1950–65, the average annual
increase in AFDC recipients was 6.7 percent; in 1965–75, 15.9
percent.[4] The number of OASDHI beneficiaries, on the other hand,
increased at an average annual percentage of 5.4 percent in 1965–75.

The reasons for this 1965–75 welfare explosion included federal
efforts to respond to the demands of the civil rights movement and
to quiet urban unrest (Piven and Cloward 1971). Similarly then, in
the late 1960s and early 1970s as in the 1930s, expanded social
welfare was a response to national political crisis.

It is important to note that the considerable growth in social welfare
has apparently not reduced inequality in the distribution of national
income. With regard to the general effects of the welfare state on
income distribution, Wilensky (1975:95) says that "assertions about
the long-run impact remain highly speculative." Between 1950 and
1976, the percentage of aggregate income received by the lowest two
fifths of United States families rose only insignificantly, from 16.5
percent to 17.2 percent (U.S. Bureau of the Census 1977:443).

End of Growth?

There are preliminary indications that after 1975 the growth in social
welfare began to taper off. Beneficiaries of federal income-mainte-

nance programs declined to 58.2 million in 1978 from a high of 58.5 million in 1977. In 1977, for the first time in more than two decades, there was a decline in the percentage of GNP represented by public social welfare expenditures. Also, the yearly percentage increase in public social welfare expenditures was down to 9.2 percent in 1977, from 14.4 percent in 1976 and 21.2 percent in 1975 (McMillan 1979:8). Finally, the marked expansion of AFDC has ended. AFDC reached its peak caseload in 1975, with 11.4 million recipients; in 1978, it had declined to 10.3 million.

If social welfare growth has indeed leveled off, it may be attributed to several factors, including the end of mass political unrest in the late 1960s and early 1970s, the fiscal crisis of the state, and the tax revolt.

Prospects

In the future, we can expect contradictory pressures to expand and to contract social welfare. One stimulus for further expansion comes from demographic trends. The proportion of the population which is 65 years old and over continues to grow. This is an important social welfare constituency, as Wilensky (1975:47) concluded in his study of 60 nations: "If there is one source of welfare spending that is most powerful—a single proximate cause—it is the proportion of old people in the population." In the sixty years between 1870 and 1930, the percentage of the population in this age group rose from 3.0 percent to 5.4 percent. However, in the shorter span between 1930 and 1976, their proportion rose to 10.7 percent. By 1990, the aged will represent 12.2 percent of the population and by 2020, 15.5 percent (U.S. Bureau of the Census 1975:19; U.S. Bureau of the Census 1977:6, 327). In 1978, the "societal dependency ratio" (persons 65 years old and over per 100 persons 18–64 years old) was 18. By 1990, it is projected to be 20; by 2020, 26 (U.S. Bureau of the Census 1979:335).

An important source of change in social welfare is the economic condition; for example, the Great Depression led to 1930s reforms. Also, changes in social welfare are often responses to political activism, as in the 1960s when grass-roots insurgency stimulated the War on Poverty. Currently, rising costs of health care and increased political demands make possible the implementation of a new policy, national health insurance—a policy likely to stimulate further growth and federalization of social welfare.

Simultaneous pressure to expand and to contract social welfare is engendered by the fiscal crisis, which is apparently national and long-term (O'Connor 1973). The fiscal crisis and tax revolt exert pressure to cut public social welfare budgets, as with California's Proposition 13 in 1978 and similar initiatives. However, at the same time, recurrent recession and increased surplus labor demand more public expenditures for those unemployed or unable to work at reasonable pay. While the political momentum for change generated in the late 1960s and early 1970s may have slowed (or decreased in visibility), its effects remain in the heightened expectations of poor and working people and their organizing efforts. Finally, it is important to note that social welfare in the United States functions within a structural framework, perhaps best described, politically, as welfare-state liberalism, and economically, as monopoly capitalism. It is increasingly open to challenge as a result of contradictions brought on by the fiscal crisis and demographic trends.

NOTES

1. The 1935 Social Security Act divided public income-maintenance programs into social insurance and public assistance. Social Security was the major social insurance program, beginning as Old Age Insurance. Survivors and Disability were added in 1939 and Health (Medicare and Medicaid) in 1966, making present-day OASDHI. As public assistance programs, the act created Old Age Assistance (OAA), Aid to the Blind (AB), Aid to Families with Dependent Children (AFDC), and General Assistance (GA), with varying degrees of federal participation. Aid to the Permanently and Totally Disabled (APTD) was added in 1950. OAA, AB, and APTD became Supplemental Security Income (SSI) in 1974.

2. A representative comment on this major transformation: "The chain reaction of bank failures and the collapse of the credit structure undermined the sources as well as the spirit of private charity. In the meantime the ability of the local communities to bear the relief burden decreased, as a result of a shrinking tax base and of mounting tax delinquencies. There could be no more convincing argument for discarding the time-honored reliance on the local community. Nor were the individual states capable of meeting the financial crisis. The resources of the national collectivity had to be mobilized" (Rimlinger 1971:198).

3. Skolnik and Dales (1976:11) make a similar point: "In the public aid category, the long-term growth masks the short-term movement within the period. The proportion of total social welfare expenditures that went for public aid declined steadily from 1950 through the early 1960s before the trend was reversed with the introduction of Medicaid, expansion of work and training and antipoverty programs, growth of the food stamp program, and, most recently, launching of the SSI program."

4. Other data emphasize this point. Between 1950 and 1965, the number of AFDC children per 1,000 children under 18 years of age increased at an average annual percentage of 2.2 percent. In 1965–75, the increase was an average annual percentage of 16.2 percent (U.S. Bureau of the Census 1977:345).

[28]

SOCIAL SERVICES FOR ALL?

Alfred J. Kahn and Sheila B. Kamerman

O RDINARY people in the United States are being deprived of constructive solutions to problems in daily living, to those "normal" problems that arise out of societal change. Indeed, the term "problems" is probably inaccurate, since the programs involved represent appropriate, accepted responses to widely shared experience. The lag will get worse, and we will pay a price unless we can offer a more hospitable environment to social invention.

We must begin by facing ideological blocks. Programs and benefits should and can be available to average people to meet normal living needs. They must be organized by both government and the voluntary sector (profit and nonprofit) so as to achieve social objectives other than those of the marketplace. The United States has some social services for all people. We need to become more comfortable in facing their normalcy if we are to improve and expand the components. Certainly such services for members of all social classes are no less essential to a society than the more traditional public welfare underpinnings for the poor and the deviant. Certainly this is no less attractive morally than governmental incentives, supports, and rescue operations for the business sector. All are, or can be, guided by shared overviews of the public interest and launched through democratic political process.

We believe in public education, yet we somehow cannot give public support to high-quality community living and care arrangements for the aged. We apparently consider it legitimate, whether in the interests of the economy or of equality of the sexes, to open broader opportunities for women in the labor force, yet we do not face

From Alfred J. Kahn and Sheila B. Kamerman, *Not for the Poor Alone: European Social Services* (Philadelphia: Temple University Press, 1975), pp. 171–79. Reprinted by permission; copyright © 1975 Temple University Press.

rapidly and thoughtfully the need for a parallel child-care policy, fearing apparently that its outcome will be to "federalize" the children. We bemoan alienation and drug addiction in young people, yet we make no serious large-scale efforts to offer wholesome living arrangements for them when they are away from their families. Only in recreation have we made headway; for about a century we have provided free, low-cost, and expensive summer camps for city children from all social classes.

Part of the rationale behind such half-measures and inconsistency is stated in the December 10, 1971, veto message in which President Nixon rejected large-scale child-development legislation:

All other factors being equal, good public policy requires that we enhance rather than diminish parental authority and parental involvement with children—particularly in those decisive years when social attitudes and a conscience are formed and religious and moral principles are first inculcated. . . .

For the federal government to plunge headlong into supporting child development would commit the vast moral authority of the national government to the side of communal approaches to child rearing over against the family-centered approach.

This president, this government, is unwilling to take that step.

What the Europeans apparently know but what Americans do not yet perceive is that social services may support, strengthen, enhance the normal family—and that failures in social provision may undermine our most precious institutions and relationships. The issue is not whether or not government will intervene. It will. The question is: Will it intervene for enhancement and prevention or to respond to breakdown, problems, and deviance alone? Will we create a sufficient supply of *public social utilities*, as we seek to create a supply of other public utilities? Or will we limit public provision to rescue operations, *case services*, helping and therapeutic arrangements for those in difficulty? Will we continue to pretend that only the "inadequate" need the services or face the universality of new social circumstances?

Whether programs foster dependency depends upon how they are administered and the nature of the entitlements. Are they beneficence, charity, given upon condition of subservience to those defined as weak? Or are they rights, seen as meeting widespread need, delivered with dignity, to a user who is seen as citizen, taxpayer, and policy-maker? They need not be free services: minimum fees, graduated fees, partial fees are easily arranged for those with funds. College tuition may cover only 40 percent or 50 percent of costs—or be very, very low—yet no college student feels that he is a public assistance client.

It needs to be said more often, and understood by more people, that the assignment of general tax revenues for social programs is morally no different—if the services are in the public interest—from tax revenue for roads, canals, guns, or forest-fire fighting. Each social program can be analyzed to assure that payment methods and eligibility rules create the incentives, entitlements, and participation which our society chooses. Whether government programs create independence or dependence—or, for that matter, whether they create urban amenity, a sense of fairness, and dedication to one's neighborhood and peers—will depend upon how they are done, by whom and for whom, how they are administered and how paid for. Why ignore all of this in the debate about government?

Yet we fear to experiment, to discuss, and to consider the consequences. In all of this we preserve some myths, justify some suffering and deprivation, and avoid facing social realities. The posture may appear to save money but it also reinforces costly inequities and creates a less attractive society for every one of us. It is a policy which undercuts unnecessarily the living standards both of working people and of the middle class. If we really look at the daily lives of children, young people, houseparents, workers, and old people—in short, of all Americans, whether living in families or living on their own—we will not sustain such a policy.

Trends

This is not the place for a full tract of social trends, but a few illustrations may suggest the urgency of the message. We direct the spotlight toward everyone, the universal experience, *not* to the sick, the poor, the troubled, the deviant.

The dependency ratio in the United States has gone up. Together, those considered too young for the labor market (under eighteen) and those encouraged to stop work (over sixty-four) constitute 44 percent of the population. In 1950, they constituted 39 percent. Put differently, in 1973 the average American family had 3.5 members, of whom 1.3 were under eighteen, 2.0 were eighteen to sixty-four, and 0.3 were over sixty-four. Society cannot sustain the inevitable needed, appropriate biological dependency (the very youngest children), encourage more dependency (extended education in the young), and indeed mandate it (retirement at a time when body and mind are still willing) without giving each type of dependency institutional form and the required benefits and program budgets. Nor will we do well unless each category, while perhaps economically and in some sense physically dependent, is permitted to develop a socially respected role which, in turn, enhances development, socialization, and social contributions.

While retirees and preschoolers constitute a larger population bloc and pose a clear challenge, opportunities in the marketplace, a quest for equality, and the decline of domestic farm labor have taken many women in the productive ages into the labor force, where once they worked at home or on farms, or were dependent members of a leisure class. Mothers of many young children now work full time. The number of children with working mothers increased by 650,000 between 1970 and 1973 (at a time when there were 1.5 million fewer children in families). Of 64.3 million children under eighteen in March, 1973, 26.2 million had mothers in the labor force. Some 6 million of these children were under age six (almost one third of all children under six). Of those mothers with children under six, 45 percent worked; of those whose children were six to seventeen years old, 57 percent worked. Nor are the female workers largely unmarried, separated, divorced, or widowed. Half of all wives (50.5 percent) living in households with husbands present worked during 1972. The rate was almost as high for white wives alone (49.6 percent). Even those with children under three are increasingly in the labor force (29.0 percent in March, 1973). Wives with children three to five years of age and with no children under three are even more likely to be at work (38.3 percent). In short, ever larger numbers of mothers of young children work all year round, full time, and the trend line is up. Society cannot ignore the question of who takes care of the younger children.

The labor market picture is not the only reason to raise the childcare question. Some even question any effort to associate the issues. There are many women who do not hold jobs who think it good for their children to have group experiences and good for themselves to have opportunity for other activity. Besides, many Americans feel that those mothers of young children who are receiving financial assistance should place their children in daytime care, take training, and work. We would also like to offer programs to children from deprived backgrounds, most of them members of ethnic and racial minorities, on the assumption that such programs will overcome the consequences of deprivation. In short, the rearing of very young children has ceased to be a household monopoly.

While American day care supply data are incomplete and outdated, there is widespread evidence of shortages in many places. Long-term needs will be even greater if projected labor-force trends and changes in women's roles continue. (In Swedish terms, the equality movement has hardly begun in the United States.) Moreover, evidence is available of considerable below-standard daytime care of infants, very young children, and school-age children and even of noncare, despite increased American investment in several categories of early childhood programs: day care, Head Start, preschool programs in the school system for deprived children, private nonprofit nursery schools, proprietary day care, publicly subsidized family day care, franchises, and so on. Moreover, what exists is costly and often has disappointing results. The excessive program and child categorizations are exasperating and the programming debate intensive. It is a movement needing new direction. And yet there remain those who would "abolish" it.

For the aged, the United States has concentrated on income security and health coverage, and has made progress despite major scandals and disappointments. Noting that there are now more than 24 million Americans aged sixty-five and over—over 10 percent of the total population—and that many will be isolated and unable to manage without some help, United States policy-makers have begun to face the obvious questions: Where will they live? What services will they need? What do they want? Are some programs more effective, more humane, cheaper? Can we do better than the reported horrors of some 23,000 private nursing homes, largely publicly supported at a cost of $4.5 billion annually (Gray 1974)? Most people retire at sixty-five. In 1940, life expectancy at birth was 60.8 years for men and 65.2 years for women. By 1973 it had become 67.4 years for men, 74.9 years for women. The questions, in short, pertain to the welfare of large numbers of average Americans over significant proportions of their lifetime.

One further illustration. In 1974, a census expert told a Senate subcommittee: "Particularly impressive has been the rapid increase over the past decade in the number of young adults who have been maintaining their own households apart from relatives." It would be difficult to find an expert who would not agree that in cities throughout the country there are thousands of such young adults who lack satisfactory living arrangements. Except for the YMCA and YWCA hotels, whose roles are declining, and for a limited number of other facilities, there are few who attempt to meet this need.

But there is a stronger, more central trend: we cannot but wonder about the quality of child life, family life, life in the retirement years, as we note the decline in large households and the shift of family tasks to other institutions and as we observe the limited resources of some families in coping with all this. Supermarket and laundry room replace the "big kitchen," and the telephone cuts distances and facilitates a new style of "visiting" and relationship. Yet it is hardly clear that the needs of young children or old people get adequate attention in the family time-and-money "budget." Does the family need to be further strengthened in its new tasks, featuring nurture, socialization, development, emotional satisfactions?

There are, after all, more separations, divorces, remarriages, unmarrieds "living together" than before. Young people leave home to work elsewhere in the country—or just to live more independently. Relatives are sometimes far from young couples. Family members have less time together.

The concern with these and similar trends is premised on the assumption that family life is good for developing children or retired old people and that, therefore, family life should in some way be approximated, and strengthened, as it shifts its specific character. Or, in the absence of a "full family" or traditional family forms, those individuals who are living apart—or together—should be assured familylike social supports, or at least what sociologists call "primary group" experience. Nor is the case one of social altruism: society has interest in the ultimate environment which gives sustenance to individuals because society has a stake in mental health, social adjustment, the quality of life, the caliber of its growing generations. Even those who fear excessive involvement cannot argue against a floor, a minimum, a protected border, if only for the children.

Policy

The response will be inadequate if it is limited to noting needs and creating specific programs to meet them. Such remedial, serial, incremental (and often grudging) acknowledgment ignores the need for plan, choice, and coherence.

The observer of domestic policy developments in Western societies recognizes many difficult issues. Communities need public services, even some social services available to all, but these must be balanced against personal disposable income. If given a choice, American citizens, at least, do not vote for "in-kind" benefits until they have a minimum of cash. Many Americans also prefer that the retired, the disabled, and the poor also have some cash. Similarly, despite acknowledged need for services which make it possible for old people to continue their lives in the community and not in closed institutions, as long as possible, there is also need for basic medical services; indeed, money, medical care, and housing policy are the foundation of all living and care arrangements.

One should not think only of the aged, however, ignoring the children; or only of the retired, ignoring the housewife. Personal social services should not develop at the expense of education, or housing arrangements at the expense of manpower and employment.

These are all limited and illustrative comments. Domestic social programs, while not completely indivisible, have major interdependencies and constraints. They also face resource realities. There are issues of balance. Thus, to deploy resources strategically and in a specific sequence, there is need for continuing research and discussion, to define preferences and needs, and for planning, to assure optimal resource deployment at appropriate times and in desirable interrelationships. If this is to be productive, imagination and innovation must be encouraged.

Government and voluntary social welfare agencies do some things to and for families deliberately and specifically: daycare, general social services such as child welfare and family counseling, income maintenance, family planning, some tax benefits, some housing activities, and so forth. These may be thought of as a subcategory of overall social policy: *explicit family policy*. There are also many activities, policies, and programs which are addressed to other targets but which affect families. The family impacts may be visible, predicted but secondary to the primary objective, or they may be unintended or even unrecognized impacts—unrecognized, that is, until felt and investigated. These are elements of *implicit family policy*: tax law, housing programs, trade and tariff regulation, road building, industrial location decisions, working hours, the organization of medical practice (to offer a partial listing).

Out of respect for our traditions and legitimate concern that damage not be done to our fundamental institutions, family policy has not been discussed or debated much in the United States. In fact, when the phrase is used many think that it refers only to population policy or to family planning. Clearly there is a gap between social change and social policies in this realm. Americans have a stake in making the needs, problems, risks, and alternatives visible. We need a family policy debate in the context of our overall domestic social policy explorations. It should be as open, widespread, and heated (but as serious about trends, needs, alternatives) as Sweden's equality discussion. It belongs within the domestic political process and can only benefit from adequate attention there. A few voices have recently been heard in debate, but the range of content is narrow and the volume low.

The United States has not, of course, stood completely still. People in this country have applied dedication and imagination to childcare, community facilities for the aging, school meals, health services, residences, and other essential areas. Nothing described lacks an excellent American counterpart, somewhere. But we in the United States have problems of coverage, quality, eligibility, and program aura (stigma or privilege?). These problems will remain unless we also deal more systematically with issues of policy and commitment.

Optimism about long-term prospects may be built on the record of social innovation, on available precedent, and on the knowledge that if a program is a good one, it is utilized. Encouragement also may be taken from the recognition by private enterprise that there are social programs so essential and so responsive to widespread need that they may even do well in the marketplace. (We refer to franchise day care, proprietary residential communities for the aged, commercial housing for the single, and so on. Here the problem is coverage, eligibility, and the balance between money-making and program quality.) Moreover, as industrial productivity increases everywhere, more and more members of the labor force are eligible for employment in the service sector, both profit and nonprofit. There will be personnel to man the services if we can decide how to pay for them. Finally, the need for social services—a specialized segment of the service sector—is increasingly recognized. Humane impulses have increased somewhat the public commitment to case services, the helping and therapeutic-rehabilitative social service programs for the troubled, hurt, deviant. Now similar investment is needed in *public social utilities*, basic services for average people in response to daily needs.

Recognition of need expands and is seen daily in the media, but just how potent that recognition has become is not yet fully clear. Reporter E. J. Kahn, interpreter of the U.S. census, has noted in the *New Yorker* (October 22, 1973, p. 122) that in 1970, in Tunica County, Mississippi, the poorest county in the poorest state in the United States, 61 percent of households had washing machines, 61 percent had cars, and 86 percent had television sets. Ours is a luxury-loving, high-consumption society. Ultimately there must be a balance between increasing the distribution of such factory-built amenities—or converting to color TVs and new cars, or enjoying trips, restaurants, better clothing—and the costs of more extensive social programs. We do not expect the American taxpayer to vote "yes" for even a very modest decrease of personal disposable income in exchange for social services unless he believes that his own life, and the lives of his family, will be enriched thereby. We doubt that he will do it out of charity for the deviant and unfortunate, whatever the average level of generosity in the society. But we also believe that the argument for self-interest looms large.

The aged, the mothers, the unattached young people, the children, the families of whom we have written here are by no means only the poor, the deviant, the troubled, of our societies. They are everyman— and are increasingly recognized as such. Domestic social policy and social invention would do well to attend to this fact. Explorations of developments in several European countries suggest that without ending democracy, individual initiative, or personal responsibility, government can contribute to amenity, enriched living, and social integration—and that all of us might benefit from the process.

The word "welfare" is often reserved in the United States for the public assistance recipients, the "welfare" poor. Elsewhere, in the "welfare state" context (why not the "consumer" or "service" state?), it has a deeper meaning. Since we have referred, among others, to Swedish programs, which expand despite costs, we end with a quotation from Sweden's prime minister:

We have to show the viability of the welfare state . . . show that democracy can handle it. We must stand or fall in an industrial society. We can't do away with it or we'd be back in the Middle Ages. We are trying to renew it from within.

Society is about homes, people, their loneliness and their need of community with others. The trouble is we have still too little welfare permeating society.

Many Americans are afraid of words such as these and are often turned away from needed programs by them. But we, too, have needs: homes, income, services, problems, loneliness, community.

[29]

THE FISCAL CRISIS OF THE STATE

James O'Connor

THERE is no way to measure the total number of people who are related to each other through the state budget, and who are dependent on the budget for their material well-being; everyone is in part dependent on the state, and for millions of poor people, minority people in particular, this dependence runs very deep. Perhaps one quarter to one third of the labor force is wholly dependent on the state for basic necessities. And, historically, more and more people have looked to the state for that which they cannot provide themselves. Schools and colleges are bulging at the seams, the welfare roles steadily expand, and state employment holds out the only hope of employment for millions of blacks, young people, retired workers, and women—between 1950 and 1966 the state sector accounted for 25 percent of the total growth of employment in the United States.

During the same period that a rising portion of the labor force has been employed by the state, real wages, salaries, and incomes of state workers have declined, first, relative to incomes in the private sector, and second, in absolute terms, predating by half a decade the decline in real wages in the private sector (which, in turn, began in 1965). (This suggests that although the state employs many workers with the same kind of skills required in the private sector there is little competition for state jobs originating from the work force in the private sector.) Better known is the fact that federal, state, and local welfare, health, and education budgets are being frozen or cut across the entire country. And the growing poverty of the state spills over into the private sector, not only in the form of rising prices for services. Owing to the absence of new facilities constructed by the

From *Socialist Revolution* (January–February 1970), pp. 14–17 and (March–April 1970), pp. 42–46, 82–94. Reprinted by permission.

JAMES O'CONNOR

state, for example, hospital fees rose by 100 percent from 1957 to 1967, and were expected to rise more than 200 percent from 1968 to 1975 (*Missouri Teamsters*, April 5, 1968).

Progressively tighter budgets, falling real wages and salaries of state employees, and declining welfare expenditures and social services in general have unleashed a torrent of criticism against the state by employees, dependents, and others. Public employee unions grow by leaps and bounds. The American Federation of State, County and Munipical Employees grew from 150,000 members in 1950 to 400,000 in 1970. Unions are calling more strikes, and strikes are fought for longer periods: in 1953 there were only 30 strikes against state and local governments; in 1966 and 1967, 152 and 181 strikes, respectively. In 1967–68 the American Federation of Teachers alone conducted 32 major walkouts and mini-strikes which involved nearly 100,000 teachers (*American Teacher*, June 1968). In Massachusetts, state employees have created an organization which cuts across occupational and agency lines, and which has mounted a demand for a 20 percent wage and salary increase. In New York 25 percent of the city's union membership are public employees. In the past few years, whole towns and cities have been brought to a standstill as a result of general strikes of municipal employees.

Practical criticism of the state has not been confined to local general strikes, and still less to traditional labor union activity. State clients and dependents have been compelled to conduct their struggles around budgetary issues in highly unorthodox ways. Today, there are few sectors of the state economy which remain unorganized. Welfare recipients have organized hundreds of welfare rights groups; student organizations have conducted a militant struggle in small or large part over the control of the state budget for minority studies programs, student activities, and so on; blacks are struggling in countless ways to force the state to intervene on their behalf; public health workers, doctors, probation officers, prisoners, even patients in public mental hospitals have organized themselves, and seek better work facilities or better treatment and more finances and resources for themselves and the people whom they serve. And in New York there is growing collaboration between state workers and clients in the form of common, militant action against the state by welfare workers and welfare recipients.

On the other side, there is developing a serious revolt against high taxation. The forms of the present tax revolt are many and varied;

the core cities are demanding that suburban commuters pay their "fair share" of city expenditures, and the suburbanites are resisting attempts to organize their communities into metropolitan governments; working-class residential districts organize tax referendums against downtown business interests; and property owners vote into office politicians who promise to reduce property tax burdens.

All of these activities—the demands mounted by state workers and dependents, on the one hand, and the tax revolt, on the other—both reflect and deepen the fiscal crisis of the state, or the contradiction between expenditures and taxation. Yet, by and large, these struggles have not been fought along class lines, and therefore do not necessarily pose a revolutionary challenge to the United States ruling class. In fact, the popular struggle for the control of state expenditures has been led by liberal forces, and, to a much lesser degree, by militant black and radical forces. And the tax revolt has been all but monopolized by the right wing.

Nevertheless, the state has been unable to develop traditional administrative solutions to these struggles, struggles in which the state itself is one of the contending parties. The state has not yet been able to encapsulate these struggles, nor has it been able to channel frustration, anger, and energy into activities which potentially do not threaten ruling class budgetary control.

The political containment of the proletariat requires the expense of maintaining corporate liberal ideological hegemony, and, where that fails, the cost of physically repressing populations in revolt. In the first category are the expenses of Medicare, unemployment, old age, and other social insurance, a portion of education expenditures, the welfare budget, the antipoverty programs, nonmilitary "foreign aid," and the administrative costs of maintaining corporate liberalism at home and the imperialist system abroad—the expenses incurred by the National Labor Relations Board, Office of Economic Opportunity, Agency for International Development, and similar organizations. The rising flow of these expenditures has two major tributaries.[1]

In point of time, the first is the development of the corporate liberal political consensus between large-scale capital and organized labor. (The 500 largest mining and manufacturing corporations employ roughly 65 percent of total mining and manufacturing workers.) Through the nineteenth century, private charity remained the chief form of economic relief for unemployed, retired, and physically disabled workers, even though some state and local governments occasionally allocated funds for unemployed workers in times of severe crisis. It was not until the eve of the twentieth century that state and local governments introduced regular relief and pension programs. (The first comprehensive use of state and local government funds for economic relief was in Ohio, which in 1898 authorized pensions for the blind, the deaf, and the mentally retarded, needy children, and widows with children.) Until the Great Depression, however, welfare programs organized by the corporations themselves were more significant than government programs. Economic prosperity and the extension of "welfare capitalism" throughout the 1920s made it unnecessary for the federal government to make funds available (in the form of loans to the state) for economic relief until 1932 (Weinstein 1968).

The onset of the Great Depression, the labor struggles that ensued, and the need to consolidate the corporate liberal consensus in order to contain these struggles, all led finally to state guarantees of high levels of employment, wage advances in line with productivity increases, and a standard of health, education, and welfare commensurate with the need to maintain labor's reproductive powers and the hegemony of the corporate liberal labor unions over the masses of industrial workers.

The need for this consensus, always threatened by the expansion and increasing alienation of the proletariat, is rooted in the antagonistic production relations. But the imperatives of the consensus are constantly changing under the impact of the developing forces of production. Today, the advance of modern technology reduces the relative number of workers in goods-producing industries, and the absolute number of workers in mining and certain key manufacturing industries. In turn, "technological unemployment" potentially threatens labor bureaucracy control over rank-and-file unionists. The big unions are under constant pressure from their membership to fight for programs that will protect unemployed workers, members forced into early retirement, and others whose normal work life is subject to profound convulsions arising from capital accumulation, the introduction of new technology, and rapid changes in the composition of demand. Unable to win adequate retirement benefits, guaranteed annual wages, and funds for other compensatory programs from the corporations themselves, the unions turn to the state, constituting themselves as the chief lobbies for expanded social insurance. The human costs of capital accumulation—unemployment, retirement, sickness, and so on—are shifted to the state budget, that is, to the taxpaying working class as a whole. (Social insurance represents a "forced savings"—to cite Oscar Ewing, Federal Security Agency administrator under President Truman—imposed on the working class as a whole.) In this way, the corporations successfully defend their profits, the unions conserve their hegemony, and redundant union labor receives material relief. And social insurance outlays continue to rise, limited only by the limits on the industrial application of modern technology.

The second tributary runs parallel with, but runs faster and stronger than, the first, and flows from the same source—the development of modern technology. Corporate capital at home and abroad increasingly employs a capital-intensive technology, despite a surplus of unskilled labor, partly because of relative capital abundance in the advanced economies, and partly because of the ready supply of technical-administrative labor power. From the standpoint of large-scale capital, it is more rational to combine in production technical labor power with capital-intensive technology than to combine unskilled or semiskilled labor power with labor-intensive technology. As we have seen, the fundamental reason is that many of the costs of training technical labor power are met by taxation falling on the working class as a whole.

Advanced capitalism thus creates a large and growing stratum of untrained, unskilled, white, black, and other Third World workers that strictly speaking is not part of the industrial proletariat. (One half of all welfare recipients in three major suburban New York counties are white [New York *Times*, August 17, 1969].) The relative size of this stratum does not regulate the level of wages, because unskilled labor power does not compete with technical labor power in the context of capital-intensive technology. This stratum is not produced by economic recession and depression, but by prosperity; it does not constitute a reserve army of the unemployed for the economy as a whole. Unemployed, underemployed, and employed in menial jobs in declining sectors of the private economy (e.g., household servants), these workers increasingly depend on the state. "Make-work" state employment, health, welfare, and housing programs, and new agencies charged with the task of exercising social control (to substitute for the social discipline afforded by the wages system itself) proliferate. The expansion of the welfare rolls accompanies the expansion of employment.[2] For the first time in history, the ruling class is beginning to recognize that welfare expenditures cannot be temporary expedients but rather must be permanent features of the political economy: that poverty is integral to the capitalist system. Thus, the ruling class is beginning to experiment with "negative income taxes" and similar schemes that represent permanent concessions to the poor. Complementing these concessions with programs that tie welfare payments to work (e.g., the Nixon proposal), the ruling class may be able in the future to expand welfare spending without dangerously undermining the social discipline of the wage system.

Further, there is every reason to expect an expansion of other programs—particularly in the areas of education and health—designed to soften the impact of poverty. And the system of higher education, in this respect inseparable from the state bureaucracy, will expand its budget, because it is becoming more and more preoccupied with questions of "social stability," "law and order," and "social reform."

Abroad, in all of the urban centers of the underdeveloped economic colonies and semicolonies of the United States, there is a vast and growing impoverished population, unable to find employment in the capital-intensive branch plants and subsidiaries of the international corporations. This increasingly restless, potentially revolutionary population is a growing source of concern for the corporate and government leaders charged with administering the empire—a concern that is translated into requests for more "foreign aid," loans, grants, and technical assistance. The general aim of "foreign aid" programs is to maintain the world capitalist social order intact, and to create the conditions for its further expansion. The need for welfare programs, "wars on poverty," "foreign aid," and other ameliorative programs knows no limit, or, more accurately, is limited only by the boundaries on the application of modern technology and the spread of capitalism itself.

Partly a reflection of the tax revolt and partly deepening the fiscal crisis that is producing the tax revolt, is the practical activity—union organizing, day-to-day agitation, strikes, demonstrations—of employees and dependents of the state. On the one hand, the developing awareness of state employees and dependents that they are subject to a gradual erosion of material standards is crucial to a general understanding of their socioeconomic condition and political future.

On the other hand, employees, dependents, and clients of the state are also subject to profound *qualitative* changes in their relations with state administrators, politicians, and the corporate ruling class. In actual struggles against the state, quantitative and qualitative issues interpenetrate. The struggle for black studies programs is at once an attempt to win control over state expenditures and to produce fundamental changes in the nature of school curriculum and social relations. Teachers' unionism weaves the issues of control of the schools, curriculum development, programming of classroom time, and racism into the traditional themes of wages and hours (*American Teacher*, September 1969). In brief, the *social* meaning of the fiscal crisis goes well beyond immediate budgetary issues. For purposes of exposition, however, the two basic themes—the quantitative and qualitative—are analyzed separately, first in relation to state employees, and second in relation to state dependents and clients.

The most important response to the deterioration of wages and salaries of state workers is trade unionism, including strike activity, slowdowns, and other traditional weapons of organized labor. Labor union activity in both the state and private sectors of the economy aims to *protect* the standard of living and conditions of work; that is, unions function essentially as defensive organizations. Thus, for example, the American Federation of Teachers proposes collective bargaining as an answer to such problems as keeping salary schedules in line with those in private industry and insuring that teachers maintain their "fair share" of control of the schools.

The uncritical acceptance by state employees of traditional modes of organization and struggle is easily understood; the themes of "economism" and corporate liberal reform have monopolized labor struggles, and state workers, no matter how militant or radical, have no alternative traditions. Yet traditional unionism is bound to fail the state employee, not only in the profound sense that the labor movement has failed workers in the private economy by binding the working population hand and foot to the corporate-dominated political consensus, but also in the immediate sense that state unionism increasingly will be unable to win wage advances and "deliver the goods."

The reason is that private workers and state workers occupy different places in the society. In the short run, the large corporations pass on wage increases won by private workers to consumers in the form of higher prices. State administrators do not have any equivalent indirect "taxing" mechanism. Instead, wage and salary increases must be absorbed by the taxpayer. In the long run, the corporations have responded to the militant economism of traditional unions by accelerating labor-saving technological change, lowering costs, and augmenting productivity. The corporations have protected profits directly by raising prices and indirectly by raising productivity, and hence over many years have contributed greatly to the absolute volume of goods and services available to the population. In other words, traditional labor struggles have forced the corporations to advance productivity, and, indirectly, real wages, in order to maintain and expand profits. As we have seen, state administrators are unable to increase productivity in the state sector. On the contrary, some are even under pressure to retard the application of modern technology to the state sector, and, in any case, they do not have any operative profitability criteria to guide decision-making. In short, there is no way for wage struggles in the state sector to "pay for themselves."

Therefore, the state normally resists state unionism in general, and wage demands in specific, more adamantly than private corporations oppose private unions. (The resistance to unionization offered by some competitive and low-productivity industries and businesses operating on small profit margins in the private sector is an exception.) Labor struggles in the state sector are increasingly opposed by the taxpaying working class as a whole, and, as a result, the traditional conduct of these struggles tends to *worsen* the condition of state employees precisely because they worsen the fiscal crisis itself. Finally, state unions ordinarily must stay on the defensive, in so far as economic demands are concerned. In the private sector, traditional unions regularly demand that workers get their "fair share" of increases in corporate income arising from productivity increases. Owing to the fact that the income of the state is dependent on the tax rate and tax base, state employee unions are unable to go on the offensive.

To the extent that state workers confine their activity to traditional economism, they are fighting a losing struggle. As yet, there is no general understanding of the function of the state, and especially of the fact that state employees are employed not by the people but by capital as a whole. That is to say, there is no general understanding that the growing antagonism between state employees and state administration conceals an objective antagonism between wage labor and private capital.

The state administration is still seeking a coherent response to the economic demands of state unions. "The problem of finding a mechanism for dealing with public employee unions and locking them firmly into the system as an ally instead of a disruptive force," Aronowitz (1968) writes, "has occupied sophisticated liberals for the past several years." The "problem" is basically unresolvable because the "mechanism" is nonexistent. In the private sector, labor and capital have learned to accept government mediation in labor-management conflicts. In the state sector, there is no organ to mediate between the *government* and the state unions. Further, local and state governments cannot afford to "lock" state workers into the "system." Even compulsory arbitration of wage disputes has failed to keep wage demands in line with the fiscal capabilities of local governments. (As a result of the compulsory arbitration of disputes by policemen and firemen in Pittsburgh, the city was in "serious financial difficulty" [Douds 1969].) Doing so would require no-strike pledges and abolition of "free" collective bargaining.[3] This obviously raises the whole range of political issues: the right to organize unions, right to strike, freedom of assembly, and so on.

The state's reply to state unionism has been a mixture of old and new tactics. An example of the former is the massive propaganda effort aimed at convincing the public of the "sanctity of public service"—that public employment carries with it responsibilities and duties very different from private employment. Divide and conquer is another example of the use of traditional antiunion tactics. To date, twenty-seven states have some form of collective bargaining law for state employees, but there is a wide divergence within nearly every state with regard both to categories of work affected and to the extent to which the law requires the stage to bargain (Rubin 1968). The remaining states have no relevant statutes, the question of whether or not state agencies are required to bargain being up in the air, and it is unlikely that coherent rulings will be soon forthcoming from the states' attorneys general and judiciaries. Local and state governments have also adopted the relatively new approach of "kicking the problem upstairs." Local politicians dependent on the political support of organized labor, and states in which the courts are ruling in favor of state unions, use the salary demands of employees to pressure state and federal governments for redistribution of tax monies through grants-in-aid.[4]

No matter what the response of the state administration to unionism, trade union activity can take any number of directions. Union militancy in the state sector has radical potential; for example, unlike private unions, state labor organizations do not justify wage demands on the basis of rising profits, but rather in terms of the need for better "public services," "quality education," and so on. Union militancy can also place state workers on the wrong side of issues such as racism, control of the schools and "professionalism." The experience of the New York City teachers provides abundant evidence of this danger. Even in the state sector, unions are poor instruments of social change because they must rely on the union shop, tight organizational structures and disciplined rank-and-file activity, and play down political education and mass activity at the base.

The key question is: What are the tendencies within the state sector and social economy as a whole that hold out radical promise? Central to this question are the social contradictions in advanced capitalist economies of the proletariat. In the state sector, particularly in relation to service workers such as teachers, welfare workers, probation officers, city planners, and public health employees, these contradictions express themselves in many different ways. On the one hand, the education of service workers consists largely of technical-scientific training; as students they are taught the rudiments of the scientific method, the history of their "profession," and so on. Service workers acquire many of the skills and practical experience that can enable them to comprehend the political economy as a system of social relations that can be modified or totally transformed. On the other hand, the fusion of economic base and superstructure and the fiscal crisis have led to the "rationalization" of state jobs, the introduction of efficiency criteria, and the transplantation of capitalist norms from production to the state administration. Thus, school-teachers who view themselves as educators are required to patrol school halls and cafeterias as policemen and generally perform social control functions that many teachers find incompatible with their own self-image.[5] College professors accustomed to "campus autonomy" are subjected more and more to the authority of the trustee, regent, or legislator. Probation officers are faced with more red tape and control from the top; welfare work is everywhere being "modernized"; and nurses are compelled to work at many tasks that traditionally have been accomplished by aides and volunteers. In short, state technical and service workers are being *proletarianized* in the context of a fiscal crisis that inhibits compensatory wage and salary increases. Further, the expansion of careers and jobs in the state sector—even though the jobs are relatively underpaid and working conditions are gradually deteriorating—reduces the dependency of workers on private capital, and tends to reinforce feelings of hostility toward the business and commercial world.[6]

Contradictions within society are reflected in conflicts within individuals. Service workers, in particular, are beginning to attempt to resolve the conflicts they feel in the course of their day-to-day work.[6] State workers are nominally in the service of "society," "the public welfare," "quality education," "public health," and so on—these are the words originally used to describe the functions of the state administration. However, service workers quickly learn, precisely because they have been trained to think in terms of social relationships, that they are in fact in the service of the state administration and private capital and that their jobs really consist of establishing the preconditions for profitable business, training "human capital" rather than educating human beings, and exercising control over subject populations. To put it another way, a contradiction forms between the formal and informal requirements of their employment. One response has been a *redefinition* of their jobs, the development of a new kind of job consciousness, and an attempt to really serve the people. In short, the education that younger state workers receive, together with the practical experience they acquire, tends to turn them against the real goals and practices of the state administration (even though older workers tend to remain loyal to "city hall" and the traditional political bosses). For this reason, service workers are able to relate easily to one another as "oppositionists" independent of their specific position within the state bureaucracy.

Service workers also relate to each other in that they require budgetary resources from the state for both their real and nominal functions. But when they take their nominal function seriously, they are at once faced with a gross shortage of resources—classroom space, buildings, hospital beds, land, welfare funds, training funds, and so on—that is, their nominal function requires far more resources than their real function. Thus, service workers easily relate to each other over questions of staffing, funds, and facilities. Needless to say, a similar conclusion may be drawn with regard to their dependence on the state budget to meet their own individual needs.

As yet, there is of course no general consciousness of the broader relations into which service workers enter. Only the welfare workers in New York City have made a qualitative leap, beginning to develop alliances with their clients. Yet there are signs that other service employees in other branches of the state economy are developing this kind of historical self-consciousness. The American Federation of Teachers, for example, is self-consciously developing social unionism. One reason is that traditional trade unionism cannot speak to their needs as *social* workers; another reason is that state unions cannot take the *economic* offensive (see above), and thus fresh militancy must, of necessity, center on qualitative issues. And, once the leap is made between state workers and state dependents, then the development of a proletarian consciousness as a whole is rendered less difficult.[7]

At this point, we can tie together some of the themes already developed. Labor strikes are only effective when they stop the flow of profits and hence threaten the social existence of the ruling class. Strikes in the state sector cannot possibly be effective in this sense; state unionism thus cannot uncritically apply the experience of private unionism. Strikes in the state sector merely raise production costs for capital as a whole—leading to increases in prices and inflation—or lower the real wages of the taxpaying working class, or both. Strikes conducted by state unions, thus, always hold the potential of dividing the working class, and delaying the development of proletarian consciousness. Objectively, therefore, there is no successful reformist, economistic strategy available to state workers. The only way for state workers even to win substantial material gains is to radicalize themselves. And to radicalize themselves requires that they seek alliances with other workers, especially workers in other branches of the state economy. It is too early to predict the nature of these alliances, the form they take, the issues on which they will revolve, and their general political thrust. One of two conclusions, however, can be drawn from existing practice. It must be emphasized that traditional economic struggles mounted by state employees cannot be expected to win the support of the taxpaying working class; from a narrow economic point of view, the interests of private and state employees are opposed, precisely because the socialization of production costs and of the expenses of maintaining the social order, including the evolving corporate liberal consensus, tend to worsen the material condition of state employees. Alliances are more likely to be forged over qualitative issues, even given the great difficulties involved.

There is no easy way for the state administration and ruling class to contain the struggles of state employees. In their frustration and disillusionment, the state workers may line up solidly behind the ruling class (as the police are doing now in many cities) and voluntarily adapt to the right-turning corporate liberal consensus. But this danger is minimal. It is impossible to train a person to perform an essentially *social* function, and arm him with the rudiments of critical thought, and subsequently expect him to be oblivious to the essentially *private* character of state power, particularly in a social milieu in which traditional labor organization and activity are largely irrelevant.

If state employees have the possibility of developing socialist consciousness, their potential is nothing beside that of state dependents: the mass of students, blacks, other Third World groups, and the poor in general. Also difficult to contain are those in motion around the issue of environmental destruction, another movement that both reflects and deepens the fiscal crisis.

Needless to say, collective bargaining does not afford a solution to the problems of state dependents if only because of the impossibility of defining appropriate bargaining units. There is no traditional way to formalize, administer, and neutralize these struggles, in particular, the struggles of those sections of the black and student movements that have already adopted an anti-imperialist, anticapitalist perspective. The corporate ruling class has begun to take the only available course of action. In the schools, it has mounted an attack on the traditional student-teacher relation, and has sought to substitute a system approach to education in order to increase its control over the student population. In the black ghettos, it is circumventing both the local and federal bureaucracies and beginning to deal directly with the black militants, especially on the crucial issue of jobs. Politically, it is adopting a divide-and-conquer strategy; on the one side, it is trying with some success to coopt sections of the black nationalist movement; on the other side, it is trying to smash the revolutionary socialists.

The movements of dependents and clients have many sources. This is not the place for a detailed investigation of them, but only for an analysis of the relation between these movements and the fiscal crisis. In the first place, these movements, in so far as they are a response to declining material conditions, obviously reflect the fiscal crisis. In so far as they raise budgetary demands, they clearly deepen the crisis. And, in so far as they are redefining the meaning of material and social well-being, their activities may deepen the crisis (for example, demands for free clinics provided by the state) or leave it unaffected (for example, emphasis on self-help, new life styles).

In the narrow material sense the activities of state dependents and state employees, to the degree that the latter are struggling for more resources to serve the people, are in no sense antagonistic, but rather perfectly complementary. Alliances between teachers and students, welfare workers and clients, and public health workers and those who use public medical facilities are possible and likely. Unity among those who are directly or indirectly dependent on the state will sharpen the contradiction between taxation and expenditures and thus deepen the fiscal crisis.

The problem arises from the intermingling of quantitative and qualitative demands. Students in the fight against authoritarianism must confront their immediate "enemy"—the teacher. City planners, whose technical solutions to problems of renewal, relocation, zoning, housing, and so on are frustrated by profit-seeking businessmen, confront those in the community who pose a third solution—planning by, for, and of those who reside in the community. Public health personnel trying to protect their "professional" status from the attacks by state administrators confront patients who demand not only technically competent medical services, but also *human* service. Professors struggling to maintain faculty "autonomy," "open campuses," and their traditional scholarly prerogatives confront black students and others who want to develop their own curricula and control their own faculties, and, indeed, redefine the meaning of traditional education.

Of all the service workers, probably the social and welfare workers, whose jobs put them constantly in touch with the lowest income groups, have learned most about dealing with their own authoritarianism. Yet, even welfare workers struggling to redefine their jobs and seek ways to help their clients, and not control them, confront masses of welfare clients with their *own* ideas about welfare and social work. And throughout the state economy, it is more difficult for employees to fight against their own racism because black people and other minorities are typically "clients to be looked after" rather than job peers, as in private production.

In short, state service workers are being proletarianized from above, and socialized from below. Under two general sets of pressures, one seeking to transform them into various kinds of "human capital," the other seeking to humanize them, service workers are subject to contradictory sets of conflicts. The only way for them to negate their proletarian condition is by helping to make a socialist revolution; the only way to participate in a socialist revolution is to fight against their own professionalism, racism, and authoritarianism; and the only way to fight these evils is to relate organizationally to those "below" them—that is, relate as equals, not as professionals, to their clients, as they must in the context of the structure of the state bureaucracy.

Seen in this framework, it is no wonder that the response of state employees to pressures from above and below has been confused and irrational. It is no wonder that the development of class consciousness is uneven, irregular, and uncertain. It is no wonder that the exclusive repetition of themes of antiracism, anti-imperialism, and anti-authoritarianism alone has not radicalized masses of service workers. And it is no wonder that in the absence of a specifically socialist perspective—indeed, in the absence of a keen comprehension of the basic contradiction between social production and private ownership itself—unionists, organizers, and demonstrators necessarily function in a vacuum. A socialist perspective can help people comprehend the class nature of budgetary control, the determinants of state expenditures and the nature of tax exploitation, the process by which the uses of technology itself is decided by struggle. In the absence of this kind of general historical consciousness, how is it possible for all those in motion to come to grips with even the immediate material, budgetary questions, not to speak of the questions of authority, control, professionalism, and service or, finally, the question of what will be the new material basis of social existence itself?

NOTES

1. A standard argument is that the rapid growth of social welfare programs is due to economic growth and the progressive income tax. For example, increases in tax revenues out of proportion to rises in income have made it possible to finance social insurance schemes that could not have been introduced otherwise owing to taxpayer resistance. This kind of argument ignores the reality of political threats to corporate rule. It tells us only that the state has the resources to finance social insurance, not why the state has chosen to use expanded revenues for these purposes.

2. This is a tendency that began in 1960. The increase in the number of welfare recipients in New York City from 1966 to 1969 was about one million, double the increase in the preceding two decades.

3. According to one labor mediator, "If freedom from public employee strikes is earnestly sought . . . the public employee organization must be given a *quid pro quo* for its no-strike pledge" (Weisenfeld 1969:27). But nowhere is it suggested what *quid pro quo* might be.

4. The dynamics of a Chicago teachers' strike suggests a pattern that may be repeated in future struggles. Following a strike in May, 1969, the teachers won a monthly salary raise of $100. The implementation of the increase rested on the approval of a large rise in state aid to the schools by the Illinois General Assembly. In the fall of the year, the teachers were told that the aid was not forthcoming and that the schools were forced to hold the increase to $50 monthly.

5. Teachers, in particular, are under severe pressure because the traditional analyses and solutions to economic disruption, social crisis, poverty, war, and so on are wrong or ineffectual precisely because of the bankruptcy of bourgeois theory and ideology. For those engaged in reproducing ruling class ideas and for others, this is another source of bewilderment, irritation, frustration, and disillusionment. It is interesting that those teachers with the highest "professional orientation" tend to have slightly higher "conflict rates" than the typical teacher, according to a survey of faculty members in twenty-eight public schools in the Midwest. Information courtesy of Steve Smith.

6. The following analysis is based on the author's experience with state employees. The generalizations are based on discussion and activity with a very limited, yet fairly representative group of workers in the Bay Area of California.

7. The process of proletarianization and resistance must be seen in the context of the Vietnam war, the black revolution, and the growing pressure from below—the movement of welfare clients, the student movement, and so on. All these related tendencies obviously had the effect of speeding up the process, and polarizing attitudes and behavior around the issues of the budget, job control, control of the schools, as well as general political issues. It is too early to know precisely how a mass movement will develop. In fact, organized workers in different branches of the state economy acting independently are placing more and more budgetary demands on the state, and thus are engaging in a common project, although as yet there is no widespread consciousness of this. State workers also have relations with each other that are entered into consciously, as a result of the day-to-day requirements of work. Some of these develop organically from the requirements of their real functions (e.g., city planner consultations with social workers in connection with the problem of relocating populations displaced by urban renewal). Some of these develop organically from the requirements of their nominal functions, made real through resistance. These relations are at present highly underdeveloped. For example, there are no joint plans of school and college teachers to extract more resources from the state in order to conduct better day-to-day resistance. Resistance, job control, control over the work place—these require an expanded consciousness of those broader relations that workers enter into independent of their will. This determines the role of theory. The role of practice is determined by the contradiction between nominal and real functions of the state.

REFERENCES

Aaron, Henry. 1967. Social security: international comparisons. In Otto Eckstein, ed., *Studies in the Economics of Income Maintenance*, pp. 13–48. Washington, D.C.: Brookings Institution.

AAWB Proceedings. 1905–62. American Association of Workers for the Blind.

Ackoff, Russell L. and Fred E. Emery. 1972. *On Purposeful Systems*. Chicago: Aldine-Atherton.

Addams, Jane. 1961. *Twenty Years at Hull-House*. New York: Signet.

Agento, R. C. 1970. Behavioral expectations as perceived by employing agencies. *Public Welfare* 28:209–13.

Aiken, Michael. 1970. The distribution of community power: structural bases and social consequences. In Michael Aiken and Paul E. Mott, eds., *The Structure of Community Power*, pp. 487–525. New York: Random House.

Aiken, Michael and Robert R. Alford. 1968. Community structure and mobilization: the case of the War on Poverty. Madison: University of Wisconsin Institute for Research on Poverty.

—— 1970. Community structure and innovation: the case of public housing. *American Political Science Review* 64:843–64.

Aldrich, H. E. 1974. An interorganizational dependency perspective on relations between the employment service and its organization-set. Presented at Research Conference, Graduate School of Business, University of Pittsburgh.

Alford, Robert R. 1969. With the collaboration of Harry M. Scoble. *Bureaucracy and Participation: Political Cultures in Four Wisconsin Cities*. Chicago: Rand McNally.

Alford, Robert R. and Roger Friedland. 1975. Political participation and public policy. *Annual Review of Sociology* 1:429–79.

Alford, Robert R. and Eugene C. Lee. 1968. Voting turnout in American cities. *American Political Science Review* 62:796–813.

Anderson, O. W. and R. M. Anderson. 1972. Patterns of use of health services. In Howard E. Freeman, Sol Levine, and Leo G. Reeder, eds., *Handbook of Medical Sociology*, pp. 386–406. Englewood Cliffs, N.J.: Prentice-Hall.

Ardant, G. 1975. Financial policy and economic infrastructure of modern states and nations. In C. Tilly, ed., *The Formation of National States in Western Europe*, pp. 164–242. Princeton, N.J.: Princeton University.

Arlidge, John T. 1859. *On the State of Lunacy and the Legal Profession for the Insane*. London: Churchill.

Aronowitz, Stanley. 1968. Public workers are sold out. *National Guardian*, February 24.

Attewell, Paul A., Lewis L. Judd, and Dean R. Gerstein. 1976. A client evaluation of involuntary detoxification from methadone. *Proceedings of the National Conference on Drug Abuse*. New York: M. Dekker.

Ausubel, David P. 1966. The Dole-Nyswander treatment of heroin addiction. *Journal of the American Medical Association* 195:949–50.

Bailey, W. 1758. *A Treatise on the Better Employment and More Comfortable Support of the Poor in Workhouses*. London.

Bailis, Lawrence N. 1972. Bread or justice: grass roots organizing in the welfare rights movement. Ph.D. dissertation, Harvard University.

Baldridge, J. Victor. 1971. *Power and Conflict in the University*. New York: Wiley.

Banfield, Edward C. and James Q. Wilson. 1963. *City Politics*. Cambridge, Mass.: Harvard University Press.

Barker, R. L. and R. B. Briggs. 1969. Perspectives on social work manpower in service delivery approaches. In T. Carlson, ed., *Social Work Manpower Utilization in Mental Health Programs*, pp. 15–24. Syracuse, N.Y.: Syracuse University Press.

Bartol, Kathryn M. 1977. Success in our jobs: what the research shows. In Bette Ann Stead et al., eds., *Women in Management Day: Proceedings*. Houston, Texas: University of Houston College of Business Administration.

Bartol, Kathryn M. and Max S. Wortman, Jr. 1976. Sex effects in leader behavior self-descriptions and job satisfaction. *Journal of Psychology* 94:177–83.

Barton, Allen. 1975. Consensus and conflict among American leaders. *Public Opinion Quarterly* 38:507–30.

Bass, Bernard M., Judith Krusell and Ralph A. Alexander. 1971. Male managers' attitudes toward working women. *American Behavioral Scientist* 15:221–36.

Becker, Howard S. 1952. The career of the Chicago public school teacher. *American Journal of Sociology* 57:470–77.

—— 1963. *Outsiders: Studies in the Sociology of Deviance*. Glencoe, Ill.: Free Press.

Becker, Howard S. et al. 1961. *Boys in White*. Chicago: University of Chicago Press.

Belknap, Ivan. 1956. *Human Problems of a State Mental Hospital*. New York: McGraw-Hill.

Bellers, John. 1696. *Proposals for Raising a College of Industry of All Useful Trades and Husbandry*. London.

Benson, J. K. 1975. The interorganizational network as a political economy. *Administrative Science Quarterly* 20:229–49.

Bentham, Jeremy. 1791. *Panopticon; or The Inspection House*. London: Payne.

—— 1797. *Pauper Management*. London.

—— 1843. *Works*, J. Bowring, ed. Vol. 10. Edinburgh.

Berkanovic, Emil and Leo G. Reeder. 1974. Can money buy the appropriate use of services? *Journal of Health and Social Behavior* 15:93–99.

Berleman, William C., James R. Seaberg, and Thomas W. Steinburn. 1972. The delinquency prevention experiment of the Seattle Atlantic Street Center: a final evaluation. *Social Service Review* 46:323–46.

Beveridge, William. 1942. *Social Insurance and Allied Services*. London: His Majesty's Stationery Office.

Bidwell, Charles E. 1970. Students and schools: some observations on client trust in client-serving organizations. In W. R. Rosengren and M. Lefton, eds., *Organizations and Clients*, pp. 37–69. Columbus, Ohio: Merrill.

Billingsley, Andrew. 1964. Bureaucratic and professional orientation patterns in social casework. *Social Service Review* 38:400–407.

Binzen, Peter. 1970. *Whitetown, U.S.A.* New York: Vintage.

Bishop, G. A. 1967. *Tax Burdens and Benefits of Government Expenditures by Income Class, 1961, 1965*. New York: Tax Foundation.

Blau, Peter M. 1955. *The Dynamics of Bureaucracy*. Chicago: University of Chicago Press.

—— 1964. *Exchange and Power in Social Life*. New York: Wiley.

Blau, Peter M. and W. Richard Scott. 1962. *Formal Organizations*. San Francisco: Chandler.

Bogardus, Emory S. 1919. *Essentials of Americanization.* Los Angeles: University of Southern California Press.

Booms, Bernard and James R. Halldorson. 1973. The politics of redistribution: a reformulation. *American Political Science Review* 77:920–33.

Booth, Charles. 1892. *Life and Labour of the People of London.* London: Macmillan.

Bornschier, Volker and Thanh-Huyen Ballmer-Cao. 1979. Income inequality: a cross-national study of the relationships between MNC-penetration, dimensions of the power structure, and income distribution. *American Sociological Review* 44:487–506.

Boston Women's Health Book Collective. 1976. *Our Bodies, Ourselves.* 2d ed. New York: Simon and Schuster.

Bowles, Samuel and Herbert Gintis. 1976. *Schooling in Capitalist America.* New York: Basic Books.

Brager, George and John Michael. 1969. The sex distribution in social work: causes and consequences. *Social Casework* 50:595–601.

Braude, Lee. 1961. Professional autonomy and the role of the layman. *Social Forces* 39:297–301.

Brecher, Edward M. and the Editors of Consumer Reports. 1972. *Licit and Illicit Drugs.* Boston: Little, Brown.

Bremner, Robert. 1956. *From the Depths: the Discovery of Poverty in the United States.* New York: New York University Press.

Brill, Leon. 1973. Introductory overview: historic background. In C. D. Chambers and Leon Brill, eds., *Methadone: Experiences and Issues,* pp. 5–40. New York: Behavioral Publications.

Brill, Leon and Carl D. Chambers. 1973. Summary and conclusions. In C. D. Chambers and Leon Brill, eds., *Methadone: Experiences and Issues,* pp. 347–65. New York: Behavioral Publications.

Brody, Stanley, Harvey Finkle, and Carl Hirsch. 1972. Benefit alert: outreach for the aged. *Social Work* 17:14–23.

Brown, Claude. 1965. *Manchild in the Promised Land.* New York: Random House.

Browne, W. A. F. 1837. *What Asylums Were, Are, and Ought to Be.* Edinburgh: Black.

—— 1864. *The Moral Treatment of the Insane.* London: Adlard.

Buckley, Walter. 1963. On equitable inequality. *American Sociological Review* 28:799–801.

Bucknill, J. C. 1880. *The Care of the Insane and Their Legal Control.* London: MacMillan.

Byrd, Doris Elaine. 1974. The social organization of a psychiatric clinic. Ph.D. dissertation, University of Chicago.

Caplow, Theodore. 1954. *The Sociology of Work.* Minneapolis: University of Minnesota Press.

Carlson, R. O. 1964. Environmental constraints and organizational consequences: the public school and its clients. In *Behavioral Science and Educational Administration,* pp. 262–76. Chicago: National Society for the Study of Education.

Carter, E. E. 1971. The behavioral theory of the firm and top-level corporate decisions. *Administrative Science Quarterly* 16:413–28.

Carter, Richard. 1961. *Gentle Legions.* Garden City, N.Y.: Doubleday.

Cartwright, Dorwin and Alvin Zander. 1960. *Group Dynamics: Research and Theory.* 2d ed. Evanston, Ill.: Row, Peterson.

Chadwick, Edwin. 1842. *Report on the Sanitary Condition of the Labouring Population of Great Britain.* London.

Chafetz, Janet Saltzman. 1972. Women in social work. *Social Work* 17:12–18.

Chalmers, Thomas. 1832. *On Political Economy in Connection with the Moral State and Moral Prospects of Society.* New York: Daniel Appleton.

Chambers, Carl D. and Leon Brill, eds. 1973. *Methadone: Experiences and Issues.* New York: Behavioral Publications.

Chambers, Carl D. and W. J. Russell Taylor. 1971. The incidence and patterns of drug abuse during maintenance therapy. Presented at Annual Meeting, Committee on Problems of Drug Dependence, National Academy of Sciences, Toronto.

Chambliss, W. 1964. A sociological analysis of the law of vagrancy. *Social Problems* 12:67–77.

Chase-Dunn, Christopher. 1975. The effects of international economic dependence on development and inequality. *American Sociological Review* 40:720–38.

Chevigny, Hector and Syndell Braverman. 1950. *Adjustment to Blindness.* New Haven, Conn.: Yale University Press.

Clark, Burton R. 1956. Organizational adaptation and precarious values. *American Sociological Review* 21:327–36.

—— 1960. *Open Door College.* New York: McGraw-Hill.

Clark, Terry N. 1968. Community structure, decision-making, budget expenditures, and urban renewal in 51 American communities. *American Sociological Review* 33:576–93.

Cloward, Richard A. and Richard M. Elman. 1966. Advocacy in the ghetto. *Transaction* 4:27–35.

Cloward, Richard A. and Irwin Epstein. 1967. Private social welfare's disengagement from the poor: the case of family adjustment agencies. In George Brager and Francis Purcell, eds., *Community Action Against Poverty*, pp. 40–63. New Haven, Conn.: College and University Press.

Cloward, Richard A. and Frances Fox Piven. 1965. The professional bureaucracies: benefit systems as influence systems. In Murray Silberman, ed., *The Role of Government in Promoting Social Change.* New York: Columbia University School of Social Work.

Cohen, J. 1969. Race as factor in social work practice. In R. Miller, ed., *Race, Research, and Reason: Social Work Perspectives.* New York: National Association of Social Workers.

Cohen, John. 1960. *Chance, Skill and Luck: the Psychology of Guessing and Gambling.* Baltimore: Penguin Books.

Cohen, Michael D. and James C. March. 1974. *Leadership and Ambiguity: the American College President.* New York: McGraw-Hill.

Cohen, Michael D., James G. March, and Johan P. Olsen. 1972. A garbage can model of organizations. *Administrative Science Quarterly* 17:1–25.

Cole, Joan. 1975. Institutional racism in a community mental health center. Ph.D. dissertation, Wright Institute, San Francisco.

Coleman, James S. 1957. *Community Conflict.* Glencoe, Ill.: Free Press.

—— 1966. Foundations for a theory of collective decisions. *American Journal of Sociology* 71:615–27.

Commager, Henry Steele, ed. 1967. *Lester Ward and the Welfare State.* Indianapolis: Bobbs-Merrill.

Committee for the Rights of the Disabled. 1966. *Newsletter.* Berkeley, Calif., November 2.

Conolly, J. 1830. *An Inquiry into the Indications of Insanity.* London: Taylor.

Conviser, Richard H. 1973. Toward a general theory of interpersonal trust. *Pacific Sociological Review* 16:377–99.

Crain, Robert L., Elihu Katz, and Donald B. Rosenthal. 1969. *The Politics of Community Conflict.* Indianapolis: Bobbs-Merrill.

Crain, Robert L. and Donald B. Rosenthal. 1967. Community status as a dimension of local decision-making. *American Sociological Review* 32:970–84.

Crawford, F. R. 1969. Variations between Negroes and whites in concepts of mental illness, its treatment and prevalence. In S. C.

Plag and R. B. Edgerton, eds., *Changing Perspectives in Mental Illness*. New York: Holt, Rinehart & Winston.

Crozier, Michael. 1964. *The Bureaucratic Phenomenon*. Chicago: University of Chicago Press.

Cumming, Elaine. 1967. Allocation of care to the mentally ill, American style. In Mayer N. Zald, ed., *Organizing for Community Welfare*, pp. 109–59. Chicago: Quadrangle.

—— 1968. *Systems of Social Regulation*. New York: Atherton.

Cutright, Phillips. 1963. National political development: measurement and analysis. *American Sociological Review* 28:260–64.

—— 1965. Political structure, economic development, and national social security programs. *American Journal of Sociology* 70:537–50.

—— 1967. Inequality: a cross-national analysis. *American Sociological Review* 32:562–78.

Cyert, Richard M., W. R. Dill, and James G. March. 1958. The role of expectations in business decision-making. *Administrative Science Quarterly* 3:307–40.

Cyert, Richard M. and James G. March. 1963. *A Behavioral Theory of the Firm*. Englewood Cliffs, N.J.: Prentice-Hall.

Dahrendorf, Ralf. 1959. *Class and Class Conflict in Industrial Society*. Stanford, Calif.: Stanford University Press.

David, M. S. 1968. Variations in patients' compliance with doctors' advice: an empirical analysis of patterns of communication. *American Journal of Public Health* 58:279–86.

Davis, Fred. 1959. The cab driver and his fare. *American Journal of Sociology* 65:158–65.

Davis, Kingsley. 1938. Mental hygiene and the class structure. *Psychiatry* 1:55–56.

Davis, Kingsley and W. Moore. 1945. Some principles of stratification. *American Sociological Review* 10:242–49.

Dawson, Richard and James Robinson. 1963. Interparty competition, economic variables, and welfare politics in the American states. *Journal of Politics* 25:265–89.

DeLeon, Richard E. 1973. Politics, economic surplus, and redistribution in the American states: a test of theory. *American Journal of Political Science* 4:769–81.

de Schweinitz, Karl. 1943. *England's Road to Social Security*. New York: Barnes.

Diaz, William A. and Stephen M. David. 1972. *The New York City*

Addiction Services Agency 1971–1972. New York: Fordham University Institute for Social Research.

Dobb, M. 1963. *Studies in the Development of Capitalism.* New York: International Publishers.

Dole, Vincent P. and Marie E. Nyswander. 1965. A medical treatment for diacetylmorphine (heroin) addiction: a clinical trial with methadone hydrochloride. *Journal of the American Medical Association* 193:646–50.

—— 1966. Narcotic blockade: a medical technique for stopping heroin use by addicts. *Archives of General Medicine* 118:304.

—— 1967. Heroin addiction: a metabolic disease. *Archives of General Medicine* 120:19.

—— 1976. Methadone maintenance treatment: a ten-year perspective. *Journal of the American Medical Association* 235:2117–19.

Domhoff, G. William. 1970. *The Higher Circles.* New York: Random House.

Douds, Charles T. 1969. The status of collective bargaining of public employees in Pennsylvania. *The Economic and Business Review* 21.

Douglas, Dorothy J. 1969. Occupational and therapeutic contingencies of ambulance services in metropolitan areas. Ph.D. dissertation, University of California.

Dumont, Matthew P. 1974. The junkie as political enemy. *Journal of Alternative Human Services* 1:16–25.

Durkheim, Emile. 1947. *The Division of Labor in Society.* Glencoe, Ill.: Free Press.

Dutton, Diana B. 1978. Explaining the low use of health services by the poor: costs, attitudes, or delivery systems? *American Sociological Review* 43:348–68.

Dye, Thomas R. 1968. Urban school segregation: a comparative analysis. *Urban Affairs Quarterly* 4:141–65.

Edwards, Allen E. 1954. *Statistical Methods for the Behavioral Sciences.* New York: Holt, Rinehart & Winston.

Emerson, R. 1962. Power-dependence relations. *American Sociological Review* 27:31–41.

Engels, Frederick. 1969. *The Condition of the Working Class in England.* London: Panther.

—— 1972. *The Origin of the Family, Private Property, and the State.* New York: Pathfinder.

Erbe, William. 1964. Social involvement and political activism: a replication and elaboration. *American Sociological Review* 29:197–215.

Espada, Frank. 1977. Contemporary government policy: response. *Proceedings of the National Conference on Drug Abuse.*

Etzioni, Amitai. 1960. Interpersonal and structural factors in the study of mental hospitals. *Psychiatry* 23:13–22.

—— 1961; 1975 rev. *A Comparative Analysis of Complex Organizations.* New York: Free Press.

—— 1964. *Modern Organizations.* Englewood Cliffs, N.J.: Prentice-Hall.

European Communities Statistical Office. 1972. *Sozialkonten, 1962–70.* Luxembourg: European Communites.

Evan, William. 1966. The organization-set: toward a theory of interorganizational relations. In James D. Thompson, ed., *Approaches to Organizational Design,* pp. 173–91. Pittsburgh: University of Pittsburgh Press.

Fairchild, Henry Pratt. 1926. *The Melting Pot Mistake.* Boston: Little, Brown.

Federal Register. 1973. Service programs for families and children and for the aged, blind, or disabled. Washington, D.C.: U.S. Department of Health, Education, and Welfare.

Fessler, A. 1956. The management of lunacy in seventeenth-century England. London: *Proceedings of the Royal Society of Medicine,* p. 49.

Festinger, Leon. 1957. *A Theory of Cognitive Dissonance.* Evanston, Ill.: Row, Peterson.

Finney, Graham S. 1975. *Drugs: Administering Catastrophe.* Washington, D.C.: Drug Abuse Council.

Fischer, Glen. 1974. *The Politics of the Purse.* Urbana: University of Illinois Press.

Fischer, Joel. 1969. Negroes and whites and rates of mental illness: reconsideration of a myth. *Psychiatry* 34:428–46.

Fischer, Joel et al. 1976. Are social workers sexists? *Social Work* 21:428–33.

Fortune. 1961a. July: 168–83.

—— 1961b. August: 132–44.

—— 1963. *Plant and Product Directory of the 1000 Largest U.S. Industrial Corporations.*

Foucault, Michel. 1965. *Madness and Civilization.* New York: Mentor.

Franzen, Thomas, Lovgren Kerstein, and Irene Rosenberg. 1975. Redistributional effects of taxes and public expenditures. *Swedish Journal of Economics* 77:31–35.

Freidson, Eliot. 1961. *Patients' View of Medical Practice*. New York: Russell Sage Foundation.

—— 1970a. Dominant professions, bureaucracy, and client services. In W. R. Rosengren and M. Lefton, eds., *Organizations and Clients*, pp. 71–92. Columbus, Ohio: Charles E. Merrill.

—— 1970b. *Profession of Medicine*. New York: Dodd, Mead.

Fried, Robert C. 1975. Comparing urban policy and performance. In Fred I. Greenstein and Nelson W. Polsby, eds., *Handbook of Political Sciences*, Ch. 6. Reading, Mass.: Addison-Wesley.

Friedland, Roger. 1977a. Class power and the city. Ph.D. dissertation, University of Wisconsin.

—— 1977b. Class power and social control: the case of the War on Poverty. *Politics and Society* 7:459–89.

Friedland, Roger, Frances Fox Piven, and Robert R. Alford. 1977. Political conflict, urban structure, and the fiscal crisis. In Douglas Ashford, ed., *Comparative Public Policy: New Approaches and Methods*, pp. 197–224. New York: Sage Foundation.

Fritchey, Clayton. 1971. U.S. treats poor scornfully, meanly. Detroit *Free Press*, June 15.

Fry, Brian R. 1974. An examination of the relationship between selected electoral characteristics and state redistributive efforts. *American Journal of Political Science* 18:421–31.

Fry, Brian R. and Richard F. Winters. 1970. The politics of redistribution. *American Political Science Review* 49:508–22.

Fry, Lincoln J. and Jon Miller. 1974. The impact of interdisciplinary teams on organizational relationships. *Sociological Quarterly* 15:417–31.

—— 1975. Observations on an emerging profession. Unpublished.

Furniss, E. 1965. *The Position of the Laborer in a System of Nationalism*. New York: Kelly.

Galbraith, John Kenneth. 1958. *The Affluent Society*. Boston: Houghton Mifflin.

Galper, Jeffry H. 1973. Private pensions and public policy. *Social Work* 18:5–12.

Gamson, William A. 1968. *Power and Discontent*. Homewood, Ill.: Dorsey.

Gans, H. 1971. Preface to Colin Greer, *The Great School Legend*. New York: Basic Books.

Gartner, Alan, ed. 1969. New ideology of new careers. *New Careers Newsletter* 3. New York: New York University Press.

Gellman, I. P. 1964. *The Sober Alcoholic*. New Haven, Conn.: College and University Press.

Gerstein, Dean. 1975. Heroin in motion: a working paper in the theory of action. Ph.D. dissertation, Harvard University.

—— 1976. The structure of heroin communities (in relation to methadone maintenance). *American Journal of Drug and Alcohol Abuse* 3:571–87.

Ghent, William J. 1902. *Our Benevolent Feudalism*. New York: Macmillan.

Glaser, Barney and Anselm Strauss. 1964. The social loss of dying patients. *American Journal of Nursing* 64:119–21.

Glassman, Carol. 1970. Women and the welfare system. In Robin Morgan, ed., *Sisterhood Is Powerful*, pp. 102–15. New York: Vintage.

Glazer, Nathan and Daniel P. Moynihan. 1963. *Beyond the Melting Pot*. Cambridge, Mass.: M.I.T. and Harvard University.

Glenny, Lyman A. 1959. *Autonomy of Public Colleges: the Challenge of Coordination*. New York: McGraw-Hill.

Goffman, Erving. 1959. *The Presentation of Self in Everyday Life*. Garden City, N.Y.: Doubleday.

—— 1961. *Asylums: Essays on the Social Situation of Mental Patients and Other Inmates*. Garden City, N.Y.: Doubleday.

Gold, David. 1969. Statistical tests and substantive significance. *American Sociologist* 4:42–46.

Gold, Raymond L. 1964. In the basement—the apartment-building janitor. In Peter L. Berger, ed., *The Human Shape of Work*, pp. 1–49. New York: Macmillan.

Goldner, Fred H., R. Richard Ritti, and Thomas P. Ference. 1977. The production of cynical knowledge in organizations. *American Sociological Review* 42:539–51.

Goode, William J. 1961. Encroachment, charlatanism, and the emerging professions: psychology, sociology, and medicine. *American Sociological Review* 25:902–14.

Goodman, J., ed. 1972. *Dynamics of Racism in Social Work Practice*. Washington, D.C.: National Association of Social Workers.

Gordon, Laura Kramer. 1974. Bureaucratic competence and success in dealing with public bureaucracies. *Social Problems* 23:197–208.

Gordon, M. S. 1963. *The Economics of Welfare Politics*. New York: Columbia University Press.

Gough, Ian. 1979. *The Political Economy of the Welfare State*. Atlantic Highlands, N.J.: Humanities Press.

Gould, Leroy et al. 1974. *Connections: Notes from the Heroin World.* New Haven, Conn.: Yale University Press.

Gowman, Alan. 1957. *War Blind in American Social Structure.* New York: American Foundation for the Blind.

Gray, Susan. 1974. Waiting for the end: on nursing homes. New York *Times*, March 31.

Greenfield, Paula. 1976. Why women work. In Meg Gerrard et al., eds., *Women in Management*, pp. 3–22. Austin: University of Texas Press.

Greenley, James R. and Stuart A. Kirk. 1973. Organizational characteristics of agencies and the distribution of services to applicants. *Journal of Health and Social Behavior* 14:70–79.

Greenstone, J. David. 1969. *Labor in American Politics.* New York: Knopf.

Greenstone, J. David and Paul E. Peterson. 1968. Reformers, machines, and the War on Poverty. In James Q. Wilson, ed., *City Politics and Public Policy*, pp. 267–92. New York: Wiley.

Greenwood, Ernest. 1957. Attributes of a profession. *Social Work* 2:45–55.

Grier, W. and P. Cobbs. 1968. *Black Rage.* New York: Basic Books.

Grønbjerg, Kirsten A. 1977. *Mass Society and the Extension of Welfare, 1960–1970.* Chicago: University of Chicago Press.

Grønbjerg, Kirsten A., David Street, and Gerald D. Suttles. 1978. *Poverty and Social Change.* Chicago: University of Chicago Press.

Gubrium, Jaber F. 1975. *Living and Dying at Murray Manor.* New York: St. Martin's Press.

Gursslin, Orville, Raymond G. Hunt, and Jack L. Roach. 1959. Social class, mental hygiene, and psychiatric practice. *Social Service Review* 33:237–45.

Gusfield, Joseph R. 1963. *Symbolic Crusade: Status Politics and the American Temperance Movement.* Urbana: University of Illinois Press.

—— 1967. Moral passage: the symbolic process in public designations of deviance. *Social Problems* 15:175–88.

Hallowitz, David and Albert V. Cutter. 1954. Intake and the waiting list: a differential approach. *Social Casework* 35:439–45.

Hamison, J. B. 1880. *Certain Dangerous Tendencies in American Life.* Boston: Houghton, Osgood.

Harris, Larry. 1967. Communicating with the culturally disadvantaged. In *Rehabilitating the Culturally Disadvantaged*, pp. 45–49. Mankato, Minn.: Mankato State College Press.

Hasenfeld, Yeheskel. 1972. People processing organizations: an exchange approach. *American Sociological Review* 37:256–63.

Hasenfeld, Yeheskel and Richard A. English, eds. 1974. *Human Service Organizations*. Ann Arbor: University of Michigan Press.

Haug, Marie R. and Marvin B. Sussman. 1969. Professionalism and the public. *Sociological Inquiry* 39:57–64.

Hausknecht, Murray H. 1962. *The Joiners*. Totowa, N.J.: Bedminster.

Haveman, Robert and R. D. Hamrin. 1973. *The Political Economy of Federal Policy*. New York: Harper and Row.

Hawley, Amos H. 1963. Community power structure and urban renewal success. *American Journal of Sociology* 68:422–31.

Heclo, Hugh. 1974. *Modern Social Politics in Britain and Sweden*. New Haven, Conn.: Yale University Press.

Heilbroner, Robert L. 1970. Benign neglect in the United States. *Transaction* 7:15–22.

Helfgot, Joseph. 1974. Professional reform organizations and the symbolic representation of the poor. *American Sociological Review* 39:475–91.

Henry, Jules. 1957. Types of institutional structure. In M. Greenblatt, O. J. Levinson, and R. H. Williams, eds., *The Patient and the Mental Hospital*, pp. 73–90. Glencoe, Ill.: Free Press.

Henslin, James. 1968. Trust and the cab driver. In Marcello Truzzi, ed., *Sociology and Everyday Life*, pp. 138–58. Englewood Cliffs, N.J.: Prentice-Hall.

Heraud, Brian J. 1970. *Sociology and Social Work*. New York: Pergamon.

Hewitt, Christopher. 1977. The effect of political democracy and social democracy on equality in industrial societies: a cross-national comparison. *American Sociological Review* 42:450–64.

Hicks, Alexander M. 1979. The political economy of redistribution: the case of the American states between the Great Depression and the Great Society. Ph.D. dissertation, University of Wisconsin.

Hicks, Alexander M., Roger Friedland, and Edwin Johnson. 1976. Democratic competitive mobilization. Unpublished.

Hickson, D. J. et al. 1971. A strategic contingencies' theory of intraorganizational power. *Administrative Science Quarterly* 16:216–29.

Hill, G. N. 1814. *An Essay on the Prevention and Cure of Insanity*. London: Longman.

Himes, Joseph S., Jr. 1951. Some concepts of blindness in American culture. In *Attitudes toward Blindness*, pp. 10–22. New York: American Foundation for the Blind.

Hinings, C. R. et al. 1974. Structural conditions of intraorganizational power. *Administrative Science Quarterly* 19:22–44.

Hobsbawm, E. J. 1968. *Industry and Empire*. London: Penguin Books.

Hobsbawm, E. J. and G. Rude. 1969. *Captain Swing*. London: Penguin Books.

Hofferbert, Richard I. 1972. State and community policy studies: a review of comparative input-output analysis. In James A. Robinson, ed., *Political Science Annual: an International Review*, pp. 3–72. Vol. 3. New York: Bobbs-Merrill.

Hofstadter, Richard. 1955. *Social Darwinism in American Thought*. Boston: Beacon.

Hollingshead, August B. and Frederick C. Redlich. 1958. *Social Class and Mental Illness*. New York: Wiley.

Hollis, Florence. 1972. *Casework: a Psychological Therapy*. 2d ed. New York: Random House.

Holsendolph, Ernest. 1974. Social action hit by financial woes. New York *Times*, November 8.

Holzman, Paula and Irving E. Lukoff. 1976. A plea for the long route: an evaluation of methadone maintenance and other short cuts to the cure of heroin addiction. Unpublished.

Horkheimer, Max. 1947. *Eclipse of Reason*. New York: Oxford University Press.

Horwitz, J. J. 1970. *Team Practice and the Specialist*. Springfield, Ill.: Thomas.

Howard, Jan. 1975. Humanization and dehumanization of health care. In J. Howard and A. Strauss, eds., *Humanizing Health Care*, pp. 57–102. New York: Wiley.

Howe, Louise Kapp. 1970. *The White Majority*. New York: Vintage.

Huaco, George A. 1963. A logical analysis of the Davis-Moore theory of stratification. *American Sociological Review* 28:801–04.

Hughes, Everett C. 1958. *Men and Their Work*. London: Collier-Macmillan.

—— 1963. Professions. *Daedalus* 92:655–68.

Hunt, Leon and Carl D. Chambers. 1976. *The Heroin Epidemics*. New York: Spectrum.

Isbell, Harris and Victor H. Vogel. 1949. The addiction liability of methadone (amidone, dolophine, 10820) and its use in the treatment of the morphine abstinence syndrome. *American Journal of Psychiatry* 105:909–14.

Jackman, Robert W. 1974. Political democracy and social equality: a comparative analysis. *American Sociological Review* 39:29–45.

—— 1975. *Politics and Social Equality.* New York: Wiley.

—— 1980. Socialist parties and income inequality in Western industrial societies. *The Journal of Politics* 42:135–49.

Jackson, Maurice. 1963. Their brothers' keepers. Mimeographed. Berkeley, Calif.: Pacific School of Religion.

Jacob, Herbert and Michael Lipsky. 1968. Outputs, structure, and power: an assessment of the changes in the study of state and local politics. *Journal of Politics* 30:510–38.

Jacobs, D. 1974. Dependency and vulnerability: an exchange approach to the control of organizations. *Administrative Science Quarterly* 19:45–59.

James, Dorothy Buckton. 1972. *Poverty, Politics and Change.* Englewood Cliffs, N.J.: Prentice-Hall.

Janowitz, Morris. 1975. Social control and macrosociology. *American Journal of Sociology* 81:82–109.

—— 1976. *Social Control of the Welfare State.* New York: Elsevier.

Johnson, Edwin. Forthcoming. The political economy of public policy: a model of organized labor and state economic policy. Ph.D. dissertation, University of Wisconsin.

Joint Economic Committee. 1972. *The Economics of Federal Subsidy Programs.* Washington, D.C.: U.S. Congress.

Jones, B. et al. 1970. Problems of black psychiatric residents in white training institutes. *American Journal of Psychiatry* 127:798–803.

Jones, Maxwell. 1968. *Beyond the Therapeutic Community.* New Haven, Conn.: Yale University Press.

Judd, Lewis L. and Dean Gerstein. 1975. *Follow-up and Evaluation Study of the UCSD-San Diego County Narcotic Treatment Program, 1970–1974.* San Diego: Department of Substance Abuse.

Kadushin, Alfred. 1976. Men in a woman's profession. *Social Work* 21:440–47.

Kadushin, Charles. 1969. *Why People Go to Psychiatrists.* New York: Atherton.

Kahn, Alfred J. 1970. Perspectives on access to social services. *Social Work* 15:95–101.

Katz, Alfred H. 1961. *Parents of the Handicapped.* Springfield, Ill.: Thomas.

—— 1965. Self-help groups. In Harry Lurie, ed., *Encyclopedia of*

Social Work, pp. 680–83. New York: National Association of Social Workers.

Katz, Daniel and Robert Kahn. 1966. *The Social Psychology of Organizations.* New York: Wiley.

Katz, Elihu and Brenda Danet. 1966. Petitions and persuasive appeals: a study of official-client relations. *American Sociological Review* 31:811–22.

—— 1968. Communication between bureaucracy and the public: a review of the literature. Mimeographed. Jerusalem: Hebrew University.

—— 1973. *Bureaucracy and the Public.* New York: Basic Books.

Katz, Elihu and S. N. Eisenstadt. 1960. Some sociological observations of the response of Israeli organizations to new immigrants. *Administrative Science Quarterly* 5:113–33.

Katz, Jack. 1977. Cover-up and collective integrity: on the natural antagonisms of authority internal and external to organizations. *Social Problems* 25:3–17.

Kennedy, Ruby J. Reeves. 1944. Single or triple melting pot. *American Journal of Sociology* 49:331–39.

Key, V. O. 1956. *Politics in the American States.* New York: Knopf.

Kotz, Nick and Mary Lynn Kotz. 1977. *A Passion for Equality.* New York: Norton.

Kramer, Morton, Beatrice M. Rosen, and Ernest M. Willis. 1973. Definitions and distributions of mental disorders in a racist society. In Charles V. Willie, Bernard M. Kramer, and Bertram S. Brown, eds., *Racism and Mental Health: Essays,* pp. 353–459. Pittsburgh: University of Pittsburgh Press.

Krause, A. Elliot. 1966. After the rehabilitation center. *Social Problems* 14:197–206.

Kravis, Irving B. 1960. International differences in the distribution of income. *Review of Economics and Statistics* 42:408–16.

Krebbs, R. 1971. Some effects of a white institution on black psychiatric outpatients. *American Journal of Orthopsychiatry* 41:589–96.

Kroeger, Naomi. 1974. Bureaucracy, social exchange, and benefits received in a public assistance agency. *Social Problems* 23:182–96.

Kuhn, Alfred. 1974. *The Logic of Social Systems.* San Francisco: Jossey-Bass.

Kuznets, Simon. 1963. Quantitative aspects of the economic growth of nations: 8. Distribution of income by size. *Economic Development and Cultural Change* 11:1–80.

Larkin, Ralph W. 1975. Social exchange in the elementary school classroom: the problem of teacher legitimation of social power. *Sociology of Education* 48:400–410.

Lasswell, Harold D. 1936. *Politics: Who Gets What, When, How.* New York: McGraw-Hill.

Lefton, Mark and William R. Rosengren. 1966. Organizations and clients: lateral and longitudinal dimensions. *American Sociological Review* 31:802–10.

Leichter, Hope and William Mitchell. 1967. *Kinship and Casework.* New York: Russell Sage Foundation.

Lenski, Gerhard. 1966. *Power and Privilege.* New York: McGraw-Hill.

Levens, Helene. 1968. Organizational affiliation and powerlessness: a case study of the welfare poor. *Social Problems* 16:18–31.

Levine, Jack and Gerald Taube. 1970. Bureaucracy and the socially handicapped: a study of lower status tenants in public housing. *Sociology and Social Research* 54:209–19.

Lichtenberg, Phillip, Robert Kohrman, and Helen Macgregor. 1960. *Motivations for Child Psychiatry Treatment.* New York: Russell and Russell.

Lindesmith, Alfred. 1965. *The Addict and the Law.* Bloomington: Indiana University Press.

Lineberry, Robert L. and Edmund P. Fowler. 1967. Reformism and public policies in American cities. *American Political Science Review* 61:701–16.

Lipset, Seymour Martin. 1963. *The First New Nation.* New York: Doubleday.

Litwak, Eugene and Lydia Hylton. 1962. Interorganizational analysis: a hypothesis on coordinating agencies. *Administrative Science Quarterly* 6:395–420.

Lockard, Duane. 1959. *New England State Politics.* Princeton, N.J.: Princeton University Press.

Loewenberg, Frank M. 1970. Toward a systems analysis of social welfare manpower utilization patterns. *Child Welfare* 49:252–53.

Lofland, John and Rodney Stark. 1965. Becoming a world-saver: a theory of conversion to a deviant perspective. *American Sociological Review* 30:862–75.

Long, Norton. 1958. The local community as an ecology of games. *American Journal of Sociology* 64:251–61.

Lowi, Theodore J. 1964. American business, public policy, case studies, and political theory. *World Politics* 16:677–715.

—— 1969. *The End of Liberalism.* New York: Norton.

Lubove, Roy. 1969. *The Professional Altruist.* New York: Atheneum.

Lukoff, Irving F. and Martin Whiteman. 1963. Attitudes and blindness. Mimeographed.

Macarov, David. 1970. *Incentives to Work.* San Francisco: Jossey-Bass.

McCarthy, John D. and Mayer N. Zald. 1973. *The Trend in Social Movements in America.* Morristown, N.J.: General Learning.

—— 1977. Resource mobilization in social movements: a partial theory. *American Journal of Sociology* 82:1212-41.

Maccoby, Herbert. 1958. The differential political activity of participants in a voluntary association. *American Sociological Review* 23:523–32.

McConnell, Grant. 1966. *Private Power and American Democracy.* New York: Knopf.

MacDonald, Dwight. 1967. Our invisible poor. In Jeffrey K. Hadden, Louis H. Masotti, and Calvin J. Larson, eds., *Metropolis in Crisis.* Itasca, Ill.: Peacock.

MacFarlan, J. 1782. *Inquiries Concerning the Poor.* Edinburgh: Longmans and Dickson.

McKinlay, John B. 1972. Some approaches and problems in the study of the use of services—an overview. *Journal of Health and Social Behavior* 13:115–52.

McKinlay, John B. and S. M. McKinlay. 1972. Some social characteristics of lower working class utilizers of maternity care services. *Journal of Health and Social Behavior* 13:369–81.

McKinney, John C. and Charles P. Loomis. 1970. The typological tradition. In Albert N. Cousins and Hans Nagpaul, eds., *Urban Man and Society*, pp. 63–72. New York: Knopf.

McMillan, Alma. 1979. Social welfare expenditures under public programs, fiscal year 1977. *Social Security Bulletin* 42:3–12.

Malthus, Thomas R. 1798, 1826. *An Essay on the Principle of Population.* 1st, 6th eds. London.

Mandell, Arnold J. 1971. The sociology of a multimodality strategy in the treatment of narcotic addicts. *Journal of Psychedelic Drugs* 4:132–37.

Mandell, Betty. 1971. Welfare and totalitarianism. Parts 1 and 2. *Social Work* 16:17–26, 89–96.

Mannheim, Karl. 1936. *Ideology and Utopia,* tr. Louis Wirth and Edward Shils. New York: Harcourt, Brace & World.

—— 1940. *Man and Society in an Age of Reconstruction.* London: Kegan Paul.

Manpower Report of the President. 1972. Washington, D.C.: U.S. Departments of Health, Education and Welfare, and Labor.

Mantoux, P. 1928. *The Industrial Revolution in the Eighteenth Century.* London: Jonathan Cape.

March, James G. and Johan P. Olsen. 1976. *Ambiguity and Choice in Organizations.* Oslo: Universitetsforlaget.

Marcus, P. M., A. W. Sheldon, and M. J. Adams. 1974. The dynamics of interorganizational networks: some empirical results. Presented at Annual Meeting, North Central Sociological Association, Windsor, Ont., Canada.

Marcus, Steven. 1975. *Engels, Manchester and the Working Class.* New York: Vintage.

Marrett, C. B. 1971. On the specification of interorganizational dimensions. *Sociology and Social Research* 56:83–99.

Marshall, D. 1926. *The English Poor in the Eighteenth Century.* London: Routledge.

Marshall, T. H. 1950. *Citizenship and Social Class.* Cambridge, England: University of Cambridge Press.

Martin, George T., Jr. 1966. Two historical responses to the question of community responsibility in social welfare financing. Unpublished.

—— 1972. The emergence and development of a social movement organization among the underclass: a case study of the National Welfare Rights Organization. Ph.D. dissertation, University of Chicago.

Marx, Karl. 1967. *Capital: a Critique of Political Economy,* ed. Frederick Engels. Vol. 1. New York: International Publishers.

Marx, Karl and Frederick Engels. 1968. The communist manifesto. In *Selected Works.* New York: International Publishers.

Mechanic, David. 1969. *Mental Health and Social Policy.* Englewood Cliffs, N.J.: Prentice-Hall.

Merton, Robert K. 1957. *Social Theory and Social Structure.* Glencoe, Ill.: Free Press.

Messinger, Sheldon. 1955. Organizational transformation: a case study of a declining social movement. *American Sociological Review* 20:3–10.

Meyer, John W. and Brian Rowan. 1975. Notes on the structure of educational organizations. Presented at Annual Meeting, American Sociological Association, San Francisco.

—— 1977. Institutional organizations: formal structure as myth and ceremony. *American Journal of Sociology* 83:340–63.

Michels, Roberto. 1949. *Political Parties*. Glencoe, Ill.: Free Press.

Mill, John Stuart, 1848. *Principles of Political Economy with Some of Their Applications to Social Philosophy*. London: Parker.

Miller, Leonard S. 1976. The structural determinants of the welfare effort: a critique and a contribution. *Social Service Review* 50:57–79.

Miller, Walter B. 1958. Inter-institutional conflict as a major impediment to delinquency prevention. *Human Organization* 17:20–23.

—— 1959. Implications of urban lower class culture for social work. *Social Service Review* 33:219–36.

Mills, C. Wright. 1943. The professional ideology of social pathologists. *American Journal of Sociology* 49:165–80.

—— 1959. *The Sociological Imagination*. New York: Oxford University Press.

Moch, Michael and Louis R. Pondy. 1977. The structure of chaos: organized anarchy as a response to ambiguity. *Administrative Science Quarterly* 22:351–62.

Moffett, J. T. 1971. Bureaucracy and social control: a study of the progressive regimentation of the Western social order. Ph.D. dissertation, Columbia University.

Mogulof, Melvin B. 1970. Black community development in five Western model cities. *Social Work* 15:12–18.

Mohr, Lawrence B. 1969. Determinants of innovation in organization. *American Political Science Review* 63:111–26.

Morely, Eileen and Alan Sheldon. 1973. Work systems and human behavior: towards a systems-theoretic approach. In F. Baker, ed., *Organizational Systems*, pp. 141–50. Homewood, Ill.: Irwin.

Morgan, James N. et al. 1962. *Income and Welfare in the United States*. New York: McGraw-Hill.

Morrison, Denton E. and Ramon E. Henkel. 1969. Significance tests reconsidered. *American Sociologist* 4:131–39.

Mott, Paul E. 1970. Configuration of power. In Michael Aiken and Paul E. Mott, eds., *The Structure of Community Power*, pp. 85–100. New York: Random House.

Moynihan, Daniel P. 1965. The professionalization of reform. *Public Interest* 1:6–16.

—— 1969. *Maximum Feasible Misunderstanding*. New York: Free Press.

Mullen, E. J., R. M. Chazin, and D. M. Feldstein. 1972. Services for the newly dependent: an assessment. *Social Service Review* 46:309–22.

Munson, Carlton E. 1976. Professional autonomy and social work supervision. *Journal of Education for Social Work* 16:98–100.

Musgrave, R. A. and J. M. Culbertson. 1953. The growth of public expenditures in the United States, 1890–1948. *National Tax Journal* 6:97–114.

Musgrave, R. A., K. Case, and H. Leonard. 1975. The distribution of fiscal bureaus and benefits. *Public Finance Quarterly* 2:259–312.

Musto, David. 1973. *The American Disease: Origins of Narcotic Control.* New Haven, Conn.: Yale University Press.

Naparstek, Arthur J. and George T. Martin, Jr. 1965. Welfare problems of the cities. *Current History* 55:341–45, 369.

National Center for Health Statistics. 1964, 1972. *Vital Statistics for the United States.* Vol. 3. Washington, D.C.

Nelkin, Dorothy. 1973. *Methadone Maintenance: a Technological Fix.* New York: Braziller.

Newby, I. A. 1965. *Jim Crow's Defense.* Baton Rouge: Louisiana State University.

New York *Times.* 1972a. Big pension rise for lowest paid gains in Senate. March 28.

—— 1972b. Senate panel moves to cut off relief funds for some addicts. June 1.

—— 1972c. Wider birth curb aids backed by Senate panel. June 8.

—— 1972d. Major provisions of Senate bill on Social Security and welfare. June 14.

—— 1972e. Social Security rise becomes a nightmare for many. October 3.

—— 1973. Suit asks Department of Labor to halt alleged peonage in mental institutions. March 14.

Nicolson, J. L. 1974. The distribution and redistribution of income in the United Kingdom. In Dorothy Wederburn, ed., *Poverty, Inequality, and Class Structures*, Chap. 3. Cambridge, England: Cambridge University Press.

Nie, Norman H. et al. 1975. *SPSS: Statistical Package for the Social Sciences.* 2d ed. New York: McGraw-Hill.

Novak, Michael. 1971a. *The Rise of the Unmeltable Ethnics.* New York: Macmillan.

—— 1971b. White ethnic. *Harper's* 243:44–50.

Obermann, C. Esco. 1965. *A History of Vocational Rehabilitation in America.* Minneapolis: Denison.

O'Connor, James. 1973. *The Fiscal Crisis of the State.* New York: St. Martin's Press.

Orshansky, Mollie. 1965. Who's who among the poor. *Social Security Bulletin* 28:3–32.

Oshima, H. 1962. The international comparison of size distribution of family income with special reference to Asia. *Review of Economics and Statistics* 44:439–45.

Osofsky, Howard J. 1968. The walls are within: an exploration of barriers between middle-class physicians and poor patients. In I. Deutscher and E. J. Thompson, eds., *Among the People: Encounters with the Poor,* pp. 239–58. New York: Basic Books.

Park, Robert E. and Ernest W. Burgess. 1921. *Introduction to the Science of Sociology.* Chicago: University of Chicago Press.

Parry-Jones, W. L. 1972. *The Trade in Lunacy.* London: Routledge and Kegan Paul.

Parsons, Talcott. 1956a. Illness and the role of the physician. In Clyde Kluckhohn, Henry A. Murray, and David M. Schneider, eds., *Personality in Nature, Society, and Culture,* pp. 452–60. New York: Knopf.

—— 1956b. Suggestions for a sociological approach to the theory of organizations. *Administrative Science Quarterly* 1:63–85, 225–39.

—— 1970. How are clients integrated into service organizations? In W. R. Rosengren and M. Lefton, eds., *Organizations and Clients,* pp. 1–16. Columbus, Ohio: Merrill.

Paske, Victor and Walter Weiss. 1965. *Fritidsun Der Sogelsen.* Mimeographed. Copenhagen.

Pearce, Diana and David Street. 1979. Welfare in the metropolitan area. In David Street and Associates, *Handbook of Contemporary Urban Life,* pp. 319–51. San Francisco: Jossey-Bass.

Pearl, Arthur and Frank Riessman. 1965. *New Careers for the Poor.* New York: Free Press.

Perkin, H. 1969. *The Origins of Modern English Society, 1780–1880.* London: Routledge and Kegan Paul.

Perlman, Helen Harris. 1963. Some notes on the waiting list. *Social Casework* 44:200–205.

Perrow, Charles. 1961. The analysis of goals in complex organizations. *American Sociological Review* 26:854–66.

—— 1965. Hospitals: technology, structure, and goals. In James G. March, ed., *Handbook of Organizations,* pp. 910–71. Chicago: Rand McNally.

—— 1970. Departmental power and perspective in industrial firms. In Mayer N. Zald, ed., *Power in Organizations*, pp. 59–89. Nashville, Tenn.: Vanderbilt University Press.

—— 1972. 1979 rev. *Complex Organizations*. Glenview, Ill.: Scott-Foresman.

—— 1978. Demystifying organizations. In Rosemary C. Sarri and Yeheskel Hasenfeld, eds., *The Management of Human Services*, pp. 105–20. New York: Columbia University Press.

Peters, Guy. 1974. Income redistribution: a longitudinal analysis of France, Sweden, and the United Kingdom. *Political Studies* 25:311–23.

Pettes, Dorothy. 1967. *Supervision in Social Work*. London: Allen & Unwin.

Pfeffer, J. and G. R. Salancik. 1974. Organizational decision-making as a political process: the case of a university budget. *Administrative Science Quarterly* 19:135–51.

Philadelphia Inquirer. 1971. City to reward "good" tenants in its projects. October 26.

Pilati, Joe. 1969. The hospitals don't belong to the people. *Village Voice*, February 6.

Pinard, Maurice. 1963. Structural attachments and political support in urban politics: a case of a fluoridation referendum. *American Journal of Sociology* 68:513–26.

Piven, Frances Fox and Richard A. Cloward. 1971. *Regulating the Poor: the Functions of Public Welfare*. New York: Pantheon.

—— 1977. *Poor People's Movements*. New York: Pantheon.

Polanyi, Karl. 1944. *The Great Transformation*. Boston: Beacon.

Pondy, L. R. 1970. Toward a theory of internal resource-allocation. In Mayer N. Zald, ed., *Power in Organizations*, pp. 270–311. Nashville, Tenn.: Vanderbilt University Press.

Poor Law Report. 1834. *Report of the Royal Commission on the Poor Laws*. London: Royal Commission on the Poor Laws.

Pratt, Lois. 1970. Optimism-pessimism about helping the poor with health problems. *Social Work* 15:29–33.

Pressman, Jeffrey L. and Aaron B. Wildavsky. 1973. *Implementation*. Berkeley: University of California Press.

Proceedings of the National Conference on Methadone Treatment. 1971. Washington, D.C.: U.S. Public Health Service.

—— 1972. New York: National Association for the Prevention of Addiction to Narcotics.

Pryor, Frederick. 1968. *Public Expenditure in Capitalist and Communist Nations.* Homewood, Ill.: Irwin.

Public Policy and Private Pension Programs. 1965. Washington, D.C.: President's Committee on Corporate Pension Funds and Other Private Retirement and Welfare Programs.

Quarterly Review. 1857. Lunatic asylums. 101:353–93.

Rapoport, R. N., R. Rapoport, and I. Rosow. 1960. *Community as a Doctor.* London: Tavistock.

Rauch, Julia B. 1970. Federal family planning programs: choice or coercion? *Social Work* 15:68–75.

Reich, Charles A. 1965. Individual rights and social welfare: the emerging legal issues. *Yale Law Journal* 74:1245–57.

Reid, J. 1816. *Essays on Insanity.* London: Longmans.

Reid, William J. 1964. Interagency coordination in delinquency prevention and control. *Social Service Review* 38:418–23.

Rein, Martin. 1964. The social service crisis: The dilemma—success for the agency or service to the needy? *Transaction* 1:3–8.

Remmen, E. et al. 1962. *Psychochemotherapy: the Physician's Manual.* Los Angeles: Western Medical Publications.

Reynolds, Bertha Capen. 1963. *An Uncharted Journey.* New York: Citadel Press.

—— 1965. *Learning and Teaching in the Practice of Social Work.* New York: Russell and Russell.

Reynolds, Morgan and Eugene Smolensky. 1974. The post-fisc distribution: 1961 and 1970 compared. *National Tax Journal* 27:515–30.

—— 1977. *Public Expenditures, Taxes and the Distribution of Income; the U.S.: 1950, 1961, 1970.* New York: Academic Press.

Richmond, Mary E. 1917. *Social Diagnosis.* New York: Russell Sage Foundation.

Riessman, Frank. 1965. The "helper" therapy principle. *Social Work* 10:27–32.

—— 1969. *Strategies against Poverty.* New York: Random House.

Rimlinger, Gaston V. 1966. Welfare policy and economic development: a comparative historical perspective. *Journal of Economic History* 26:556–71.

—— 1971. *Welfare Policy and Industrialization in Europe, America, and Russia.* New York: Wiley.

Rischin, Moses. 1965. *The American Gospel of Success.* Chicago: Quadrangle.

Rist, Ray C. 1970. Student social class and teacher expectations: the self-fulfilling prophecy in ghetto education. *Harvard Educational Review* 41:411–51.

Ritti, R. Richard and Drew W. Human. 1977. The administration of poverty: lessons from the "welfare explosion" 1967–1973. *Social Problems* 25:157–75.

Robb, J. H. 1961. Family structure and agency coordination: decentralization and the citizen. In J. L. Roberts, ed., *Decentralization in New Zealand Government Administration*, pp. 33–55. New York: Oxford University Press.

Roberts, Pearl R. and Joseph W. Eaton. 1964. Council house, a psychiatric volunteer demonstration project. Mimeographed. Pittsburgh: National Council of Jewish Women.

Robinson, Virginia P. 1936. *Supervision in Social Case Work*. Chapel Hill: University of North Carolina Press.

—— 1949. *The Dynamics of Supervision under Functional Controls*. Rev. Philadelphia: University of Pennsylvania Press.

Rock, Paul. 1974. The sociology of deviancy and conceptions of the moral order. *British Journal of Criminology* 14:139–49.

Romanyshyn, John M. 1971. *Social Welfare: Charity to Justice*. New York: Random House.

Rosengren, William R. and Mark Lefton, eds. 1970. *Organizations and Clients*. Columbus, Ohio: Merrill.

Roth, Julius A. 1963. *Timetables*. New York: Bobbs-Merrill.

—— 1972. Some contingencies of the moral evaluation and control of clientele: the case of the hospital emergency service. *American Journal of Sociology* 77:839–56.

Roth, Julius A. and Elizabeth M. Eddy. 1967. *Rehabilitation for the Unwanted*. New York: Atherton.

Rothman, David. 1971. *The Discovery of the Asylum*. Boston: Little, Brown.

Rubin, Richard S. 1968. *A Summary of State Collective Bargaining Laws in Public Employment*. New York: New York State School of Industrial and Labor Relations.

Rubington, E. 1973. *Alcohol Problems and Social Control*. Columbus, Ohio: Merrill.

Rubinson, Richard. 1976. The world-economy and the distribution of income within states: a cross-national study. *American Sociological Review* 41:638–59.

Rubinson, Richard and Daniel Quinlan. 1977. Democracy and social inequality: a reanalysis. *American Sociological Review* 42:611–23.

Rushing, W. A. 1971. Individual resources, societal reaction, and hospital commitment. *American Journal of Sociology* 77:511–25.

Russett, Bruce M. et al. 1964. *World Handbook of Political and Social Indicators.* New Haven, Conn.: Yale University Press.

Ryan, William. 1969. Community care in historical perspective: implications for mental health services and professionals. *Canada's Mental Health,* Supplement No. 60.

—— 1971. *Blaming the Victim.* New York: Random House.

St. Luke's Hospital. 1750. Considerations upon the usefulness and necessity of establishing an hospital as a further provision for poor lunaticks. London. Unpublished manuscript.

Salancik, G. R. and J. Pfeffer. 1974. The bases and use of power in organizational decision-making: the case of a university. *Administrative Science Quarterly* 19:453–73.

Samuelson, Paul. 1973. *Economics.* 9th ed. New York: McGraw-Hill.

Saucier, Anne. 1971. The qualifications and activities of caseworkers in a county welfare department. *Social Service Review* 45:184–93.

Schattschneider, Elmer Eric. 1960. *The Semi-sovereign People, a Realistic View of Democracy in America.* New York: Holt.

Scheff, Thomas J. 1964. The societal reaction to deviance: ascriptive elements in the psychiatric screening of mental patients in a midwestern state. *Social Problems* 11:401–13.

—— 1966. *Being Mentally Ill.* Chicago: Aldine.

Schein, Virginia Ellen. 1973. The relationship between sex role stereotypes and requisite management characteristics. *Journal of Applied Psychology* 57:95–100.

—— 1975. Relationship between sex role stereotypes and requisite management characteristics among female managers. *Journal of Applied Psychology* 60:340–44.

Schorr, Alvin. 1968. *Explorations in Social Policy.* New York: Basic Books.

—— 1969. Editorials. *Social Work* 14:2, 128.

Schorr, Alvin and Edward Baumheier. 1971. Social policy. *Encyclopedia of Social Work.* New York: National Association of Social Workers.

Schumpeter, Joseph. 1942. *Capitalism, Socialism, and Democracy.* New York: Harper and Bros.

Scoles, Pascal and Eric W. Fine. 1971. Aftercare and rehabilitation in a community mental health center. *Social Work* 16:75–82.

Scotch, C. Bernard. 1971. Sex status in social work: grist for women's liberation. *Social Work* 16:5–11.

Scott, Robert A. 1967. The selection of clients by social welfare agencies: the case of the blind. *Social Problems* 14:248–57.

—— 1969. *The Making of Blind Men*. New York: Russell Sage Foundation.

Scull, Andrew T. 1974. Museums of madness: the social organization of insanity in nineteenth-century England. Ph.D. dissertation, Princeton University.

—— 1975. From madness to mental illness: medical men as moral entrepreneurs. *European Journal of Sociology* 16:219–61.

—— 1976. Mad-doctors and magistrates: English psychiatry's struggle for professional autonomy in the nineteenth century. *European Journal of Sociology* 17:279–305.

—— 1977. *Decarceration: Community Treatment and the Deviant—a Radical View*. Englewood Cliffs, N.J.: Prentice-Hall.

Seeley, John. 1967. The problem of social problems. In *The Americanization of the Unconscious*, pp. 142–48. New York: International Science.

Seeley, John R., Bulford H. Junker, and R. Wallace Jones, Jr. 1957. *Community Chest*. Toronto: University of Toronto Press.

Segal, Arthur. 1970. Workers' perceptions of mentally disabled clients: effect on service delivery. *Social Work* 15:39–46.

Selznick, Philip. 1949. *TVA and the Grass Roots*. Berkeley: University of California Press.

Sharkansky, Ira. 1972. *The Maligned States*. New York: McGraw-Hill.

Sherif, Carolyn Wood. 1976. On becoming collegial while being woman. In Meg Gerrard et al., eds., *Women in Management*. Austin: University of Texas Press.

Shenker, Israel. 1969. Students take over, but it's all academic. New York *Times*, March 7.

Shils, Edward A. 1962. The theory of the mass society. *Diogenes* 39:45–66.

Shlonsky, Hagith. 1971. Welfare programs and the social system. *Social Service Review* 45:414–25.

Shonfield, Andrew. 1966. *Modern Capitalism*. London: Oxford University Press.

Sills, David L. 1957. *The Volunteers*. Glencoe, Ill.: Free Press.

Sjoberg, G., R. A. Brymer, and B. Farris. 1966. Bureaucracy and the lower class. *Sociology and Social Research* 50:325–37.

Skolnik, Alfred M. and Sophie R. Dales. 1971. Social welfare expenditures, 1970–71. *Social Security Bulletin* 34:3–16.

—— 1976. Social welfare expenditures, 1950–75. *Social Security Bulletin* 39:3–20.

Slater, Miriam K. 1969. My son the doctor: aspects of mobility among American Jews. *American Sociological Review* 34:359–73.

Smigel, Erwin. 1964. *Wall Street Lawyer.* New York: Free Press.

Smith, Adam. 1776. *The Wealth of Nations.* New York: Modern Library.

Social Service Review. 1968. Index. Vol. 42.

—— 1972a. Child development plan vetoed. 46:108–11.

—— 1972b. Brownie point welfare. 46:111–13.

Soloway, Irving H. 1974. Methadone and the culture of addiction. *Journal of Psychedelic Drugs* 6:91–99.

Spencer, Herbert. 1864. *Social Statics.* New York: D. Appleton.

Spradley, J. P. 1970. *You Owe Yourself a Drunk: an Ethnography of Urban Nomads.* Boston: Little, Brown.

Srole, Leo et al. 1962. *Mental Health in the Metropolis.* Vol. 1. New York: McGraw–Hill.

Stack, Steven, 1978. The effect of direct government involvement in the economy on the degree of income inequality: a cross-national study. *American Sociological Review* 43:880–88.

Stagner, R. 1969. Corporate decision-making: an empirical study. *Journal of Applied Psychology* 53:1–13.

Stanton, Alfred and Morris Schwartz. 1954. *The Mental Hospital.* New York: Basic Books.

Stark, W. 1810. *Remarks on the Construction of Public Hospitals for the Cure of Mental Derangement.* Glasgow: Hedderwick.

Steger, Emil. 1931. Intake policies in family case work. In *National Conference of Social Work,* pp. 189–97. Chicago: University of Chicago Press.

Steinfeld, Melvin. 1970. *Cracks in the Melting Pot.* Glencoe, Ill.: Free Press.

Stephen, Leslie. 1900. *The English Utilitarians.* Vol. 1. London: Duckworth.

Stiles, Evelyn et al. 1972. Hear it like it is. *Social Work* 53:292–99.

Stouffer, S. 1963. *Communism, Conformity, and Civil Liberties.* Gloucester, Mass.: Peter Smith.

Straits, Bruce C. 1965. Community adoption and implementation of urban renewal. *American Journal of Sociology* 71:77–82.

Strauss, Anselm. 1969. Medical organization, medical care, and lower income groups. *Social Science and Medicine* 3:143–77.

—— 1979. *Negotiations: Varieties, Contexts, Processes, and Social Order.* San Francisco: Jossey-Bass.

Strauss, Anselm et al. 1964. *Psychiatric Ideologies and Institutions.* Glencoe, Ill.: Free Press.

Street, David. 1967. Educators and social workers: sibling rivalry in the inner city. *Social Service Review* 41:152–65.

Street, David, George T. Martin, Jr., and Laura Kramer Gordon. 1979. *The Welfare Industry: Functionaries and Recipients in Public Aid.* Beverly Hills: Sage Publishing.

Street, David, Robert D. Vinter, and Charles Perrow. 1966. *Organization for Treatment.* New York: Free Press.

Suchman, E. A. 1965. Stages of illness and medical care. *Journal of Health and Social Behavior* 6:114–28.

Sudnow, David. 1967. *Passing On.* Englewood Cliffs, N.J.: Prentice-Hall.

Syzmanski, Albert. 1972. Trends in class structure. *Socialist Revolution* 2:101–22.

Szasz, Thomas. 1960. The myth of mental illness. *American Psychologist* 15:113–18.

Szasz, Thomas and Marc H. Hollender. 1970. The basic models of the doctor-patient relationship. In H. W. Polsky, D. S. Claster, and C. Goldberg, eds., *Social System Perspectives in Residential Institutions*, pp. 119–31. East Lansing: Michigan State University Press.

Taeuber, Karl E. and Alma R. Taeuber. 1965. *Negroes in Cities.* Chicago: Aldine.

Teele, James E. and Sol Levine. 1968. The acceptance of emotionally disturbed children by psychiatric agencies. In Stanton Wheeler, ed., *Controlling Delinquents*, pp. 103–51. New York: Wiley.

Temple, William. 1770. *An Essay on Trade and Commerce.* London.

Terreberry, Shirley. 1968. The evolution of organizational environments. *Administrative Science Quarterly* 12:590–613.

Tessler, Richard C. and Norman A. Polansky. 1975. Perceived similarity: a paradox in interviewing. *Social Work* 20:359–63.

Thibaut, John W. and Harold H. Kelley. 1959. *The Social Psychology of Groups.* New York: Wiley.

Thomas, A. and S. Sillen. 1972. *Racism and Psychiatry.* New York: Brunner/Mazel.

Thompson, E. P. 1963. *The Making of the English Working Class.* New York: Vintage.

Thompson, James D. 1962. Organizations and output transactions. *American Journal of Sociology* 68:309–24.

—— 1967. *Organizations in Action.* New York: McGraw-Hill.

—— 1968. Models of organization and administrative systems. In *The Social Sciences: Problems and Orientations,* pp. 95–405. The Hague: Mowton/UNESCO.

Thompson, James D. and William J. McEwen. 1958. Organization goals and environment: goal setting as an interaction process. *American Sociological Review* 23:23–31.

Thompson, James D. and Arthur Tuden. 1959. Strategies, structures, and processes of organizational decision. In James D. Thompson et al., eds., *Comparative Studies in Administration,* pp. 195–216. Pittsburgh: University of Pittsburgh.

Titmuss, Richard M. 1950. *Problems of Social Policy.* London: His Majesty's Stationery Office.

—— 1958. *Essays on the Welfare State.* London: Allen and Unwin.

—— 1962. *Income Distribution and Social Change.* Toronto: University of Toronto.

Tonnies, Ferdinand. 1957. *Community and Society,* ed. Charles A. Loomis. East Lansing: Michigan State University Press.

Townsend, Joseph. 1786. *A Dissertation on the Poor Laws, by a Well-Wisher of Mankind.* London.

Tracy, Phil. 1972. Working for welfare. *The Village Voice,* February 24, June 22, June 29, July 6.

Tropman, John E. 1971a. Benign neglect. *Transaction* 8:6, 8.

—— 1971b. Public welfare appropriations, utilization, change, and service. Unpublished.

Tuite, Matthew, Roger Chisholm, and Michael Radnor. 1972. *Interorganizational Decision-making.* Chicago: Aldine.

Turk, Herman. 1970. Interorganizational networks in urban society: initial perspective and comparative research. *American Sociological Review* 35:1–19.

Turner, Ralph H. 1966. Modes of ascent through education—sponsored and contest mobility. In R. Bendix and S. M. Lipset, eds., *Class, Status, and Power,* pp. 449–58. Rev. New York: Free Press.

—— 1967. *On Social Control and Collective Behavior.* Chicago: University of Chicago Press.

Ullman, Alice et al. 1971. Activities, satisfaction, and problems of social workers in hospital settings. *Social Service Review* 45:17–29.

United Fund of Greater Chattanooga. 1973. *Know Your United Fund.* Chattanooga, Tenn.: United Fund.

United Way of America. 1971. *United Way Directory, 1971–1972.* Alexandria, Va.: United Way.

U.S. Bureau of the Census. 1950–1964, 1973–1979. *Statistical Abstract of the United States.* Washington, D.C.

—— 1962b, 1963b, 1973b. *County and City Data Book.* Washington, D.C.

—— 1966. *Census of Manufacturing.* Washington, D.C.

—— 1969. *Current Population Reports.* Series P-60, no. 59. Washington, D.C.

—— 1970, 1975b. *Historical Statistics of the United States.* Washington, D.C.

U.S. Department of Health, Education, and Welfare. 1961. *Social Security Programs Throughout the World, 1961.* Washington, D.C.

U.S. Department of Justice. 1961, 1967. *Uniform Crime Reports for the United States.* Washington, D.C.

U.S. Department of Labor. 1965. *Survey of Consumer Expenditures: 1960–1961.* Washington, D.C.

U.S. Food and Drug Administration. 1970. Conditions for the investigational use of methadone for narcotics addicts. Washington, D.C.

U.S. Office of Labor-Management and Welfare-Pension Reports. 1960. *Register of Reporting Labor Unions.* Washington, D.C.

U.S. Social and Rehabilitation Services. 1971. *Overview Study of the Dynamics of Worker Job Mobility.* Washington, D.C.

U.S. Social Security Administration. 1965. International comparisons of ratios of Social Security expenditures to gross national product. Washington, D.C.

Van Ness, Edward H. 1967. The regional medical program in heart disease, cancer and stroke. In *Utilization of Rehabilitation Manpower in the Community Setting,* pp. 75–79. Mankato, Minn.: Mankato State College.

Ventre, Francis T. 1966. Local initiatives in urban industrial development. *Urban Affairs Quarterly* 2:53–67.

Vinter, Robert D. 1963. Analysis of treatment organizations. *Social Work* 8:3–15.

—— 1974. The social structure of service. In Paul E. Weinberger, ed., *Perspectives on Social Welfare*, pp. 453–71. New York: Macmillan.

Vinter, Robert D. and R. C. Sarri. 1966. The juvenile court: organization and decision-making. In *Juvenile Court Hearing Officers Training Manual*, pp. 173–320. Vol. 2. Ann Arbor: University of Michigan Press.

Vontress, Clemmont E. 1971. Racial differences: impediments to rapport. *Journal of Counseling Psychology* 18:7–13.

Wadsworth, H. G. 1970. Initiating a preventive-corrective approach in an elementary school system. *Social Work* 15:60–66.

Wagner, Jon. 1977. *Misfits and Missionaries: a School for Black Dropouts*. Beverly Hills, Calif.: Sage Publications.

Wakefield, E. 1812. Plan of an asylum for lunatics, etc. *Philanthropist* 2:226–29.

Wallerstein, Immanuel. 1974. *The Modern World System*. New York: Academic Press.

Walsh, J. L. and R. H. Elling. 1968. Professionalization and the poor: structural effects and professional behavior. *Journal of Health and Social Behavior* 9:16–28.

Warren, Roland L. 1967a. Interaction of community decision organizations: some basic concepts and needed research. *Social Service Review* 41:261–70.

—— 1967b. The interorganizational field as a focus for investigation. *Administrative Science Quarterly* 12:396–419.

—— 1973. Comprehensive planning and coordination: some functional aspects. *Social Problems* 20:55–64.

Wasserman, Harry. 1970. Early careers of professional social workers in a public child welfare agency. *Social Work* 15:93–101.

—— 1971. The professional social worker in a bureaucracy. *Social Work* 16:89–95.

Webb, Eugene J. et al. 1973. *Unobtrusive Measures*. Chicago: Rand McNally.

Webb, Sidney and Beatrice Webb. 1927. *English Poor Law History*. London: Longmans, Green.

Weber, A. F. 1899. *The Growth of Cities in the Nineteenth Century*. New York: Columbia University Press.

Weber, Max. 1930. *The Protestant Ethic and the Spirit of Capitalism*. London: Allen and Unwin.

—— 1946. *From Max Weber: Essays in Sociology*, ed. Hans Gerth and C. Wright Mills. New York: Oxford University Press.

—— 1961. *General Economic History*. New York: Collier.

—— 1968. *Economy and Society*. Vol. 1. Totowa, N.J.: Bedminster.

Weick, Karl E. 1976. Educational organizations as loosely coupled systems. *Administrative Science Quarterly* 21:1–19.

Weiner, Hyman J. et al. 1971. *The World of Work and Social Welfare Policy*. New York: Columbia University School of Social Work.

Weinstein, James. 1968. *The Corporate Ideal in the Liberal State 1900–1918*. Boston: Beacon.

Weisenfeld, Allan. 1969. The New Jersey Employer-Employee Relations Act of 1968. *Economic and Business Bulletin* 21.

Wenocur, S. 1975. A political view of the United Way. *Social Work* 20:223–29.

Wheaton, William L. C. 1964. Integration at the urban level: political influence and the decision process. In Philip E. Jacobs and James V. Toscano, eds., *The Integration of Political Communities*, pp. 120–42. New York: Lippincott.

Wheeler, Stanton. 1966. The structure of formally organized socialization settings. In O. G. Brim and S. Wheeler, eds., *Socialization After Childhood*, pp. 51–116. New York: Wiley.

White, Joseph. 1970. Guidelines for black psychologists. *Black Scholar* 1:52–57.

White, Paul E. 1974. Resources as determinants of organizational behavior. *Administrative Science Quarterly* 19:366–76.

Whitaker, William H. 1970. The determinants of social movement success: a study of the National Welfare Rights Organization. Ph.D. dissertation, Brandeis University.

Whittaker, James K. 1972. Group care for children: guidelines for planning. *Social Work* 17:51–61.

Wilder, John R. 1963. Self-help in mental illness. *The Medical Practitioner* 2:14–18.

Wilensky, Harold L. 1975. *The Welfare State and Equality*. Berkeley: University of California Press.

Wilensky, Harold L. and Charles N. Lebeaux. 1965; 1975 rev. *Industrial Society and Social Welfare*. New York: Free Press.

Williams, Martha, Liz Ho, and Lucy Fielder. 1974. Career patterns: more grist for women's liberation. *Social Work* 19:463–66.

Williams, Robin M. 1961. *American Society*. New York: Knopf.

Williamson, Mary. 1961. *Supervision*. New York: Association Press.

Wilson, James Q. 1966. Innovation in organization: notes toward a theory. In James D. Thompson, ed., *Approaches to Organizational Design*, pp. 193–218. Pittsburgh: University of Pittsburgh Press.

Wilson, James Q. and Edward C. Banfield. 1964. Public-regardingness as a value premise in voting behavior. *American Political Science Review* 58:876–87.

Winch, Robert F. and Donald T. Campbell. 1969. Proof? No. Evidence? Yes. The significance of tests of significance. *American Sociologist* 4:140–43.

Wiseman, Jacqueline P. 1970. *Stations of the Lost*. Englewood Cliffs, N.J.: Prentice-Hall.

Wittenberg, Rudolph. 1954. *So You Want to Help People*. New York: Association Press.

Wolfinger, Raymond E. and John Osgood Field. 1966. Political ethos and the structure of city government. *American Political Science Review* 60:306–26.

Wood, Arthur Lewis. 1967. *Criminal Lawyer*. New Haven, Conn.: College and University Press.

Zald, Mayer N. 1970a. *Organizational Change: the Political Economy of the YMCA*. Chicago: University of Chicago Press.

—— 1970b. Political economy: a framework for comparative analysis. In Mayer N. Zald, ed., *Power in Organizations*, pp. 221–61. Nashville, Tenn.: Vanderbilt University Press.

—— 1977. Demographics, politics, and the future of the welfare state. *Social Service Review* 51:110–24.

—— ed. 1965. *Social Welfare Institutions: a Sociological Reader*. New York: Wiley.

Zald, Mayer N. and Roberta Ash. 1966. Social movement organizations. *Social Forces* 44:327–41.

Zald, Mayer N. and Patricia Denton. 1963. From evangelism to general service: the transformation of the YMCA. *Administrative Science Quarterly* 8:214–34.

Ziegler, Luther Harmon. 1969. *Lobbying: Interaction and Influence in American State Legislatures*. Belmont, Calif.: Wadsworth.

Zietz, Dorothy and John L. Erlich. 1976. Sexism in social agencies: practitioners' perspectives. *Social Work* 21:434–39.

CONTRIBUTORS

Michael Aiken   Department of Sociology, University of Wisconsin, Madison

Robert R. Alford   Department of Sociology, University of California, Santa Cruz

Paul Attewell   Department of Sociology, University of California, Santa Cruz

Richard A. Cloward   School of Social Work, Columbia University, New York

Joan Cole   Organizational Consultant and Psychotherapist, Berkeley, California

Phillips Cutright   Department of Sociology, Indiana University, Bloomington

Roger Friedland   Department of Sociology, University of California, Santa Barbara

Lincoln J. Fry   Social Science Research Institute, University of Southern California, Los Angeles

Jeffry H. Galper   School of Social Administration, Temple University, Philadelphia

Dean R. Gerstein   National Academy of Sciences, Washington, D.C.

Nathan Glazer   Department of Sociology and Graduate School of Education, Harvard University, Cambridge, Massachusetts

Yeheskel Hasenfeld   School of Social Work and Department of Sociology, University of Michigan, Ann Arbor

Marie R. Haug   Department of Sociology and Center on Aging and Health, Case Western Reserve University, Cleveland

Alexander Hicks   Departments of Political Science and Sociology, Northwestern University, Evanston, Illinois

Morris Janowitz	Department of Sociology, University of Chicago, Chicago
Edwin Johnson	Department of Sociology, University of Wisconsin, Madison
Alfred J. Kahn	School of Social Work, Columbia University, New York
Sheila B. Kamerman	School of Social Work, Columbia University, New York
Alfred H. Katz	Schools of Public Health and Social Welfare, University of California, Los Angeles
Anthony Leong	Center for the Study of Neuroses, University of California, San Francisco
George T. Martin, Jr.	Department of Sociology, Montclair State College, Upper Montclair, New Jersey
Jon Miller	Department of Sociology and Laboratory for Organizational Research, University of Southern California, Los Angeles
Carlton E. Munson	School of Social Work, University of Houston, Houston, Texas
James O'Connor	Department of Sociology, University of California, Santa Cruz
Jeffrey Pfeffer	School of Business, Stanford University, Stanford, California
Marc Pilisuk	Department of Applied Behavioral Sciences, University of California, Davis
Frances Fox Piven	Department of Political Science, Boston University, Boston
Sonia Rosenbaum	Investment Consultant, Northampton, Massachusetts
Julius A. Roth	Department of Sociology, University of California, Davis
William Ryan	Department of Psychology, Boston College, Chestnut Hill, Massachusetts
Robert A. Scott	Department of Sociology, Princeton University, Princeton, New Jersey
Andrew T. Scull	Department of Sociology, University of California at San Diego, La Jolla
David Street (deceased)	Department of Sociology, University of Illinois at Chicago Circle, Chicago

Marvin B. Sussman	Individual and Family Studies, University of Delaware, Newark
Daniel Thursz	B'nai B'rith International, Washington, D.C.
John E. Tropman	School of Social Work and Institute of Gerontology, University of Michigan, Ann Arbor
Joseph L. Vigilante	School of Social Work, Adelphi University, Garden City, New York
James D. Wright	Department of Sociology, University of Massachusetts, Amherst
Mayer N. Zald	Department of Sociology and Center for Research on Social Organization, University of Michigan, Ann Arbor

NAME INDEX

SUBJECT INDEX

AAWB (American Association of Workers for the Blind), 269, 275, 278, 280–82, 284n
Accountability, 3, 58, 485–86
Administration: of asylums, 29; centralization of, 14, 210, 215–19, 492–94; fragmentation of, 474, 480; innovation in, 29; of methadone programs, 112–17, 119; and professionals, 343–45; rationalization of, 14, 29–30, 292–95; of self-help, 437; and sexism, 355–57, 365–67; of the state, 529–35; of universities, 347; of welfare, 263–64, 285–99, 474, 480; of the welfare state, 14, 198. *See also* Social service administration
Adoption services, 83, 236–37, 292
AFDC. *See* Aid to Families with Dependent Children
AFSCME (American Federation of State, County, and Municipal Employees), 524
AFT (American Federation of Teachers), 524, 529, 534
Aged: communities for, 520; and the mobility ethic, 100; numbers of, 511, 517; as problem area, 59–60, 236, 511, 517; programs for, 512n; and social insurance, 76, 148; social worth of, 324; and welfare, 156. *See also* Age structure; Medicare; Social Security
Agencies: allocations to, 208, 246–62; client relations of, 4, 103, 301–21, 349, 452–55; coordination of, 233–45, 299n, 407–11; and "creaming," 455; critique of, 450–73; goals of, 263–92, 393–410, 474, 482; and paraprofessionals, 116–19, 349;

record-keeping of, 461–62; sectarian, 96; sexism in, 358–67; social control by, 527; and social work students, 455; supervision in, 358–67. *See also* Organizations; Social services
Agency for International Development, 525
Age structure, 2, 10, 43, 197, 511, 517
Aid to Families with Dependent Children (AFDC), 383, 512n; benefits of, 186; caseload increase of, 156–58, 505, 510–11; as exceptionalistic program, 77–78; keeping people off, 192; and poverty, 93; and social work students, 459–60; and stigma, 65; and welfare rights, 488–89, 494–95, 497, 501n. *See also* Welfare
Alcohol abuse, 110, 173, 285, 382; emergency room treatment of, 326–28, 335; innovative clinic for, 393–411, 411n; moral evaluation of, 326–28; and unemployment, 457; by youth, 60
Alcoholics Anonymous, 394, 398, 406–7, 441n
Alienation, 2, 17, 59, 124–25, 129, 188, 349, 399–400, 514, 526
Altruism, 14, 121, 342, 440–41
AMA (American Medical Association), 475
American Association of Workers for the Blind (AAWB), 269, 275, 278, 280–82, 284n
American Federation of State, County, and Municipal Employees (AFSCME), 524
American Federation of Teachers (AFT), 524, 529, 534